THE RETIRED MINISTER

HIS CLAIM
INHERENT, FOREMOST, SUPREME

BY
JOSEPH B. HINGELEY

THE ABINGDON PRESS
NEW YORK CINCINNATI

Price, $1.00 net; postage, 15 cents. Address orders to the
BOARD OF CONFERENCE CLAIMANTS
1018 South Wabash Ave., Chicago, Ill. Orders filled also by
THE ABINGDON PRESS
150 Fifth Ave., New York
THE METHODIST BOOK CONCERN and its DEPOSITORIES;
and by DENOMINATIONAL PUBLISHING HOUSES
and BOOK DEALERS generally

TO MY FATHER

THE REV. EZRA HINGELEY, D.D.
1825–1894

The Church's Wish for the Veterans

Voiced by Bishop Quayle

May the heat not be too great for them, nor the winter too cold, because of the eternal summer in their hearts.

....

The Old Circuit Rider

....

....

Unpacking His Saddle Bags

....

The Retired Minister
His Claim Inherent, Foremost, Supreme.

......

"I have fought a good fight, I have finished my course, I have kept the Faith."

FOREWORD

The supremacy of the claim of the Veteran Preacher is being recognized by all the Churches. The new adjectives applied to the claim are significant: "Inherent," "Foremost," "Supreme."

The General Conference of the Methodist Episcopal Church in 1908 declared the claim of the Retired Minister to be *"inherent."*

The Presbyterian Church in 1909 adopted Dr. A. T. Pierson's word and declared that the claim was *"foremost."*

The National Convention of Laymen held in Indianapolis in 1913 called it "the *supreme* claim of the Retired Veterans."

The Bishops of the Methodist Episcopal Church in session at Washington, D. C., on October 29, 1914, demanded that the

Supreme claim should be given the Supreme Place, and closed their Address and Appeal to the Church as follows:

"We pledge ourselves and, as far as we may, pledge the whole Church to full and loyal cooperation to bring in this new and better day for the Church we love and the men we honor."

This book contains addresses made at the Inauguration Convention by men to whom the Churches have committed this great Cause, as well as by other leaders whose hearts are full of affection for Retired Ministers and whose minds and hands are employed in seeing that the Veteran Clergyman comes to his own.

As you read you will discover enthusiasm, optimism and a resolve that aged ministers of the Gospel shall not be provided for as objects of charity; but that the laymen of the Churches in whose service they have wrought, shall fulfill the promise of a comfortable support made to them when they took their ordination vows, and shall *"see them through."*

We are under special obligation to distinguished leaders of great Churches, and representatives of great business corporations whose illuminating articles give breadth and interest to this book by informing us as to what other institutions are doing to provide for the faithful and aged. Especially are we indebted to the Rev. Alfred J. P. McClure, D.D., of the Episcopal Church, the Rev. William H. Foulkes, D.D., of the Presbyterian Church, the Rev. Samuel Lane Loomis, D.D. and the Rev. W. A. Rice, D.D., of the Congregational Church, the Rev. J. R. Stewart, D.D., of the Methodist Episcopal Church, South, the Rev. W. B. Matteson of the Baptist Church, the Rev. Henry H. Sweets of the Southern Presbyterian Church, the Rev. Denis Wortman, D.D. of the Reformed (Dutch) Church, the Rev. W. R. Warren, D.D., of the Disciples of Christ and to the many other contributors, ministers and laymen, whose labors have made this book possible.

In the name of the Retired Ministers we extend our grateful thanks to Charles Scribner's Sons, The Continent, The Altemus Co. and others, who permit the use of copyright matter; and to men of large affairs like Mr. Renner of the Pennsylvania Lines, Mr. Pew of the Youngstown Steel Company, Mr. Campbell of South Bend, Judge Oliver H. Horton of Chicago, and others who have rendered valuable service. Their willingness to share their time and labors in such a Cause is an indication of the hold which the retirement competency idea has upon the business world. The Rev. J. Clayton Youker reported the several addresses and assisted in the preparation of the book, and the Rev. M. E. Snyder, Ph.D., and the Rev. Charles R. Oaten, secretaries, rendered valuable and distinguished service.

We have added chapters which have appeared in the columns of the "*Veteran Preacher*" and in Church periodicals; also music and poetry and statistics, with the intention of making this book a Compendium to which the laity and ministry may turn for information as to the Cause of the Retired Minister.

The Abingdon Press has given to this book a printed form worthy of its subject matter; for we expect that "The Retired Minister" will be welcomed to the shelves of ministers' libraries and to the homes of Christian people.

JOSEPH B. HINGELEY.

Evanston, Illinois.

CONTENTS

PART I. THE CLAIM INHERENT

CHAPTER I. THE MERITS OF THE CASE

CHAPTER II. OLD AGE

PART II. THE CLAIM FOREMOST

CHAPTER I. THE CHURCH'S PROGRAM

CHAPTER II. THE PROGRAM OF BUSINESS

CHAPTER III. POST-MORTEM DISTRIBUTION OF WEALTH

PART III. THE CLAIM SUPREME

CHAPTER I. EPISCOPAL LEADERSHIP AND CONFERENCE

CHAPTER II. THE 1915 CAMPAIGN

CHAPTER III. AGENCIES

CHAPTER IV. HISTORICAL

PART IV. THE CLAIM ILLUSTRATED

CHAPTER I. SCRIPTURAL TREATMENT

CHAPTER II. STORY AND SONG

A RETIRING COMPETENCY FOR THE RETIRED MINISTER

PART I

THE CLAIM INHERENT UNDERLYING PRINCIPLES

The Church's Recognition that the Right to a Comfortable Support Inheres in the Gospel Ministry, is Justified by the Character of the Ministry, the Demands Made on it, and the Service it Renders; and calls for an adequate Retiring Competency for the Old Age of Ministers of Christ.

CHAPTER I. THE MERITS OF THE CASE

THE TASK GOLDEN

BISHOP
WILLIAM A. QUAYLE, D.D., LL.D.

It is lovely to be at the vortex of things. It is rather radiant to be at the center of the storm; and I confess in the privacy of this presence that I fellowship with Brother Berry in his delight in magnitudes.

Looking After Our Immortality

To get hold of a thing that is big enough to get hold of us is magnificent. To go winking and blinking around about little business is not worth the winks and the blinks; but to get hold of a sea and tuck your fingers into its mane, and see the thing leap and want to be riderless, and for you to sit and ride it to the shore, O that is worth while. It is worth while to be in a great Church with a great God steering to a great eternity; and the thing I think of pretty often is: Who is going to keep us to our immortality? Who is going to keep us to our bigness? Who is going to look after our vastnesses? Who is going to tell us with insistent voice that we are sublime? Who is going to tell us that death does not count any, if we live a right life? Who is going to point the finger at the majesty we are and the majesty we are to be? Who is going to help us look after our immortality?

There are many who will help us to look after our mortality: the grocer will help us, and the doctor will help us, and the shoe merchant will help us, and the railroad man will help us, and the statesman will help us, and the educator will help us, and the college will help us; but who is going to help us look after the Godward? Who is going to help us look after our everlastingness? Answer: The preacher is going to help us; he is the man that keeps tune with the infinite; he is the man who, though he may not spell the best and though he may not be educated the most, has heard in his own heart the deathless music, and pitches the tune. What people need is the tune of their everlastingness. I remember so many times when people would say to me, "Preach on the things of the day; preach on the things that people are thinking about during the week"; but I never did, because they thought about those things themselves and did not need to have me help them. But on Sunday I began to take up the harp of life and smite upon some of the strings with what little might I knew, and began to make men dream of deathlessness; and then men got religion. The thing we are after is to get hold of our own souls; to know that life leads us so long a distance, that the run is so very far, so very expeditious, and so very glorious. O my heart, canst thou take to the race? O my heart, canst thou make the run? O my heart, who is going to get thee to the summit of the sky, and O my heart, who is going to get thee back behind the stars, and O my heart, who is going to get thee over where the angels stay, and O my heart who is going to get thee where Christ walks the road every day and bringeth a morning to every shadowy night? Who is going to get thee there? And the answer is: The preacher is going to help us, and so the preacher is the most manifest majesty of all men.

The Preachers

I think of the funny men I have had preach to me, and I remember how they did tear the beautiful garment of dramatic expression into small ribbons and did not care about the ribbons at all; and I remember when I heard them fall on the "whoms" and the "whos," and all the ridiculosities of speech; yet I remember some of those men, who could not get it arranged whether they should say "who" or "whom," who brought you up until you fell on the outstretched Hand, and caught the foot of the cross of God. I would not say that I like people to be ungrammatical, but I would rather hear some people who are ungrammatical and divine, than hear other people who are grammatical and utterly human. The preacher that came over to me and said, "Billy, you belong with Jesus," that is the fellow. He was a kind of a farmer fellow, and he grew all crops but hair, and he wore farmer clothes, and spoke about farming and sowing; and he said that there was a sower who went out to sow, and there was a great harvest; and everybody paid heed. And then he came and put his hand on my shoulder and said, "Billy, God wants you to be one of His farmers," and I came up the aisle of the schoolhouse, not to the chancel—there wasn't any—there wasn't anything but a dictionary in the schoolhouse, so I came up and bowed at the dictionary; and, O me, the wind was wild that night, it was as stormy as on the wide sea, the storm that beat upon that prairie schoolhouse; the wind had its chance, and blew like it did on the Sea of Galilee; and Christ came over and said, "Boy, what do you want down here?" and I said, "I want Thee, O Christ." And He said, "I have come."

Oh, people, there isn't anybody who ever drew breath, that knew how to draw the bow of steel and aim the arrow of strange words, golden and beautiful, who can use words beautiful enough for the preachers of God; and though they had small salaries and large families and few belongings and scant wealth, they had God. In their dreams they talked about God. Said an old preacher, in my hearing at a Conference, "Brother Quayle, I am so old, and have no business to be here; I have been superannuated for years, and I cannot preach; and O," he said—and his voice was as wistful as a mother's calling the name of her dead daughter; if you have ever heard that you will never forget it—"Brother Quayle, sometimes in my sleep in the night I awaken myself from my slumber because I dream I am preaching."

Thanks be to God for the preachers who thought so little of themselves because they thought so much of Christ! Thank God for the preachers who had not more sense than to go around visiting everybody, and did not know that anybody was lowly, did not know that there were lowly people in the world, but thought that there were only high people in the world because Christ died for them, and said to every one, "Brother, Christ spoke your name in my ear; and He said, 'He knew you all; come on over, come on over!'"

A Task Worth While

Brother Cranston, I think it is perfectly beautiful to consider this last thing which we have tackled. We have tackled everything we could think of, and something else. If there is anything we have not tackled I wonder what on earth it is. We take a collection for every sort of thing, and even for the folk that represent the illimitableness of the unknown we take a collection. Preachers take all the collections for everybody else, but never take a collection for themselves. They have been so busy caring for other people they forgot themselves. I think that is the greatest credential a Methodist preacher ever had: He was busy at the Task Golden. An old man who had whiskers long enough to anchor by put both hands into his whiskers and said, "Brother Quayle, I have been preaching sixty odd years, and for over fifty-eight years I never came home but a woman I loved met me at the door; and now," he said, with a great gasp and sob, "nobody meets me at the door"; and he said, "Brother Quayle, I did not have enough money to pay for her funeral; but if I had all the money that the churches I have served owed me and did not pay me, I would have ten thousand dollars, plus." O Church of the living God, we have got to be honest; we have got to be square for the sake of ordinary virtue, but O, we have got to do the square thing!

At a certain foreign-speaking Conference I was guest in a certain preacher's house. I felt that it was an imposition; and after a moment I said, "Living is up, politicians notwithstanding to the contrary; let me go." "No, you must stay here," he said; "my wife is the daughter of a Methodist preacher, and she says you have to stay here." So I said, "What your wife says stands; I will stay," and soon we were talking about her father, the preacher, and about her mother, the preacheress, and she said this thing which I thought was sweet. She said that her mother was dying with inflammatory rheumatism, and they moved her from room to room downstairs, and the pain was so terrible she could not stay in one room long, and they moved her around so tenderly, and she said, "One day mother said, 'Take me upstairs.' And the preacher said, 'Why, mother, sweetheart, we cannot take you upstairs; the doctor says the least jar might send the rheumatism to your heart.' She said, 'Take me upstairs.'" Women do not consider what the doctors say nor what the preachers say; when they want to do a thing that is the thing they want to do. The father said to the daughter, "You speak to your mother"; and the daughter said, "Mother, we cannot take you up"; and not any of them would touch her to take her up; so, being a woman, she went upstairs. The husband and the daughter came tagging after and said, "Mother, you will die on the stairs"; and she panted away on the stairs, but never turned back—did a woman ever turn back when she had set her heart on going? Finally she got upstairs, and went into a little room that had only one window; and they expostulated, "What makes you go into the poorest room in the house?" And she smiled. It transpired that the next day was Sunday, and it transpired that that little window looked straight into the back of the church and through that church up to the pulpit, and so that when she was lying in bed, propped up on the pillows, and her husband came into the pulpit on Sunday morning, she could see him. And she had climbed the stairs in jeopardy of her life that she might see her husband climb into the pulpit and stand behind the holy desk and open the Holy Book; and she lay there smiling, and the next day she was in the kingdom of God.

O Church of our supreme love, watch your minister climb into the pulpit and open the Holy Book! O Methodist Church, climb the stairs and watch your preacher preach, because, peradventure, he will open the truth of God so that mortality shall be swallowed up of life, and things little shall look large, and the glory of God shall come upon the heart. I think the Methodist Church is going to love its preacher in the pulpit out loud so he will know that somebody is hungry to see him and hungry to hear him and hungry to love him; and by and by, when he is clean tired out, will give him a chance to rest, and say to him, "Beloved, sit down and rest a while, until you get so rested up that you can climb the stairs yourself and land at the top in the arms of God."

William A. Quayle.

St. Paul, Minn.

The Preacher's Call

"The Spirit of the Lord God is upon me, because the Lord hath anointed me to preach."—Isa. 61. 1.

"Unto me is this grace given that I should preach."—Eph. 3. 8.

LOST MAGIC

The Bells of Louvain, cast a century ago by the famous molder, Van Den Steyn, had long since lost their sweetness, before they were destroyed in the ruined Belgian city.

Sadly he shook his frosted head,
  Listening and leaning on his cane.
"Nay, I am like the bells," he said,
  "Cast by the molder of Louvain."

Often you've read of their mystic powers,
  Floating o'er Flanders' dull lagoons;
How they would hold the lazy hours
  Meshed in a net of golden tunes!

Never such bells as those were heard
  Echoing over the sluggish tide:
Now like a storm crash, now like a bird,
  Flinging the carillons far and wide.

There in Louvain they swing to-day,
  Up in the turrets where long they've swung;
But the rare cunning of yore, they say,
  Somehow has dropped from the brazen tongue.

Over them shines the same pale sky,
  Under them stretch the same lagoons;
Out from the belfries, birdlike, fly,
  As from a nest, the same sweet tunes.

Ever the same, and yet we know
  None are entranced these later times
Just as the listeners long ago
  Were with the wonder of their chimes.

Something elusive, as viewless air,
  Something we cannot understand
Strangely has vanished of the rare
  Skill of the molder's master hand.

So when you plead that life is still
  Full as of old with tingling joy,
That I may hear its music thrill
  Just as I heard it when a boy,

All I can say is: "Youth has passed;
  Master of magic falls and swells,
Bearing away the cunning cast
  Into the molding of the bells."

PAVING THE LAST MILE FOR THE ITINERANT

THE REV. FREDERICK T. KEENEY, D.D.
President Permanent Fund Commission
Central New York Conference

God has a care for preachers. He has a special care, I think, for all whom He calls to special tasks of holy service. It began long ago, as is shown by the provision which He made for the Levites. They had no land, as had the others; but they had what was better than land, a place in the hearts of the people. God cared so much for them that He counted the neglect of the Levite as one of the chief sins of Israel. When the Israelite withheld his support, God withheld His crops, but when he cared for the Levite, God filled his granaries. The provision for the Levite's need was by divine appointment; and to it was ever linked a promise. The statute ran: "The Levite and the stranger, and the fatherless, and the widow, which are within thy gates, shall come, and shall eat and be satisfied; that the Lord thy God may bless thee in all the work of thine hand which thou doest."

If you would know God's richest blessing, give heart-room to the stranger, the fatherless, the widow, the Levite and the prophet. Until the Most High revokes His promise, no man is poorer for sharing the best he has with those who are the subjects of God's special care; to this the Shunnamite woman and the widow of Zarephath bear testimony.

The same truth is emphasized in the New Testament. Christ, the Good Shepherd, had special promises and tender messages for those whom He called to represent Him as under-shepherds of the flock. They came closer to His heart than did any others, and were more often in His prayers. They, too, had neither lands nor houses. They were to go forth without scrip or purse. There was need of neither, for Christ had provided for them a richer legacy—the hearts of those to whom they ministered. You might have thought them poor, but they were not. It might have seemed that they were having a hard time; but it was a triumphant journey all the way. True, there was many a paradox. They, like Paul, were sorrowful, yet always rejoicing; poor, yet making many rich; having nothing, and yet possessing all things; unknown, and yet well known; dying, yet very much alive; chastened, but not killed.

God's ministers in every century have been in this "apostolic succession." No life has more of paradoxes than that of the Methodist itinerant. There are the hard places, and there are the Mountains of Transfiguration; there are days of humiliation and defeat, and days of victory; there are days when one might wish to die, and there are days when one might wish to live a thousand years. There are joy-days enough, so that I ask no one to shed tears or to give a feather's weight of sympathy to the Methodist itinerant until he comes to the last mile. Then, if you can lighten the load a bit or help pave the way, you are doing a service so Christlike that angels well might covet the task. I speak of the last mile out of the fulness of an overflowing heart. I entered the Methodist itinerancy when I was two months and thirteen days old. I have lived under a parsonage roof through all the intervening years. Sometimes the roof has leaked, but more often not. Sometimes it was so low that there was not much room between one's head and the rafters; but usually it was high enough. Sometimes father's purse was so thin that one did not need an X-ray to see through it; but usually there was a ham or a spare rib hanging in the woodhouse. Sometimes the boys used to plague me because the knees of my trousers were patched; and said that the reason lay in the fact that my father made me pray so much that I wore them through prematurely; but I was always sure of at least one pair of pants, so long as father had some old trousers which could be made over, and mother did not lose her skill with the needle.

Father and I began preaching in 1863, when the price of everything was high, except the price of preaching. That was kept down to a strictly gold standard throughout the Civil War. During the first year of father's ministry he was the junior preacher on a large circuit. The Conference Minutes for that year report the salary received by both ministers as $200, with a donation of $260; but the Minutes do not tell how this sum was divided. Inasmuch, however, as the senior minister had five children, and years of experience, while my father had only a pair of twin baby boys, it is fair to assume that the junior preacher had the smaller share. In those days farmers were coining gold from the war prices, while from his meager income father was paying twenty dollars a ton for hay to feed his horse; for the itinerant who did not have a good horse was always subject to censure. The following year the Minutes are more definite, and disclose the fact that father received $162 salary and a donation of $214. But he preached five years before his salary and donation combined reached $500; as did many another itinerant who is now, staff in hand, wearily marching the last mile.

Father was a revival preacher and pastor of the old type who took God at His word, and who never knew that the fight was either long or hard until after the victory was won. Like many another, he could preach, exhort and pray until the morning, without weariness, if there was a seeking soul at the altar to be "prayed through." During the first winter of his ministry he held revival services continuously for five months at the various appointments on the circuit, and preached every night, without once undressing for a night's rest. For mother was not strong. My twin brother and I, less than a year of age, were companions in sorrow as in joy. If one cried, the other invariably joined him in vocal sympathy. During the day mother would care for us and look after the house, while father prepared for the evening service and made necessary calls. After his return from the evening service late at night, mother, worn with the day's work, retired; and father secured such rest as he might while lying upon the couch, ready to put wood on the fire frequently, to keep the old parsonage warm for the babies, and to care for them as occasion might require. When we slept well, he slept also; but if either of us awoke there was sure to be a wakeful company of three. I once asked him: "Father, would you enlist in the itinerancy over again, if the years were rolled back and you had the chance to begin again? Would you leave the old homestead, where four generations of our kindred have been born, and become a Methodist minister, moving here and there at the will of the Bishop and the people, and be glad to go, in the consciousness that God had called you to the ministry?" Then my father, four-score years old and helpless with paralysis, from the wheeled chair where he had been enthroned for five years made answer: "Fred, I would not wait a second to decide. I would rather spend my life as a Methodist minister than be a king." That day I realized, as I had never done before, that I had royal blood coursing through my veins.

I grant that it is not easy for a man with a heart to be moved every year or two or three, as these Veterans had to be under the time limit; or as pastors even now have to do all too frequently. It isn't easy to pull the heart up by the roots and transplant it to new soil, to say good-by to tried old friends, and look strangers in the face on the first Sunday after Conference knowing that if you learn to love them, some day you must say good-by to them also and move on. This is not a pleasant experience for a man with a heart; and the minister who has not a heart had better dig ditches than attempt to preach. But, nevertheless, there are so many compensations; so many good people whom the itinerant comes to know, so many hearts and homes open to take him in, so many precious promises, tested under a great variety of circumstances, that I ask no sympathy for the Methodist itinerant until he comes to the last mile. It is then that he needs heartening, and in most cases his purse needs to feel the touch of silver.

If one could always remain the pastor of one congregation he would have both love and coin sufficient to pave the last mile of the journey. He and the people would grow old together, and his gray hairs and advancing years would come on so silently as scarcely to be noticeable. Those whom he had led to Christ would not forget him; those whom he had joined in matrimony would remember him; and the children whom he had baptized would grow up ready to share with him, as long as they had aught to share with any one. But most men in the Methodist ranks come to retirement as the pastor of some little church where they have been known but a brief time. In their prime they may have served strong Churches. But the fever of haste is upon us, and the activities of Church life are so many, that the old man finds it difficult to keep the pace, and he has to ask for lighter work.

Often on the smaller charge, where the later years find him, he is not welcome. The church had asked the Bishop for a young man; and when a preacher nearing retirement was sent, though rich in both experience and years, it was but a scanty welcome that awaited him. In a year or two the people decide that they must have a change; and the Bishop is compelled to tell him that no charge wants him, and that nothing remains for him but retirement. It is then that I have seen the Veterans hurry out of the Conference room to hide their tears; and when their eyes were dry, I have known that their hearts were weeping. It is then that I pray God and the Church, in their pity for the preacher, to lighten the load and help pave the last mile of the way.

Did you ever hear an old preacher say that he wanted to "die in the harness"? I have heard it from the lips of scores. Do you know what he means? He means that some day he would like to bring a gospel message to some waiting congregation, look once more into their faces and feel the thrill of rapture coming back from their countenances, quickening his heart beat; at the close of the service pray with some seeker at the altar, and then lie down to sleep and wake up in glory. If ministers had their way there would never be a Retired Preacher. But God knows that we younger men need these old heroes to cheer us on and pray us through and hold up our hands, and knowing this, He sometimes delays their coronation.

Did you read that poem, inspired by the life of Amzi Smith, a Newark Conference pastor, who went home to glory after forty-three years' service on little country charges in Northern New Jersey? The son of another preacher paid tribute to his memory in words that might be written of many a hero in any Conference:

"Six hundred dollars was the most he earned
In any year, so far as I'm aware;
For two and forty years he lived on that,
Or less. Riches unsearchable he preached,
And drew this pittance for his household's needs.
And yet he seemed to think it was enough.
I do not know that ever he complained.
Perhaps it was enough, for he was fed
And clothed. His wife, the boys and girls, the horse,
All had enough. He had his work to do,
And did it faithfully, as unto God.

And where he labored hungry hearts were blest,
Sinners became good men. The village smiled
Where Amzi Smith abode.
As God blessed Obed-Edom and his house
The while the ark was there, so did He bless
The towns and fields and hamlets where this man
Dwelt, with God's glory in his humble soul.

O God, let not that race of giants die;
Give us more men like them, old-fashioned, brave,
True to the truth; men that have made the Church
Mighty, and glad, and songful in the past."

When these noble spirits come to the last mile, we are less than men, less than Christians, less than followers of John Wesley, if we do not pave it with our prayers, and with our love and gifts. When God calls men, and sets them apart as watchmen upon the walls of Zion, His call is for life. He wants no divided life nor service; and the Church wants no pastor whose one business is not to preach the gospel. If the minister gives himself wholly to the Church for his whole life, the Church is in honor bound to provide for him; not only during the years of his active service, but also when he is too old and feeble to work. Support for the last mile is as imperative as for the first. God might never have laid this honor and responsibility on the Church. He might have sent ravens to provide for His ministry as He did for Elijah. He might have sent angels to preach the unsearchable riches of Jesus Christ. But He knew that men were better.

I do not plead at this time for larger salaries, although in many cases they are pitifully small. Most churches mean to be generous, and to pay their pastor according to their ability and the light they have. But in some places the light is exceedingly dim. In too many cases the support promised is not paid. Throughout the entire denomination the deficiencies during the last fifty years total $5,000,000, and they have fallen upon the men who could least afford to bear them.

With a given salary, a minister cannot save as much as other men on the same income. No matter how small his salary may be, he must dress neatly and well, for no church wishes a "seedy" looking pastor. He must have a larger library than most men in his congregation; he must take more periodicals; he must travel more extensively; he must attend more conventions; he must be interested in every organization in his church, and be a contributor to each one. Sometimes by his own generosity he must shame wealthy and stingy laymen into giving. When Syracuse University was founded pastors who were receiving only $500 subscribed $500; and others on a salary of $1,000 subscribed $1,000; and they paid seven per cent interest until they could pay the principal.

Often the little that the minister has saved disappears through poor investments before he reaches the last mile; this is not strange. He does not have enough to invest to really learn how to invest, and often he secures his experience at the cost of his savings. He is honest himself and thinks that other people are, until he learns that much advice concerning investments is not devoid of self-interest. The nightmare of a preacher's dreams, whether waking or sleeping, is to provide for his loved ones and himself for the last mile.

The Church has been slow to recognize the fact that when the preacher comes to the last mile she should not treat him as a pauper but as a pensioner. She should not wound his spirit and break his heart by a dole of charity; but should count it a high honor and a joyous privilege to help make his last mile the brightest and the best. I am glad that we live at a time of enlarging vision, when the last mile of the itinerant's journey is appealing strongly to the Church; and when the men whose prayers and faith made possible the prosperity of the present, shall not only know that God has not forgotten them, but that the Church does not forget. The dawning of this new day for the Conference Claimant has been long delayed, but the sun is now up and is hastening toward the meridian. In the Central New York Conference it required twenty-four years to add $1,300 to the Permanent Fund for Conference Claimants. But during the last decade the funds have leaped from $17,000 to $200,000; and the slogan now is, "Three hundred thousand dollars by October 1, 1915." A mighty impulse was given to the movement four years ago when the son of one of our retired ministers presented the Conference with $50,000 in honor of his father and mother, who had spent their lives serving the smaller churches of the Conference. Had the father preached one hundred years the total salary received by him would not have exceeded the amount which his generous son gave in a single year. And, thank God, Methodism has many sons who are rich not only in gold but richer still in love for the Church, who will help pave with their gold the highway on which the itinerant travels his last mile.

Methodism is rich to-day, not alone in gold, but also in the lives of those whom God has called into her ministry, and in the memories that linger, like a golden halo, about the lives of those whom He has promoted to the Church Triumphant. No Annual Conference is without its heroic Veterans, who opened the way for us younger men to come into the Conference and share their honors; men who built the churches where we preach and the parsonages where we live; who led our fathers and mothers to Christ, and taught them the alphabet of prayer. We will not forget. The Church will not forget. God helping us, we will free the itinerant's last mile from anxious care, and so pave it with love as to make it the best mile of the entire journey, as he mounts up the steeps toward the city with sure foundations.

Syracuse, N. Y. FREDERICK T. KEENEY.

OLD AGE

HENRY WADSWORTH LONGFELLOW

It is too late! Oh! nothing is too late.
Till the tired heart shall cease to palpitate,
Cato learned Greek at eighty; Sophocles
Wrote his grand "Œdipus," and Simonides
Bore off the prize of verse from his compeers,
When each had numbered four score years;
And Theophrastus at four score years and ten
Had but begun his "Characters of Men."
Chaucer at Woodstock, with the nightingales,
At sixty wrote "The Canterbury Tales."
Goethe, at Thelmar, toiling to the last
Completed "Faust" when eighty years were past.

What then! Shall we sit idly down and say,
The night has come; it is no longer day?
The night has not yet come; we are not quite
Cut off from labor by the failing light;
Something remains for us to do, or dare
Even the oldest trees some fruit may bear;
For age is opportunity no less
Than youth itself, though in another dress;
The sky is filled with stars invisible by day.
Fast as the evening twilight fades away.

THE ROAD OF THE LOVING HEART

MILDRED WELCH

That it was they called it, the simple, Samoan Islanders, who built the road for their friend, Robert Louis Stevenson, "a name that brings us, as it were, a breeze blowing off the shores of youth."

The road was cut through the brush with much labor and toil, that, unhindered, the beloved story-teller might come and go between his house in the woods and the beach.

Along that road there came at sunset all his "friendly helpers in a foreign isle," to join with him and his family in the simple evening worship that bound all hearts together beneath the peace of his roof.

Fame, honor, wealth, and the love of unnumbered hearts, followed him. He, at least, could say that life had given him what he asked: "That he might awake each day with morning face and morning heart, eager to labor, eager to be happy if happiness should be his portion; and if the day were marked for sorrow, strong to endure it."

The day came at last when the Samoan chiefs carried him out by the Road of the Loving Heart to the crest of the hill that looks ever to the restless sea, and the storm-swept reefs, and there they laid him to rest, and on the stone they graved his own sunny-hearted words:

"Glad did I live and gladly die
  And I laid me down with a will.
Home is the sailor, home from sea,
  And the hunter, home from the hill."

The Road of the Loving Heart—how good it is that it was granted to one man, at least, to go home that way.

Do we ever think of a class of men, whom we send to their Father's House by the Road of the Sorrowful Way?

Men who, though lacking the special genius of Robert Louis

Stevenson, lack nothing of his courage, his patience, his sunny-hearted sacrifices.

Instead of fame, wealth, honor, they have long years in destitute home mission fields, long watches by the bed of the sick and the side of the dying, long rides in heat of summer and storm of winter. Have you ever seen them—that thinning line of old ministers, their shoulders stooped, their hair white, their eyes dimmed, their faces marred with others' sorrows?

One of them went home not long ago by the Road of the Sorrowful Way. When he died, many articles were written about him and his praises were sounded far and wide, but while he lived, he was in abject poverty and sometimes in humiliating need.

"I am sorry," he wrote, when he acknowledged the receipt of a pittance from the Relief Fund, "to have caused so much trouble, and ere another collection comes around I will be where the wicked cease from troubling and the weary are at rest."

Soon after the old Minister entered in "where beyond the voices there is peace."

The days slip by and our old ministers are going home. We choose the path they tread. Shall it be the Road of the Sorrowful Way, or do they enter that land where none shall say: "I am old," by the Road of the Loving Heart?

AN OLD MINISTER

SAMUEL McCOY

In hours when I review that one dear life—
  The life of that one Man whom most I owe—
And ponder whether rich or vain his strife,
  His toil repaid with bitter wage or no,
Day hardly softened, though it be near done,
I cry in pity. Yet the westering sun,
  With glory not of earth, lights up his face,
And heaven hallows him as who has won
  His earthly fight, far beyond power to trace
My helpless love; and peace rests in his eyes,
  And God's high calling is his matchless prize.

FANNY CROSBY'S OFFERING

FANNY CROSBY

94 Years Young

LOVE'S RECOMPENSE

AN APPEAL IN BEHALF OF RETIRED MINISTERS

There is a work of love and duty
  That devolves upon us all.
There is a tender, pleading message,
  And its tones like music fall:
Help our weary Veteran Preachers,
  Scatter roses o'er their way:
Rally round them, hasten quickly—
  Not to-morrow, but *to-day.*

From the well of deep affection
  Now their hearts with gladness fill,
Do not wait their names to honor,
  Till the pulse of life is still.
Break the box of alabaster,
  Pour its oil upon them now,
Make their dwelling bright and happy,
  Wreathe in smiles each furrowed brow.

They have borne the royal standard
  Of our Master and our Lord.
From the time of early manhood
  They have preached His Holy Word.
But their strength has lost its vigor,
  And their cheek its youthful glow;
For the frost of age has touched them
  And their locks are white as snow.

Watchman on the walls of Zion
  Though their feet no more will stand,
From the top of Pisgah's mountain
  Faith beholds the promised land.
Soon triumphant like an army
  Marching through the realms above,
They will shout the grand old story,
  Robed in white and crowned with love.

Fanny J. Crosby—blind, bowed with age, but yet clear of mind—gave expression to the following rich sentiment at her home in Bridgeport, Conn., on her ninety-fourth birthday:

"As for my age, it doesn't seem to me that I am in the nineties, and I attribute my good health and long life to the fact that I never let anything trouble me, and to my implicit faith, my implicit trust in my heavenly Father's goodness. If I didn't get the thing I wanted to-day, well, I'd get it to-morrow; if not then, I realized that it wasn't good for me to have it. Everybody is born for something, has a talent for something, and with a little patience will find his or her place in the world. You will conquer only by love. Love is the great engine which is going to reform the world."

Blind, we call her? She reverses the declaration of the Lord addressed to the Pharisees—she *not* having eyes, seeth.

What a remarkable life she has lived! We cannot hope to have her with us long; but her philosophy of sunshine, of trust, of love, will abide as long as hearts are hungry and men seek the truth.

Frances Ridley Havergal's question and answer give the larger meaning of the life of our Sweet Singer:

"How can she sing in the dark like this?
What is her fountain of light and bliss?
O, her *heart can see*, her heart can see!
And its sight is strong and swift and free!"

When we planned our program in behalf of the old preachers we wrote to her, asking for a song, and were told "that she would be pleased to write a hymn for so worthy a cause." We assured her that such a service would be greatly appreciated, especially by the Retired Ministers, the widows and orphans, and in due time received the following letter:

Bridgeport, Conn., August 24, 1909.

Dear Dr. Hingeley:

I trust you will allow me to substitute a poem for the song I promised you. It seemed to me that I could better present a plea in a poem to be read than in a song. I have written the same and enclose it herewith.

Could I voice my inmost thoughts in words I am sure the appeal would touch every member of the Church. I pray that what I have written will touch many.

Sincerely, FANNY J. CROSBY.

A RETIRING COMPETENCY AND THE CALL TO PREACH

THE REV. L. J. BIRNEY, D.D.
Dean Boston University School of Theology

The strongest appeal made to strong men is not that of the sovereignty of God, but of the dependence of God. The amazing extent to which God has made Himself dependent upon men for the consummation of His plans captures the loyalty of great souls. The revelation of divine dependence grows with every new discernment of the laws that control the moral elevation of life. Every point of contact between divine and human life reveals it. We desire to speak of one of the most significant of these; the point at which God endeavors to lift a life into the prophetic character and function.

The Call

The very existence of the apostolic order, as inseparable from the whole plan of redemption, vividly reveals how God must wait upon the aid of man in seeking highest ends. He can make mountains and moons without him, but without him He cannot morally change the humblest countryside. The calling of the twelve is the symbol of a perpetual process.

But the divine dependence is not seen best in the fact that He must call prophets, but rather in the countless human elements and influences upon which the effectiveness of that call depends. A recent writer on the call to preach says that one characteristic of the call to the ministry is that it is always effective, that everyone whom God would call to preach will eventually preach. That is not true. One wonders if the writer ever mingled closely with men.

It would be as reasonable to say that no one ever enters the ministry except those really chosen of God; a claim which with difficulty would win the assent of the Pew. This very hour there are hundreds of men, busy in trade and profession, whom God intended for the ministry and who would have wrought mightily as prophets of the Most High. That this is true is witnessed by the repentant confession of many; though not less sad is the fact that others will be unconscious of it to the end of the day. For God's call to the ministry comes more often in the still small voice, which may be lost in the din of world voices, than in earthquake or fire; and, as the Christian ideal becomes more dominant and universal, the still voice becomes more and more, and the earthquake less and less, the means divinely used. A very large percentage of the most effective prophets of our time received no irresistible call, but a quiet conviction in an open mind that life would mean most for God and humanity if spent in the ministry.

The Call Obscured

Among the influences which tend to obscure the call, what of the meager and pitiful provision for the closing years? And at once we say, and with emphasis, that the young man to whom the call comes with clear and unmistakable conviction, who seeing the meager income that makes saving almost impossible, and years of probable penury at the close, and because of that alone turns back to this present world as Demas did, is no better than Demas was. In him is no stuff of which heroes are made, and the loss is not great. We doubt indeed if there are many whom God has called and chosen, and in whose souls that call rings clear, who are turned back by the threatening lion of want. But whenever that does occur, the Church will share the guilt. For a great Church like ours has no moral right thus to create a purely artificial and wholly unnecessary hardship. It is vastly different from the hardships and the perils that face the pioneer, or the missionary to a savage people who are ruled by savage ideals. That kind of hardship is as inseparable from the process of human redemption as was the cross. But the suffering of which we speak comes from those who have accepted all the vast benefits of the gospel truth, who do understand its message of love. It originates in the ingratitude and selfishness of those who have received that message; and it falls heavily upon the life of those whose feet, now weary, were once beautiful upon the mountains, as they brought the glad tidings of peace. The burden falls upon them on account of the neglect of a great

Church, which has power with ease to lift the last burden from the last years of the last man who has labored long and well in the great world task. The Church must share the guilt of the man whose unwillingness to bear the fruits of her negligence closes his eyes in disobedience to the heavenly vision.

But the greatest loss is not among those in whom the call has matured to unmistakable conviction. The real mischief is done long before the call is realized, and in a far more insinuating, subtle and effective way. It is done by seriously prejudicing the mind of the youth of the Church against a calling which the Church permits to be surrounded too often by an air of pauperism and want. Every call to preach has a psychological background, upon which the call is dependent to an undreamed-of extent. Ninety-five per cent of those who have heard and heeded the call to preach spent their childhood and youth in an atmosphere where the ministry was honored and that call not opposed. Upon that background God is largely dependent for His ministry. That law works as readily in the opposite direction. The influences that tend to make the ministry unattractive to youth, lowering its dignity and strength, tend to make a mental background against which it is exceeding difficult for the Holy Spirit to place His call with power; just as the attitude of a home in opposition to the Church or to the Christian life creates in the child of the home a mental attitude through which it is vastly more difficult for the Spirit to bring conviction.

Prejudicing Youth

Among the influences that create early prejudice against the highest of all callings, the failure of the Church to give that calling a self-respecting freedom from the fear of want is by no means the least. I will never be able to eradicate the impression made upon my mind by the annual presentation of the "worn-out preachers' cause," as it was then called, and by two or three examples of aged need and dependence, creating as they did not only a sense of pity, but as in every healthy lad, a sense of injustice and revolt. The heroism and sacrifice called for in the life and work of a minister appeal to the soul of the normal lad. These need never be minimized. But to place the minister in the position of a suppliant, a beggar, and a dependent disgusts the normal youth, and all unconsciously lays a foundation of opposition to influences human and divine that would lead him to choose that work.

The Church of Christ has no moral right to allow the greatest calling God ever permits men to enter, to be compromised in the minds and hearts of the youth of the Church just at the time when ideals are taking their deepest root, when ambitions are shaping, and just at the time when the dignity and strength of a life work makes its strongest appeal. Prejudice the mind of the boy at that age and we add inexpressibly to the difficulty with which the Spirit of God will reach him for the ministry. Not the veteran worn with the toil of the years, who thrills his heart like the uncertain steps of an old soldier, but the position of mendicancy in which the man who has bravely done his work is placed—that is what helps to close the heart of many a youth against the Spirit's voice.

The Lure of Other Callings

The dignity and importance of the ministry suffer further, in comparison with the substantial appeal made to the youth of the Church, by other callings, and the community attitude toward these. The teaching profession is being more and more placed upon a basis of ample provision for the final years, not as a charity but as a just compensation for service rendered the community. Its importance to society and its essential greatness are thereby attested. The ministry is far more fundamental to world uplift, but the present provision of the Church for the man who has given his life to it does not certify that fact to the youth of the Church. A provision which secures the comfort of the minister in the years when his strength has been spent, and secures it on a basis of self-respect, will more convincingly evaluate to the rising generation the dignity of apostleship than any eloquence poured out to establish its greatness.

One of the first duties of the Christian layman is to place the ministry upon a basis that will say, not in word but in substantial fact, to every youth seeking the place in which to invest his life, "Here is a task we hold to be above every task in dignity of its own and in the significance of its results. If God will let you enter it, His Church will see to it that your every care and energy may be spent for His Kingdom and not in anxious solicitation concerning the years ahead."

The Minister's Hearthstone

There is another word that must not be left unsaid. Every minister has sacred right to the hearthstone and the dear faces around it. That he may come near the heart of the race, love and home are God's sweet gifts to him. While no woman is worthy a place at the side of God's chosen prophet, who is not willing to suffer with him to the end, if need be, yet no man is worthy either to be the prophet of God, an example to the people, or the husband of a noble woman, who is willing to see her suffer. And in many a brave young man's heart there is at this point a moral struggle that breaks up the very deeps of his life. As fine and sweet a bit of unheralded heroism as I know is where two souls, in the face of promised worldly comfort and plenty in other tasks, and with examples of aged penury for the prophet, go out together accepting if need be the latter rather than lose the heavenly vision. But the Methodist Episcopal Church has no moral right to darken that sacred experience in the life of God's chosen prophet by the cloud of fear and apprehension for the future; no moral right to place in the path at that holy moment the terrific temptation to retreat by creating a struggle between love and duty. As clear and as definite as is God's call to the two who stand thus at the altar to go forth, even at the risk of want, is God's call to the great and wealthy Church to whose service they consecrate their lives, to see to it that there shall be no want to fear, and that such a struggle shall be forever unnecessary.

Rural Ministry

The call to certain specific types of ministry, of greatest importance, is seriously affected by the failure of the Church to provide amply for the final years. The rural ministry is the very hope of the Church and indeed of Christian civilization. Three fourths of the leaders of all the great professions and industries were born and reared in the rural sections. A very large percentage of the urban Church membership came from rural churches and received their first religious impressions there; and over 80 per cent of our whole Methodist membership is now in the country and the lesser cities. That field under modern conditions and with modern methods is becoming increasingly attractive. It is imperative that there be raised up a trained rural ministry which shall volunteer for life work in that vast and important field. This the schools of theology are endeavoring to do. Few things will help more effectively to create such a ministry than will the assurance that when work is done there shall be no wolf at the door. Ministerial support in the rural work must in the nature of the case continue to be small, and little or nothing can be laid by. Much of the eagerness to pass from the country to the city pastorate originates in the desire to provide for the future. Better far that the Church provide for the future and send a host of strong, well-trained men to perform that most significant of tasks.

City Problems

This is not less true of the pioneer sections where vast harvest fields will wave white for the reaper in the not distant future if the planting is done before the tares have choked the ready and fertile soil. Numberless villages are springing out of the earth at the touch of the magic wand of "profit," centers of coming empires. To-day is the critical time which will decide the type of their coming civilization. To-day is the time when they should receive the indelible stamp of Christian ideals, which will only be given by the man sent of God and the Church. It is a heroic task, done in a noble fashion by our fathers in the faith. But the conditions that face the prophet to-day are vastly different from those under which our fathers toiled. It is an age which not only lifts the standard of comfort and respectability and decency far higher, but likewise an age when the purchasing power of the ministers' pittance is far less than it was then. God would call to that heroic task some of the most virile and stalwart youth in the Church. It will help Him beyond estimate, if His Church will stand with Him and pledge these modern pioneers that their faithful toil of to-day in those fields of meager remuneration will lay up for them treasures on earth as well as in heaven, which the Church will give to them in the years of rest and setting sun. All we have said of these two special forms of the ministry is equally true of the ministry whose gigantic task it is to evangelize the vast multitudes from foreign shores.

Even though it were true that none whom God may call would hesitate because of the Church's failure to provide, yet the Church has no moral right to capitalize devotion to duty. Yonder across their early teens comes shouting and glad a mighty company whose faces are beautiful with hope. With them comes One upon whom all hopes depend. He is choosing as he walks with them, with voice so still they scarce can hear it, choosing those who are to go forth with Him to the conquest of the world. And as He chooses, I think I hear Him say to His Church in a voice that has accent of command, "See to it, O Church of Mine, that these I choose may go with me in a devotion undivided, a consecration untormented by fears of the future, for it is because of my faith in my Church that I bid them 'Come with me, and be not anxious for to-morrow.'"

Boston, Mass. L. J. Birney.

A PASTOR

Dr. John G. Holland

He knows but Jesus Christ, the crucified.
Ah, little recks the worldling of the worth
Of such a man as this upon the earth!
Who gives himself—his all—to make men wise
In doctrines which his life exemplifies.

The years pass on, and a great multitude
Still find in him a character whose light
Shines round him like a candle in the night;
And recognize a presence so benign.
That to the godless even it seems divine.

He bears his people's love within his heart.
And envies no man, whatsoe'er his part.
His church's record grows, and grows again,
With names of saintly women-folks and men.
And many a worldling, many a wayward youth,
He counts among the trophies of his truth.

O, happy man! There is no man like thee,
Worn out in service of humanity.
And dead at last, 'mid universal tears,
Thy name a fragrance in the speaker's breath,
And thy divine example life in death.

"A RIPER, MORE TRANSCENDENT YOUTH"

Just sixty-two? Then trim thy light,
And get thy jewels all reset;
'Tis past meridian, but still bright,
And lacks some hours of sunset yet.
At sixty-two
Be strong and true,
Scour off thy rust, and shine anew.

'Tis yet high day; thy staff resume,
And fight fresh battles for the truth;
For what is age but youth's full bloom,
A riper, more transcendent youth?
A wedge of gold
Is never old;
Streams broader grow as downward rolled.

At sixty-two life is begun;
At seventy-three begin once more;
Fly swiftly as you near the sun,
And brighter shine at eighty-one.
At ninety-five,
Should you arrive,
Still wait on God, and work and thrive.

Keep thy locks wet with morning dew,
And freely let thy graces flow;
For life well spent is ever new,
And years anointed younger grow.
So work away,
Be young for aye,
From sunset, breaking unto day.

A RAIN OF THE ROSES

ROBERT LORRMAN

"It isn't raining rain to me,
It's raining daffodils;
In every dimpled drop I see
Wild flowers on the hills.
The clouds of gray engulf the day
And overwhelm the town;
It isn't raining rain to me,
It's raining roses down.

"It isn't raining rain to me,
But fields of clover bloom,
Where every buccaneering bee,
May find a bed and room;
A health unto the happy,
A fig to him who frets,
It isn't raining rain to me,
It's raining violets."

A RETIRING COMPETENCY AND MINISTERIAL EFFICIENCY

BISHOP
FRANCIS J. McCONNELL, D.D., LL.D.

I was very much impressed once when I heard Dr. Hingeley say that he thought the emphasis on the old preacher as a subject for benevolence had been overdone, and I was very much pleased when in the *Veteran Preacher* he quoted a remark of a Bishop to the effect that he had never known of a Retired Minister of the Gospel starving to death. I am glad that the accent is being placed at another point. As a matter of fact, when you look up the history of the Church not any of them have starved to death. They have been pretty well taken care of, but it has not been done in a systematic way, nor according to a regular plan; and we have begun to place the accent on inherent right and justice under the compelling motive of gratitude.

For myself, I am not so very much impressed when a man says, "We must make some kind of a retiring fund in order to make the proper appeal to young men." There is something in it, perhaps, but if that is what young men are thinking of they are not exactly of the type that have gone before them. I can see force in the argument that we are in line with the great social movement. In these days we are insisting more and more that organizations of all kinds shall prepare for and anticipate the needs of the old age of those who serve in the day of their strength. But it seems to me there is one line of argument in these days that we cannot sufficiently stress, important as the other lines may be, and that is the need of making the present ministry more effective.

Old Age Investments

There are some things of a very simple kind that, as far as my limited observation goes, do cut into the effectiveness of Methodist ministers, and one thing is the temptation to make some kind of an investment out of their limited salaries, that will surely provide for old age. One picture in my mind here to-night is the picture of a Methodist Bishop, not now living, who once, when I was a good deal younger than I now am, came to me to consult about his finances. He said, "If you had any money to invest how would you go about it?" I was a good deal in the position of a colored brother who was asked to change a ten-dollar bill, who said, "I cannot change the bill, boss, but I thanks you for the compliment." I felt a good deal like that when talking to this venerable Bishop, and said this perfectly commonplace thing, "If I had money to invest I would put it in sure bonds, yielding four or four and a half per cent, and if I could get five per cent, I would take that." There is something pathetic in the picture of that man saying, "I do not dare to do that. I do not care to have my wife thrown on the generosity of the Church when I am gone, and I have to take some risk; so my money is in stocks." If we could gather before us the Methodist ministers who have tried to make investments in order to care for their old age, we would find a great host; and may be I am touching a tender spot to-night; but really this thing, insignificant as it may appear at first glance, does cut into the effectiveness of ministers. They do make investments. Some smooth man tells them all is right, and the first thing they know everything is gone. If that does not cut into the effectiveness of a Methodist minister I do not know what will.

I have a book at home that tells how to promote certain speculative enterprises. I did not get it because I desired hints in that direction. It tells what classes of persons to send circulars to, and it groups ministers in two classes. It says that in some denominations the preachers receive larger salaries than in the others, and—I use its language—it tells how to get at the "easy marks." In the first group are the Presbyterians and the Episcopalians, and in the second group are the Methodists and Baptists. They put us in the second class because we do not have large sums of money to invest, not because we are any the less eager to invest. It is apparently an insignificant thing, but, nevertheless, one of the best ways to increase the effectiveness of a Methodist minister is to give him no excuse to worry about investments.

Giving All to the Work

There is another duty that occurs to me, and it has nothing to do with the benevolent phases of the problem but only with the effectiveness of the present ministry, and that is the doing of all we can to keep the ministers from getting into outside enterprises, and to keep them where they will be giving all their thought as well as their time to the service of the kingdom of God. Another man comes to my mind who graduated from an Eastern university and afterwards went into the ministry, and took the very largest appointments in a great Conference in the Central West, and was really a great man until he began to get interested in all manner of side enterprises. I remember that at one time he had managed to get together a great deal of money, and went into a farming enterprise, investing all his money in what Dr. Borden P. Bowne used to call "the inhabitants of the sty." After he had invested all his money in them, forgetful of the fact of their liability to infirmities, one night they woke up squealing, and two or three days afterward ceased to squeal, and all his money and the money of several other preachers had gone. They were doing what the Bishop said he had to do—they had been taking risks. Soon things were made uncomfortable for him in his Conference. That man to-day, with a long and successful career in the pastorate behind him, is selling odds and ends in a Western city. I would not say that his worry over the future had everything to do with this, but it grew from that start.

If we wish to keep men down to the right kind of preaching, let their minds have nothing to do with worry for the future; and if we wish to keep men to a bold utterance, make it possible for them to keep these things out of mind. When men go into the Methodist ministry they know that they will not receive such salaries as other men receive, and that they will not retire on a large pension, but if you make it sure that they need not worry about the future it will all come back in the effectiveness with which they work. A certain great military hero was sent to do a singularly hazardous piece of work. He came back alive, and somebody, anxious to know the thrill he had, asked what his feelings were as he went forward to that fearfully hazardous task. He replied that "the greatest feeling of satisfaction I had was the knowledge that in case I went down, I had the future arranged for, so far as my own private affairs were concerned, and that the government of the United States would care for those dependent upon me. These were the things in my mind as I went into that place of danger."

Ministerial Boldness

Wendell Phillips was once asked what he thought of the ministry. He said, "I think the ministry is ill prepared in one way. The ministers ought to be so provided for that they will have no thought concerning financial worry. A minister ought to be a man for whom in that sense of the word somebody will provide, so he can speak the truth with the utmost boldness, without any fear of consequences." In these days, when men have to rebuke evils and to deal faithfully with those committed to their care, at least this much of certainty ought to be in their minds, that if they will stand like prophets of the living God and speak forth words of prophecy, they need not worry concerning the future. We are to follow in John Wesley's footsteps and be men of one work, and if we lose a certain boldness and begin to care for the things of this life, a large part of the effectiveness of the ministry of the present day to the present generation will be gone.

I am glad that we are getting the emphasis off poverty and are ceasing to talk of the hardships of the older ministers, and are placing the Veterans' Cause on a systematic basis and getting down to the fact that what we are after all along the line is an effective ministry. We are beginning to get hold of the young because we know how much depends upon them, and we are training them from the start; and we try to get hold of the young men and to train them from the start for an educated ministry, and we are doing this other thing, not merely because of the justice of so doing, but for the practical success of the ministry in this day of the world, and to make it a more effective instrument, so that Methodist preachers can give themselves whole-heartedly to the entire work to which they are sent, by being relieved of care for their future old age.

Denver, Colo. Francis J. McConnell.

SAVING vs. EFFICIENCY

THE REV. J. W. VAN CLEVE, D.D.
Vice-President Board of Conference Claimants

LARGE SALARIES OR PENSIONS. The words which form the title of this paper define a real and vital issue. In the matter of caring for Retired Ministers we are shut up to a choice between two possible solutions. One is to pay the preacher a salary with a liberal surplus above living expenses and then leave him to his own devices. Whether he shall spend his old age in comfort or in penury is to depend wholly upon his own frugality and wisdom. If he fails to save his money and to keep it, then he is to be left to suffer the consequences of his neglect, precisely as other shiftless people do. This policy makes a fine superficial show of wisdom and justice, of the distinctively worldly type, but from the higher viewpoint it discloses discouraging gaps. The alternative is to pay the minister a fair working salary, while he is fit for work, and to encourage him to spend his salary for his equipment and development by providing a comfortable pension for his failing years. It is almost the reverse of the other plan in that it makes the future of the minister depend wholly upon his ministerial service.

COMBINATION POLICY FALLACIOUS. The time-worn policy of trying to combine these two into a scheme which offers neither sufficient savings nor sufficient Church support, and pieces out a little savings from a slender salary, with a little giving from the Church later on, cannot be accepted as a real solution. It is a perpetual temporizing without either a rational basis or an adequate result. No solution can be acceptable or final, which does not, in its general outlines, commend itself to the men who are most deeply and directly concerned in it as just and equal. No such conviction of substantial justice can ever be produced by this policy of patchwork. The very attempt to administer such a policy involves us in immediate perplexity over questions concerning relative economic deservings—questions that will not be pushed aside, but which cannot well be answered.

The Question of Frugality. Should the man who has neglected to save money receive for that reason a larger allowance, so that he may live as comfortably as his more frugal brother? If we have supplied a man with an income that would enable him to save, and have done this in order that he might save, ought he not to be required to save or be penalized for his failure so to do? Should not the frugal man profit by his frugality? If they are to receive an equal allowance, shall it be large enough to provide a reasonable degree of comfort for the improvident man, or just enough to afford a bare subsistence for the man who has lived frugally? If the former of these standards is adopted, then, in a way, we shall be paying both men twice, when one of them does not need it; if we adopt the latter we shall have the unedifying spectacle of an old Methodist preacher in want, a thing which we never shall be able to justify to the world. If the question of relative frugality and wastefulness is to be considered, how shall it be determined? If a man were to ignore the needs of his own kin—parents, brothers, sisters—because they were not of his immediate household, we would hardly commend him for his prudence; and yet on just such prudence might depend the margin between a surplus and a bare balancing of receipts and expenditures. Sometimes a large factor in what passes for economy and thrift is a species of shrewd bargaining which at least contributes nothing to ministerial efficiency. Furthermore, the temptation to cross the line between a fair bargain, and what is popularly known as a "great bargain" is not always resisted. Ministers with a little surplus cash have been known to take advantage of the necessities of the unfortunate in ways, that, while technically honest, were nevertheless calculated to cast a lasting shadow of reproach upon the Church and the ministry. Again, what calls itself by the name of economy may be a lack of liberality. No small hindrance to the benevolent work of the Church has come from the penuriousness of well-to-do preachers. The matter of frugality is far from being as simple as it looks.

How will it be possible among so many factors to decide whether a man is to be accounted as frugal or as something less commendable? Every man is convinced that he has used all possible diligence and frugality, and will feel that he has been unjustly dealt with unless treated accordingly.

THE QUESTION OF SALARIES. It is the same issue which appears in the question, "Ought not the man who has received a smaller salary to be correspondingly favored in the distribution to Conference Claimants?" The minister who has received $1,500 ought to have saved more, and should therefore be less needy, and receive a smaller allotment than the one who has never received more than $1,000. This also is only a superficial securing of justice. Differences in salary may count for something, but often they do not. Always they count for less than is popularly supposed, and they are by no means conclusive in individual cases. Size of income is only one factor in making up the account. The situations which offer the larger salaries usually impose a higher standard of living; the size of a salary cannot be considered wholly apart from the number of people it is to support; the variant of perquisites evades all calculations, sometimes being a negligible quantity and sometimes a noticeable addition to the income; a family handicapped by the frequent or continuous illness of some of its members is not on equal terms with one in which health is practically unbroken; some men have a positive genius for attracting gifts and donations outside of the salary, which is lacking in other men who are equally good and efficient. These considerations are quite enough to show how indefinite and unsatisfactory must be any distribution which can be made under this patchwork combination of personal savings and Church contributions.

DESERVING OR NECESSITIES. Further confusion and difficulty are introduced into the problems by the commingling of deservings and necessities. Neither under this plan can be entirely left out of the accounting. The plan rests upon the assumption that the minister has earned a life-time support, a part of which is still due and unpaid. The only tangible evidence that he has not received it is the fact that he does not have it. This fixes as the actual basis of his claim, not his past services or his past receivings but his present poverty. No matter how we try to disguise it, this scheme makes the

Retired Minister an object of the charity of the Church. It will be difficult, if not impossible, to obtain an adequate support upon such a plea. Men do not feel toward their charities the compelling sense of obligation which binds them to the payment of their debts. Furthermore, we shall not be able to secure for any man, however worthy, who is an object of charity the respect which is freely accorded the man who lives upon an income which is justly and securely his own. Under such a system, the preacher must not only expose his poverty, but he must justify it in order to establish his claim to support. Before the equity of his claim can be fully recognized, he must set at rest all the questions heretofore enumerated, which relate to the wise and frugal use of his money. They may not be asked explicitly and officially, but they will be implied in the minds of his brethren, and cannot be ignored by those who are to adjust his claim. In some way or other it will be inquired whether or not he is really poor and in need; how poor he is, and how he came to be so poor. This system converts what ought to be a Roll of Honor into something not far from a roll of dishonor. It tends to defeat itself by weakening the incentive to save. It is a policy which never arrives anywhere. Instead of solving the problem it effectually blocks the way to a solution. One of the two propositions already stated must be definitely adopted and definitely worked out in order that we may have a consistent policy that we can follow to the end.

An Expensive Policy. I present the proposition to solve the problem by paying such salaries as will afford a good margin for savings, because sometimes it seems to be offered in all seriousness by men who are sincere and liberal. Too often it is offered by men who show no disposition to provide the liberal salary required. The emphasis seems to be on the savings and not on the salaries, as if the end really sought were to get rid of responsibility for the support of Retired Ministers. No thoughtful man offers this plan as a measure of economy. It is the most expensive proposition ever propounded, if it is to be made genuinely effective. A salary which, by pinching economy under favorable conditions, will yield some little savings for a very frugal man is not enough. For this plan a salary must be paid which will permit the ordinary man without cutting his living expense below the level of efficiency to lay up enough to keep him in comfort after his working days are over. If the minister has saved enough to keep him in comfort then it is because the amount over and above a comfortable living has been paid him by the Church. It is held in his own name as his own possession and at his death passes to his heirs. In this way the Church loses all further benefit from it, and must immediately begin to provide a like sum for the man who follows him. If the Church either as an organization, or by its individual members, holds this sum in its own possession, paying the income of it to the Retired Minister, then at his death it may begin to use the same funds for the support of another man.

EMBARRASSING GAPS. This proposition is not only expensive but displays embarrassing gaps. It misses the case of the man who lacks the gift to save. Such a man is not to be reproached for his deficiency in this respect any more than is the man who lacks eloquence to be reproached for his deficiency. In spite of admonitions and reproaches some men seem never to acquire the gift of acquiring. Other men are the victims of persistent or repeated misfortunes which make savings impossible. If a policy were possible which would leave each man to care for himself with his own savings, it would simply condemn all men in these two classes to inevitable want. In spite of its outward show of justice, we somehow cannot help feeling that for a Methodist preacher, who has been a faithful servant of God and of the people, to be in want for the ordinary comforts of life, or to spend his last days in a poorhouse, or to be placed in the position of becoming a dependent upon charity, would be an unseemly thing.

THE EFFICIENCY TEST. But pass by these considerations and put the issue between these two policies squarely upon the point of efficiency.

I quote from an article relative to teachers' pensions, contributed to the Outlook by Martha Bensley Bruere. We need scarcely do more than substitute "preacher" for "teacher" in order to make the article serve the purpose of this discussion, for the principle is identical and the facts parallel.

TEACHING EFFICIENCY MARRED. "I have before me the family budgets of a series of high school teachers and college professors, men on salaries ranging from $1,200 to $4,000 a year, and living across the country from Maine to California.

In every case but one it is easy to see how old age and the fear of it is like a paralyzing hand to mar the efficiency of their homes. The fear of the future drives these men to save as the only way to provide for the future, and tends to reduce below the efficiency line the amount of money they are at liberty to spend on their homes and their professional equipment."

Two items from the budget of a high school teacher receiving a salary of $1,800 a year are Insurance $140, Savings Bank $325. These represent the drain on the family income in order to provide for the future. The insurance is a slight defense for the family in case of death of the bread-winner, and would probably yield scarcely enough to provide a home. The bank item represents a provision for old age none too large for its purpose. If it were to continue for thirty years, with no draft for sickness, non-employment, accident or other emergency, it would scarcely amount to more than enough to provide an income of $400 a year. Over against these items put the following from the same budget: "Food, $180; Papers, Magazines, etc., $7; Vacation, $50."

From the letter of a professor's wife which accompanied her budget the following excerpts are taken:

"You will see from this schedule that it is absolutely necessary that I should do all my work, including my laundering. Trying to put our children through Eastern Colleges was too much for some of us, for I have been under a severe mental strain, and our daughter has been in a sanitarium for months because of a nervous break-down." "After my husband outlives his usefulness he and I will have to live on $250 a year."

The writer of the article asked the head of a great school system this question: "If you knew that you would have a pension for your old age, and that your family would be provided for if you died, would it make any difference in your work?" His answer was, "It would make me thirty—no, forty—per cent more efficient right now. The thought of what might happen to them, if I were scrapped, is a ball and chain on my foot holding me back from no end of things I might and ought to do." Dr. Henry D. Pritchett is quoted as saying: "A large proportion of the teachers in American Universities are engaged in turning the grindstone of some outside employment with one hand while they carry on the work of teaching with the other."

One Exception. The one exception found by the writer of the article, in which efficiency was not being paralyzed by fear of the future, or fettered by the struggle to save, was that of a teacher receiving only a moderate salary who was entitled to a competent pension, with a half allowance for his wife in case of his death, so that he was perfectly free to invest the whole of his salary in equipment and development.

Preachers and Teachers. Every consideration which this article advances relative to the efficiency of teachers applies to the minister with equal or even greater force. The average salary of the teachers of the country is slightly in advance of that of the ministers. Proportionally a larger number of teachers are unmarried than of ministers; while the longer vacation of the teacher offers an economic opportunity which the minister does not have; but nevertheless the whole relation between savings and efficiency for the minister is fairly set forth in these extracts.

Efficiency Waste. Their first suggestion is, that it is not wise to raise the issue, much less to force the issue, between the hoarding of money for future necessity and its use for present efficiency. If we leave a man to depend upon his savings for his comfort in retirement, inevitably we raise this issue. No one really expects the salaries of the rank and file of the ministers to be raised to such a figure as will enable them to provide for all reasonable demands for ministerial equipment, and at the same time to lay up a sum that will enable them to secure their future beyond peradventure. There will be a constant tendency to pare down investment in efficiency to the lowest possible limit in order to allow increased investment in savings. The loss in efficiency which results from the diversion of money to the savings account is only a part of the loss. There is a savings policy which involves a certain efficiency waste. I do not undervalue or oppose economy. A wise and well-directed economy is in itself a wholesome exercise. But it must have behind it not the lash of a motive which is a consumer of nerve force, but the exhilarating push of a motive which of itself is an inspiration. An economy over-driven by the fear of want is likely to waste over savings, time and energy that ought to be expended in production. In the period of my ministerial apprenticeship a young man came to my study with the familiar hard-luck story, "Out of money and out of work." His immediate needs were met. He claimed to be a carpenter, and I persuaded a good-natured contractor to give him a job. A few days later I asked him about the young man. "That fellow!" said the contractor. "I fired him." "What for?" I asked. "Wasn't he a good workman?" "He was a good enough workman. I fired him for picking up nails. Every time he dropped a nail he stopped to pick it up. I told him to let the nails go, for his time was worth more to me than the nails. After I had told him about a dozen times and he kept on, I fired him. I couldn't afford to pay a man carpenter's wages to pick up nails." It is no exaggeration to say that to-day our churches are requiring the preacher to provide for his own comfort by "picking up nails." The proper direction for the preacher's economy to take is the effective investment of his salary for the enrichment of his ministry. His salary ought to be estimated with that in view. Any considerable amount beyond that is almost sure to result in the impairment of ministerial life and service. As the soldier, so the minister ought not to carry too many *impedimenta*. Brethren, if we wish to claim a soldier's pension, we must accept the conditions of a soldier's service.

Nervous Waste. Close to this lies the vivid suggestion in almost every one of these extracts of the superior efficiency of the man who is freed from anxiety as to the future comfort of himself and his family. The minister's efficiency depends ultimately upon the condition of his nervous system. A few men may scout this statement as failing to give due honor to the Holy Spirit; but only a few and they have not wisely considered this matter. There is no way by which the Holy Spirit can come into a man's life and be passed on to other lives without being transmitted over that mysterious complex of living wires, the nervous system. If they are worn or broken or grounded, the transmission of the divine message will be obstructed. We have to consider not only the familiar physical truth that whatever consumes nerve-force or depresses nervous vitality lowers both mental and physical efficiency, but also the surprising spiritual truth, that the waste or weakening or breaking of the nervous system hinders the working of the Holy Spirit by marring the instrument through which He must operate. The way to avoid this impairment of efficiency is to lift the burden of support in age from the minister's mind by pledging the Church for it and backing the pledge with the necessary cash.

Divided Interest. Let us apply to this problem another familiar fact, the loss of efficiency through a division of interest and attention. If the minister must provide in any considerable part for his old age he cannot have an undivided mind. At this point we are confronted by the fact that for the average minister to provide for himself through his savings only is practically impossible. Men do not come to the possession of a competency by the mere accumulation of savings, but by the growth of savings through profitable investment. Savings alone are not sufficient. This is why the man who has only his savings to depend upon never quite gets fear out of his heart. The profitable investment and management of savings divides time and energy. The minister who is involved in business enterprises and loaded with business anxieties cannot give himself wholly to the work of the ministry. The drag of the outside interest never ceases. If the minister seeks to unload this burden by commending the management of his savings to some one else, he will still need to be on his guard lest the manager shall manage to absorb the bulk of the profits, to say nothing of the original investment. One of the saddest chapters in ministerial life is that which contains the record of the tragedies and failures that have resulted from attempts of ministers to build up their pitiful little savings into a competency—men who have been stripped of their savings, men who have been stripped of reputation and men who, retaining a measure of both, have been lured on until their lives were emptied of spiritual power while they, like Samson, "wist not that their strength was departed from them." The tragedy of the men who have sought to escape poverty over this road is more bitter even than the tragedy of those who, knowing and single-hearted, have gone steadfastly on, not pleasing themselves.

Concentration. Not least of all, though often least considered, is the result of the continuous concentration of life into the minister's one great business. Every backward pull of dread of the future upon a man's nervous and spiritual energy, every bestowment of interest upon a rival enterprise, has retarded the growth of ministerial power, and hastened that staying of progress which proclaims the crossing of the dead-line. I have in mind a minister, one time a leader in his Conference, who when in his prime began to provide for his old age. In a few years his acceptability and usefulness were gone, and he lives discontented and unregarded, but *rich;* and I have in mind another minister whose hair is white, and who walks about in a body that shows in every attitude and movement the traces of age, but who seems destined to preach with acceptability and power until he falls in the midst of his work. He has poured his whole life into his one sacred business and he is as useful and happy and *poor* as any minister has a right to be. The plan which compels a man either to forego comfort in age or to use up life in the attempt to build his savings into a comfortable fortune; which cuts off a man's efficiency just when he ought to be at the zenith of his usefulness, thus robbing the Church of years of service, is not economy. Not only in length of service do we lose, but also in its intensity and fulness. A life which is divided in its interests and activities loses momentum every time it turns aside. When it resumes its course, it does so with a slower rate of motion; and not until after a considerable time does it recover what has been lost, and the gain which should have been made will never be recovered. A life divided and wavering between two interests never comes to its best. But a life which with perfect abandon pours its full intensity of concentrated energy into the work of the ministry experiences an accumulation of power until the body begins visibly to fail.

CONCLUSION. We conclude that the long-tried, patching-out policy is impossible of adjustment, humiliating to the ministry, unworthy of a great and self-respecting Church, and ought to be abandoned as speedily as possible; that the policy of requiring the minister to care for his own comfort with his savings will either seriously reduce ministerial equipment and efficiency without really providing an adequate support, or will require an increase of salaries which passes the bounds of reasonable expectation; and that the only righteous way out is to pay the minister a good working salary while he works and a living pension when he becomes old.

JOSEPH W. VAN CLEVE.

Decatur, Ill.

THE DEBT OF THE NATION TO THE MINISTRY

THE REV. ISAAC H. LIDSTONE
Treasurer Board of Trustees, East Maine Conference

It ought not to be a difficult matter, in the Capital of the Nation, to discover the amount of the national debt, even though the sum total of that indebtedness is so large that the ordinary man finds difficulty in comprehending it. It would be, also, an easy matter to find out how this great debt was incurred; some of it charged to the Mexican War, other vast sums to the Civil War, another sum to the late war with Spain; and still other millions to the exigencies of administration, or maladministration, as the case may be, when the income of the nation did not equal its expenditures. But there is a debt which no man has measured, a thing indeterminate, which the most skillful accountant cannot compute—the debt of which we speak at this time—the Debt of the Nation to the Ministry. It would be comparatively easy to tell of national obligations to the few who, like Saul the son of Kish, tower above their fellows, but who can tell the story of the influence exerted by the obscure and inconspicuous toiler in the kingdom of Christ! I desire to recall the nation's obligations to them, "lest we forget, lest we forget."

Foundations

We are not far from magnificent structures dedicated to the uses of the republic. Like the disciples of old, we might say, "See what manner of buildings are these!" We are filled with admiration for the skilled artisans who wrought to the end that symmetry and strength and beauty should be combined in these splendid buildings. We regard with pleasure the harmony in coloring, the beauty of pillar and capital, the appropriate frieze, the mural decorations, and the inanimate loveliness of the artist's dream which has become visible in granite and marble. But who among us gives a thought to the massive, unseen stones of the foundation? Hidden from the gaze of men, these stones are as fine in grain and as enduring as those which adorn the superstructure; but the skill of the artificer was not lavished on them. Yet if the rugged stones of the foundation should fail, ruin would come to the building. There are ministers who, like the stones in the foundation of the Capitol, are unseen by the crowd, and known to but few master builders of foundations, for whom awaits a crown of eternal rejoicing.

The beginnings of this republic were essentially religious. The Puritan was a mighty man in war, a splendid pioneer, and undoubtedly pious, but he was also the personification of militant intolerance. He hated Baptists, witches and Catholics; and later, when he had the opportunity, he showed but little affection for the Methodists. He had many virtues, although they were at times obscured by external unloveliness. He built his churches on the hill-top, and beside the church he built a school-house for the instruction of his sturdy offspring. How did it come to pass that the Pilgrim and the Puritan came to the rugged coast of Massachusetts? The *minister,* John Robinson of Delft, was the dominating spirit, the mainspring of the whole movement which resulted in the voyage of the Mayflower and the founding of the new state. As Bishop Quayle has put it, "The clergyman was in the veins of American life. He was not injected. He was and always will remain a constituent of the blood."

The religious element is one of the most prominent features in the founding of all the colonies. Roger Williams, a preacher, flees for his life, finds an asylum and founds a new State in Rhode Island. William Penn, another preacher, founded the great commonwealth of Pennsylvania. It would be difficult to find anyone more thoroughly religious than the Roman Catholic, Lord Baltimore. The Dutch Protestants founded New Amsterdam, and Governor Oglethorpe brought John Wesley to America in order to implant the gospel leaven among the citizens of Georgia. The Huguenots, persecuted for righteousness' sake, settled the Carolinas. Only in Virginia was the Church an afterthought, when it had been discovered that it required more than the valor of a John Smith to establish order and justice among men.

The Knight of the Saddlebags

But this is not the end of the matter by any means. The knight of the saddlebags was no mean factor in making civilization real in the West as well as in the East. To read the story of Bishop Asbury is to become acquainted with the means used to make this a Christian nation instead of a nation according to the ideals of Paine and Voltaire. The pioneer preacher, who endured poverty and perils of every sort that he might bring the good news to those who were scattered abroad in the wilderness and on the prairies of the great western domain, was not always polished in speech and manners. He could fight as well as exhort. He knew Christ and his sins forgiven, and preached a believable doctrine, which President Hyde of Bowdoin College characterized as follows: "Methodism was the revival of grace, when *law had lost its grip and love was dragging her anchor.*" The picture which Peter Cartwright draws for us of the conditions of Rogues' Harbor was true to life in other parts of the frontier than Illinois. These men were heroes without knowing it, knight errants of the cross of Christ! They were the real conquerors of the wilderness. They attended *"Brush College."* The wilderness was their Alma Mater; the Bible, the Discipline, Fletcher's Checks, and the writings of John Wesley constituted their biblical and theological library; they loved God, believed in a very real devil, hated sin and loved sinners. In the words of an ancient doggerel we may say:

"The circuit riders of that day were not so very grand.
They took degrees at rolling logs and clearing up the land.
But when they rose to preach it seemed that you could smell
The fragrant flowers of heaven and the stifling smoke of hell."

Certainly they were the rough stones in the foundations of empire. They belonged to a class of men of whom the world was not worthy; and a fitting characterization of them would read like the eleventh chapter of Hebrews. The itinerant ministry became cultured without losing its old-time stamina, and is still preaching the gospel in the demonstration of the Spirit and of power. The wilderness is no longer the problem, but newer and more difficult problems have arisen amid the complexities of modern life, which try the souls of men and their capacity to meet them, as certainly as the fathers had to meet the old problems which tried their souls.

The Preacher a Moral Force

Let me speak now of the preacher as a force in the realm of morals. I am not yet fifty years old, but I have seen some things which strengthen my faith in the power of the gospel when it is preached by a man who is unafraid and whose heart God has touched. I once knew a community whose immoralities were most striking and disheartening. So low were its ideals that two men swapped wives without the formality of a divorce, one man giving the other an ox chain to boot. A Baptist preacher came to that town and though amazed by what he saw, he believed that the gospel could do what the law had failed to do, and began a campaign for the salvation of that community. He consorted with the lowly, and like his Master became the friend of the outcast. Presently some were convicted of sin and turned to the Lord. The good work went on, the Sunday school became a popular institution, and the prayer meeting a place of amazing interest and power. Respectable folk saw what God had wrought and turned to the Lord. That was yesterday. What are the conditions to-day? "Old things have passed away, behold all things have become new." Honesty and chastity prevail and the local magistrate, once so necessary, has disappeared. I preached in a Methodist church in that region and saw a number of these people, "clothed and in their right mind." That Baptist minister had done what the law had failed to do. He belongs to a brotherhood who constitute the militant phalanx of the kingdom of heaven.

I live in the State of Maine. I love every crested hill of her rugged landscape. I love her forests, aglow with the glories of autumn and rioting in gold and crimson amid the deep green of the firs. I love her rugged sea-coast in all its moods of storm and calm. I love the salt breath of the ocean when Boreas and Euroclydon crest every rugged reef with spume until they foam like the frothing of some fabled monster. But that which makes me proud of Maine is not her wealth or scenic beauty, nor her abundant harvests, her orchards, lakes or hills, her happy homes, her prosperous and growing cities or splendid institutions. I love the Old Pine

Tree State, because of the fact that no saloon keeper or brewer can look me in the face and say, "I am doing business with the sanction of the law." But there was a time when the conscience of Maine slept, while iniquity was sanctioned for a price, and law was nullified by the aid of legal devices; when political parties came together in convention and declared their fervent allegiance to the prohibitory law, and then forgot it, being in favor of the law but against its enforcement. Then came a man who reached Holland's ideal:

"God give us men! A time like this demands
Strong minds, brave hearts, true faith, and ready hands.
Men whom the lust of office cannot kill;
Men whom the spoils of office cannot buy;
Men who have opinions and a will;
Men who have honor and who will not lie;
Men who can face the treacherous demagogue,
And damn his flatteries without winking;
Tall men, sun-crowned, who live above the fog
In public duty, and in private thinking.
For while the rabble with their thumb-worn creeds,
Their large pretensions and their little deeds,
Mingle in selfish strife, lo! Freedom weeps,
Wrong rules the world, and waiting justice sleeps."

Wilbur F. Berry, a Methodist preacher, was that man. He came to us with a message. He woke us from our decade-long sleep. He showed us the majesty of the law and the relation of the citizen to its enforcement. He laughed our cowardice to shame; and Maine awoke. He has a jail sentence hanging over him, but he does not go to jail; for sometimes the devil is wiser than we think. That is the reason that Dr. Berry does not go to jail. We still have our prohibitory law, and from the life and lips of a Methodist preacher we are learning that the price of liberty and sobriety is eternal, sleepless vigilance.

This is but one instance of many that I could cite in which the minister has saved the day for law and order and awakened communities to the peril of lawlessness. For good morals are as nearly related to economics as to righteousness. Sin is a burden not only to the soul, but on the taxpayer. The true minister is a constructive statesman. He is a builder of citizens in the truest sense of the word; for history bears witness to the fact that morals are not self-propagating, and that behind every system of efficient morality there must be the support in some form of religion.

The Minister's Family

In a marked degree the nation is in debt to the minister's family. Take one conspicuous instance: At the American Institute of Instruction, held in Halifax, N. S., in 1900, there was given a series of sketches of some fifteen hundred descendants of Jonathan Edwards, who was born in 1703. Out of the fifteen hundred descendants there were only six criminals. There was not a single pauper, imbecile or insane person; but in railroading, mining, medicine, law, literature, statesmanship and theology, the descendants of Jonathan Edwards have been prominent in the country at large. Two hundred and eighty-three of the fifteen hundred were college graduates, and thirteen were college presidents. Our limits forbid any attempt at a comprehensive statement, but we will give a few names of preachers' sons whom we delight to honor, and whose memory is like incense: Henry Clay, the great compromiser; Fitz-Greene Halleck; Oliver Wendell Holmes; James Russell Lowell; Frederick Lawrence Knowles; Richard Watson Gilder; the last two coming from Methodist parsonages, as did also the late Senator Dolliver and United States Senator Bristow. The Field family, including Henry M., the editor, David Dudley and Stephen J., lawyers, and Cyrus, of Atlantic cable fame, lend distinction to the family of every preacher in the United States. To these we may add the names of Henry Ward Beecher, and his gifted sister, Harriet Beecher Stowe, Louis Agassiz the scientist, Samuel F. B. Morse the inventor, and the Wright brothers, the perfecters of the heavier-than-air flying machine. The honored President of this great Republic, Woodrow Wilson, is a preacher's son, as were also Presidents Arthur and Cleveland.

In the world of education it would be difficult to find a college or university that was not in some large measure indebted to a minister. He is and always has been preeminently the friend of education. It is a source of astonishment to many people to learn how large a percentage of the students in the colleges at the present day are sons of ministers. In Methodism's oldest college there are sixty. Rev. John Howard founded Harvard University; Dr. Leonard Wood founded Andover Theological Seminary; Dr. Dempster, Dr. Barrows and Bishop Baker founded Garrett Biblical Institute; Rev. Thomas Kirkland founded Hamilton College; Rev. John Livingstone founded Rutgers College; while Goucher College, Baltimore, betokens the foresight and genius of Rev. John Goucher. Dartmouth College was born in the heart of the Rev Eleazar Wheelock, pioneer of the Christian education for the Indians of New England. We add the names of some great college presidents, who have enhanced the glories of the institutions over which they have presided, and we have such men as Jonathan Edwards, Drs. Witherspoon and McCosh. No wonder that Princeton glories in the fact of their presidency of that great school. Williams had Mark Hopkins, of whom it is said that James A. Garfield on one end of a log and Dr. Mark Hopkins on the other constituted a university. At this point again the ministry gets near to the presidency, for Mark Hopkins did more to shape Garfield's life than any other person, excepting his devoted and heroic mother. To these add Eliphalet Nott, sixty-two years a college president, Francis Wayland, John Price Durbin, Wilbur Fisk, Stephen Olin, Nathan Bangs, Cyrus D. Foss, E. O. Haven, William F. McDowell, Matthew Simpson, Thomas Bowman, John P. D. John, Dr. Gobin, Edwin H. Hughes, J. R. Day, Herbert Welch and others; some of whom went from the college presidency to the episcopacy.

In the realm of literature there are so many names of ministers that I can scarcely give you a list of them without making it the merest catalogue. Here are such names as Abel Stevens, Daniel Curry, Gilbert Haven, D. D. Whedon and that versatile and discriminating editor of the *Methodist Review,* William V. Kelley. To these add that robust thinker and indefatigable debater and controversialist, Dr. James M. Buckley; and the splendid and efficient journalist who has made New England wiser and better for a quarter of a century, Dr. Charles Parkhurst, of *Zion's Herald,* and his associate, Dr. E. C. E. Dorion. Others who are aspiring to fame in the realms of Methodist literature will not be envious at the mention of these names. I wanted to say these things while these men are living; for thank God, all of the worthies of the editorial sanctum are not dead!

Lyman Abbott, Henry Ward Beecher, Washington Gladden,

A. T. Pierson, Henry van Dyke, Newell Dwight Hillis, Edward Everett Hale and many others might be mentioned.

The Minister a Patriot

In conclusion let me say that the minister is ever a patriot. In the days when the fate of the Union trembled in the balance there were two men who were conspicuous in their services to the country: Matthew Simpson, Methodist, and Henry Ward Beecher, Congregationalist. While Bishop Simpson flamed up and down the land, kindling the fires of patriotism in thousands of American hearts, and sustaining in prayer and fellowship the Great Heart at the White House, Beecher went to England to state the case to the British. It was no small task. It demanded a high type of courage and skill to face the hosts of Englishmen whose families were hungry because of the embargo on cotton. But Beecher won the day. On the night of his first great victory the audience was filled with the mob spirit, but Beecher conquered, and tradition says that on the next day there was taken from the hall a dray-load of brickbats which had been intended for the American preacher. And what shall I say for the thousands whose names are not mentioned, men for whom the wilderness and the solitary place have been glad and under whose cultivation the desert has rejoiced and blossomed as the rose? The Nation is their debtor, a tardy debtor, it is true, but we believe that the better day is coming for those who have borne the burden and the heat of the day, and that the time is hastening when this great Church, which came into being at the time the Nation was born, and which received its constitutional form at the time the American Constitution was being formulated, will properly care for the widow and the orphan, and will make life's eventide bright for the Veteran of the cross. Bishop Cranston had a prophet's vision when he said:

"The world will never pay its debt to these men. But *the Church will not repudiate their Claim.*"

Then there will be no more the specter of want to alarm them, nor the feeling of sadness that the Church has forgotten its obligations, but a glad sense of security in the providence of God and the honesty of his people.

Isaac H. Lidstone.

Danforth, Me.

THE CHURCH'S DEBT TO THE PASTOR'S FAMILY

THE REV. GEORGE M. STONE, D.D.

Late of Hartford, Conn.

The justice of the claim of aged and disabled ministers upon the Church, for sympathy and aid in their time of need, involves a plea in behalf of other members of the minister's family. The wives, and sometimes no less the children of Christian pastors, have always been, in the Protestant economy of the pastoral office, no inconsiderable element in their success. The tactful service of the pastor's wife has frequently perpetuated his term of office on a difficult field. Her consecration has as frequently shielded him from adverse criticism where, perhaps, it may have been deserved. All the more does her relation to the minister's home deserve recognition, because it has been in her life work so many times unrecognized. Her hints and suggestions regarding literary faults of the preacher, her vigilance over his personal appearance, her subtle and womanly insight into social forces, never appear in the memorial notices of the pastor's work.

The Protestant idea of family life gets expression in the pastoral office. No contrast in church-life is more significant than the home of the Protestant pastor and the domicile of the priest of the Roman Church. This contrast is an ever-present object lesson to emphasize the sanctity of marriage, and its equal spiritual purity with the state of celibacy.

The early charter of Christian liberty included the life of the family, as is clear from the questions of Paul, "Have we no right to eat and to drink? Have we no right to lead about a wife that is a believer, even as the rest of the apostles?"

The Fathers of the Nicene Council repelled with indignation the proposition to enforce celibacy upon Christian pastors. When in the eleventh century, after many previous struggles in the Church, the iron heel of Hildebrand stamped out the family and the home from the life of the minister, he admitted to those altars one of the most serious menaces to the purity and the power of the Church itself. The Greek Church has carried over from the primitive mold of church-life the right of marriage for its pastors.

The Reformation of the sixteenth century, logically and naturally, restored marriage to the minister. When in 1525 Martin Luther led Catherine Von Bora to the altar as his wife, and with her founded a happy Christian home, he inaugurated a new and noble chapter in the history of the home-life of the world. How widely has the family life of Christian pastors since molded the domestic conditions of the nations of the earth! How many pictures of homes in Germany, England, Scotland and America are recalled by the mere mention of the manse, the rectory and the parsonage!

The minister's home owes much to the widows of pastors, because they have contributed in so large measure to purify the family circle in places where they have been known. It is time that we should repudiate the cynical estimate of the waywardness of ministers' sons. The fact is to-day that the sons of Christian pastors constitute a large part of the moral strength and fiber of the best communities East and West. It has been said that every President of the United States had a praying mother. Some one has said, "When we educate a man, we educate an individual; but when we educate a mother, we educate a family." In many communities the pastor's family is the model for others. A subtle but pervasive influence goes out from it, elevating other lives and giving them permanent direction.

There is an uncomputed service rendered by pastors' wives in the training of men for the Christian ministry. Everywhere about us are pastors' sons in the ministry. Of Dr. Storrs it was said that "he was ancestrally preordained to the Congregational Ministry." His father, grandfather and great-grandfather were in this hereditary line. The history of the women who wrought side by side with these illustrious men has not been written; but who shall deny to them a definite and perhaps preponderating share in the turning of their sons toward the calling of their fathers? The fame of Jonathan Edwards filled two continents, but the quiet, household sway of Sarah Pierrepont Edwards was scarcely less a blessing to the world.

One President of the United States was the son of a Baptist minister. The best positions in civil and social life are filled to-day by the sons and daughters of Christian pastors. The widows of our pastors deserve honor and reward, because of their practical ability and skill in the economic administration of the household. We hear now-a-days much of great financiers. The frugality and good management of some of the women in the humble parsonages of the land would rival that of the most noted men of affairs in the centers of trade. Large families have been raised and educated upon six hundred dollars salary per year. They tell in New England of the housewives of a hundred years ago who made one paper of pins last a lifetime. There are pastors' wives still living who would, I think, be quite equal to this degree of economy.

In considering our debt to the widows of pastors, due emphasis should be placed upon the uncertain lot of such women in case of the untimely death of the husband. The change made in such cases is frequently greater than in the more common vocations of life. Not long since I was in a sad home, where the pastor, a popular man, had been stricken down suddenly in comparatively early life. The widow, with her little family, was soon to go out of their home. Of course, the library must be sold. The death of the pastor involved not only a change in the social position of the wife, but also brought about new and painful conditions in every aspect and hope of her life. Even though the pastor's wife may have left a home of independence to become her husband's helpmeet, such are the vicissitudes of life that she may not return to it in her day of bereavement. It would be difficult to imagine a situation more trying and precarious than that of a pastor's widow under said circumstances.

The Church should exercise a constant solicitude over them as co-workers with her ministers and missionaries. "The graves of all the saints are blest," but while no conspicuous shafts of marble mark the resting-places of the band of consecrated women, the earth has no more sacred dust than theirs. The grave of Sarah Boardman Judson, at St. Helena, joins together the continents which hold the dust of Ann Hasseltine on one side, and Emily Chubbuck on the other. The entire Church of God has paid its tribute to these handmaids of the cross. Our plea to-day is in behalf of that numerous company whose services in an humbler sphere have been under "the Great Taskmaster's Eye," and have met His divine approval. In pleading for these, we plead for the silent. They suffer, and make no sign. It is said in one of the most beautiful Psalms, the sixty-eighth: "She that tarried at home, divided the spoil."

The well-earned reward of Christian women is recognized by the Master Himself that it may be by us also. The emphatic recognition of the service of Mary in the breaking of the alabaster vase upon the person of Christ is perhaps our clearest and highest warrant for conscientious solicitude over the temporal needs of the widows of our pastors. When gifted women have entered Christian service, partial friends have said, "To what purpose is this waste?" When Fanny Forrester became the wife of Dr. Judson in the flowering time of her literary genius, the worldly public were thrown into something like a panic over what they thought "an unparalleled and senseless sacrifice." It was the common talk that the brilliant authoress was throwing herself away. Already, however, her Master had said of one of her predecessors, "Wheresoever this gospel shall be preached in the whole world, there shall also this, that this woman hath done, be told for a memorial of her."

Many years ago, I stood on the deck of an outward-bound steamer in the harbor of New York. Among the groups on the deck, saying farewells, were a young bride and her husband, starting out as missionaries to South Africa. The bride had been reared in one of the most affluent homes of the great city. The step she was taking in leaving it for service and suffering in the dark continent was inexplicable to some of her friends. Her clear-sighted faith left her without doubt of her course, and enabled her to act upon the higher motive and finally to give up life for it.

The Protestant idea of the faithful pastor's family life has created a sphere for the exercise of a wide variety of woman's gifts. Martha served the Master as truly as Mary, though after a different manner. Each held by her special gift, and met a felt want of the Lord during His earthly life. And still the varied needs of His people require services widely different. The *chef* of the Parker House, Boston, and the president of Harvard College received the same salary. But confusion twice confounded would ensue if they changed places for a single day. Martha had no sentiment. But sentiment has its legitimate place in the Church, and Mary brings it to her altars. "She bows, she bathes the Saviour's feet with costly spikenard, and with tears." Of her practical sister, it is written, "They made him a feast at Bethany, and Martha served." For He was hungry betimes, and knew the difference between a savory meal and one prepared without the skill of woman's native art. There are different gifts, but the same spirit, and both man and woman serve best who hold fast to their own gifts with true self-reverence and steadfast faith that God has woven into them the qualities which pleased Him.

Finally, there is a cloud of witnesses on earth and in heaven, who could speak of the unpaid debt owed to pastors' wives; the pastors themselves. Principal Fairbairn, in the dedication to his noble book, "The Place of Christ in Modern History," says: "This book is dedicated to my wife, whose quiet helpfulness and fair companionship have made the twenty-five years of our wedded life years of happy labor and gracious peace." The classic verse of Old Testament love is: "And Jacob served seven years for Rachel; and they seemed unto him but a few days, for the love he had to her." This is love before marriage, but the sober word of the wise man in past marriage life is: "Her price is far above rubies. The heart of her husband doth safely trust in her, so that he shall have no need of spoil. She will do him good and not evil all the days of her life. She openeth her mouth with wisdom; and in her tongue is the law of kindness. She looketh well to the ways of her household, and eateth not the bread of idleness. Her children arise up, and call her blessed; her husband also, and he praiseth her."

High encomiums should fall upon living ears. There is too much post mortem appreciation of the value of pastors' wives. Let us see to it that we fail not in honor and care for the living. I had rather have a single violet on my study-table today than a whole bank of flowers on my casket after death. On His cross our blessed Lord provided a home for His mother in the sheltering love of His dearest disciple. What shall be our response to the known need of our own homeless sisters of the same Lord?

ARMY CHAPLAINS NOW RETIRED PREACHERS

1. The Rev. C. H. McDermond, Missouri Conference, Chaplain of the 194th Pennsylvania U. S. V.

2. The Rev. William H. Thomas, New England Conference, Chaplain of the 4th New Hampshire U. S. V.

3. The Rev. Ezra R. Lathrop, Minnesota Conference, Chaplain of the 10th Minnesota U. S. V.

4. The Rev. Joseph Henry James, New England Southern Conference, Chaplain of the 3d New Jersey U. S. V.

5. The Rev. Isaac E. Springer, D.D., Detroit Conference, Chaplain of the 3d Wisconsin U. S. V.

WHY A SERVICE PENSION?

THE REV. C. W. MILLER, A.M.
Pittsburgh Conference

Why should the Church contribute to the support of the Retired Minister? Is there any obligation beyond that of support for those who are in active service? What is meant by the expression *"supporting* the ministry"? If it means that the service rendered, the responsibility borne, cannot be measured by financial standards, that *remuneration* is impossible, that all we can do is to sustain the soldiers of the cross so that they do not go a warfare at their own charges, then the word is well chosen. No wage can *pay* the soldier for the risk taken and the service rendered in defense of the nation's life and honor, for supreme devotion in the hour of the nation's supreme need. So also the high service of humanity, which true gospel ministry involves, can have no financial equivalent.

But if it means that the ministry is a non-producing class, a burden and tax upon society, without the rendering of equivalent service, then the use of the word is ill-considered and misleading. In this objectionable sense we might as well speak of supporting the officers of the government, physicians, lawyers, teachers, merchants, mechanics, farmers and laborers, for when we pay the doctor's bill, the lawyer's fee, the teacher's salary, the mechanic's wage, we are supporting them as truly as we are supporting the minister when we pay his stipend; and when we expend one hundred dollars for groceries, dry goods, clothing or shoes we contribute ten or more dollars to the support of the seller.

Judged by mere financial standards the Church pays. It is cheaper and more efficient for good order and popular well-being than the city government; and the average minister contributes as much to the support of others as they do to his. No doubt the majority of ministers could say, with

Dr. Adams of the Brick Church, New York, "I have paid more for the privilege of preaching the gospel than any of my parishioners has paid for the privilege of hearing it"; and we may safely say that the Church at large has had her ministerial service at less than cost. But to our question,

"Why Should the Church Contribute to the Support of the Retired Minister?"

First, *The term of financially productive activity is short.* Taking into account the preparation demanded, few men can enter the ministry under twenty-five years of age—some are thirty years or beyond. By this time men in other pursuits have given five or ten years to their chosen line of work.

But not only does the active career begin later, it closes earlier. When the hair begins to turn, the minister is suspected of growing old, though his physical force may not be noticeably abated, and though his mental grasp may be broader and his spiritual insight be deeper than ever before. He is no longer in demand just when other professional men are reaping the rewards of mature powers and wide experience, and just when he is better equipped than ever before to be the spiritual guide of a congregation.

Second, *The pecuniary rewards are small.* The time required for a liberal education is from five to seven years and the cost may be estimated at three thousand dollars—by no means an extravagant figure. Add to this the financial return for these years if they had been devoted to a handicraft or business, and the capital invested is considerable. Clerks and apprentices receive wages while learning their handicraft or business, but an education involves outlay from start to finish. The comparison is with the skilled artisan, the business man, the man in other lines of professional or semi-professional work, for we need the skilled workman in the pulpit and the parish as much as in any other field of human effort. And the Church is looking for her brightest and best equipped young men for the service of the sanctuary, realizing that a ministry which would command respect must be competent to lead and instruct the people, and that no other profession or calling makes such demands on mind and heart. Is it any wonder that young men of ability, and natural ambitions, knowing in advance that they will be shut up to an uncertain "comfortable support" and may be foredoomed to scant fare, should hesitate to enter the ministry unless compelled by an overmastering sense of duty or love for the work! Yet instances are not at all rare of men who have turned away from flattering prospects and profitable engagements to enter the ministry, and who could vastly improve their worldly circumstances by returning thereto.

But the Church, while regarding the "call to the ministry" as imperative, has often forgotten that "the Lord hath ordained that they who preach the gospel should live of the gospel." And might we not take less counsel of our fears of a secularized ministry and think more on the sins of omission of an unduly and unwisely economical Church? As a rule, no man who could not have commanded more in another calling is fit for the ministry; and no man is fit for it who does not feel that the holy service is above financial considerations, and who does not enter upon it, "not for filthy lucre, but for the gospel's sake," out of love for the service itself. No man can acquire wealth from his ministry—I do not think that he should—I want one human activity to have upon it the stamp of a divine calling rather than the mint-mark of the secular government. Wealthy ministers are rare, and their wealth has come from other sources than their ministry. The vast majority fail of a competency for their simple needs when retired from active work. Even those salaries which the Church calls large are but a fraction of the incomes of the leaders in commerce, finance and industries. Beecher was as great in his line as Morgan and Carnegie in theirs. Bishop Merrill would have been a great lawyer. Yet what is the salary of a bishop compared with the salaries of out-standing men in the professions!

Third, *The financial demands on him are greater than on any other man of equal income.*

The larger expense attendant on his preparation accompanies him to the end of his active career. He is expected to be abreast of the thought of the day, to be equal to the best informed in the pews. The lay-worker is useful but *the preacher is indispensable,* and the minister who would command respect must be the teacher of his people, "able by sound doctrine both to exhort and to convince the gainsayers." "*Beaten oil* for the sanctuary" involves expense of both labor and money. He must feed his mind if he would have it healthy and vigorous; he must reap in many fields of knowledge; he must read the kind of reading that costs. His congregation demands that he shall maintain what they consider a respectable style of living and dress for himself and family. In the struggle to do this on inadequate means, and to do for children what educated parents feel it worth many privations to do, many a faithful wife's health has broken and she has gone, too soon, to her coronation. He is expected to lead, and as a rule does lead, in the benevolences of the Church and must be in the front rank of every public and private charity. Every one, from the agents of great religious or educational enterprises down to the ill-favored and malodorous tramp at the back door, selects him as the first victim. The entertaining of the congregation, so far as it has religious, charitable or reformatory aspect, falls to his lot. He must keep "open house" as well as open heart to every good cause; and apparently no one ever thinks of the cost!

With the demand for charity, with the standard of living fixed for him by the people, with books and other literature for himself and for his family and with the education of children, to meet the demands of the situation and save anything from the ordinary salary is a fine problem in finance.

The Methodist Ministry

These things are true of the ministry in general, and up to this point all ministers share in experiences incident to their calling. But there are some features of the position of a Methodist preacher of which I wish to speak particularly.

First, *The Methodist Preacher is an ecclesiastical soldier, pledged to "come" and "go," "do this" and "do that" at the bidding of another.*

No other minister is in this position except the Roman Catholic priest. But unlike the soldier who is educated, paid and pensioned by his government, and unlike the priest who is educated and provided for by his Church, the Methodist minister must provide his own education and equipment and has no definite assurance of support. He has no vote or voice as to his field of labor or the adjustment of his salary, and no recourse at law if the salary is not paid. In other communions the local church issues a call which the minister may entertain or not, as he pleases. If he entertains it, he is a party to the conditions under which his service shall be rendered, and if these do not suit him he may decline to serve; if the call is accepted, the church is bound to the fulfillment of the obligations assumed in the arrangements made. But the Methodist minister is in the hands of the powers that be, the Bishops, who, with the advice of the District Superintendents, appoint him to "do that part of the work which we advise, at those times and places which we judge most for His glory." These powers often "gird him and carry him whither he would not." Arriving at his destination he is in the hands of the arbiters of his fate for the ensuing years who "do unto him whatsoever they list." Apparently the local church is the only party in interest, and decides his "allowance." He has neither vote nor veto as to the conclusion reached, nor appeal from it, nor recourse if his "allowance" is defaulted. He is an itinerant whose principal duty is to itinerate whenever a dissatisfied parishioner suggests it—a kind of Wandering Jew, whom any one at any time may command to move on. Pains and penalties are for him if he refuses or abandons the work assigned him, but there are no pains and penalties for the church which refuses to receive or to support him, unless it be the report of a "deficiency" and a change of preachers.

The usage of a century has dulled our appreciation of the magnitude of this self-surrender; but if any man thinks it a small affair to put the direction of his life and the comfort and the well-being of his family at the disposal of another, *let him try it!* He can doubtless find a "captain of industry" willing to employ him on these terms, to come and go at command, to do such work and receive such pay at such time and in such measure as may suit the employer's fancy.

Second, *Other churches have sustentation and home mission funds to assure the worker a definite support while he is developing new work.*

Methodism is evangelistic; it is a great missionary movement which is not delayed until the development of bases of supply. It does not wait for calls from organized churches with stipulated salaries, but goes out into the highways and hedges, into the mountains, the wilderness and the plains, to call men to salvation and to organize them into churches. In this way it has won the victories of the past and is to-day pushing its conquests among the scattered populations on the frontier, in mining and lumber camps and among the unchurched masses in our populous cities and their suburbs. Men of all creeds admit that Methodism is the most profound and potent fact in twentieth century Christianity. Even secular historians eulogize it; it is the very romance of religious history. From an obscure society in the Established Church of England it has developed into a religious "world power" whose influence is upon every other communion, whose agencies of conquest are in every land, and which must be reckoned in every list of the forces by which the kingdoms of this world shall become the kingdom of our Lord and of His Christ.

Who made it? The itinerant preachers who, in apostolic fashion, went everywhere preaching the Word; the men who are now called "worn-out," "superannuated," "retired," "Conference Claimants"; who could always say of themselves with Paul, "As poor yet making many rich." The Methodist itinerancy is a matchless system of ministerial supply, but it is expensive; because a moving army cannot be subsisted at the same cost as a settled community of the same number of men. It was not devised to care for weak ministers but to help weak churches and create new churches; and the heaviest burden and expense has fallen on the workers themselves. It is to be hoped that our great-hearted laymen will remember this, and when they glorify our itinerancy and clamor for a restoration of the time-limit will reflect that these things seem much easier when some one else is between the millstones and must bear the expense, and endure the hardship and the heart-break. In addition to this, our pastoral support is conceded to be below the average of other churches. Some of our ministers have largely increased their financial receipts and their opportunity to work out large plans for effective church work, and perhaps many more could have done so, by going into the pulpits of other churches, while very few come to us. We appear to have the most expensive system of ministerial supply at the least expense to the churches.

Third, *The Methodist Episcopal Church is more fearfully afraid of worldliness in her minister than any other Church.*

The monastic "vow of poverty" is presumed to be on him and what is esteemed a virtue in other men is considered a discredit in him. Numerous doors to personal profit are open to men in all other professions or callings; and in other denominations the acquisition of property is not regarded with jealousy as it is among us. The injunction that Methodism lays upon her minister is, "Spend and be spent in this work; give thyself wholly to it; no man that warreth entangleth himself with the things of this life, that he may please Him who hath called him to be a soldier." She demands that he shall be "a man of one work"; that he shall not dabble in business or speculation; that he shall use his business ability in building and improving churches and parsonages and paying old debts, and the Church does not refuse the preachers financial help in doing these things. She is even somewhat jealous of the increase of his private means by legitimate investment or natural growth of his own or his wife's patrimony; apparently fearing that God may not be able to keep him humble unless he is kept becomingly poor. The law of the Church, the traditions of more than a century, personal and popular sentiment and much itinerating combine to discourage business ventures for his own profit, so that it is the rare exception when he has been able to save enough to buy a home for himself and his aging wife; still rarer when, in addition to owning his house, he is able to meet their simple needs when retired from service; and should he have managed to save something, it is always tremendously overrated in the public mind.

We need to divert our thought from the exceptional salaries, including those of the Bishops, who are worth all they receive, and direct it to the "average," all the time remembering that most salaries are below the average. In the leading Conferences embracing the large cities, the "average salary" is not above the comfort line, and the "ordinary salary" is much below the safety line. In every State, even in the great cities, earnest and faithful preachers are trying to live on sums which would be rejected by the hod-carriers.

Fourth, *In the matter of age the Methodist Itinerant is at a disadvantage as compared with the settled pastor.*

The settled pastor ages *with* his congregation, without exciting special comment; he has aged *in the service* of his congregation, has baptized their children, married their young people and received them into the church, comforted their sick and dying and buried their dead. He is a personal friend as well as a spiritual adviser, and none but the coarsest would object to him on account of his gray hairs. But the Methodist itinerant stands revealed in all his grayness on the first Sunday after Conference, and the shock is sometimes too severe to be recovered from. He is a stranger who has worn himself out in serving others, and the age objection comes with ease and bluntness, "We don't want that old man!" and the judgment is seldom reversed. I do not insist that he should be kept beyond his year, though his ministry might be the best blessing kind Heaven could send them; I only ask that he shall be given "fair-play," and that he shall not be driven to "the Common." In the settled pastorate one may save something even from a small salary; but our itinerancy has begotten a desire for change for the mere sake of change, and frequent removals make it impossible to acquire a competency even by rigid economy, the savings of one pastorate being consumed in removing to another. Nowhere else in our own Church is the age-limit so early or so mercilessly drawn as in the pastorate. Men may serve acceptably as Bishops or district superintendents, as editors or secretaries, long after they have passed the dead-line of pastoral acceptability. A Bishop may become venerable, but the pastor becomes antiquated. When signs of age appear the demand for young and more athletic men crowds him back into smaller charges and poorer pay under the specious pretext of "lighter work," in which the only lighter thing is the salary; for there is no harder work than that of cheering a small or discouraged charge on to a solid footing and self-respect. So when the last charge has been served, the preacher is usually without income or property, and without the relationships that give standing in the community. He is a man without a home and almost without a country!

If the Church demands this kind of service, and keeps her ministers on the narrow margin of "a comfortable support" (*of the sufficiency of which the Church is sole judge*), then she ought to continue the "comfortable support" in the years of enforced retirement. The soldier of the Church, who has separated himself from the affairs of this life "that he may please Him who hath chosen him to be a soldier," who has turned away from other employments, however lucrative or pleasant, who has surrendered his right to go where he pleased, to do what he pleased, and to make the best bargain he could; who has given his life to the service of the Church in return for whatever the Church saw fit to give him, ought to be well cared for when his failing powers and "the good of the service" compel him to stand aside; and until that is done the Church has no right to object to him on account of his age. When such provision has been made he can be retired at a specified age, as in the case of the Bishops; for there are men who ought to be enjoying a well-earned rest, who are holding on to work beyond their powers, in preference to the semi-pauperism and semi-starvation of the "necessitous fund." Men who in the vigor of their manhood's powers rode forth to conquer the world for Christ, and on many a hard-fought field have won the spurs of the noblest knighthood, in the evening of life are reduced to the pitiful pass of saying, "Put me, I pray thee, into one of the priests' offices that I may eat a piece of bread!"

The readjustment of ministerial support, due to changed financial conditions, has resulted in betterment for the man in active service. His claim receives consideration, his rights are more firmly settled, and default in payment of promised support has been recognized as a shame. But it has been disastrous to the Retired Ministers. They were overlooked and neglected so long by their brethren that they are supposed to have no right of ministerial support—nothing but the appeal of poverty to generosity. They have been considered "necessitous cases" and their claims have been administered on the basis of need in disregard of immemorial rights and in defiance of ancient law and custom. They have been asked to come before quarterly conference and the Conference stewards and establish their "necessity" in order that they may receive their "allowance." How humiliating it is to compel one to sound the depths of his poverty, to make display of the leanness of his larder, the bareness of his wardrobe and the emptiness of his purse that he may be fed with the crumbs that fall from the table of a rich, powerful and prosperous Church, to whose interests he has given his best years and his best service. It is not charged that the people generally regard his support as a charity or contribute grudgingly to it. The ministers are worse offenders than the people; and as long as his claim is based on necessity rather than on service, and he must prove his need in order to make good his title to support, and receive his dole from a necessitous fund, it is not easy for him to avoid disquieting and humiliating thoughts. This condition has come about, not because any one purposed it, but through lack of consideration, "For evil is wrought by want of thought, as well as want of heart." It is the usual fate of him who is not present to look after his own interests. Being "out of sight," the Veteran Preacher has been "out of mind."

When Bishops Bowman and Foster were retired in 1896 they were deeply moved; and a great wave of sympathetic feeling swept over the Church. This was not strange, for it is no small thing to lay down a loved life-work. But these Bishops retired, not only with the love of the Church and with her honors thick upon them, but with the assurance of worldly comfort for their remaining days. A similar scene, but with more elements of tragedy in it, is silently enacted every year by less prominent characters on a less conspicuous stage, when men no less tried and true, no less worthy of the love of the Church, lay down their life-work in the Annual Conferences to face the future with the certainty of scant comfort in their declining years. Is it asking too much of the Methodist Episcopal Church, which, more than any other Church since the days of the apostles, owes her success to the labors and sacrifices of her ministry, that those who can no longer bear the burden and heat of the day shall be adequately provided for?

We are not pleading for the endowment of a charity, but for partial payment of a debt on which judgment has been confessed by the Church. From 1876 to 1900 the Pittsburgh Conference reported $140,000 in deficiencies of salary, or, with interest on defaulted payments added, $250,000; and this Conference ranks with the best! And these deficiencies were charged up to men who were doing hard service on small salaries and to whom the loss of even a small sum required stern self-denial and suffering, to men whose inconspicuous and ill-requited toil built up and strengthened the more prosperous churches.

The Remedy

The remedy. Almost a generation ago there began to be a profound and widespread conviction among thoughtful ministers and laymen that the provisions for the support of Retired Ministers were not only a humiliating experience for the ministers themselves, but a dishonor to the Church which they had served so faithfully and with such scant financial recognition; and also that the methods by which their claims were ascertained and administered were as futile as the results were inadequate; so they began to plan to remedy this shameful condition, rescue the claimant from his enforced position as a mere dependent, restore him to his birthright as a member of the ministerial force, and reestablish his right to a comfortable ministerial support. As a result many Annual Conferences devised plans for providing annuities based on years of service, with incidental help in all cases of emergency. From time to time the General Conference took a hand, until in 1904 a commission of picked men was ordered to study the subject and report at the ensuing session. With patient and painstaking labor they built up a system which was embodied in their report and adopted in 1908. This system provides annuities based on years of effective service as its main feature; as Mr. Marvin Campbell well says, "putting a premium on *continuing in the service* rather than on entering it." While we urge every one not to postpone his giving, but to be "his own executor," yet we hope to be remembered in the last wills of many.

We need a better sense of proportion in our giving. Though no other cause outranks this in the justice of its claim, yet in the past it has been postponed for every other cause. Within little more than a generation gifts to benevolences increased 1,420 per cent in the Pittsburgh Conference; pastoral support, 365 per cent; distribution to claimants, 435 per cent; a large part of such increase coming from the dividends of The Book Concern, Chartered Fund and the

Board of Conference Claimants, and from the income of our invested funds. Increase of ministerial support will be a great blessing to the Church in the improvement of ministerial service; for the greatest menace to the effectiveness of the Methodist minister is not laziness nor worldliness, but the fact that, with only a bare "support" during active years and with the certainty of scant fare when retired, he becomes the prey of distracting thoughts; the needs of his family diverting him in part from the duties of his calling. The Church will never get the best service of a man in the pulpit or in the homes if he must be perpetually wrestling with financial problems, or be haunted with the specter of scant fare when his working days are ended; but with *sufficient* provision for his active service and assured comfort in retirement, the Church will have a right to demand that her ministers be "separated" men, given wholly to the work of God.

We should evangelize the heathen world, but we ought not to forget those who evangelized us, or who are now seeking the lost sheep of the house of Israel. We should pay our church-debts, but we should discharge in larger measure our debt to those "who through labor and travail preached unto us the gospel of God." We ought to give liberally to education that "the coming man" may be fully equipped for the great day in which God shall give him his opportunity, but we ought not to neglect those who "with bare hands," mighty toil and heroic endurance prepared the way for him.

The Methodist Episcopal Church, youngest but not least of ecclesiastical world-powers, cannot afford to have it said, "The hire of the laborers who have reaped down your harvests, which is of you kept back, *crieth.*"

Washington, Pa. CHARLES W. MILLER.

REQUISITES OF A PREACHER

A father's tenderness, a shepherd's care,
A leader's courage which the cross can bear;
A ruler's awe, a watchman's wakeful eye,
A pilot's skill, the helm in storms to ply;
A fisher's patience and a laborer's toil;
A guide's dexterity to disembroil,
A prophet's inspiration from above;
A teacher's knowledge and a Saviour's love.

—*Bishop Ken.*

A DEPENDABLE PENSION

MR. MARVIN CAMPBELL

South Bend, Indiana, Treasurer of the Board of Conference Claimants

A LAYMAN'S VIEW

As a layman I approach the most important interest of the organic Church, its preachers. For every five effective preachers there are one Retired Minister and one widow. The interests of those five effective preachers are so closely allied to those of the two Conference Claimants as to be almost inseparable. The Retired Minister or other Claimant should and *can* have his full disciplinary allowance, and not be compelled to be content with sixty per cent of it as now.

ANNUAL CONFERENCE RESPONSIBILITY

Responsibility for the care of the Retired Ministers rests almost wholly with the Annual Conferences; because, in providing for them each Annual Conference is a little dominion of its own clothed with autocratic power. It determines who are Claimants; fixes its own rules or conditions as to retirement; and may apportion to the churches any amount it may deem necessary for the support of its Claimants. No preacher can be retired except by Conference action. This applies to no other department of the Church; and if *Claimants are not fully paid, the responsibility rests almost wholly on the Annual Conference.*

The law gives to the superannuate *more* consideration than to the effective minister, but he does not get as much consideration. The Annual Conference can apportion to the pastoral charges for the superannuates whatever amount it will, though it cannot fix or even suggest the amount for the support of the pastor, who must take his chances with the quarterly conference.

PAYMENT OF A DEBT

The superannuate and the widow are as surely entitled to payment as the effective Minister. There is no higher duty than the honest payment of honest debts. The disciplinary allotment to the Claimant is a debt, a part of the debt for ministerial support. We have no religious right, no honest right, to refuse payment except on account of our absolute inability. But we have the ability both as to wealth and liberality; and although we have not yet fully demonstrated our ability as to organized and systematized methods, it is both fair and gratifying to be able to say that we are in better condition, much better condition, than we were four years ago.

SERVICE ANNUITIES

The Discipline does not define the conditions which entitle Claimants to a service annuity. Each Annual Conference should establish clean cut rules for its action. There should be well-defined conditions as to annuities, and they should be rigidly observed. The *option* to make a distribution based upon service or to make a distribution based on necessity could not be justified if all were entitled to years of service annuity; for to take away the right from those who have met annuity conditions would be unjust. It would create a deplorable uncertainty as to the annuity, no matter how faithful or how long the service had been.

Each necessitous case must be passed upon individually, but it should not be provided for by taking money from entitled annuitants. Annuities are paid in spirit and fact as ministerial support. Necessitous payments are in spirit and fact benevolences, commendable indeed, but nevertheless benevolences. Annuitants should not be taxed for benevolences. These should be met from other sources. The spirit of the annuity is not that of reward for having been a preacher, but rather for having *continued to be a preacher* until unfitted for the itinerant service.

THE PREACHER ALONE INDISPENSABLE

We can dispense with tall steeples, ornamented windows, elaborate decorations, carpeted aisles, rich-toned organs and paid choirs. We can dispense with any or all of these and still, if we have a preacher, we can have a church. Indeed we can dispense entirely with the church edifice, and if we have a preacher may hold meetings in school houses, public halls, parlors or kitchens. *We can do without everything else, but we cannot do without the preacher.* He is the one, and the only indispensable factor in the organic Church.

Without fair assurance that they will not die paupers, the time may come when we will have a dearth of preachers; indeed I am not sure but it has come already. The average salaries of Methodist Ministers permit no savings, and the secular world will not give employment to men of advanced years. Generally the service annuity is the only hope of income after old age retirement. To enter the itinerant life with no fixed home is sacrifice, but to end such a lifework with no visible support is *to be sacrificed.*

The budget for ministerial support, in which are included both the effective minister and the superannuate, is the most important fund of the whole Church, because it secures and insures the one and the only indispensable factor of the organic Church. Lay hold of this fact. Take it home to your Annual Conference: The most important part of the budget of your church, the one indispensable fund in the whole Church is that for ministerial support, which includes the support of the Veteran Ministry.

CAN THE SERVICE ANNUITY BE PAID IN FULL?

Well, can *we* do what others have done, and are doing? The Methodist Church, Canada, the United Methodist Church and the Wesleyan Methodist Church of England, the Australian Methodist Church, pay full annuities to their Conference Claimants and have done so for many years. There is absolutely no failure.

If we are as loyal to our Church, if we are as just to our Retired Ministers, if we are as capable administratively as are the Methodists of Canada, England or Australia, then the full annuity can be paid by us; for it is paid by them. We must admit indifference or imbecility or both unless we grant that this can be done. Take this home to your Annual Conference and see to it that it meets its responsibility.

The churches to which I have referred have well-defined conditions as to annuity. They also have a necessitous fund; but it is not created by taking money from the annuitant. The three hundred and fourteen superannuates of the Methodist Church, Canada, average thirty-four years of service. Some of our Annual Conferences average as low as twenty-six years, while others are as high as thirty-three years. In the Canadian Church no man retires upon annuity except after forty years of service, unless unfitted for itinerant work.

Let me repeat, payment cannot be made to the one not entitled to an annuity except by taking money from those who are entitled. What stronger call for systematic method as well as for the increase of funds?

INDIANA METHODISTS

Indiana Methodists will illustrate the average situation. They are listed as paying annual grand total of $400,000 to the various benevolences, yet the shortage due Conference Claimants last year was $23,000; a deficit of thirty-five per cent. A membership that pays $400,000 to various and, some of them, remote benevolences, can and will pay this $23,000 *debt* if it is properly brought to their notice with anything like the insistence or system of secular business. I question the religious right to pay the $400,000 to benevolences until the $23,000 debt to Conference Claimants has been paid; but all can be paid.

Business prudence, common justice, respect for the law of the Church, fidelity to the aged fathers in Israel, all demand *a full and dependable annuity.* Then why are not sufficient funds provided? Simply because of lack of method.

I am told of a Methodist layman, much interested in Conference Claimants, who pays to various benevolences more than a thousand dollars per year and to Conference Claimants, five dollars and thirty-eight cents per year. He pays more than this to the Humane Society. He pays to the various benevolences because they are brought to his notice by earnest field agents. He pays to the Claimants his ratio share of the budget of his Church. Nobody asks him to pay more. He would undoubtedly pay liberally, if asked. There are hundreds of such cases; able to give, ready to give, but uninformed.

A CONFERENCE CLAIMANTS' STEWARD

Let me make a practical suggestion, which is by far the most important thing I have to say: Have a Laymen's Aid Society or, what is more practicable, broaden the scope of your Preacher's Aid Society or other Annual Conference organization and especially the work of the field agent, so as to give him not only the power to solicit endowment, but also to raise a current budget to meet the entire claimants' deficit that is not met by the apportionment. He will easily find ways to prevent any annual deficit and at the same time be more efficient as to endowments. Place upon your field agent the double duty of securing a present budget for the deficit as well as that of securing endowment, and your problem is solved.

In every quarterly conference there should be a Conference Claimants' steward. A Claimants' steward is even more logical than a district steward. There are thirteen times as many Conference Claimants as district superintendents. Why not have a steward to look after the thirteen aged and infirm Claimants as well as a steward to look after the one district superintendent? All are in the same class, and upon the same pay roll, that of ministerial support.

ENDOWMENTS NECESSARY

Endowment investment is needed for the Superannuate as surely as church and parsonage investment is needed for the pastor; the one for income, the other to save rent. The Methodist Episcopal Church has more than $225,000,000 invested in churches and parsonages, and less than $4,000,000 invested as endowments for three thousand Retired Ministers and three thousand widows. This is but two per cent of the investment for twenty per cent of the ministers; or if all the Claimants are counted (widows and orphans as well as Retired Ministers) for *thirty* per cent of all.

I say that endowment is needed; but do not depend upon endowment income, for it may be many years before this will be sufficient. The Claimant must be provided for by the budget plan as surely as must the pastor, and a part of it at least must be raised upon the "ability to pay" plan, just as the salary of the effective preachers is raised upon the "ability to give" plan. A flat assessment upon all of the churches of the Conference is right in part, but the whole amount cannot be secured in this way, since some poor churches cannot give more than they are now giving.

WILLS AND LIFE ANNUITY BONDS

Wills and after death bonds are desirable, very desirable, but don't neglect the righteous poor while waiting for the death of the godly rich.

SUMMARY

In conclusion: We do not lack money. We do not lack loyalty to the Church. We do not lack solicitude for the superannuate. But we do lack method and an intense purpose to see the Retired Preacher through. Take this home to your Annual Conference and see to it that it exercises its autocratic power and establishes right methods.

THE NATIONAL CONVENTION OF LAYMEN

summoned "The Whole Church to its Whole Task," and called for

"The hearty and full support of those Boards which are created by the Church as the proper instruments for the application of the benevolences of the Church to the world's need."

There is no greater or more important Benevolent Board in Methodism than the Board of Conference Claimants, and pastors and pastoral charges as well as Methodist laymen will fail to do their whole task, unless they give to this Board their hearty and earnest support.

The Convention recognized

"THE SUPREME CAUSE OF THE RETIRED VETERANS FOR AN ADEQUATE SUPPORT IN THEIR OLD AGE."

As a layman and speaking for and to the laymen I say with the Bishops:

"Let the supreme cause have the Supreme Place in 1915."

Marvin Campbell.

South Bend, Ind.

THE CHURCH'S OBLIGATION TO THE VETERAN MINISTRY

THE REV. HENRY H. SWEETS, D.D.

Secretary Ministerial Relief
Presbyterian Church in the U. S.

Justice Demands It

It is not a charity. When the Church ordains a man to the work of the ministry, she says, "Separate yourself from the sources of worldly gain. Minister to us in spiritual things and we will minister to you in material things."

Judge Beaver well says: "When a minister has been solemnly ordained and thereby adopted by the Church, and has, by his ordination vows, voluntarily closed the avenues by which men ordinarily acquire a competency, and afterward becomes physically or mentally disqualified for the proper discharge of the duties of his high office, or after a half century of devoted service is laid aside by the infirmities of age, he has a right morally—aye, and *just as much right legally in the truest sense*—to claim from the Church such provision at least as at the time of his ordination was made for those in like circumstances."

Honor Enforces It

The Church cannot afford to break this solemn pledge. A successful business man wrote: "I think we all appreciate to some extent this privilege and duty that God has laid on us, of taking care of His aged and infirm servants and their dependent ones, but I am afraid we fail to appreciate our individual responsibility in this matter. *Our names are all on the bond and our Master is our endorser. Do we propose to let His note go to protest?*"

Dr. Pierson says: "It is an insult to call this charity. It is in the very highest sense a *debt,* and should be so honored as an imperative obligation owed to those who used their days of strength in the service of our Lord; and no blessing can be expected on a Church which allows the veteran soldier of Christ to go down to his grave a dependent on charity, looking for a miserable pittance bestowed as on a beggar, for the bare subsistence of life."

Gratitude Compels It

The ministers who are on our rolls have turned their backs upon inviting fields. They have made themselves poor for the sake of Christ and His Church. The lonely widows and orphans have shared these privations with those who have fallen in the strife. They have sown the seed in hard and ofttimes unpromising fields and we to-day are reaping the splendid harvest. They laid the foundation deep and strong upon which we are erecting the temple of God.

Self-Respect Requires It

The farmer cares for the faithful old horse which has served him well. The house dog is fed from his master's table, even after he is too old to watch. "Soulless corporations" are setting aside vast sums of money from which they are pensioning those who have assisted them in gaining their wealth. And shall not His Church, which professes to have His spirit, minister to the needs of God's aged saints who have denied themselves in the days of their strength in order that they might care for the poor, seek the lost, relieve the sorrowing, and lead to a blessed hope in God?

Expediency Suggests It

It is not expedient for the Church to let her worn-out servants come to pinching need and humiliating poverty. The Presbyterian General Assembly declared: "This is the day of opportunity. If the Church does not act promptly, not only will the cause of Ministerial Relief suffer, but the supply of candidates for the ministry will be seriously affected. If the father lies wounded on the field of battle uncared for, can we expect the son to fill his place in the depleted ranks?" And where could you find a missionary, either at home or abroad, laboring on an insufficient salary, who, should he know that if he fall by the way, the loving arms of the Church would be placed beneath him; or if he be called to his reward, his wife and his little ones would be cared for by the Church, would not have more heart and zeal to put into his exacting labor?

Sympathy Directs It

The loneliness of these brave old warriors, shut up ofttimes within the four walls of their rooms, and the dependence of the widows and orphans who have shared the privations of those whose tired bodies rest in "the bivouac of the dead," is a pathetic, mute appeal. They are not laggards. Gladly would they be again in the forefront of the battle. But God has shut them in. Added to their weakness and pain of body is the thought, which sometimes must come, that they are forgotten—orphaned by the Church.

Religion Urges It

It is of the very essence of Christianity. "Pure religion and undefiled before God and the Father is this: To visit the fatherless and widows in their affliction, and to keep himself unspotted from the world." To plead for these Veterans is not begging. It is counsel to do right that the people need —counsel for the lack of which the Church is daily forfeiting the blessings of duty done. Therefore, to the ministry, we would say: *Shake off your false modesty. Help the Church to do right.* Your aged brethren are suffering through a neglect for which the people are not responsible, since they do not know the facts. It is in your power to make the facts known, and so to help them. *"Whoso seeth his brother have need, and shutteth up his compassion from him, how dwelleth the love of God in him?"*

Obedience Enjoins It

The support of the ministers of the gospel is not a matter left to the whims of men. It is according to the Divine order. God means that no minister shall be "entangled in affairs of this life," and to prevent this He made abundant provision for those set apart to the service of the sanctuary. Having no inheritance among the children of Israel, the Levites were assured from want from the cradle to the grave, and their widows and orphans after them. The abundant tithes and offerings, the levitical cities and their suburbs, and the sacredness of their calling assured to all those who stood before the Lord to minister to Him, the most ample, continuous, and unfailing supply for all their wants.

God declares through the apostle Paul: "Do ye not know that they which minister about holy things live of the things of the temple? And they which wait at the altar are partakers with the altar? Even so hath the Lord ordained that they which preach the gospel should live of the gospel." Time and again God said, "Take heed that thou forsake not the Levite so long as thou livest in the land."

Lord, God of Hosts, be with us yet, Lest we *forget!*

The Love of Christ Constrains Us

We cannot now see Him with our eyes, or minister to His bodily needs, but He has identified Himself with His disciples. Then shall the King say, "Come, ye blessed of my Father, inherit the kingdom prepared for you from the foundation of the world: for I was an hungered, and ye gave me meat; I was thirsty, and ye gave me drink; I was a stranger, and ye took me in; naked, and ye clothed me; I was sick, and ye visited me; I was in prison, and ye came unto me. Inasmuch *as ye have done it unto one of the least of these my brethren, ye have done it unto me."*

The Example of Jesus Guides Us

Our Saviour taught by His life as well as by the words of grace that flowed from His lips. He left a striking example in His care for His own mother. See Him on the cross enduring suffering, pain, death; dying for the sons of men. As He looks out over the vast crowd, His eye falls upon His mother. He sees the days of loneliness and want that must come to her. Hear His tender words, "Woman, behold thy son. John, behold *thy* mother." If the Saviour, in anguish and pain and death, recognized His mother's need and made provision for it, should not the grateful Methodist Episcopal Church in these days of wonderful material prosperity care, even with lavish hands, for those who, in a special sense, are the mothers and brothers and sisters of our Lord Jesus Christ?

HENRY H. SWEETS.

Louisville, Ky.

THE SHEPHERD WHO WATCHED BY NIGHT

THOMAS NELSON PAGE

From "The Land of the Spirit," Copyright, 1913,
by Charles Scribner's Sons
Illustrations by Paul Julien Meylan

The place had nothing distinguished or even perhaps distinctive about it except its trees and the tapering spire of a church lifting above them. It was not unlike a hundred other places that one sees as one travels through the country. It called itself a town; but it was hardly more than a village. One long street, now paved on both sides, climbed the hill, where the old post-road used to run in from the country on one side and out again on the other, passing a dingy, large house with white-washed pillars, formerly known as the tavern, but now calling itself "The Inn." This, with two or three cross-streets and a short street or two on either side of the main street, constituted "the town." A number of good houses, and a few very good, indeed, sat back in yards dignified by fine trees. Three or four churches stood on corners, as far apart apparently as possible. Several of them were much newer and fresher painted than the one with the spire and cross; but this was the only old one and was generally spoken of as "The Church," as the rector was meant when the people spoke of "the preacher." It sat back from the street, in a sort of sordid seclusion, and near it, yet more retired, was an old mansion, also dilapidated, with a wide porch, much decayed, and to the side and a little behind it, an out-building or two, one of which was also occupied as a dwelling. The former was the rectory, and the smaller dwelling was where the old woman lived who took care of the rectory, cleaned up the two or three rooms which the rector used since his wife's death, and furnished him his meals. It had begun only as a temporary arrangement, but it seemed to work well enough and had gone on now for years and no one thought of changing it. If an idea of change ever entered the mind of any one, it was only when the old woman's grumbling floated out into the town as to the tramps who would come and whom the preacher would try to take care of. Then, indeed, discussion would take place as to the utter impracticability of the old preacher and the possibility of getting a younger and livelier man in his place. For the rest of the time the people were hopeless. The old preacher was not only past his prime but his usefulness. Yet what could they do? No one else wanted him, and they could not turn him out. He was saddled on them for life. They ran simply by the old propulsion; but the church was going down, they said, and they were helpless. This had been the case for years and now as the year neared its close it was the same.

Such was the talk as they finished dressing the church for Christmas and made their way homeward—the few who still took interest enough to help in this way. They felt sorry for the old man who had been much in their way during the dressing, but sorrier for themselves.

This had been a few days before Christmas and now it was Christmas eve.

The old rector sat at his table trying to write his Christmas sermon. He was hopelessly behindhand with it. The table was drawn up close to the worn stove, but the little bare room was cold, and now and then the old man blew on his fingers to warm them, and pushed his feet closer to the black hearth. Again and again he took up his pen as if to write, and as often laid it down again. The weather was bitter and the coal would not burn. There was little to burn. He wore his old overcoat, to save fuel. Before him on the table, amid a litter of other books and papers, lay a worn Bible and prayer-book open, and beside them a folded letter on which his eye often rested. Outside, the wind roared, shaking the doors, rattling the windows and whistling at the key-holes. Now and then the sound of a passing vehicle was borne in on the wind, and at intervals came the voices of boys shouting to each other as they ran by. The old man did not hear the former, but when the boys shouted he listened till they had ceased, his thoughts turned to the past and to the two boys whom God had given him and had then taken back to Himself. His gray face wore a look of deep concern, and, indeed, of dejection, and his eye wandered once more to the folded letter on the table. It was signed "A Friend," and it was this which was responsible for the unwritten Christmas sermon. It was what the world calls an anonymous letter and, though couched in kindly terms, it had struck a dagger into the old man's heart. Yet he could not but say that in tone and manner it was a kind act. Certainly it had told the truth and if in tearing a veil from his eyes it had stunned him, why should he not face the truth!

He took the letter up again and reread it, not that he needed to read it, for he knew it by heart. Every sentence was seared into his memory.

He reread it hoping to find some answer to its plain, blunt, undeniable statements, but he found none. It was all true, every word, from the ominous beginning which stated that the writer felt that he had "a clear duty to perform," down to the close when with a protestation of good-will he signed himself the old man's friend.

"You must see, unless you are blind," ran the letter, "that your church is running down, and unless you get out and let the congregation secure a new and younger man, there will soon be no congregation at all left. No men come to church any longer and many women who used to come now stay away. You are a good man, but you are a failure. Your usefulness is past." Yes, it was true, he was a failure. His usefulness was past. This was the reason doubtless that no Christmas things had come this year—they wanted to let him know. It pained him to think it, and he sighed.

"You spend your time fooling about a lot of useless things," continued the anonymous friend, "visiting people who do not come to church, and you have turned the rectory into a harbor for tramps.

"You cannot preach any longer. You are hopelessly behind the times. People nowadays want no more doctrinal points discussed; they want to hear live, up-to-date, practical discourses on the vital problems of the day, such as the Rev. Dr. —— delivers. His church is full." This also was true. He was no longer able to preach. He had felt something of this himself. Now it came home to him like a blow on the head, and a deeper pain was the conviction which, long hovering about his heart, now settled and took definite shape, that he ought to get out. But where could he go? He would have gone long since if he had known where to go. He could not go out and graze like an old horse on the roadside. There was no provision made for such as he. No pensions were provided by his church for old and disabled clergymen, and the suggestion made in the letter had no foundation in his case: "You must or, at least, you should have saved something in all this time."

This sounded almost humorous and a wintry little smile flickered for a moment about the wrinkled mouth. His salary had never been over six hundred dollars, and there were so many to give to. Of late, it had been less than this amount and not all of this had been paid. The smile died out and the old man's face grew grave again as he tried to figure out what he could do. He thought of one or two old friends to whom he could write. Possibly, they might know some country parish that would be willing to take him, though it was a forlorn hope. If he could but hold on till they invited him, it would be easier, for he knew how difficult it was for a clergyman out of a place to get a call. People were so suspicious. Once out, he was lost.

At the thought, a picture of a little plot amid the trees in the small cemetery on the hill near the town slipped into his mind. Three little slabs stood there above three mounds, one longer than the others. They covered all that was mortal of what he had loved best on earth. The old man sighed and his face in the dim light took on an expression very far away. He drifted off into a reverie. Ah, if they had only been left to him, the two boys that God had sent him and had then taken back to Himself, and the good wife who had borne up so bravely till she had sunk by the wayside! If he were only with them! He used to be rebellious at the neglect that left the trains so deadly, but that was gone now. He leant forward on his elbows and gradually slipped slowly to his knees. He was on them a long time, and when he tried to rise he was quite stiff; but his face had grown tranquil. He had been in high converse with the blessed of God and his mind had cleared. He had placed everything in God's hands, and He had given him light. He would wait until after Christmas and then he would resign. But he would announce it next day. The flock there should have a new and younger and abler shepherd. This would be glad tidings to them.

He folded up the letter and put it away. He no longer felt wounded by it. It was of God's ordaining and was to be received as a kindness, a ray of light to show him the path of duty. He drew his paper toward him and, taking up his pen, began to write rapidly and firmly. The doubt was gone, the way was clear. His text had come to his mind.

"And there were in the same country shepherds abiding in the field, keeping watch over their flock by night, and lo, the angel of the Lord came upon them, and the glory of the Lord shone round about them; and they were sore afraid. And the Angel said unto them, Fear not: for behold, I bring you good tidings of great joy, which shall be to all people. For unto you is born this day in the city of David a Saviour, which is Christ the Lord. And this shall be a sign unto you; Ye shall find the babe wrapped in swaddling clothes, lying in a manger."

Unfolding the story, he told of the darkness that had settled over Israel under the Roman sway and the formalism of the Jewish hierarchy at the time of Christ's coming, drawing from it the lesson that God still had shepherds watching over His flocks in the night to whom He vouchsafed to send His heavenly messengers. On and on he wrote, picturing the divine mission of the Redeemer and His power to save souls, and dwelling on Christmas as the ever recurrent reminder of "the tender mercy of our God whereby the dayspring from on high hath visited us."

Suddenly he came to a pause. Something troubled him. It came to him that he had heard that a woman in the town was very sick and he had intended going to see her. She had had a bad reputation; but he had heard that she had reformed. At any rate she was ill. He paused and deliberated. At the moment the wind rattled the shutters. She did not belong to his flock or, so far as he knew, to any flock, and once when he had stopped her on the street and spoken to her of her evil life, she had insulted him. She had told him that he had better look after his own people instead of lecturing her. He turned back to his paper, pen in hand; but it was borne in on him that he was writing of watching over the flock by night and here he was neglecting one of his Father's sheep. He laid aside his pen and, rising, took down his old hat and stick, lit his lantern, turned on his lamp, and, shuffling through the bare, narrow passage, let himself out at the door. As he came out on to the little porch to step down to the walk, the wind struck him fiercely and he had some difficulty in fastening the door with its loose lock; but this done he pushed forward. The black trees swayed and creaked above him in the wind, and fine particles of snow stung his withered cheeks. He wondered if the shepherds in the fields ever had such a night as this for their watch. He remembered to have read that snow fell on the mountains of Judea. It was a blustering walk. The wind felt as if it would blow through him. Yet he stumbled onward.

At length he reached the little house on the back street in the worst part of the village, where he had heard the sick woman lived. A light glimmered dimly in an upper window and his knocking finally brought to the door a woman who looked after her. She was not in a good humor at being disturbed at that hour, for her rest had been much broken of late; but she was civil and invited him in.

In answer to his question of how her patient was, she replied shortly: "No better; the doctor says she can't last much longer. Do you want to see her?" she added presently. The old rector said he did and she waved toward the stair. "You can walk up."

As they climbed the stair she added: "She said you'd come if you knew." The words made the old man warmer. And when she opened the door of the sick-room and said, "Here's the preacher, as you said," the faint voice of the invalid murmuring, "I hoped you'd come," made him feel yet warmer.

He was still of some use even in this parish.

Whatever her face had been in the past, illness and suffering had refined it. He stayed there long, for he found that she needed him. She unburdened herself to him. She was sorry she had been rude to him that time. She had been a sinful woman. She said she had tried of late to live a good life, since that day he had spoken to her, but she now found that she had not. She had wanted to be a believer and she had gone to hear him preach one day after that, but now she did not seem to believe anything. They told her that she must repent. She wanted to repent, but she could not feel. She was in the dark and she feared she was lost. The old man had taken his seat by her side and he now held her hand and soothed her tenderly.

"Once, perhaps," he said doubtfully, "though God only knows that, but certainly no longer. Christ died for you. You say you wanted to change, that you tried to ask God's pardon and to live a better life even before you fell ill. Do you think you could want this as much as God wanted it? He put the wish into your heart. Do you think He would now let you remain lost? Why, He sent His Son into the world to seek and to save the lost. He has sent me to you to-night to tell you that He has come to save you. It is not you that can save yourself, but He, and if you feel that it is dark about you, never mind—the path is still there. One of the old Fathers has said that God sometimes puts His children to sleep in the dark."

"But I have been— You don't know what I have been," she murmured. The old man laid his hand softly on her head.

"He not only forgave the Magdalen, for her love of Him, but He vouchsafed to her the first sight of His face after His resurrection."

"I see," she said simply.

A little later she dozed off, but presently roused up again. A bell was ringing somewhere in the distance. It was the ushering in of the Christmas morn.

"What is that?" she asked feebly.

He told her.

"I think if I were well, if I could ever be good enough, I should like to join the church," she said. "I remember being baptized—long ago."

"You have joined it," he replied.

Just then the nurse brought her a glass.

"What is that?" she asked feebly.

"A little wine." She held up a bottle in which a small quantity remained.

It seemed to the old preacher a sort of answer to his thought. "Have you bread here?" he asked the young woman. She went out and a moment later brought him a piece of bread.

He had often administered the early communion on Christmas morning, but never remembered a celebration that had

A PATCH OF WHITE BECAME . . . . A FACE AND, BELOW, A SMALL BUNDLE CLASPED TO HER BREAST TOOK ON THE LINES OF A BABE

seemed to him so real and satisfying. As he thought of the saints departed this life in the faith and fear of God, they appeared to throng about him as never before, and among them were the faces he had known and loved best on earth.

It was toward morning when he left; as he bade her good-by he knew he should see her no more this side of Heaven.

As he came out into the night the snow was falling, but the wind had died down and he no longer felt cold. The street was empty, but he no longer felt lonely. He seemed to have got nearer to God's throne.

Suddenly, as he neared his house, a sound fell on his ears. He stopped short and listened. Could he have been mistaken? Could that have been a baby's cry? There was no dwelling near but his own, and on that side only the old and unoccupied stable in the yard whence the sound had seemed to come. A glance at it showed that it was dark and he was moving on again to the house when the sound was repeated. This time there was no doubt of it. A baby's wail came clear on the silence of the night from the unused stable. A thought that it might be some poor foundling flashed into his mind. The old man turned and, stumbling across the yard, went to the door.

"Who is here?" he asked of the dark. There was no answer, but the child wailed again and he entered the dark building, asking again, "Who is here?" as he groped his way forward. This time a voice almost inarticulate answered. Holding his dim little lantern above his head, he made his way inside, peering into the darkness, and presently, in a stall, on a lot of old litter, he descried a dark and shapeless mass from which the sound came. Moving forward, he bent down, with the lantern held low, and the dark mass gradually took shape as a woman's form seated on the straw. A patch of white, from which a pair of eyes gazed up at him, became a face and, below, a small bundle clasped to her breast took on the lines of a babe.

"What are you doing here?" he asked, breathless with astonishment. She shook her head wearily and her lips moved as if to say, "I didn't mean any harm." But no sound came. She only tried to fold the babe more warmly in her shawl. He took off his overcoat and wrapped it around her. "Come," he said firmly. "You must come with me," he added kindly;

then, as she did not rise, he put out his hand to lift her, but, instead, suddenly set down the lantern and took the babe gently into his arms. She let him take the child, and rose slowly, her eyes still on him. He motioned for her to take the lantern and she did so. And they came to the door. He turned up the walk, with the babe in his arms, and she going before him with the lantern. The ground was softly carpeted with snow, the wind had died down, but the clouds had disappeared and the trees were all white, softly gleaming, like dream-trees in a dreamland. The old man shivered slightly, but not now with cold. He felt as if he had gone back and held once more in his arms one of those babes he had given back to God. He thought of the shepherds who watched by night on the Judean hills. "It must have been such a night as this," he thought.

As they reached his door he saw that some one had been there in his absence. A large box stood on the little porch and beside it a basket filled with things. So he had not been forgotten after all. The milkman also had called and for his customary small bottle of milk had left one of double the usual size. When he let himself in at the door, he took the milk with him. So the shepherds might have done, he thought.

It was long before he could get the fire to burn; but in time this was accomplished; the room grew warm and the milk was warmed also. The baby was quieted and was soon asleep in its mother's lap. And as the firelight fell from the open stove on the child, in its mother's arms before the stove, the old man thought of a little picture he had once seen in a shop window. He had wanted to buy it, but he had never felt that he could gratify such a taste. There were too many calls on him. Then, as she appeared overcome with fatigue, the old man put her with the child in the only bed in the house that was ready for an occupant and, returning to the little living-room, ensconced himself in his arm-chair by the stove. He had meant to finish his sermon, but he was conscious for the first time that he was very tired. But he was also very happy. When he awoke he found it was quite late. He had overslept and though his breakfast had been set out for him, he had time only to make his toilet and to go to church. The mother and child were still asleep in his room, the babe folded in her arm, and he stopped only to gaze on them a moment and to set the rest of the milk and his breakfast where the young mother could find it on awaking. Then he went to church, taking his half-finished sermon in his worn case. He thought with some dismay that it was unfinished, but the memory of the poor woman and the midnight communion, and of the young mother and her babe, comforted him; so he plodded on bravely. When he reached the church it was nearly full. He had not had such a congregation in a long time. And they were all cheerful and happy. The pang he had had as he remembered that he was to announce his resignation that day was renewed, but only for a second. The thought of the babe and its mother, warmed and fed in his little home, drove it away. And soon he began the service. He had never had such a service. It all appeared to him to have a new meaning. He felt nearer to the people in the pews than he ever remembered to have felt. They were more than ever his flock and he more than ever their shepherd. More, he felt nearer to mankind, and yet more near to those who had gone before—the innumerable company of the redeemed. They were all about him, clad all in white, glistering like the sun. The heavens seemed full of them. When he turned his eyes to the window the whole earth seemed white with them. The singing sounded in his ears like the choiring of angels. He was now in a maze. He forgot the notice he had meant to give and went straight into his sermon, stumbling a little as he climbed the steps to the pulpit. He repeated the text and kept straight on. He told the story of the shepherds in the fields watching their flocks when the Angel of the Lord came upon them, and told of the Babe in the manger who was Christ the Lord. He spoke for the shepherds. He pictured the shepherds watching through the night and made a plea for their loneliness and the hardship of their lives. They were very poor and ignorant. But they had to watch the flock and God had chosen them to be His messengers. The wise men would come later, but now it was the shepherds who first knew of the birth of Christ the Lord. He was not reading as was his wont. It was all out of his heart and the eyes of all seemed to be on him—of all in pews and of all that innumerable host about him.

He was not altogether coherent, for he at times appeared

"DON'T YOU HEAR THEM SINGING? . . . YOU MUST SING TOO." . . . BEFORE THE HYMN WAS ENDED THE OLD SHEPHERD HAD JOINED THE HEAVENLY CHOIR to confuse himself with the shepherds. He spoke as if the message had come to him, and after a while he talked of some experiences he had had in finding a child in a stable. He spoke as though he had really seen it. "And now," he said, "this old shepherd must leave his flock, the message has come for him."

He paused and looked down at his sermon and turned the leaves slowly, at first carefully and then almost aimlessly. A breath of wind blew in and a few leaves slid off the desk and fluttered down to the floor. "I have been in some fear lately," he said, "but God has appeared to make the way plain. A friend has helped me, and I thank him." He looked around and lost himself. "I seem to have to come to the end," he said, smiling simply with a soft, childish expression stealing over and lighting up his wan face. "I had something more I wanted to say, but I can't find it and—I can't remember. I seem too tired to remember it. I am a very old man and you must bear with me, please, while I try." He quietly turned and walked down the steps, holding on to the railing. As he stooped to pick up a loose sheet from the floor he sank to his knees, but he picked it up. "Here it is," he said with a tone of relief. "I remember now. It is that there were shepherds abiding in the fields, keeping watch over their flocks by night, and the light came upon them and the glory of the Lord shone round about them and they were sore afraid, and the Angel said unto them:

"'*Fear not: for behold, I bring you good tidings of great joy, which shall be to all people. For unto you is born this day in the city of David a Saviour, which is Christ the Lord.*'"

They reached him as he sank down and, lifting him, placed him on a cushion taken from a pew. He was babbling softly of a babe in a stable and of the glory of the Lord that shone round about them. "Don't you hear them singing?" he said. "You must sing too; we must all join them." At the suggestion of some one, a woman's clear voice struck up, "While shepherds watched their flocks by night," and they sang it through as well as they could for sobbing. But before the hymn was ended the old shepherd had joined the heavenly choir and gone away up into Heaven.

As they laid him in the chamber on the hill opening to

the sunrise, the look in his face showed that the name of that chamber was Peace.

They talk of him still in his old parish, of the good he did, and of his peaceful death on the day that of all the year signified birth and life. Nothing was ever known of the mother and babe. Only there was a rumor that one had been seen leaving the house during the morning and passing out into the white-clad country. And at the little inn in the town there was vague wonder what had become of the woman and her baby who applied for shelter there that night before and was told that there was no place for her there, and that she had better go to the old preacher, as he took in all the tramps.

THE VILLAGE CLERGYMAN

GOLDSMITH

"A man he was to all the country dear,
And passing rich with forty pounds a year;
Remote from towns he ran his godly race,
Nor e'er had changed, nor wished to change his place;
Unpracticed he to fawn, or seek for power,
By doctrines fashioned to the varying hour,
For other aims his heart had learned to prize,
More skilled to raise the wretched than to rise.

"His house was known to all the vagrant train,
He chid their wanderings, but relieved their pain;
Careless their merits or their faults to scan,
His pity gave ere charity began.
Thus to relieve the wretched was his pride,
And e'en his failings leaned to virtue's side;
But in his duty, prompt at every call,
He watched and wept, he prayed and felt for all;
And, as a bird each fond endearment tries
To tempt its new-fledged offspring to the skies,
He tried each art, reproved each dull delay,
Allured to brighter worlds, and led the way.

"At church, with meek and unaffected grace,
His looks adorned the venerable place;
Truth from his lips prevailed with double sway,
And fools, who came to scoff, remained to pray.
E'en children followed, with endearing wile,
And plucked his gown, to share the good man's smile.
His ready smile a parent's warmth expressed,
Their welfare pleased him, and their cares distressed;
To them his heart, his love, his griefs were given,
But all his serious thoughts had rest in heaven."

SHOULD MINISTERS MARRY?

MARION HARLAND

Paul, the itinerant missionary, contends stoutly for his right to lead about a wife (inferentially, if it should please him so to do), quoting in his support of the claim the example of Cephas, etc. That the right was admitted without cavil in the early church we gather from further remarks relative to the wives of bishops and deacons.

Martin Luther gave unequivocal testimony to his views upon the subject of a married clergy by wedding a nun who had, like himself, abjured the conventual life. From that day onward the theory of the protesting Church has not wavered with respect to the right and practice. Suggestions from irresponsible sources to the effect that he wars most effectively who carries light impedimenta are frowned down when directed churchward. An unwritten law encourages, if it does not enjoin upon, the young minister to take unto himself a wife betimes as part of his equipment for the home or foreign field.

The consensus of parish or community is that the ministry of reconciliation—the noblest of what are classed as the "learned professions"—is involved with social and domestic obligations that pertain to no other calling. For the right discharge of these, we are informed by the Church at large and by individual members, a married man is better fitted than a bachelor. The minister's wife is his helpmeet in an especially sacred sense. The Christian home ruled by the united twain is an object lesson no congregation should lack.

A FINE THEORY

So far, so fair! From the Protestant viewpoint the theory is flawless, the world and human nature being not many degrees from the status of Paul's times. Will the reader who is supposed to be versed in the Scriptures bear with me when I ask him to read as for the first time the advice in detail given by the chiefest of apostles to his "own son in the faith" called through his instrumentality to the bishopric of Ephesus?

A PERFECT PARSON

"A bishop, then, must be blameless, the husband of one wife, vigilant, sober, of good behavior, given to hospitality, apt to teach; not given to wine; no striker; not greedy of filthy lucre, but patient; not a brawler; not covetous; one that ruleth well his own house, having his children in subjection with all gravity (for if a man know not how to rule his own house, how shall he take care of the house of God?). Not a novice, lest being lifted up with pride he fall into condemnation of the devil. Moreover, he must have a good report of them which are without, lest he fall into reproach and the snare of the devil."

The whole epistle is a masterpiece of sound common-sensible counsel, informed with paternal tenderness. Student and licentiate of the twentieth century can find nowhere a better manual of faith and practice. Yet we catch ourselves speculating as to the probabilities of Timothy's marriage. There is no fatherly word for the bride among the greetings to Aquila and Priscilla and other friends in the second letter.

However this may have been, the picture of the well ordered parsonage and the portrait of the master thereof have not been improved upon by modern writers upon clerical life and clerical manners. Happy is that parish that hath such!

MUZZLING THE OX

We have no allusion to the high price of foodstuffs in Ephesus, yet practical Paul does not omit the truth that human life requires material sustenance. Harking back, once and again, to the Mosaic injunction, "Thou shalt not muzzle the ox when he treadeth out the corn," he declares plainly: "The laborer is worthy of his hire," and "They which preach the gospel shall live by the gospel." Lest there may be some misapprehension as to the source from whence this same "living" is to come, we are admonished in another epistle: "Let him that is taught in the word communicate to him that teacheth in all good things."

Why multiply texts to prove what is theoretically a foregone conclusion? The obligation of the Church to provide for those who minister unto them in holy things has been recognized in all ages. The right of the minister to marry is as frankly acknowledged. In a majority of churches the expediency of his marriage is openly urged. Almost as binding in civilized communities is the demand that the pastor shall be an educated gentleman, and his wife a woman of culture and refinement. Paul sets the pace here, too. "He must have a good report of them which are without." The parish must never be ashamed of him or his family. Have you ever thought of the deep meaning wrapped up in the phrase "given to hospitality"? We express it in part when we say that "the minister keeps an open house."

A MIRACLE OF GRACE

To condense the requisitions: He must live in a house large enough to accommodate wayfaring brethren and their families; to entertain church societies and "delegates." He must set a decent table; his children must be as well clad as their playfellows and attend good schools. The parsonage is a city set on a hill, and the walls might be of glass, so open to the eye of all men and women are the movements and manners of the inmates.

Yet let me quote from a paper issued by the church sustentation society of a leading denomination in America and abroad:

"Every minister who is duly installed over a church and congregation of our communion is promised a 'competent worldly maintenance that he may be free from worldly cares and avocations.'" It is significant that the word "avocations" is used in its legitimate meaning: "The act of calling aside, or diverting from one's proper calling or business."

EIGHT HOURS AND OVERTIME

"The competent worldly maintenance" is to secure all the energies and time of the laborer for the vineyard he is hired to tend. Your mill hand "knocks off" your work at 5 or 6 o'clock, and if he be a wide-awake fellow, he turns many an honest penny during the evenings and half holidays. The bookkeeper may, without let or hindrance, write up other ledgers than your own at home. There are scores of ways by which the professed hireling may eke out his wages. Physicians, lawyers and merchants ask nobody's permission as to the employment of their spare hours. "One man, in his time, plays many parts"—and perchance quadruples his income, but our ordained and installed Ixion is bound to the wheel of his "sacred office" until his "period of usefulness is at an end." (O, familiar and fateful phrase!)

We have, then, a finely tempered instrument of the most approved pattern, which is not to be diverted to any use other than that designated in the contract. The natural sequence would seem to be that a fair and equitable price should be paid for it. In reply, I append the comment of another writer upon this topic: "There is bitter humor in the 'Form of Government' just quoted when the 'competent worldly maintenance' is a third less than a mechanic's wage."

NEARING THE BREAD LINE

The bitterness is made pungent and the humor of the situation lessened by the statement drawn from the circular letter put forth by the secretary of a ministerial relief association connected with an influential and, in the main, wealthy communion: "The average salary paid to our ministers in the active pastorate is $600 per annum."

Of course he cannot support life upon that unless he be a bachelor and his residence be in a mining camp or a mountain region where the barest necessaries of life must suffice to supply his wants. If a family man must get along upon less than a mechanic's wage, he is helped out by donation parties and occasional boxes of cast-off clothing from richer churches. In plain English, he and his are paupers as essentially as if they were lodged in the almshouse. Said a rich woman to me with the air of one who, by her deeds of mercy, makes her calling and election sure: "I always give liberally to the Church and other worthy charities. You know, 'Whoso giveth to the poor lendeth to the Lord.' As I often say to my husband, 'We cannot ask better security.'"

"Church and other charities!" That is oftener the tone of the rank and file of Protestant Church members than we are willing to admit. All that they contribute to the pastor's support over and above the meager stipend we have indicated is set down to the Lord's account—and on the debit side of the sheet. Interest is compounded according to a system patented by themselves.

LAGGING BEHIND THE WORLD

Philanthropists write and declaim from the rostrum against the penuriousness of a government that pays its armed defenders a "beggarly pittance." The soldier grumbles less loudly in the knowledge that half pay awaits him at the close of his term of service and a pension for his family at his death. Our minister may be turned out of office many years earlier than his blue-coated brother, and absolutely penniless so far as any provision made by the Church goes. By sailing closely to the wind he may have kept his family in food and clothes. He has not been able to save a dollar even from the stray checks and greenbacks doled out to him patronizingly by friend and parishioner. In his most prosperous estate, he and his thrifty helpmeet have achieved only shabby gentility. For the remainder of their days they drop the tattered cloak of gentility and settle down to the unequivocal squalor of confessed poverty. And this at an age when his college mates are touring the continent in their motor cars and eating the plum cake of carelessness!

Do not plead that the Church, as a whole, is ignorant of the enormity of this injustice. The Church does not concern itself with improvident families unless they belong to the "interesting poor"—the class for which we build settlement houses and association halls and welfare work homes.

FOR LOVE OR MONEY

If poor young ministers will marry poor girls they must take what is coming to the educated improvident. After all, the outspoken old minister was not so far wrong as we are inclined to think—or say—who advised the graduating class of theologues to pick out wives who are "pious and have a little property." It is fast becoming fashionable to deprecate the marriage of ministers who have nothing but their salaries to depend upon. Careful students of varied economies do not hesitate to point out the superior efficiency of Roman Catholic missionaries, and to attribute their success to their celibacy. There is no disguising the fact that wives and children are impedimenta that cannot be cast aside when duty calls to another field. These are spokesmen whose deliverances are not indorsed by the Church. On the contrary, we still swear audibly by Paul and content our consciences with spasmodic relief of suffering consequent upon ill-advised wedlock. Is it possible that underlying the apparent apathy lurks the belief that more and better work is accomplished by the celibate than by the married minister? That, instead of overt advocacy of a tenet that might scandalize oldtime Christians and cause the enemy to blaspheme, we foresee that the end will be as surely gained by slow starvation?

MUSIC AND MINISTRY

Before I, who write thus, am accused of treason to my faith and Church, look the ugly facts square in the face and say upon what other hypothesis they may be explained away. Protestants are not niggardly in other directions. There is hardly a church in any city that does not expend more upon music in one year than it subscribes in three years for "ministerial relief and the ministers' widows' fund." A single memorial window that is criticized as a blotch upon the wall of the sanctuary costs treble the sum asked for by the incumbent who demurs in spirit at the task of soliciting funds for the "sustentation" of his needy brethren. May be because an echo of the old epitaph sounds through the chambers of his soul: "As we are now, so must you be!"

Denis Wortman, D.D., the able secretary of the Society for Ministerial Relief of the Reformed (Dutch) Church in America, has a pertinent and feeling word upon the unwillingness of the clergyman to press home upon the hearts of his hearers the plain truth of the attitude of the Church upon this subject: "Do you know that it does grind upon us to be asking help for men in our own profession? It seems to humiliate! It seems to lower the dignity of the ministry! Possibly with some it seems to bring our sacred calling into contempt. We are exposing poverties many of our clergy are painfully endeavoring to conceal for the Master's sake."

EARLY RETIREMENT

From a report compiled by the same writer, I quote: "The number of annuitants increases from year to year, and will continue to do so with increase of prices of living and the earlier retirement of ministers from active service."

There is pregnant meaning in that last clause. It is set forth, without apology for the bald statement, in a government report issued by the Bureau of Education. It is headed boldly by the journal copying the report: "Number Who Seek Protestant Pulpits Constantly Decreasing. A remarkable decrease in the number of Protestant ministers graduated from the universities of the country is shown in a current report of the United States Bureau of Education.

"It is plain, says the report, that educated men no longer seek the cloth as they did when the nation was younger. It may mean much or little that the percentage of ministers among the graduates of typical colleges has declined from a proportion of sixty or seventy per cent to less than ten per cent. An examination of the figures collected at the close of the nineteenth century from thirty-seven representative colleges discloses the fact that the ministry takes between five and six per cent of the university graduates, which marks the lowest point for that profession during the two and one half centuries of American college history."

Put side by side with these statements the certainty that the decrease in the number of candidates for work in a fast widening field, white for the harvest, is as well known to the aforesaid Protestant Church as the simplest fact in natural history, and that it does not incite it to amendment of the wrong which has brought it about—what deduction can be drawn from such knowledge and apathy? As a body, the Church is determined not to maintain married men in the ministry. Actions, more eloquent than protestations, give the lie to the professed approval of home sketched by Paul and nominally indorsed by professors of the Protestant faith.

CROWNED WITH CARE

It is a favorite trick of business and political organizations to "freeze out" unpopular members rather than eject them openly. A Church that affects to condemn papal principles and usages is quietly freezing out the married clergy in its own faith. Without abating one jot or one tittle of belief in the obligation to spread the gospel of salvation to earth's remotest bounds, we insist, practically, that such work must be done by a man who is willing to resign the joys of home, the companionship of wife and child, and to bring personal requirements down to hermit fare and squatter's hut, while he is adjudged capable of discharging "acceptably" the duties of the sacred office. It has passed into a proverb that the pastor crosses the dead line at fifty. His hoary head is disgrace and displacement instead of glory.

RESIGNATION OR WHAT

"We kinder lost our relish for our preacher," said the deacon of a colored church, "so we done sent in his resignation." The same is done in effect yearly in hundreds of Protestant churches made up of his superiors in race and education. Freezing him out is equivalent to sending in his resignation. If he be celibate, he may have taken out a "limited insurance policy" upon his life and scraped together the premium year by year. He has timed it to fall due at fifty, or thereabouts, and (if he be single) he may have enough to keep the life in him for the rest of his weary, because idle, days.

The tale is trite, but none the less pitiful because it is so often told. Sensational newspapers set "scareheads" above announcements of the rapidly thinning ranks of the Church militant. The Church is itself apparently content to let the logic of events demonstrate the necessity of a celibate clergy, if the evangelization of the world is to go on.

NATIONAL MONUMENTS

HENRY VAN DYKE

Count not the cost of honor to the dead!
  The tribute that a mighty nation pays
  To those who loved her well in former days
Means more than gratitude for glories fled;
For every noble man that she hath bred,
  Immortalized by art's immortal praise.
  Lives in the bronze and marble that we raise,
To lead our sons as he our fathers led.
These monuments of manhood, brave and high,
  Do more than forts or battle ships to keep
Our dear-bought liberty. They fortify
  The heart of youth with valor wise and deep;
They build eternal bulwarks and command
Eternal strength to guard our native land.

NOT CHARITY BUT JUSTICE

RETIRING PENSIONS AND ORGANIZED CHRISTIANITY

BISHOP
RICHARD J. COOKE, D.D., LL.D.

I have been a Gospel Minister for forty years and know the hardships of the itinerant's life. After I had been preaching for thirty years, if anything had happened to me there would not have been a roof to cover my wife and children. I worked for small pay, and on my first circuit, which was nearly one hundred miles long and as wide as I cared to make it, my horse died in the cotton field, and I walked. We had no members and I had to make them, and received as salary fifty dollars and a pair of socks. I do not need to have my sympathies stirred; memory will do that for me.

I would change the emphasis in pleading for the Retired Ministers from charity to justice. The provisions for their comfort are now placed upon the ground of support, though for a long time it was put on the ground of charity; an appeal which Preachers learned to scorn. What the Retired Ministers need is not charity, but justice.

I would go further and say that it is not so much a question of the support of the ministry as it is a question of the maintenance of organized religion. When you sift it down to the real basis of the proposition, this will stand out clearly to every thinker who studies the processes and workings of social forces. The question of a dependable pension for Retired Ministers concerns the permanence of organized religion.

It is a platitude that there never was an age like this; but it is a tremendous platitude. There never was an age when so much was required of human brain and nerves and energy as is required to-day. There never was a time when there was such a demand for men of brains and parts and power and energy and efficiency; resourceful men, men who are never defeated; men of quality, ability and power; men of thought and of vision. The whole world is flung wide open to the man who has energy, thought and insight; who neither sees ghosts nor fears the lions in the way, but goes straightforward; who when difficulties are in the way makes himself difficult to the difficulties. Vast fortunes are being made, and vast opportunities are offered in every line. No department of human thought or activity is shut to men of brains and power. To-day demands in our civil governments and national Congress men of prophetic power—not mere politicians, men who can get elected merely, but men with prophetic vision, who study the ongoings of Divine Providence and the play of the social, political, national and international forces; who study humanity, and think and plan for humanity. Such is the growth of government and intelligence, and such are the demands on the human spirit, that nobody to-day can aspire to national fame or to be a statesman, who does not have keen perceptions of the mighty movements of humanity and who is unable to adjust human laws and forces to events which will as surely happen as that the stars will roll in their orbits.

Not only in politics, national and international, and in great industrial enterprises and constructive schemes; in great affairs relating to the reclamation of lands, the tunneling of mountains, the building of railroads, and the bridging of streams, but also in the Christian Ministry men of the largest ability are required. There never was a time when there was such a demand for men of the highest ability in the pulpit of the living God as this very day, for the simple reason that this day is like no other day. There never was a time when there were so many school-houses, colleges and great universities, or such great teachers in them; and there never was a time when the accumulated wisdom of all the ages was so concentrated in institutions of original research, scientific and sociological, concerning everything that pertains to the human spirit and the growth and development of humanity. Your children and the children of the people to whom you preach are in the public schools, which, by reason of their development under the care of scientific men, are equal to the first class colleges of thirty years ago. These young people are getting ready for world ventures. Their minds have been opened, and throb with tremendous energy as they go out to the work that is before them. If they go to the Church of God, and, instead of finding a man of brains, who has a grip on things and himself, a man as equal to his place as a preacher as the teacher, scientist and statesman are to theirs, they find a man who is not able to lead them anywhere, one who had no outlook, no teaching nor informing power, no inspiring or uplifting vision, and not a single cell in heart, soul, mind and spirit vibrating by the vivid truth which he proclaims, where in a short time will these young people be, and where will the Church be?

The Church says to the young man coming out of her schools and colleges, and beginning the ministerial life, "You will have a small salary compared with what you can earn. You have ability to go into civil engineering, or medicine or jurisprudence, or into large industrial enterprises and prosper; but as a Minister of Jesus Christ there will be but a pittance for you throughout your life. The time will come when your wife will walk timidly and humbly down the aisle and quickly draw her poor, faded skirts into the pew lest people should see how shabbily she is dressed, her womanly instinct revolting at the difference she feels in her sensitive nature between her clothing and that of the women of the parish. Your little girl will be comparing her clothes with the nicely embroidered dresses of the little girls at their side, and your little boy will look at his thick shoes and compare them with the soft kid of the little boy next door; and you will live that sort of a life not because you are not the peer of their fathers in intelligence or capacity, but because you cannot compete financially with the men who are doing the larger material things in life. In college perhaps you hobnobbed with these fellows on the terms of intellectual and social equality, but you find yourself as a Minister stinted in income, and at the end of your active life what prospects have you for peace, comfort and satisfaction when the day's work is done and you shall sit down in the twilight to look into the long unknown?"

In the presence of such questions how many men of brains, power and energy are going to sacrifice themselves to that kind of life? And then how will the Church of God be able to adjust itself to meet the religious problems of to-morrow, and to relate itself to the scientific revelations which lie ahead of us? And how can the Church relate itself to the philosophic outcome of the human spirit produced by the cultural forces? How can the Church become the great leader of humanity and set the tune for the world to sing by unless she has preachers who can pitch the key and command the respect and reverence of men who come out of great institutions into our churches? The result will be that your children will lose respect for the Church and its leadership and scholarship and spirit, and will turn aside to other agencies which minister to the spirit, in order to develop the cultural content of their inner life.

It is a remarkable fact that in the conflict between the Church of Rome and the French Legislature, this strange thing happened, that notwithstanding the fact that the aristocracy of France supported the Church with the prestige of their names and gave their money, yet they failed to put their sons into the Ministry, which was recruited from the peasants of Brittany and southern France. What was the result? The time came when the Church was face to face with conditions which the thinkers of the nineteenth century had produced. Renan had done his work throughout France, and the works of the English philosophers and of the German Strauss had been translated into French, and had become the common property of the intellectual men of France; and in the Senate there were the sharp, incisive, scientifically trained skeptic, the enemy of the Church, and the keen-witted, sarcastic politician, both pointing the finger of scorn and blurting with sarcastic tongues, while the Church stood like a fat ox, helpless under the fatal blows. The Church that quivered under the thunder of the Christless statesman of France had not a single soul of power and ability who in the hour of Rome's night was able to stand up and defend the Church of his fathers; and down she went under the scorn and contempt of the nation, separated forever from the life of the nation, because there was nobody to compete with those men on the "Left," nobody to answer their arguments, no one scientifically trained, no one with the world view, no one who had been bred in the modern atmosphere, no one able to cope with them in oratory or thought or influence. So in the long run, unless we get men of ability and culture and provide that such men shall give all the energies of their lives to the Church, the time will come when Protestant America will find itself in a tremendous emergency with no one able to defend it as it ought to be defended.

You say that if men be really touched by the Holy Ghost they will go into the Ministry of the Church; that no man will resist the call of the Spirit; that if the love of Christ is in his heart, the young man will enter the Ministry ready to sacrifice himself for the Church. I want to say that there are millions of men who to-night would shed the last drop of blood for Jesus Christ and rejoice in doing it, who would not crook their little finger for a Church that violates the first principles of the gospel of Jesus Christ and forgets the old age or disabilities of its ministers. Not all good men consider that this, that or the other organization is necessary to Jesus Christ; and you will find them going into Y. M. C. A. work, and into various kinds of associational Christian work, without throwing themselves into the work of the Ministry. Men of brain and power and culture and ability and influence will not find their way in, if the Church of God starves them out, and gives them no chance to raise their families as the families next door are raised. They will not go into the Church if their boy will feel that it is a misfortune to him that his father was a Christian Minister, and will say, "I did not have the chance in the world that you had, nor your opportunity for education because my father was a Minister of Christ." The result will be that you will get weaklings into the pulpit, and men who seek it for a living.

The Church must have preachers who will stand on their own feet and succeed on their own merits; men who go out into the world to preach the gospel of Jesus Christ because the gospel is a power in their own lives, and the fire so consumes them that they must preach it; who feel, "Woe is me if I preach not the gospel!" When a man has that in him and preaches the gospel with power, vigor, strength, and conviction, the Spirit of God will honor him; that is why He abides in His Church. We should put this question of a dependable pension for Retired Ministers before the people everywhere because the cause of religion and the permanence of organized Christianity are at stake; and when our people grasp the thought that it is for the sake of religion itself that we plan great things for the Retired Ministers, then the Church will continue the royal race of prophets of God and spiritual leaders of Humanity.

Portland, Ore. RICHARD J. COOKE.

WHY DON'T YOU SPEAK FOR YOURSELF, JOHN?

"Still John Alden went on, unheeding the words of Priscilla,
Urging the suit of his friend, explaining, persuading, expanding.
But as he warmed and glowed, in his simple and eloquent language,
Quite *forgetful of self*, and full of the praise of his rival,
Archly the maiden smiled, and, with eyes overrunning with laughter,
Said, in a tremulous voice, '*Why don't you speak for yourself, John?*'"

O YE FORGETFUL PREACHERS, pleading for schools and colleges, for Missions and hospitals—for black men and yellow men and red men and brown men—ministers whose sympathies go out to the ends of the earth—composites of John Baptist, John Knox, John Calvin, and John Wesley—*WHY DON'T YOU SPEAK FOR YOURSELVES?*

The income required to meet the needs of the Retired Ministers is not large enough. But it will be large enough just as soon as the PASTORS SPEAK OUT WITHOUT APOLOGY, WITHOUT HESITATION, WITHOUT FALSE MODESTY.

Look at the reports of your Connectional Relief Boards. See how Veterans fared whose term of service was the same as yours. Put yourself on the list; or put your wife on the list. Then try to make the mental adjustments of your life and hers to the condition of retirement; and see how it will clear your throat and how your voice will ring out in behalf of your disabled brothers and sisters.

You do not hesitate to plead for China and Africa and Korea; for Belgium and France and Germany. Why fail to CRY ALOUD TO YOUR PEOPLE for your own brothers and sisters who received so little for their support last year?

The laymen are puzzled, however, because preachers hoarse from shouting for the heathen can scarcely speak above a whisper in behalf of the Retired Ministers. Pastors must come to self-consciousness and self-assertiveness in this their own cause. Do a little courting on your own account.

STOP! LOOK! LISTEN!

THE REV. JOSEPH B. HINGELEY, D.D.

Corresponding Secretary Board of Conference Claimants

STOP!—"THINK ON THESE THINGS"

To earnest-minded Men and Women I would speak earnest, personal words concerning the needs of the Retired Ministers, and the widows and dependent orphans of deceased Ministers, especially those of the Methodist Episcopal Church.

1. *No other church demands so much of its Ministers and their families.* They are not allowed to choose where they should go, or whom they should serve, or what financial support they shall receive. Surrendering themselves wholly to God and His work, they not only devote themselves entirely to His cause, but devote all they have or can secure. They not only preach the Gospel of Liberty, but the path to the parsonage door is worn by the feet of the sorrowing and the needy. They not only urge liberality to every good cause, but they are themselves examples of liberality. They are royal givers.

2. *On entering the Ministry they took this Pledge:*

"To employ all their time in the Work of God."

"To be merciful for Christ's sake to Poor and Needy people and to all Strangers destitute of help."

"To give themselves wholly to their Office and to apply themselves to this one thing."

"To search for the Sick, Poor and Impotent that they may be visited and relieved."

In fulfilling these Christly duties enjoined by their Ordination Vows they are not mere almoners of others' wealth, but they draw on their own slender purses.

With the scanty support our Aged Ministers received they needed no exhortation against laying up treasures on earth, for earthly treasures were not theirs.

3. *I need not remind you how faithful they were to their trust.* Your memory enshrines them.

They were Friends of your Childhood.

They led you to Christ.

They sanctified your Marriage Vows.

They fought life's hardest battles at your side.

They walked with you amid the shadows.

Their Prayers lifted up as on eagle wings your sainted Father and Mother, and brought smiles to the faces of your Triumphant Loved Ones.

Their tears mingled with yours as they fell on the graves of Your Dead.

4. *They were good business men,* as ten thousand churches and hundreds of Colleges, Hospitals, and Homes for the poor and needy erected by them show. BUT THEIR BUSINESS WAS NOT TO MAKE MONEY. IT WAS TO SAVE AND MAKE MAN; and in doing this task nothing was held in reserve—time, talent, means.

While you were growing *rich* on the well-earned increment of your honest toil, and through the increment of an atmosphere and conditions which they created, they were giving themselves to you and yours. They saw the country change from conditions of struggle and poverty to conditions of wealth and plenty. As the cost of living increased, their little stipend diminished or ceased altogether, until they now stand old, penniless, helpless; with courage to do, but without strength to perform their holy offices.

Strange indeed would it be if you, who owe so much to them, should leave them to poverty and neglect. Stranger still, if you to whom these words come should fail to help them in their pressing needs, or hesitate to strengthen hands which often strengthened you.

LOOK!

1. HOW MANY THERE ARE

In round numbers there are

3,181 Retired Ministers,
3,123 Widows of Deceased Ministers,
285 Orphan Children.

A total of 6,589 Conference Claimants in whom the

Methodist Episcopal Church declares "the claim to a comfortable support rightly inheres." (Discipline ¶ 323.)

In addition to these there are also 500 Retired Ministers who relinquished their claims in the interests of their less favored brethren.

This would be a large number of a *small* Church, but it is *not* large for the Methodist Episcopal Church with twenty thousand ministers, three and one half million members, fifty million dollars annual expenditure, and three hundred millions of property.

Nor is it strange that there should be 3,200 Retired Ministers out of a total 20,000—one out of seven. A regiment of soldiers with only fifteen per cent incapacitated for duty is unknown in days of peace; and in time of war scarcely one out of two can be brought to the firing line.

Cannot the Methodist Episcopal Church, which places fifty million dollars on God's altar each year, spare at least two millions—a nickel out of each dollar—for the Veterans who made it, and for the Widows and Children of the fallen?

2. WHAT DO THEY RECEIVE?

Only thirteen Conference Claimants receive more than $500 a year.

Only one hundred and forty receive more than $400.

Only five hundred receive more than $300.

Of the remaining six thousand;

Twelve hundred receive less than $50 each.

Fifteen hundred receive less than $100.

Thirty-six hundred receive less than $200.

3. HOW DOES THIS LOOK TO YOU?

If you are not familiar with the work that is now being done for the Aged Minister you will be woefully discouraged and ashamed. But when you learn what your brothers and sisters are doing to better the condition of the Retired Ministers, and the widows and orphans, you will thank God that their condition has improved greatly since the Board of Conference Claimants was organized in their behalf, and they were given a voice to speak for them.

Since 1908 one hundred thousand dollars has been added

each year to the amount distributed to Conference Claimants. But not until half a million dollars more has been added to the present annual distribution can a self-respecting Church join in the Doxology.

LISTEN!

Many agencies are providing help for the Retired Ministry: The CHARTERED FUND; The BOOK CONCERN; ANNUAL CONFERENCE FUNDS; and direct contributions from the churches which by law goes to them.

But the authorized organization which correlates the entire work and conducts an inspirational and educational Campaign in behalf of the Veteran Preachers is "THE BOARD OF CONFERENCE CLAIMANTS OF THE METHODIST EPISCOPAL CHURCH," now in its fifth year, which has given $175,000 to needy cases and is now creating a Connectional (that is general) Permanent Fund of $1,000,000; the income of which, together with other moneys secured by the Board, helps those Retired Ministers, Widows and Orphans everywhere whose needs are greatest.

THE BOARD OF CONFERENCE CLAIMANTS

is the *agent of the entire Church in behalf of all needy claimants, without reference to Annual Conference boundaries.* Its money is first distributed to necessitous cases within the bounds of the weaker Conferences, and afterward to those within the stronger Conferences. The Board is thus the great equalizer between the poorer and the more prosperous fields. Its purpose as expressed in the Discipline is, that "A more equitable and generous support may be secured for the Retired Ministers and other Conference Claimants, *especially for those in the more needy Conferences.*" (¶ 471.) *Conferences and churches cooperate* in providing the Board with money for such distribution, and Methodist people everywhere are asked to become contributors to the Connectional Permanent Fund of the Board.

To the Board of Conference Claimants has been given not only the duty of building up and administering this Connectional Permanent Fund, but also that of "Increasing Revenues for the benefit of Conference Claimants."

The Board is therefore a great inspirational organization. It publishes a quarterly magazine, *The Veteran Preacher;* it provides tracts for general distribution; it maintains a valuable literature covering important phases of the work. It issues Life Annuity Bonds, and urges the making of Wills in favor of the Retired Preachers and Widows. Through its representatives it keeps in touch with Annual Conferences, and it cooperates in every possible way with all agencies employed by the Church to advance the cause of the Retired Ministry.

The Connectional (or general) Permanent Fund is for perpetual investments, *the income only being used* to help those Claimants who are in the greatest need. The General Conference authorized the *"Jubilee Gift for Conference Claimants,"* thereby celebrating the Sesqui-Centennial, or 150th Anniversary of American Methodism, expecting that at least a Million Dollars of it should go into the Connectional Permanent Fund of the Board.

ANNUAL CONFERENCE FUNDS

THESE EARNEST WORDS are addressed to you—a *personal message from me,* to whom in a special way the Cause of the Retired Ministers, Widows and Orphans has been committed. But I speak not only for the Board of Conference Claimants alone but also in behalf of all ORGANIZATIONS AND ANNUAL CONFERENCES which represent this Cause in its nearer relations. God has raised up threescore Conference agents and representatives who are serving the Church and the Veteran Ministry by securing much needed funds. I speak also for them. Their names will be found on page 289. They ask you to help the Retired Ministers you know, and the widows and children of men who served in your own Conference. Whatever organization you use in helping the veterans I ask that *you join in the holy purpose* of providing for the Aged Ministry; and I solicit from you—even as though I were speaking to you face to face—a Gift—*a liberal gift*—if possible, a GREAT GIFT for this Cause; a gift which will represent, at least in part, your duty in so administering your affairs that you may know, that the aged Minister may know, that God may know that you have administered your estate in His Way.

Should you desire to communicate with me or with your Conference representative, write fully and freely. Should you desire to see us, let us know and we will come to you, Messengers of Divine Opportunity, glad to return as Messengers of your bounty to his needy servants.

Every day a new earth mound covers the wearied, worn body of an aged Methodist Minister. Yesterday you might have helped him. To-day you cannot. I do not appeal for him. His reward is ample. But I do appeal for his comrade who survives, for the aged companion of his trials and triumphs, and for the dependent orphans, whose tears fill the eye of God. Their needs furnish your highest opportunity for holy service.

The *best way for you,* and the *best way for the Old Preachers,* who are with us to-day but who to-morrow will have gone to their reward, is to *make a Gift* to them, to be *forever invested* in their behalf and in behalf of successive generations of Aged Ministers.

Do not say, as Festus did of Paul, "Thou art beside thyself! Much learning of the needs of the Veterans doth make thee mad!" This Cause has been on my mind and heart for years. If you realize the need and will contribute to relieve "the necessities of the Saints"—the Aged Ministers and Widows—I am sure that you will agree that "I speak the words of truth and soberness."

Chicago, Ill. JOSEPH B. HINGELEY.

VETERANS OF THE CROSS

V. A. COOPER, D.D.

Church of the living God, arise!
Your army peoples earth and skies;
Veterans of the living host,
Borne down with age at duty's post,
Worn out with toil not counted loss,
Come bending low beneath the Cross.

O Church of God, your Heroes greet
Who lay their trophies at your feet!
Let not the nation put to shame
The gratitude they justly claim.
Their wants relieve, your bounty give
And make them happy while they live.

PART I. THE CLAIM INHERENT

CHAPTER II. OLD AGE

GIVE THEM THE FLOWERS NOW

Closed eyes cannot see the white roses,
Cold hands cannot hold them, you know;
Breath that is stilled cannot gather
The odors that sweet from them blow.
Death, with a peace beyond dreaming,
Its children of earth doth endow;
Life is the time we can help them,
So give them the flowers NOW.

Here are the struggles and striving,
Here are the cares and the fears;
Now is the time to be smoothing
The frowns and the furrows and tears.
What to closed ears are kind sayings?
What to hushed heart is deep vow?
Naught can avail after parting,
So give them the flowers NOW.

Just a kind word or a greeting;
Just a warm grasp or a smile—
These are the flowers that will lighten
The burdens of many a mile.
After the journey is over,
After tired hands drop the plow,
What is the use of them, tell me?
So give them the flowers NOW.

Blooms from the happy heart's garden,
Plucked in the spirit of love;
Blooms that are earthly reflection
Of flowers that blossom above—
Words cannot tell what a measure
Of blessing such gifts will allow
To dwell in the lives of the Veterans,
So give them the flowers NOW.

SOME ADVANTAGES OF GROWING OLD

THE REV. W. H. THOMAS, D.D.

New England Conference

Just now it is the fashion to be young. The crowds on the streets appear to be young, and the profusely advertised lotions and treatments and devices to keep one looking young indicate that youth is the fashion.

A little while ago it was the fashion for one to appear to be old. "Tonsorial artists" in the eighteenth century frosted every head with silver. They did not then with evil pride seek to conceal old age. The people did not so much pretend to be young as to look old. Only white heads of hair were in style and could be admitted to court. I mention this to disarm young people's prejudice in favor of youth by calling to mind that age can be fashionable, and so perhaps persuade them to consent to grow old; or at least to look kindly on the old, old fashion, ever new, of growing old; that fashion that elevates one to the only real and natural aristocracy in the world, the aristocracy of old age.

One day Dr. Holmes said he was contemplating writing a book that would supplement his Autocrat of the Breakfast Table by treating of matters as over the supper table, showing how the same things looked when the day was done. His quaint, cheery, and unconquerable spirit is to be found in his last book, Over the Tea Cups.

Max Mueller quotes with approval the Bishop of London's statements:

"Men judge more wisely of what is essential and of what is indifferent in the quiet sunset of life than in the heat and burden of the day; and Richter says:

"Like a morning dream life becomes more and more bright the longer we live, and the reason for everything appears to be clear. What has puzzled us before seems less mysterious, and the crooked paths look straight as we approach the end."

That would be a sorry arraignment of Providence which made life continue while taking away its advantages, leaving a man poorer for all he has toiled, studied and suffered; so that you may well expect other advantages to replace those taken away by age. If youth takes away precious things as it departs, growing old brings other precious things that can only come with the years. For the years are not robbers. Though they take from us they give us more than they take, and we are the richer for them.

Age has its own beauty. If the promise on the face of youth is beautiful, the achievement, the maturity on the face of age is likewise beautiful. We have seen sweeter smiles on the face of seventy than on the face of seventeen. There is a beauty one makes for one's self. All life's good or evil that enters the soul of man is at work chiseling and molding the face. Ah! that wonderful sculptor within us, who is silently day by day molding our outward man to the likeness of the inward man. The beauty of matured character; the beauty of the holiness the years have molded; the beauty that goodness brings, appear mostly when the evening rain of memory falls on the furrowed cheek.

By growing old a man gets acquainted with himself—usually the last one to get acquainted with and the most difficult acquaintance to secure. We are taught that memory is the proof of identity; that although every particle of body and brain that were me have gone, yet I am "I" still. But there is an element deeper than memory. Memory may be destroyed, yet personality goes on, all the influence of its forgotten past molding it. As one grows older he finds that the "I" has survived all changes of body, mind or character, and of the years. This inner selfhood of the soul is like the clear daylight. It is given us to see with or by, but we cannot see it. The camera or the artist can make a picture with or by daylight, but to make a picture of daylight is impossible.

Growing old permits us to see how much better the world is becoming. Law is being modified to be more just; governments are less tyrannical and more humane; comforts are multiplying and being more widely diffused; science is bringing to light what has long been hidden in darkness. There are those to whom life seems all askew and worse every day, who mournfully ask what the world is coming to. We reply that you have only to grow old and see what it is coming to, and be glad.

Religion may change its form of expression. The present ecclesiastical system was no more to be found in the first century than was the present civilization. When I go about among the churches and listen to a belated young preacher trying to run his mill with water that went by years ago, and to dreary repetitions of obsolete commonplaces that try the patience of the saints, I am not discouraged, for I have looked in our schools and seen the faces of the coming men. What a great thing it is to send out to every community a man who consents to a poorly paid calling, yet is refined, intelligent and quietly happy in self-denying work; "poor, yet making many rich" in places where money is made the standard of respectability, influence, happiness and intelligence. Every parsonage with its limited financial circumstances is proclaiming the right value of life to those whose minds the god of this world has blinded. The great German says:

"Ye great or blessed spirits above us! When a man here, under the poor clouds of life, throws away his fortune because he prizes it less than his heart, then is he as blessed and as great as you." Sadly Walt Whitman wrote, "I am tormented day and night by three demons, ill-health, poverty and old age," but the Veteran Ministry, that company of the noble army of martyrs, endures without complaint. We congratulate the Church that the unrighteous, ungenerous treatment of them is passing away and that better conditions are coming.

Growing old enables us to laugh when the mourners go about the street crying, "Christianity is a failure." "Christianity a failure!" said Dr. Bartol. "It has never been tried." Men are not tired of Christianity. They have never found enough Christianity to get tired of it. We have been exasperatingly complacent about it, counting our numbers, boasting our wealth, not knowing how poor and blind and naked we were. But Christianity has not been outlived; it has not been lived enough. The Christian ideal has not been tried and found wanting. It has been found difficult, and tried feebly; but we are just beginning to see that the teachings of Jesus are gathering force while other things are falling into contempt.

The unrest of the Church is a sign of improvement. In all

ages the prophets and priests have been at war. We know that religion is not theology. It may be lived under many theologies. Religion is not ecclesiasticism. It lives under many forms of Church organization. Religion abides; theology and ecclesiasticism need periodical revision.

"It is the strangest of paradoxes in history that religion loses itself without the Church, and its fineness is always destroyed *within* the Church." The prophet appears rousing and firing the hearts of the people for advance, but without the priest and the Church, he ends as a voice crying in the wilderness. The priest, as Jesus said, slays the prophet and by-and-by debases the Church. Yet the Church is the refuge of religion until the time comes, as it inevitably comes, when it bursts out as a pent-up fountain and will not be confined. Then the priest and the Church begin to make amends by rearing handsome sepulchers to slain prophets. The experiences of the years lead us surely to expect that in the end true religion will be the gainer.

The relations of science and religion have changed with the years for the better. There is no feud between science and religion any more than there is between science and life. They travel on parallel roads. Science has to do with nature's processes. Religion has to do with the consummation of the processes of nature and life, character, perfection.

Growing old brings the surer faith, because established on the facts of our own experience. By seeming necessity, every once in a while men put their theories and beliefs into the melting pot to reassay them and put new values on them. It would be unaccountably sad indeed if God had so fixed it that the world must depend for its religious faith on the disputed opinions of the few. He did not do so. Jesus said, "If any man will do His will he shall know the doctrine"; and the experience of doing His will brings a basis for a satisfactory faith.

Long years ago a very old man went up on a mountain to die. He had put into the melting pot Egyptian beliefs and the beliefs of the Hebrew patriarchs; his own hands were blood-stained; his life strenuous. He had refused a throne from principle, and had led a people out of bondage. He had talked with God until his face shone. He had given God's law to men, that remains to this day. Yet he had been discouraged with the waywardness and sins of the people. His fondest hopes, his life's labors were unfulfilled. He was to die, as so many do, in sight of the promised land. Yet when he went to his death with everything dear to him vanishing from his sight, his death song was,

"Underneath are the everlasting arms."

His life's problems had been transmuted into experience. The evening mists of old age and death gathered thicker and thicker around him, but in the darkening of life his heart felt itself embraced more closely by the everlasting arms.

He who spake as never man spake said, "Love your enemies; bless them that curse you; do good to them that hate you; pray for them that despitefully use you and persecute you." He tells us to do what is against our nature and practice. Laws and governments are against it. It is easy to prove that society could not go on bound by His teaching, and yet in our innermost nature we recognize that He is right, and that the highest soul must live by His teaching.

He said, "He maketh His sun to rise on the evil and the good." We are confused and say, "Light is for the good and darkness for the evil; rain for the just, but the parching desert for the unjust." But when He adds, "Ye shall be perfect as your heavenly Father is perfect," we feel that He opens the door to a life higher and wider and nobler, and our spirits respond thereto.

Paul called Jesus the "Yes" of the promises of God. Christ's teaching is the affirmation of the aspirations in the heart of man. Divine suggestions come to human consciousness, and we realize that we are allied to a being who guarantees the ultimate goodness of existence.

Growing old brings us where we affirm God with every breath; and every act of disinterested goodness proves our sense of oneness with that Spirit whose claims are absolutely imperative; while underneath us are the everlasting arms. That sea captain a thousand miles from land, suffering with ptomaine poisoning, sent a wireless call for a physician and a prescription, and through hundreds of miles of darkness the answer came fitting his needs. His agony abated, his life was saved. So we in our sore needs send out our cries into the darkness for help, and the answer comes telling us what we must do to be saved. It brings relief from sin, comfort in sorrow and communion with an intelligence and helpfulness that is out of sight. As we grow old we know by long experience that there is a divine help that responds to our cry of need. This experience becomes as much a reality as life itself or feeling or thought, and brings a defensible faith, "For faith is the giving substance to things hoped for; a test of things not seen"; so that with Jesus we may say, "We speak that we do know, and testify that we have seen." These experiences cost us our days, our energies and our illusions, but they brought us to the place where—

"The steps of faith
Fall on the seeming void
And find the rock beneath."

They bring us where we can say, "O how melodious sound around me the evening bells of life."

The florist opens a box brought from the far tropics, and brings to view a gnarled, earthly bulb. He puts it into favorable conditions, its face turned toward the light, and by and by there hangs the exquisite exotic orchid. How wonderful that so much rare beauty should spring from so much uncouthness; that the continual experience of the light and warmth of passing days should bring from the root that had no beauty such a transcendent flower of supernal beauty. Something like that has happened to us with the growing years. We have been persuaded to come out of the dark prison of sordidness, to cast off the cerements of sin and to lift up our souls into the light of God. Something has been unfolding in us after a hidden pattern. We would not dare say it, but the apostle does:

"We all with unveiled faces beholding as in a mirror the glory of the Lord are transformed into the same image, from glory to glory, even as from the Lord, the Spirit."

If that is the interpretation of our life's experiences with God, then hopefully, cheerfully may we still go forward with the years. By growing old we graduate from the sad, pathetic, longing cry of the King James Version, "My heart and my flesh cry out for the living God," into the experience represented by the Revised Version,

"My heart and my flesh sing for joy for the living God."

South Norwalk, Conn. W. H. Thomas.

SEVEN AGES OF A MINISTER

EZRA SQUIER TIPPLE, D.D.
President Drew Theological Seminary

I. The Divine Summons

The awakening voice: "I heard the voice of the Lord, saying, Whom shall I send, and who will go for us?" *Inward struggles:* Men preach not because they want to preach, but because they *must*. "Woe is me if I preach not the Gospel." *Dawning convictions:* "Behold, to obey is better than sacrifice, and to hearken than the fat of rams." *Worldly ambitions laid upon the altar. The sacrifice complete.*

My life, my blood, I here present,
If for thy truth they may be spent;
Fulfill thy sovereign counsel, Lord;
Thy will be done, thy name adored.

II. Sharpening the Sword

Days of preparation: A long journey over a rough way. *Hard work, much of it:* Sacrifices for the sake of an adequate equipment daily. *Patient effort, long continued:* The preacher must get some word from God before he speaks it.

"Clearly he has a task which will need an undivided attention and a complete absorption in its fulfillment. He is to climb Sinai with its ring-fence of death, and on the summit speak face to face with Him whom no one can see and yet live. He is to push through the wilderness, eating angels' meat or nothing, and scale the crags of Horeb, where in a great hollow, shadowed by a hand, he may, through earthquake, wind, and fire, discern the still small voice. What a venture it is for him! No sphere of human activity is to be compared with the exigencies of this endeavor."—*Horton.*

Days of waiting, as in the upper room in Jerusalem; desert days, as to John; *days of want and penury even,* but days of heroic ideals and high hopes.

III. On the Skirmish Line

When, at one of the early Conferences of the Church, Bishop Asbury called for a volunteer to go to some desert region in the far South, "the region of many diseases and broken constitutions," as he said, Enoch George sprang to his feet and cried, "Here am I; send me." *This has ever been the spirit of the Methodist preacher.* An apostle "by the will of God," he has gone to Hardscrabble Circuit, or other difficult field, with courage and gladness of heart. *Salary small,* $400 *or* $500 *perhaps,* but he is not of those prophets who, according to Amaziah's scornful judgment, preach in order to earn their bread. Anyhow, many churches seem to believe that ministers ought not to expect to live by bread alone, and furnish a more ethereal diet. *So there is a continuation of the story of hardships and sacrifices.*

IV. In the Heat of the Conflict

Sun at meridian; battle at high tide; the exhilaration of victory felt; all the powers of mind and heart at full play.

'Tis not a cause of small import
  The pastor's care demands;
But what might fill an angel's heart,
  And filled a Saviour's hands.

Yet all the while continued sacrifices. Rigid self-denial the rule of the household; children to be educated; an example of benevolence to be shown; appearances to be kept up; a thousand demands on the preacher's income. What of the rainy day? Or old age? But why have anxious thought of the morrow? Has not this preacher the divine promises and the pledge of a great Church?

V. The Turn of the Tide

Scarcely perceptible at first, but the tide is going out now. He is stronger and better equipped than at any time in his life, but fewer churches seem to desire him. O the shame of it! There is a touch of gray in his hair, and church committees turn from him as "too old." He knows how false it is; his soul protests against the injustice of it all; but, but —why kick against the pricks? *The tide is at the ebb now.*

VI. The Lengthening Shadows

The years multiply. Forty of them perhaps have now been given to the Church. They have indeed been years of hardship and sacrifice, but glad, happy years of blessed service. *Salaries have never been large,* but there has been no complaint. He did not enter the ministry to make money—that question was settled in those far-off days when he heard the voice of the Lord. He has preached, not for money, but that he might have the seal of God's favor and the approval of his own conscience. *Souls have been his hire.* Neither God nor the Methodist Church has yet failed him. Why should he doubt or fear now, when he walks with faltering step, when work is becoming too heavy a burden for him to carry much longer?

VII. Superannuation

The preacher's Gethsemane, too often, alas! The fateful hour, towards which he has sometimes looked with mysterious dread, has come. He is no longer in "active" service. *Another has taken his place on the firing line.* He watches the conflict from a distance. O the anguish of this, when his heart still beats with courage and the song of battle is still on his lips! Few realize the agony and bitterness of this experience. But, anyhow, he is *comfortable,* you say. *Is* he? IS he comfortable?

What was it Cardinal Wolsey said, in his fall from power? "Had I but served my God with half the zeal I served my king, he would not in mine age have left me naked to mine enemies." This man, this Methodist preacher, has been serving God these many years. He has given to the Church all his affection, energy, thought and devotion. God has been his master; the Church has been the field of his unremitting toil. Now that he has come to old age, will the Lord cast him off? Never. God's promises are sure. They have not been revoked. What is this that He pledges? "I will in nowise fail thee, neither will I in any wise forsake thee."

E'en down to old age all my people shall prove
My sovereign, eternal, unchangeable love;
And when hoary hairs shall their temples adorn,
Like lambs they shall still in my bosom be borne.

God must make good His word to the old preacher, but how? God works through his people. *The Church must make good the pledges of the Almighty.* The Lord has laid upon the Church this solemn duty. The Church is the bank where God's promises to the old preacher must be cashed. Archangels will not be sent from heaven with currency as long as the Church has an abundance. *God is pledged to the support of His sons who trust in Him, and we are His chosen agents to do His will toward them.* We must not fail Him, lest those whom He loves and whom we love and honor, and to whose fidelity and labors the Church and, it may be, our own soul owes so much, when in their old age they ask for bread are given a stone, or for fish are given a serpent. The Church must, in the name of Christ, care for the preacher who in the journey of life has come to the last inn on the road and *"superannuated,"* waits the royal summons.

Madison, N. J. EZRA S. TIPPLE.

THE SENIOR RETIRED METHODIST MINISTER

THE REV. DAVID JORDAN HIGGINS, D.D.—97 YEARS OLD

Dr. Higgins was born at Gorham, Me., on September 18th, 1817. He pursued his studies at Wesleyan University for three years and entered the Maine Conference in 1842.

At the outbreak of the Civil War, he raised a company and was made its Captain, and quickly won his way to promotion, being commissioned Colonel of the Twenty-fourth Ohio Volunteer Infantry. Physically disabled by the hardships of the service, he resigned his commission and soon after reentered the Methodist ministry in Minnesota. He took a Retired relation in the Northern Minnesota Conference in 1899.

Dr. Higgins has been a student all his life. Two years ago he completed a four years' course in advanced philosophy in the University of California, and is now taking a course of study for the degree of Doctor of Philosophy. He has written recently *American Life in the XIX Century,* and *The Problem of Christianity.*

Concerning his books, he wrote:

"I make these studies for my physical benefit, for I find that my physical energy depends largely upon my mental activity."

Dr. Higgins is also a Bible student and has made it his daily practice for years to read a chapter of the Bible in the Greek or Hebrew text. He is a standing rebuke to any young minister who thinks that he has completed his studies when he has finished his Conference Course. Though almost a centenarian, his mental activities are keen. At the request of Dr. Hingeley he prepared the following article:

DOES THE MINISTRY PAY?

THE REV. DAVID JORDAN HIGGINS, D.D.

Seventy years in the ministry of the Methodist Episcopal Church furnishes a whole volume of reminiscences; especially because no organization affords such variety of life experiences as does the Methodist Itinerancy. In the early days the pastorate of one-year limit kept the preacher busy night and day. What he did must be done rapidly, for the "Itinerant Wheel" revolved as regularly and inexorably as the earth, and he must move on, his work completed or not. His one work was evangelizing sinners, with but small opportunity to make himself felt as a factor in social or civic life. His salary of $100, if paid in full, provided his clothing and supplied him with the few books necessary for the "Conference Course of

Study." But his food and that of his horse was abundant and of the best quality; for the mothers and sisters of the Church displayed the best specimens of their culinary art when the preacher came around, for his special good or harm; often for his harm, for many a favorite preacher owed his untimely death to the rich food urged upon him by the good sisters. What a picture, that home, where the preacher was entertained: The best room; the nice warm bed; the cozy open fire; the brooding mother, and the smiling daughters.

The scene changes and the pastorate lengthens to two years, and the salary is raised to $200. A parsonage is supplied, and the preacher's bride fills it with sunshine. What a joy animates the heart and life of the preacher, when the choicest maiden of the whole country comes to the parsonage! No matter now, how long the rides between appointments, or how cold the storm that beats in his face, there is a home awaiting him with the welcoming kiss and loving greetings.

The children come, blessed children! Their clattering feet, and ringing voices seem like angel wings, and the sweet melody of heaven. The cunning fingers of the wife and mother cut and stretch the scanty cloth for the children's garments, and mend the socks of the husband; and, best of all, she sits at his side and helps to untangle the knotty dogmas of Paley, Butler or Watson, or suggests a needed thought for next Sunday's sermon.

The years pass; and the comfortable, neat church, with its steeple, takes the place of the rough school house. The pipe organ is substituted for the bass-viol and flute. The Conference Seminary rises, and the children finish their education or prepare for college. The grand old Church of the preacher's love and care grows in strength and wealth. The pastorate lengthens, the time limit dies out, and the preacher stays at his work as long as all parties agree; long enough to become a felt factor in social and civic life. He is no longer a "Traveling Preacher." He has become a "Settled Pastor." The Church becomes institutional, rather than evangelistic, as when he began his ministry. The work of the preacher becomes educational rather than revivalistic, and his worth is gauged by his ability to build imposing church edifices, and to raise money for the conservation of the institutions of the Church. The wealthy churches elect their pastors by committee with the approval of the appointing power. Education, with its wider range of study, is the spirit of the times.

Meanwhile the average preacher receives his appointment as in the older time, and lives on the "ragged edge" of apprehension as to what he will do when he is old and must retire from active work; for after educating his children and living decently among his parishioners, he has no margin to save for the future.

At last the time comes for him to retire. His gray hairs tell of passing years, and the young people want young ministers, who can more readily sympathize with their tastes, and are "up-to-date." So he retires from the work which he has loved, and in which he has found his highest joy, into the seclusion of superannuation.

The children have gone out and made homes for themselves. With his gracious wife, who has borne with him the burdens of itinerant life, and feasted on the riches of sweet communion with the parishioners, he finds a home for himself, relying on the pension, that the Church is bestowing, and which is increasing annually. They retire into the bosom of some local Church and thank God that they have been honored with the privilege of serving the Church and humanity, within the limits of their ability, and of associating with the highest and noblest class of people human life has produced.

Does the itinerant ministry pay? Are there compensations for whatever extra labor and privation the calling involves? For answer: Think of the rich inheritance of benefits which have accrued from the passing years, and have accumulated into a fund of experiences. The elevating influence of pastoral intercourse with the cleanest class of human beings. The invigorating exchange of high thought with fellow ministers. The necessity of large and close study of the developing knowledge of the age. The call for constant intimacy and communion with the Divine for inspiration to understand the message he is to deliver to the people. All these, and unspeakably more of inflowing results, have poured in to make his character. No preacher of sober mind, reviewing his ministerial experiences, can fail to rejoice that he was called to be an "Itinerant Preacher."

David J. Higgins.

Pasadena, Cal.

GROWING OLD

Dr. A. V. Barnes, in The Christian Advocate

A little more tired at the close of day,
A little less anxious to have our way;
A little less anxious to scold and blame,
A little more care for a brother's name;
And so we are nearing the journey's end,
Where time and eternity meet and blend.

A little less care for bonds of gold,
A little more zest for the days of old,
A broader view and a saner mind,
And a little more love for all mankind;
And so we are faring down the way
That leads to the gates of a better day.

A little more love for the friends of youth,
A little more zeal for established truth;
A little more charity in our views,
A little less thirst for the daily news;
And so we are folding our tents away
And passing in silence at close of day.

A little more leisure to sit and dream,
A little more real the things unseen;
A little nearer to those ahead,
With visions of those long loved and dead;
And so we are going where all must go,
To the place the living may never know.

A little more laughter, a few more tears,
And we shall have told our increasing years.
The book is closed, and the prayers are said,
And we are part of the countless dead.
Thrice happy, then, if some soul can say,
"I live because he passed my way."

WILL THE LIGHTS BE WHITE?

Cy Warman

Oft when I feel my engine swerve,
As o'er strange rails we fare,
I strain my eyes around the curve
For what awaits us there.

Swift towards life's Terminal I trend,
The run seems short to-night.
God only knows what's at the end;
I hope the lamps are white.

THE OLD MAN AND THE CHILD

THE REV. THOMAS TIPLADY
London, England

The modern Church has ignored those in life's second childhood. The commercial world regards a man as "too old at forty," and "fires out" its gray-haired ones, and unfortunately, the Church has accepted the world's estimate. There are monthly sermons to young men and women, but I have never seen any advertisement of monthly sermons to old men and women. The idea would be laughed at. I don't know why. Probably old men need comforting, as often as young men need inspiring; but the young men are placed in the center of the Church and the old men are left out in the cold—and old people are susceptible to cold. The old man looks back wistfully to the days when white hairs were regarded as a halo of glory, and often, when the preacher has forgotten him, there has been "a door opened in heaven" and he has seen there One Whose "hair was white as white wool, white as snow."

Forces

Old men cannot hustle and make things hum; therefore it is concluded that their work is done. But Mr. Worldly Wiseman and Mr. American Hustle have yet to learn that it is not so much what we do that counts, as what we are. The mightiest forces in grace, as in nature, are often quiet and still.

A Child's Vision

The Church, by accepting the commercial world's estimates of human life, has cut itself off from its chief reservoirs of spiritual power. The most spiritual people in the world are the children and the aged, and the most worldly are the middle-aged. A child's life is full of the spiritual and romantic. The world to him is full of fairies, angels, devils and, above all, God. Heaven is as real to him as England, and more real than France. He believes in immortality, but not in death. He believes in prayer. It is as natural as talk. He walks with sure step in the spiritual world, and talks intimately and naturally about it. He has not merely ideas but knowledge, not merely belief but vision. He renews the faith of his parents, as quietly and surely as spring renews the face of nature.

Extremes Meet

It is the same with the aged. They are in life's *second* childhood. The extremes of age meet, and human life becomes a perfect circle. The old man has sailed round the world of human experience, and finds himself back in the harbor from which he sailed as a boy. He set out to prove what he already knew by intuition. Columbus had discovered America before he sailed from Europe. He sailed the Atlantic to prove the truth of that which had already been revealed to his mind. The child knows, but has not proved his knowledge. The old man has proved what the child knows by intuition. The middle-aged is in mid-Atlantic beset with doubts and fears. He has not the unwavering faith with which he started, nor the absolute assurance with which he will end.

Youth and Age Lovers

Only the child and the old man are sure. They see the same things and subscribe to the same creed. Children and old folk love the same objects and treasure the same ideals. That is why children and old people become chums, and never quarrel. They understand one another. The middle-aged understand neither of them. It is always the grandparents who spoil the children, and the children who spoil the grandparents. Leave the young and the old together, and they are as happy as the day is long.

Aged Simeon and the Babe

It was, of course, two old people who first discovered the Babe Jesus in the temple. Old Simeon and Anna were the first to bless the Child and to praise God for Him. The picture of old Simeon with the Babe Jesus in his arms shows the eternal relationship of childhood to old age. An old man always feels like singing the Nunc Dimittis when he has a child in his arms. He feels that, at last, he is understood; that he is no longer among strangers, but at home; at last all is harmony. The child and the old man are alike—gay, careless, romantic and devout. There is merriment when they meet. Life is always dull when you have sent the children to the boarding-school and the old folk to the workhouse.

Mid-Life Least Spiritual

It is in mid-life that we are least spiritual and keep closest to the earth. We walk the midmost years with leaden feet. The middle-aged has to bear the burden and heat of the day. He has to provide for the little children and the old folk, as well as for himself. He has to enter into the thick of the fight, and his eyes are blinded by the battle-smoke and his ears deafened by the sound of blows. He turns from poetry to prose, and from romance to what he calls reality. He gets so near to life that he becomes short-sighted. He lacks vision. He cannot see the woods for the trees. He begins to despise his early ideals: and to call himself a "practical man." In the Church his bent is toward business and organization, and he makes a splendid Church officer; but he is inclined to leave the more spiritual work to the young folk and the old folk. To him the Church is a machine, and he wants to "run" it on up-to-date business lines; but to the old man and the youth the Church is a living thing—a plant, or vine, that needs loving and tending.

Lack of Vision

Now, it is evident that if the Church's life is to be full and complete we must have youth, mid-life and old age evenly balanced. If youth predominates there will be too much of the ideal and too little of the practical; if the middle-aged predominate there will be too much organization and too little of the ideal and spiritual; and if the old folks predominate there will be spirituality, but the organization will fall to pieces. In the Church of to-day the middle-aged predominate, and there is a consequent lack of vision. The machine is perfect, but we do not know what to do with it. Our gun is perfect, but we do not know how to point it.

Having no vision, we cannot see where the enemy is. The middle-aged are the hands of the Church, but the young and the aged are the eyes and ears.

Listen and be Reverent

We need not only hands to fire the gun, but eyes to direct it. We need the aged Moses on the hill-top praying, if the younger Joshua is to fight successfully in the valley. It is the young men who see visions and the old men who dream dreams; and it is the middle-aged that work them out. Joseph dreamt in his youth, and worked out his dreams in mid-life. The need of to-day is vision, and it will come when we lead back the children into the pews and the old people into the counsels of the Church. The child and the old man each live on the border-land of the eternal world. The child comes to us with trailing clouds of glory from heaven which is his home, and the old man stands at the bounds of the west gazing on the City of God. The child is bathed in the beauty of the dawn, and the old man is lit up with the glory of the sunset. Let us be reverent before them, and honor whom God honors. Let us listen to the voices which come to us from the extreme bounds of life. Let us listen, for the child's voice is weak and the old man's tremulous, and we may miss that which belongs to our peace.

Thomas Tiplady.

London, England.

SERENE OLD AGE

The Rev. J. W. Adams, D.D.

Serene I watch Life's setting sun:
The twilight scarcely seems begun.
I still can see afield to go;
And still I joy to reap and sow;
And so, at threescore years and ten,
I'm happy as I've ever been.

I'm learning where are pastures green,
And waters still that lie between.
With shepherd's crook and shepherd's pride,
My trusting little flock I guide.
Of all the years which I recall,
The seventieth has been best of all.

WILLIAM'S SUPERANNUATION

FROM "THE CIRCUIT RIDER'S WIFE"

BY CORRA HARRIS

Permission of The Altemus Co., Philadelphia

William was failing fast and he came down with sciatica that spring. He had been in bed a month. The people on the circuit began to show that they were disappointed in not having an active man who could fill his appointments. . . . I was sitting in the kitchen door one morning wondering what God was going to do about it; for I knew that we could not expect help from any other source. The agnostics may say what they please, but if you get cornered between old age and starvation you will find out that there is a real, sure-enough God who numbers the remaining hairs of your head and counts the sparrow's fall. William and I tried Him and we know. There were terrible times toward the last, when we never could have made it if it had not been for just God.

William never recovered from that attack of sciatica. His legs got well, but he did not. He was different afterward, as if he had fallen into a trance. He filled his appointments after a fashion during the remainder of the year, but became increasingly forgetful. The people did not like it and the presiding elder called for his superannuation at the Conference on the ground of "failing powers."

William was too dazed by the misfortune of his superannuation to think or plan for the future. For him there was no future. He sat in the chimney corner, following me about the house with his vacant eyes, but really grieving for one of the choice, hard circuits, with its dried fruit salary, such as he had received for years; or remembering the good pastoral times he had in this or that year.

I have sometimes wondered what would be the moral effect upon a church community if an old and helpless preacher like William should be sent to it with the understanding that the church should minister to him instead of him ministering to the church; that every saint and sinner should be invited to contribute to his peace and comfort, even as for years he had labored for them. There would be less preaching, of course, but more development in real Christian service.

Within a month the horse and buggy were sold, the cottage at Redwine rented, and we settled in it like two crippled birds in a half-feathered nest. Now, for the first time since I left Edenton, a happy, thoughtless bride, I had leisure to think just of ourselves. And I found that we were two human numerals added together for a lifetime which made a deficit. Yet we had not been idle or indifferent workers. For thirty years William had been in the itineracy, filling nearly every third and fourth class appointment in the Conference. He had preached three thousand sermons, baptized more than four hundred infants, received nearly four thousand souls into membership. He had been untiring in his efforts to raise his assessments, and had paid more pastoral calls than half a dozen doctors do to become famous and wealthy.

Time changed us; we grew old. I abandoned my waist line to Nature's will and my face settled into the expression of a good negative that has been blurred by too long exposure to strong light. Toward the end William looked like the skin-and-bones remnant of a saint. His face was sunken and hollowed out till the very Wesley in him showed through. His beard was long, and had whitened, until it gave his Moses head the appearance of coming up out of a holy mist. To make things worse William took on a weary look after his superannuation like that of a man who has made a long journey in vain. This is always the last definition the itineracy writes upon the faces of its superannuates. They are unhappy, mortified, like honorable men who have failed in business. They no longer pretend to have better health than they really have, which is the pathetic hypocrisy they all practice to the last when they are in annual fear of superannuation. So I looked at our deficit and knew that something was wrong.

I have never doubted the goodness of God, but things being as they are, and we being what we are, it takes a long time for

Him to work it out for us, especially in any kind of a Church. Meanwhile I tried to find some of our old friends, only to discover that most of them were dead. I planted a few annuals, set some hens, and prepared to cultivate my own peace.

But William was changed. He had lost his courage. Whenever the rheumatism struck him he gave in with a groan. Then he took up with Job and before we had been back long enough for the flowers to bloom, he just turned over on his spiritual ash-heap and died. He was buried in the little graveyard behind Redwine Church, along with the men and women to whom he preached thirty years ago.

I can feel that I am not setting things down right, not making the latitude and longitude of experience clearly so you can see, as I can when I close my eyes, the staggering tombstones in the brown shadows behind the little brown church.

I used to wonder why Paul, passing through all the grandest cities and civilizations of his times, never left behind him a single description of any of their glories. But I know now. Paul lost the memory of sight. He had absent-minded eyes to the things of the world. So it is with the itinerant. The earth becomes one of the stars. I cannot remember roads and realities. I recall most clearly only spiritual facts, like this: Timothy Brown was a bad man, soundly converted under William's ministry; but how he looked, on what circuit he lived, I have forgotten long ago.

The very scene of his passing floats a mist in memory. I know he lay in the same house where he had brought me on our wedding day. Through the window in the pearl light of the early morning there was the same freshness upon the hills, the same streams glistening like silver maces between them; there was the same little valley below, fluted in like a cup filled with corn and honey and bees and flowers. The same gray farmhouses brooded close to the earth, with children playing in the dooryards. It was all there the morning he died, as it had been that blue and glad morning thirty years before; but I could not see it or feel it with him lying stretched and still upon the bed. It is dim and blurred, and I cannot think it or write it properly. There seemed a rime upon the window-panes; the hills were bare, and the cup of the valley lay drained and empty before me, with the shadow of death darkening all the light of the day. I remained in the little house between the hills, walking about, attending to my few wants, receiving an occasional visitor in a sort of trance of sorrow. William had meant more to me than heaven. I had endured poverty, prayers, persecutions and revivals for his sake. And now I had lost him. I missed him when I looked down the bridle path into the valley, and I missed him when I looked at the stars. Nothing meant anything to me without him.

WHY DO WE WAIT?

Why do we wait till ears are deaf
  Before we speak our kindly word,
And only utter loving praise
  When not a whisper can be heard?

Why do we wait till hands are laid
  Close-folded, pulseless, ere we place
Within them roses, sweet and rare,
  And lilies in their flawless grace?

Why do we wait till eyes are sealed
  To light and love in death's deep trance—
Dear wistful eyes—before we bend
  Above them with impassioned glance?

Why do we wait till hearts are still
  To tell them all the love that's ours,
And give them such late meed of praise,
  And lay above them fragrant flowers?

How oft do we, careless, wait till life's
  Sweet opportunities are past,
And break our "alabaster box
  Of ointment" at the very last!

O, let us heed the living friend
  Who walks with us life's common ways,
Watching our eyes for look of love,
  And hungering for a word of praise!

—British Weekly.

PART II

THE CLAIM FOREMOST

THE CHURCH'S PROGRAM AND BUSINESS

The Declaration of the Church that the Claim of the Retired Minister is Foremost in the Churches has resulted in the creation of regularly established Boards to enable the Church to meet its just Obligation to provide a Retiring Competency. The fact that the Business World recognizes the Principle of Old Age Pensions for Employees reacts helpfully on the Churches.

CHAPTER I. THE CHURCH'S PROGRAM

THE FOREMOST CLAIM

THE REV. ARTHUR T. PIERSON, D.D.

There is singular unity in the work of the Church not always apprehended even by her members. The manifoldness of that benevolent work all finds a center of revolution in the ministry. If the aged servants of God, those prematurely disabled, or the families of those who have died in the work, are left to want and destitution, our whole system is wretchedly and inexcusably defective.

The Hebrew economy was in advance of anything that has thus far characterized the Christian Church. The Levites, set apart to the service of the sanctuary, were provided for on a magnificent scale. Having no proper inheritance among the Children of Israel, they nevertheless were assured from any possible want from the cradle to the grave, and their widows and orphans after them. The abundant tithes and offerings, the levitical cities and their suburbs, and the sacredness of their calling, assured to all those who stood before the Lord to minister to Him, the most ample, continuous, and unfailing supply of all their wants.

For Ourselves We Regard This as Foremost in Its Claim on the Churches.

A candidate for the ministry in his vigor may manage so as to supplement parental aid by the work of his own hands, or, even without any outside help, carry on his studies; and his youthful energy may bear the strain. The minister, in the prime of his powers, may be able to supplement a small salary by the work of his brawn or brain, or by rigid economy make a little suffice. But when old age or premature decay of his powers disables him from work with mind or muscle, who shall then care for him but the Church he has served?

We honestly believe that to-day nothing hinders young men of promise from entering the ministry more frequently than the prospect of no provision for old age, or of a family left in premature dependence without a head! A business man out of his business success gathers a provision against these exigencies. But most ministers, by far the majority, have barely enough to support their families, and cannot lay up against the future. They ought not to be compelled to do so.

In the nature of the case the ministry can never be and ought never to be a money-making profession. We believe God never meant the place of a minister to be ordinarily one of ample means or elegant luxury; but He does mean that no minister should be "entangled in affairs of this life"; and to prevent *this,* it is more important than any other one thing to assure every servant of God that whatever self-denial may be incident to the days of his actual and active labor, when the day of work is over he shall not suffer want for the necessities of life, or, if prematurely called hence, shall not leave a wife and children to be cast on the charity of the very Church he has self-denyingly served.

It is an insult to call this *charity.* It is in the very highest sense a *debt,* and should be so honored as an imperative obligation owed to those who use their days of strength in the service of our Lord; and no blessing can be expected on a Church which allows the veteran soldier of Christ to go down to his grave like an inmate of a poorhouse or a dependent on charity, looking for a miserable pittance bestowed as on a beggar, for the bare subsistence of life.

"They served us without asking any questions, in the performance of a duty which is laid upon us as well as upon them. Their duty had nothing to do with them or with their own personal and peculiar interests. They did not give their lives for themselves; they gave their lives for us. That is the way in which men grow distinguished, and that is the only way—by serving somebody else than themselves. A war of service is a war in which it is a proud thing to die."

No; President Wilson was not speaking of Retired Ministers. He was speaking of the Vera Cruz heroes. But he might have said all that, and more too, of the Veteran Preachers and their "Cause of Justice and Benevolence."

THE CHURCH'S PROGRAM

THE PROTESTANT EPISCOPAL CHURCH

THE REV. A. J. P. McCLURE, D.D.

Treasurer and Financial Agent
General Clergy Relief Fund

Dr. Agnew of the Presbyterian Church was almost accurately truthful, as well as brilliant and witty, when he said that the clergy are idolized at 30; criticized at 40; ostracized at 50; Oslerized at 60 and canonized at 70. Such a pithy sketch of a Minister's career deserves a place in our anthology of American epigrams.

You have asked me "to state what is being done by the Protestant Episcopal Church to provide for the aged and disabled clergy, and the widows and orphans." I answer briefly.

Early Organization

The Episcopal Church in this country began very early to consider this important matter. Indeed, the first general meeting of Bishops, clergy, etc., was called to consider ways and means to this end.

As a result of this early Conference, semi-insurance organizations diocesan and mutual contributing societies of various kinds sprang up. I mention a few as types of the way men's minds were working. "The Corporation for the Relief of the Widows and Children of Clergymen in Communion with the Church of England in America," was chartered in 1769 in the Province of New York. The title was changed later so as to read: "The Corporation etc. in the United States of America." Still later the title was changed so as to apply only to the Diocese of New York. This old society, requiring dues from the clergy, is still in active existence, and like others of the same kind, which split off from the original organization as new dioceses were formed required a contribution or a payment of a specific amount from church or clergy, or the payment of dues. Other societies were organized as insurance or semi-insurance companies. Many of these are still in existence, as for instance in the Dioceses of Connecticut, New York, Pennsylvania, New Jersey, Maryland, Chicago, South Carolina, etc. All are more or less limited both geographically and in their application to clergy, widows and orphans. As a rule they are unprogressive and the amounts granted are inadequate; usually about one hundred dollars per annum. One of the best of these old societies is still in existence in the Diocese of Pennsylvania. It bears a tremendous name, as was the fashion in those days: "The Corporation for the Relief of the Widows and Children of Clergymen in Communion with the Protestant Episcopal Church in the Commonwealth of Pennsylvania." It was organized in 1769, and has built up a large capital fund. It grants insurance to clergymen for their widows and children on premiums which are about one half those required by regular insurance organizations. Although this corporation is pursuing a most generous and liberal policy, permitting the payments of premiums to cease after fifteen years and making grants out of the surplus to especially needy widows and orphans without regard to the amount of the original insurance, the clergy as a whole do not take large advantage of this cheap and safe insurance. The clergy are and ought to be other-worldly minded, but one suspects that some of them drift along rather helplessly and do not exercise ordinary exemplary thrift in these matters.

When dioceses began to form and split off throughout the Church they made provision for those within their bounds by recommending or directing that an annual offering be taken in all the parishes and missions usually at Christmas time; and in time this offering came to be known as the Christmas Fund. In many dioceses this fund was divided into two parts, under two Boards, permitting a choice of offering on the part of contributors *i. e.,* a fund for the old and disabled clergy, and a fund for the widows and orphans. At one time there were as many of these societies as there were dioceses in the Church. Another type of society, bearing the title, "The Clergyman's Retiring Fund Society of the Protestant Episcopal Church in the United States of America," was founded in 1874. Its benefits apply only to the clergy who reach the age of 60; not to sick and disabled clergymen or to widows and orphans; nor even to the clergyman's estate. The dues are $12, $24 or $36 per year, and the Society pays to its members when they reach the age of sixty a portion of the interest upon accumulated funds and contributions, in accordance with the dues paid and years of membership. If the man dies before sixty neither his widow nor his orphans, nor his estate benefit by his connection with the society. As is evident the scope of the society is limited, but it justifies itself by declaring, "This one thing we do." It has among its membership a goodly number of Bishops and clergy who pay annual dues, and has gathered to itself a permanent fund of nearly $400,000. Another type of clerical help is that represented by the "Clergymen's Mutual Insurance League," incorporated in 1869. Any clergyman over forty-five years of age and in good health may become a member. Upon the death of a member, all contribute an assessed sum to be given to the widow.

Clergy Homes

Besides these organizations, we have also various homes, and plans for homes and rest houses, and lands for clerical cottages, as for instance, the splendid location at Pacific Grove, California, under the auspices of the Diocese of California, where cottages can be built on land furnished by the association. There is also the modest clergy house at Saluda, North Carolina; and the plans for a Clerical Village to be built in connection with the Cathedral at Washington; a scheme very dear to my heart and the outgrowth of my own suggestion. A large sum of money has been left by a benevolent lady for carrying out this idea. The plan is to have a series of cottages within the Cathedral Close, built in harmony with the Cathedral architecture, into which may be translated aged clergymen, who will be given honorable connection with the Cathedral staff, and take such services and morning and evening prayer work as may be possible for them to do; while at other times they may fill their declining days with much interest through having access to the great libraries, the meetings of Congress and other events in the capital of the Nation.

In this sketch it has already become evident that the Episcopal Church has been multiplying organizations according to many ideas. There have been and still are in all parts of the Church systems and schemes supplementing and overlapping clergy help and relief. In spite of what I am about to tell you, conditions are still rather chaotic, unbusinesslike, unjust to the clergy and confusing to the ordinary churchgoer, who is not sure to what he is giving, or to what local or general or special or insurance or general society he ought to contribute.

General Clergy Relief Fund

And this leads me to speak of "The General Clergy Relief Fund," in the shaping of whose methods and policy and work I have had much to do. As the Church grew and spread to missionary fields, foreign and domestic, it became evident that some general provision ought to be made for the whole Church, looking toward larger cooperation and greater justice, and providing for those in missionary jurisdictions, which are not able to have local funds. Therefore, in 1853 there was instituted a general society, covering the whole Church and bearing the cumbersome but descriptive name: "The Trustees of the Fund for the Relief of Widows and Orphans of Deceased Clergymen, and of Aged, Infirm and Disabled Clergymen of the Protestant Episcopal Church of the United States of America." This General Society with its long, cumbersome, descriptive name was not popular, because it seemed to conflict with diocesan and other societies that were seeking contributions for their own local funds. It was not pushed; it was not known and did not get large contributions. By the time of the Civil War it was almost extinct and forgotten. But the problem of the poorer dioceses and the missionary jurisdictions, and the multiplied chaotic, unchristlike and unbusinesslike situation still remained. In 1871 at the General Convention of the Church, the copyright of the new Hymnal together with the royalty upon its sales was turned over to the General Society, and the trustees were made a committee to revise and prepare the new Hymnal for publication. Some of the older clergy even began to call the General Society, "The Hymnal Fund Committee"—an easier task than attempting to remember the long legal name. The royalty on the Hymnal brought in quite a sum of money, and the General Society was given a new start. But there was still the conflict of interest between the General Fund and the diocesan funds. The local funds in order to protect themselves provided certain eligibility tests. A clergyman must have been in a diocese a certain number of years; he must have been officially connected with the diocese; he must have had a church in the diocese; he must have had a seat or vote in the Diocesan Convention; he must have had a record of a series of annual contributions, etc., etc. Failing in any one of these, the clergyman or the clergyman's widow and children found themselves at the critical period unable to receive help from the fund they had helped build up.

Unification of Societies

About fourteen years ago the writer of this paper became the active agent and treasurer of the General Society. His first effort was to point out the advantages of the unification of all societies in the Church and the injustice of the diocesan system; and to urge inclusiveness and brotherly ideals such as should animate Christians in doing this great and necessary work for the whole Church. He urged the fact that the clergy are ordained to the ministry of the whole Church, not to a diocese. He established correspondence between the general fund and all kindred funds and societies in the Church, to the end that there might be an understanding and a practical cooperation between all the agencies, and a general bureau which should record all that was done by the Church in the matter of clergy relief, in order that everything should be done intelligently and in the most efficient way. The diocesan or local system was vigorously attacked, and to-day, after unaccountable opposition here and there, sixty-seven of the eighty-odd dioceses and missionary jurisdictions have merged with the General Society, and depend on it for pension and relief.

The next move was to get rid of the old and cumbersome title which had caused no end of confusion in legacies and bequests and to adopt the simple and inclusive title which the General Society now bears, viz: "The General Clergy Relief Fund."

The advantages of unity have been manifested by a finer and more catholic and Christian spirit in the whole business; greater definiteness, system and unity in pressing the matter upon the whole Church; larger interest and larger offerings; less expense in management; but above all in a simple, just and uniform system of making grants and providing pension and relief. In making grants the trustees assume a definite responsibility to provide a definite sum. This means that there must be definiteness and even superfluity of resources. Offerings from individuals and churches and dioceses fluctuate. Hard times or local depression lessen the amount of the offerings. Legacies and bequests are irregular. An endowment fund was necessary and was agitated for years. Finally, in 1907, a commission was created to raise an Endowment Fund of five million dollars for the whole of clergy relief, that is, for the old and disabled clergy, the widows and orphans of clergy, the family unit, and for pensions at sixty-four years, as the canons specify.

Automatic Pensions at Sixty-Four

Some years before the Convention which took this action, the present Treasurer and Financial Agent had discovered a desire on the part of some to contribute to a fund to be set aside by the General Society, the interest to be used solely as a pension for every clergyman who had reached the age of sixty-four, without regard to disability or other limitation, and had inaugurated such a fund, and called it "The Fund for Automatic Pensions at Sixty-Four." Shortly after the commission appointed to raise the five million dollar endowment began work, it decided to use the money so raised simply for Automatic Pensions at Sixty-Four, making the effort a straightout pension proposition. But the Church was not ready to devote so large a sum to that one purpose. The ideal, no doubt, was fine, but the current needs of the disabled clergy, widows and orphans were pressing and besides a more definite system was required for the whole business. Consequently, the effort did not meet with the success expected, and at the last General Convention in New York the commission asked to be excused, in view of the new and comprehensive plan which will be explained later.

How is the money provided for the current work of the General Clergy Relief Fund? After years of agitation and suggestion the General Convention ordered that every parish, mission and congregation should take up an annual offering. This requirement is more or less observed throughout the Church; but, alas, there is neither penalty nor sufficient authority to compel contributions! Many of the dioceses, while adopting the order and recommendation of the General Convention, have retained their old custom of an offering at Christmas time. Others have selected Thanksgiving; some Quinquagesima or Charity Sunday because of the Collect used on that day; others Good Friday, Easter or All Saints Day. This irregularity is rather an advantage as it brings in money throughout the year, making it easier to send appeals to the churches, to circularize the clergy and to do the accounting work. It also provides money at desirable intervals for quarterly payments to beneficiaries. Another provision of the General Convention was to recommend that a certain percentage of the communion alms received at every administration of the Holy Communion be set aside and sent to the treasurer of the General Clergy Relief Fund. These offerings, together with the royalties on the standard Hymnal and on the Mission Hymnals, are the sources of income.

Beneficiaries

As to who may be pensioners or beneficiaries, the canon or system of rules under which the trustees work reads:

"The widow of any deceased clergyman, remaining unmarried, the children of any deceased clergyman until they have reached the age of twenty-one years, unless they shall have married before that age, and any clergyman permanently disabled, or having reached the age of sixty-four years, shall be entitled in the discretion of the trustees to share in the benefits of this fund. All applications to the trustees shall have the written recommendation of the Bishop, or, in case there be no Bishop, of the clerical members of the standing committee of the diocese or missionary district to which the applicant may belong."

The procedure is something like this: A clergyman or widow or orphan applies or application is made for them by the Bishop or by some clergyman or friend, and a form for information is sent to the applicant to be filled and sent to the Bishop for his endorsement. It then comes before the trustees, and a grant is made as speedily and as generously as the funds permit. Grants up to six hundred dollars per year for current need (disability through sickness of young or old clergy, and to the widows and orphans) go out to any reputable clergyman of the Episcopal Church in quick response to the call, and they go into all dioceses and into several foreign countries in which the applicants are living. There is but little red-tape and a maximum of humanity, Christianity and helpfulness. There are no fees, no dues, no geographical limitations, no physical examinations nor age requirements; except that the interest-pension checks from the special fund for Automatic Pensions at Sixty-Four go out only to men who are sixty-four years old or over, without regard to need but only to years of honorable service.

The General Society is doing a wide and gracious work which is abundantly certified to by thousands of grateful and appreciative letters. It has awakened the Church, and indeed other Christian bodies, to an active interest and effort to solve the whole problem of clerical support and pension and relief. The present condition of the General Clergy Relief Fund is indicated by the following statement of one of the trustees made to the last General Convention. I quote:

"It is the most encouraging report that we have ever presented to any General Convention. We call especial attention to the total receipts of $678,243.44, to the total appropriations to beneficiaries of $306,882.40, and to the low ratio of expense of administration—five and eight tenths per cent. When the present treasurer began his work we were receiving from churches and individuals about $43,000 in three years; now a total from all sources of nearly $700,000. When the present treasurer began we were paying about $76,000 in three years to beneficiaries; now, over $306,000. During the term of the present treasurer we have paid to beneficiaries a total of over $800,000 and nearly a million and a half dollars have passed through the treasurer's hands for current pension and relief, and for investment. In fact, receipts and payments to beneficiaries have nearly been doubled in every report made to the General Convention during his term. The capital funds of $90,000 are now over $600,000. The beneficiaries on the list, then about 80, are now 669. Then no dioceses had merged; now 67 are depending entirely upon the General Clergy Relief Fund."

Church Pension Fund

In conclusion, let me outline briefly the scientific and business plan which has been prepared by our new Commission and which is now before all the dioceses for adoption or rejection. All our efforts have been working up to this plan. The dioceses have been merged, the work has been unified and Christianized, that is, made less selfish and local; the vision of a service pension has been thrown before the eyes of the Church in the phrase, "Automatic Pensions at Sixty-Four"; the awkward name changed to the unifying inclusive one, "The General Clergy Relief Fund"; and knowledge and high ideals have been implanted. The new, all-embracing scientific plan has been widely noticed and heralded as epoch making. The commission appointed by our General Convention in 1910 "to consider the whole problem of clerical support, pension and relief" had the good fortune to secure an expert from the Carnegie Foundation, and the whole subject has been thoroughly worked out upon the basis of facts secured by the commission from the clergy and others, upon which are based the actuarial calculations. It is proposed under the new system to make all grants of pension and relief under exact rules, not only in order that every clergyman may receive his pension provision without sacrifice of dignity, and that all suspicion of partiality may be removed from the pension administration, but in order that the Church may know exactly what its pension budget will be, and so provide resources which will meet the needs. A fundamental proposition of the commission is that pension and relief must not be considered as a subsidiary or a by-work of the Church, but must be considered as *a vital and considerable part of all direct salaries and support*. Therefore, inasmuch as pension and relief require a considerable portion of the active salary, this proportion must be provided in the same manner that the salary is provided; that is, that every organization in the Church, parochial, diocesan or otherwise, that pays a salary or a stipend or a remuneration to a clergyman must automatically increase its appropriations by a certain fixed percentage, the increase to provide a pension for the clergyman and his family. By such a method when money is needed to pay the pension, the money will be on hand.

The retirement age is set at sixty-eight and the pension provision is one and one fourth per cent of the average stipend received by the clergyman since the time of his ordination multiplied by the years of stipend. This means in general about half the average stipend for those clergymen who are ordained at the usual age, and reach sixty-eight years of age and have work and place during that time. The system provides also that for those disabled before the retirement age a pension shall be granted amounting to forty per cent of the last stipend. To the widow of a clergyman it is proposed to grant an annuity equal to one half the pension the husband would have been entitled to during marriage, with a minimum of $300 per year, provided that the marriage took place before the husband's retirement. For minor orphans of clergymen it is proposed to pay $100 for each child under seven years; $200 for each child between seven and fourteen years; and $300 for each dependent minor over fourteen years old.

Sufficient money for this system, it is estimated, will be provided by assessing about seven and one half per cent on the salaries of all clergy, to be paid into the central pension fund not by the clergy themselves but by the dioceses. A very original feature is the sharp segregation of what is called "The Fund for Accrued Liabilities" from "The Fund for the Continuing Liabilities," which is only for those who are ordained after the plan is put in operation.

In other words, the complete, scientific and self-supporting pension system will apply only to those men who are ordained after it goes into operation. The present clergy upon the list are to be provided for by a lump sum of three and a half millions of dollars raised for what has been called the "Accrued Liabilities." The insistence upon the separation of the "Accrued Liabilities" from the "Continuing Liabilities" has been unflinching, because careful investigation has shown that most pension systems have had hard sledding at the eleventh year after their establishment. At that time there is such an accumulation of accrued and continuing liabilities as to make it necessary either to raise more money or adopt a new system. The "Accrued Liabilities Fund" will not provide as large a pension as the pension system itself when it fully gets into operation; and alas! even under this latter one and one fourth per cent of the salaries of the clergy divided by the years of service will not bring in a sufficient pension allowance before twenty-five or thirty years. Such is the penalty of delay in adopting a system that will stand alone and grow as the Church grows. A minimum pension of six hundred dollars per year and a maximum of two thousand dollars has been ordered; the average will be about eight hundred or nine hundred dollars.

The new Church Pension Fund, built upon these lines, proposes to deal with the dioceses in making the required assessments; emphasizing the fact that if there is no pay there will be no pension. A record and account will be kept with every clergyman as to his age at ordination, date of marriage, wife's age, number and ages of children, salary at each period, when employed, etc., etc. Each diocese will be notified annually from these statistics and from actuarial calculations of the men in the dioceses who will reach the retiring age, the number of widows and orphans, the number permanently disabled, etc. In other words the financial requirement for the year will be accurately indicated to each diocese, and the diocese must assess this amount upon its churches, reducing its assessment by the interest upon any endowment funds it may have. If there is a deficit on the part of some of the churches it will reduce the pension and relief grants to individuals in that particular diocese by so much.

Such is only the barest outline of an admirable piece of work by the commission and its expert secretary. The scheme has been presented in part to the various dioceses and until the meeting of the General Convention in 1916 it will be carefully considered. The whole scheme is scientific and businesslike and seems from the scientific point of view to be perfect and without an alternative. The immediate inference from this statement of the new Church Pension Fund scheme is that those who have small salaries will receive small pensions, and that those who receive large salaries will receive large pensions, and, therefore, the question will arise whether it will not produce self-seeking and work as a penalty upon self-denial, and the willingness of men to go to hard places where salaries are small and irregular, even though the harvest is great. It is a question, also, whether this essentially Christian enterprise can safely be taken out of the realm of practical Christian charity and made simply a scientific, mechanical business matter, observing only the hard natural law of supply and demand: "To him that hath shall be given."

Perhaps in the Church we need to remember and observe a higher spiritual law, namely, "Bear ye one another's burdens and so fulfill the law of Christ." Of course, all we do in the Church should be done with regard to strict business efficiency and integrity, but the Church is not a business enterprise as is a railroad or a corporation in the sense of being a money-making organization or in having a regular scale of salary for officers of different grades. However, it may be found that there is more justice and humanity, as a whole, in the definiteness and liberality which will be provided by an adherence to strictly scientific and business methods. It would seem, however, that even after the Church has provided pension and relief for the clergy and widows on the basis of years of service and the amount of their salaries while in service, there will still remain special requirements which may justly arouse generous impulses and call for special help.

Vision of Unity

My brethren, I bid you Godspeed and success in your own great enterprise. You will succeed, I am sure. The vigorous, virile, energetic way you Methodists have of attacking this and other problems is stimulating and worthy of imitation. Your Church has grown greater and more effective in many respects than its mother, and I am glad and proud to have the approval of such a Church by your workers in the same line, through the use of many of my circulars and leaflets and writings, and by the honor of this call to stand before you and tell you of our efforts and accomplishments in the Protestant Episcopal Church. Perhaps before long this intercommunication will lead us to larger, finer and more truly Christian things. I wish I had the time and the eloquence to tell you of the noble vision of largeness and unity which a half dozen or more of us, representatives of clergy relief societies in various denominations, were permitted to see and live with for a whole winter, as we met under the call and plan and stimulus of your Dr. Crandall J. North. The story has never been told in public. Methodist, Baptist, Lutheran, German Reformed, Presbyterian, Episcopalian secretaries and treasurers and other representatives doing this same work in our separate bodies, met in New York and prayed and talked and devised a large scheme for a great Union Foundation to be established for all churches; a plan which if we could have carried it through would have done more for Christian unity than many loose federations. O, that the Lord had opened the eyes of the rich men and women we appealed to and had permitted them to see this vision and what it would lead to aside from the material plans for help. It was a great vision. My honored friend, Dr. North, may yet be canonized for this at 70 if he is not Oslerized before that time.

It was a delight and inspiration to work and think, if only for a few hours each week, with men of one mind, filled with earnestness on this subject. We railed and declaimed, without quit or hindrance of missionary boards or of the sound of the grinding of the ecclesiastical machinery, at the curious Christianity that was all the time asking for more money to send more men to the front, and was forgetting or neglecting those who had been at the front, but who are now on the Honor Roll of the invalid corps. But through it all we caught the vision of what was to be when God's kingdom should come.

Philadelphia, Pa. ALFRED J. P. McCLURE.

Prayer for the General Clergy Relief Fund

O Lord Jesus Christ, Thou gracious Shepherd and Bishop of our souls, we beseech Thee for Thy ministering servants, now aged and infirm, and no longer able to work as active laborers in Thy vineyard. Leave them not, neither forsake them in this their hour of temporal want and distress. Open the hearts and hands of Thy people for their support and comfort, that their pathway to the grave may be free from all worldly cares and anxieties. Let the fund which Thy Church has established for their relief be increased many fold, that neither they nor their helpless widows and orphans may ever come to want or have cause to complain of our neglect, but as the members of one family and household of faith, may we rejoice together in Thy love shed abroad in our hearts through the same Jesus Christ, our most Blessed Lord and Saviour. Amen.

MINISTERS AND HORSES

It pays better to be a faithful horse than a faithful minister when old age comes on. "Many a man," said the Rev. J. H. McIlvaine, addressing Episcopal laymen at Pittsburgh, "makes better provision for an old horse than is made by the Church for her old ministers." As this is not hyperbole, but literal truth, it is a severe indictment of the churches. Dr. McIlvaine cited his own denomination—the Protestant Episcopal—which, though not the largest numerically, is one of the wealthiest in the country, and yet which gives only nine or ten cents per member to the support of its old and worn-out clergy. He welcomed the coming of the business man to the front in our churches, because in this way finances would be put on a business basis. Would it not be possible to interest the laymen in these old soldiers of the Church, who have fought their last fight, but who ought to be able to spend the few remaining years of life without coming to actual want?

We are busy discussing pensions for school teachers, public servants and veteran workers of all kinds. Would not an agitation for better pensions for old preachers be in order? Surely the ministry is not a more selfish or remunerative calling than the others. Thirty men, contributing outright $3,000,000, have established in New York the New Theater, designed to cultivate the highest and best in dramatic art, free from any sort of influence from the box office. No dividends are to be paid, but any profits accruing are to go toward a permanent fund devoted to the enlargement of the original enterprise. The drama needs to be fostered in just the way the New Theater plans to do it, and we have no criticism of the princely philanthropy back of the project. But we raise the question, If thirty men in New York can give $3,000,000 for the stage, are there not throughout the country one hundred millionaires who could together put up a $10,000,000 fund to pension old and needy ministers? Business men of the churches, here is a practical proposition. We believe you can put it through.—*Leslie's Weekly.*

THE CHURCH'S PROGRAM

THE PRESBYTERIAN CHURCH

THE REV. W. H. FOULKES, D.D.

General Secretary Ministerial Relief and Sustentation

For nearly two centuries, the Presbyterian Church has given attention to this fundamental Cause which represents the duty of the Church of Christ to the Retired Ministry.

In Colonial days the dreadful distress of many honored men of the Ministry, who were left in their old days without any means of support, and the special distress of the widows and orphans of the faithful servants of the Church, appealed strongly to the sense of justice and duty in the hearts of God's people, and many were seeking some practical means of doing what all felt should be done for the honor of the Church and the relief of her suffering servants.

At the first meeting of the Synod of Philadelphia in 1717, "A Fund for Pious Uses" was established. A treasurer was elected to receive contributions, and the Synod disposed of the money at its own discretion. This Fund was intended for Home Missionary work, to aid a school in Philadelphia, for such other objects as the Synod might determine, and for the relief of disabled Ministers and their families, and the first appropriation from the Fund, of which we have any record, was made in 1721 for the relief of two widows of Ministers.

Board of Relief

After a century and a half of loosely organized work, on May 29, 1876, the General Assembly organized the Board of Ministerial Relief, which has for its cumbersome title, the caption "The Presbyterian Board of Relief for Disabled Ministers, and the Widows and Orphans of Deceased Ministers." The purpose for which this corporation was formed was to receive, hold and disburse such real and personal estate as may be given to it for the relief and support of disabled Ministers and the needy Widows and Orphans of Deceased Ministers of said Church. From the date of this organization until this day, the Board of Relief has grown in favor with the Church. Its appeal has been one that has touched the heart of Presbyterianism. Its policy has been to secure, by means of annual contributions from the Church, legacies and individual donations, a sufficient sum of money to meet in some way the need of the aged and disabled servants of the Church; but while the Board of Relief has thus, to a certain extent, met the need of the disabled ministry of Presbyterianism, it has never overtaken that need. It has attempted to do an impossible thing, namely, to meet relative need upon the basis of annual appeals therefor.

Sustentation

As a result of this failure and, in part, as a result of conservative policies on the part of the Board, the General Assembly in 1909 organized the Ministerial Sustentation Fund, which embodied the contributory pension idea, and which permitted Ministers, by making a regular annual, semi-annual or quarterly payment, to provide in part for their own day of disability. The maximum benefits of the Sustentation Fund are $500 a year during lifetime for every man who has reached the age of seventy and who has served the Presbyterian Church thirty full years. For the Minister who has reached the age of seventy, without having served thirty full years in the Presbyterian Church, a maximum pension of $100 for the first five years of his ministry, plus $10 for every year's service thereafter. For the Minister who has become disabled, whatever his age, a maximum pension of $100 for the first five years of his ministry, plus $10 for every additional year. A maximum pension of three fifths of the amount to which her husband would have been entitled or was receiving is to be paid to every widow, or if no widow survive him, to be divided between the dependent children, if any, of the deceased member of the Fund. The principle of the Fund is that the Minister's own payments provide one fifth of the maximum pension, and the contributions of the churches, by means of gifts to the Endowment Fund and otherwise, are made to swell the total annuity up to the maximum amount. Already the Church has provided enough money on the basis of nearly a thousand Ministers who are paying rates to the Sustentation Department to make possible the payment of 60 per cent of the maximum pension to the disabled members of the Fund.

For a number of years after the formation of the Sustentation Fund there was, I regret to say, friction between these two agencies, each of which was seeking the same general result, though in different ways, but in 1912 the General Assembly combined these agencies under the title of "The Presbyterian Board of Ministerial Relief and Sustentation"; both charters remaining intact and both corporations being administered in law by the same Board of Directors and the same executive officers. To-day Presbyterianism faces its great task of providing for its aged and disabled servants with a harmonious and complete plan; on the one side Relief, which is the ambulance at the foot of the hill which will continue to provide for those who may have need in the day of their dependency; on the other hand Sustentation, which will growingly assist men now young to provide in part for their disability or old age, thus building a fence around the top of the hill of disability.

Relief

The Relief Department of the Board of Relief and Sustentation is organized to give gracious relief to those who in their service have come to need. There is no badge of shame in their necessity. It is the brand of the Lord Jesus. Those Christians who speak contemptuously of the "poor minister" may well ask themselves whether after all they are not merely "badge wearers," while the Minister is a branded servant "drinking His Lord's cup" with Him. For over a hundred years the Church has gathered and has given this sacred relief. It has never met all the absolute need of the Veterans of the cross. They have borne the most of it themselves. The Church has measurably met relative need. The Board of Relief has gathered what the Church would give and has given it as widely as it could, but the Church has never given one tenth enough to meet the need fully and honorably. The gifts of the Church have never overtaken the wants of the saints. The Presbyterian Church last year provided for practically two thousand dependent Ministers, missionaries and their families, seven hundred of whom were widows.

During the current year the Relief Department has appropriated approximately $30,000 more than last year, while the Church has only given approximately $7,000 more than last year. It would be the height of folly to deprive those who are now disabled in order to provide for the Ministry of a half century hence. The disabled Ministry of to-day must be cared for *now* and *first*. The fact that last year only four churches out of ten gave to the relief of these disabled servants indicates that the Presbyterian Church must "go on to perfection." The Pension Department of Ministerial Relief and Sustentation is steadily growing. If the Church were to attempt to establish in one year a pension plan to protect all her Ministers, and were able to compel every Minister to contribute his part, she would have to invest many millions of dollars all at once. By the present plan, however, she makes it possible for her to build up her part of the pension as rapidly as she will, the minister only receiving a pro rata share of the pension according to the measure of her gifts. There are those in the Presbyterian Church who think that it is enough to relieve need as it arises and as largely as possible. The Church, however, has determined to test her own mettle and to prove the promises of God by attempting to do both; first and foremost, to relieve the need that now exists or that will yet be met; second and equally vital, to build up a reserve fund so generous in its proportions and so constantly enriched that as its bounty is drawn upon from year to year it will be constantly replenished. A Relief Department alone would continue to meet relative need, but would never overtake it. A Pension Department alone would gradually build up an adequate support in the days of their disability for those uniting with it, but would overlook both those now disabled and those who, for years to come, would be unable or unwilling to contribute toward its upbuilding. The Relief and Sustentation Department working together as the Assembly has directed, each supplementing the other, each vital to the Church and both supported by the Church, constitute the solution of the problem which, in the words of our own Robert E. Speer, is its "holiest and most sacred privilege and duty."

$10,000,000 Fund

The General Assembly has undertaken the task of raising a permanent Endowment Fund of $10,000,000 by means of which to accomplish this task. Even this amount will not be adequate if the Church desires to accomplish, upon an actuarial basis, the whole task. I am glad to report that as a result of steady accumulations during the years and of some generous gifts recently, we have invested now approximately $3,000,000, and we have great encouragement to believe that the Church will so respond that we will have the total sum eventually raised. We are at present conducting campaigns in various centers of Presbyterianism. One that was carried on last November, in the Presbytery of Pittsburgh, brought us in subscriptions approximately $125,000, and also, what was of more importance, gave us access to the hearts and consciences of Presbyterian people. Our plans for such campaigns reach several years into the future.

We also depend as a Church upon annual gifts from our congregations for the current work of Relief, and are using every effort to stimulate that source of income so that those who are now aged and disabled may not be abandoned in the effort to establish a statesmanlike plan. The largest sums will come to us in legacies. God does not expect the average man of means to deplete his capital, any more than he expects the average carpenter to sell his hammer or saw, but to use them; to give an account of income now and to give on that day, when every one of us shall stand before the Great White Throne, a full and itemized account of capital.

A Great Legacy

I want to tell you the story of one legacy; that of Lady Martha Ellen Kortright, who was a Philadelphia Presbyterian girl. She married Lord Kortright and moved with him to England; and survived him without children. She wrote two wills; one an English will, leaving all her English property to English charities; the other, an American will, leaving her American property to four Presbyterian Institutions—the Board of Home Missions, the Board of Education, the Board of Relief and the Presbyterian Hospital of Philadelphia. The British Government, however, with those qualities that sometimes are admirable and sometimes the reverse, levied an income tax upon the whole estate; and since it could not collect it from the American estate it collected it *all* from the British estate and practically wiped out the entire British legacies. Then the British heirs sued the American heirs, trying to recoup themselves for this loss. The American heirs contended that they should not be compelled to suffer on account of the rapacity of the British Crown. The Pennsylvania Supreme Court finally handed down its decision which said that these four Presbyterian Institutions had a right to the property, and our genial and efficient Treasurer, Dr. Heberton, went over to the Trust Company one day with his little satchel and brought to our office the sum of $318,066.69, our share of the residue of the estate; $48,000 of which was accrued interest. There is a rule of the Assembly which says that we shall not hoard our interest, we must spend it. So the question immediately arose as to how we could spend our interest in the quickest and best way possible. It would have taken a whole year to have heard from the Presbyteries recommending increases. We felt that the $48,000 belonged to our annuitants, and we had a special meeting of the Board, found a resolution that gave us ample power, and we voted to send, without their knowledge or expectation, a Christmas gift of twenty-five dollars to each of the 1,251 annuitants then upon our roll.

I wish that I could share with others the deep and unutterable joy that has come to me from the reading of those legacies of love that have come to us from the annuitants. Our gifts were sent the week before Christmas. One recipient wrote the day before Christmas: "Yesterday my little boy came to me and said, 'Mother, are we going to have any Christmas?' I had just spent my last twenty-five cents and I said to him, 'My boy, God has never forsaken us, and I know He never will.'" And then she added, "When your letter came with its check for twenty-five dollars it seemed as if Jesus Himself had come into my home."

Of those to whom we sent the gift, not a few sent back a tithe to the Board! One widow wrote and said: "When your letter came I was in the deepest dungeon of distress. No one knows the desolation and loneliness of my soul; and when I saw that the old Church really cared for me because of what my husband did, I was like a bird let loose from a cage.

True to the practices of my sainted husband, I am sending you back $2.50 for your work." Such is heroism!

Advance Program

The Presbyterian Church is moving forward to the accomplishment of this holy task for six reasons.

First. The care of the aged or disabled servants of any society or organization, by that society or organization, is universally recognized as a paramount duty. Men everywhere point the finger of scorn at those institutions which enrich themselves on the fruitage of human toil, and then cast aside the toiler in the day of his old age or disability. This duty is both economic and moral. The producer of values, whether spiritual or material, deserves a fair share of that which he produces. It is his due. Both from an economic point of view which regards an old age pension as a "wage earned during productive years and wisely deferred for payment to the years of disability," and from a moral point of view which regards the obligation to care for dependent classes as fundamentally just, the duty is paramount. All of this applies fully as much to the Church as it does to an industrial concern.

Second. The adequate care of the disabled servants of the Church is one of the clearest duties outlined in the Word of God. The support of the Levite was both sufficient and permanent. The prophet summed up God's requirements as these: "to do justly and to love mercy and to walk humbly before thy God." The widow of the Gospel Minister or missionary, who is really the heart of the whole task, is singled out in Scripture as the special recipient of divine tenderness and favor. The prophet pictured Jehovah as the "Judge of the widow and the Father of the fatherless," while the Apostle James tested the Apostolic Church by the standard of pure religion which consists in "visiting the fatherless and the widows," as well as "keeping himself unspotted from the world." Presbyterians boast themselves of their adherence to the Pauline doctrines; they may well ask themselves how they are measuring up to the duties outlined by the Apostle James.

Third. The demands which the Church makes upon her ministers enforce the reasonableness and the importance of this service. She asks that they be men set apart from a secular to a sacred calling. She encourages them to undergo a long period of preparation which involves a constant outlay of money without any appreciable return as income during the days of apprenticeship. She bids them give her their unstinted energy and their undivided time. She looks with suspicion upon any diversion of their talents or time into channels of material prosperity for themselves. She rewards them with a bare competence, which, when it is averaged with the returns in any other high calling, falls fearfully below the level, and which is scarcely on the plane of those forms of labor whose economic standard is not half so high. She pleads with them to establish Christian homes in which children may grow up. She points with pride to some of the choicest products of her ministers' homes, men, who are found in Presidents' chairs, in cabinet offices, on Judges' benches, in all the walks and stations of life, occupying worthily the highest positions. If she makes all these demands upon them, she owes it to them that they may be fully provided for in the day of their old age and disability.

Fourth. The needs of her disabled servants rise to-day to the Lord God of Hosts as a cry for justice. Honored Ministers who have served humbly and fruitfully for three and four decades are suffering the pangs of want. Aged women who have been left desolate by the death of those, the burdens of whose Ministry they have shared, are to-day tasting the "inside of the cup" and are finding it bitter. Our Board cannot share with the Church all the intimacies of the suffering servants of God. There are aged Ministers who have not sufficient or reasonable clothing suitable for the simplest services in the House of God. There are widows with growing children who, toiling day and night with the needle and sometimes over the washboards, are not able to keep pace with the high cost of living, and are compelled to take promising lads out of high school and to deprive them of needed education; when in some cases the faces of the deceased Ministers' sons have been set toward the Gospel Ministry, despite all the hardships they have encountered at home. There are old couples drawing near the evening of life, without children or near relatives upon whom to lean, with barely enough to provide the commonest necessities of life and without one of its luxuries. The cry of all these is loud in the ears of the living and Eternal God. He is challenging His Church today, "Give ye them to eat!"

Fifth. The mission of the Church to evangelize the world, so clearly recognized as her supreme duty and so imperfectly fulfilled, demands new efficiency in the leadership of the Church. She will not, cannot rise higher than the levels of her ordained leadership. If she will release her Ministers from the bondage of fear over approaching old age, she will unlock treasuries of power for herself. She will, by this, prove to a gainsaying world, that she believes in her mission and in her power to fulfill it. Every great economic, social and moral challenge which is so distortedly voiced in the unrest of the world, and which is so violently set forth in those fundamentally fallacious schemes of life that threaten to engulf the nation, comes eventually to the Church for its solution. Every great moral reform and all the redemptive forces of the race must be kindled into a glow at the altar of the Church. If her priests are heavy with the sleep of burdens unjustly borne, are full of fear because of the specter of want that will not down, her fires will flicker dimly. If she turns aside from her ordained leadership in the days of its adversity, the choicest flower of her youth will not offer themselves for leadership in the days of their prosperity.

Sixth. The approval of her Lord awaits her fulfillment of His imperative command. He who said, "Go into all the world," also said, "I was hungry and ye gave me to eat. Inasmuch as ye did it unto one of the least of these, my brethren, ye did it unto me." It is well for Christian men and women to give largely to build, maintain and endow great institutions, libraries and art institutes, universities and hospitals, associations for young men and young women. These and a hundred other things are worthy of those who seek the approval of Christ. But if the Church shall do all these things, "even giving her body to be burned," and have not that sweet and gracious charity, that grace of love for those who have served her, it "will profit her nothing." "The Lord is mindful of His own," and if the Church has the mind of Christ she will seek the welfare of those who most clearly, although all too imperfectly, represent Him on earth.

WILLIAM H. FOULKES.

Philadelphia, Pa.

TABLES OF RATES PRESBYTERIAN SUSTENTATION FUND

The minister continues to pay the rate corresponding to his age at entrance.

Age	Annual	Semi-Annual	Quarterly	Single Payments
21........	$17 13	$8 52	$4 54	$351 67
22........	16 89	8 70	4 40	345 88
23........	16 80	8 65	4 37	342 92
24........	16 82	8 51	4 38	341 84
25........	16 93	8 72	4 49	342 14
26........	17 11	8 81	4 54	343 58
27........	17 35	8 94	4 60	345 76
28........	17 67	9 10	4 68	348 66
29........	18 04	9 29	4 78	352 15
30........	18 46	9 51	4 89	356 45
31........	18 93	9 75	5 02	361 28
32........	19 47	10 03	5 16	366 29
33........	20 06	10 33	5 31	372 54
34........	20 69	10 66	5 50	378 75
35........	21 40	11 02	5 67	385 41
36........	22 16	11 41	5 87	392 50
37........	22 99	11 84	6 09	399 99
38........	23 89	12 30	6 33	407 81
39........	24 81	12 78	6 57	415 32
40........	25 89	13 33	6 86	424 48
41........	27 01	13 91	7 16	433 21
42........	28 44	14 65	7 54	442 29
43........	29 55	15 22	7 83	451 80
44........	30 97	15 95	8 21	461 50
45........	32 52	16 75	8 62	471 59
46........	34 21	17 62	9 07	482 17
47........	36 06	18 57	9 56	493 02
48........	38 08	19 61	10 09	504 39
49........	40 29	20 75	10 68	516 41
50........	42 74	22 01	11 33	528 95
51........	45 45	23 41	12 04	542 58
52........	48 44	24 95	12 84	556 21
53........	51 77	26 68	13 72	570 86
54........	55 53	28 60	14 72	586 12
55........	59 77	30 78	15 84	602 16
56........	64 61	33 27	17 12	618 76
57........	70 19	36 15	18 60	635 95
58........	76 71	39 51	20 33	653 78
59........	84 42	43 48	22 37	672 55
60........	93 69	48 25	24 83	692 39

THE CHURCH'S PROGRAM

THE PRESBYTERIAN CHURCH IN THE UNITED STATES

(SOUTHERN PRESBYTERIAN CHURCH)

THE REV. HENRY H. SWEETS, D.D.
Secretary Education and Ministerial Relief

I count it a rare privilege to have some part in the statesmanlike and far-reaching movement in which the Methodist Episcopal Church is engaged.

Too long the enfeebled Veterans of the Ministry have been neglected. Too often we have been so busy in leading on the victorious host to greater victory and wider conquest that we have forgotten the command of the great King:

"Take heed to thyself that thou forsake not the Levite as long as thou livest upon the earth."

We congratulate the great Methodist Episcopal Church upon her determination to remove this reproach. We have come to know and to love your leader. With a mind to comprehend the abiding principles of justice and truth; with a heart to feel the burdens of "the saints who are in need" and to call forth the sympathy and help of the able and strong; and with such energy and enthusiasm thrown into the work, under the blessings of God, you cannot fail. The success and blessing that will surely come to you will encourage the rest of us, and in the lives of all our veterans will hasten the fulfillment of the promise, "At evening time it shall be light."

The Presbyterian Church in the United States, commonly called the Southern Presbyterian Church, came into being in 1861. On account of the great crisis through which our country was passing at that time, the Church was poor, business activity was at a standstill, and after the close of the war, her territory was impoverished and her securities worthless. So many were the demands made on the new Church in attempting to overtake the vast destitution that abounded on every hand, that the new, struggling organization had little opportunity or means to care for its enfeebled ministers or their destitute families.

Organizations for Ministerial Relief

In 1867 the committee of Home Missions was authorized to appropriate five per cent of all its receipts to the relief of the destitute widows and children of ministers and to ministers in infirm health. The next year a collection was ordered from all the churches for the Relief Fund, to be handled by the treasurer of Home Missions. The day for this collection was the first Sabbath in July, and this day was retained until 1911. The amount received from this collection in 1869 was $3,624; in 1879, $8,381; in 1889, $12,965; in 1899, $14,384; in 1909, $35,035; in 1914, $57,300.

Not until 1901 did the General Assembly erect a separate agency for the conduct of this work. The Executive Committee of Ministerial Relief began its labors in that year; the main stress being placed upon the annual offering for Ministerial Relief, the help being given to needy ministers and the families of deceased ministers on the basis of age, need and service to the Church.

In 1904 the General Assembly consolidated the causes of Education for the Ministry and Ministerial Relief, and in 1911 a further consolidation was effected of all the executive agencies of the Church. The work of the Church is now carried on through four executive committees or boards—Foreign Missions, Home Missions, Sabbath Schools and Publications, and Christian Education and Ministerial Relief.

In 1869 another plan was suggested to the General Assembly for the "Relief of the Families of Deceased Ministers," and during the next year an elaborate scheme was formulated for the relief of both disabled ministers and the needy widows and orphans of deceased ministers. In furthering this plan the following statement was made:

"The scheme under consideration, unlike life insurance, makes no discrimination on account of age, health or the number of years that a minister may have been engaged in preaching the gospel. The ministers are all regarded as officers of the Church and servants of the Lord Jesus Christ, and their families, in consequence, as clearly entitled to the beneficent provisions of the general arrangement. The only limitation or discrimination will be in relation to the number of annual payments that must be made by the Church before a minister's family can be entitled to the full amount."

The plan then worked out was not based upon sound, business principles, and both ministers and churches failed to contribute the necessary amounts. After many changes, in 1885 the business was transferred to the "Clergy Friendly Society," a voluntary organization of business men of Baltimore. In 1890 these gentlemen signified their desire to relinquish the trust, and the next year the funds were placed in the "Presbyterian Ministers' Fund" of Philadelphia.

Growth of Resources

How our ideas and the resources of the Church have grown! In 1882 the General Assembly was informed that "the late Rev. Stuart Robinson, D.D., of Louisville, Ky., had shown princely liberality, so characteristic of his noble nature, in a munificent donation of $25,000 as a permanent endowment fund for this cause." But the time was not ripe for such a forward movement, and in 1884 the General Assembly withdrew all claims to this bequest because the way was "not clear to enter upon an organized effort to increase the endowment of said fund to $100,000, which was evidently contemplated by this venerable servant of God." In 1901 a movement was finally launched looking to the establishment of a permanent fund, the interest of which should be used in relieving the necessities of infirm ministers and needy widows and orphans. In 1902 this Endowment Fund was $298.30. In 1906 an elder in the First Presbyterian Church, Atlanta, Ga., offered to give the sum of $100,000 to the Endowment Fund, provided $125,000 was added to the $25,000 which was the amount of the Endowment Fund at that time. In a short time this condition was met, and the Endowment Fund immediately increased to $250,000.

In more recent years the Church has constantly been disturbed by a heavy debt resting upon the Foreign Mission Committee and, with other urgent matters on hand, the time never seemed propitious for a church-wide campaign for the enlargement of the Endowment Fund. Some amounts have been added through bequests. A few churches, Sunday schools and societies have contributed small amounts, and a few interested persons have made annual contributions to it. The fund now amounts to $326,000.

The Presbyterian Church in the United States is composed of 3,430 churches, 1,819 ministers and 311,000 communicants. We have on the roll of Ministerial Relief 62 ministers, 146 widows and 20 orphans. In the 228 homes of these beneficiaries are many invalids and 65 little fatherless children under 14 years of age. In 1913 we gave to the support of all these claimants of the bounty of the Church, $38,725.

When a minister reaches the age of seventy and has served the Church for thirty years, he is entitled to be placed on the "Roll of Honorably Retired Ministers." There are now twenty-eight ministers so enrolled, who received an average last year of $270; the largest amount appropriated to any one being $600. The average amount paid the other thirty-four ministers whose names were not on that Roll was $215. The average amount received by the widows was $150. The average assistance given to each of the 228 homes represented by beneficiaries was $170 per annum.

Plans for Ministerial Relief

We are relieved from the difficulties faced by many Church Boards which have several agencies trying to solve the same problem. All funds for disabled ministers and their families are handled by this one agency, "The Executive Committee of Ministerial Relief," which has adopted the following plans for increasing the amounts to be provided for the beneficiaries.

1. The Assembly's Budget. When the Church adopted the every-member canvass plan and apportioned amounts to the various synods and presbyteries for the general work of the Church, fourteen per cent of the offerings were assigned to Christian Education and Ministerial Relief. The amount asked for the work for 1915 is, therefore, $172,666. Inasmuch as great efforts are being made to push this financial plan, there is every reason to believe that we will receive for this work a much larger amount than that contributed last year. About two thirds of this amount ($100,000 to $120,000) will go to the department of Ministerial Relief.

2. Annual Collections. The months of April and December have been set apart by the General Assembly for instruction as to this work and as the time for offerings to

it. We are carefully informing the churches of the needs through the pastors, getting the people more interested in the work by means of carefully prepared leaflets, and are seeking to secure offerings in those churches that have not yet fully adopted the financial plan of the every-member canvass.

3. WOMEN'S SOCIETIES. The General Assembly has urged all the women's societies, including the Pastor's Aid and the Missionary Societies, to interest themselves in *all* the work of the Church. They have been requested to give fourteen per cent of their contributions to the work of Christian Education and Ministerial Relief. This gives us access to one of the most important agencies of the entire Church. The women are studying the matter, using carefully prepared programs, prepared by our committee and their own auxiliary, and are not only giving far in excess of their former offerings, but are doing much to interest the whole Church in the work.

4. THE SUNDAY SCHOOLS. Owing to the fact that the month of December has been assigned to our work, we have the privilege of preparing the Christmas exercise for use in the Sunday schools. The tender but sane appeal of this sacred cause is presented in attractive exercises which call forth the sympathy and help of the officers, teachers and pupils of the Sunday schools. Inasmuch as the pupils are soon to take their places as the leaders in the Church and are to become the financiers of the country, we consider this one of the most helpful and hopeful parts of our entire campaign for the enfeebled veterans of the Church.

5. PUBLICITY CAMPAIGN. Some time ago the Church decided to consolidate the magazines published in the interest of foreign missions and home missions and to combine them into a magazine which would represent the four great agencies of the Church. Through the columns of this magazine we have the privilege of making known to the women's societies the best forms of programs and keeping constantly before the Church and our people the needs of our beneficiaries and the sacred claims of this work. In addition to this all the Church papers of the South open their columns for brief articles, attractively prepared, by which means we are able to reach thousands of our people with the latest information and the most attractive appeals.

6. Future Plans. By direction of the General Assembly we are now entering upon a vigorous campaign to increase the Endowment Fund to at least $500,000. In addition to this we have been directed to put forth every effort to increase the annual offerings to this cause. While the Church has never adopted the idea of "pensions" for her ministers, she has definitely assumed the task of caring for the disabled ministers, and the needy widows and orphans. Every dictate of justice, honor, gratitude, self-respect, expediency, sympathy, religion, obedience to the great Head of the Church, love to Christ and the example of Jesus enforce this demand —that those who minister in spiritual things shall not be allowed to suffer and render inefficient their ministry on account of lack of material support. The Church has at last awakened to the fact, that regardless of salaries paid, there will still be needs, definite and certain, in many ministers' homes, and she is now endeavoring through the Endowment Fund to render less uncertain the means of support for the unfortunate ones.

We do not propose to make the interest from invested funds the sole means of meeting this obligation. We want the people to have the joy of taking upon themselves *"the fellowship of ministering to the saints,"* and to feel the duty of supporting the ministers of the Church, whether active or retired, by their loving gifts. Trusting in the great God of Elijah and the sense of justice in the hearts of our people, we are planning better and nobler things for them.

Ministerial Relief and the Ministerial Supply

Since our work concerns also the recruiting of the Ministry, we have made careful study of the reasons why the Church is not furnishing a sufficient supply of capable leaders for the ever-widening work of the Church, both at home and abroad. I do not believe that many young men are kept out of the Ministry because of the hardships they must encounter, and the lack of provision for the days of need, though this may serve to turn some of our boys aside. If the Church permits her faithful leaders to lie wounded and uncared for on the field of battle, or to struggle along unaided after they have been retired from labor and from income, can she rightfully expect the son to rush forward to take the place of the father in the depleted ranks of the ministry?

Most of the boys at the time of decision know little of these sad trials, but God knows them every one. May it not be that because the Church has shown so little appreciation of the faithful ministers He has called to her service that God for a time is withholding these priceless gifts! I long to live to see the day when these wrongs shall be righted, and to have some part in bringing fuller justice to our ministers and richer blessing to the Church.

We thank you, our warm-hearted brethren of the Methodist Episcopal Church, for the determination and vim with which you have attacked this problem. There is urgency in the call to go forward. Many of those whose cause we plead will be with us but a very short time. Their gray hairs and bended forms betoken they are much further from the bounds of infancy, than from the gates of death. With wasted forms and feeble strength they can only sit and wait the summons that will soon come to call them into His presence. *What we do for them must be done in this generation,* nay, must be done *now*. What a joy to labor for these lonely men, and to remember that as we seek to minister to them we are ministering unto Him.

"Yes, we believe Thy Word,
Though dim our faith may be,
Whate'er we do for Thine, O Lord,
We do it unto Thee."

Louisville, Ky. HENRY H. SWEETS.

A SUNSET SONG

THE REV. E. STUART BEST, D.D.

The eightieth milestone's close at hand,
The pearly gates I see,
I hear the harps of an angel band,
They sing sweet songs to me.
"No more the dreary desert roam,
Thy Saviour comes to lead thee home."

I'm willing, Lord, to labor here,
Keep toiling till the sun goes down,
'Midst cherished friends and loved ones dear,
'Tis joy to gain a fadeless crown.
Then, Saviour, when the prize is won,
Oh, let me hear Thee say, "Well done!"

VETERANS OF THE WORLD'S GREATEST ARMY

THE ATLANTA CONSTITUTION

It is the practice the world over to provide liberally for the old age or the indigence or the disability of the men who, in large and little wars, have freely periled life and health in the service of their country. We are just beginning to awake to the infinitely more sacred obligation we owe the worn or crippled veterans of religion; the men who in the service of the Cross sacrifice health, comfort and convenience, not for an inspiring four years, but for the entire term of their mature activities.

The cause is one which should appeal to the most generous instincts of men and women of every denomination, as well as those whose reverence for religion is of a non-sectarian character, for these men are, as a matter of plain fact, veterans in the greatest army of the world.

They enter most intimately and personally into the sanctity of our homes, in the hours when joy rings its highest cadence or when grief shadows the fireside like an impenetrable pall. The physician safeguards the material health, saving our strength that we may expend it for the sake of those for whom self-sacrifice is a luxury, and we are likely to compensate him in liberal measure. The minister of the soul, who gives consolation when the office of the physician has become of no avail, and who stands unmoved by our side if despair or disgrace should drive thence our dearest companions, too often is dismissed with a miserable pittance. It too frequently happens that he is so inadequately paid that he must deprive his family of the necessities and advantages of life, and he is as likely as not to reach the age for retirement without a penny against the inevitable rainy day.

Happily, we are rousing to the inadvertent cruelty and injustice of this custom, and denominations throughout civilization are taking steps to repair their neglect of the past and forestall its perpetuation in the future.

THE CHURCH'S PROGRAM

THE METHODIST EPISCOPAL CHURCH, SOUTH

THE REV. J. R. STEWART, D.D.
Secretary Superannuate Endowment Fund

For many years past, in the Methodist Episcopal Church, South, references to the meager support of Conference Claimants have been punctuated with regretful remarks and apologetic hesitation. This paper is a candid attempt to set forth our successes and failures in the management of this important matter. The interesting and contradictory nature of existing facts eludes satisfactory analysis. Free and frequent expressions of sincere deprecation of this state of affairs are heard within and even beyond our Church circles. Inconsistency or indifference might be suggested as applying to those who feel so deeply and yet act so tardily; but such judgment may properly be suspended until the real situation is carefully reviewed. Our belief is strong that if our Methodist constituency could be furnished with full information, forcefully presented, concerning the prevailing and often distressing needs of Conference Claimants, the solution of our problem would soon be in sight.

Darkness begets indifference. Ignorance concerning the merits of any good cause is its worst enemy. Sympathy would be moved and interest stirred into activity if the light of intelligence were flashed upon the situation. The real conviction of the Church has not been practically expressed on this subject, nor its strength delivered. With us, the desultory and haphazard manner of handling this great interest has been its defeat. Strange to say, even the *popularity* of the Claimants' Fund has exposed it to neglect and abuse. We have relied entirely too much upon a general and somewhat vague impression that our Retired Ministers, widows and children, so much honored and beloved and so worthy of a competency, are as a matter of course provided for; that the Conference Claimants' Fund is the easiest of all to secure, that it will surely be paid, and that in any event, the good people will not allow the Claimants to be in want. Not only have authorized agents relied upon the popularity of the cause to secure the payment of these claims, often without adequate presentation, but they have made the *popularity* of the cause the basis of appeals to secure the payment of *other connectional claims.* Our Claimants have not had a "square deal" at the hands of their friends.

Annual Conference Agencies

Until within very recent years the Annual Conferences have been solely responsible for the support of their Claimants. That the Conferences have never been able, for some reason not clearly apparent, fully to discharge this responsibility, by current collections, is a depressing fact of common knowledge. This is indicated by numerous organizations consisting of aid societies, endowment funds, superannuate homes, and lastly, our Superannuate Endowment Fund, all of which are intended to be supplementary to the regular line of support. These are so many confessions of the inability of the Annual Conferences to discharge this responsibility. It should be stated, however, in the interest of fairness, that a small number of our Conferences have gone far in advance of others in the support of their Claimants, but the number of those which have been successful is very small, not exceeding a half dozen. The maximum sum paid in these Conferences does not exceed five hundred dollars, and there are comparatively few who receive as much as four hundred dollars per annum. The true situation, however, is better realized when we strike an average of the amount paid the representative of each superannuate family; which, counting all that is received from every source, has not yet reached one hundred and fifty dollars, and quite a number of our superannuates decline to receive anything in deference to the interests of others, because of their greater need.

Our Annual Conference organization charged with the duty of making provision for Claimants is the Joint Board of Finance, composed of an equal number of ministers and laymen. This Board fixes assessments, subject to ratification by the Conference. Preachers in attendance on the Board meetings are almost invariably in the majority, so that the actual responsibility has rested largely on them. The question then arises, Why have not the clerical members, being in the majority, provided adequately for the maintenance of those who naturally hold such a warm place in their sympathetic esteem? Is it a matter of undue modesty? Can it be due to lack of business earnestness and foresight? Have they felt their responsibility duly? It is evident and must be confessed that our preachers have not used, to the full extent, the opportunity they possess for providing the needed support. Their unselfishness and modesty may be admired even though their business methods be subject to criticism. The shortest and easiest way to reach the goal of long-cherished desire is through ample assessments for the annual collections, so presented that the people may see their responsibility and opportunity. It is our conviction that if this had been done, our great problem would have received satisfactory solution long ago. But we are now under necessity of providing the support largely by indirection, since we have failed to do it by direct methods.

Endowment Funds

Through indirect agencies and organizations considerable sums have been contributed to the general cause. There are twelve or fifteen Annual Conferences which have established interest bearing funds, the largest of these scarcely exceeding one hundred thousand dollars. The income from these funds has been a valuable aid. There are also a few preachers' aid societies, which exist for a similar purpose. Then, in addition, there has been developed within the past fifteen years, in some dozen or more Conferences, the Superannuate Home movement. The pioneer in this form of activity has succeeded in securing more than thirty of these homes and has attained the largest success in this form of enterprise.

But the most ambitious attempt was the launching of our Superannuate Endowment Fund, with the avowed purpose of raising a minimum sum of five million dollars. As far as we are advised, the agitation of this matter was begun very properly by prominent laymen, the leader being the late Mr. W. F. Vandiver of Alabama. Discussion of this subject was held in private circles at the General Conference of 1898, but nothing further was done. In 1902, in the Episcopal Address, written by Bishop Hendrix, which contained strong and definite recommendations on the subject, our Bishops expressed their desire for such a movement. Great interest was manifested in the committee when the plan of organization was formulated, and its recommendations were adopted by the General Conference without opposition and on a full tide of enthusiasm. Immediately there was a spontaneous subscription of ten or twelve thousand dollars.

The Board of Trustees of the Methodist Episcopal Church, South, a corporation already existing, was made custodian of the fund under certain general directions. A field agent was employed who spent two years in visiting Annual Conferences and churches, soliciting subscriptions. He met with encouraging success, and then tendered his resignation, believing that his special line of work was completed. Knowing the great loss that is incident to the collection of popular subscriptions and realizing the fact that a better business foundation should be laid for the accumulation of a great fund, the trustees began seriously to consider the modification of plans. By this time they realized that the accumulation of a large fund would require the faithful operation of wise and well matured methods for a period of years. At the beginning, some with vivid imagination could see the great fund leaping into form and fact in an incredibly short time. Others were altogether doubtful of final success. Still others looked with large hope to the munificent benefactions of wealthy members of the Church for the building of this endowment. A yet larger number believed that the difficulties of the task would certainly yield, sooner or later, to persistent effort and that the noble undertaking would be crowned with success.

Direct Contributions from the Churches

Preparation for inflowing beneficence through the regular channels of the Church was not overlooked. Provision is made for receiving aid from the membership at large by requiring every pastor to present the subject annually to each congregation and to receive voluntary contributions. It is evident that the founders of the fund regarded this source of growth with large expectation, but we are sorry to be compelled to state that the failure of the pastors to take these offerings was a sore disappointment. Easy as it may be to confess the shortcomings of others, it really requires something of an effort to state the plain fact, that only a very few of our preachers ever attended to the performance of this duty. The Board exhausted whatever ingenuity it possessed to induce them to do so, but with incredibly small success. They simply would not stand for this method. We again came up against that subtle, indefinable, paralyzing influence which makes our preachers measurably incompetent to deal with this problem. Their finer sensibilities and stalwart, independent manliness forestalled them. Their itinerant training had been on a different line. They had been schooled to self-denial and self-respect, and refused to go before the public and practically plead their own cause. Our Board became thoroughly convinced that we need not expect them to take this collection, though, almost to a man, they were deeply interested in the success of the movement, as demonstrated by the fact that they were large personal contributors.

General Conference Assessments

Realizing that there was a great problem to be solved and knowing that the men in the ministry had possession of the slate, the Board began devising measures to set them to work. Convinced that no connectional enterprise could have large success independent of the active agency of the preachers, the expedient of an assessment was resorted to. The Board, being without power to fix assessments, appealed to Annual Conferences to assume them: a line of effort which frequently met stern opposition and was sometimes defeated, but finally prevailed in nearly all the Conferences. The General Conference of 1910 was memorialized to give the desired relief by authorizing a uniform assessment, but through a conjunction of unfortunate circumstances the effort failed. The work, however, was continued along former lines with increasing encouragement throughout the following quadrennium. Three plans for enlargement were presented for the consideration of the General Conference of 1914. Two of them were quite comprehensive in scope, though widely different; one of them being presented by the Board which is custodian of the fund. These progressive plans were promptly turned down by the committee, but a more conservative recommendation of the Board was promptly approved and enacted into law. This provision is in part as follows: "To further provide for the enlargement of this fund, an assessment shall be made on all Annual Conferences of a sum not less than one per cent of the amount paid for ministerial support." From this one source the fund should receive not less than fifty thousand dollars annually at the beginning and the amount should increase with the normal growth of the Church. Three fourths of the net income of this is disbursed annually to claimants through the several Annual Conferences, on the basis of the number of claimants, while one fourth is retained for increase of the Fund. The disbursement this year approximates nine thousand dollars; and will increase annually. After the fund shall have been completed the entire net income will be available for distribution. Some real estate has been deeded to the Board for the fund, with retention of life interest by the donor. By this commendable method one can practically administer on his own estate and be better assured that his purpose will be carried out after his decease than he could be by making a will. One such provision made recently will yield from fifteen to twenty thousand dollars.

Bequests

Since this fund has been in existence, a number of bequests have been made from which a considerable aggregate has been realized. Bequests are provocative of law suits and not infrequently the Church loses. We have one such suit now pending in a higher court involving an interest in a large coal land estate. We are expecting, also, that suit may be brought at any time in another case involving fifteen thousand dollars. We look with large favor on the purchasing of Life Annuity Bonds by those who have money they would like to put into this sacred cause and need the income from it during life. This line of contribution has been given great encouragement of late and with gratifying success. Fifty thousand dollars have been secured by this means, and our donors seem highly pleased with their investment. We expect large increments from this source. Our ministers have splendid opportunities, by cooperation with us along these lines, to render large and valuable service to the cause which should be dear to them.

The gathering of a five million dollar fund would be a short and easy task for our two million members if everybody was busy at the task. Yet that great achievement, as an accomplished fact, seems far in the future. A friend who was kneeling close beside the preacher who was praying too loud whispered, "Don't pray so loud. The Lord is not deaf." Without subduing his tones the man responded: "I know the Lord is not deaf; but He is a long way off from this place." So, we are compelled to admit that the Five Million Dollar Fund seems a long way off. But we are pressing on to the goal, and as long as we are proceeding there is a prospect of arriving. With $325,000 in cash holdings, and about $425,000 in total assets, we realize that our growth has been slow. It is not necessary to detail our hindrances, but only sufficient to say that these obstacles are fast disappearing. Our fund never before had as fair a prospect as at present. During the last quadrennium the cash assets almost doubled. We have every reason to believe that during the present quadrennium the sum will again be quite duplicated; a faith founded upon the legitimate expectancy of growth, as well as on the knowledge of other sources from which we are hopeful of receiving large additional amounts.

Justice and Fair Dealing

We are coming more and more to realize that a comfortable support for our claimants *must be provided,* by whatever honorable means. The justice and fairness of a guarantee of life-long sustenance for those who have consecrated themselves to a life-long service of religious leadership is so apparent that it scarcely needs to be stated. The vast majority of the preachers in our Church receive only a meager living, and many are pressed financially to the last limit in order to be able to continue their labors through the active period of their lives. It is impossible out of their small salaries to save anything for old age and disability. Honestly construed, life-time surrender to a great public life-service means life-time support. There are those who tell us that unless our ministry, both active and retired, are more comfortably maintained, we shall soon be without men to fill our itinerant ranks. We are not greatly alarmed at this warning, and thank God for that spirit in our itinerants which savors not of the things that be of men. They are held to their serious calling by conscientious convictions. They are not hirelings. Like the great Japanese Christian, the late Joseph Neesima, "They have a plow on their hands." As long as they believe that they are called of God to this ministry they will be found faithful, regardless of the hardships they may have to endure. With all this we realize that some may be deterred from entering the ministry, and others diverted to other lines of religious activity.

Gratitude

The well-informed among us are filled with regret and shame as they recall the fact that so many preachers and their families are kept on the depressed plane of embarrassing poverty. But when they realize the heroism which makes such a ministry possible, their sense of shame disappears in gratitude to God for the noble men and women "who count not their lives dear unto themselves, so that they may finish their course with joy, and the ministry which they have received of the Lord Jesus." The heavy hand of inadequate support falls with crushing weight upon many circuit preachers in country places and mountain districts. The Church's greatest debt of gratitude is due these earnest preachers for the splendid service they render in directing the doubtful feet of the inexperienced to the safe paths of gospel peace. With no prospect or opportunity of providing for the proverbial "rainy day," these men of faith move quietly and sublimely onward "making many rich," yet themselves remaining poor. Sooner or later they reach the inevitable day of retirement from both service and salary to a mere annual pittance, and to a trust in a merciful providence. How unfortunate it is when age and want, unseemly yoke-fellows, must be coupled together!

During the recent session of my Conference I visited the reputed spot where that young Southern hero, Sam Davis, was executed in 1863. He rose to posthumous fame because he chose to surrender his life rather than divulge the name of the person who had confided to him certain information which was found on his person. To the reluctant officers who did everything possible under the military restrictions to save his life, urging him repeatedly, even when he stood upon the death scaffold, to divulge the name of his informant, he replied: "Had I a thousand lives I would give them up before I would betray the confidence of a friend." As I looked on the scene of that tragedy I thought of the honor and heroism of that youth whose name will be handed down to coming generations. And I thought also, of the noble, self-sacrificing men and women in our itinerant ranks, whose unheralded names are worthy to be recorded in the heroic annals of the ages with those of the great men and women of the Republic.

The time is coming when a just and righteous people will honor and reward such Christlike service as our itinerant preachers are rendering, and will count it a privilege and a pleasure to make their old age an evening time of delight. The churches have slept long beyond their wakening time, but are now putting on their working apparel for an earnest and strenuous day's toil, the closing of which shall witness that in the future there shall be always an ample competency for the weary ministers, the lonely widows and the dependent orphans of Methodism.

Nashville, Tenn. J. R. STEWART.

WORN-OUT PREACHERS

BISHOP O. P. FITZGERALD

"Worn-out Preachers"—that is the right word. They are not tired out; they are not driven out because of any wrongdoing; they are not drawn out by any hope of worldly gain or ease. The law of the Church says: "A Superannuated Preacher is one who is worn out in the itinerant service." I recently looked upon the picture of one of them, the face of a good man whom I have long known and highly esteemed. The face bore the marks of physical pain and of weariness under the burdens he was carrying. In its expression I did not read discontent or complaint, but a longing for the call to go home where the weary rest. This thought came into my mind: "If we had before us in one group all our worn-out preachers, what a study it would present!" Broken and stooped, with wrinkled faces, whitened hair, and eyes that are dimmed—some things about them remind us who these men are. They are the servants of God who have fought a good fight, men who have performed the labor of love, and are exercising now the patience of hope. The sight of them would recall their lives, their heroism that was unflinching, their self-denial that was not merely a rhetorical expression, their patience and fortitude, which they practiced themselves as they had preached it to others. They are good faces—the faces of good men. Some one has said: "There are no happy old men among the servants of Satan." These worn-out preachers are happy in God in the midst of their distress and under the privations which have fallen to their lot. And their wives—mothers in our Israel, holy women who have shared their toils, who have kept step with them as their traveling companions in their itineracy—the picture would be incomplete without them. For the most part their names are unknown in the world. They have prayed and toiled and ministered with no thought of fame or worldly profit of any sort, but the blessings of God have followed their tracks. Their names are written in God's book of remembrance with those recorded in the Epistle to the Hebrews.

THE SUPERANNUATE ENDOWMENT FUND

Bishop E. E. Hoss

Let us imitate here the wisdom of the Roman Catholics, who have learned how to wait. They expect to be here next year, and lay their plans accordingly. If Methodism is to abide, it must do the same thing. The day has passed for mere temporary expediencies. We must take the ages into account.

Surely there is no class of men who better deserve to have their old age protected from want than the average itinerant preacher. Except in rare instances they do not, even in their prime, receive more salary than is sufficient to meet the current expenses. Many of them fail to fare even that well. Only the most rigid economy and self-denial keep them out of debt. In nearly every case they come to old age with but scant financial resources. Ofttimes they are forced to drop out of the ranks homeless and penniless. It is not pretended that the collections made in the Annual Conferences furnish enough to meet their actual wants.

This is the thing, as many have bitterly learned, that makes the coming of superannuation such a dreadful thing. After a man has been thirty or forty years a Methodist Minister he is virtually unfitted for any other work. And who wants to have an old preacher? What place is there left for him in the world? With thousands of eager and efficient young men seeking employment, he is simply crowded out. To me it is a pitiful spectacle. Once in a while I meet a venerable brother who has been a little more fortunate or a little more provident than the rest of his comrades and is spending a happy and comfortable old age under his own vine and fig tree, and I am always happy at such a sight. The plea I now make is for those who are, if not down and out, at least in great straits. If I were younger, I should like to lead a crusade in their behalf.

THE CHURCH'S OBLIGATION

Bishop Collins Denny

We cannot shut our eyes to the fact that we have grown to be a great people, amply able to care for those who are legitimately dependent upon us. Any lack of appreciation on our part for these Veterans is a serious reflection on the Church. Long ago we should have devised and pressed some wise plan for a better care for these old preachers. Any steps that we can now take which will accomplish this result ought to be taken with gladness, indeed, with enthusiasm. We are far behind our English brethren in this matter. God has greatly blessed us not only in giving us increase of membership, but also in increasing the resources of our people. Such provision as we make for those who have turned away from secular pursuits to serve Him cannot but meet His blessing.

OLD AGE, THE INDIAN SUMMER OF LIFE

Annual Report, Methodist Episcopal Church, South

God designs old age to be the Indian summer of life, the gentlest, the tenderest, the most beautiful of all life's seasons; for he says: "And even to your old age I am he; and even to hoary hairs I will carry and will deliver you." God's special care and love for old age marks it as the Indian summer of earth's pilgrimage.

Crowned Veterans
"So Great a Cloud of Witnesses"

THE CHURCH'S PROGRAM

THE BAPTIST CHURCH

THE REV. W. B. MATTESON, D.D.
Secretary Baptist Ministers' Home Society

I am a convinced Baptist and believe in liberty, democracy and independency. I am not, however, alone among Baptists in realizing that we pay a great price for our liberty. Perhaps we value it the more because we pay so much, but we are not blind to the advantages of more centralized methods. Democracy, either in political or ecclesiastical affairs, is not synonymous with the greatest immediate efficiency, and therefore in recent years our denomination has made a serious effort to secure closer cooperation without abating our independency. In 1908, we created the Northern Baptist Convention as an instrument of common expression and united action. The Convention has no authority but—what we think is better—great influence. Although at first looked upon with much suspicion—Baptists are preternaturally afraid some one is going to try to "boss" them—this organization has already led the way to important changes, and increasingly commands our respect and confidence.

At no point, perhaps, has our polity worked to greater disadvantage than in the problem of ministerial relief. The status of a Baptist minister is peculiar. He is ordained by the local church, subject to its discipline and to its discipline alone. So long as his people are loyal, a Baptist minister is a king on his throne, "his right there is none to dispute"; but apart from the local church, he is a waif and a stray. He hardly belongs to a denomination. The denomination did not ordain him, exercises no real supervision over him, and, naturally enough, has felt no great responsibility as to what became of him. The chief reason for the laggard's place we Baptists occupy in the work of ministerial relief lies in these characteristics of our polity. Our people are kind and generous; they are quickly responsive to any call of real suffering; but in the absence of a common plan or general supervision relief has been given in a haphazard way, as a sort of occasional and incidental charity; with little appreciation of the real dignity and importance of the cause.

Early Organizations

The first considerable organization among us for this work was "The Baptist Ministers' Home Society," organized in 1882 and working in New York, New Jersey and Connecticut. A few other organizations followed; but up to a very few years ago the situation was chaotic. In addition to the society just named, we had a similar organization in the central West covering five States; some States had funds; some associations had small funds; the German and Danish Baptists did something among themselves; but there were great gaps in between where nothing was being done in any organized way; and such organizations as existed were, for the most part, feeble and their work ineffectual. One of the very first things done by the newly created Northern Baptist Convention was the appointment of a Ministers' and Missionaries' Benefit Board, charged with the express duty of overseeing this work, filling in the gaps, unifying and harmonizing existing agencies, and pushing forward the whole work to greater achievement. The Board called to its secretaryship Dr. E. T. Tomlinson, and in 1911 raised an endowment of $250,000. The Convention in June,1914, authorized an additional million. The cause is now, for the first time, recognized as one of our great denominational causes, and is regularly put on the apportionments. This new standing has already secured for it wider recognition and more generous support.

Ministers' Homes

We have experimented with institutional methods. Our first considerable society, "The Baptist Ministers' Home Society," as its name suggests, was organized about the idea of a Home. I have heard it claimed that this was the first Home established in this country expressly for old ministers; a doubtful honor. Our next most important society, the one in the central West, also centered in a Home. Through the munificence of Mr. George Nugent, a magnificent Home with generous endowment, was established in Germantown, Pa., and a fourth Home has been completed recently in Southern California. Altogether they represent a property investment of $180,000 and endowments of $315,000. The Home is a beautiful and appealing idea, and will always have a real place in this work, for cases will occasionally arise that cannot otherwise be as well provided for; but as a method of dealing with the real problem of ministerial relief, we soon found it inadequate to the point of futility. We have, I imagine, done more than any other denomination in the way of such Homes, and less for our old ministers! Over-emphasis on Homes has tended to blind us to the real problem, and has delayed our recognition of the actual conditions.

Relief Plans

Our principal method has been that of relief. The societies which were originally centered in Homes soon undertook outside relief; the New York society practically abandoned its Home; the Michigan society does much more outside than inside. Most of the State and associational funds were never otherwise used. Our aim has not gone beyond that of preventing or relieving actual suffering. The usual way has been to grant a monthly allowance, of from ten to twenty-five dollars per month, conditioned on a minimum of honorable service, but otherwise solely determined by the needs of the particular case. We have pensioned old ministers and given allowances to those who were disabled, and to the widows and orphans of those who died. This method is the most economical and adaptable of all. It has worked fairly well, and we have never turned a deaf ear to anyone in real distress. The chief difficulty has been that our ministers often object to it as savoring of alms, and so being humiliating and pauperizing. The old minister who wrote me that "he had rather die than accept our help," spoke for many. There has thus grown up among us a strong demand for some method less offensive to the self-respect, and many ministers have expressed a desire for a contributory plan, by which they could be helped to help themselves. So our Benefit Board in 1914 at the June meeting of the Northern Baptist Convention, brought forward a "Proposed Plan for the Pensioning of

Baptist Ministers," substantially identical with that which is being put into operation by the Congregationalists; and very similar to that which was inaugurated six years since by the Presbyterians. Though called a "pension" plan, it would be more accurately described as an insurance plan. Ministers are to pay annual premiums, scaled to age, sufficient to earn annuities of one hundred dollars by the time they are sixty-five years old, and the Church proposes to increase this annuity to a maximum of five hundred dollars, as soon as it can secure the necessary funds. Lesser benefits are offered to disabled men; and still less to widows and orphans. The advantages of the plan are obvious. The ministers do their fair part, and this in itself constitutes a strong appeal to the Church to do its fair part. The relation is strictly contractual; the Church agrees to do a certain thing upon condition that the minister does a certain other thing. No humiliating questions need be asked. Need has nothing to do with it. Those who go in purchase insurance at eighty per cent discount. Aside from the fact that the plan would not be safe and workable without large endowments the disturbing doubt with us is as to the possibility of enlisting our ministers generally in support of such a plan. All experience seems to be against the success of contributory plans, when the contribution is voluntary, and there is no way of exercising compulsion. Mr. Lewis, in his work on "State Insurance" says, "It is generally agreed that plans for old age relief which are purely optional fall far short of reaching the evils which they seek to alleviate." The failure does not lie in any lack of benefit for those who go in; but in the fact that so many, and those generally the men on the smaller income, who most need protection, feel unable to pay the premiums, and so do not go in. Such experience as we have had confirms our fears. Contributory plans tried by German Baptists and in some southern States have failed of any great success.

In Massachusetts we have some approach to a truly pension system, chiefly through the generosity of Mr. Ford, of Youth's Companion fame, who bequeathed nearly $200,000 to the State Ministers' Conference. It is proposed to pay to every Baptist minister, who has given at least ten years of honorable service in that State and who has reached the age of sixty-two, a pension of $20 for each year of service up to twenty-five years, with a maximum of $500. At present the allowance is $15 per year, a maximum of $375. Nineteen men are now thus pensioned in amounts ranging from $155 to $375. The Conference recognizes, however, that brethren in need have a first claim upon the funds, and twenty-two were so helped last year. Until the fund has been increased to at least a half million dollars they will be unable fully to carry out their purpose.

Summary

Our work is being done through so many different and unrelated organizations, and with so much diversity of method, that it is very difficult to summarize the results. So far as I have been able to ascertain, the Baptists of the North have property dedicated to this cause valued at $170,000 and endowments amounting to $1,270,000. Last year they cared in all for 404 beneficiaries (800 if all members of the families helped are included), and expended $88,567. The Baptists of the South have $170,000 in endowment, and expended last year $44,418 for 416 beneficiaries. Taken all together we Baptists have in property and endowment $1,612,000, and cared last year for 820 persons, at an expense of $132,986. Our Baptist experience is peculiarly conditioned; but, for that reason has its contribution to make to the problem.

1. Small Salaries. We find that the underlying condition of dependency is inadequate salaries. The chief reason why ministers or their families become dependent is simply that salaries are commonly so small that few ministers are able to provide against "the rainy day," or to save enough to be independent in their old age. We cannot hope, therefore, to finally solve the problem of relief, until we have in some way secured, especially for the smaller salaried men, a substantial increase of income. We have, unfortunately, no real statistics of our own respecting salaries, but according to the United States Census Bulletin, we rank fourth among the greater denominations; below the Episcopalians, Presbyterians, Congregationalists and just above the Methodists; paying an average salary of $833, or, outside of the large cities, $683. But, as these statistics are based on reports from only sixty per cent of our churches, and it is the smaller churches that have generally failed to report, the figures

given are probably considerably above the mark. I believe it to be a very generous estimate to say that one Baptist minister in ten has over $1,000; three in ten over $750, and that much more than half receive less than $600. Of the service actually rendered by the beneficiaries of the Baptist Ministers' Home Society in New York State over a period of thirty-two years, sixty-three per cent was in churches which raised for all home purposes last year less than $1,000. The great majority of our beneficiaries are men who never had a salary of over $600 per year. They did not save because they could not save.

2. MISFORTUNES. But, although small salaries condition our problem, they are not the active causes of dependency. Over seventy per cent of all dependency is due to misfortune, sickness, unemployment and permanent disability; not so much to old age as to the infirmities of old age; and for the family, to the death of the wage earner. The average annual cost of sickness in the United States is estimated at $100 per family, and ministers do not escape their share. Some startling statistics in the last Presbyterian report show that the loss in that denomination through unemployment would amount to a reduction of over $300 (or more than twenty-five per cent) in the average salary. Both these risks, sickness and unemployment, would be included in any complete plan of protection. They are not included in any plan we know, chiefly because of their cost. Not to include them is not to eliminate the cost, but simply to refuse to distribute is to let it lie where it falls; and, where it does fall, it seriously affects the possibility of saving. A year without employment would be a nearly fatal blow economically to many of our ministers; and in actual practice, men so affected among us are likely to leave the ministry entirely, which is the solution of despair! Though we have only very incidentally and indirectly dealt with these risks, we have sought to protect our ministers and their families against the major misfortunes of complete disability, old age and death. The minister who says, "What we need is not pensions but larger salaries" is right in his affirmation. But he is entirely wrong in his implication that, if salaries were increased, the need for pensions would disappear. Let salaries be increased beyond any reasonable hope, and the five great misfortunes, with others

of less virulence, still lie in wait to devour his hopes. With a larger salary the minister could a little better protect himself, the proportions of the problem would be somewhat reduced, but protection would still be greatly needed. Men being what they are and life what it is, no increase in salary will eliminate nor even greatly reduce the need of relief.

3. The Rural Problem. Our Baptist problem is, in a large measure, a problem of the rural church. We, like Methodism, are a country Church, and our strength is in the towns, villages and rural districts. Seventy-three and four tenths per cent of our total population dwell outside of large cities; but eighty-six per cent of the Methodists and eighty-eight per cent of the Baptists dwell there. In New York State twenty-one per cent of the population live in communities of less than 2,500 inhabitants; but this twenty-one per cent supports sixty-four per cent of our Baptist churches. When the rural church declines, we die at the roots, and we know how serious the situation is to-day in the country churches. All agree that the only possible solution is to put trained and efficient men on these fields. But to find such men and keep them there is the great difficulty. This is a matter of providing decent maintenance. Conditions of ministerial life in the country have greatly changed and all for the worse. Among us, at least, salaries are nominally less than they were thirty or forty years ago. In actual purchasing power, when everything is taken into consideration, the country minister's income has declined nearly half. The pastor of the small church in the small village, on a small salary, is the crux of our situation. The point here at issue is of great importance to our ministers; but it is vastly more important to our Church. We shall stand or fall with the rural church. We must stand by the country pastor.

4. Disability and Widowhood. A careful study of the records of the Baptist Ministers' Home Society, during a period of thirty-two years, shows that we have helped more ministers than widows and orphans. This is, I believe, contrary to the usual experience. It is contrary to our own in later years. But even with this unusual preponderance of ministers the chief cause of dependency, in the experience of this society, has not been ministerial old age: forty-four per cent has been due to the death of the wage earner; forty per

cent to ministerial old age; nine per cent to permanent disability; seven per cent to various causes, of which prolonged sickness and lack of employment are chief. Without attaching undue importance to figures based on so limited an experience, the fact, confirmed by all that I have been able to learn of the experience of other similar organizations, seems to be that the greatest need is not pensions for old age but protection against disability and widowhood. The common practice of giving a lesser benefit to the widow than to the disabled minister is based neither on justice nor correspondence with the real need. To minimize this phase of our work in order to emphasize old age benefits is to lose touch with the facts; to stress the lesser and remoter need at the expense of that which is both greater and nearer. It is also to weaken greatly the strength of our appeal to the ministers themselves. We are all invincible optimists as regards the risks of life. Others may be hit; we expect somehow to escape. Especially is a young man likely to be optimistic as regards the risk of a dependent old age; old age is so far away, and dependency is to vigorous youth so utterly unthinkable! So many things may happen before that! He may die; half of us do; and a considerable part of the other half drop out. The average age of those who have entered the Presbyterian pension plan is stated to be 48. Present protection makes a much stronger appeal than future pensioning and is more needed.

5. Our Obligation to care for our ministers is more than sentimental. It is primarily a matter of obedience to the first Christian injunction, to love one another and to care for the brother in need; an obligation of peculiar emphasis when the "brother" concerned is one who has devoted his life to the service of the Church. We shall never get beyond this obligation of love, nor do we wish so to do. But, the first implication of love is justice. Love should go far beyond justice, but it is less than love, until it has attained to justice. And we are beginning to see that we have no right to take the lives of men, consume their strength and devour their years, and then, when we have squeezed the last drop of vitality out of them, cast them out upon the rubbish heap and forget that they ever were! If we fail to recognize this, we are in the way of being sharply reminded. The underlying principle of all modern social insurance—a movement with a long

history abroad, but now just beginning to be felt in America —is that every industry must care for its own waste, the waste of men as well as the waste of material. If that principle ever becomes established in this country—and it certainly will—the recently adopted workingmen's compensation laws pointing that way, the time will come when Society will say to the Church, "We refuse longer to permit you to cast upon us the burden of caring for your broken men. You shall have no ministry, unless you undertake to care completely for your ministry." Such a demand would be as just, as it would be humiliating. Love, justice, self-respect and an awakening sense of social obligation demand that we care for our own.

6. THE YOUNG MINISTER. The real aim of all our plans is not, when all is said, to help the old minister, but the young; the ultimate beneficiary indeed is not the minister at all but the Church. Our problem is a part of the great problem of securing a proper maintenance for our ministry, and that is the greatest of all our problems, underlying all others, involving, as it does, the efficiency of both the Church's present and future leadership. It is as hopeless as it is cruel to expect efficient service on beggarly wages. The minister's wife who recently told me: "My husband could preach better sermons if he did not have to worry so about those coal bills," spoke a parable of wide application. We do not ask the Church to make our ministers rich; we prefer them poor; but, there is a point of income, widely variable in particular cases, below which the minister, cankered with care, burdened with material anxieties, ground down by poverty, unable to travel or buy books or otherwise keep himself at his best, begins to lose efficiency. Oppressed with present anxieties, he is gripped with fear for his future. What would become of his family if he were to die to-morrow? What would become of himself or of them if he were to be permanently incapacitated or to live on beyond the years when the churches would accept his services? We, who are laboring at this problem of protection, do not directly deal with the salary problem; but we do touch it, and that at its sorest point. Our aim is to persuade our people to say to the minister in active service to-day, "Give yourself whole-heartedly to the work; spend yourself freely; be not afraid; we do not pay you such salaries as we should, but this at least we do solemnly promise, 'We

will stand back of you; if you fall in the work we will care for you; if you die, we will not permit your family to suffer; if you grow old in it, we will comfort your declining years.'" If we could but so say that as to carry conviction to the men on the hard fields and the small salaries, we should put new heart and hope into them; we should vastly increase their efficiency; and the Church would be the real beneficiary.

7. "Called, Chosen, Faithful." I am now in the fourth year of service in this cause, and am glad to confess that the greatest thing these years have brought me is a new appreciation of our ministers. Many of them are not great men, but the most of them are good men, faithful and hard working. I think often of this incident. A London preacher went down to a little country hamlet to dedicate a tablet placed in the chapel in memory of a recently deceased pastor, who for many years had labored, unnoted and unsung, in an obscure country village. Arriving early, the London preacher entered the little building and stood before the tablet. Upon it were inscribed the name of the pastor, the date of his birth, the date of his death and only these further words: "Called, Chosen, Faithful." As he stood pondering the inscription an old man and his wife came and stood beside him silently looking. After a little, the old man said with trembling lips, "We all loved him, and our lives are better because he lived among us!" Who of us would not be proud, indeed, if we were secure of such an epitaph—"Called, Chosen, Faithful," with the commentary in the hearts of our people, "We all loved him, and our lives are better because he lived among us"? I do not simply believe, I know, that many such men are numbered among our pastors. They live in small places; the world little notes them; the Church bestows upon them no honors; they bear hardships as good soldiers of Jesus Christ; they know poverty and want and the lack of all things; but they have been Called and Chosen and they are Faithful. Their people love them and are indeed better for their having lived among them. "I honored a faithful minister in my heart," said Governor John Winthrop, "and could have kissed his feet." The words are no longer extravagant. To help such men is our high privilege: we could ask no more joyful service.

Mt. Vernon, N. Y. W. B. Matteson.

THE CHURCH'S PROGRAM

RELIEF IN CONGREGATIONAL CHURCHES

THE REV. WILLIAM A. RICE, D.D.
Corresponding Secretary Congregational Board of Ministerial Relief and Annuity Fund for Congregational Ministers

It was not until 1886 that the national movement for the care of aged ministers was inaugurated by the National Council of The Congregational Churches of the United States. Prior to that time several State organizations for Ministerial Relief had been making a very small and inadequate provision for widows and Ministers. Before the division of the Congregational Church into the Unitarian and Orthodox branches a considerable fund had been gathered in Massachusetts, exclusively for widows of ministers. This fund, amounting to about $160,000, is still intact and is administered by a joint Board of the two Churches for the benefit of both denominations. There are fourteen State Relief Societies of which the oldest, New Hampshire, will celebrate its one hundredth anniversary in 1915. Several State Societies have merged with the National Society. The fourteen State Societies now hold permanent endowment funds of nearly $400,000 and annually distribute about $35,000 to over 200 families.

The National Board

The National Board, now in its 28th year, has gathered an Endowment Fund of about $300,000 and annually receives from all sources an average of $50,000. It has more than 200 families on its roll and gives to them over $30,000 a year.

These combined forces represent endowments of about $700,000 and annual receipts, including interest and gifts for endowment, of about $85,000. They distribute about $65,000 to over 400 families, representing approximately 700 dependent ministers and their wives, widows and orphans.

In addition to the work of these Boards of Relief the National Council at its meeting in Kansas City in October, 1913, adopted a general plan for Ministerial Annuities, and committed the inauguration, perfecting and promotion of the plan to the Board of Relief which has secured a separate charter for this work, known as

THE ANNUITY FUND FOR CONGREGATIONAL MINISTERS

The object of this endeavor is to provide at the age of sixty-five or seventy an annuity of five hundred dollars for the remainder of the minister's life, or three fifths of this sum for his widow. There is also a disability annuity in case the minister is totally disabled before reaching the annuity age; also a provision for the minor children until they become of age. The annuity provision applies only to those Congregational ministers, who became members of the Fund by making annual payments of premiums which according to actuarial estimates will yield one fifth of the amount of the old age pension or its prior provisions. That is, the minister purchases one fifth and the churches undertake to purchase four fifths; or for every dollar the minister puts into the Fund, the churches are to be asked to put in four dollars. The provisions of the Annuity Fund are applicable mainly to the younger ministers. The rates are very reasonable for the men who are under forty, though they are available for men older, up to fifty-five and even more.

The Annuity Fund has just been inaugurated and therefore has not had time for growth. No statistics can be given. It promises, however, to be one of the greatest achievements of the denomination.

In the Congregational churches there are some 6,000 ministers. The average salary is probably about $800. This means that there are many who receive much less. There are over 1,300 churches which pay salaries of not over $500. It is absolutely necessary, therefore, for the churches as a whole to make more adequate provision for the periods of old age, infirmity, sickness and incapacity. Our churches are awakening to this responsibility as never before and are endeavoring to accomplish this end through their Boards of Relief and the Annuity Fund.

WILLIAM A. RICE.

New York.

THE CHURCH'S PROGRAM

THE CONGREGATIONAL CHURCH

THE REV. SAMUEL L. LOOMIS, D.D.

Trustee Annuity Fund for Congregational Ministers

We Are Proud of Our Kindred. The Congregational body is sometimes spoken of as one of the oldest branches of the Church of Christ in America, and looks back with what we hope may be considered a pardonable pride upon our spiritual ancestry. She may be, perhaps, a bit over-conscious that,

"Still she keeps the ancient stock
And stubborn strength of Pilgrim Rock,"

yet I assure you that she takes much greater pride and satisfaction in contemporary kindred than in remote ancestry; and in no member of the family does she have greater joy than in the vigorous, abounding life, astonishing progress and mighty achievement of her younger sister, The Methodist Episcopal Church.

We Are Rich in Hope. Beware, little sister, that you do not think of us as old, even though we have seen a few more summers than you; for our eyes are not yet dim, nor our natural force abated, and above all we are supremely rich in that quality which is the characteristic sign of youth, Hope.

I remember once hearing a charming after-dinner speech by Joe Jefferson, who said that old men are sad, not so much because of weakness and infirmity, but for lack of that most enjoyable factor of life: Hope. Old men, having little or nothing to look forward to, live in the past. He therefore recommended gardening "because it is always pointing forward, always giving one something to expect." When you hear about our work you will realize that in the Department of Ministerial Relief, at least, we show no signs of senility;

for though we have little to boast of by way of achievement, we are exceedingly rich in expectations.

A SYSTEM OF PENSIONS. The Congregational Board of Ministerial Relief has two functions which, though kindred in nature, are entirely separate and distinct.

In the first place, by a system of modest pensions it provides for the necessities of those Veteran Ministers who have been unable to make adequate personal provision for old age and infirmity. While these pensions do not go to all aged ministers, but only to the small number whom the evening of life finds in special want, we are careful to emphasize the fact that this money is not to be thought of as a charitable gift, but rather as a well-earned and honorable reward offered by the Church to disabled but unconquered soldiers of the cross. This part of our work has been going on for many years and will doubtless be continued for years to come. In thirteen States it has been carried on by local societies for ministerial relief in cooperation with the National Board. Besides providing the required pensions, we have made a fair start in the direction of endowment, having raised $670,000 for this purpose. We feel keenly that the pensions hitherto provided are quite too small. Three hundred dollars, in some States four hundred dollars, is our maximum. We have great hope that this sum may be increased 30 or 40 per cent.

AN ANNUITY FUND. A second function of the Board of Ministerial Relief is that of establishing and conducting an Annuity Fund for the benefit of all Congregational ministers who are willing and able to comply with its conditions. This is a new task. In 1913 we presented to the National Council of Congregational Churches a report touching the economic condition of our ministers and their necessities, together with a practical plan for their relief.

THE MINISTER'S ECONOMIC CONDITION. The Board pronounced it a matter of imperative importance that some effective measures for the relief of our ministers be set on foot. At once upon entering the ministry a man gives up the usual opportunities of making money, and the hope of possessing many of the luxuries or larger comforts of life, things which by education and culture he is fitted to appreciate. These he cheerfully surrenders for Christ's sake and the gospel's. In return for such sacrifice, it is only right, if he be a faithful man of fair ability, that his profession should afford him a living of secure and moderate comfort up to the very end of his days. This was the idea of our fathers, and it accords with the Master's teachings that the laborer is worthy of his hire. In the life of the modern Protestant Church we have, however, fallen far below this ideal. Professor Rauschenbusch affirms that our ministers properly belong to the proletariat; their wages rarely ample, generally meager and often pitifully small; their employment irregular, uncertain, and, as they advance in years, increasingly difficult to find; many of them having no fixed abode, but drifting from city to city and from village to village, with but the slightest opportunity of saving for themselves; dependent for support in old age upon children, kindred or friends.

The Present Situation is Deplorable. The average salary is barely a thousand dollars. Multitudes of faithful men receive much less than that, and only thirteen out of every hundred exceed fifteen hundred dollars. The attempt to live and provide for a family upon such incomes, especially within the past few years, can mean but one thing, that for thousands of our preachers life is a steady fight with poverty, a struggle that bears with special severity upon ministers' wives. And this is not the worst of it. The average minister has before him the cheerless prospect that at the portals of old age, even this meager income will cease, and he, whose narrow means have made saving almost impossible, having no further opportunity to earn a living by his chosen profession, will be thrown into a position of humiliating dependency. Such conditions are alike unjust to the Christian minister and discreditable to the Church.

Society, long committed to the principle that the old age of public servants should be provided for, has in recent years been giving wide extension to that principle. Pensions are granted to-day, not to old soldiers only, but to railroad employees, to veteran police and firemen, to teachers and professors, and to employees of great corporations. It is high time for the Church to begin treating with more systematic and considerate care the old age of Veteran Preachers.

Usefulness of Pensions. Such provision should increase a minister's efficiency. To be assured that he has something coming to him in the day of need would release a man from anxiety, afford him a comfortable sense of security, and enable him to give an undivided mind to his great work. Relieved from the necessity of saving every possible penny against the evil day, he might have somewhat more to spend on the necessities of life, the wholesome and abundant food that makes one fit for work, the decent clothing required both for self-respect and the respect of the community, and the books that are the essential tools of the preacher's trade.

Such provision should also tend to lengthen the period of his activity in pastoral service. Our present method of dealing with ministers is unspeakably wasteful. On the one hand, we complain of the meager supply of preachers, and plead with young men to enter the profession, while on the other we are throwing away, by scores and hundreds, fully trained and equipped men at the very summit of their power. A minister at fifty years of age, if his health be unimpaired and if, escaping the snares of indolence, he has been giving his whole heart to his calling, is worth much more to any church than he was worth at forty, and immeasurably more than at thirty. Any loss of youthful ardor is much more than replaced by his increased richness and ripeness of mind, his practical wisdom, his growth in tenderness of heart and in spiritual power. Yet, these fundamental facts of ministerial experience very frequently have no weight whatever with churches; for if, for any reason, the minister of fifty or more loses his pulpit, he finds it extremely difficult to find another. Churches seeking for a man of his very type will pass him by without consideration, their dominant reason being the fear that if they take him they may in a few years "have an old man on their hands."

At whatever age he may have been called to a church, it must certainly be a disagreeable task to dismiss a worthy and beloved pastor because he is too old to serve efficiently, especially when he has no competence beyond his salary. Few churches can afford to retire him on half-pay. It is deemed simpler, in order to avoid all such embarrassments, to choose a younger man as minister and then let him go before he becomes old. However strongly one may disapprove this policy, he must recognize the fact that the condition exists, and there is reason to believe that proper provision for the minister's old age will, in a measure, serve to rectify it. If the Church could feel that his old age was partly provided for there might be greater willingness to employ him in the later and more effective years of his maturity. On the other hand, by tending to enhance the dignity and security of the ministerial office such provision would be influential in persuading young men to enter the ministry. The clergyman's unfortunate economic condition has doubtless had no small influence in withholding them from the profession. It is not that our youth lack the heroic spirit, the willingness to make sacrifices; but it is one thing to sacrifice yourself and quite another to sacrifice your wife and children. Not every sacrifice is noble. That which involves the crippling of one's powers, the narrowing of one's opportunities, and the diminution of one's influence is always of questionable wisdom. If we wish to secure for the Christian ministry the best of our young men, we must take all possible pains to make the minister's place one of dignity and genuine opportunity.

The Proposed Plan. In view of these facts and conditions, the Board of Ministerial Relief presented to the National Council a definite, practical plan to be known as "The Annuity Fund for Congregational Ministers," by means of which a certain modest provision might be made in the future for any and every Congregational minister who should find himself willing and able to enter into the proposed arrangement. This plan was adopted by the Council by a practically unanimous vote. The Board was directed to take such steps as might be necessary to set it on foot and make it effective, and was authorized to undertake the raising of a two million-dollar fund, the income of which should be applied to this purpose. The plan rests upon three fundamental principles:

1. That every minister for whom an annuity is to be provided should himself help to provide it by regular payments during the productive period of his life;

2. That every church should be taught to regard its fair share of the necessary cost of properly providing for the old age of Congregational ministers as a part of its ordinary fixed expenses;

3. That every man of ample means among us should be made acquainted with this fund as affording one of the safest, sanest and best investments for the kingdom of God.

We append the table of rates of ministers' payments for annuities to begin at age of sixty-five.

RATES OF PAYMENT FOR ANNUITIES CONGREGATIONAL CHURCH

Annuity Payment to Ministers to begin at sixty-five.

Age	Annual	Semi-Annual	Quarterly	Age	Annual	Semi-Annual	Quarterly
21	$21.47	$11.05	$5.69	39	$36.36	$18.72	$9.63
22	21.52	11.08	5.70	40	38.22	19.68	10.13
23	21.57	11.11	5.71	41	40.25	20.73	10.67
24	21.77	11.21	5.77	42	42.48	21.88	11.26
25	22.13	11.39	5.86	43	44.93	23.14	11.91
26	22.57	11.62	5.98	44	47.64	24.53	12.62
27	23.09	11.89	6.12	45	50.61	26.06	13.41
28	23.70	12.21	6.28	46	53.93	27.77	14.29
29	24.38	12.56	6.46	47	57.64	29.68	15.27
30	25.15	12.95	6.66	48	61.77	31.81	16.37
31	26.00	13.39	6.90	49	66.45	34.22	17.61
32	26.93	13.87	7.14	50	71.77	36.96	19.02
33	27.96	14.40	7.41	51	77.84	40.09	20.63
34	29.08	14.98	7.71	52	84.86	43.71	22.49
35	30.28	15.59	8.02	53	93.02	47.91	24.65
36	31.62	16.14	8.24	54	102.66	52.87	27.20
37	33.06	17.03	8.76	55	114.22	58.82	30.27
38	34.63	17.84	9.18				

Rates for annuities to begin at age of seventy.

Age	Annual	Semi-Annual	Quarterly	Age	Annual	Semi-Annual	Quarterly
40	$25.89	$13.33	$6.86	51	$45.45	$23.41	$12.04
41	27.01	13.91	7.16	52	48.44	24.95	12.84
42	28.44	14.65	7.54	53	51.77	26.68	13.72
43	29.55	15.22	7.83	54	55.53	28.60	14.72
44	30.97	15.95	8.21	55	59.77	30.78	15.84
45	32.52	16.75	8.62	56	64.61	33.27	17.12
46	34.21	17.62	9.07	57	70.19	36.15	18.60
47	36.06	18.57	9.56	58	76.71	39.51	20.33
48	38.08	19.61	10.09	59	84.42	43.48	22.37
49	40.29	20.75	10.68	60	93.69	48.25	24.83
50	42.75	22.01	11.33				

SAMUEL L. LOOMIS.

Westfield, N. J.

THE CHURCH'S PROGRAM

DISCIPLES OF CHRIST

THE REV. W. R. WARREN, D.D.

Secretary Board of Ministerial Relief,
The Church of Christ

In the beginning, and for the first seventy-five years of their history, most Ministers among the Disciples supported themselves wholly or in part by work in other callings. This was comparatively easy, since they were largely a rural people. Possibly this compelled them to be a rural people. Alexander Campbell himself was a prosperous farmer, as well as a successful publisher, along with his distinguishing labor as preacher, educator and writer.

The persistence of the type was strengthened by the reaction against the distinction between clergy and laity; and the natural instinct of economy mightily reinforced the rebellion against a "hireling ministry." The doctrine of plain meeting house and unsalaried preacher was full of comfort to the thrifty soul. But as the farmer of the Middle West was also a hospitable soul, the churches multiplied through the upper Mississippi Valley.

Of course many churches were planted at an early date in cities and towns. These were strengthened and others were started by the general urban trend of population. Increasingly the larger churches thus developed required the full time and undivided attention of their Ministers. The first salaries were small, and as the men approached retirement it became manifest that some provision must be made for their old age, as well as for disasters that might sooner overtake them. So in 1885 the General Missionary Convention undertook to effect a national organization of the work that was already being done locally in many quarters and by the whole State of Missouri.

Not until 1895, however, was a permanent organization formed, through the Board of Ministerial Relief of the Church of Christ, incorporated in 1897 with headquarters in Indianapolis. In its Permanent Fund are two items that commemorate the earlier efforts: "The Missouri State Fund, $800" and "Scott Fund, held in Trust by the American Christian Missionary Society, $2000." The latter came from a bequest paid in 1887.

The prime mover in establishment of the Board was Mr. A. M. Atkinson, a business man of Wabash, Indiana. Together with W. S. Priest, W. F. Cowden, W. F. Richardson and N. S. Haynes, he was appointed on the Committee on Ministerial Relief at the International Convention of 1894, in response to a memorial from the State Convention of Colorado, where Mr. R. H. Sawyer had agitated the question. During the year ex-Governor Ira J. Chase, one of Indiana's greatly admired preachers, died suddenly, leaving his wife totally blind and helpless. Mr. Atkinson at once raised a fund for her support, and while doing so, became so deeply impressed with the necessity of general and concerted action that he devoted the rest of his life and much of his means to the cause, dying in 1899, during the Cincinnati Convention at the close of an impassioned address to a group of fellow business men, his last words being, "Quit you like men!"

After Mr. Atkinson, the leadership fell to Mr. Howard Cale, a prominent lawyer of Indianapolis, the generous efforts of Chaplain J. B. McCleery, U. S. A., retired, having been cut short by death. When Mr. Cale died, in 1904, the Rev. A. L. Orcutt, a highly esteemed Indianapolis minister, succeeded him as President of the Board, having served several years as its Secretary.

For two years the work was carried on, as best it could be, in connection with his pastorate, and then he was asked to give his full time to the effort of promoting the cause from the office, with but little expense of travel. The operation of the law, "To him that hath shall be given," was not yet on the side of the Board. Its small outlay brought meager increase of receipts from year to year, and though the expense was held down to the minimum the percentage was ruinously high. The first year's receipts, 1896, were $5,340. In 1910, they were $14,306.

But information was spreading and conviction ripening for a more marked advance, which was started by another devoted business man, who in 1911 generously proposed that, if the Brotherhood would raise $20,000 the next year, he would add twenty per cent to it, and in the same proportion up to $30,000, and would continue to do so for five years. When it proved impossible to bring this challenge home to the people effectively from an office, the Board called W. R. Warren to become Secretary, in the belief that his four years' experience as Centennial Secretary would assure prompt success. Eleven months had brought in only a little over $8,000, leaving $12,000 to get in one month in order to secure the $4,000 extra. By providential intervention and extra effort the goal was reached. Every one of the three State Conventions, three churches and one hundred and seven individuals that were seen responded generously, while only one of the sixty letters written brought an offering, and that from a member of the Board. In 1913 $5,325 was received on the twenty per cent proposition and in 1914, the full $6,000.

In the two years during which the Board has been in the field with but a minimum equipment for a continental work, the total receipts have grown from $17,317 to $39,686, and the Permanent Fund has increased from $31,514 to $69,274. At the same time we have had full fellowship with the other national boards in the Men and Millions Movement, which is expected to add $200,000 to our Permanent Fund.

From the first the rule has been to add to the roll every applicant who on investigation was found: *First,* To have given his life wholly to the ministry, any other work having been only incidental; *Second,* To have lived "as becometh the Gospel"; *Third,* To be without other sufficient support. Until the advance of two years ago this kept the maximum payment down to $25 or $30 per quarter. The revival of interest, it develops, came just in time to meet greatly increased demands, and has been strong enough to enable us to increase payments to as high as $25 and $30 per month, and in one instance, $40.

In 1913 the retired missionaries of both the Foreign Christian Missionary Society and the Christian Woman's Board of Missions were added to the pension roll, payments being made through those boards, which in many instances add an allowance out of their own treasuries.

On September 30, 1914, the pension roll carried 111 names: 60 ministers, 43 widows and 8 missionaries, a net gain of 26 during the year. The total of pensions paid was $19,356, a gain of $5,590. The average was $190, a gain of $62 in two years. One received $435; sixteen, $300 to $360; nineteen, $200 to $295; thirty-nine, $120 to $180; nineteen $60 to $80; and seven, smaller sums for parts of the year.

The average age of ministers pensioned on account of old age is 74 years; of those pensioned for other disabilities, 51 years; of the whole list, 70 years; of the widows, 65 years. The average ministerial service of the ministers on the roll was 33 years; of the widows, 30 years; the total ministerial work represented by the 111 names being 3,539 years.

Money received from Annuity Bonds, Bequests and the larger individual gifts is added to the Permanent Fund, which is loaned at 6 per cent on improved real estate in and near Indianapolis, where it is exempt from taxation and can be looked after by the Board's officers.

The Sunday before Christmas is the regular day for the presentation of the work in the churches. Better results are coming from the Every-Member Canvass and the Missionary Budget. The number of contributing churches and Sunday schools in 1914 was 910, a gain of 105. For 1915 the Board has united with the other national societies in presenting a joint apportionment to about 8,000 churches. Considerable interest is being taken by the Sunday schools in our suggestion that they adopt the "White Gifts for the King" Christmas service and devote their "Gifts of Substance" to "Ministerial Relief; for those who, having given self and service fully until disabled, should be made guests at the King's table." The supplies are furnished free to such schools as promise to give their offerings to the fund.

The custom of our Annual International Convention is to make an offering to Ministerial Relief in the Sunday afternoon Communion service. At the Centennial in Pittsburgh, in 1909, this amounted to $2,619. In Toronto in 1913, on the statement that half of the amount received would be used for the benefit of the three sons of Mr. and Mrs. Eldred, missionaries who had both died in Africa during the year, $3,623 was given. Shortly afterward Doctor and Mrs. Hugh T. Morrison, of Springfield, Ill., undertook the full care and expense of rearing the boys in their home and as their own.

A notable example of the work's beneficence was furnished last year in the case of a prominent minister, whose health broke so completely that it was thought he could never preach again. The relief from anxiety and the sense of fellowship, which the assurance of a monthly pension brought, enabled him to recover so rapidly and completely that after two payments he took a less exacting charge, in which he has been richly blessed. His son had been taken out of college to earn the family's living, but on receipt of the pension, went back, is now preparing for the ministry, and preached his first sermon on the Sunday of the Atlanta International Convention.

COMPARATIVE FINANCIAL STATEMENT

Receipts

Sources	1911	1912	1913	1914
Churches	$7,500	$8,982	$13,141	$15,528
Individuals	2,394	4,055	2,648	2,455
Bequests	3,219	6,112	6,312	300
Annuities	1,600	1,100	2,700	5,800
Conventions	768	10	1,039	3,367
Miscellaneous	35	4	784	2,750
Total	$15,516	$20,263	$26,624	$30,200
The 20 Per cent Proposition	....	4,053	5,325	6,000
Interest and Rent	1,800	1,666	2,011	3,486
Total	$17,316	$25,982	$33,960	$39,686

Pensions

Names on Roll	71	75	85	111	26
Amount Paid	$8,816	$9,540	$13,760	$19,356	$5,590

William R. Warren.

Indianapolis, Ind.

THE TOUCH OF A VANISHED HAND

JOHN TROLAND

We sigh for the touch of a vanished hand—
 The hand of a friend most dear,
Who has passed from our side to the shadowy land;
 But what of the hand that is near?

To the living touch is the soul inert
 That weeps o'er the silent urn?
For the love that lives in our hand alert
 To make some sweet return?

As the days go by, are our hands more swift
 For a trifle beyond their share
Than to grasp—for a kindly, helpful lift—
 The burdens someone must bear?

We sigh for the touch of a vanished hand,
 And we think ourselves sincere;
But what of the friends that about us stand,
 And the touch of a hand that's here?

THE VETERAN'S HAND

After fifty years in the Baptist ministry the Rev. B. T. Welch, in a half-playful, half-rapturous manner, would hold up his thin, trembling, palsied hand and say to it:

"Old Hand, what ails you? Cannot you be still for a moment? Seventy and six years have left their marks on you. But bless the King in Zion this day for all the service you have been able to render Him. How often have you handled the sacred pages of His Word! What use you have been in preaching His gospel! How often you have baptized loving disciples! How many you have received into fellowship into His Church! For how many you have broken the emblem of His broken body! Poor old hand! I remember when you were fair and young and strong.

"Never mind the past. Thanks to my loving Lord, it will not be long before you will put your fingers into the print of the nails in His hand; not long before you will lay a crown at His feet; not long before He will stretch out His own hand, mighty to save, and grasp you and greet you, and His touch will heal your palsy and send immortality thrilling through your every vein and fiber. Be of good cheer, old Hand! You shall soon touch more than the hem of His robe, His robe, and are healed forever!"

THE CHURCH'S PROGRAM

REFORMED (DUTCH) CHURCH IN AMERICA

THE REV. DENIS WORTMAN, D.D.

Secretary Ministerial Relief, Reformed (Dutch) Church in America

The Reformed Church has two methods of Ministerial Relief, the Disabled Ministers' Fund and the Widows' Fund. They are alike in this, that ministers, their widows and orphans may receive this greatly needed benefit; they both have a partial endowment, the churches are supposed to make an annual offering for both funds; both deserve and require larger endowment and larger annual sustainment. They differ only in methods and measures of help; the former being a blessed beneficence, the latter a happily combined beneficence and insurance.

The Disabled Ministers' Fund, started in 1854 and reconstructed in 1863, is for relief of Disabled Ministers, and their widows and orphans in honorable need. Assistance is unfortunately limited, on account of lack of funds, to $200 a year; and may be given only as recommended by Classis, and year by year. We seek larger annual offerings and worthier endowment, so we be not limited to such miserly amounts. The annual offering has now increased from $3,900 to $8,535; which must be increased to $10,000, and be kept there, at the least. The Fund has an endowment of $101,000, which we must increase to $250,000 at least, for which we ask and entreat large gifts and legacies from the rich. Eighteen ministers and thirty-six widows are now enjoying this relief. Meanwhile the number of annuitants increases from year to year, and will continue to do so with increase of prices of living and the earlier retirement of Ministers.

The Widows' Fund is a combined beneficence and insurance, and I think a unique and inviting one. If the minister begins insurance at thirty-five years of age or under, his premium is $20 a year for life; if he begins between thirty-five and forty-five, it is $30 a year; if between forty-five and fifty-five, it is $40; if between fifty-five and sixty, it is $45. After sixty it is too late. The annuity to the widow of the insurer is $200 during her lifetime; and at her death her children, under sixteen, receive a percentage. If there is not sufficient money for the $200, the annuity is proportionate to money in the treasury. This year it is $185. The minister himself may receive this aid, when recommended by Classis, upon two physicians' certificates that he is permanently incapacitated for ministerial service.

The present endowment of this Fund is only $114,000, and the General Synod urgently calls for its increase to at least $250,000. This last church-year ministers gave toward their own insurance $2,200, and two thirds of our churches (the others not strong ones, but largely missionary) gave $5,550; which latter figure ought to be $10,000. The present annuities of $185 should be $300, if we would be in line with kindred denominations. There are now on this fund twenty-one ministers and fifty-seven widows. Some others should be receiving this relief who are deterred from asking because of the stringency of our funds. The increasing expenses of living, the fateful shortening of ministers' terms of service, the deplorable extent to which churches and ministers are in jeopardy of a shortening service, imperil the prosperity of the churches as well as the prolongation of gracious pastorates and discourage strong and energetic young men from perilous pastorates, short and precarious. These considerations summon men and women of wealth to the handsome endowment of these precious funds.

For all Thy reverend servants, Lord,
  Who long have served and bravely borne,
Who well have taught and wrought Thy word,
  Whose virtues still Thy Church adorn,
We bless Thee, and implore Thy grace
Till, past dark death, they see Thy face.

Surcease be theirs from fears and tears
  While through these earthly wilds they roam,
And grateful thoughts of well-spent years
  While gazing toward their nearing home;
And ours the children's heritage
Of sweetening their declining age.

We thank Thee for their lives sincere
  That warned and wooed away from sin,
For words of wisdom and of cheer
  That helped us worthier wealths to win;
Lord, may we save from care and loss
The saints that led us to the Cross!

May we who follow in their train
  Their virtues view and deeds outdo,
And like them strive the world to gain
  For Him who to its rescue flew;
Him and them may we join, among
Thine aged made forever young!

DENIS WORTMAN.

East Orange, N. J.

GERMAN BAPTISTS OF AMERICA

For many years the German Baptist Conferences have come to the aid of their aged and infirm ministers as their condition required. The General Missionary Committee began in a humble way aiding a few until to-day the appropriations amount to $2,475 annually. Thanksgiving Day or New Year's Eve offerings have been devoted to this cause, and in churches which have introduced the duplex envelope a certain percentage is designated to this purpose. Sixteen ministers receive an annual allowance of from $50 to $250. Last year $3,556 were disbursed for relief to ministers and their families.

Several years ago a legacy of $2,000 was left, the interest of which was to be used for ministerial relief to be known as the "Martha E. Miller Fund." Mrs. Miller had been a minister's wife; her husband had been compelled to leave the ministry on account of ill-health. He prospered in business and devoted much money to God's kingdom and remembered his brethren during his lifetime and gave this legacy through his wife. The German Baptist Publication Society voted $500 of its profits in 1910 and the same amount in 1911 for ministers' pension or ministerial relief. This was to inspire people to create a permanent fund.

At the General Conference in 1910 a committee of representative men was appointed to devise plans for a more thorough and extensive Ministerial Relief Fund, to report at the next General Conference.

The ministers themselves have for many years sustained a Society known as "The Mutual Aid Society of German Baptist Ministers of North America." It was incorporated without capital and strives to enlist all the younger ministers. It has a membership of 137 at present. The average assessment is $10 per year, and the benefit in case of death is $250, if the minister should die within five years of his membership, and $500 after that term. This Society has aided thirty-one ministers' widows or their families during the past fifteen years.

THE NEW ZEALAND SUPERANNUATION FUND

Each minister pays an annual subscription of $41, and the circuits pay for each minister $56 yearly. The annuities range from $150 per annum to ministers superannuated after five years' service, to $700 to those who have labored forty-four years. The secretary recently said, "The next General Conference ought to be able to declare an appreciable increase to the annuities. The capital now stands at $2,225,000, and 52 per cent of the annual income is being added to the accumulated capital."

WESLEYAN SUPERANNUATES

The report of our Wesleyan brethren on the Worn-Out Ministers' Fund has just been made, showing a healthy condition. There are nearly nine hundred ministers and ministers' widows having claims on the fund, and the leaders of the Church hope that the increased donations are a recognition of the claims of the fund and likely to continue. The average term of service in the Wesleyan ministry is thirty-eight years, and the average grant for supernumeraries is $5 per week, and for widows in the neighborhood of $3.

The Methodist Recorder, commenting upon this, delivers itself in words that could apply with equal propriety to American Methodism. It says:

"Let our readers consider what it means—that after near forty years' service in our ministry there is a pension of one pound a week! We are all hearing of the increased cost of living, but we have heard of very few ministers' stipends that have increased. There are thousands of generous people in Methodism who are sometimes distressed because it is difficult to find cases in which they can be sure their gifts will be rightly applied. We would suggest to them this fund. 'Charity' is not the word. The brethren are of our own household, and cannot be disregarded because they are old. We know a kind-hearted master by his affection for his old servants, a loyal-hearted man by his love for his old teacher; may we not know a Christian Church by its care for its old ministers?"

JEWISH RABBIS

In Jewish reformed congregations, the highest salary is $18,000 per annum, the next $15,000, there being quite a few at $10,000 and $12,000, while salaries of $5,000 and upward are common. The leading Jewish congregations in Cincinnati pay their ministers $7,000 and $10,000 respectively, and in addition these gentlemen receive fees amounting to several hundred dollars more. But even at these figures there are not enough graduates from the American Jewish theological schools to properly supply the increasing demand, and the average salary tends to become larger.

"Reading such figures, some financially-hard-pressed ministers might be just a little tempted to say, '"Almost thou persuadest me to be"—a Jew!' That even with such salaries there are not enough young rabbis for the demand would indicate that among both Jews and Gentiles the financial consideration is not the foremost element in the call to preach."—*Western Christian Advocate.*

SUPERANNUATE HOMES

The North Alabama Conference of the Methodist Episcopal Church, South, has an agent for Superannuate Homes, and has provided for thirty-two families since the movement was inaugurated. The Homes are proving a great blessing to the claimants, and a blessing to the communities.

There are thirty Homes valued at $67,000.

The California Conference has twenty Conference Claimants' Homes all occupied.

THE METHODIST EPISCOPAL CHURCH

The following general statement is of interest:

The full account of the methods and institutions employed by the Methodist Episcopal Church in securing the money needed to pay in full the inherent, foremost and supreme claim of its Retired Ministers will be found in Part III.

The following general statement indicates progress:

THE GIST OF IT

I. $4,000,000 raised for distribution from 1908 to 1913.

II. $2,500,000 added to Investments since 1908.

III. $1,500,000 *additional increase* distributed to Claimants during the last five years as compared with any previous five years.

IV. $500,000 increase in *annual* distribution in 1914 as compared with 1908.

V. Number of Claimants in 1913 was 6,589: 3,181 ministers, 3,123 widows, 285 orphans.

VI.	879	Claimants received less than $50 each.			
	1,171	Received from	$51	to	$100.
	1,200	" "	101	to	200.
	1,171	" "	201	to	300.
	411	" "	301	to	400.
	127	" "	401	to	500.
	13	" "	501	to	600.

(Children not included.)

VII. Average salary, $720; average Disciplinary rate, $10.25.

VIII. Average Annuity rate paid, $5.25; 51% of the full Disciplinary rate.

IX. MONEY NEEDED Each Year to Pay All Claims, $1,600,000.

X. For the twenty years prior to 1907 direct contributions from pastoral charges increased at the rate of $9,600 a year. Since 1908 the *increase* has been $30,000 a year.

Let us devoutly say, *"What hath God wrought!"*

XI. The total revenue for distribution in 1913 represents a five per cent income on $22,000,000. To meet its obligations the Methodist Episcopal Church needs an annual revenue equal to five per cent of $32,000,000. Hence the need of the 1915 CAMPAIGN for $10,000,000 additional Endowment.

THE CHURCH'S PROGRAM

THE METHODIST EPISCOPAL CHURCH

THE REV. J. B. HINGELEY, D.D.
Corresponding Secretary
Board of Conference Claimants

The movement for providing for Disabled Preachers in the Methodist Episcopal Church dates back to Revolutionary days when the inquiry was made at the Conference of the little band of Wesleyans as to what could be done for the preachers who were worn out in the service. At that time all the Methodists in America could have been accommodated in any church in Washington.

In those early days, the Methodist organization was communistic. Each preacher received the same salary and the provision for the care of the superannuated preacher was the same as that for the men in the active ranks. The oldest institution of organized Methodism is the "Chartered Fund," which still exists and contributes $3,600 a year to the support of Claimants, even though the contributors to the original Fund have been dead a century or more.

From the very beginning the chief source of income for the Retired Preacher has been the contributions from the churches, which to-day amounts to half a million dollars.

The Book Concern makes the Retired Preachers beneficiaries of its income, the amount paid for the care of the aged ministers, widows, and orphans, now being $300,000 per year.

Most Annual Conferences have Permanent Funds, varying from $10,000 to $300,000. The income of this money is applied to the relief of Claimants. In 1908 the Church provided a connectional, or general board, known as the Board of Conference Claimants, to care for the general interests of the Retired Ministers, and to create funds for the special care of those who are in the poorer sections of the country. Since the organization of the Board of Conference Claimants, there has been an annual increase of the distribution throughout the Church of $500,000. This legislation marks an era of advance along this line. In 1912 the General Conference asked for an additional five million dollars for investments. The campaign to secure this money is known as the "1915 CAMPAIGN." Each Conference is projecting a campaign for enough funds to meet its own obligations, and the Board of Conference Claimants is seeking additions to its funds.

In April, 1914, the Bishops appointed a special Committee, consisting of Bishops McDowell, Berry, and Quayle, to prepare an Address and Appeal to the Church in behalf of a $5,000,000 Fund, the appeal to be presented at a special meeting to be held in Washington during their fall meeting. On Thursday night, October 29, 1914, this

ADDRESS AND APPEAL TO THE CHURCH

was delivered in the presence of representatives of thirty Conferences, and a large gathering of local Methodists. The Inauguration Meeting was fittingly held in the Metropolitan Church at the capital of the Nation.

The program for the Convention was prepared with great care, all the men upon the program being familiar with the special topics to be presented. On Tuesday afternoon and Wednesday morning there was a review of the present provisions made for the care of Retired Ministers. On Wednesday afternoon, plans for the intensive and cooperative Campaign were discussed. On Thursday, Dr. McClure, of the Protestant Episcopal Church, Dr. Foulkes, of the Presbyterian Church, Dr. Stewart, of the Methodist Episcopal Church, South, Dr. Loomis, of the Congregational Church, Dr. Sweets, of the Southern Presbyterian Church, and Dr. Matteson, of the Baptist Church, told what was being done in these great Churches to provide suitably for the Retired Preachers.

Mr. J. W. Renner, Secretary of the Pension Department of the Pennsylvania Railroad, presented an instructive address as to what is being done by that great railroad to provide for aged employees. There were also special addresses on the Pensions by Corporations, Wills, Life Annuity Bonds, and other topics of vital interest to the cause.

"The Veterans of the Cross Fellowship," is an organization of the Retired Preachers, for the purpose of cultivating fellowship and bringing them into closer touch with the Church's work. Dr. Varnam A. Cooper, the President of the National organization, as well as a great many of its members, are Veteran Soldiers, and naturally enough, the language of the campaign and the camp is the language of this delightful Fellowship. There is no lack of numbers sufficient for such an organization. We are accustomed to large numbers in connection with all things Methodistic, but are perhaps surprised to learn that in the Methodist Episcopal Church alone, there are 3,181 retired preachers; 3,123 widows of preachers, and 500 dependent orphans, making a total of almost 7,000 Claimants, whose claim to a comfortable support is recognized.

Since the claim of each widow is one half that of a Retired Minister of the same length of service; and the claim of the dependent orphan child is one fifth of what his father's claim would be; it follows that the full claims of these 7,000 Claimants in the different classifications are equal to the full claims of 5,000 Retired Ministers. Such a statement of the case may add clearness of understanding to friends of aged ministers who are not familiar with Methodist terminology.

THE CLAIM

The Methodist Episcopal Church recognizes a twofold obligation toward the Retired Minister.

First, an Annuity, or Pension, based upon the length of service. The amount of this Annuity varies in different Conferences, in proportion as the average salaries vary. The standard is the same relatively in all Conferences, namely, that the Retired Minister who has fulfilled thirty-five years of service is entitled to an amount equal to one half of the average salary of the active men in his Conference. The average salary varies greatly throughout the Church, but the ratio for the support of the Retired Preacher is the same, namely, that he shall have half as much as the average pastor. For example, in the Baltimore Conference, the average salary is $1,050; the half salary, $525. The Retired Minister who has fulfilled thirty-five years of service in that Conference is entitled to a pension of $525, and if he has served a longer or shorter time than thirty-five years, he would be entitled to such proportional share of the amount.

Second: An additional amount, when necessary, is provided to relieve needy cases. The annuity or pension would make reasonable provision for a minister of long service, but only an inadequate provision for one of short service. Hence in addition to the money to be distributed on the basis of service as annuities or pensions, the Church provides money which may be added to the amount of the annuity or pension.

THE BOARD OF CONFERENCE CLAIMANTS

The Board of Conference Claimants was constituted in order to provide this additional amount, but until funds in the hands of the Board are sufficient to do so, Conferences may apply part of their revenues to help needy cases. Because of the necessity of so providing for necessitous cases the Baltimore Conference, whose legal annuity is $15 a year, pays but $10 a year. The 1915 CAMPAIGN is for the purpose of so increasing the revenues of the Board of Conference Claimants that its funds may be sufficient to provide whatever additional help may be needed throughout the Church; and also to increase the invested funds of Annual Conferences to an amount sufficient to enable them to meet their annuity obligations.

All departments of the Church are interested in this 1915 CAMPAIGN. The Bishops have written earnestly in behalf of it. Letters from the entire Official Family of Methodism, urging the fulfillment of the Church's obligation toward the Retired Preachers are printed in this volume. Bishop Oldham has just written a most attractive booklet entitled, "We'll Do It," taking for his text the statement of Dr. V. A. Cooper, of the New England Conference, who when speaking of the vows taken by the ministers, and the promise of the laymen of a comfortable support, said of the laymen, *"They took us for life, let them see us through!"*

The work of the Board of Conference Claimants is world-wide. It receives money from every continent on the globe and extends help to Retired Methodist Preachers in China, India, South America, Africa, and to the warring nations of Europe; and when the carnage shall cease the Board will be the organized hand of the Church to relieve the distress of the aged ministers, the widows and orphans of Europe's stricken Methodism.

LITERATURE

The Board of Conference Claimants has an extensive Literature, and publishes a Magazine, *The Veteran Preacher,* which is filled with items concerning his care.

The Board of Conference Claimants has secured some fine music for the Cause. Dr. W. J. Kirkpatrick wrote the music for "Veterans of the Cross"; Thoro Harris, of Chicago, wrote music for Mrs. Smith's poem, "Remember the Faithful." Dr. Hingeley has a song entitled, "The Veteran's Camp Fire," sung to the tune, "Tenting To-night." Mr. and Mrs. Martin, authors of the familiar song, "God Will Take Care of You," wrote for the Board the words and music of "Scatter the Flowers Now"; and Fanny Crosby, at the request of Dr. Hingeley, wrote the beautiful poem entitled, "Love's Recompense." (See INDEX and TABLE OF CONTENTS.)

EPISCOPAL AREAS

The last General Conference of the Methodist Episcopal Church assigned the Bishops to the supervision of Annual Conferences in definite areas during the quadrennium, believing that there will be a stronger sense of responsibility and a stronger administration by this method.

Bishop Burt has already organized the Buffalo Area in the interests of Conference Claimants. Each of the six Conferences in his area has a separate organization to help raise the amount of money needed, and, beside that, these six Conferences have formed an organization for mutual assistance. Since the problem in this area will be to raise more than a million and a half dollars, such an organization can be made very effective.

Chicago, Ill. JOSEPH B. HINGELEY.

SOME BEGINNINGS

In 1763 a Fund for worn-out preachers was inaugurated by Mr. Wesley.

In 1774 the second American Conference ordered an Easter collection for needy itinerants.

In 1784 a Preachers' Fund was instituted, to be kept up largely by a ministerial tax. This was afterwards merged into the Chartered Fund.

In 1789 the Disciplinary plan of raising a Fund for the Superannuated Preachers, and the Widows and Orphans of Preachers was as follows:

Ques. 1. How can we provide for Superannuated Preachers, and the widows and orphans of Preachers?

Answ. 1. Let every Preacher contribute two dollars yearly at the Conference.

2. Let every one when first admitted as a Traveling Preacher, pay twenty shillings, Pennsylvania currency.

3. Let the money be lodged in the hands of the Presiding Elder, or lent to the College; and an account thereof kept by the Deacon.

N. B. The application of the money shall rest with the Conference.

4. Out of this fund, let provision be made, first, for the worn-out Preachers, and then for the widows and children of those that are dead.

5. Every worn-out Preacher shall receive, if he wants it, not usually more than twenty-four pounds annually, Pennsylvania currency.

6. Every widow of a Preacher shall receive yearly, if she wants it, during her widowhood, twenty pounds.

7. Every child of a Preacher shall receive once for all, if he wants it, twenty pounds.

8. But none shall be entitled to any thing from this fund, till he has paid fifty shillings.

9. Nor any one who neglects paying his subscription for three years together, unless he be sent by the Conference out of the United States.

10. Let every assistant, as far as possible, bring to the Conference the contribution of every Preacher left behind in his circuit.

In 1908 the Church began to do business for the superannuates along tried and successful lines by establishing the general or connectional Board of Conference Claimants.

PART II. THE CLAIM FOREMOST

CHAPTER II. THE PROGRAM OF BUSINESS

A UNIQUE PAY ROLL

With 2,040 active employees who have been in service forty years or longer, and with 1,572 men who served forty years or more and are now receiving pensions, the Pennsylvania Railroad has a unique pay roll, with 489 men who have been in its service more than fifty years. The employees in the service fifty years or longer are as follows:

1 employee 66 yrs.,	7 employees 59 yrs.,	42 employees 54 yrs.
3 employees 64 yrs.,	23 employees 58 yrs.,	39 employees 53 yrs.
5 employees 62 yrs.,	20 employees 57 yrs.,	53 employees 52 yrs.
3 employees 61 yrs.,	27 employees 56 yrs.,	93 employees 51 yrs.
8 employees 60 yrs.,	41 employees 55 yrs.,	124 employees 50 yrs.

Pennsylvania employees are blessed with longevity, for it has in active service, 4,717 employees who are between the ages of 60 and 70. The Carlisle tables of mortality show the expectancy of a man 21 years of age to be 40.75 years; but the Pennsylvania Railroad has 4,015 employees who exceed this. The following figures show the employees between 60 and 70 years:

Age	No. of Employees	Age	No. of Fmployees
60	702	65	455
61	607	66	347
62	637	67	325
63	570	68	318
64	540	69	216

There were living in 1912 eight Pennsylvania Railroad employees who are over ninety years of age, all of them receiving regular pension payments from the company.

WHAT RAILROADS ARE DOING

PENNSYLVANIA LINES

MR. JOHN W. RENNER
Secretary Pension Department, Pennsylvania Lines

The request for information as to the pension system in effect on the Pennsylvania System Lines contained two specific inquiries: first, as to pensions for those retired from service on account of age or incapacity; and, second, as to provision for the maintenance of dependents of deceased employees.

The analogy between the railway service and church work may be considered as fairly close in the case of those in either line of work remaining in active service until reaching a pensionable age; for employees in either service have as a rule given all, or a large proportion of their working years to the service. But there is no such analogy in the matter of providing for dependents of the deceased. In railway work, only the employee himself performs any service for his employer, and it is therefore but fair that the employee should bear the expense of insurance for his family, at least so far as death from natural causes is concerned. In church work, the pastor's family is usually as actively engaged as is the paid minister, and it would seem entirely proper that the employer, the Church, should make provision for their maintenance in case of the death of the head of the family.

In its arrangements for pension and relief payments, the practice of the Pennsylvania System has been very largely followed by other railroads, and while the details of the application of the principles involved have varied more or less on the several roads, to suit the conditions there existing, the basis adopted on the Pennsylvania System may be taken as fairly typical of what the railroads are doing.

Many other industries, public service utilities, corporations, banks, etc., have pension and relief plans suited to their own conditions and needs.

First, the PENSION PLAN of the Pennsylvania System Lines.

All employees who attain the age of seventy years, and those who may be incapacitated upon or after attaining the age of sixty-five years, are retired from active service, and paid a monthly pension allowance. This pension payment is based on the plan of allowing annually for each year of service, one per cent of the average wages received during the ten years last preceding retirement. Thus, a man who entered the service at twenty years of age, and was retired at seventy, would receive 50 per cent of his average pay for the ten year period immediately preceding his retirement.

For the calendar year 1913, the Pennsylvania System Lines paid out in pensions under this plan a total of $1,165,996.33, and had on the pension roll at the close of the year 2,846 ex-employees who were seventy years of age or older, and 1,129, between the ages of sixty-five and seventy—a total of 3,975 pensioners. The average pension paid during that year, therefore, was $294 a year, or $24.50 a month. Inasmuch, however, as the length of service was in some cases as low as from fifteen to twenty years, ranging from that to 55 years, and as some employees had earned comparatively little wages in the ten years next preceding retirement, it is apparent that the average payment to those with a full term of service is very much above $294.

Since the inauguration of the plan, January 1, 1900, to September 1, 1914, there has been paid in pension allowances a total of $10,342,092.99, to a total of 8,293 retired employees. Of these 4,060 have died during this period, leaving on the pension roll on September 1, 1914, 4,233 retired employees.

This pension list is customarily referred to as the "Roll of Honor," and each month a bulletin is published giving the names, occupation and length of service of all who were retired in that month, with a biographical sketch of those with a service of fifty years or more.

Second, the RELIEF DEPARTMENT of the Pennsylvania System Lines, that is, the provision made for financial assistance to families of deceased employees, and to employees incapacitated through sickness or injury.

This department was inaugurated on the Eastern lines in 1886 and on the Western lines in 1889. Prior to that time, when an employee died, or was seriously incapacitated, a subscription paper was circulated among his fellow employees, and each subscribed what he felt like giving, the company frequently supplementing this by making a further contribution, particularly in cases where the disability or death resulted from injury received in the service. To replace this uncertain and unsatisfactory plan, the company organized and has since maintained, a "Voluntary Relief Department," into which those employees who desire to become members pay monthly a contribution based on the benefits which they elect to receive for disability or death, the company contributing the entire cost of operation, including the salaries of the staff of medical and supervising officers, and making up any deficits that may arise through the operation of the fund, which is operated and disbursed jointly by a committee or board consisting of representatives, respectively, of the company and the employee members, each having equal representation on the committee of management.

The maximum class of membership which may be taken by any employee is governed by his monthly rate of pay, and the class of membership taken by each determines the rate of benefit payments to be made on account of the disability or death of the member. The following table exhibits the amounts of the contributions and benefits of the several classes:

	1st Class	2d Class	3d Class	4th Class	5th Class
Highest monthly pay for each class.....	$40.00	$60.00	$80.00	$100.00	over $100.00
Rate of contribution per month........	.75	1.50	2.50	3.00	3.75
Disablement benefits, per day:					
First year.........	.50	1.00	1.50	2.00	2.50
After first year....	.25	.50	.75	1.00	1.25
Payments in the event of death..........	$250.00	$500.00	$750.00	$1,000.00	$1,250.00

In addition, any member in insurable health may obtain additional death benefits, in multiples of $250, until the total death benefit is double the normal death benefit as shown in the above table, the additional contribution to be made on this account being graded according to the class taken and the age of the member at the date the additional death benefit is secured. Thus the maximum death benefit that can be taken by an employee whose compensation is over $100 per month is $2,500, the contribution for which, up to forty-five years of age, is $5.25 a month for death benefit and accident and health insurance.

Employees have very generally availed themselves of membership in this provident feature of the service, especially in those branches of the service where the employment is practically permanent or the risk of health or accident greatest. On June 30th of this year, 81.1 per cent of the employees of the lines west of Pittsburgh were members of the Relief Department. On the system lines, east and west of Pittsburgh, there are now about 155,000 employees with membership in the Relief Department.

During the year 1913, the contributions of members to this fund totaled $2,881,307.29, and this large sum was supplemented by contributions of the companies aggregating $408,895.82, which, with $143,008.55 interest on surplus funds, made the total receipts for the year $3,433,211.66. Out of this fund benefits were paid as follows:

Death benefits to beneficiaries of deceased employees	$855,331.91
Disablement benefits to members	1,818,601.78
Superannuation benefits to retired employees in addition to pension, on lines east of Pittsburgh only	98,153.19
Total benefits paid to members and their beneficiaries	$2,772,086.88
Operating expenses paid by the companies	408,895.82

There being no operating cost to the insured, and no profits to be paid to the insurer, and as the accumulation of a large reserve is not necessary (the companies, as stated above, making up any deficit), it is apparent that the rates of contribution to this fund bring greater returns in disablement and death benefits to the company's employees than could be obtained in any other way from a like expenditure.

Reverting again to the pension plan, a few of the rules

adopted by railroads generally in the administration of these funds should be mentioned. To prevent the payment of pensions to men of very short service, it is necessary to establish an age beyond which no new employees will be taken into the service, or a minimum length of service after which a pension will be paid, and some roads have both requirements. On the Pennsylvania System, the maximum age for taking new employees into the service has been fixed at 45 years. All employees reaching the age of 70 years are retired regardless of their length of service, and pensioned. Those incapacitated between the ages of 65 and 70 are pensioned only after 30 years' service, it being understood that most of the employees are members of the Relief Fund, their disability benefits carrying them to pension age if incapacitated. Some roads have fixed the maximum age for entering the service as low as 35 years, some as high as 50, but the majority of them have adopted 45 years. The number of years' service after which a pension is paid for age or incapacity varies on the different roads from 10 years to 30 years. One road has made it optional with its employees to retire at the age of 60, and a few others at 65, whether they be incapacitated or not, if they have been in the service a specified number of years.

The suggestion is often heard that after a certain number of years of service, say thirty-five or forty, an employee should be given a pension if he desires to retire from active service. This is frequently done in European countries, where the pension funds are provided by joint contributions of the men and their employers, but so far the rule has not been adopted by any railroad in this country, where the pension funds are provided entirely by the employer.

It has been the aim in this paper to give such information concerning the retirement and relief plans of the Pennsylvania System as might be of assistance in planning similar features in the work of the Church. The great mass of detail involved in the formulation of equitable rules of administration can well be omitted from consideration until the general principles have been determined, and, accordingly, only these general principles have been here considered. If further study of the subject leads you to desire information as to the working rules and regulations of these departments of railway service, it will be gladly furnished in such detail as may be practicable.

In closing I quote from an address made some time ago on the subject of Pensions, before a convention of the Railroad Young Men's Christian Association, by Mr. John Hurst, a member of my official staff, as follows:

"Throughout all the centuries men have dreamed of the Brotherhood of Man. In a competitive and commercial age like this, when the struggle in every line of endeavor grows more intense from year to year, the ideal of a human brotherhood such as Christ lived and preached, and such as Tennyson sings of in his 'Locksley Hall', seems very far away. But step by step, slow, toilsome steps at times it is true, we are advancing in the direction of a wider recognition of the rights of man. One step is the pension scheme, which has in it this supremely Christ-like feature: it takes care of a man when he is too old or infirm to take care of himself."

JOHN W. RENNER.

Pennsylvania Station, Pittsburgh, Pa.

RAILROAD PENSION SYSTEMS

COURTESY OF DR. W. H. FOULKES

COMPANY	Pension Fund Established	Age of Retirement		Years of Service Required	Average Yearly Pension
		Voluntary	Compulsory		
B. & O.	1884	65	70	10	$235.00
C. & N. W.	1900	65	70	20	251.00
Penna.	1900	65	70	30	241.00
Phila. & R.	1902	65	70	30	362.00
D., L. & W.	1902	60	70	25	275.00
So. Pac.	1903	65	70	20	......
Union Pac.	1903	65	70	20	314.00
Santa Fe.	1907	65	..	15	255.00
Omaha.	1910	..	70	20	......
N. Y. Cent.	1910	..	70	10	312.00

The pension is generally figured as 1% of the average monthly wages for the last 10 years for each year of service. Illustration: If the average wages were $100, and the service 30 years, the pension would be $30 a month.

Eighteen other railroads have pension systems, all of them non-contributory, that is, the company pays all.

The latest—the Boston & Maine—is contributory, half and half; the men pay half and the company pays half.

Nearly all of the railroads have benefit associations, to which employees contribute; most of them have a relief department also.

CHICAGO & NORTHWESTERN RAILWAY COMPANY

Employees who have attained the age of *seventy* years, and who have been *twenty* years in the service shall be retired and pensioned, except executive officers appointed by the Board of Directors. Employees who have been twenty or more years in the service, and who have become permanently disabled, may be retired and pensioned at any time. Length of service is computed from the date of entry into the service to the date of retirement, and the forcible retirement of employees becomes effective on the first day of the calendar month following their seventieth birthday.

The monthly pension allowance is determined on the following basis: For each year of service, one per cent of the average regular monthly pay for the ten years next preceding retirement; provided, that the minimum amount shall be $12 per month. The annual pension disbursement cannot exceed two hundred thousand dollars, and should it do so, a rate is established proportionately reducing all allowances.

An example: If the average monthly pay for the last ten (10) years of a man's service with the company has been sixty dollars per month, one per cent of the monthly pay would be sixty (60) cents; and if he has served the company twenty (20) years his pension would be twenty (20) times sixty (60) cents, or twelve dollars per month, and each additional year of service would add one (1) per cent of his monthly pay.

Length of service alone does not constitute the basis for a pension. Age and length of service are combined. The candidate for a pension not only must have served the company at least twenty (20) years, but he must have arrived at a pensionable age. Pension allowances are paid monthly, until the death of the beneficiary; provided, however, that the company may withhold its stipend in case of gross misconduct. The acceptance of a pension does not debar any retired employee from engaging in any other business which is not prejudicial to the interests of the company, but he cannot reenter its service. The pension system confers no legal claim to a pension allowance.

A Pension Board, composed of five officers of the company, appointed by the Board of Directors, serves under the direction of the President.

INDUSTRIAL PENSION SYSTEMS

COURTESY OF DR. W. H. FOULKES

COMPANY	Pension Fund Established	Age of Voluntary Retirement	Age of Compulsory Retirement	Years of Service Required	Employees' Contribution	Annual Pension
American Express	1875	60 (?)	60 (?)	20	....	One half average pay for last 10 years; maximum, $500
Wells Fargo Co.	1903	60	70	25	....	1% average pay last 10 years for each year of service
Procter & Gamble	1904	..	..	7	1 hour's wages every 4 weeks—3% per month	75% average pay last 2 years
Pitt Coal Co.	1907	..	..	10	....	$10 per month
International Harvester Co.	1908	65	70	20	....	1% average pay last 10 years for each year of service. Minimum, $18; maximum, $100 per month
Morris & Co.	1909	55	..	20	3% of wages	2% of last salary for each year of service. Maximum, $5,000
Armour & Co.	1911	60	65	20	3% of wages	2% of last salary for each year of service
U. S. Steel	1911	60	70	20	....	1% average pay last 10 years for each year's service. Minimum, $12; maximum, $100
American Telegraph & Telephone Co.	1912	50-55	55-60	30-20	....	1% average pay last 10 years for each year's service. Minimum, $20

AGED AND DISABLED PRINTERS

The International Typographical Union has 60,000 members, composed of printers, mailers, newspaper writers, etc.

It maintains in Colorado Springs, Colo., the Union Printers' Home and Tuberculosis Sanatorium, where it cares for aged and disabled members, and especially provides for the treatment of those members who are afflicted with tuberculosis.

It pays to those who have reached the age of sixty years and have been members for twenty years or more, and who are unable to earn a living at the trade, a pension of $5 per week, $260 per year. It also pays burial benefits.

It maintains a school for the technical instruction of apprentices and printers, which can be taken advantage of without interference with the regular work and at a small cost.

WHAT CORPORATIONS ARE DOING

MR. JOHN O. PEW
President and General Manager
Youngstown Iron and Steel Company

The "pension habit" is growing. Governments are pensioning their veterans and corporations are rewarding their employees for long and faithful services. Soldiers and sailors retire on three-quarters pay. Nearly everybody, it would seem, lives and works in the blessed hope of a "comfortable support" upon retirement from active work; and while humanitarian reasons may have much force in bringing about pensions for aged and faithful workers, it ought to be said that there are other important reasons which are inducing corporations to take care of their employees in old age. The slogan of this materialistic age is "Efficiency"—how to get the greatest amount of work out of a plant or a worker with the greatest amount of profit. There are "efficiency experts" whose sole business it is to show corporations how greater efficiency can be secured by new systems of management, new machinery, the standardization of supplies, the decrease of motions in the performance of a given task. Even the bishops are holding efficiency conventions in their Episcopal Areas in order to get better results out of the efforts of preachers and laymen—to make them more "efficient" for the profit of the Church and the kingdom.

Corporations are finding out that when faithful servants can look forward to a pension in old age, they are more contented in their work, have a more personal interest in the business, and prefer to stay on their job and give their best to the work to which they have been assigned. They become more "efficient." One great reason why corporations are giving old age pensions is because employees become more efficient, their earning power becomes greater, and the money invested in pensions brings splendid returns.

American Telephone Company

The subsidiary companies of the American Telephone and Telegraph Company are pensioning their 175,000 employees, about 130,000 of whom are in the employ of the Bell Telephone Company. The total yearly pay of the whole group is about $115,000,000, about $80,000,000 being paid out by the Bell Company alone. A fund of $10,000,000 has been provided, made available on January 1, 1913, for pensions, sick benefits and life and accident insurance. This fund will be made good from year to year through appropriations by the various subsidiary companies. Employees *will not be called upon to contribute one cent.* The pension plan with the insurance and disability plan provides for a pension of one per cent per annum of the annual average pay during the ten years next preceding retirement, multiplied by the number of years of service. For instance, a man with thirty years of service behind him would receive a pension equal to thirty per cent of the average amount earned by him during the ten years preceding his application for the benefit. Disability during the performance of duty will be met with full pay for thirteen weeks; and half pay until the employee is able to earn a livelihood, the time not to exceed six years, Disability not in the performance of duty will be met with a graduated compensation, depending upon length of service. Employees having relatives depending upon them will be entitled to insurance against death by accident, occurring in and due to the performance of work for the companies, in the sum of three years' wages not to exceed a total amount of $5,000. All employees having relatives dependent upon them, and who have been five years in the service, will be entitled to an insurance against death in a sum equal to six months' wages, when the term of employment has been from five to ten years. When the term of employment has been ten years or more, the insurance paid will be one year's wages, the maximum paid being $2,000. With these plans to take care of their employees in their old age, these companies show a determination to reward faithful service and at the same time secure greater "efficiency."

Armour & Company

Armour & Co., the great packing house, has established a

pension fund for the benefit of its 15,000 employees throughout the United States. Ogden Armour, the head of the company, gave a million dollars to this pension fund. The fund is created for the benefit of salaried employees who have reached the age of from fifty to sixty-five and who have been employed twenty years or more in the service of the company. Employees must pay into the fund three per cent of their salaries annually. Employees on retirement receive two per cent of the salary paid them at the time of their retirement for each year of service—that is, an employee having served twenty-five years will receive during every year of his retirement fifty per cent of the salary received by him when retired. Such employee receiving a salary of $2,000 at retirement will receive after retirement a pension of $1,000 per year. Women employees are eligible to the pension fund; but a clause provides that upon marriage they are to receive back all the moneys they have paid in. All employees who leave the service will receive back the amounts paid in. Pensioned employees may engage in other business or accept other employment so long as it is not of the same character as that conducted by Armour & Co.

United States Steel Corporation

For a number of years the United States Steel Corporation has been pensioning its employees. The first year of operation of the pension plan showed 1,606 beneficiaries. $12,000,000 has been set aside for the pension fund. During the first year, the average age of those pensioned was sixty-six; the average years of service were forty; and the average monthly pension $20.75.

What need I say more of the pension funds of great corporations! Time would fail me to tell what the Chicago Tribune, The First National Bank of Chicago, The International Typographical Union, The Old Merchants Relief Fund of Philadelphia, The First National Bank of New York, the Carnegie Foundation and other institutions are doing for their pensioners. All recognize not only the pensioners' need of a pension but their need of an efficient worker. While the outlay is great they are more than compensated by increased faithfulness and the fine feeling of fraternity which is produced by the pension system.

What corporations are doing, the Church must do, not as charity but as an investment for "efficiency." But the Church should be moved by a still greater motive. *An irresistible law, the higher law of the eternally just,* compels the Church to take care of its veteran workers in their old age.

JOHN O. PEW.

Youngstown, Ohio.

THE FIRST NATIONAL BANK, CHICAGO

The First National Bank of Chicago was a pioneer in pensions. The Bank Pension Fund was established in 1899.

The fund is known as "The Bank Pension Fund." It was optional with officers and clerks whether they should enter the fund at its inception, but all subsequent employees are required to enter the fund, if eighteen years of age or over, and to pass a medical examination prior to such entry.

The officers and employees contribute to the fund three per cent of their salaries, payable monthly and deducted from the monthly pay. No clerk is allowed to marry on a salary of less than $1,000 per year, without the consent of the bank, under penalty of dismissal and forfeiture of his rights to the fund. In case of voluntary resignation or dismissal all payments into the funds are returned without interest. As a general rule no pension is granted unless the officer or employee shall have completed not less than fifteen years of service and attained the age of sixty years. If an officer or employee shall die prior to fifteen years' service and no pension is granted, the amount contributed is returned to his legal representative with interest at four per cent. On attaining the age of sixty years and having fifteen years' service a member may retire on a pension, or may be required to retire; on attaining sixty-five years he shall retire, unless specially requested to remain. An officer or employee who before attaining the age of sixty years shall be incapacitated for work by ill-health or affliction shall be permitted to retire and take the benefits provided. Officers and employees whose term of service shall have been under twenty-five years shall not be entitled to a pension for a longer time than their term of service; if such service has reached twenty-five years or more they shall be entitled to such pension for life.

The amount of pension allowed officers or employees shall be on the basis of one fiftieth of their salary at date of retirement for each year of service; thus if they have fifteen years of service to their credit, they will receive fifteen-fiftieths of their salary, if twenty-five years, twenty-five fiftieths, or one half. The maximum pension is subject to the following limitations: In no case shall it exceed thirty-five fiftieths of their salary. On a salary not exceeding $10,000, it shall not exceed $4,000. On a salary not exceeding $15,000, it shall not exceed $5,000. On a salary exceeding $15,000, it shall not exceed $6,000. If a clerk enter the service of the bank prior to eighteen years of age his term of service shall commence at the date of his first payment to the fund at eighteen years of age. The widow of a deceased officer or employee shall be entitled to receive half the amount to which her husband would have been entitled; but she shall not receive a pension for a longer period than her husband's term of service. The pension shall cease if she remarries. At her death, if she leaves any children her pension shall be paid to them or to trustees for them until the youngest child shall reach the age of eighteen years; each child's interest to cease as he or she reaches that age or marries prior to that age.

The funds are invested by the bank's officers. The policy of the bank has been to build up a strong fund. A contribution of $25,000 was made at the beginning and subsequent contributions have averaged about six per cent of the salary total. The interest earnings have so far met all pension requirements and left a surplus of profit to the fund. There are no expenses for administration. The membership of the fund and pensioners have been as follows:

	Members	Pensioners		Members	Pensioners
1899	243	0	1907	524	15
1900	307	4	1908	541	18
1901	335	8	1909	548	17
1902	417	10	1910	558	22
1903	430	10	1911	581	24
1904	447	10	1912	607	27
1905	474	13	1913	646	30
1906	500	13			

If an officer or employee shall be in receipt of a pension at the time of his death, the period for which he shall have received a pension shall be deducted from the period during which a pension shall be paid to his widow. The children of a deceased officer or employee whose wife died before him shall receive one half of the pension to which he would have been entitled, to be divided among them.

It would be difficult to estimate the value of the Bank Pension Fund to the employee. The sense of security which it affords, taking the place of worry for the future, for the employee's old age and for the family which survives him, should he be taken away or incapacitated, is fully appreciated. The mental strain is thus relieved, and greater energy and efficiency is encouraged. The older men are more loth to leave and accept other positions, and are generally better satisfied. Employees are permitted to purchase stock of The First National Bank and have it carried for them by the fund, by paying $10 per share down and $5 per share per month.

These pension features and the provisions for the comfort, amusement and welfare of employees develop a spirit of fidelity and fraternity which brings results in efficiency and loyalty to the bank.

CARNEGIE FOUNDATION FOR TEACHERS

The Carnegie Foundation for the Advancement of Teaching has an endowment of $15,000,000 to provide retiring allowances for teachers and officers of higher educational institutions, and distributed $2,936,927 during the first eight years.

The 1913 report showed that $579,440 was distributed to professors and $80,949 to their widows; a total of $660,389.

The number of new allowances was thirty-three, making the total allowances now in force 403. The average annual payment to pensioners was $1,703.

COLLEGE PENSIONS—THE CARNEGIE FUND

Courtesy of Dr. W. H. Foulkes

Includes seventy-two colleges and universities.
Retirement Age: 65.
Service Required: 15 years as professor, or 25 years as instructor and professor.
Incapacity: After 25 years as professor, or 30 years as instructor and professor.
Pension: One half average salary last five years, plus $400. Widow receive one half of what would be her husband's allowance.
Average Retirement Pension for 1912: $1,678.66.
Average Widows' Pension for 1912: $912.11.
Average Age of Retirement: 69, 70, 71 in different years.

RETIREMENT OF TEACHERS
IN NEW YORK CITY

DR. CHARLES S. HARTWELL, M.A.
Eastern District High School

The Board of Retirement for teachers in New York City was first organized July 10, 1905. It consists of the President of the Board of Education, the chairmen of the Committee on Elementary Schools and on High Schools, the City Superintendent and three members selected from the principals and teachers of the public day schools. The teacher members are elected for three years by representatives of the teachers elected by each district in the city.

The Retirement law set aside eight hundred thousand dollars, ($800,000) standing to the credit of the teachers' fund on December 31, 1904, as a permanent fund, the principal of which should not be encroached upon. To this is added annually "five per cent of all excise moneys or license fees belonging to the City of New York and derived or received by any commissioner of excise or public officer from the granting of licenses or permission to sell strong or spirituous liquors, ale, wine or beer in the city of New York, under the provisions of any law of this state authorizing the granting of such license or permission."

To the amount of thirty dollars in one year, for teachers and principals, and forty dollars, for supervising officials, the law authorizes the deduction of one per cent from the salaries of all from the city superintendent to the new teacher entering the system. This is added to the Retirement Fund.

All money deducted from salaries of teachers because of unexcused absences also becomes a part of this fund. Donations, legacies and bequests are placed in the fund.

On recommendation of the Board of Retirement the Board of Education has power to retire at the beginning of each semester, by a two-thirds vote of all its members, any member of the teaching or supervising staff, who may apply for retirement, provided he or she has been engaged in teaching or in school or college supervision for a period aggregating thirty years, fifteen of which shall have been in some of the institutions of New York City. The Board of Education may retire any member of the teaching or supervising staff who has reached the age of sixty-five years.

The amount to be paid upon such retirement, whether voluntary or otherwise, shall be not less than one half the annual salary paid to such person at the time of retirement; but, except in the case of professors of the Normal College, shall not exceed, in the case of a teacher or principal, the sum of fifteen hundred dollars per annum, and in the case of a supervising official, two thousand dollars per annum. In no case shall the amount be less than six hundred dollars per annum. Any person retired after twenty years of service, but with less than thirty years of service shall receive an annuity which bears the same ratio to the annuity provided for on retirement after thirty years of service as the total number of years of service of said person bears to thirty years. These annuities, like salaries, are paid in monthly instalments.

The number of persons retired is limited in any one year, so that the entire amount of the annuities to be paid for that year shall not be in excess of the amount of the retirement fund applicable to the payment of annuities for that year.

Retired persons are eligible to reappointment in the schools.

Principal Lyman A. Best of Brooklyn, N. Y., who has been Secretary of the Board of Retirement since its organization in 1905, has issued a series of annual reports of the greatest value. For ten years previous to that time there had been a teachers' pension fund.

Between 1895 and 1913 there have been 1927 retirements, an average of 107 per year; of whom 1,404 were on the rolls on July 31, 1913. The number of teachers in New York City at the same time was 19,681.

The total income of the Retirement fund from 1894 to 1913 was $12,911,703, and the balance on hand on December 31, 1913, was $1,095,255.

An effort is being made to secure a unification of retirement regulations for the various branches of the city service and important changes in existing laws are imminent.

Brooklyn, N. Y. CHARLES S. HARTWELL.

TEACHERS' PENSION FUNDS

Courtesy of Dr. W. H. Foulkes

STATES WHICH AUTHORIZE TEACHERS' PENSIONS

1894—New York.
1895—Michigan.
1896—New Jersey, Ohio.
1907—Illinois, Indiana, Pennsylvania, Rhode Island, Utah.
1908—Massachusetts.
1909—Minnesota, Nebraska, Colorado, Wisconsin.
1910—Virginia, Louisiana.
1911—Connecticut, Kansas, Oregon.
1913—Iowa.

In seven States all teachers are included: New York, New Jersey, Virginia, Iowa, Rhode Island, Maryland, Wisconsin. In two cases all the funds are provided by the State: Maryland, Rhode Island. All the others are contributory—the teachers pay part.

CITY	Fund Established	Years of Service Required	Age Retirement	Teachers' Contribution Per Year	Yearly Pension
New York	1894	30	65	1% of salary—not over $30	Half pay—$600 to $1,500
Chicago	1895	25	..	$5 to $30	$400
San Francisco	1897	30	..	$12	$300 or more
Cincinnati	1897	30	..	$20	$300
New Orleans	1902	15	60	1% of salary	Half pay
Sacramento	1905	20	60	2% of salary	Half pay
Memphis	1907	30	..	1% of salary	About $300
Indianapolis	1907	25	..	1% or 2% of salary—not over $20	$15 for each year of service—not over $600
Omaha	1909	40	..	1% of salary	$500
Minneapolis	1909	20	..	$5 to $25	$16.67 for each year of service—not over $500

The average years of service are thirty.
The pension varies from $200 to $2,000, or one half of the average salary during the last five years.

CITIES WHICH HAVE TEACHERS' PENSION FUNDS

1894—New York, Washington.
1895—Brooklyn, Chicago, Detroit.
1896—Buffalo.
1897—Albany, Cincinnati, Providence, San Francisco, Syracuse.
1898—Charleston.
1899—Saint Louis.
1900—Boston, New Orleans.
1905—Rochester.
1906—Troy, Cleveland.
1907—Philadelphia, Schenectady, Elmira, Indianapolis, Memphis.
1908—Harrisburg, Springfield, O., Yonkers, Salt Lake City.
1909—Columbus, Denver, Omaha, Milwaukee, Baltimore, Saint Paul, Minneapolis.
1911—New Haven.
1912—Louisville.

This Is a Partial List Only

The first teachers' pension bill was passed by the New York State legislature in 1894.
About 30% of all the public school teachers in the United States are now under pension systems.
About 15% are non-contributory systems, in which the teachers pay nothing.
About 17% are mutual benefit associations, in which the teachers pay all.
About 68% are contributory associations, in which the city pays part and teachers part.

"THE PENSION HABIT"

The Telephone Company has followed the fashion in instituting a pension system for employees. We are getting quite in the pension habit. A great many big business concerns in some way share their profits with employees, or bestow reward for long and faithful service.

Nearly everybody, it would almost seem, lives and works in the happy advance rays of a sunset of "retirement." The soldier and sailor are to retire on three quarters pay. Considering their troubles, the hello girls ought to be worth as much consideration.

An irresistible law, the higher law of the eternally just, has compelled all this. And we have yet seen only the beginning.

Who would have dreamed of this pension tendency fifty years ago? The clergymen did not, as they went out to preach righteousness on pitiful pay. And it is noteworthy that these very preachers are about the only workers now left without adequate pension. The school teacher, the college professor, Mr. Carnegie has pensioned. It might be worth while for the Church, the richest institution in all the land, to do the right thing by her old preachers.

These men, however, who did so much to bring about this new day, are not advancing their claim.

—*The New York Mail.*

TRANSMUTING THE TRUTH INTO GOLD

Leslie's Weekly is never more pleased than when it renders service to the churches, and particularly when such assistance is in the line of aid to the old and faithful ministers of the Church. In a recent editorial we advocated a better and more adequate system of pensioning those who had worn themselves out in the service of the churches. In addition to much favorable comment by the religious press, we are glad to note that the national board of the Methodist Episcopal Church is sending the editorial as a leaflet throughout the denomination. The secretary of the board, in a personal letter to the editor, says, "We greatly appreciate your editorial, and are hoping that your message will be transmuted into gold for the Veteran Preachers." We hope so, too.

—*Leslie's Weekly.*

OLD-AGE, MOTHERS' AND GOVERNMENT PENSIONS

THE REV. STEDMAN APPLEGATE, D.D.
New Jersey Conference

It has long been the custom of Christian nations, in consideration of past services of government employees, to grant an income or pension, to take effect on retirement. It is usual to define such pension as being given in consideration of past service. This has led to the statement that pensions are given by a government, corporation or private employer in the nature of deferred pay. While this is true, there is another thought that should not be overlooked. The object of attaching a pension to a post is not merely to reward past service, but to secure continuity of service as well as to enable the employer to dispense with the services of an employee without hardship to him, should old age or infirmity render him inefficient.

The granting of pensions was first applied to the army and navy, and to persons who had become disabled while in the military service of their respective countries. With the increase of national wealth and government responsibilities there has come a demand for expert service; and this has necessitated the enlarging of the pension system, so that the departments through which pensions are dispensed are now as follows, Army, Navy, Civil Service and Judicial.

England has taken the initiative in pensioning the veteran citizen—the old man—and now dispenses pensions through the civil list as well as through the political and ecclesiastical list. The civil list pensions are given in England to the following classes of persons, on recommendation to the Crown by the First Lord of the Treasury: those who may have just claims on the royal beneficence by their personal services to the Crown, or their performance of duties to the public; those who by useful discoveries in science or by attainments in literature or art have merited gracious consideration.

The ecclesiastical pension is granted to bishops, deans, canons, and incumbents who may become incapacitated by age or infirmity for the discharge of their ecclesiastical duties, such pensions to be a charge upon the revenues of the see or cure vacated.

Germany, Italy, Switzerland and a few other countries have introduced a system of government insurance which requires that an amount proportioned to the individual wage shall be paid by the insured person, the government also paying a proportionate amount; thus giving stimulus to the individual, and to the government control and general supervision. When from old age, or other causes, it becomes necessary for the insured to retire from active service, the government, through this system of insurance, provides a yearly allowance for the veteran citizen, the old man.

While the legal enactment for the care of government employees is eminently commendable, it has remained for our modern Christian civilization to discover the factors of strength, glory and national greatness in the form of the noble and loyal citizenship, self-respecting, self-sacrificing motherhood, and to grant pensions to old men and mothers. These citizens by their thrift and consecrated energy, by their noble and heroic sacrifices, and by their united devotion to national standards, have contributed to the greatness and glory of their nation. Therefore, they are sustained when incapacitated for further service, or when overtaken by untoward circumstances over which they have no control, from the bounty which they helped to create.

It is a very pleasing fact to note that our Government now grants a pension to dependent motherhood, because of a deceased son who may have been the support of such mother. The wisdom of many of our State Legislatures in enacting a law pensioning widowed motherhood, is highly commendable. The wise, the humane, and Christian character of such a law, can be seen in the lessening of crime, the introducing of a higher morality, and the giving of strength to the State and nation. The amount given such a widow is paid by the State where she may reside, in proportion to the number and age of her children. The child labor law of many States also provides that where the labor of a child is necessary to the maintenance of the home, the amount of wage the child could earn is paid to the family by the State, and the child is kept in school, in training for efficient citizenship. This at first was considered as charity; but self-respecting and honorable families were loath to receive such charity, and to overcome such embarrassment the money is now provided as a scholarship for the child.

Another pleasing feature in connection with the pension idea is that many of the States and cities of our Republic recognize the necessity and value of the work of education and public instruction and are retiring public teachers on a pension.

Much might be said in commendation of various public service institutions which are creating retirement funds for faithful employees. It would seem that an awakened conscience is recognizing the worth of the Master's statement over nineteen centuries ago, that "the laborer is worthy of his hire" and that the hire is more than the daily wages.

In introducing these humane conditions the ethics and altruism of Jesus Christ are very prominent. While the commendable conditions of our social system are constantly assuming new proportions, it is a lamentable fact that the Church of Jesus Christ, an institution of no mean proportion, prospering under the leadership of men who have in their manhood, the elements of courage, heroism and self-sacrifice and who are faithfully presenting the economic, social, and spiritual teachings of Jesus Christ, has failed to provide a reasonable average support for the active minister, and a worthy amount for the Retired Veteran.

The granting of pensions by governments, corporations and private individuals, is based upon the character and relationship of the pensioned to society or governments. If this principle of reward of position and merit were applied to the character and value of church work, and the relationship sustained to such work by the faithful pastor and preacher, as it is applied to society and its workers, there would not be one poorly paid minister or one veteran without a reasonable pension; indeed, if the scriptural injunction to stewardship were obeyed, there would be no need of mentioning, much less of pleading for, such a worthy cause.

The Word of God is rich in promises to the man who meets the obligation of stewardship; Proverbs 3. 9, 10, "Honor the

Lord with thy substance, and with the first-fruits of all thine increase, so shall thy barns be filled with plenty, and thy presses shall burst out with new wine." In Malachi 3. 10, 11, we have a command, with a promised blessing: "Bring ye all the tithes into the storehouse, that there may be meat in mine house, and prove me now herewith, saith the Lord of hosts, if I will not open you the windows of heaven, and pour you out a blessing, that there shall not be room enough to receive it. And I will rebuke the devourer for your sakes, and he shall not destroy the fruits of your ground; neither shall your vine cast her fruit before the time in the field, saith the Lord of hosts."

Christianity repudiates the pagan doctrine of ownership and recognizes possession as the token of confidence on the part of the divine owner. Stewardship is not a natural human conception; the unaided human instinct will not discover it. The recognition of stewardship marks the supremacy of the spiritual man. The divine ownership of the land was recognized by the Israelites, based upon the statement of God's Word, "The land shall not be sold forever: for *the land is mine;* for ye are strangers and sojourners with me" (Leviticus 25. 23). As an acknowledgment of divine ownership, a tenth of the product of the soil was set aside to maintain the worship of Jehovah. The Jews were also required to tithe their annual increase in order to meet the expense of those religious and social festivals whose purpose was to exalt patriotism and to maintain friendship among the people, as well as to care for the poor. When Christians learn that "the earth is the Lord's and the fullness thereof," ingrained human selfishness will disappear, and instead there will be the outflow of human gratitude, love and sympathy, and a ready response to the sense of obligation. Then God's Church and ministry will be sustained according to the divine plan, not as a charity, not as a pension, but as a divinely appointed support, not from the people but from God, whose portion is in their hands.

The Church a Social Asset

There are some who harp on the inefficiency of the Church, but such people do it ignorantly, and therefore may obtain mercy. The educating of the conscience and the improving of the morals, which is the work of the Church, with her teaching of truth respecting God and man, sin and righteousness, life and death, heaven and hell, are responsible for our beautiful towns, with their excellent moral tone; which else would be hotbeds of vice and crime. Church members are not often criminals; neither are all non-church-going people criminals, but the vast majority of such come from the latter class. Every person in a community profits by the presence of the church in that community.

We are told that crime costs the nation more than seven hundred million dollars each year. Without the Church of Jesus Christ, this would be multiplied many times. The Church not only curbs crime, protects society, checks disorder and wards off barbarism, but it nurtures childhood, redeems men from sin, and inspires them with lofty purposes and high ideals. She preaches the goodness of God and the brotherhood of man.

In many communities the Church has been living largely as a charity. The consecrated preacher, too modest to plead his own cause and too self-sacrificing to allow other interests not to appear prominent, has taken an insufficient stipend for the generous services bestowed, and has made a charitable donation to churches of the balance that was due him. O, that the eyes of the laymen might be opened, and that they might see that Christ's honor is at stake and that the first obligation is to God the giver! The individual, the Church, or the nation lacking this element of honor will not long continue to prosper. O, that our people might see the horsemen and chariots of God who have fought their battles for them amid trouble and sorrow, whose great victories for temporal prosperity, home and heaven have been ushered in by these battalions of God! Then the laborer would be considered worthy of his hire, and the mouth of the ox that treadeth out the corn would be unmuzzled; young men would be cheered and inspired in their labors, old men would be comforted, widowhood would be sustained, and God's Church would be eminently successful in her varied labors for saving men.

STEDMAN APPLEGATE.

Ocean Grove, N. J.

ILLINOIS PENSIONS MOTHERS

The Illinois law provides for the partial support of mothers with children under fourteen years of age. Any mother who is a citizen of the United States, who has resided in the county for three years, whose husband is dead, or whose husband has become permanently incapacitated for work, is entitled to the benefits of the law for her children upon complying with its requirements. The assistance allowed to each mother cannot exceed $15 a month where there is but one child, and shall never exceed $50 a month for one family. The pensions are awarded by action of the Juvenile Court, attached to which is a pension department created for the purpose of investigating applicants.

PENSIONING MOTHERS IN OHIO

More than six hundred applications have been made for pensions under the Mothers' Pension Act of Ohio. A special tax levy is made. In Hamilton County (Cincinnati) the commissioners recently appropriated $60,000 to be used for these pensions. Those eligible for pensions are "women whose husbands are dead, imprisoned, permanently disabled for work by reason of mental or physical infirmity, and deserted women when the desertion has extended over a period of three years." The women must present a clean moral record, and give evidence of the school attendance of their children and of actual poverty. They must have been residents of the county for at least two years, and, as beneficiaries, must not perform labor outside of their homes, except with the consent of the court. The maximum allowance amounts to $15 a month for a woman with one child, and $7 a month each for other children.

OLD-AGE PENSIONS

Editorial, Philadelphia Ledger

Whatever opinion one may hold as to the economic effect of the various forms of old-age pensions which are in operation in the world, whether voluntary or as part of governmental systems, the subject is one which is commanding an increasing attention at the hands of legislators and students of social science. The association of the subject with the extreme programs of socialism has tended to divert the interest of many who would otherwise give the problem the study which its importance deserves, though it is a singular fact that the present German law of compulsory insurance, was enacted through the influence of Bismarck, who hoped by thus forestalling the Socialists to check the spread of that party.

In America the subject has never been seriously considered as coming within the scope of practical or desirable legislation. The nearest approach to governmental old-age pensions is the retirement on part pay of certain officers who have given their lives to the public service, but the extension of the system to the general civil service has always been promptly negatived whenever seriously proposed. On the other hand, the system has been applied to a larger extent than is generally appreciated by railways and corporations.

The Massachusetts Bureau of Statistics of Labor has lately issued a special report on this subject, which sums up not only the salient facts about the old-age pension plans in operation abroad—not omitting, of course, the system in New Zealand, that land of social experiments—but gives the essential features of the various plans which have more or less seriously been suggested. Taking the statistics of Massachusetts for the purpose of comparison, the compiler of this report shows that in a recent year the aggregate expenditures by the State, cities and towns and by individuals and corporations for charitable purposes and soldiers' relief were $10,-948,868, or an average benefaction per capita of $3.90.

To this computation were added the figures from the census of the persons over sixty years of age, the statistics of deaths and the expectation of life as computed by insurance actuaries, so that the author of the report was in a position to estimate the amount of money that would be required to pay old-age pensions in that State. It is declared that the sum now expended in charity would pay an annual pension of two hundred and sixty dollars to one fourth or one fifth of the persons in the State sixty-five years of age and over; and that as the experience abroad is that not more than one fifth of those beyond sixty or sixty-five apply for the old-age pensions, the feasibility of old-age pensions in Massachusetts is thereby established. The assumption is that old-age pensions would do away with the necessity for charity.

TWO WORKMEN: LIKENESS—CONTRAST—REASON

A Likeness

Preachers and Bricklayers both have honorable vocations.

Preachers and Bricklayers both do constructive work.

Preachers and Bricklayers both earn honest livelihoods.

Preachers and Bricklayers both support families and uphold society.

A Contrast

The Preacher	The Bricklayer
Receives an average salary of $600.	Receives $5 per day, $1,500 per year.
Requires seven to ten years' preparation.	Serves a three-year apprenticeship.
Buys books costing from $200 to $300 annually.	Buys tools costing $30.
Buys working clothes costing from $40 to $60.	Buys working clothes costing $20.
Makes his home a social center.	Regards his home as his castle.
Occupies a movable "tent or cottage."	Has a fixed home and may own it.
Is paid irregularly and uncertainly.	Has an honest lien for his wages.

The Reason

The expenses of ministers are necessarily larger than those of the majority of an average congregation.

The parsonage must be in such a condition as to be open to all at all times.

The dress of the minister and his family must be such as will bear inspection.

The mechanic, the farmer, and most persons who labor for a living have special garments to be worn while they work; but the minister must be ready to visit the sick, or to receive a person who may call at his residence, at all hours, even in small communities.

He is frequently appealed to by the poor, and he must give to everything for which appeals are made in the Church.

He is expected to entertain both the officials of his own Church and the general officials.

In purchasing, a minister cannot make a close bargain without the loss of prestige.

The minister must buy books and be a constant reader. One man of influence in his congregation can injure his reputation by charging him with being illiterate.

He must pay traveling expenses to Conventions, Synods and Conferences.

Many cures are proposed for the condition of inadequate support; but there is none so wise, so philosophical, so effective as for the Church to see to it that, whatever present sacrifices she may require of her Ministers, they may know that in Old Age they will be sufficiently provided for.

MOTHERS' PENSION FUNDS

Courtesy of Dr. W. H. Foulkes

Mothers' Pension Funds are established by law in—

California	Michigan	Pennsylvania
Colorado	Minnesota	Utah
Idaho	Missouri	Washington
Illinois	Nebraska	Wisconsin
Maine	New Jersey	Iowa
Massachusetts	Ohio	Oregon

For example: Ohio gives a pension of $15 a month to a dependent widow with one child under 14 years of age; and a pension of $7 a month for each additional child under 14 years of age.

UNITED STATES PENSIONS

During the fiscal year from June 30, 1913, to June 30, 1914, the United States paid out $172,417,546 in pensions, says Pension Commissioner Saltzgaber in his annual report. This compares with $174,171,660 in 1913, the largest amount ever paid out. The commissioner points out that the maximum expenditure has been reached and a decrease may be expected to continue. The grand total of expenditures for pensions from 1866 to and including 1914 was $4,633,511,926.

The number of pensioners of all classes on the rolls for 1914 was 785,239, against 820,272 in 1913. The number of Civil War pensioners was 728,129, compared with 762,439 in 1913. The largest number ever on the rolls was in 1902, when there were 999,466.

From July 1, 1790, to June 30, 1865, there was distributed for pensions the sum of $96,445,444, while from July 1, 1865, to June 30, 1911, the total disbursements for pensions were $4,133,936,286. The grand total expended by the federal government for pensions, including cost of administration, has been $4,351,252,591.

HOLLAND'S PENSIONS FOR OLD AGE

The Old Age and Invalidity Pension Act in Holland aims at three things:

1. To assure pensions to those who have become permanently unfit to earn their own living.
2. To assure pensions to every man and woman of seventy years and more whose yearly income has amounted to $480.
3. To grant annuities to the orphans of those insured under the pension act until they shall have reached the age of thirteen years.

The objection that seventy years is very old and that most laboring people do not reach that age cannot be urged against this measure, because it is coupled with the invalidity act, which extends the same pension as the old age act, to all those insured under its provisions. So when a laborer through ill health or weakness can no longer earn his bread he (or she) can draw a pension. It is immaterial whether that pension is called "invalidity" or "old age."

PART II. THE CLAIM FOREMOST

CHAPTER III. POST-MORTEM DISTRIBUTION OF WEALTH

PAGE

INFLUENCE MADE IMMORTAL

BISHOP HENRY W. WARREN, D.D., LL.D.

Last year 45,737 members of the Methodist Episcopal Church were transferred from the church militant to the church triumphant. Some thousands of these had property which they had a right to dispose of to loved ones by will. We wish to commend a more general *inclusion of the Lord among the loved ones.*

This is a matter of justice and obligation. While men own and personally possess property, they are simply stewards as related to God, who giveth the power to get wealth, and hence should be considered in its use and disposal. This justice and obligation also is evident from the fact that the general community has been a factor influential in making the getting of wealth possible. Men are actually indebted to many public causes for their wealth. There is the university that gave him his education at about ten per cent of its cost. There is the Church that made character possible. There is the cooperation of the customers with the tradesman, and there is the unearned increment on many an investment in real estates, etc. It is right that *these aids to getting wealth should share in its distribution.*

This disposal greatly affects the estimation in which the legatee is held. Everybody loves the posthumous benefactor of the lowly and needy children of earth. Even the other heirs see that their friend has higher ideas than mere money-getting and broader sympathies than one's own family.

It also affects one's own sense of relation to God.

As life draws toward the close one wishes that his usefulness might be prolonged. It can be and should be made perpetual by will.

Ministers should make it a part of their business to instruct the people in regard to their high privileges in this matter. Pope Leo XIII has no delicacy to prevent him from performing his duty in that respect. In an encyclical letter he urges all who have received divine bounties, either external or gifts of mind, to employ them as a steward of Providence for the benefit of others. In the time of Christ there were no general agencies by which one could benefit the world. Hence He highly commended and commanded alms giving to one's neighbors, and wonderfully enlarged the meaning of that word.

WILLS

OLIVER H. HORTON

For Sixteen Years Judge Circuit Court, Chicago
For Three Years Judge Appellate Court, Illinois

I. HAVE YOU MADE YOUR WILL?

To ask this may seem a delicate matter; but to make a Will does not shorten life, and you alone know to what cause you wish to leave your property. It is possible to do good perpetually by a wise bequest.

If you have not made your Will, should you not do so now?

If you have already made your Will, please read these pages and then consider whether it is as you wish it to be.

Believing that he was doing a lasting favor to godly and benevolent people, the writer has prepared these suggestions and forms.

Let me first state some facts about Wills, make some suggestions as to their form and the mode of executing them, name a most worthy beneficiary, and then "show unto you a More Excellent Way."

The general or local Church Representatives are always ready to furnish legal advice and forms for those who desire to make their Wills, and to inform them more fully as to this important matter.

Bishop Warren said:

"Generous legacies and bequests should lift the Cause of the Retired Ministers to a basis of adequacy and dignity which will react upon the Church and fill the hearts of workers in all hard places with courage and hope."

Hoping that by doing so we may aid the friends of Veterans, who may be making bequests, we state some principles and rules which are applied in the interpretation of Wills and give some forms and suggestions as to making and executing them.

II. YOU MAY BE YOUR OWN EXECUTOR

Before explaining Wills let us urge that, as far as practicable, you be your own Executor. The Board of Conference Claimants and other Church organizations[1] present a safe and simple aid to this. We trust that it would give you pleasure to assist the Veteran Preachers. To enable you to do so, in case you can not forego the income during life, the different Church Boards issue Life Annuity Bonds which pay you a liberal annuity, semi-annually, quarterly or monthly for life. Payments thus provided for are secured beyond all question. Such LIFE ANNUITY BONDS not only provide an income for life and guard effectually against uncertainties and unfortunate investments, but they remove all doubts and uncertainty in reference to the execution or interpretation of Wills, and save court fees and other costs.

There is no safer investment and no better mode of securing beyond all doubt a definite income for life than is offered by these Life Annuity Bonds. And further, you will rejoice that when you no longer need the income the money will go on doing good in your name perpetually.

III. INTENT OF TESTATOR

The controlling rule in Courts of last Resort is to ascertain what the Testator (that is the one who makes the Will) intended. When such purpose is ascertained the meaning of the Will is determined thereby. But this purpose must be *ascertained usually from the Will itself,* not from outside evidence.

OUTSIDE EVIDENCE

There are some exceptions to this general rule. For instance, if a Will should contain a bequest of a farm containing 160 acres in a certain township, and it should appear that the Testator owned *two* farms in that township, with different acreage, testimony outside of the Will may be taken to show which of the two farms contained the number of acres mentioned in the Will. It would thus be determined which of the farms was meant by the Testator.

Or, the Will might devise the farm upon which the Tes-

[1] For names of other Church organizations which receive gifts on the life annuity basis see page 289.

tator resided without giving a description of it. Outside proof may then be offered to determine where the Testator resided at the time of executing the Will.

These illustrations indicate the character of evidence outside of the Will which may be offered to aid in its construction, but, generally speaking, as above stated, the meaning and intent of the Testator must be ascertained from the Will itself. Hence the need of special care in making a Will.

WITNESSES

Some states require three witnesses, though generally only two are required. We advise that there always be *three* witnesses and thus make the Will good in this respect in all states. Where states require only two witnesses there is no objection to having three, and in case of the death of a witness, it would be convenient to have two surviving witnesses to testify to the execution of the Will rather than to be compelled to prove the handwriting of a deceased witness.

A Benevolent Board lost over $100,000 in a state which required three witnesses, because there were only two witnesses.

Note this: A beneficiary under a Will cannot be a legal witness of the Will. There should be three *disinterested persons* as witnesses.

One of our Conferences lost a bequest of $50,000 because a trustee of the Society to which a bequest was made had witnessed the Will.

TIME LIMIT

In some states a Will must be made at least sixty days before the death of the Testator, which is a strong reason for immediate attention to the making of your Will. Have you any assurance of living two months?

A great University lost half a million dollars for endowment because the Testator delayed, and died within a month of the time he made his Will.

IV. VARIOUS FORMS FOR WILLS

Assuming that it is your purpose to make a bequest in favor of the Superannuated or Retired Preachers and the Widows and Orphans of deceased Ministers of the Methodist Episcopal Church, you could use one of the following forms:

FORM OF WILL

Know all men by these presents that I..................... of .... County of .... State of .... being of sound and disposing mind and memory do make, publish and declare this my last Will and Testament as follows:

FIRST, I will and direct that my funeral expenses and my just debts be paid by my executor.

*SECOND, I give, devise and bequeath to...............
....
(Here describe special bequest of money or personal property, or if real estate, give the correct description thereof.)*

THIRD, I give, devise and bequeath to the (Board of Conference Claimants of the Methodist Episcopal Church, a corporation created and existing under and by virtue of the Laws of the State of Illinois, for the benefit of the Connectional Permanent Fund)[1] *the sum of.............Dollars ($.............) and the receipt of the treasurer of said Board shall be a full and sufficient discharge of my executor for the same.*

*FOURTH, I hereby designate and appoint ....
..........................executor of this my last Will and Testament and direct that he (she or they) be not required to give any bond or security for the performance of the duties of such executor .*

*In witness whereof I hereunto set my hand and affix my seal this .... day of .... A. D. 19....
(Sign here)......................[Seal]
Signed, sealed, published and declared by.........
...............................as and for his (or her) last Will and Testament; and we at his (or her) request in his (or her) presence and in the pres-*

[1]In case the bequest is to be made for the benefit of Conference Claimants in an Annual Conference, or for the Retired Ministers of another Denomination, be sure to get the proper legal title of the Conference or Society which is to administer the money. See page 289.

ence of each other hereby subscribe our names as witnesses this ....day of...............
A. D. 19....

....

....

....

CODICIL

(An addition to or change in a Will already made).

I .... of ....
being of sound and disposing mind and memory, do hereby make, publish and declare this Codicil to my last Will and Testament which bears date ....A. D. 19....,
that is to say:

I give, devise and bequeath to the (Board of Conference Claimants of the Methodist Episcopal Church, a corporation created and existing under and by virtue of the Laws of the State of Illinois, for the benefit of the Connectional Permanent Fund)[1] *the sum of .... Dollars ($......) and the receipt of the treasurer of said Board shall be sufficient discharge to my executor for the payment of the same.*

I hereby ratify and confirm my said Will except as hereby modified and altered.

In witness whereof I hereunto set my hand and affix my seal this ....day of................A. D. 19...
(Sign here)..........................[Seal]

(Note Form for witnessing to Codicil is the same as that to the original Will.)

CODICIL FOR REAL ESTATE

Paragraph to be inserted in Will or Codicil for real estate:

[Number] I give, devise and bequeath to the (Board of Conference Claimants of the Methodist Episcopal Church, a corporation created and existing under and by virtue of the Laws of the State of Illinois, for the benefit of the Connectional Permanent Fund)[1] *the following lands and premises,*

[1] See note at bottom of page 266.

that is to say...... (Here insert location and correct legal description)...... to have and to hold the same with the appurtenances thereunto belonging to said Board of Conference Claimants, its successors and assigns forever.

CODICIL FOR RESIDUARY ESTATE

PARAGRAPH TO BE INSERTED IN WILL OR CODICIL DEVISING ALL OR A PART OF THE RESIDUARY ESTATE:

[Number] I give, devise and bequeath to the (Board of Conference Claimants of the Methodist Episcopal Church, a corporation created and existing under and by virtue of the Laws of the State of Illinois,)[1] *all (or a stated fractional part) of the rest, residue and remainder of my estate, real, personal and mixed of which I may die seized or possessed or in which I have any interest.*

SPECIAL NOTE:

(a) Let the details of witnessing the Will or Codicil be followed EXACTLY AS STATED IN THE ABOVE FORMS. In many states, and perhaps in all, if the witnesses are not ALL PRESENT TOGETHER AT THE TIME of the execution of the Will by the Testator, the Will will not be probated or held to be valid.

(b) Any of the gift clauses of the above form of Will or Codicil may be omitted or others inserted. In either case the numbers of the clauses should be consecutive.

(c) Some states require three witnesses. Therefore in all states let there be three witnesses if practicable. In most states only two witnesses are required.

(d) In some states it may be necessary to have a seal of some special form, but generally the word "seal" written with a pen with a scroll around it is sufficient.

V. BENEFICIARIES

In these forms we have named as beneficiary the Board of Conference Claimants of the Methodist Episcopal Church.[1] This is the great connectional or general organization of the Church which looks after Retired Ministers (Superannuates),

[1]See note at bottom of page 266.

the Widows of deceased ministers, and their dependent children under sixteen years of age. The number of such beneficiaries is almost 7,000, of which number almost 4,000 are *"necessitous cases,"* that is, those who have larger needs than can be provided for by the Annual Conference. Such necessitous cases are found in substantially every Annual Conference, and many of them are found in the poorer conferences on the border or frontier, where adequate provision can not be made by the Annual Conference for the Veterans and Widows.

The Methodist Episcopal Church not only has the general organization named above, the "BOARD OF CONFERENCE CLAIMANTS OF THE METHODIST EPISCOPAL CHURCH," but many ANNUAL CONFERENCES HAVE INVESTED FUNDS held by Trustees or Preachers' Aid Societies, the income of which goes to the Retired Preachers and other Claimants who are related to the Annual Conference. It is very important that in any case the exact legal name of the beneficiary organization be used.[1]

VI. REASONS FOR MAKING A WILL.

(1) If you do not make a Will the court must appoint an administrator to settle up your affairs. This person will have charge and control of your property for at least one year after your death, and may be a stranger or an inexperienced person in whom you would not confide while in life; or, if a relative or friend be appointed, he or she will be put to the trouble of giving a bond, and in some cases may be wholly unable to obtain the bond required by law.

(2) If you leave no Will and have minor children, the shares of such minors will have to go to a guardian, who may also be a stranger whom you yourself would not have chosen; and, during the minority of your children, the provision for them, earned by you through years of care and labor, may be endangered.

(3) By making a Will, you can select your own executor, and nominate, if you like, a guardian for your minor children.

(4) By making a Will, you can divide your property in a way which shall, under all the circumstances, seem most just and equitable, and make gifts to others than your heirs at law.

---

[1] For the names of such Annual Conference organizations see page 289.

(5) By making a Will, you can make trust arrangements for children and loved ones.

(6) The making of a Will is not a difficult or troublesome matter, nor is it expensive if attended to in a business-like manner.

VII. MAKING A WILL A CHRISTIAN'S DUTY

Dr. M. J. Dubois

Protestant Episcopal Church

A duty? Yes, indeed, the neglect of which is disobedience to the command, "Be ye therefore ready." Imagine a soldier not ready to start at the bugle call, or a clerk whose accounts are not ready for inspection whenever his employer calls for them! Yet thousands of Christians are as unprepared for death! Stewards of the Master, they are not ready to give an account to Him; resting in false security and letting the weeks and years slip by rarely if ever giving a thought to the time when they shall be called to account.

"Ready" should be the Christian's answer at any time. And there is no excuse for us, even were the call to be very sudden, leaving to others the deciding of what to do with our belongings. If this is true of the man with ten talents, it is just as true of the man with one. If the millionaire must dispose of millions, then those who have but little are under even stronger obligation to leave everything in perfect order.

In the minds of some persons there is a kind of superstition about making a Will which makes them put it off indefinitely. They are afraid. Yet what splendid preparation it is for the Christian. To review all that God has given him. To realize while assigning earthly possessions to others that as "we brought nothing into this world it is certain we can carry nothing out." To loosen the tendrils of selfishness which have been growing steadily and imperceptibly, until the entrance to our heart is choked by them! Reopen the entrance. Loosen the hold earthly possessions have upon you and let the True Vine grow unhindered. Be strong and face death, which must come to all and which will not be hastened by making your Will. Make your Will quietly, carefully and prayerfully. Then you will look on the things around you as yours for a short time only; the idea of stewardship will grow, and when the Master calls, you will gladly "leave all and follow Him."

* * *

These are earnest words by Dr. Dubois. While their inspiration is on you please remember that providentially there is a *"more excellent way"* of fulfilling the Christian's duty as steward of God's manifold mercies by securing a Life Annuity Bond, and, as executor of your own estate, seeing with your own eyes the accomplishment of your purpose of helping the aged ministers.

VIII. "A MORE EXCELLENT WAY"

It is the LIFE ANNUITY BOND way. Let us explain it.

A Life Annuity Bond is an Insurance Policy "turned 'round!" In life insurance you pay an uncertain number of *small* amounts, and one *large* amount is paid at death.

In a LIFE ANNUITY BOND you pay a large amount *once,* and receive a number of small amounts annually, semi-annually, quarterly or monthly, until death.

A person who must have an *absolutely sure,* fixed income until the last day of life, or who desires to make a benevolent distribution of his property without litigation, expense or failure will buy a LIFE ANNUITY BOND. The money is at once carefully and safely invested by the General Benevolent Board of the Church, or the Annual Conference and the holder of the Bond receives regular, fixed and assured payments during life. When the annuitant dies the interest will provide perpetually for Veteran Preachers and Widows and Orphans.

LIFE ANNUITY BONDS pay a higher rate than the current interest because the claim of a Life Annuity Bond terminates with the death of the annuitant, and a conservative and economical management of business without commissions or heavy expense assures a sufficient income.

The rate paid to an annuitant on a LIFE ANNUITY BOND is determined by the *age* of the annuitant, the older the person the higher the rate. *No medical examination is necessary.*

LIFE ANNUITY BONDS may be purchased for any amount, and upon the life of one or more individuals, or for one or more beneficiaries designated by the purchaser.

LIFE ANNUITY BONDS are not experimental. They date back to the days of the Roman Empire. The British Government and other nations have issued such Bonds for more than a century.

LIFE ANNUITY BONDS pay the interest at any interval desired by the annuitant—yearly, semi-annually, quarterly or monthly.

LIFE ANNUITY BONDS ARE SAFE: for back of them in the Methodist Episcopal Church is the Board of Conference Claimants or the Annual Conferences and back of these the *General Conference* which authorized them. Back of these is the *Methodist Episcopal Church,* with its three and a half millions of members, and with that habit of financial responsibility and intelligent cooperation which has made its great Boards and Business enterprises the admiration of the world, and has given to them the very highest commercial rating. Back of all these are *invested resources many times* the amount of bond liability, with investments rapidly increasing. The same statement holds true of any other Denomination. For list of organizations see page 289.

Investments are mainly in loans secured upon real estate. The loans and investments are made and approved by such experienced and successful business men and financiers.

Had the Methodist part of the $120,000,000 paid to Life Insurance Companies for Life Annuities since 1890 been invested in the LIFE ANNUITY BONDS of the *Board or of Annual Conferences* those millions would be to-day and forever serving the Veteran Preachers.

IX. A GENERAL CONFERENCE ORGANIZATION

One purpose in establishing the Board of Conference Claimants and similar general organizations is in order that through its agency the great and well-to-do Conferences and great-souled laymen might render assistance to the Retired Ministers in the hard places. Thus the Pioneer Preacher, carrying the message of the Cross to new fields, has a loving recognition of his service, the home church helping him in his old age. The general or connectional Boards are the agents *of the Entire Church,* projecting plans for the benefit of the Retired Ministry and Widows and Orphans of deceased Ministers.

THE PURPOSES OF THE BOARD

(1) To seek an Endowment for the PERMANENT FUND and for Annual Conferences.

(2) To agitate, inspire and instruct, that there may be sufficient in God's house for His aged servants.

(3) To cooperate with Annual Conferences in every practicable way.

HOW ARE MONEYS RAISED?

(1) BY GIFTS FROM GOD'S PEOPLE. They love the Old Preachers and Love loosens the purse-strings.

(2) BY THE SALE OF LIFE ANNUITY BONDS which at the same time absolutely and perpetually secure the Gift for the benefit of Conference Claimants without possible litigation or loss, and provide a fixed income for life for the donor or for a relative, or for some Veteran Preacher or other friend chosen by him.

(3) BY SECURING WILLS WITH BEQUESTS IN FAVOR OF THE RETIRED MINISTER.

As to Wills, Bishop Warren wrote a few days before his death:

"An army of 45,000 Methodists is sent over every year to follow Him who rides the white horse of victory on the other side. Probably a fourth of these dispose of their property before going. Nearly every one of them should remember some phase of the cause of God in that final disposition. It adds rest and satisfaction to the dying bed of the Testator and thrilling emotion to the welcoming 'Well Done' of the Master."

ANNUAL CONFERENCE ORGANIZATIONS

Besides the connectional Board of Conference Claimants, almost every Annual Conference has an organization for administering funds in behalf of their Conference Claimants. The legal title of such incorporated Boards will be found on page 289. Be sure to use their exact legal title in wills and all legal documents.

OLIVER H. HORTON.

42 Dearborn St., Chicago, Ill.

NOTES CONCERNING WILLS

AN AUTHORITY ON WILLS

Daniel S. Remsen of the New York bar, an authority on the post mortem administration of wealth, told the members of the Pennsylvania Bankers' Association that the wills of Harriman, Bostwick, Yerkes, Plant, Mrs. Mary Baker Eddy, and other prominent persons were unsafe models to follow. As a type of the "safe and sound" will he cited that of J. Pierpont Morgan.

The way to get better wills is to make them. Lawyers are able and willing if the service was demanded. The client must give his lawyer a fair chance and demand his best service. When the will is complete he must demand that it be tested while he is alive and able to repair any defects or ambiguities that may be discovered. This method produced the will of Mr. Morgan.

A "safe" will Mr. Remsen defined as one free from danger. The word "sound," he said, meant "without a flaw." A safe will was one so written as to insure the fulfillment of the maker's wishes. A sound will was one that could be enforced even though it might not insure the result the maker wished. The Harriman will, he asserted, was "sound" but "unsafe." The will of Samuel J. Tilden was cited as a conspicuous example of the will that was both unsafe and unsound. All wills may present objectionable features when used as precedents without competent legal advice.

But there is "a more excellent way" than that of disposing of your property by Will: Administer your own estate. Do your giving *now;* or if you must protect your life income, do your giving by means of a LIFE ANNUITY BOND.

This will determine the post-mortem use of your money without possible failure and will furnish an unchallenged "safe" and "sound" income during your life and the lives of your loved ones.

BETTER THAN A WILL

Money left in wills may never reach the persons or institutions for whom it was intended. Many wills have been broken and moneys diverted. Dr. Holmes in *"Parson Turrel's Leg-*

acy" tells us of a legacy given to Harvard College that caused a great deal of trouble. In concluding the story the doctor says:

"God bless you, Gentlemen! learn to give
Money to colleges while you live.
Don't be silly and think you'll try
To bother the colleges when you die
With codicil this and codicil that,
That knowledge may starve while law grows fat;
For there never was a pitcher that wouldn't spill,
And there's always a flaw in a donkey's will."

PROVIDES FOR HORSE IN WILL

Capt. Holly P. Nickell, a Confederate veteran of Lee's Summit, Mo., made careful disposition in his will of his old saddle horse, Pinto. A clause of the will reads:

"It is my wish that my old horse, Pinto, shall be well taken care of. His shoes shall be taken off and he shall be turned out to grass and pass the rest of his days in comfort."

GETTING AND SPENDING

Deep problems of finance, national and international, are full of complexity, but popular interest in money, as related to individuals, is chiefly concerned with two very easily understood questions: *how to get it* and *how to spend it.* Few persons care much about keeping it. There are abnormal individuals called misers who are inspired with a sinister purpose to hoard; and there are ill-advised people who wish to build great fortunes for their children, thus providing them an opportunity for selfish living and consequent destruction of character. But in general the world is not anxious to keep money, knowing that it must be surrendered anyhow within a few years, when death will step in and cry, "Your money *and* your life!"

The majority of people seek to retain only a sufficient amount of money to maintain life in comfort to the end of the chapter and make provision for those having claims upon them. There is wisdom in this policy. To hoard money is as foolish as to attempt to hoard time. You cannot lay up either and draw from the accumulation when the term of life is exhausted.

The best investment to-day is the Life Annuity Bond; as far ahead of other bonds as the present mode of travel is ahead of the old time prairie schooner.

A person who must have an *absolutely sure,* fixed income until the last day of life, or who desires to make a benevolent distribution of property before death without litigation, expense or failure, will buy a LIFE ANNUITY BOND. The money is carefully and perpetually invested and the buyer receives regular, fixed and assured payments during life. When the annuitant dies, the interest provides perpetually for Veteran Preachers, widows and dependent orphans.

ILLUSTRATIONS

1. A widow had $1,500. She needed the income during life but was distressed as to its safe investment, and wanted the money to go to Retired Preachers after her death. So she paid the money to the Board of Conference Claimants, and now receives $45 every six months, until God shall give to her His welcome and crown.

2. A husband and wife had $5,000 which they had set aside for aged ministers, but needed the income. They paid the $5,000 to the Board of Conference Claimants; and as long as they or either of them shall survive will receive $150 every six months. When they are called Home successive generations of Retired Methodist Preachers will call them "Blessed." They administered their own estate and saw their money in the hands of the Board for perpetual investment.

3. A Christian woman who, on account of age and ill health lived in California, had a house in an eastern city, which brought to her an uncertain income and all sorts of expense and trouble with tenants and agents. She deeded the property to the Board of Conference Claimants; and now, without further expense, trouble or loss on the first day of each month she receives a draft for $30. The rentals go to the Board, and when her home in Heaven opens its doors to receive her, the income from her earthly home will continue, and provide comfort for the Aged Preachers.

—*The Christian Advocate.*

NOTE.—Many Annual Conference organizations issue satisfactory Life Annuity Bonds. For addresses of representatives and legal titles, see page 289.

UNITED STATES OF AMERICA.

INCORPORATED UNDER THE LAWS OF THE STATE OF ILLINOIS

Board of Conference Claimants

OF THE

Methodist Episcopal Church

ANNUITY BOND

No. ______________ $______________

Whereas, ______________
(hereinafter called Annuitant) of ______________
in the County of ______________ and State of ______________,
has this day made a gift to the Board of Conference Claimants of the Methodist Episcopal Church, a corporation organized and existing under and by virtue of the laws of the State of Illinois, U.S.A. and located at Chicago, in said State, of the principal sum of ______________ Dollars ($______),
subject to the terms and conditions hereinafter set forth, and;

Whereas, said corporation has accepted said gift subject to such terms and conditions;

Now, Therefore, said Board of Conference Claimants in consideration of the premises and for other good and valuable considerations, the receipt whereof by it is hereby acknowledged, hereby promises and agrees to pay on demand an annuity of ______________ Dollars ($______)
to be paid to ______________ in semi-annual installments of ______________ Dollars ($______)
each, during the life of said annuitant, commencing on the ______________ day of ______________ A.D. One Thousand Nine Hundred and ______________
(if said annuitant is then living), and terminating with the last payment preceding the death of said annuitant, and upon the death of said annuitant said gift shall be and become absolute and unconditional, and said Board of Conference Claimants be released from all obligations incurred under this agreement.

It is understood and agreed that said principal sum shall be and remain part of the Permanent Fund of said Board of Conference Claimants, the net income from which shall be used toward the support and in the interest of Conference Claimants in the Methodist Episcopal Church.

This contract is issued upon the application of said annuitant, a copy of which application is made a part hereof, and is accepted by said annuitant upon the express conditions:

(1) That said annuitant at the last anniversary of h___ birth, was then not less than ______________ years of age, which, if found to be untrue, this contract shall thereupon cease, and be cancelled, and said Board of Conference Claimants shall have power to make an equitable settlement for payments already made thereunder.

(2) That said Board of Conference Claimants shall be furnished at every annuity payment with satisfactory evidence that said annuitant is living.

In Witness Whereof, the Board of Conference Claimants of the Methodist Episcopal Church has caused these Presents to be signed by its Vice-President, and attested by its Secretary, and its corporate seal to be affixed hereto, this ______________ day of ______________, A.D. One Thousand Nine Hundred and ______________

Board of Conference Claimants of the Methodist Episcopal Church.

Attested: ______________ Secretary.

By ______________ Vice-President.

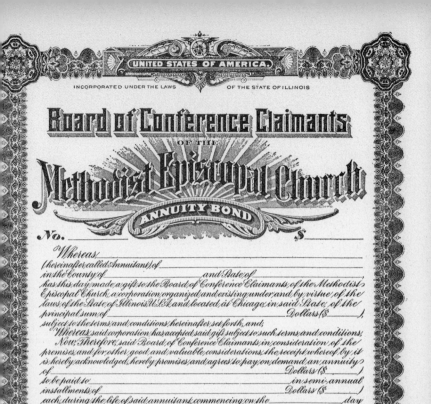

APPLICATION BLANK

(For A Joint Life Annuity Bond Some Verbal Changes Would Be Made)

To the Board of Conference Claimants of the Methodist Episcopal Church, 1018 So. Wabash Ave., Chicago, Ill.

I.......................................in the county of ....and State of........................ (applicant), being desirous of aiding said Board to assist in the support of Conference Claimants, and desiring at the same time to purchase from said Board an annuity of.............Dollars ($.................), to be paid to.......................... ....(annuitant), in semi-annual installments, do hereby declare that..he was born at.. on the...........day of...........................in the year One Thousand, Eight Hundred and....................., and agree that if the above statement as to the date of annuitant's birth be untrue, the gift of..........................Dollars ($...........), made by me to you shall be and become absolute and unconditional, and that the annuity contract issued by you upon this application shall cease and be canceled, and no longer of any effect. Annuitant's father's name was.................. and h...... mother's maiden name was......................

IN WITNESS WHEREOF, I have hereunto set my hand and affixed my seal this..........day of..................A. D. One Thousand, Nine Hundred and..................

(Signature of Applicant)

..................................[SEAL]

(Signature of Annuitant if other than the Applicant)

..................................[SEAL]

WITNESS:

....

....

Note.—For the names of other Church organizations which receive gifts on the life annuity basis see page 289.

BANKER OLIVER'S INVESTMENT

A STORY

HENRY ALBERT COLLINS

"The Life Annuity Man"

After working in his garden until nearly noon John Donaldson, a retired farmer, donned his coat and was starting downtown to get his mail and make inquiries whether any more bodies had been recovered from the coal mine explosion, when he saw James Oliver, the banker, coming up the road in his electric.

Mr. Oliver stopped at the gate, alighted and came toward the house.

"Good morning, James," said Mr. Donaldson.

"Fine morning, John," replied the banker.

After comfortably seating himself on the porch Mr. Oliver said, "John, it occurred to me that you might like to invest the money you received from the sale of that fifty-five acres of ground to the Central Railroad Company in something that would give you a large rate of interest."

"Yes, that was our desire," said Mr. Donaldson.

"John," said Mr. Oliver, "they are getting up a company to develop a large mine in the Island of Batavia. Immense quantities of gold and silver have recently been discovered there. This company has the first option on this mine."

"What rate of interest will this company pay?"

"That has not been fully decided yet, anywhere from ten to fifty per cent a year, I have been told."

"Have they sold many shares of stock?"

"Well, from what I have heard," said the banker, "they are selling like hot cakes. Shall I put you down for twenty thousand dollars' worth of stock?"

Before answering the question Mr. Donaldson went into the house and consulted his wife. Returning to the porch he said, "James, you and I have grown up together here. You have been very prosperous. Our tract of land which we sold for twenty-two thousand and five hundred dollars was all the property Mary and I possessed."

"You have that other twenty-five acres and the house here," interrupted Mr. Oliver.

"That is true, but wife and I have decided to give that twenty-five acres to the town for a cemetery. With the big railroad shops and other factories coming here our town will be likely to grow. You know the town has only a small cemetery which will soon be outgrown, and being so close in, it is likely to be condemned."

"Why don't you offer to sell the strip to the town?"

"For the reason that the best things are always given away," said the farmer. "You have read the stanza:

'Wisest he in this whole wide land,
Of hoarding till bent and gray;
For *all you can hold in your cold dead hand*
Is what you have given away.' "

"Yes," said Mr. Oliver. "How much stock will you take in the new company?"

"James, will you give Mary and me a bond that you will refund to us any losses that this new company may cause us?"

The banker shifted his chair and replied, "I cannot do that. My money is all out on mortgages or invested in real estate."

Mrs. Donaldson came out on the porch, shook hands with the banker, asked after the health of himself and household; then excused herself and returned to the kitchen.

"James, did you hear Dr. Hingeley preach yesterday?" asked Mr. Donaldson.

"No, I never go to church since my wife died," said the banker.

"Well, he gave us a fine sermon about being useful in this world."

"O, I suppose so. You know that I am so busy during the week that I have to run out to the farms on Sunday and see if everything is all right."

"James, let me tell you something. Last Saturday Dr. Hingeley of Chicago came to town and induced us to put ten thousand dollars on the Life Annuity plan into the treasury of the Board of Conference Claimants of the Methodist Episcopal Church, the connectional or general organization of which he is the secretary, and ten thousand dollars into the Preachers' Aid Society of our Annual Conference."

"You're an idiot!" exclaimed the banker, rising from his chair and reaching for his hat.

"Wait a minute, James, and let me say something more."

"Well, out with it," said the banker.

"James Oliver, you know that Mary and I have given each of our three children a good education. Paul has a fine position on the Northwestern Railroad, which pays him a salary of five thousand dollars per year. Esther's husband has a larger income. Martha will soon marry a man who is richly endowed with this world's goods. It is true we deposited twenty-two thousand and five hundred dollars in your bank, but on last Saturday Mary and I gave Dr. Hingeley a check for twenty thousand dollars for these Life Annuity Bonds."

"Let me see them," said Mr. Oliver.

While waiting for the banker to read the bond, Mrs. Donaldson brought out a big pitcher of fresh buttermilk and a plate of hot gingerbread. The two men helped themselves to the tempting lunch.

After the banker had carefully read the Life Annuity Bonds he said, "What new scheme is this to get money?"

Mr. Donaldson replied, "It is not a new scheme. History tells us that hundreds of years before Christ the old countries were receiving money on this plan. In the year 40 B. C the Roman government enacted the law governing the annuity business. This law, which has been greatly improved, is still in force. For more than two hundred years this annuity business has been growing larger each year. One insurance company, which also does annuity business, reports having over one hundred million dollars in annuities on which they are paying interest. A number of other Annuity Companies report having from one to forty million dollars each."

"Where did you first hear about this plan?" said Mr. Oliver.

"My wife," said the farmer, "visited her aunt last Thanksgiving, and while there she heard of two cases where Annuity Bonds had been of wonderful value."

"Tell me about them," said the banker.

Mrs. Donaldson, overhearing their conversation, came out on the porch and said, "May I tell you about these cases?"

"Certainly," exclaimed both men.

"Some three years ago a well-appearing, educated young man went to Riverview, where my aunt lives. The man attended church and took a prominent part in the social life of the town. He became acquainted with the church organist, the daughter of a millionaire, and after a short courtship they were married. In a few months the husband came home drunk, after having spent the night gambling in a saloon. The millionaire threatened to turn the young man out on the street, but the daughter pleaded for mercy and her father relented. Seeing the unhappiness caused by strong drink, in order to put temptation out of the way of his only son, a delicate lad of seventeen, who was easily led by his associates, the father put seventy-five per cent of his property into Life Annuity Bonds for the benefit of himself, his son, and daughter, but he did not mention this fact to anyone except his banker.

"In about a year the father died. In the meantime the daughter's husband had apparently reformed, but after the funeral went on a protracted spree, came home frenzied by drink and tried to kill his wife. Thinking that he would soon get control of his wife's property the husband made his boast of what he would do with it, and when he learned that the estate had been disposed of on the Life Annuity plan he became furious and threatened to bring suit to recover the money paid for the Life Annuity Bonds. Finding that it was impossible to recover money paid for these Bonds, he said, 'Well, I guess father was right after all.' This man reformed, and to-day is living an honorable, useful life in Riverview. The health of the millionaire's son failed and he is still living at a well-known sanitarium. Having read a circular about life annuities I suggested that John write to Dr. Hingeley for further information, and he came at once to see us as John has told you."

Mrs. Donaldson invited the banker to stay to dinner and he accepted the invitation.

"John," said the banker, "I see by this Bond that you get a good rate of interest, which is paid semi-annually. What induced you to put your money into the Board of Conference Claimants?"

"Do you remember the pastor of our church who died some ten or twelve years ago? He was never paid enough money to support himself and family decently, to say nothing of saving anything for the 'rainy day.' He and his wife skimped along in order to help out with our annual missionary collections—for you know the minister always sets the example for liberality—until they often went hungry. The minister attended a funeral one cold winter day and, being underfed and thinly clad, he took cold and soon after died with pneumonia. His wife went back to her folks, an object of charity."

"Yes, I remember him. That funeral was my wife's. I paid the preacher two dollars for preaching the sermon. Perhaps I did not give him enough. You know I used to give ten dollars a year to the church for my wife."

Mr. Donaldson arose from his chair and coming closer to his visitor said:

"J a m e s, don't you want to join your wife when you leave this world?"

The banker attempted to speak but could not utter a word, and bowed his head on the arm of the chair.

"My wife was the best woman that ever lived," he sobbed.

"You have been true to her memory all these years, James. God has given you many blessings and much wealth. He has raised you up from your recent bed of sickness. Is it not a good time to give yourself to Christ who died for you? Will you not enlist in His service and be true to Him the balance of your days?"

"I will," said the banker.

Then the men bowed in prayer, and when they arose from their knees the banker said, "John, I'm so happy. I never felt this way before. I wish that my wife were here."

"Doubtless your wife's spirit is here, James. Her prayers for you are answered. You are 'a new creature in Christ Jesus; old things have passed away; behold, all things have become new.' "

Mrs. Donaldson wisely refrained from announcing the noonday meal until the men had risen from their knees. She then rang the bell for dinner, and the men entered the house and sat down at the table.

After the blessing had been asked, while partaking of the appetizing food, Mr. Oliver said, "John, what are you going to do with that twenty-five hundred dollars in the bank?"

"That belongs to the Lord. Wife and I are tithers. We always set aside for the Lord the first tenth of all the money we receive. He has not shown us yet where He wants this money used."

"What about the security of the money you gave away for the Life Annuity Bond?" the banker asked.

"That is perfectly safe," replied the farmer. "The Methodist Episcopal Church handles the money through the Permanent Fund of the Board of Conference Claimants, an institution authorized by the General Conference and incorporated by the State of Illinois. The Annual Conference also is regularly incorporated and duly authorized. We will draw the annuity interest semi-annually as long as Mary or I live, and after our death the income of our purchase money will help support Conference Claimants as long as the Methodist Episcopal Church and this Republic lives."

"Conference Claimants!" said the visitor, "who are they?"

Mr. Donaldson replied, "This Permanent Fund is for the worn-out preachers, and the widows and orphans of deceased Ministers, who are called 'Conference Claimants' because the Church recognizes that on account of their sacrifices and services they have an inherent *claim* for a comfortable support as long as they live. They are to be paid a reasonable annuity or pension yearly, and an additional amount when needed.

"O, I see. Not a bad idea, and an honor to a great Church. Our bank is just organizing a pension retirement fund, and I will have to talk it over with Dr. Hingeley. He must be quite familiar with the problem. What about taxes on the Life Annuity Bond?" inquired Mr. Oliver.

"Annuity Bonds are not taxable," replied the farmer.

"You are getting old, John. Suppose both of you die soon, don't you see that then the Board will get all the principal of the money you gave them and will only have paid back the interest to you?" said the banker.

"Yes, that is what we want," said the farmer, "but it is said to be a positive fact, borne out by experience, that annuitants usually live longer than other people."

"How do you account for that?"

"Simply because a Life Annuity gives a stated income as long as the annuitant lives; all financial worry is removed; the interest always comes promptly; there is no money lying idle to reduce the income; no commissions or expenses for making new investments; no grudge against any one who advised a bad investment; no breaking of a will; no court costs or guardian's fees to pay after death, and the delight which always comes when we invest money with God."

"Do your children approve of your giving away this money for benevolent objects?" asked Mr. Oliver.

"Mary and I talked with our children about it and they agreed that whatever we did with the money would be all right as far as they were concerned. I believe you know what we did with the money you paid us for that north eighty acres?"

"Yes, I saw by your checks that you gave five hundred dollars toward building the parsonage and most of the balance to your children," said the banker.

The banker seemed in no hurry to leave. He moved a chair into the shade and sat down, and when Mr. Donaldson returned to the porch said, "John, do you know whether the people who invest their money in Life Annuity Bonds are satisfied with their investment?"

The farmer replied:

"It is a fact that those who buy one Annuity Bond nearly

always buy more. Dr. Hingeley tells me that one man has purchased five Bonds from the Board and that quite a number have two and three each. Many purchasers do as I have done and get the bonds of several strong organizations."

"The twenty thousand dollars which you paid for the Life Annuity Bonds is a big sum," said Mr. Oliver. "Do you know whether any one else ever paid so much for those Life Annuity Bonds?"

"O, yes, quite a number of bonds have been issued for fifty thousand dollars to one hundred thousand dollars each, and some have been issued for very much larger sums.

UNITED STATES OF AMERICA

INCORPORATED UNDER THE LAWS OF THE STATE OF ILLINOIS

Board of Conference Claimants

OF THE

Methodist Episcopal Church

ANNUITY BOND

No. ________ $ ________

Whereas ________ (hereinafter called Annuitant) of ________ in the County of ________ and State of ________ has this day made a gift to the Board of Conference Claimants of the Methodist Episcopal Church, a corporation organized and existing under and by virtue of the laws of the State of Illinois U.S.A. and located at Chicago in said State, of the principal sum of ________ Dollars ($ ________) subject to the terms and conditions hereinafter set forth, and

Whereas said corporation has accepted said gift subject to such terms and conditions.

Now Therefore, said Board of Conference Claimants in consideration of the premises and for other good and valuable considerations, the receipt whereof by it is hereby acknowledged, hereby promises and agrees to pay on demand an annuity of ________ Dollars ($ ________) to be paid to ________ in semi-annual installments of ________ Dollars ($ ________) each, during the life of said annuitant, commencing on the ________ day of ________ A.D. One Thousand Nine Hundred and ________ (if said annuitant is then living) and terminating with the last payment preceding the death of said annuitant, and upon the death of said annuitant said gift shall be and become absolute and unconditional, and said Board of Conference Claimants be released from all obligations incurred under this agreement.

It is understood and agreed that said principal sum shall be and remain part of the Permanent Fund of said Board of Conference Claimants, the net income from which shall be used toward the support and in the interest of Conference Claimants in the Methodist Episcopal Church.

This contract is issued upon the application of said annuitant, a copy of which application is made a part hereof, and is accepted by said annuitant upon the express conditions:

(1) That said annuitant at the last anniversary of h__ birth, was then not less than ________ years of age, which, if found to be untrue, this contract shall thereupon cease and be cancelled, and said Board of Conference Claimants shall have power to make an equitable settlement for payments already made thereunder.

(2) That said Board of Conference Claimants shall be furnished at every annuity payment with satisfactory evidence that said annuitant is living.

In Witness Whereof, the Board of Conference Claimants of the Methodist Episcopal Church has caused these presents to be signed by its Vice President and attested by its Secretary and its corporate seal to be affixed hereto this ________ day of ________ A.D. One Thousand Nine Hundred and ________

Board of Conference Claimants of the Methodist Episcopal Church

Attest: ________ Secretary. By ________ Vice President.

Reduced facsimile of Life Annuity Bond

"We know of one case when a man thirty times a millionaire, who desired to have an unquestioned support for his children, placed almost $600,000 in one of Methodism's institutions, believing that, though great business corporations might fail, the Methodist Church would not fail. But of course most of the bonds are taken by persons in moderate circumstances who can pay only from one hundred dollars to a few thousand dollars for a Bond."

Mr. Oliver then asked:

"What about the medical examination before getting a Life Annuity Bond?"

"No medical examination is required," said the farmer, "and the older the applicant the higher the amount paid."

"What do you know about the management of the funds

of the Board of Conference Claimants' Fund?" asked the visitor.

Mr. Donaldson replied:

"An economical and personal management of the business is assured. There are no commissions to be paid to agents, no heavy expenses in the management, and no watered stock in the Life Annuity System, and for every dollar of liability the Board has an investment of twenty-five dollars."

Mr. Oliver was silent for a time and then asked, "John, is Dr. Hingeley still here?"

"I think so. He and our pastor were going to call on several persons in regard to Life Annuity Bonds. I will 'phone the parsonage and inquire."

Returning to the porch, the farmer said, "Yes, he and our pastor are at Andy Campbell's for dinner."

Mr. Donaldson reported to the banker that the meeting had been arranged, as requested, and said that Mr. Julian, the miller, had bought a Life Annuity Bond for his wife, as a perpetual birthday gift.

"What is Dr. Hingeley's address?" asked the banker.

Handing him a card, Mr. Oliver read, "Joseph B. Hingeley, Corresponding Secretary of the Board of Conference Claimants, Room 400, 1018 South Wabash Avenue, Chicago, Illinois."

"Thank you," said the banker. "I must go now."

James Oliver shook hands with the farmer, thanked him for his hospitality, entered his car and said:

"If my visit with Dr. Hingeley turns out as I hope it will I may have something else to tell you to-morrow. Good-by, John. God bless you!"

Havana, Ill. HENRY A. COLLINS.

LIST OF ANNUAL CONFERENCE ORGANIZATIONS AND THEIR OFFICIAL REPRESENTATIVES

CONFERENCE	LEGAL NAME OF SOCIETY AND OFFICIAL REPRESENTATIVES
Arkansas	Conference Trustees of the Arkansas Conference. Thomas Mason, Treasurer, Siloam Springs, Ark.
Baltimore	Preachers' Aid Society of the Baltimore Conference. Hugh Johnston, Endowment Fund Secretary, Preachers' Aid Society, Baltimore, Md., 3010 North Calvert St.
California	The Conference Claimants' Endowment Board of the California Annual Conference of the Methodist Episcopal Church. J. H. Wythe, Agent of Conference Claimants' Endowment Fund, San Jose, Cal., 100 Minnesota Ave.
California German	Board of Trustees of the California German Conference of the Methodist Episcopal Church. George Guth, Treasurer of Board of Trustees, South Berkeley, Cal., 3342 California St.
Central German	Mutual Preachers' Aid Society of the Central German Conference of the Methodist Episcopal Church. John Mayer, Secretary Mutual Preachers' Aid Society, Toledo, O., 523 Segur Ave.
Central Illinois	Conference Claimants' Society of the Central Illinois Conference of the Methodist Episcopal Church. J. W. Pruen, Secretary Conference Claimants' Society, Lewistown, Ill.
Central New York	The Trustees of Central New York Conference. Theron R. Green, D.D., Secretary of Permanent Fund, Syracuse, N. Y., 201 Clarendon St.
Central Pennsylvania	Annuity Fund of the Central Pennsylvania Annual Conference. B. H. Hart, Treasurer Board of Trustees, Harrisburg, Pa. The Preachers' Aid Society of the Central Pennsylvania Conference. E. M. Stevens, President of Preachers' Aid Society, Williamsport, Pa., 523 Market St.
Central Swedish	Trustees of Central Swedish Conference. C. J. Nelson, Secretary of Trustee Board, Moline, Ill.
Chicago German	Ministers' Relief Association. H. C. Lemcke, Financial Agent and President, Milwaukee, Wis., 3317 McKinley Boulevard.
Colorado	The Methodist Episcopal Colorado Conference Preachers' Aid Society. John Collins, Secretary of Preachers' Aid Society, Denver, Colo., 2224 South Ogden St.
Columbia River	Conference Claimants' Endowment Association of the Columbia River Conference. W. E. Armfield, Corresponding Secretary of Conference Claimants' Endowment Association, Spokane, Wash., 02227 Hamilton St.
Dakota	Conference Claimants' Endowment Fund of the Dakota Conference. M. E. Nickerson, Secretary of Conference Claimants' Endowment Fund, White, S. D.
Delaware	Board of Conference Claimants of Delaware Conference. J. H. Nutter, President, Marion Station, Md.
Des Moines	Preachers' Aid Society of the Des Moines Conference
Detroit	Superannuated Preachers' Aid Society of the Detroit Annual Conference. John Sweet, Secretary and Treasurer of Superannuated Preachers' Aid Society, Detroit, Mich., 1179 Fourth Ave.
East German	Mutual Benefit Society of the Members of East German Conference. Henry Miller, Treasurer of Mutual Benefit Society, Brooklyn, N. Y., 1169 Green St.
East Maine	Preachers' Aid Society of the East Maine Conference. S. M. Bowles, Secretary of Preachers' Aid Society, Fort Fairfield, Me.

CONFERENCE	LEGAL NAME OF SOCIETY AND OFFICIAL REPRESENTATIVES
Erie	The Erie Annual Conference of the Methodist Episcopal Church. R. S. Borland, Commissioner of Permanent Annuity Fund, Mercer, Pa.
Genesee	Permanent Fund Board of the "Genesee Annual Conference of the Methodist Episcopal Church." S. A. Morse, Conference Secretary of Permanent Fund, Buffalo, N. Y., 37 Minnesota Ave.
Georgia	Annuity Fund Society of the Georgia Conference. W. A. Parsons, Secretary of Annuity Fund, South Epworth, Ga.
Gulf	Executive or Legal Board of Stewards of the Gulf Conference. C. A. King, President of Executive or Legal Board of Stewards.
Idaho	Conference Board of Trustees of Idaho Conference. Thomas Johns, Secretary of Conference Board of Trustees, Mackay, Ida.
Illinois	Preachers' Aid Society of Illinois Conference. Robert Stephens, Field Secretary of Preachers' Aid Society, Danville, Ill.
Indiana	The Preachers' Aid Society of the Indiana Conference of the Methodist Episcopal Church. James A. Sargent, Secretary and Field Agent, Indianapolis, Ind. 905 Fletcher Saving and Trust Building.
Iowa	Permanent Fund of the Iowa Conference. J. C. Kendrick, Financial Secretary of Permanent Fund, Ottumwa, Ia.
Kansas	Permanent Fund of the Preachers' Aid Society of the Kansas Conference. J. B. Gibson, Field Agent of Permanent Fund, Topeka, Kan.
Kentucky	Preachers' Relief Association of the Kentucky Annual Conference of the Methodist Episcopal Church F. W. Harrop, Secretary of Preachers' Relief Association, Covington, Ky.
Lexington	Preachers' Relief Association. W. H. Pope, Field Secretary, Louisville, Ky., 320 Jackson St.
Maine	Preachers' Aid Society of Maine Conference. W. Canham, Secretary of Preachers' Aid Society, Farmington, Me.
Michigan	The Twentieth Century Endowment Fund for Conference Claimants of Michigan Conference. L. E. Lennox, Secretary, Kalamazoo Mich.
Minnesota	Conference Claimants' Endowment Fund for the Minnesota Conference. Peter Clare, Corresponding Secretary, Hamline, Minn.
Missouri	Preachers' Aid Society of Missouri Conference. T. J. Enyeart, Secretary of Preachers' Aid Society, Bosworth, Mo.
Nebraska	Conference Claimants' Endowment Fund of the Nebraska Conference. C. M. Shepherd, Field Secretary, Lincoln, Neb.
New England	Preachers' Aid Society of the New England Annual Conference of the Methodist Episcopal Church. V. A. Cooper, Agent of Board of Stewards, Roxbury, Mass., 1 Kensington Park. Joel M. Leonard, Agent of Board of Stewards, Melrose, Mass, 177 Bellevue Avenue.
New England Southern	Conference Claimants' Fund of "The Trustees of the New England Southern Annual Conference of the Methodist Episcopal Church." Edward C. Bass, Financial Agent of Conference Claimants' Funds, Providence, R. I., 145 Cranston St.
New Hampshire	Preachers' Aid Society of New Hampshire Conference. Elwin Hitchcock, Field Agent, Bradford, Mass., 268 Salem St.
New Jersey	Centenary Fund and Preachers' Aid Society of the New Jersey Annual Conference of the Methodist Episcopal Church. Stedman Applegate, Corresponding Secretary of Centenary Fund and Preachers' Aid Society, Ocean Grove, N. J., 92 Embury Ave.
New York	Permanent Commission on Annuity and Invested Funds. Corresponding Secretary on Annuity and Invested Funds, Milton, N. Y.

CONFERENCE	LEGAL NAME OF SOCIETY AND OFFICIAL REPRESENTATIVES
New York East	The New York East Annual Conference of the Methodist Episcopal Church. New York East Conference Endowment Fund Commission. C. J. North, Corresponding Secretary, Auburn, N. Y., 138 East Genesee St.
Newark	Centenary Fund and Preachers' Aid Society of the Newark Conference. G. C. Wilding, Secretary of Centenary Fund and Preachers' Aid Society, 33 Emerson Ave., East Orange, N. J.
North Dakota	Conference Claimants' Endowment Fund of the North Dakota Conference. James Anderson, Treasurer of Conference Claimants' Fund, Jamestown, N. D.
North Indiana	Preachers' Aid Society of North Indiana Conference of the Methodist Episcopal Church. J. W. Cain, Secretary, Marion, Ind., 1702 South Booth St.
North Montana	Board of Trustees of North Montana Conference. O. A. White, Secretary of Trustee Board, Polson, Mont.
North-East Ohio	Annuity Endowment Fund of North-East Ohio Conference. M. E. Evans, Field Agent and Financial Secretary.
Northern German	Preachers' Mutual Aid Society, Northern German Conference. G. Raihle, Treasurer and Field Agent of Preachers' Mutual Aid Society, North Minneapolis, Minn., 1602 Dupont Ave.
Northern Minnesota	Conference Corporation, The Northern Minnesota Conference. J. W. Robinson, Agent and Collector, Minneapolis, Minn.
Northern New York	Preachers' Permanent Fund of the Northern New York Conference of the Methodist Episcopal Church. S. J. Greenfield, Field Secretary of Preachers' Permanent Fund Commission, Utica, N. Y., 530 State St.
Northwest German	Permanent Fund of Northwest German Conference. E. W. Henke, Treasurer, Charles City, Ia.
Northwest Indiana	Preachers' Aid Society of Northwest Indiana Conference. A. C. Shafer, Field Agent of Conference Claimants' Funds, South Bend, Ind.
Northwest Iowa	Conference Claimants' Permanent Fund of Northwest Iowa Conference. O. P. Miller, Treasurer, Rock Rapids, Ia.
Northwest Kansas	Preachers' Aid Society of Northwest Kansas Conference. C. M. Snyder, Secretary of Preachers' Aid Society, Plainville, Kan.
Norwegian and Danish	Preachers' Aid Society of Norwegian and Danish Conference. E. T. Schollert, Secretary, Minneapolis, Minn., 2923 Aldrich Ave.
Ohio	Preachers' Mutual Relief Association of the Ohio Conference. W. H. Miller, Field Secretary of Conference Claimants' Commission, Columbus, O., 1442 Highland St.
Oklahoma	Preachers' Aid and Annuity Association of Oklahoma Conference. J. A. Ferguson, Secretary, Tecumseh, Okla.
Oregon	Conference Claimants' Permanent Fund of Oregon Conference of the Methodist Episcopal Church. G. F. Hopkins, Financial Secretary of Conference Claimants' Permanent Fund, Portland Ore., 63 East Humboldt St.
Pacific German	Conference Trustee Board of Pacific German Conference. George Hartung, Conference Agent for Permanent Fund, Portland, Ore., 345 Graham St.
Philadelphia	Preachers' Aid Society of Philadelphia Conference of the Methodist Episcopal Church. J. S. Hughes, Treasurer and Corresponding Secretary of Preachers' Aid Society, Philadelphia, Pa., 2016 North Twelfth St.
Pittsburgh	Permanent Annuity Fund of Pittsburgh Conference. W. D. Slease, Secretary of Conference Permanent Annuity Fund, Pittsburgh, Pa., 3119 Kelvin St.
Puget Sound	Preachers' Aid and Permanent Fund Society of the Puget Sound Conference. H. Williston, Secretary, Camas, Wash.

CONFERENCE	LEGAL NAME OF SOCIETY AND OFFICIAL REPRESENTATIVES
Rock River	Superannuates' Relief Association of the Rock River Conference. C. A. Kelley, Corresponding Secretary of Superannuates' Relief Association, Chicago, Ill., 1020 South Wabash Ave.
Saint Louis	Trustees of the Permanent Fund of Saint Louis Conference for Conference Claimants. W. R. McCormack, Secretary of Trustee Board, Kansas City, Mo., 2009 Spruce St.
Saint Louis German	Permanent Fund of Saint Louis German Conference. H. Zimmermann, President of Trustees, Warrenton, Mo.
Southern California	Annuity Endowment Fund of Southern California Conference. Wesley K. Beans, Secretary of Conference Funds, Los Angeles, Cal., 1671 West Twenty-third St.
Southern German	Preachers' Aid Society of Southern German Conference. H. Schmalz, Secretary of Preachers' Aid Society, Hilda, Tex.
Southern Illinois	Conference Claimants' Society of Southern Illinois Conference. F. M. Van Treese, Corresponding Secretary, McLeansboro, Ill.
Southwest Kansas	Permanent Fund of Southwest Kansas Conference. John A. Cragun, Secretary of Board of Stewards, Kingman, Kan.
Troy	Conference Claimants' Endowment Fund of "The Trustees of the Troy Annual Conference of the Methodist Episcopal Church." W. H. Hughes, Corresponding Secretary, Mechanicsville, N. Y.
Upper Iowa	Conference Claimants' Fund of Upper Iowa Conference. J. W. Bissell, Agent of Conference Claimants' Fund Commission, Waterloo, Ia.
Vermont	Preachers' Aid Society of Vermont Conference. W. W. Roberts, Secretary, Williamston, Vt.
West German	Superannuates' Relief Society of West German Conference. Edw. Sallenbach, Secretary, Omaha, Neb., 3031 Leavenworth St.
West Ohio	Conference Endowment Fund of West Ohio Conference. U. G. Humphrey, Corresponding Secretary, 220 West Fourth Street, Cincinnati, O.
West Virginia	Permanent Trust Fund Association of West Virginia Conference. G. W. Kepler, Field Secretary, Sistersville, W. Va., 112 East St.
West Wisconsin	Superannuated Preachers' Fund of the West Wisconsin Conference. F. E. Bauchop, Field Secretary, Madison, Wis.
Wilmington	The Board of Stewards of the Wilmington Conference of the Methodist Episcopal Church. W. G. Koons, Chairman, Lewes, Del.
Wisconsin	Wisconsin Conference Board of Trustees of the Methodist Episcopal Church. Walter A. Hall, Secretary, Fond du Lac, Wis.
Wyoming	Preachers Aid Society of Wyoming Annual Conference. Austin Griffin, Secretary of Preachers' Aid Society, Oneonta, N. Y.

PART III

THE CLAIM SUPREME

PROGRAM OF METHODISM

Laymen declared at the National Convention of Methodist Men that the Claim of the Veteran Preachers was Supreme. Methodism, voiced by its Bishops, declares that "The Supreme Claim shall be given the Supreme Place."

The 1915 Campaign for $10,000,000 will assure a Retiring Competency for every Minister, Minister's Widow and dependent Orphan.

The Recognition of this Claim as Inherent, Foremost and Supreme involves the adoption of adequate Ways and Means, so that the Claim may be met. A great Judge declared:

"*Our names are on the bond, and our Master is the endorser. We do not propose to let His note go to protest.*"

CHAPTER I. EPISCOPAL LEADERSHIP AND CONFERENCE

The Bishops of the Methodist Episcopal Church

John H. Vincent	William A. Quayle
Earl Cranston	Charles W. Smith
David H. Moore	Wilson S. Lewis
John W. Hamilton	Edwin H. Hughes
Joseph F. Berry	Frank M. Bristol
William F. McDowell	Homer C. Stuntz
James W. Bashford	Theodore S. Henderson
William Burt	William O. Shepard
Luther B. Wilson	Naphtali Luccock
Thomas B. Neely	Francis J. McConnell
William F. Anderson	Frederick D. Leete
John L. Nuelsen	Richard J. Cooke

Wilbur P. Thirkield

The Bishops' Address
and
Appeal to the Church

One hundred and fifty years ago the Methodist itinerant began his work in America; began to create our Church; to help build the Republic and to assist in establishing Christ's Kingdom in the world. The history of this itinerant is full of heroism and self-sacrifice, of achievement and victory for righteousness. In the early heroic days the superannuated preacher and the effective preacher shared alike in the modest support then allowed to preachers and their families. Afterward came a changed basis for the Superannuate. He was granted what the Church chose to give, the collection being regarded as a benevolence and its apportionment made on the basis of the supposed necessities in each case. To-day our Church, acting in increased generosity and larger justice, declares that—

"The Claim to a Comfortable Support Inheres in the Gospel Ministry"—

That this claim is not a gratuity nor a charity, and is not forfeited by retirement from active service.

The Methodist Episcopal Church now puts its retired minister upon a half-pay basis, reckoned on the years of service, and thus stands alongside those governments and corporations which grant old age or service pensions to those faithful servants who through age or illness are unable to do the work they love.

The General Conference of 1912 authorized a general and thorough canvass of the Church during this quadrennium for a Jubilee Gift of Five Million Dollars to the funds of the various Annual Conferences and to the Permanent Fund of the Board of Conference Claimants. The year 1915 has been chosen as the year for the Veterans' Jubilee. The words can be calmly written, but this bare statement is thrilling and inspiring beyond all words. In our wide reach we have three thousand retired ministers, men who received the Church from the heroic past and handed it down to us. Their day of active toil is past; their day of suitable recognition is at hand. We have on our Roll of Honor an equal number of women, the widows of men who have fallen, women whose services have often equaled and whose sacrifices have equaled and often surpassed the services and sacrifices of their husbands. In addition to this we have more than five hundred minor orphans to whom the Church stands, in God's name, as "Father to the Fatherless." These all constitute the beloved company for whom the Church now inaugurates this new Campaign.

Their Just and Proper Annual Claims, estimated on the Disciplinary plan, amount to one million six hundred thousand dollars. The aggregate seems very large, but the average pitifully small. To meet this, the Church now raises one million one hundred thousand dollars annually as follows: The Chartered Fund, the oldest institution of Methodism, provides $3,600; the Book Concern, the magnificent sum of $300,000; the Board of Conference Claimants, $25,000; annual contributions from the churches, $500,000; Annual Conference endowments, $150,000; and from miscellaneous sources amounts are provided which bring up the total assets to $1,100,000; leaving a net annual liability of $500,000. This is so nearly perfect that we ought to go on to perfection.

We gladly report that since 1908 the annual distribution to Conference Claimants has increased half a million dollars, from $600,000 then to $1,100,000 now. But the Church is still half a million dollars below the moderate standard of "comfortable support," and as yet not one Retired Preacher in ten receives as much as $300. Our task as a Church is to provide $1,600,000 annually, the sum necessary to meet what the Laymen at Indianapolis called—

"The Supreme Claim of the Retired Veterans."

While there is a continued increase of income from sources enumerated above, the Campaign of 1915 is intended to add at least $5,000,000 to the permanent investments held by the Annual Conferences and by the Board of Conference Claimants. The successful issue of this Campaign, together with the normal increase from other sources, will enable Annual Conferences to provide the full legal Annuity for all Claimants. To raise such an amount would be a large task for a small Church, but it is only a good day's work for the Methodist Episcopal Church. If entered upon with zeal, enthusiasm, and intelligent cooperation, it can be completed during the Sesqui-Centennial Year.

The Laymen at Indianapolis declared this to be "the supreme claim of the Retired Veterans for an adequate support in their old age." If this be true, then the supreme claim should for once be given the supreme place. Its fundamental righteousness, its appeal to our finer sympathies and affections, its immediate urgency ought to give it such place in 1915 that the "Supreme Claim" shall be fully met.

This, then, is our Appeal to the Church in behalf of our Veterans.

The Church which does not look after its youth will shortly have no adults to look after.

The Church which neglects the education of its youth will shortly lose its place of leadership and power in the world.

The Church which educates its ministry and then discards or casts it off as soon as old age comes will shortly have no ministry, and the Church will be gone.

God gave the Gospel, but it was brought to our homes and hearts by devoted, self-denying messengers of His grace. The world will never pay its debt to these men. But the Church will not repudiate their claim. The debt is just. It is long overdue. Let us make 1915 memorable for the Veterans!

And as we thus appeal to the Church we pledge ourselves and, as far as we may, pledge the whole Church to the full and loyal cooperation with the Board of Conference Claimants and the Annual Conferences in their plans and efforts to bring in this new and better day for the Church we love and the men we honor.

William F. McDowell,
Joseph F. Berry,
William A. Quayle,
Committee.

Adopted by the Board of Bishops in session at Washington, D. C., October 29, 1914.

(Signed) Luther B. Wilson,
Secretary.

EPISCOPAL ADDRESSES TO GENERAL CONFERENCES

THE ADDRESS AND APPEAL TO THE CHURCH in behalf of the Retired Ministers and Widows was a statement of mature convictions, as is indicated by previous declarations made to the General Conference. The address of 1904 was prepared and delivered by the imperial Bishop Foss; that of 1908, by the truly and tenderly great Goodsell; and that of 1912, by the statesman-like Cranston, who has been with the Advance Movement for his aged brethren from the very beginning of the newer and better things and whose term as Senior Bishop should see the climax of the Church's achievements for the Veteran Ministry.

The brief letters from the Bishops, which make a kind of "Round Robin" in behalf of their brothers in the retired ranks, are preceded by some words from Bishops who though dead still speak in terms of love for the aged brethren; and will be followed by letters of inspiration and approval from the entire Methodist official family.

Episcopal Address, 1904

We bring before you in review a host of Veterans of the great army of itinerant Preachers of the Methodist Episcopal Church, who have served thirty, forty or even fifty years.

Their work challenges the admiration of the Church and the respect of mankind. They went into wildernesses and frontiers, into spare and poor communities and into difficult mission fields, into poor parts of cities and planted the Church.

These are the men who created the Church, carried it out of the barns and kitchens and housed it in consecrated buildings which they had caused to be built.

These are the men who, hearing the voice of God, turned their backs on preferment, left lucrative engagements, stopped their ears to the promises of ambition and their eyes to the allurements of luxury, and took up the burdens of an itinerant life, counting all things but loss for the excellency of the knowledge of Christ.

THESE ARE THE MEN WHO BROUGHT THE GOOD NEWS to you or to your fathers and persuaded them to be reconciled to God. They may well be called 'camels journeying through the desert, browsing on thistles, laden with jewels.'

IT IS THE SUPREME COMMAND of civilization that these men be properly cared for.

EPISCOPAL ADDRESS, 1908

A plan, carefully worked out by our commission, for the better support of our superannuates, their widows and orphans, will be laid before you. God grant that it may prove to be a method so wise, acceptable and adapted to all sections that our men may work in the certainty that when age and illness destroy their pastoral activity they will have their necessities met by a grateful Church.

EPISCOPAL ADDRESS, 1912

The Board of Conference Claimants and its active Secretary have been loyal to the system outlined in the new law, and the outcome of their work is exceedingly gratifying. No more vigorous campaign has ever been waged in any interest of the Church than that carried forward during the last three years in behalf of the Fund for Conference Claimants.

The response of the Church has been prompt and generous. Including the Book Concern dividends, almost a million dollars were given for the year 1911, and a total of two and a half millions distributed in the three working years since the Board was organized—besides $1,300,000 permanently invested. We give thanks to God for this auspicious advance toward the full discharge of a sacred obligation. It is a pleasure to know that the basis of the plan is sound in principle and that its details have been so generally approved by the Conferences. We have reached sixty per cent of all claims. Now for full payment! With this assured, our faithful pastors and their dependent families will no longer dread retirement, and the Church will no more be ashamed of its ingratitude to the men who have given their lives to its service.

VOICES SILENT BUT PERSUASIVE

Though Dead, They Still Speak

Bishop Merrill

The superannuated relation is not appalling. I like the word 'superannuated' better than the word 'non-effective.' It is a good Methodist word, sanctioned and sanctified by long usage. The relation is an honorable one, and I cannot see why anyone entitled to enter it should hesitate on the threshold or dread the relation or the name of it. It is simply the recognition of the facts in one's life which have brought him up to it.

One of the weaknesses of our superannuate plan appears to be in reaching the needs of the workers who break down on the frontiers or who superannuate in the border and weaker Conferences. There seems to be no way of putting them on an equality with their brethren who work in more favorable places and superannuate in larger Conferences. The question of the support of our Conference Claimants will never be settled until a large Connectional Fund is raised, in whose dividends all the Conferences share. A Church which can give a twenty million dollar Thank Offering in three years and which contributed $35,000,000 in a single year can, and some day will, make adequate provision for the comfortable support of all her Veterans.

Bishop Warren

The Methodist Church was the first institution of any kind to establish a pension aid for its Veterans. It was begun by Asbury as the Chartered Fund. This Church far surpasses any other in the care of its heroes, and thus meets a high privilege and a solemn duty.

Bishop Walden

In 1889 I stated three things: *First,* the sacred duty of the Church to furnish the Conference Claimants with "a comfortable support"; *second,* that their right to such a support was as just as that of the Pastor, the Presiding Elder, or the Bishop; *third,* that, for these reasons, the Claimants should have a pro rata share of the amount raised for pastoral support.

It is not a new cause; it antedates the Christmas Conference; and the Disciplinary place it has always had in Annual Conference matters has held it close to the preachers. Believing that spiritual and secular affairs are so interrelated that they must be advanced together, I seized the opportunity of bringing this sadly neglected obligation to the attention of the Preachers. This was one among the many efforts by which the Church has been led to see her duty and to improve the methods for securing an ample support for Conference Claimants.

Bishop Smith

No cause before the Church is more worthy or more urgent than the support of Conference Claimants. These heroic men and women have done work for the Church for which they can never be fully paid. The least we can do for them is to give them a comfortable support in their old age. To make this support sure no method is so good as that of creating permanent funds to bring a regular income which can always be depended on.

Bishop McIntyre

Who said there is no aristocracy in Methodism? I say there is! Have I not felt that wave of holy emotion that sweeps over the Conference when the warrior of many battles unlaces his armor saying, "Bishop, I am ready to retire. Put me on the last list; last and *best!*"

Yea, with wet eyes we have watched you go from the front line to the shade of the trees, and have said, "These are our heroes. This is our 'Hall of Fame.'"

As sure as His eternal word is sure, your patience, valor, faith and service are not lost. We will love you more and more as we fare down the hill together, and on the river's brim will shout you over to Him who loved you first and will love you last, whose greeting will be, "Servant of God, well done."

I am deeply interested in all our Church work, but in my thirty years' pastorate this was always first, the Retired Preachers' Fund. If we forget them God will forget us.

THE EPISCOPAL ROUND ROBIN

VOICES PLEDGED TO THE "NEW AND BETTER DAY"

Bishop Vincent

After the Bishops' Conference had unanimously endorsed the plans for an intensive, general, cooperative campaign in 1915, we dropped a line to Bishop Vincent to inform him as to what had been done. He replied as follows:

"Any service I can render I shall be most happy to offer. Am ready to write or speak as you direct."

Bishop Cranston

God gave the Gospel, but it was brought to our homes and hearts by devoted, self-denying Messengers of His grace. The world will never pay its debt to these men, but the Church will not repudiate their claim. The debt is just. It is long overdue. A Jubilee of debt paying! Good for the General Conference. Let us make 1915 a memorable year for the Veterans.

The Board of Conference Claimants and its energetic Secretary well deserve the thanks of the entire Church for the zeal and success with which they have pressed their important trust upon the attention of the people. The Bishops are in position to know the degree and frequency of the compulsory hardships which seem to be inevitable to the itinerant Ministry, and to realize the justice of the claim conceded by the Church to the Retired Minister. It is cheering news indeed that there will be such a creditable advance over the distributions of previous years. Surely the Church will not leave these dependent men and their families to eke out an existence on two thirds of what is absolutely necessary for their support. With every honest and loyal Methodist this cause will plead for itself.

Bishop Moore

I did my best to leaven the Conference with the Cause of the Superannuates. O how I prayed that the seed might fall into good ground! God bless you in your great work more and more.

Bishop Hamilton

You know my interest in this cause and it is scarcely necessary for me to add a word to what you have said in bringing the matter to the attention of our pastors.

Bishop Berry

The Board of Conference Claimants has made a great beginning. Even its most sanguine friends scarcely expected so much to be accomplished so soon. Now a strong pull and a pull all together will send it forging ahead in glorious style. It is a cause which appeals directly to every Minister who will surely be its ardent friend. The laymen are showing deep interest. Some are giving and others will give if the cause is presented, and I bespeak cordial and united support in all the Conferences now under my care.

By action of the Bishops, you have right of way this coming year. I discover quite a strong revival of interest in Conference Claimants and their claims. You are certainly pushing a vigorous crusade, and it will tell.

Bishop McDowell

The Church which educates its ministry and then discards it or casts it off as soon as old age comes will shortly have no ministry, and the Church will be gone.

I am very glad of an opportunity to join in the message of good cheer to the Retired Ministers and widows, not alone and not chiefly because of the increased funds distributed to those who have nobly served the Church, but because of the increased interest in the servants of the Church which this fund represents. If the Church gave its Retired Ministers more money and less love at the same time, no true minister would care for it; for after all, our great earthly reward is the love of the brethren; just as our high heavenly reward is the love of our Father.

Bishop Bashford

The proper care of the veterans of the nineteenth century gives the best assurance of recruits for the still more tremendous battles of the twentieth century.

Bishop Burt

One of the most inspiring and helpful hours in all my Conferences is when I call the Roll of the Veterans. I invite them to the front and ask them to speak in order that their example and messages may kindle enthusiasm in the young men. There is just one regret present on every such occasion, and that is the little we have to give to these heroic men, and to the widows and orphans of those who have been called up higher. The one cause that the Church cannot neglect and maintain its self-respect is that of the Veterans.

Bishop Wilson

America has not yet recognized its obligation to the early itinerants who, in the days of the fathers wrought the mighty elements of conscience and faith into the fabric of our national life. Those heroic itinerants have traveled on and passed within the City. But it must never be said that the Methodism of the Twentieth Century is forgetful of them or indifferent to the obligation which the present sustains to the past. It is not too much to ask that this unpaid debt to the fathers be transferred to their successors, and that this obligation be met, as we meet the other honest claims which are upon us. The service which these men of God have rendered is of such nature that there are no equivalents for it in monetary values; and because of this it may seem scarcely proper to attempt expression of indebtedness in such sordid things as silver and gold. The fact is that neither here nor elsewhere is it possible to pay for love and sacrifice; but it is the common instinct of humanity to recognize even debts we cannot pay, and, as nearly as we may, interpret sentiment in substantial offerings. It will be conceded perhaps that from the beginning the acceptance by the Church of ministerial service involved the guarantee of fair support to those who served; but far beyond such formal debt—which some might deem explicit and others inferential—is the real claim which every honest soul in Methodism must recognize, and which we must in some appropriate way try to meet now that we are called to consider it and the opportunity for suitable expression is presented. As members of a great communion let us give worthy response to the call which Methodism is sounding through the Board of Conference Claimants in the 1915 Campaign.

Bishop Neely

You can count on the Bishops for leadership or anything else they can do to forward the great work of securing an adequate support for Conference Claimants. They will take any burden that you may put on them that they can possibly carry. The churches and the laymen must underwrite the guarantee to a comfortable support by providing sufficient permanent investments to secure a dependable pension.

Bishop Nuelsen

The Methodist Veterans of Europe sent hearty greetings to their Brothers beloved in America. There are fifty-five Retired Methodist Ministers in Europe, scattered over the Continent from the land of the midnight sun to sunny Italy. They represent eight Annual Conferences, seven nationalities, and as many languages. A noble band of workers they are. They belong to the first generation of European Methodists, who laid the foundations. They were pioneers.

How their hearts are cheered, when at the Annual Conferences I present to them your affectionate greetings; not so much because they receive a dividend from America—as much as they appreciate and need financial assistance—but by the assurance that the heart of the great Church is beating with theirs. The moral effect of the work of the Board of Conference Claimants on both ministers and laymen is most excellent.

It must be exceedingly gratifying for you to know how the Church rallies at your call. May God's abundant blessing be upon your work and upon the noble army of Veteran Preachers.

Bishop Quayle

A handshake with our brethren beloved who are scarred and wounded and ready in every way to die—to the Retired Ministers of our beloved Methodism. Their name is sweet and their works do follow them. Retired ministerial support is no longer benevolence but a salary for which let us thank God devoutly. As regards the building up of an adequate fund to supplement the support from the pastoral charges, the only thing to be said is that the most we can do is the least we dare to do.

May the heat not be too great for them to bear, nor the winter too cold, because of the summer in their hearts.

Bishop Lewis

The obligation created by that abandon to financial consequences characteristic of Methodist preachers in the execution of the task assigned to them by the Church; the modest needs, unsupplied, of the worthiest band of men and women in all the land; God's generous bounties distributed among a grateful people whose prosperity is in large measure attributable to faithful pastors and teachers; the unanimous voice of the General Conference inspiring, and Bishops and Secretary leading the Church to actually do that which every member knows to be just and generous, are the signs of the victory which shall be ours when a *minimum* of five millions of dollars shall be placed to the service of this noble company of Retired Methodist Preachers, their wives and their widows. I am anxious to do everything in my power to help in this worthy cause. I believe in it with all my heart and sincerely thank you for your masterful leadership.

Bishop Hughes

I have heard the words again and again, but no Methodist clergyman has ever yet gone to the poorhouse, and none ever will. To spread such false rumors is a contemptible injustice to the Church, and is not fair to its future.

I am writing to offer a very hearty second to the appeal that Dr. Hingeley makes in behalf of the brethren who are now superannuated. I urge that you put much stress on the Connectional Fund. The final and practical evidence of the close brotherhood of our Ministry, as well as our appreciation of that brotherhood, may be seen in our attitude toward this offering.

Bishop Bristol

I am in close sympathy with the work now being done to meet the demands of the General Conference for the Five Million Dollars asked for Conference Claimants, and to which the Bishops gave their unanimous approval last spring. I hope that the Conferences in the Omaha Area will take advantage of this Church-wide movement to provide sufficiently for the Retired Preachers, widows and orphans.

Bishop Henderson

What a great year 1915 promises to be in the history of the world! Men are looking forward and predicting wonderful things for the betterment of the race, because of the possibilities which they see locked up in these twelve months. We are looking for Methodism to thrive, of course. We are looking for better churches and better preachers and better members, and we are looking for better care of all our interests: our churches, our people and our preachers. What a year it will be for the Methodist preacher if the Church hears the cry for the Five Million Dollar investment for its veterans! It will be a sad year for many a man who has labored his life away for the Church and must now give place to youth and vigor; but what a difference for such a man to find that the Church will take care of him, as he has tried to take care of the Church!

Every Methodist owes much to the Methodist preacher. Some of us owe all that we are religiously to some preacher who to-day is having a few dollars doled out to him each year in return for the very best of a whole life given to the Church. For pride's sake, we should be ashamed; for love's sake, we will not allow it. The whole Church hears the call, for it comes from every quarter of the world-wide field; the whole Church must heed the call, for these are her own, who have helped to make her what she is.

Bishop Shepard

The cause of the Veteran has always seemed to me a sacred one. Love for the Master and the brethren unite to make us faithful to the men who laid the foundations.

To the older preachers of Methodism the truth was fire in their bones, and their messages burned on their lips. It was, "Woe is me if I preach not the Gospel in that schoolhouse, in that barn, on that common, two or three times a day." They were flames of fire and voices of thunder going through the land. Their history is a Book of the Acts of the Modern Apostles; a history of the campaign of the Soldiers of the Cross.

They have ceased a bit now because the silver cord is slackened and the wheel is shaky at the cistern; but they remain with us a while, lest we forget. While they remain they are the sacred wards and charge of the Church to which they gave their lives. They left their tentmaking, their nets, everything, that they might preach everywhere, almost without money and altogether without price. They left all to follow Christ and Paul and Asbury. Like their Lord, they became poor that we might be rich. Common gratitude, and above all, Christian love—love because of work's sake if we are not blessed with personal acquaintance with them—bids us remember them. Better, as sons in the Gospel we should give them their meed of reverence and the kindly care due to fathers.

Bishop Luccock

Slowly the Church is awakening to a worthy appreciation of the work of Methodist ministers and their wives in building up the kingdom of God on earth. They have been faithful toilers on the King's highway. They built themselves into the Church and into the Republic. All are "numbered with the saints," and not a few of them deserve to be enrolled among the "noble army of martyrs."

The growing solicitude of the Church for the welfare of its aging ministers is beautiful and gracious. Multitudes who, in manifold ways, have entered into the fruit of their labors, give to this fund "not grudgingly nor of necessity," but cheerfully and generously; recognizing the care of the Veterans to be a privilege as well as an obligation of love and honor. All hail! leaders and victors of the conquering host! "The Church of Christ salutes you!"

Bishop McConnell

Anxiety over material affairs can easily reach a point where it impairs the efficiency of the preacher of the truth. Wise lawyers have a saying that if a lawyer begins to "watch the ticker" he is lost—that is to say, lost as a lawyer, though he may become a success as a money-maker. If the minister has to watch the ticker or any other indication of the ups and downs of money values, he is lost as a preacher. It was this universal truth, perceived in his deep understanding of human nature that made Jesus so anxious that his disciples should not be troubled by material concerns.

I congratulate you on the work you are doing for the Retired Preachers. There is no more progressive enterprise afoot in our Church to-day than the effort to care suitably for the Retired Ministers. The movement is in line with the wisest social thinking as well as with the best Christian spirit. May you have the very largest success.

I rejoice in your success, I believe in your work not only for its direct aid to the Preachers, but because of its general social influence. The Methodist Church ought to take the lead in showing to other institutions and to the community as a whole, the duty of caring for the old age of faithful servants who in their prime wrought for the welfare of men.

Bishop Leete

None of the world's aged workers ought to be obliged to pass their final years in penury or in fear of want.

Because I believe in service pensions for all Veterans, and because I know the great sacrifices required of men in the Christian Ministry I hail the day of the generous support of Retired Preachers and their families. Teachers, firemen, policemen, soldiers and the hosts of public and private servants whose future has now been provided for and made secure are not to be considered more worthy than are the faithful souls whose toil and rigid self-denial laid the foundations and built the walls of Christian institutions, created the moral atmosphere in which alone righteous government is possible, and contributed largely to the comforts and to the safety of social life. How great a debt is due to those who have taught virtue, have led advanced movements, have comforted the sick and dying and have brought the fact of God into the lives of men.

The leaders of the Church have not amassed fortunes, acquired high stations or achieved fame. They have given their all for Christ's kingdom, and for man's good. Now care for them—the old, the weak, the gentle, loving pastors and friends of other days as well as of the present. Light up their eyes with the joy of just recognition. Smooth out the furrows of care by removing altogether the dread of indigency. Straighten bowed forms with the sense of self-respecting independence. Then add frequent tributes of appreciation and of affection, and the cup of the forgotten, the burdened, the sorrowing, will overflow with well deserved happiness.

Bishop Cooke

In pleading for Conference Claimants I would change the emphasis from charity to justice. It is not so much the question of support for the ministry as it is that of the maintenance of organized religion. How can the Church become the great leader of humanity and set the tune for the world to sing by unless she has preachers who can pitch the key, and can command the respect and reverence of men who come out of educational institutions? We should put the question of a dependable pension for Retired Ministers before the people until they grasp the thought that it is for the sake of religion itself that we are planning this great thing.

Bishop Thirkield

The report of the increased offerings for our Conference Claimants is gratifying and inspiring. When one contemplates the good cheer, comfort and help brought into the lives of hundreds of our noble army of Retired Ministers, it raises a shout of joy. A thousand blessings on the noble work of the Board of Conference Claimants.

MISSIONARY BISHOPS

Bishop Thoburn

The tendency and drift of the times is in the direction of "retired lists" for faithful workers, both within and outside the Church. It is an instinct of the age, and no Church can afford to ignore it.

BISHOP J. E. ROBINSON

Right glad I am to believe that the efforts of the Board of Conference Claimants to devise more liberal things for the proper support of the Retired Ministers of our beloved Church appear certain to meet with encouraging response. From my heart I say: Not a mite less for a single one of the Church benevolences; but more, *vastly more,* at this opportune time, to make it possible for adequate support to be secured for the good men who have valiantly borne the burden and heat of the day, into whose successful labors we have been privileged to enter.

BISHOP JOHN W. ROBINSON

He has a right to it. The Church acknowledges that right. He needs it. The Church can easily supply that need.

It is this argument, that the Retired Minister greatly needs and has a clear right to a modest livelihood in his old age, and that the Church both acknowledges that right and its ability to meet it, that is going to carry the campaign for a Jubilee endowment fund for Conference Claimants to a successful termination. So long as the Church is true to its obligations there can be no other logical outcome to the proposition.

BISHOP EVELAND

Our Nation pensions the soldiers who risked their lives for the Flag. Can the Church do less for the men who burn up their lives in its service? This generation is building upon the foundations laid by others. It must not leave these Foundation Builders to a helpless and uncared for old age. It will indeed be "A Blot upon the Escutcheon" of Methodism if we fail to make full and adequate provision for the Retired Preachers. May divine wisdom and strength be given to you to carry to complete success the great Campaign upon which you have entered.

THE INAUGURATION CONFERENCE

Convention Greetings

"Washington, D. C., October 28, 1914.

"To the Bishops of the Methodist Episcopal Church,

"Dear Brethren:

"The Convention in the interests of Retired Ministers, composed of representatives of thirty-five Annual Conferences, now in session at the Metropolitan Memorial Church, Washington, D. C., sends you greetings.

"We are glad of this opportunity of expressing to you our thanks for the leadership furnished by you in planning the 1915 CAMPAIGN for raising the $5,000,000 ordered by the General Conference, and our confidence in the success which will come to the Campaign conducted under Episcopal leadership.

"Your fidelity to this great interest has brought great joy to the Retired Ministers, who rejoice that their Chief Pastors are earnest and solicitous in their behalf.

"We anticipate with pleasurable expectation the great meeting to be held by you in the Metropolitan Church on Thursday night when the

Address and Appeal to the Church,

prepared under your direction, will be presented. We know that the Address will ring true to this Cause, and will find a glad response in the hearts of the people.

"The plan suggested at your Spring Meeting, of each Bishop organizing the work in his own Area, gives promise of large success; and we are confident that in every Area the Ministers and laymen will gladly follow the leadership of the resident Bishop.

"Should it be consistent with your other duties, the Convention will be highly honored by your presence at any time during the session, either as individuals or as a body."

Invitation to the Bishops

At the morning session of the Bishops' Conference Dr. J. B. Hingeley, Corresponding Secretary of the Board of Conference Claimants, extended to the Bishops the following formal invitation to the Inauguration Mass Meeting:

"WASHINGTON, D. C., OCTOBER 29, 1914.

"TO THE CONFERENCE OF BISHOPS,

"DEAR BROTHERS:

"Three thousand one hundred and eighty Retired Methodist Ministers will leave their gardens and the labors by which they help to keep the wolf from the door, and will assemble at the Metropolitan Memorial Church, in the Capital City of the great Nation which their labors have made secure, waiting to hear from your lips the fulfillment of this pledge made by you last April:

"*'We pledge our hearty cooperation to this Campaign in all ways.'*

"Accompanying them will come three thousand one hundred and twenty-three heroes' widows, with faces shining through their tears, in joyful expectation that the Church is about to fulfill the promises made to them of a comfortable support, while they are waiting triumphant reunion with those whom we lovingly call 'Brothers.'

"Nestling in their arms, or seated at their side, will be five hundred bereft orphan children, for whom the Methodist Episcopal Church stands as 'Father of the Fatherless.'

"All these await you in the church where the great Methodist martyr, President McKinley, worshiped, to listen to your solemn pledge of leadership in their Cause.

"We call these heroes of the Cross 'Veterans.' They long since learned to follow where the Bishops lead, and they know what it means when the Bishops of the Methodist Episcopal Church approve the 'purpose to raise Five Million Dollars for this worthy Cause during this quadrennium!'

"They know what to expect when you assign a McDowell, a Berry and a Quayle to prepare an

ADDRESS AND APPEAL TO THE CHURCH;

and they have not forgotten the many messages that the Church has already received from your pens, nor the militant words of your senior Bishop, that though

"'The world will never repay its debt to these men, the Church will not repudiate their claim.'

"To the holy fellowship of these seven thousand Conference Claimants, I invite you to-night. They are represented by the leaders of their Cause in every Conference east of

Illinois, together with some from the Pacific coast. Never before were you honored with such an invitation. The whole Church awaits you, and as it listens to the Roll Call of the Bishops, will hear also the responses of those whose words are preserved in the literature of this great Cause: McIntyre, Walden, Warren, Bowman, Joyce, Merrill—would you know the others, call the Roll of all who have gone—who have guided legislation, inspired enthusiasm and brought joy to generations of Retired Preachers. Four million Methodists will scan to-morrow's papers to read your utterance, and the entire Christian world, already attracted by the purpose of this great Convention in the Capital City, will take new courage by the emphasis you will give to the daily increasing interest in pensions for the aged.

"The laymen of the Church, who at Indianapolis called this

"*'The Supreme Claim of the Veteran Preachers'*

await your word and leadership in this great movement, which to-day is the common task of the entire Christian Church.

"Your Address and Appeal to the Church will bring the benediction of Christly joy to six thousand Claimants' homes, and to almost two-score thousand Methodist parsonages.

"The Church awaits your word, and prays that in delivering this Message the divine inspiration may make you Prophets of the Lord.

"Truly yours, in the name of all Veteran Preachers,

"JOSEPH B. HINGELEY."

THE WHITE HOUSE, WASHINGTON.
OCTOBER 1, 1914.

MY DEAR DOCTOR HINGELEY:

I have your letter of September twenty-second and I hope that you will convey my greetings to those assembled at the important meeting you are planning for the twenty-seventh, twenty-eighth and twenty-ninth of October.

I sincerely hope that the cause of justice and benevolence they will meet to consider will be carried forward with the greatest success.

Sincerely yours,

WOODROW WILSON.

WASHINGTON, D. C., OCTOBER 27, 1914.

WOODROW WILSON, PRESIDENT OF THE UNITED STATES,
WASHINGTON, D. C.

HONORED SIR:

Your gracious letter of October first to the National Convention in the interests of Conference Claimants of the Methodist Episcopal Church was read before that body this afternoon. It is with pleasure that I convey to you the following resolution which was unanimously adopted by that body:

Resolved, That the Washington Convention in the interests of Retired Ministers of the Gospel have heard with great pleasure the greetings of the President of the United States. We gratefully record our appreciation of the fact that this Christian Statesman has found time in the midst of cares and responsibilities, greatly increased by existing conditions, to recognize the "Cause of Justice and Benevolence," which we are meeting to consider, and to express the hope that the Cause will be "carried forward with the greatest success." We extend to the President our thanks for his communication, and we devoutly pray that his strength may be sufficient for his task.

Resolved, That the secretary of the Convention be directed to send a copy of this Resolution to the President.

Sincerely yours, M. E. SNYDER, Secretary.

EPISCOPAL LEADERSHIP

JOINT MEETING OF THE CONFERENCE AND CONVENTION

WASHINGTON, D. C., OCTOBER 29, 1914.

At eight o'clock the Bishops met at the Metropolitan Memorial Church, Bishop Earl Cranston, Senior Bishop, presiding.

After prayer by Bishop Burt, Bishop Cranston spoke as follows concerning the Greetings from President Wilson:

The strength of such utterances as we have just heard lies in what is back of them. There is no doubt that the words of this letter from the President of the United States represent deep convictions, based on memories of the past; memories of his preacher father and the parsonage home, and of the years recalled by every preacher's son and daughter when the table was sometimes scantily laid, and luxuries were unknown because of meager income. I believe that we all feel here to-night that we have in the President of the United States a Christian gentleman as well as a Christian statesman, whose every word has been well considered from the standpoint of a devout believer in God and His truth, and in the obligations of the world to the men who proclaim the message of grace.

Bishops' Address and Appeal

Bishop Cranston introduced Bishop McDowell, saying:

Some time ago in anticipation of this Convention and of this hour which brings the deliberations of this Convention to their culmination, a committee was appointed by the Bishops to prepare an Episcopal Address and Appeal to the Church in behalf of Conference Claimants. The committee consisting of Bishops McDowell, Berry and Quayle has prepared the Address and Appeal to the Church, and it will now be read by Bishop McDowell.

Bishop McDowell made the following statement:

The document which I now read was unanimously adopted by the Board of Bishops in their session to-day. They put on it not only their signatures, but the entire weight of their personal interest and official power. (See page 295.)

The Rev. Joseph B. Hingeley, Corresponding Secretary of the Board of Conference Claimants, formally accepted the Address in the name of the Methodist Episcopal Church, as follows:

Bishop Cranston, Bishop McDowell and Brothers of the Episcopacy: The spirit of your Address and Appeal to the Church represents the spirit of the great Convention which has just closed. I assure you that your message means a great deal to these representatives of forty Conferences who have spent three days considering the problem of an adequate support for Retired Methodist Ministers. It means a great deal to all Methodist preachers and Methodist people to know that the trained, official, normal leadership of the Church is directing this great enterprise.

It is therefore with great personal joy that we receive your message, which will go out from this historic Church to all the churches and will bring gladness and confidence into Methodist parsonages and Methodist homes everywhere. Three thousand two hundred Retired Ministers, three thousand four hundred widows of brethren whom we have loved, and five hundred of their orphan children will rejoice in the fact that the 1915 CAMPAIGN has been launched by such an effective deliverance.

Ever since last spring when the 1915 CAMPAIGN was first presented to your Board until this moment, every request that we, officially representing this connectional interest, have made to any or all of you has been granted, with manifest delight to you, as well as to the great advancement of the cause. In the name of these brethren assembled and of a loyal Church, we accept this deliverance, and we will all seek to show, as far as we can, that since you so well know how to lead, we know equally well how to follow. The General Conference asked for $5,000,000, but the 1915 CAMPAIGN has taken such strong hold on the people that the Annual Conferences are projecting Annual Conference campaigns amounting to $10,000,000. The Spring Conferences have not yet determined the amount for which they will ask, but it is evident that the 1915 CAMPAIGN will not be a campaign for $5,000,000, nor for $10,000,000, but for a good round $12,000,000 or more, the investment needed at five per cent interest to provide the $500,000 that Bishop McDowell has shown you is still needed in order to pay all claims in full. Under the leadership of Christ's modern disciples, there will be the miracle of multiplying the dollars, greater even than that of multiplying the loaves and fishes—yet it will be a multiplying of the loaves of divine bounty for the aged, the widow and the orphan.

Brethren of the convention, let us rejoice that we have a leadership which, under God, is equal to the task.

Bishop Berry most earnestly and positively committed himself, his brethren, the Bishops, and all the churches, to an intensive, triumphant Campaign. (See page 325.)

Bishop Quayle in an inimitable way aroused the enthusiasm and strengthened the determination of the assembled delegates and the visitors. (Page 13.)

Bishop McConnell emphasized the meaning of such a Campaign from the viewpoint of the largest efficiency. (Page 39.)

The Senior Bishop, Earl Cranston, addressed the Convention pledging Episcopal leadership and cooperation. (Page 321.)

INAUGURAL ADDRESS

BUILDING ON A GOOD FOUNDATION

BISHOP EARL CRANSTON, D.D., LL.D.

Every Annual Conference here represented has its own plan. The methods are not uniform but all have the same fundamental purpose; the gathering of funds which shall be safely invested, and out of which there will be an annual revenue to supplement the annual offerings of the pastoral charges. I think the outlook for this general 1915 CAMPAIGN is better than that of any other church-wide undertaking of recent years, not simply because we are going about the raising of a creditable sum of money for a great object—that might be true of many enterprises, and it has been true many times—but because we are now earnestly going about *the business of being honest.* It has been a constant reflection on the Church that it has not dealt honestly with its Ministry. Every man here who has been a Preacher for forty years has suffered by unpaid balances, to be charged to profit and loss when he left the parish where the delinquency was made. Somebody owes this.

As we are starting the 1915 CAMPAIGN let us remember that it is absolutely necessary to provide annually the sum of one million six hundred thousand dollars for what we call a "comfortable support" for our Retired Ministers. Between the sum actually available to-day and that required even for this scant support there is the startling margin of five hundred thousand dollars. Who shall carry that large deficit? That is the question for the Methodist Episcopal Church. I see a long line of 3,200 Retired Ministers, old men, broken men, men with infirm health, educated men, men trained away from the ordinary lines of self-help in order that they might serve the Church; and 3,500 women, the widows of such men; and 500 of their orphan children standing before the prosperous Methodist Episcopal Church in this long drawn out line—7,000 of them in all. Will you not try in pathetic loyalty to hold these figures in mind: 7,000 claimants; and $1,100,000 paid to redeem the Church's pledge of $1,600,000; on which in these days of high prices it is paying them only sixty-five cents on the dollar. Some of these once loved pastors are going cold this winter for want of a better overcoat; some are hardly presentable in the pulpits of the churches to which they are attached; some are able to preach as well as ever in their lives, and yet have been prematurely sent to retirement by the demand of the churches for young preachers. Surely they deserve at least a little comfort till God shall call them home.

The Honor of the Church

The question who shall hold together these two ends of the problem—the honor of the Church and the unpaid annual balance of half a million dollars—is to be now answered. Who shall pay this five hundred thousand dollars a year? This 1915 CAMPAIGN for $10,000,000 says that the Church shall pay it. The records of the past show that the old men and widows and orphans have been paying it. The enlightened conscience of Methodism declares that they shall not continue to pay it by suffering penury and want. If our thrifty people were exposed to want, and denied the blessings which they had given to thousands, they would quickly find reasons for pledging that added five hundred thousand dollars annual income —5 per cent on $10,000,000—inside of six months; and nobody would be the poorer. If the whole Church, and the District Superintendents and even one thousand of the Pastors of Methodism had been here and had received the impressions that have been made on our minds, and had caught the spirit that has come upon us at this Convention, the 1915 CAMPAIGN would be an easy as well as a glorious task.

But let me tell you what we already have; our new financial plan as adopted by the General Conference and the churches, gives promise of a larger annual offering from the pastoral charges. It now seems assured that the apportionment for worn-out preachers, as it goes out in the annual askings of the churches, will be larger and more fully met than it ever has been. Next we have the growing revenue from our great Publishing House, which was founded by the early itinerants;

and the increasing dividends of the Board of Conference Claimants which has already paid $175,000 to help where help is most needed. With these resources at hand and with a rapid, urgent, compelling campaign this program of honor and honesty now sent forth will be gloriously realized in 1915.

The Bishops' Pledge

Wing the words of our Appeal with your prayers, and wherever you speak let it be known that 1915 is the *Jubilee Year* for the long-neglected Retired Ministers of the Methodist Episcopal Church and those dependent upon us on their account. God bless you, brethren, and give you the old time Methodist "liberty" wherever you speak on this great cause.

I think it is fortunate that the Bishops can plead this cause without the handicap of seeming to beg for themselves. We have no complaint to make. The Church takes good care of us. The Bishops are free to plead for their brethren. O, that every Retired Minister might feel as restful for tomorrow as the Methodist Episcopal Church has made it possible for her Bishops to feel. And for that very reason we ought to be all the more earnest, insistent and persistent in making the 1915 CAMPAIGN a complete success.

Next to the Bishops, who stand as the natural leaders of the forces of Methodism, ought to be the laymen, the possessors of all the opportunities this wonderful age and this opulent land are giving to men of brave heart and intelligent enterprise. For the sake of Christ and the Church these Ministers surrendered all these opportunities to them. Brethren of the laity, think of that! Do not make the Preachers plead for themselves. I beseech you, do not lay the burdens of the campaign on them; but let the words of the Bishops, and the awakened conscience and zeal of the laymen make good the purpose of the Church to meet its honest obligations to the men who earned the promised support long, long ago, and too long have waited the day of payment.

OFFICERS BOARD OF CONFERENCE CLAIMANTS
METHODIST EPISCOPAL CHURCH

O. H. HORTON,
Vice-President

J. B. HINGELEY,
Corresponding Secretary

E. C. CLEMANS,
Field Representative

BISHOP W. F. McDOWELL,
President

J. W. VAN CLEVE,
Second Vice-President

MARVIN CAMPBELL,
Treasurer

J. A. MULFINGER,
Recording Secretary

A CONQUERING CAMPAIGN

BISHOP JOSEPH F. BERRY, D.D., LL.D.

DEAR BRETHREN: This is not the time to talk about ways and means. I am in the presence of experts. You have discussed already the practical phases of this 1915 CAMPAIGN. All that remains for us to do to-night is to congratulate you on the success of your Convention, and to exhort you earnestly to go out from this place to put into practice the splendid ideals that you have lifted up, and the comprehensive and inspiring plans which you have formed.

A DENOMINATIONAL MOVEMENT

I am very glad that this is to be a great denominational movement. It is more denominational than our evangelistic campaigns, for in them we go to men and women and urge them to give up sinful lives and serve Jesus Christ; and we make church affiliations and church loyalty a secondary consideration, emphasizing loyalty to Jesus and surrender to him; and that is not essentially in any strict sense a denominational crusade. But the work to which you have put your hands is distinctively and enthusiastically a great denominational movement of the Methodist Episcopal Church. I am somewhat of a Methodist, and I want the 1915 CAMPAIGN to succeed because it represents a Methodist movement. Every day I rejoice in the fact that God has given me a place in this communion and I thank Him that our great Church is in these days measuring up so well to its responsibility; and coming up to the help of the Lord in these strategic times when so much is being crowded into short spaces, and when the opportunities are so golden. I make no apology whatever for the fact that I am intensely denominational. The fact is that the man who is not intensely in love with a denomination is of very little use in the Church or the world.

The man who believes that one Church is just as good as another Church, and that it is almost sinful to emphasize denominationalism, has very little sympathy in my heart. I feel like a little girl who, with a little Catholic companion, visited a Sisters' hospital. The Sister in charge took them about the place, showing them the private and public wards and the operating room, while the little girls looked around in open-eyed wonder. As they were leaving the Sister said, "My little dear, I have been wondering what Church you belong to," and the Catholic girl said, "I belong to the Catholic Church." "Thank God for that!" said the sister. Then she asked the other, "And what Church do you belong to?" And the little Methodist girl proudly answered, "I belong to the Methodist Church—and thank God for that!" That is the way I feel; and if we are going to have a great Campaign, and if it is to be brought to a successful consummation, it must be a great denominational movement, that will take hold of the heart of Methodism and arouse a mighty enthusiasm to do the work promptly and well.

An Opportune Movement

The movement is most opportune. It is a good time to strike. We have not had so good time as this for generations. The educational campaign which has been carried on concerning our obligation to pay to God what we owe Him in a systematic way is already bearing much fruit. If I had the authority I would have an educational bureau in connection with every benevolent cause in the Church which would be educating the membership, rich and poor, concerning the obligation and opportunity of systematic and proportionate paying into the treasury of God. If we could have that for even one year the results would make earth and heaven rejoice. If our people would pay one tenth into the treasury of God, how every treasury of every benevolent board, and of this institution of yours would overflow. The problem would be, how to spend properly the money that is rolling in from the generous Church.

These are great evangelistic times? Everybody is talking about religion. Last Sunday in the city of Philadelphia we had eight hundred laymen in the pulpit exhorting sinners to forsake sin and accept the Saviour of the world. Does that mean anything? It is in the air, it is everywhere. People are talking about religion. I was in a banquet of four hundred business men a few weeks ago, and expected that the men would talk politics or business, but they spent the evening talking religion. Have you observed how during the last two years the great daily newspapers have allied themselves with the Christian forces of the Republic and are specifically doing the work of evangelism? In Philadelphia when the preachers could not agree as to holding the Sunday meetings, a great newspaper, the *North American,* chartered a great special train, and took two hundred and fifty pastors to Scranton to see Billy at work, and entertained them there for three days. On the next Monday morning the preachers' meetings by a practically unanimous vote—Baptists, Presbyterians, Disciples, Methodists and Protestant Episcopalians—invited him to come, and he is coming. If, under God, Mr. Sunday leads thousands of people into the churches of Philadelphia, to whom shall be given the credit? To the publisher of that metropolitan daily newspaper who had the courage and Christian sagacity to insist that the evangelist be invited. Evangelism is in the air. Our God is marching on. The kingdoms of this world are becoming the kingdoms of our Lord and of His Christ; and it seems to me, Dr. Hingeley, that you must have been divinely guided, just at this time to launch upon the Nation and the Church this great Campaign. The revival of systematic giving and the revival of evangelism will be the foundation for this forward movement which is to win in glorious fashion.

All hail to the Ten Million Dollar Campaign! If it had been a campaign for two and a half millions it would not have interested me so much. But this Church of ours is a great Church, and we have no business attempting small things. This big Church ought to do big things; and so we are going out in the name of God to do a great thing for our Veterans. May God speed the day when the Hallelujah Chorus will sound out in commemoration of the fact that the 1915 CAMPAIGN has been a magnificent success; and that everywhere it shall be known that in the treasury of the Methodist Episcopal Church there are millions perpetually invested for the support of the Veteran Ministry.

Philadelphia, Pa. JOSEPH F. BERRY.

ADDITIONAL MEMBERS BOARD OF CONFERENCE CLAIMANTS

B. F. Adams
G. W. Brown
James Hamilton
Perry Millar

J. E. Andrus
O. P. Miller

C. W. Baldwin
E. C. E. Dorion
M. S. Marble
J. O. Pew

WE SHALL WIN

BISHOP WM. F. McDOWELL, D.D., LL.D.

President Board of Conference Claimants

I could not let the first day of this Convention go by without coming to put my own heart into it at its very beginning, and to assure you, if you need any assurance, of my utmost sympathy with the plans that are proposed by the Board of Conference Claimants and by the Annual Conferences for this magnificent thing that we are going to do.

After I came into the pulpit to-night and found my old and very dear friend, Dr. Edmund M. Mills, presiding, there came to my mind a happy coincidence. I venture to say that in 1899 Dr. Mills was put in charge of the most impossible, in many respects the most hopeless and utterly inconceivable kind of a proposition that was ever assigned to anybody by our Church; the task of raising the Twentieth Century Thank Offering of twenty million dollars. At the close of his first speech, with some measure of enthusiasm, he expressed confidence that the Church would do it. Think of a man beginning a job with any idea that it is going to be done. That is the way he did: he began with the idea that it was going to be done before he quit. When he had finished his speech and stepped down with the feeling that a man has after he has made his first speech for the first time, a venerable Preacher said to him, "I am glad that the Church has a man like you." Of course that made Dr. Mills feel good. "I am so glad," continued this good man, "that the Church has a man who knows so little that he hopes so much."

Now, Dr. Hingeley, here are you two men on the platform, and here am I, having been related to Dr. Mills in that movement, and being related to you in this. You come not to that kind of a situation. You are a man who, partly by reason of what this other man helped to accomplish, can go on with a kind of confidence that is partly born of the success of that great movement. And, please God, you do not now have to know so little that you may hope so much; *you can hope so much now because you know so much.*

This is a great thing we are at. Every once in a while we get stirred up in our minds because we have so many things going, and we say that we cannot have a Conference Claimants' campaign because we have an educational campaign; and we cannot have an educational campaign because we have a hospital campaign; and we cannot have a hospital campaign because we have a church building campaign; and we cannot have a church building campaign because we have a foreign missionary campaign; and we cannot have a foreign missionary campaign because we have a Freedmen's Aid campaign. But that is what makes it worth while to be a Methodist.

I am getting to be one of the older Bishops in the Church, and therefore I am supposed to be fairly and reasonably loyal, but I make this declaration of principle and faith to you to-night, that if I knew a Church that had in its heart more big things to do for Christ's kingdom, and more determination to do them, and more belief that it could do them than the Methodist Church has, I would go out and get into that Church. For the joy of being a Methodist is that the Methodist Church has so many big things that it can do and wants to do. Instead of worrying because we are going to start another great campaign let us be proud of the Church that has the courage, with everything else going on, to say "We will do this." For after all one of the tests of a Church is not the limited number of things it can do, but the large number of things to which it gives its heart and hand. That is the truth of it. A Church that has only one or two things going on is no Church for a man with a lot of things in his mind.

We are going to do it. It is not any part of mine to-night to do more than simply to speak this word of committal. When I was a young fellow in the school of theology more years ago than I care to mention, one evening I read in the evening paper that Mr. George William Curtis, then editor of Harper's Weekly, was going to speak in Boston Music Hall upon civil service reform. That was the day when the principle "to the victors belong the spoils" was absolutely intrenched in American politics. I went to hear Mr. Curtis.

It was a charming address; the memory of it will live with me while I live. At the close of the address, without any fuss, without raising his voice, without any indication that he had to persuade himself by the vigor with which he shouted what he was saying, but with the perfect calmness that expresses the highest confidence, he said: "Ladies and gentlemen, civil service reform is coming and is near." Then he told this story, that in the darkest days of the Civil War, when everything seemed discouraging, he called upon Mr. Lincoln and talked with him far into the night. "When we rose to separate for the night," said Mr. Curtis, "Mr. Lincoln, remembering the discouraging conversation that we had had, turned to me and, putting his hand on my shoulder, looked down into my eyes with the most patient eyes the world has seen for eighteen centuries, and said in a voice that I shall never forget, '*Nevertheless, my son, we shall win.*'

"Now," continued Mr. Curtis, "whenever I am tempted to lose heart, with reference to any good cause, or to lose heart with reference to the cause of good itself, I feel again that hand upon my shoulder, and see again those patient eyes, and hear again that confident voice saying, '*Nevertheless, we shall win,*' for victory must be first faith, and then fact: it must first be in our hearts and then in our hands."

To-night, victory is faith; to-morrow it will be fact; to-night it is in our hearts; to-morrow, please God, victory will be in our hands.

Chicago, Ill. WILLIAM F. McDOWELL.

TWO MEN

J. L. Shepard

Two men of equal heart and mind
  Go forth into the world to fight,
To win what seems the noblest good
  And battle for the right.

One weaves the fabric of his life
  Upon the loom of wealth and power
And sows the gifts that surely reap
  The plaudits of the hour.

The other holds the souls of men
  Above the lure of fame and gold,
And, toiling, leads the scattered sheep
  Into his Master's fold.

Which won success and true reward,
  As Life's exacting path he trod?
Was it the man who served himself,
  Or he who served his God?

IT COULDN'T BE DONE

Somebody said that it couldn't be done,
  But he, with a chuckle, replied
That "maybe it couldn't" but he would be one
  Who wouldn't say so till he'd tried.
So he buckled right in, with the trace of a grin
  On his face. If he worried, he hid it.
He started to sing as he tackled the thing
  That couldn't be done, *and he did it.*

Somebody scoffed: "O, you'll never do that,
  At least no one ever has done it."
But he took off his coat and he took off his hat,
  And the first thing we knew he'd begun it;
With the lift of his chin, and a bit of a grin,
  Without any doubting or quibbling;
He started to sing as he tackled the thing
  That couldn't be done, *and he did it.*

There are thousands to tell you, "It cannot be done";
  There are thousands to prophesy failure;
There are thousands to point out to you, one by one,
  The dangers that wait to assail you;
But just buckle in with a bit of a grin,
  Then take off your coat and go to it;
Just start in to sing as you tackle the thing
  That "cannot be done" *and you'll do it.*

GREETINGS TO THE CONVENTION

JUSTICE THOMAS H. ANDERSON, LL.D.
Supreme Court, District of Columbia

Mr. President, friends and members of the Convention:

I have just come from the court-room where I have been trying to reconcile the conflicting testimony of witnesses upon the somewhat doubtful theory that each one was endeavoring to tell the truth; and to apply the law of the case upon the less doubtful proposition that the lawyers would have been in agreement with the court as to the law if they had been administering it from the bench instead of engaging in a legal combat at the bar. I come from that somewhat turbulent and heated atmosphere into this serene and restful place to extend to you on behalf of the membership of Metropolitan Church and of the members of all the Methodist churches of Washington, a most hearty greeting, and a cordial welcome to this historic church and to the City of Washington, and to assure you that we are in the heartiest sympathy with the purpose of your coming. If this Convention is to succeed and to bear the fruits for which we hope and pray, we must grasp its purpose and catch its spirit. Its purpose is plainly stated in this program: its spirit is in the heart and hopes of our common Methodism, and you will catch it a little later if the spirit of this Convention has not been tugging already at your hearts.

What is that spirit? It is the spirit of fair play, the spirit of the Golden Rule: To do unto others as we would that they should do unto us. We are commanded by the Great Head of the Church to "render unto Caesar the things that are Cæsar's and unto God the things that are God's." While He thus admonishes us of our duty to the state, He likewise admonishes us of our supreme duty to God. It is in recognition of this supreme duty, not only supreme but all-comprehensive, that we are here assembled. Within close reach of that duty stand the battle-worn Veterans of our great Church. We are here, therefore, to focus our thought and sympathy upon them and upon those who are dependent upon them, within the meaning and spirit of the Golden Rule. The commanding influence of our beloved Church as a power for righteousness and civic virtue and the uncompromising foe of men and measures inimical to the advance of Christ's kingdom and the ultimate supremacy of His reign over all peoples and all nations demands not only that our Bishops, ministers and other leaders, like the leaders of great armies and strong navies, shall be trained and disciplined for high service, and shall devote their lives and talents to that service; and also that when the years of service end—when by reason of old age or other disability, they can no longer keep step with the moving column—they shall not be permitted to suffer and to be pauperized through the indifference and neglect of the Church.

The time has come, therefore, for action. We have long since recognized the necessity for this movement, but now for the first time we are lining up to meet a great and urgent need. In doing so we are simply following the humane policy of the railroads, and other great business enterprises of this country, as well as the policy of the government of the United States itself, which already has upon its pension rolls its soldiers and its sailors, and will soon have added thereto a vast civic pension list, to the end that the men who have toiled in the service of the government until they have reached the age when they are no longer able to labor and earn a living shall not be cast out unprovided for. So should the Church, following out this humane policy and recognizing the urgent necessities of the case, be quick to respond to the needs of the situation by generous voluntary gifts from its membership. We see in England an established Church with its Bishops, Archbishops, Peers of the realm, and spiritual lords of Parliament; with great cathedrals nobly endowed, and all that, but in this country we have no such establishment; and it is to the glory and usefulness of the Church that we have not. But the necessity for suitable provision for these worthy Veterans is all the more imperative. The men who under the call of God enter the ministry and dedicate their lives to His service are dependent, as a rule, upon the meager salaries voluntarily contributed by the membership of their respective congregations, with nothing to look forward to for the support of themselves and those dependent upon them when old age overtakes them, other than the wholly inadequate provision now made under our present system. This unfortunate situation should not be allowed to continue. If the spirit of the Golden Rule and the teachings of the Sermon on the Mount are to be given practical application to the present situation, let us make haste to do unto these our brethren as we would that they should do unto us.

If we do that—and I believe we will—we cannot fail. This great Campaign, which you are here inaugurating, cannot be completed in a day nor in a year. It takes four years to organize and carry to completion a presidential campaign, and if it takes as long to complete this Campaign for righteousness and simple justice—although no such time should be required—let us see to it that we do not grow weary in the fight, but that the justice and urgent need of this movement be earnestly pressed home upon the hearts and consciences of our people, to the end that the Campaign may be gloriously and quickly won.

Washington, D. C. THOMAS H. ANDERSON.

RESPONSE TO THE ADDRESS OF WELCOME

THE REV. JOSEPH W. VAN CLEVE, D.D.

2d Vice-President, Board of Conference Claimants

It is an unprecedented thing in the history of the Church that there should be a convention of this character which will spend three days considering the interests of the Veteran Preachers. Such a thing has never been even dreamed of before, and it emphasizes the fact that the Retired Minister has won an altogether new place in the thinking of the Church. We are gathered to award to him this new place in our thinking, that a little further on we may give him the place of comfort which the Church is providing.

It has always been easy to indulge in eloquence about the worn-out preachers, every one of them invested with the pathos that hovers over any man who is close to the edge of eternity; and over the line of lonely women who at times attend our Conferences, reminding us of brethren departed. It would be easy for a man who has any gift of eloquence to be eloquent about them; to heap up invective against rich men and a neglectful Church; to draw portraits of uncomplaining poverty, or to praise the heroism of days that are past and the almost unbelievable results of the labors of these men who can labor no more. But the significance of this gathering is that we have come upon a time when we feel that such things are no longer sufficient, and that the time has come to develop a broad and a consistent business policy for their care. Such a policy has been outlined, and the directions for the forward movement have been definitely given.

We have found ourselves a little embarrassed by the multiplicity of interests that seem to converge toward this one end and which as yet do not converge accurately. We have not always been quite sure of keeping out of one another's way, and have not fully coordinated the various forces that work to this end in the various parts of our great connection. But for the time being, we have moved the Capital of Methodism to the Capital of the nation that we may take counsel together, and make large and consistent plans which may be materialized into large and consistent operations; and I trust and believe that when we shall have concluded our deliberations here we will be ready to go before the Church with such a comprehensive program as will command instant acquiescence and hearty cooperation.

One of the things which give us the largest assurance of progress and success is the response we find everywhere from the thoughtful laity of the Church, such as has just been voiced by Mr. Justice Anderson. We are very grateful for this greeting and for the privilege of meeting in this significant church of Methodism, which has so much of the historic connected with it; and we shall be glad in connection with our chief Ministers and ecclesiastical leaders to devise and plan a campaign that shall so capture the imagination and liberality of the Church that at its consummation the Veteran Preacher shall come to his own, and have such a support as will enable him to retire in both comfort and dignity; having a sense of dignity himself and a knowledge that the Church itself is being dignified by the care with which it provides for its servants in their old age.

PART III. THE CLAIM SUPREME

CHAPTER II. THE 1915 CAMPAIGN

THE UNTHINKING LAYMAN

Brother Jim Jones was a Methodist of the old school; always at his place in church ready to shout, sing or pray.

Among his stock was old Bill, a black mule with nearly a third of a century faithful service to his credit.

One morning Brother Jones hitched Bill to the plow and started across the field.

"Git up!" said Brother Jones, but Bill didn't move. He just turned his head, looked mournful like at his boss and laid down. His working days were over. Brother Jones knew that, because it was the first time that Bill had ever refused to move. As he looked into the mule's eyes he knew that Bill had done his level best, and that he hated to quit. But there was no help for it; and so he turned him out to die.

That night Joe, Brother Jones' boy, said:

"Pap, what've you done with old Bill?"

"Why, son, he fell down at the plow this morning, and I turned him out to die. Guess his working days are over."

"You turned old Bill out to die! See here, Pap; ain't he been working for you all his life?"

"He sure has, son, and he worked, hard, too."

"And you goin' to church every Sunday and singin' 'I Want to Be an Angel'? Pap, do you reckon an angel would treat old Bill that way after he'd worked for him all his days?"

This was putting the thing in a new light to the old man, and Brother Jones began to feel that he had been pretty mean to old Bill. He spoke to his wife about it, and she told him that if he didn't go out and get old Bill and bring him to the barn and feed him and treat him well from that time on, she'd leave him. Every person about the place seemed to think that Brother Jones had treated old Bill outrageously mean; and he was so ashamed of himself that he sneaked down into the woods, hunted up the old mule and brought him back.

From that time on every day was Sunday for old Bill.

Was Joe right? Were Sister Jones and the hired man and the neighbors right?

Did old Bill's third of a century of faithful geeing and hawing and plowing and mowing beget DUTY?

And I wonder if old Preacher's service begets duty.

HISTORY OF THE 1915 CAMPAIGN

Dr. Hingeley's Report, 1912

In the report made by the Corresponding Secretary of the Board of Conference Claimants at the Annual Meeting in February, 1912, the following suggestions were recorded:

The Veterans' Jubilee

The suggestion of Dr. E. L. Watson, of the Baltimore Conference, that since the next quadrennium included the Sesqui-Centennial of American Methodism, it should be made emphatic by raising a million dollars for the Permanent Fund of the Board of Conference Claimants, has been echoed in different parts of the country. Mr. J. P. Holland, formerly of Milford, Del., introduced the following resolution in the California Lay Electoral Conference, and it was unanimously passed:

"Whereas, The next Quadrennium, 1912-1916, includes the one hundred and fiftieth Anniversary of American Methodism, the tremendous growth of which has been due in the largest sense to the fidelity, energy and self-sacrifice of a Ministry which is represented to-day by the Superannuated Preachers, who have so often yielded to other causes that only during one brief quadrennium has the Church systematically and earnestly pushed their claims on the attention of our people or legislated directly in their interest. Therefore, be it

"*Resolved,* 1, That we memorialize the General Conference of 1912 to assign to the Church, during the next quadrennium, the holy task of so increasing the annual income for the superannuates that the promise of a comfortable support, sacredly made to them when they enter the Methodist Ministry, shall be fulfilled to those who are to-day in the honored ranks of the Veteran Preachers.

"2. That to secure such comfortable support for the future, we request the General Conference to call upon the Church for a Million Dollars for the Permanent Fund of the Board of Conference Claimants, that it may have ample funds available to lead the Church in this movement, and to provide for necessitous cases and needy Conferences.

"3. That we request the Bishops to include this movement

in the Episcopal Address, and to urge this program on the attention of the General Conference with such recommendation as may seem to them to be wise, to the end that the Church may graciously and sufficiently provide for the superannuates who come from the pastorate, as it does for those who enter the Honor Roll of the Veteran Ministry from the General Superintendency."

Quite a number of Annual and Lay Conferences passed similar resolutions, memorializing the General Conference to set aside the next quadrennium for Conference Claimants.

Dr. Hingeley, Corresponding Secretary, added:

"It is very fitting that the several Jubilees which have been held, for Africa, Korea, China, etc., should be followed by a great Jubilee for the cause of the Veteran Preacher; and it is hoped that the next General Conference will assign to the Board the task of leadership in this movement, and I suggest that a memorial covering the same be sent from this Board to the General Conference and that the Members of the Board who may be delegates to the next General Conference be requested to urge this matter on the attention of the delegates.

"The Hebrew Jubilee was held every fifty years. The Old Preacher has waited three times fifty years for his Jubilee. How dare we refuse him!"

The General Conference, 1912

In accordance with these suggestions, the Board memorialized the General Conference, which took action as follows:

Report No. 1, the Jubilee Gift

"Whereas, The year 1912 is the Centenary of the first delegated General Conference and opens the quadrennium in which the one hundred and fiftieth anniversary of American Methodism falls and should be fittingly observed. Therefore be it

"*Resolved,* That the General Conference authorize a general canvass of the Church, during this quadrennium, in behalf of the various endowment funds for Conference Claimants, for a Jubilee Gift of $5,000,000, the same to comprise all gifts to the funds of the several Annual Conferences, and also to the Connectional Permanent Fund of the Board of Conference Claimants."

The Action of the Board, 1913

At the Annual Meeting of the Board held in February, 1913, the Board adopted the following:

"We note with pleasure that part of the report of the Corresponding Secretary concerning his interviews with representatives of Annual Conferences, relative to cooperation between Annual Conferences and the Board of Conference Claimants, which indicates willingness on their part to engage in such combined effort. This will not only directly increase the amounts in the hands of the Board of Conference Claimants, but will enable the Board largely and effectively to promote the general cause by helping to increase the funds in the hands of Annual Conferences."

Dr. Hingeley's Report, 1914

Meanwhile the Corresponding Secretary had come into sympathetic relations with the leaders in many great Conferences, and in February, 1914, was able to report to the Board as follows:

"I believe our plans are practicable and that large results will be accomplished by cooperative effort. Nineteen hundred fourteen should be the year when the Annual Conferences shall assume their entire responsibility for Retired Ministers and other claimants and provide sufficiently for present needs. Nineteen hundred fifteen must be the year of cooperation between the Board and the Annual Conferences to bring from hiding $5,000,000 of God's money, now 'hid in napkins' and subject to moth and rust and loss; and 1916 should see the present provisions for the care of Retired Ministers and widows so far realized as to make it advisable to adjust standards of support on a more liberal basis."

After mature deliberation the Board adopted the following resolution:

"We believe that the time has come when some aggressive movement should be made to bring this Board and the secretaries or other representatives of Annual Conference Superannuate Funds, Preachers' Aid Societies and similar organizations, as well as representatives of the Conferences which have as yet no organization, into a more perfect understanding that we are working for the same end. Therefore,

"We recommend that this Board take the initiative by calling a great conference of secretaries and representatives to meet with the Board at the time most advisable. To this end the cooperation of the Bishops should be secured."

Group Meetings

The General Conference had already taken action, looking forward to an intensive campaign for Five Million Dollars as the Sesqui-Centennial Gift for Conference Claimants; and in accordance with this recommendation of the Board, Dr. Hingeley held group meetings of Conference representatives at Minneapolis, Chicago, Columbus, Cleveland, Syracuse, Boston, New York, Philadelphia and Baltimore, all of which unanimously recommended that an intensive and extensive campaign for Five Million Dollars during the year 1915 be projected, and requested the Bishops to cooperate in the arrangements and to give episcopal leadership.

Bishops' Meeting at Germantown

Meanwhile the spring Conferences endorsed the 1915 CAMPAIGN, and on April 30, 1914, a committee representing the several group meetings waited upon the Board of Bishops, who unanimously adopted the following:

"*Resolved,* That the Bishops have heard with pleasure the representations of the Board of Conference Claimants and of the several Annual Conferences, concerning the plans under contemplation for the larger and more adequate provision for the care of our Conference Claimants.

"2. That without having before us the details of plans proposed, we heartily approve the general purpose to raise the sum of Five Million Dollars for this worthy cause during this quadrennium.

"3. That a committee of three Bishops be appointed at this meeting to prepare an address to the Church to be adopted at our following meeting, for the launching of the Campaign proposed for the year 1915.

"4. That we pledge our hearty cooperation to this Campaign in all ways."

The following Committee was appointed to prepare the Address and Appeal to the Church: Bishops McDowell, Berry and Quayle.

In sending these resolutions to the Church the senior Bishop sent the following message:

"God gave the Gospel, but it was brought to our homes and hearts by devoted, self-denying Messengers of His grace. The world will never pay its debt to these men, but the Church will not repudiate their claim. The debt is just. It is long overdue.

"A Jubilee of debt paying! Good for the General Conference. Let us make 1915 a memorable year for the Veterans.

EARL CRANSTON."

During the summer of 1914 Dr. Hingeley met district superintendents, Conference agents, trustees, stewards and other representatives of thirty fall Conferences, which made recommendations for the 1915 CAMPAIGN, which were subsequently adopted by the Annual Conferences.

THE 1915 CAMPAIGN

The 1915 CAMPAIGN is not merely for $5,000,000. It is for whatever amount of money, as determined by the several Annual Conferences, is necessary in order to provide *a dependable annuity or pension for all claimants for all time to come.* On December 31, 1914, the total amount so designated exceeds $12,000,000, with several Conferences yet to report. When this amount, in addition to present holdings, is in the treasuries of the several Annual Conferences, and in the Permanent Fund of the Board of Conference Claimants, Annual Conferences will be on the one hundred per cent basis of payment, will be able to provide the full annuities as fixed by the Discipline and to add a sufficient amount in the special cases so as to insure a "comfortable support" for each of the seven thousand Claimants of Methodism.

WASHINGTON INAUGURATION CONVENTION

Such was the preparatory work which brought the Church to the Climactic Day, October 29, 1914, when, after the close of the Washington Inauguration Convention, the Bishops delivered their "Address and Appeal to the Church."

SOME NEW THINGS

THE NEW ATMOSPHERE AND PURPOSE

At the Central New York Conference I was introduced at ten o'clock, and to my question, "How much time have I?" Bishop Burt replied, "You have all the time until adjournment," two hours; and the Bishop, Dr. Keeney, Dr. Greene and myself took all the time. At two o'clock I was called to speak at a joint meeting of the laymen and preachers, and again at six o'clock at the banquet of the Laymen's Association. Do you wonder that the Campaign is progressing in the Central New York Conference when the cause of the Retired Preacher does not have to beg for a hearing, and laymen like Brother Transue bring the message of their devotion!

Area Meetings

In addition to the meeting of the representatives of the six Conferences of the Buffalo Area, called by Bishop Burt, I had held two meetings at Syracuse in preparation for the Annual Conference. Every District Superintendent of the Conference is at this Convention: Mills, Pittman, Brown, Riegel. The Conference did not beg off from their duty to their Retired Brethren, but *asked for the full disciplinary apportionment*—enough money to pay present claims in full. In this the Conferences have not been playing fair with their aged brethren. The Bishops' claim, the District Superintendents' claim and the Pastors' claim are asked for at one hundred cents on the dollar, as they should be, but the laity are being asked to pay only forty, sixty or seventy cents on the dollar of the claims of the Retired Preachers. Unless Pastors, District Superintendents and Bishops are ready to accept their own claims on the basis of forty, sixty or seventy cents on the dollar, they ought not to be willing that the Retired Preachers should have their claims discounted. This is not laying an added burden on the pastoral charges. *The obligation is now there, unmet,* and the 1915 CAMPAIGN is to help the laymen fulfill their responsibility to the entire Ministry.

On Saturday night a representative of the Washington Times came to me. He had been assigned the duty of writing the story of the Convention. After he had been given the information he came to seek, he said that he would like some "human interest" or "hard luck stories," some statement of the poverty and penury of the old Preachers. I showed him the larger vision and meaning of the Campaign, and said: "My brother, the Methodist Church is not dealing out hard luck stories. We have gone beyond that. It is true that some Methodist Preachers are poor, but they consider their poverty 'in executive session' and enjoy the luxury of keeping their poverty to themselves. We are not pleading poverty; we have no 'hard luck' stories to tell; we are a party of Christian gentlemen, ministers and laymen, members of the Methodist Episcopal Church, who have mutual obligations, which we are seeking to meet fairly and squarely, not on the basis of hard luck stories, nor the plea to pity the poor old penniless Preacher, but on the basis of the righteousness of the claims of the Veteran Ministers and the joyful willingness of the laymen of the Methodist Episcopal Church to meet in full all the obligations of the Discipline." A fine article on the retiring competency for Retired Ministers appeared the next day.

A Laymen's Movement

It is well to remember, when speaking of the Disciplinary provisions for Conference Claimants, that half of the members of the General Conference who made the legislation were laymen and that the Magna Charta statement that "the claim for a comfortable support *inheres in the ministry* and is not invalidated by the retirement," was written by a layman, Robert T. Miller. I have yet to find an intelligent layman who does not ring true on this question. I have never had any difficulty in the Lay Associations or Lay Conferences. In three instances, when Annual Conferences were asking less than the law required, memorials were sent over from the Lay Conference to the Annual Conference requesting that the full amount be apportioned.

In another Laymen's Association, when the stewards hesitated to ask for the full amount, the laymen stated that they were not begging off, and would gladly do what the law required. At the Rock River Conference a year ago, Dr.

James Rowe, since gone to his reward, asked, "Dr. Hingeley, how much money must the churches of the Rock River Conference raise in order to pay the claims in full?" They had been apportioning $15,000. I replied, "$30,000." The apportionment was fixed at $30,000, and they paid their Claimants ten thousand dollars more this year than last, and commissioned the Rev. C. A. Kelley to raise $500,000 for the Preachers' Aid Society.

The West Ohio Conference Commission recommended a campaign for $400,000. The Conference Trustees lowered the recommendation to $300,000, but the Conference made it $500,000.

Promises Realized in Cash

I hope that by the time this Convention closes every one of us will be so filled with determination and enthusiasm that the Spring Conferences will put themselves into line, and that what is needed shall be accomplished throughout the entire Church: *Enough money to meet all obligations in full.* I am thankful that we are at last seeing the whole Church moving as one body. We have the natural leadership, that of our Bishops and District Superintendents, and the whole Church, laymen and preachers, are forwarding the work, not merely because some aged or poor man needs help, but because the Methodist Episcopal Church would so meet its obligations to the Ministry that the young man who takes his first vows shall know that if he serves God in the Methodist Ministry until old age comes, the Methodist Episcopal Church has the money invested to take care of him until God shall call him home. And there will be the delightful thought for the young man that while he is waiting the eligibility of old age, the income on the money will be providing for other blessed brethren, and that when he passes along, generations of Methodist Preachers will be strengthened for their duty with the knowledge that the money is there.

The promises are good enough to rejoice the heart. Let us cash these promises, not only for the old man sitting in the front pew, but for ourselves as well, for to-morrow our dull ears will make us seek the front pews; and for generations of young preachers whom we would lure into the Ministry.

THE NEW EMPHASIS

One of the most helpful things connected with the present campaign is the fact that the emphasis is being put at a new place. The old plea, "pity the poor old preacher" on account of his poverty has been supplanted by the new plea to help enable the Methodist Episcopal Church to *make good its promises* to the Retired Preachers. The liabilities for Conference Claimants can be determined by any accountant who reads the law and understands the situation. The resources can be determined from published reports; the balance, which indicates the net liability, is a matter of subtraction of resources from liabilities; and the proposition of the 1915 CAMPAIGN is to eliminate the net liabilities by making the resources equal to the liabilities.

As far as the American Conferences are concerned the gross liabilities to-day are about $1,600,000; the gross resources are less than $1,100,000, which makes the net liabilities in excess of $500,000. On account of unwillingness to face the proposition of so great a net liability, there has been a tendency in the Conferences not to state the entire gross liability. This ostrich-like custom of burying the head in the sand has ceased, and the laymen, especially, are demanding that the full liabilities be stated, and are placing themselves on the platform of the most rigid honor and honorable dealing with all claimants. They are rebuking the foolish habit of the ministers, who alone can fix the apportionments for the pastoral charges, standing between the layman's duty and his pocketbook. They feel fully competent to defend their own purses and are saying to the ministers, "Tell us what the Veterans need and the law requires, and we will show that our professions of love to the aged Ministers are more than sentiment."

How often this note was struck at the Convention! Bishops, Preachers, laymen, all sang the song of GRATITUDE and JUSTICE in the same key. Every Bishop that spoke rang true to the fact of the Church's duty to provide for the Retired Ministers. Laymen declared that the Church was ready honestly to pay its debts to the Veterans and gratefully recognized their obligations; and the Preachers on the program, from opening to close, opened the eyes of all to the vision of the great Church recognizing its supreme obligations and meeting them in the spirit of loyal and loving gratitude.

EFFICIENCY

The relation of suitable provisions for Retired Preachers to "efficiency" of the Minister was greatly emphasized. Dean Birney, of the Boston School of Theology, presented the relation of the ministerial pensions to the call to preach. Dr. Joseph W. Van Cleve made an exceedingly strong presentation of the fact that it was far better for efficiency in the Church of God that the Church provide for the old age of its ministers and require them to make investments in themselves for a larger efficiency instead of starving mind and spiritual impulses by the processes of meager savings for the "rainy day." Bishop McConnell in his usual clear and lucid manner urged the same matter at the Inauguration Meeting.

THE CLIMAX OF THE CAMPAIGN

The General Conference assigned the Campaign for Five Million Dollars to this quadrennium, during which occurs the One Hundred and Fiftieth Anniversary of American Methodism. Nineteen hundred and fifteen has been made the Campaign Year, and the spring Conferences will have just a full year to complete their canvass. At the convention the Rev. E. L. Watson, D.D., District Superintendent of the Baltimore West District, made a very fitting suggestion that the one hundredth anniversary of Asbury's death, March 31, 1916, be set for the climactic ending of the Campaign.

Never was a suggestion more timely or more valuable or that carried in itself a larger meaning than that the one year of one hundred and fifty years of magnificent history, which is to be devoted to this *INHERENT, FOREMOST AND SUPREME* Claim should conclude with the anniversary of the death of the great founder of American Methodism.

APPROACHING A CRISIS

MR. JUDSON L. TRANSUE
Williamson, N. Y.

I am deeply interested in the care of Retired Ministers because I know what Methodist Ministers have had to undergo in order to bring to us our glorious heritage, because my father preached the blessed gospel of Jesus Christ for fifty years and never received a salary of over eight hundred dollars a year. I know what it means for a man to give his life to the Church and bring up a family of seven children on such a stipend, and I am free to confess that I do not see how it was done, except through God's help. When Christmas came I have seen the anxious look upon the faces at the head of the table, who were wondering what the little ones would have for Christmas; but I have seen these same faces light up with joy when they had given their lives to the work and had seen sinners come to the altar and yield their hearts to the Lord; and have heard them say, "It is worth all it cost; and it has not cost more than it ought to have cost." I cannot recall a single grumble through all those years, nor a single regretful expression except, "I wish we could have done more." They preached the Gospel, and, thank God! lived it.

The Methodist Episcopal Church is facing a crisis. From my outlook, which is not very great, it seems to me that the question of providing for the Veteran Preachers must be settled before we can expect God to pour out His blessings upon the Church. We stand before a neglected duty, and if we shrink back from doing it, from putting on the altar of God a sufficient sum of money to take care of these men, God will turn away from us. I have looked over the Conference minutes and counted the number of members, and have considered their efforts year after year and the very few additions to the Church, and have asked myself, "What is the matter? Something must be wrong." And as I have surveyed the field and have seen how little has been done for the aged Ministers, it has seemed to me that the Church must take care of these men or there will be no use for the Methodist Episcopal Church in the future. God will withdraw His blessing from her. We have been very careful about one thing; as a friend expressed it concerning another Church, that "the people thought the Ministry should be poor and pious, and, if the Lord would keep the Preachers pious, the laymen would attend to the other part and keep them poor."

We are facing the problem of raising five million dollars for Conference Claimants, a big sum, of course, but not a dollar a member for our constituency. I wish that when we representatives of the Conferences return home we would say: Here is the plan. Let one hundred thousand members of the Methodist Church give fifty dollars a year for five years. For I would rather have one hundred thousand members give fifty dollars than to have ten or fifteen men give the whole sum. It seems to me that in our work we have expected to get big sums from the few rather than small sums from a great many. If these men would give this money, the Lord would pour out His blessing upon them and upon the whole Church and the problem of financing all our enterprises would be settled. Fifty dollars a year from one hundred thousand members can be secured. We have two hundred thousand dollars in our Conference, and I believe that we will not stop with less than the three hundred thousand dollars and will then go on to half a million.

It can be done. I would like to see this movement sweep through Methodism. The other Boards would not become poverty-stricken, but the gifts would go next year to some other cause and the next year to another. There is nothing that opens a man's heart to the gospel so quickly or so widely as giving to the great causes of the Church. But first of all we ought to provide for the men who made it possible for us to have the Church. If one hundred thousand men during this year would lay fifty dollars apiece upon the altar for the Veterans' Cause, I believe the Lord would pour out such a blessing upon them that they could not contain it, and it would bubble over and bless others, and we would have such revival as we have not seen for generations. Let us do it!

Williamson, N. Y. J. L. Transue.

THE 1915 CAMPAIGN

THE GERMAN CONFERENCES

THE REV. J. A. MULFINGER, D.D.

Recording Secretary
Board of Conference Claimants

The ten German Conferences of the Methodist Episcopal Church in America have not been dilatory in taking up the matter of adequately caring for Conference Claimants. For a number of years they have been seeking to provide a better support for these Veterans of the Cross by organizing Preachers' Aid Societies and building up permanent funds in every Annual Conference.

The Conferences in Germany were fortunate in having men as their founders, who from the beginning recognized the importance of this cause, and who instituted a pension system by which the Conferences are able to-day to grant an adequate support based on years of service to ministers retiring from the effective ranks. The money needed to do this is derived from the income of their own Book Concern and from Permanent Funds which have been accumulating from the beginning through annual payments made by the preachers. Moneys received from other sources are distributed according to need.

The German Conferences in this country have adopted plans by which they hope to secure sufficient funds to provide fully for their Conference Claimants. There is a Permanent Fund in every Conference, the total amount in 1914 being $287,800. The income derived from these funds in 1914 amounted to $16,000; but, in spite of this, not a single Conference Claimant in the ten Conferences received last year the full annuity or pension. The average full legal annuity rate was $10, but on an average, only $3.61 a year was paid to the 267 Conference Claimants: 123 Retired Ministers and 144 widows and dependent children of deceased preachers.

The total amount needed in 1914 by the German Conferences in the United States in order to pay all claims, both for annuitants and necessitous cases, was $63,300; and the reports indicate that only $41,900 of this amount was paid, leaving a deficit of $21,500. This sum must be added to the annual resources before these Conferences can pay the claims at one hundred cents on the dollar. For this reason the German Conferences are entering enthusiastically into the 1915 CAMPAIGN. They need more money in their Conference permanent funds, producing a larger annual income for Conference Claimants; and they must have a larger income from other sources. The total amount of investments should be increased to at least $500,000; and meanwhile the apportionments to the pastoral charges should be increased to a sufficient amount to provide for the men who are now on the Honor Roll. As the endowment income increases the apportionment can be decreased. If this increase is made the Conferences will be able to fully meet all claims; but we must not overlook the fact that the number of Claimants is slowly increasing and for that reason we should greatly increase invested funds.

The German Conferences held in 1914 committed themselves to the great 1915 CAMPAIGN by unanimously indorsing the plans of the Board of Conference Claimants and by inaugurating a campaign within the bounds of each Conference for the purpose of increasing the amount of permanent funds, and also by increasing the apportionments. An agent has been appointed in almost every Conference and the ministers have pledged themselves to loyal support.

The rank and file of the German preachers have done heroic work in laying foundations and extending the borders of our great Church. The pioneers of German Methodism were heroes who dared and accomplished great things for God. Their names are worthy of being placed in the Hall of Fame of the Methodist Episcopal Church. They suffered great privations and hardships, and sacrificed their all upon the altar of God and the Church. The Church fully appreciates the value of their untiring and strenuous labors in bringing to the Germans arriving on our shores a personal knowledge of the saving power of Christ and getting them into the Church.

German Methodists are a valuable addition to the entire connection, and are numbered among the most generous supporters of all of our benevolent enterprises. The pioneer preachers received a mere pittance for support; and even at the present time the average salary of the German preachers is hardly $700. Still most of them have economized to such an extent as to become examples to their flocks in benevolent offerings; have fed and clothed their usually large families, and have managed to give to their children the advantage of a higher education. Besides this as a rule they have laid by a small sum of money or acquired a modest home for old age. We sometimes marvel and ask, "How did they ever do it?"

We would like to mention all of the names upon their Honor Roll, but space will not allow: Nast, Jacoby, Nuelsen, Riemenschneider, Plank, Mulfinger, Kuhl, Fiegenbaum, Kopp, Rothweiler, Lyons, Koch, all of whom have joined the great throng of witnesses before the throne of God and are now a part of the cloud of witnesses who rejoice in the triumphs of the Church. What a heritage they have left! What an incentive their lives have been to all! They do not need financial support; but others who served with equal heroism and fidelity have followed in their train and are now on the retired list, waiting for the call of the Master; and the Church owes to them a comfortable and generous support in old age. Are we willing to pay this debt? Will the Church respond to the Appeal made by the Bishops in their behalf? Are they at last coming to their own?

We firmly believe that this Appeal will meet with a generous and loyal response from every German member of our Church, and that the close of the 1915 CAMPAIGN will find all German Conferences in position to pay in full every claim of their Conference Claimants.

We append a table showing what the German Conferences have accomplished in providing an adequate support for their Conference Claimants and indicating their present needs.

Survey of the German Conferences, 1914

In these tables *units* are eliminated in the last column, and both *tens* and *units* in the other columns.

Column A gives the amount necessary in order to pay the full disciplinary rate shown in column D, plus the amount that would be needed for "necessitous cases."

Column B includes all amounts for distribution, whatever their source or method of distribution.

Column C is the remainder obtained by subtracting the sum in column B from the sum in column A, and indicates the shortage of the Conference, or its net liability.

Column D gives the annuity rate according to ¶ 331 of the Discipline; and column E gives the rate paid in 1914 and also the percentage of such rate to the total disciplinary rate.

Column F states the amount of the permanent endowment held by the Annual Conference, and column G the amount of the income from such endowment.

Name of Conference	A Total Liabilities	B Total Annual Assets	C Net Liability	D Disciplinary Annuity Rate	E Annuity Rate Paid. Percentage	F Annual Conference Permanent Endowment	G Income from Endowment
California	$3,000	$1,600	$1,400—40%	$10.00	$2.00—20%	$12,800	$730
Central	10,000	8,800	1,200—12%	9.00	4.00—44%	55,300	4,600
Chicago	7,800	4,400	3,400—43%	10.00	2.26—22%	49,000	1,400
East	8,400	4,700	3,700—44%	13.66	3.64—26%	33,300	2,350
Northern	7,500	3,200	4,300—57%	10.50	5.20—50%	19,400	1,030
Northwest	4,000	2,600	1,400—35%	10.00	2.08—21%	21,800	1,150
Pacific	2,100	1,300	900—43%	9.00	5.80—64%	5,200	250
Saint Louis	11,000	7,700	3,300—30%	9.00	3.50—38%	50,000	2,880
Southern	3,600	2,300	1,300—36%	9.00	4.55—50%	5,000	320
West	5,900	5,300	600—12%	9.00	3.10—35%	31,000	1,400
Total	63,300	41,900	21,500	9.91	3.61—37%	287,800	16,110

Chicago, Ill. J. A. Mulfinger.

EIN WOHLVERDIENTER LOHN

THE REV. ADAM J. LOEPPERT, D.D.

Chicago German Conference

"Was lange währt, wird endlich gut," so mag mancher ausrufen, der nun wahrnimmt, wie die Veteranen im Predigtamte der Bischöflichen Methodistenkirche zu ihrem Rechte kommen und ihnen ein wohlverdienter Lohn winkt. Die Kirche ist erwacht, wie noch nie vorher; dem verdienstvollen Veteran, der zu seiner Zeit in der Vollkraft der Jahre in den vordersten Reihen der heissen Schlacht gekämpft, dabei aber meistens sich und die Seinen vergessen hat, will sie ihre Dankesschuld bezahlen, sodass ihm der Lebensabend nicht in bangen Sorgen ins Auge starrt. Die Kirche mit ihren erkenntlichen Gliedern am Leibe Jesu Christi hat diese edlen Helden in den heiligen Dienst des Predigtamtes berufen. Dem Ruf der Kirche sowie dem unwiderstehlichen Rufe Gottes folgten sie und weihten sich ausschliesslich der heiligen Arbeit. Nie erwartete die Kirche von ihnen, dass sie sich in Verbindung mit ihrer Arbeit weltlichen Geschäften widmen sollten, denn das Predigtamt ist ganz naturgemäss kein weltlicher Beruf. Gott verstand auch nie darunter, dass seine Knechte im Ueberfluss oder gar im Luxus leben sollten, noch dass die Dinge dieser Erde ihre Zeit, Kräfte und Gedanken in Anspruch nähmen. Um das Letztere zu verhüten, ist es für unsere Kirche von grösster Wichtigkeit und ihre heiligste Pflicht, diesem dienstunfähigen Soldaten, wenn er auch in aktiver Tätigkeit viel Selbstverleugnung geübt hat, einen sorgenfreien Lebensabend zu gewähren, sodass er nicht der notwendigsten Lebensbedürfnisse wegen darben muss, oder wenn er gar schon vorzeitig von seiner Arbeit abgerufen wird, seine sich aufopfernde Gattin und seine Kinder von der Gnade und Barmherzigkeit der Kirche abhängig sind, der er selbstaufopfernd gedient hat.

Keine andere Kirchengemeinschaft fordert so viel von

ihren Predigern und deren Familien wie die Methodistenkirche, zumal wenn man das Reisepredigtamt mit seinen Freuden und Leiden in Betracht zieht. So sollte es auch gar nicht schwierig sein, die Frage aufzuwerfen und zu beantworten: "Worin bestehen die Verdienste unserer Veteranen?"

Die Methodistenprediger sind den einzelnen Seelen nachgegangen. Beobachte unsere deutschen Pioniere. Die Einwanderer waren entweder lutherisch, reformient oder katholisch; mit persönlichen Erfahrungschristentum waren sie nicht bekannt. So reiste der Prediger oft dreissig, vierzig oder gar fünfzig Meilen weit auf den Prärien und in den Urwäldern herum, suchte die einzelnen deutschen Familien auf und war zeitweilig wochenlang von seiner Familie fort. Kein Sturm und Ungemach störte ihn in seiner herrlichen Arbeit, denn "Seelen retten war sein Beruf" und "Wehe ihm, wenn er das Evangelium nicht den armen Sündern brachte." Er setzte oft sein Leben aufs Spiel in der Organisation der ersten Gemeinden und musste unermüdlich arbeiten, bis die junge, doch bald kräftige, Pflanze zum starken Baum herangewachsen war, unter dessen Schatten die heutige Generation wohnen kann. Doch darf hier nicht vergessen werden, dass es heute eben so schwer ist, den Baum zu pflegen, und die einzelnen Seelen dürfen nicht vernachlässigt werden.

Unsere Veteranen waren immer reich an Werken der Liebe und der Barmherzigkeit. Man denke doch an die Armut der Deutschen vor fünfzig Jahren. Wie gross war die Not. Die Glieder der einzelnen Gemeinden sind im Laufe der Jahre wohlhabend geworden, doch der Prediger, der seinen geringen Besitz immer wieder mit den Aermsten teilte, die an seine Türe kamen, blieb arm. Der brave Mann dachte an sich zuletzt und dann war's zu spät. Nie hat er den Bettler ein Almosen verweigert, auch hatte er stets ein Bett und Zimmer für den fremden oder befreundeten Gast, wenn man sich auch wundern musste, wo der geistliche Herr und seine Familie die Nacht zubrachten. Und wie viel hat er erst für das Werk der heiligen Mission und Wohltätigkeitsbestrebungen aller Art getan? Er hat als Mittel des Heiligen Geistes den ersten Trieb in den strebsamen Knaben hineingelegt, sich dem Werke der Heidenmission zu widmen.

Das blühende Werk in Deutschland und der Schweiz verdankt ihm seinen Anfang. Er legte den Grund zu unseren Schulen und Lehranstalten. Wer hätte an Waisenhäuser oder gar Altenheimaten gedacht und dieselben nach ihrer Gründung unterstützt und deren Interessen vertreten, wenn es nicht für jene Veteranen, die damals noch in ihrer Vollkraft des Lebens standen, gewesen wäre?

Und in den Werken der Wohltätigkeit, der Gründung von Anstalten aller Art, das jüngste Kind, die edle Sache der Diakonie, durchaus nicht zu vergessen, hat der Prediger nie kärglich gesät, noch spärlich gegeben, sondern immer über Bitten und Verstehen und häufig weit über seine Kräfte hinaus. In der Sammlung der Missionsgelder ging er mit guten Beispiel voran und in den Unterschriften für den Bau neuer Kirchen, Fundierung von Lehrstühlen und in Ausstattung von Krankenzimmern in Hospitälern stand sein Name nicht unten in der Liste.

Sie haben ihre Arbeit unter grossen Selbstverleugnungen getan. Sie hatten versprochen, zu gehen, wohin die Kirche sie sendet. Und mit dem Resultat waren sie fast ausnahmslos zu frieden. Ein andrer Arbeiter kann ja nach Belieben seine Arbeit oder seinen Wohnplatz wählen; nicht so der Methodistenprediger. Er muss bleiben. Wehe ihm, wenn er das Evangelium nicht predigt. Und wer denkt an die Verluste beim Ziehen? Wer an die Opfer der Predigerkinder in den Wechsel der Schulen und die Argusaugen, die an ihnen immer nur Zielscheiben der Kritik sehen? Wer erst an die Opfer der edlen Predigersfrauen? Und ich wage hier zu behaupten, dass ihre Arbeit und ihre Opferwilligkeit heute wie vor dreissig oder fünfzig Jahren, der ihrer Männer ebenbürtig zur Seite steht, wenn sie dieselbe in vieler Beziehung nicht gar überragt. Nimmermehr will unsere grossherzige Kirche dieser edlen Schaar der tapfersten Frauen, die je unter Christi Kreuzesfahne kämpfte, die Sorgenlast noch erschweren, sondern die Steine aus dem Wege räumen und ihnen den wohlverdienten Lohn geben. Tausende unserer besten Glieder und Familien in der Kirche haben es nächst dem lieben Gott den Predigern zu verdanken, dass sie sind, was sie sind.

Die Methodistenkirche hat etwa 3,000 ausgediente Prediger, 3,000 Predigerswittwen und 300 Predigerwaisenkinder, in runder Summe 6,300 Personen, die von der Mildtätigkeit der Kirche abhängig sind für ihren ganzen oder teilweisen Lebensunterhalt. Und wie blutet den Konferenzverwaltern oft das Herz, wenn sie nicht reichlich geben können, sondern kärglich geben müssen, da nicht Mittel genug vorhanden waren. Nun ist aber die Kirche zu ihrer Verantwortlichkeit erwacht, sodass diese Unterstützung in Zukunft keine Mildtätigkeitsgabe sondern ein wohlverdienter Lohn und berechtigte Pension ist, sodass bald ein jeder altersschwache Prediger wenigstens die Hälfte seines jährlichen Durchschnittsgehaltes auch jährlich als wohlverdienten Lohn erhalte. Die Generalkonferenz von 1912 hat einen Feldzug unternommen, die Behörde unserer altersschwachen Prediger und ebenfalls die Bischöfe haben denselben gutgeheissen, nach welchem im Jahre 1915 fünf Millionen Dollars als stehendes Kapital in den verschiedenen Konferenzen unserer Kirche gesammelt werden sollen, ein Fonds, der Zinsen genug abwerfen dürfte, um den berechtigten Ansprüchen gerecht werden zu können.

Dr. Joseph B. Hingeley, der unermüdliche korrespondierende Sekretär der Behörde für Konferenzanspruchhabende, verrichtet eine edle Arbeit und setzt sich in derselben ein Lebensmonument, indem er als weiser Stratege vorangeht, den wohlverdienten Lohn auf eine sichere Basis zu bringen. Und, Gott sei Dank, die Kirche bleibt nicht gefühllos. Die Laien sind gerne bereit, sich die Frage vorzulegen: "Was kann ich tun?" Dadurch erfüllen wir nur ein göttliches Gesetz. Vom Stamme Levi erwartete das Volk und der Herr, dass er sich vom Zehnten nähren sollte, nachdem er seine ganze Zeit und Kraft dem Dienste der alttestamentlichen Kirche weihte. Jesus sagte bestimmt: "Der Arbeiter ist seines Lohnes wert." Je näher wir diesem göttlichen Prinzipe kommen, desto eher können wir als Kirche erwarten, dass die Knechte Gottes ihre ganze Zeit und Kraft dem jetzigen Geschlecht widmen. Auch wird die Rückwirkung auf die Kirche selbst eine wohltuende sein, indem nicht nur das Predigtamt gebührend geehrt und geachtet wird, sondern unsere Jünglinge werden bereitwilliger dem Rufe Gottes folgen, ihr Leben in den Dienst des grössten Herrn zu stellen. Und wäre ein solch wohlverdienter Lohn nicht des grössten Opfers wert?

Chicago, Ill. ADAM J. LOEPPERT.

THE 1915 CAMPAIGN

THE SWEDISH CONFERENCES

THE REV. HERMAN YOUNG

Eastern Swedish Conference

We have in this country six Swedish Methodist Episcopal Conferences with a church membership of over twenty thousand; with twenty-two thousand Sunday school scholars and one hundred and sixty-seven ministers. The Conference Claimants funds of the six Conferences amount to $29,300. A great many of our Retired Ministers and many now in effective work labored for years in connection with English speaking Conferences, and when we started our own Conferences we came with empty hands. The Eastern Swedish Conference, only fourteen years old, has members who have been in effective work between thirty and thirty-eight years.

In our six Conferences we have twenty-three superannuated ministers and about the same number of widows and dependent children. The collections last year were $3,330.

The average salary of the several Conferences varies greatly; but that of all the Swedish preachers in this country is about $700, which fixes the full claim after thirty-five years of service at $350, or ten dollars per year. Most of our Conferences now pay full rate. That this is in many cases insufficient, I do not need to say, as many of our brethren have not been able to lay aside anything for old age, and most of the preachers now in the work are barely able to support their families, even by the exercise of the strictest economy. The seemingly dark prospect for the sure oncoming of old age has been the reason why several of our ministers have left our ranks, and, although we do not approve of their course, the fact still remains and the remedy must be found. We are a part of the great Church, and because Christian work must be carried on in America in the Swedish language for years to come, we believe that Methodism should not give over the field to others, but should continue to carry on our work.

The question is not whether religious work is to be carried on in America in the Swedish language, but whether the gospel according to Methodist doctrine and principles shall be proclaimed in that tongue or whether we will allow other denominations to do the work which God has providentially given us, or allow religious fakirs to ensnare our people. But in order to continue our work in the Methodist Episcopal Church the brethren who enter our ministry, many of whom are born in this country and have good opportunities in other lines of work, must feel that there is security for their future.

Because many of our people are of the toilers with little hope of independence in old age, the Claimants pension idea has not been and is not received as hospitably as it should be, but we hope that the 1915 CAMPAIGN will reach the Swedish Methodists and be the means of awakening them to their responsibilities and duty in this respect.

May 14, 1915, will be the seventieth anniversary of the day when the first Swedish Methodist minister, the Rev. O. G. Hedstrom of the New York Conference, preached his first Swedish sermon in the old Bethel ship "John Wesley" which lay in New York harbor and thereby started the work of Methodism among the Swedish people of America; and I hope that the one hundred and fiftieth year of American Methodism and the seventieth anniversary of Swedish-American Methodism may be made forever notable as the year in which the claims of all the Veteran Preachers will be met.

At a general convention of Swedish Methodist Ministers, held at Evanston, Ill., last June, and attended by representative ministers and laymen from all our Conferences, a plan was presented and discussed as to the possibility of uniting the invested funds of all our Conferences and paying claims of all our Retired Ministers according to the average salary of all the effective preachers which, as stated above, is $700. Such an arrangement would be a help in case of transfers from one Conference to another, which are more frequent among us than in the English-speaking Conferences, and would bind us more closely together in all our work. We rejoice in our membership in the Methodist Episcopal Church, and confidently expect that all our congregations will fall into line with the 1915 CAMPAIGN.

422 Dean St., Brooklyn, N. Y. HERMAN YOUNG.

VOR GJELD TIL DE UDTJENTE PREDIKANTER

H. K. MADSEN
Norwegian and Danish Conference

Fra den amerikanske borgerkrig fortelles følgende historie: En dag kom general Grant marscherende med sine batallioner forbi en liden hytte, beboet af en gammel kvinde. Da hun fik øie paa soldaterne, styrtet hun ud med ildrageren paa sin skulder og fylket sig ind i geledet. Soldaterne lo og spurgte, hvad hun vilde: "Aa," sa den gamle, "kan jeg ikke gjøre mere, saa kan jeg da vise, paa hvilken side jeg staar, for eller imod slavetrafiken." Hun tog et standpunkt, og det er ikke saa lidet. Dersom alle mennesker vilde ta et standpunket, saa vilde verdn bli meget bedre, og iser om de lig denne kvinde tog det rette.

For nerverende kalder vor elskede kirke, gjennem raadet for konferencefordringshavere, paa sine sønner og døtre for at samle et fond paa 5 millioner dollars til fordel for de udtjente predikanter og deres efterladte. De fleste af kirkens aarskonferencer har sluttet sig til denne velsignelsesrige bevegelse, der staar under den i alle henseender dygtige, og serlig for denne sag saa vel kvalificerede mands ledelse, Dr. Joseph Hingeley, hovedsekreteren for raadet for konferencefordringshavere.

Som norsk-danske methodister raader vi ikke over store midler; men om vi kun vil gjøre, som kvinden gjorde, fylke os ind i geledet, stille os paa den rette side, bli med i bevegelsen for det store maal, en sorgløs alderdom for de udtjente predikanter, og gjøre det lille vi kan, saa er det alt, som ventes af os.

Vi maa vere med. Pligten byder os; thi vi skydder de udtjente predikanter saa uendelig meget. Vi skylder dem respekt og agtelse for den store gjerning, de har udført. Vi skylder dem beundring og kjerlighed for deres store opofrelser og noble virke. Husk dog, vi skal ikke elske bare med store ord og vakre fraser, men i handling, og derfor skylder kirken dem et sorgøst livsophold paa deres gamle dage.

Tenk paa, hvad disse veteraner har ofret! De har tjent kirken og sine medmennesker hele sit liv for en liden løn, saa de ofte har maattet negte sig og sine det mest nødvendige. De fleste af dem har veret udrustet med evner og uddannelse, saa de kunde fyldt vigtige og lønnende stillinger i samfundet. Men de agtet alt for skarn at vere mod ypperligheden af at forkynde Kristi evangelium. Det er derfor kirkens usvigelige pligt at sørge for dem, naar de ikke lengere kan gjøre det selv.

Nogle vil muligens sige, de gamle prester har tjent ligesaa meget, som de fleste af os. Meget mulig; men glem saa ikke, at medens de var i arbeidet for Gud og kirken, blev mange krav stillet til dem, som var forbundet med store udgifter. De var kirkens representanter og maattee altid vere pent og anstendige kledte. Deres hjem var gjestfrie med stadig dekkede borde. Folket kom og gik. Var nogen i nød, saa gik de ikke prestens dør forbi. Til ham kom de først, og ofte maatte han laane for at hjelpe andre. Heraf forstaaes let, at det var omtrent umuligt at legge noget tilside for alderdommens dage.

De gav, hvad de havde. Muligens de ofte maatte sige: "Guld og sølv har jeg ikke; men hvad jeg har, det giver jeg dig." De gav et fuldt evangelium, som reddet mange fra synd og fattigdom, saa de er rige idag, medens mange af de gamle predikanter er lige fattige som før. De gav et rent liv, der virket som et bevarende salt i kommunen og samfundet. De gav sin sympati og kjerlighed, sine smil og sine taarer. De gav alt, sine evner og krefter for at løfte folket paa det religiøse, intllektuelle og materielle omraade. Med andre ord de gav sig selv for andres vel.

Derfor bør kirken si til disse gamle hedersmend: Guld og sølv det gir vi nu dig! saa du kan sidde lunt og ubekymret paa dine gamle dage ved din hjemlige arne og erfare sandheden af Jesu ord: "Søg først Guds rige og hans retferdighed, saa skal alle andre ting gives eder."

Saa kom da, venner, og tag et kraftig tag i det store løft for det felles maal, saa ogsaa vore egne udtjente predikanter, deres enker og barn kan se en lysere fremtid imøde.

H. K. Madsen.

2108 N. Sawyer Avenue, Chicago, Ill.

THE 1915 CAMPAIGN

COLORED CONFERENCES

THE REV. W. H. DEAN, D.D.
Washington Conference

Every race is dependent upon its leaders; no race more than ours. For our race there are few libraries, no highly developed press, no superior schools, no large learned class. Therefore, for their opinions and their religious and literary ideals, the masses are dependent upon their preachers, who are indispensable to the growth of the Church and the development of the people. The masses have been led always by a small but powerful class of thinkers, and more and more we are to be led by the men of our own race. Only trained and trusted leaders can adjust the colored race to the peculiar conditions among which their lives must be spent.

But the preacher cannot live on earth, and board in heaven. He has a right to and must have a "comfortable support." He must be able to lay by something for the "rainy day," or the Church which insists on the devotion of all his time, talent and means to its work must see that his old age is secure. He must dress himself and family, and educate his children; he must keep the choicest literature of the day in his library, and be able to study and preach without the distraction of worldly cares. Gospel ministers "must live of the gospel."

But if the man in the active ranks must be taken care of, much more must the Church provide for the minister when he is retired. This too is imperative. The Church must not let the wolf of hunger snarl at the Veteran Minister's door.

The colored Conferences, nineteen in number in this country, are doing relatively little for the support of their Conference Claimants. Claimants are many, and their needs great, but for the most part they are dependent for their support on the connectional help furnished by The Book Concern, the Chartered Fund and the Board of Conference Claimants. In the colored Conferences the permanent investments for

Conference Claimants do not amount to $1,500, and when you consider what these same Conferences do along other lines, it is clear that this ought not so to be. Dr. E. C. Clemans, field representative of the Board, is now meeting important groups of the preachers with the proposition that the colored Conferences unite to raise an endowment fund of $100,000; the money to be held in trust by the Board of Conference Claimants and to be administered in behalf of the contributing Conferences. The Board will pay at least five per cent on the money invested, the income to be paid to the several Conferences in proportion to the amount of money to their credit.

The Conferences of Methodism now have invested funds amounting to $4,000,000 and are increasing them to $15,-000,000. By the arrangement proposed, the colored Conferences also may have invested funds. The income from them will be a very helpful addition to the present income. The $100,000 invested by the Board for the colored Conferences will secure the future support of all the preachers and will mean even more to the men in the effective ranks than those who are to-day on the retired list. For example, the South Carolina Conference has been receiving a dividend from the Board amounting to $300. If that great Conference had $10,000 to its credit in the Permanent Fund, it would annually receive at least $500 in addition to the $300, making a total of $800. The perpetuity and safety of the funds would be guaranteed. The Bishops who have colored Conferences in their areas have endorsed the plan for the $100,000 endowment fund. Several Conferences have appointed commissions which are to report plans at the next session of the Conferences, so that the 1915 CAMPAIGN may begin immediately after adjournment. It is intended to raise this endowment not so much by collections as by subscriptions from the well-to-do, both white and colored, by bequests in wills, real estate holdings and by the sale of Life Annuity Bonds. In this way the colored Conferences will swing into line and will have a share in the results. The nineteen colored Conferences will surely join in this great movement; and the money will be raised. Let the slogan be: One Hundred Thousand Dollars for the Veterans of the colored Conferences.

Washington, D. C. W. H. DEAN.

COOPERATION

THE BISHOPS

BISHOP THOMAS B. NEELY, D.D., LL.D.

You do not need to be told that you can count on the Bishops for leadership or anything else they can do to forward the great work of securing an adequate support for Conference Claimants. They are already interested, and have already expressed themselves as they did at their meeting in May. They will take any burden that you may put on them that they can possibly carry. A new book by me was printed this year called the *Minister in the Itinerant System,* and the principles laid down in that book stand back of the work that you have before you at this time. A good deal is being said about the layman, and I would not discount him in any particular, but we must not discount the Minister. The Minister is the great business man of the Church, the most important factor and the only indispensable factor of the Church; and he ought to be made to know when he enters the Ministry of the Methodist Episcopal Church, that he has certain things guaranteed to him, and that the Church will keep its word to the very letter.

In the first place, he is entitled to equitable treatment in the matter of his appointment whether he has a call from an official Board or not. It is the duty of the administrator to give the Preacher his rightful place, if it is within the possibilities, and to treat him equitably in the matter of his appointment.

In the second place he has the guaranty of the Church to a fair support; not to a salary, but to a "comfortable support"; and that also means equity of treatment. He must be paid what he deserves, what his family needs, and what the people are able to give. A fair support will cover all these things.

In the third place, he has a guaranty that when he is retired he shall have an annuity or pension from the funds for the support of Conference Claimants. The Church promises this and the laymen must underwrite this guaranty by providing permanent investments sufficient to make the annuity pension promised in the Discipline a *dependable* pension. The Board of Conference Claimants and the 1915 Jubilee Gift of $10,000,000 must be underwritten by the whole Church. I frequently use the word "superannuate" because it is a notion of mine that the word "superannuate" for a Pastor is more honorable than "retired"; retired is the proper word for an officer, but it is not the proper word for a Minister who has rendered service. The word "superannuate" shows that he has rendered service for all the *years, and more,* that he was expected to give effective service; and it is therefore as Bishop Merrill declared in 1904, "an honorable title." Retired does not necessarily mean the same.

The law declares that a certain amount of money should go to a Minister as an annuity, or pension based on his years of service. The annuity or pension ought to be absolute, and just as a veteran soldier takes his pension without anybody putting him through an inquisition as to whether he has a few dollars or a shack somewhere, so should the Veteran Preacher receive annuity on years of service without any impertinent or insulting inquisition. It is not fair when the law says to the Preacher, "You will get your annuity in proportion to your service," for the Annual Conference not to let him have that amount or any amount on that basis. He may not always take it, but it is his by right, and nobody has any business to ask him to disclose how much money he may have buried in an old stocking, or invested elsewhere. The Church must see to it that when a young Minister enters the Ministry of the Methodist Episcopal Church he will be sure that nothing shall cut him out of his annuity, and that his support shall be as "dependable" as the Church of God which promised it.

Philadelphia, Pa. THOMAS B. NEELY.

COOPERATION,

DISTRICT SUPERINTENDENTS

THE REV. FRANK P. PARKIN, D.D.
District Superintendent Central District
Philadelphia Conference

Inasmuch as the 1915 CAMPAIGN for five million dollars was formally approved at the spring Conference of the Bishops held in Philadelphia, it is not inappropriate that a District Superintendent from the city of "Brotherly Love" should appear on this Inauguration Program which is so full of expressions of *love* for our Retired Ministers.

The District Superintendent becomes more and more essential to all aggressive movements in Methodism. Thoughtful and discriminating students of our history and polity, and observers of the evolution now being wrought in our Church by the assignment of Bishops to residential areas, are forced to the conclusion that this office is destined to become more and more influential.

The corresponding secretaries of all our great Church boards clearly recognize the fact. The following statement, which appears at the very head of a recent communication sent out by one of our keenest and most far-seeing secretaries, voices their attitude: "No group of men in the Methodist Episcopal Church have so signal an opportunity in this age to do the Church a great service as the District Superintendents. You are becoming increasingly the *key-men* to whom the Church must look for generalship in pushing its advance measures *into the last church.*"

Assuming, therefore, that this apt phrase *"key-men"* justly characterizes the District Superintendents of the Methodist Episcopal Church, it follows, both logically and actually, that unless they shall be genuinely and enthusiastically enlisted in this campaign, little of a practical character will be done.

What can a District Superintendent do to advance this campaign?

First. He must lay it on the heart and conscience of the

preacher-in-charge of every appointment on his district, especially on the younger men, that, ¶ 556 of the Discipline is in force: "The law of the Church in regard to the *pro rata* division of the amounts raised for ministerial support is binding, and it is incumbent on the Pastors and District Superintendents to see that such *pro rata* division be made."

A western editor in the first issue of his paper had this motto, *"Vim, vinegar and victory."* Without vim no great achievement can be accomplished. Even vinegar has its legitimate function. It was Josh Billings, that prince of all American humorists, who once said: *"Every man needs just enough vinegar in his constitution to keep the flies off."*

Second. The District Superintendent must see that the full amount apportioned to his district be reapportioned by the district stewards to the several pastoral charges on a just and equitable basis. As a preliminary to this the district superintendents should insist that the Annual Conference apportion the full amount required to pay the claims at one hundred cents on the dollar.

Third. During the year he should keep in touch with the pastors and people and *"stir up their pure minds by way of remembrance"* that the Retired Preacher must be fully recognized in the budget for "Ministerial support." Where the duplex system has not been inaugurated, "Old Folks' Day," or "Veterans' Day," will furnish a good opportunity for meeting the apportionment.

Fourth. In the quarterly conference visitation the laity should be instructed as to the justice of the Retired Ministers' claims, and the request should be openly, frankly and earnestly made that this great cause should be remembered in their wills.

Fifth. Proper provisions for the ministry in all denominations are related to the problem of Church unity, for without such provisions rivalry, spiritual inefficiency and a host of good men living on beggarly stipends, are the inevitable results, with increased demands upon Conference funds.

The District Superintendent can cooperate in every movement toward Church comity, Church federation, and Church unity in such a way as to set loose vast amounts of money for this noble fund for the aged veterans of the cross.

Philadelphia, Pa. FRANK P. PARKIN.

COOPERATION

ANNUAL CONFERENCE ORGANIZATIONS AND THE BOARD OF CONFERENCE CLAIMANTS

THE REV. S. A. MORSE, D.D.
Secretary of the Permanent Fund, Genesee Conference

When a friend expressed to Lord Kames his regret at his ignorance of a particular branch of political economy and asked for advice, his Lordship replied: "Shall I tell you, my friend, how you will come to understand it? Go and write a book upon it." Though this is not a book, it is written upon the principle expressed by the Scotch judge, for, surely, I know little about the subject. But who does know? There is no background of experience, or even of observation, for a picture of this sort. Imagination must supply the perspective. I can hope only to make a few suggestions and start a discussion from which the writer may himself receive more than his paper can possibly give.

In the first place, let me emphasize the importance of cooperation between the Conference organizations and the Board of Conference Claimants. To this end it is essential that there be a frank and full recognition of the leadership of the Board of Conference Claimants. It is only trite to say that large mass-movements require conspicuous headships—headships charged with abundant power, and clothed with the dignity of vast responsibilities. Lacking this, the masses fall apart, going their several ways, working often at cross-purposes, if, indeed, they do not actually fall to fighting each other. Lacking coherence and coordination, and the vision of the general with his glass yonder on the heights, the movement is chaotic and ineffective. Instead of Rome, Greece might have become the seat of an age-long empire had she been willing to recognize some supreme power to command and lead. Even when a common peril drove the tribes into union, democratic jealousy compelled the change of generals every day, even in the face of the foe. Methodism is an outstanding illustration of the aggressive force inhering in an organization of military-like compactness, and moving like an army under well-nigh individual control toward its objective, the conquest of the world for its Lord and Master, Jesus Christ.

The one great department of Methodism that has suffered most for lack of coordination and commanding leadership is the one which relates to the support of the Retired Ministers. No wonder that we have been confused and belated! Treated thus, where would our missionary enterprises be? If in 1819, when we began our foreign missionary work, or in 1864, when we began our work of Church Extension, we had grappled in a similar way and with like vigor with the question of the proper care of our worn-out preachers and widows, to-day no member of a Methodist Episcopal Conference, who had served even a moderate length of time, would be in danger of hearing the snarl of the gaunt wolf of hunger. The wonderfully successful enterprises alluded to above are well-entitled to the name of *movements.* But had they been treated as the cause of the claimant has been, the characterization would be grotesquely inaccurate. To illustrate the point take a few statistical facts from the annals of one Conference, representative, perhaps, of the conditions in almost any Conference of the Church, which I have denominated

Some Significant Contrasts

Genesee Conference—Full Membership: 1852, 10,135. 1913, 50,907. More than five-fold increase.

Church and Parsonage Property: 1859, $381,700; 1913, $4,608,825. More than a twelve-fold gain.

Benevolent Giving: 1850, $6,353; 1913, $125,293. Multiplied by more than 18.

Per Capita Giving for Conference Claimants: 1852, 16 cents; 1913, 28¾ cents. Only 1¾ times more.

Average Payment to Worn-out Ministers: 1852, $190.66; 1913, $219.77. Only $29.11 more to each, while cost of living has advanced at least 66 per cent.

Everything has boomed except the care of the preacher—the man who made things go.

Is this a square deal? Verily, no.

Look again at these figures exponential of growth in that

Conference, and be amazed. There are increases of five-fold, twelve-fold, eighteen-fold in certain important items, and for the men and women who have made all this possible, when retired from the firing-line an increase of but $29 per year; and that in the face of an increase of not less than 66 per cent in the cost of table necessities. Surely, this is not a square deal. It is a situation intolerable, especially in view of the fact that there has been no adequate increase in the average pastoral support.

A new era dawns. At last the Church is awake. At last we have authorized leadership, and relationships somewhat articulated. To be sure we are as yet in the infancy of the new movement, and we are toddling like babies learning to walk. But we are learning, and soon we shall walk and not be weary, run and not faint. We have leadership well-equipped and worthy to be followed. The Board of Conference Claimants is wisely planning the campaign, and is becoming a sort of clearing-house of information and the source of light and inspiration for the whole Church. The need of this has long been felt by those particularly interested in endowment work. Many of us have had a zeal not according to knowledge, devising schemes more or less fantastic and utopian. That even that aggregation of wisdom, the General Conference, has sometimes been in need of illumination is seen in the abortive legislation which had to be thrown into the junk heap; and by the method of distribution of Book Concern dividends to the Annual Conferences. Our "Witenagemōt" imposed upon the Book Committee the duty of dividing these profits among the Conferences on the basis of Conference membership; a plan which entirely ignores the crucial questions of the number of claimants, and their aggregate years of service and total annuity claims. The time of this ignorance may have been winked at, but now, with the light of experience focalized by experts, our quadrennial parliament may well be commanded to repent. In such matters as these, Conference organizations should be ready to hold up the hands of the Board of Conference Claimants and seek to make that body most efficient in its work for the worn-out men and women of the itinerancy. Not that individual judgment be suspended, or reason abdicate her throne! But, having counseled, let us all strike together for remedying evils which we see. The rules of the game of "Follow-my-leader" may be applied to the serious affairs of life.

There should be cooperation between the two parties considered herein in a matter in which the Conference organizations must be the chief gainers. I refer to the creation and distribution of an endowment literature. Neal Dow declared that, preceding the adoption of the constitutional prohibitory amendment in Maine, he "sowed the State knee-deep with literature" on the subject of intemperance. This great work of ours cannot be accomplished without liberal use of printers' ink. That is seed from which great harvests often grow. Young Erasmus in Paris wrote: "As soon as I get any money I shall buy Greek books; *then* I shall buy some clothes." Like the great scholar of the Renaissance we must put immense emphasis upon books, or, at least, upon leaflets, tracts, hot shots, printed tastefully and fired frequently. It is the age of the printer. We can do nothing without him. "Write a book," advised a great orator, "a book is the only immortality." The printed page is to be a chief portion of our campaign ammunition. I am glad that Martin Luther flung an ink bottle and not a boot-jack at the devil. Devils of opposition born of ignorance and prejudice and selfishness may be defeated by pen and ink attacks as by no other kind. Now, the Board of Conference Claimants and the local organizations may do most valuable cooperative work by uniting in the production of educative and campaign literature. The Board, for example, issues some most excellent pamphlets and leaflets which could be used with good advantage in Conference campaigns. Among these issues are *"The Banker's Investment,"* a leaflet on the life annuity plan; Marvin Campbell's able address at the Indianapolis Convention of Methodist Men; and latest perhaps, by Dr. Oldham, *"We'll Do It."* Judge Horton on "Wills" is also valuable. These all bear the imprint of the Board of Conference Claimants, but can be printed with the imprint of the Annual Conference and in such large quantities as to reduce to a minimum the cost of production for Conference organizations. I now have in my possession the very low figures quoted for the purchase of a tract by Marion Harland on *Should Protestant Ministers Marry?* circulated in large numbers by the Presbyterian Board. The last page is blank. It is my thought to accept the generous offer of that board, and use the last page to localize and make applicable to our own situation the text of the tract. This can be done at much less cost than we could possibly produce the pamphlet. Our Board can do something of this sort for the local organizations. Besides reducing the printing bill of the local organizations this plan would tend to supply the Conferences oftentimes with better "stuff" than would otherwise be circulated; and would tend to ally the general and the local forces in such a way as to make the impression of strength, allaying possible jealousies that might arise from the seeming conflict of the local forces with the general board. It is just possible, on the other hand, that the Conference organizations may sometimes print productions which the Board would be wise to use and to give a wider distribution through its great circulatory system.

These principles apply to that excellent quarterly, *The Veteran Preacher*. My own belief is that we cannot anywhere conduct a campaign with the greatest success without the aid of a periodical issued monthly, or at least quarterly. We must get into contact regularly and frequently with our constituencies if we are to gain final victory and reach it soon. It ought to be possible to publish monthly *The Veteran Preacher* having, say, half of the contents of a character applicable to the situation as a whole and the other half made up of matter particularly interesting to the people of the Conferences using the plan. Of course, this would be upon an equitable basis as to cost. With cheap freight rates and parcel post charges, this scheme must be practicable. Is it too much to hope that some practicable plan may be set afoot soon looking to the covering of our whole territory by an educational and campaign periodical such as I have spoken of?

There is another feature of possible cooperation which, on the surface, looks very feasible. I refer to the organization, through the careful consultation of the board with local organizations, of a lecture bureau, a corps of men who through practice and native ability have become experts in our propaganda, and who could be called upon at almost any time for aid in Conference campaigns. This suppositive flying squadron might be chiefly limited to the several episcopal areas in the interest of economy. Of course, there is already some interchange in the services of such men, but it is upon no organized basis such as would make it most efficient. Such a list of available men might be on file in Dr. Hingeley's office, and their names published in *The Veteran Preacher*. Of course, no man would make money out of the plan, but be content with his expenses. We can never repay the men who went before us, building a highway for us to travel on, and who made the franchise of Conference membership of almost inestimable value to us. We are their debtors as those who come after us will be indebted to us. Glorious debt! I would like to make it measurelessly large. These are but hints, and experience will be required to demonstrate their value or otherwise.

If in this paper I have seemed to emphasize the ways in which the Board of Conference Claimants may operate to help the local organizations, it is perhaps because this lay in the nature of the case. I can at least here record my own grateful appreciation of the work of Dr. Hingeley, who is sparing neither time nor effort to serve the cause in and through the various Conference organizations. Our presence here is but one of the many proofs of this. We are glad to learn that Conferences are seconding his motion in respect of the full apportionment for Conference Claimants. He has had to do much preaching to bring about this result. It is well that he is persistent. Through this one move alone our claimants throughout many sections of the Church will share more abundantly than ever before in the benefits resulting from an aroused conscience on the subject of what is due our pastors emeritus, our *corps of honor*. This is taking a long stride toward the happy time when the great majority of our retired men and women will be on the annuity list only, and all relief cases will be amply cared for by distribution from the general office in Chicago.

S. A. Morse.

27 Minnesota Ave., Buffalo, N. Y.

CAMPAIGN LEADERSHIP: CONFERENCE REPRESENTATIVES

THE REV. W. D. SLEASE, D.D.
Secretary Permanent Fund, Pittsburgh Conference

Every enterprise is dependent upon its leadership. If the enterprise is laudable and the leadership competent success is almost certain; but however laudable the enterprise, if the leadership be weak, failure will be the result. The greatest enterprises are the salvation of humanity, the lessening of human ills, and the elevation of the moral life. Such leadership was committed to the apostles and their successors, the ministers of the gospel of the Son of God, who are the accepted coworkers with God in saving the world and building the kingdom of heaven. Since the Church is the greatest institution, "an everlasting kingdom," its establishment and enlargement is the greatest work committed to men. The greatness of this world enterprise demands that its builders be of the highest type, the best trained workmen that nature, culture and grace can produce. The Church says to its young men who are called to become its spokesmen, "Give me all your strength, all your talent, all your culture, all your heart, all of yourself, and I will give you a comfortable support throughout your life." There are certain demands in ordinary life, and certain limitations to human ability, for which God has provided. But He demands that His chief builders shall not be handicapped in their great work by being compelled to go into the business marts to compete for the necessary things of ordinary life because He needs all their talent, time and effort for the work of His Church. This underlying principle of the divine economy is manifested in both the old and new covenant systems of building up the kingdom of God.

In the old theocratic economy God made magnificent provision for the temporal support of his priests and Levites as is shown by the ordinances promulgated by Moses. The same economic principle is shadowed in the long neglected covenant of the Methodist Episcopal Church which promises its ministers "a comfortable support." After a century of neglect the sense of responsibility to God and of obligation to its Veteran Ministers has been revived and Methodism is launching a church-wide campaign to enable it to meet its obligation, having for its slogan, "Five million dollars for perpetual investment in behalf of the Retired Ministers, widows and orphans." The enterprise is cooperative and intensive and extensive, and will surely succeed if its leadership is equal to the task. The Board of Conference Claimants originated the movement, and must continue in its leadership. For this is a world-wide movement of the whole Church and by the whole Church, and for the whole Church, though the work will be largely done in and by Conferences. The Church has its untiring and indefatigable leader in the person of the Corresponding Secretary of the Board of Conference Claimants, the Rev. Joseph B. Hingeley, D.D. Most Annual Conferences have agents in the field, and all must have. Upon these, to a large extent, will depend the success of the movement. If these agents are competent, intensive and industrious, then the movement will be widely effective, and the century-old pledge of the Church for a comfortable support, so long unredeemed through lack of sufficient assets, will become effective in both spirit and letter.

To be practical rather than theoretical I would say that these Annual Conference agents should be men with large visions of Christ and the Church, with a profound sense of their responsibility to God, and their duty to their retired brethren. They must be men who not only see visions, but who dream dreams and make their dreams come true; men who keep step with the advanced public sentiment as to the reasonableness of all old age pensions, especially to those which are inherent in the gospel ministry. They must be men of faith, and loyal-hearted, and experienced with faith in God, faith in the Church and its loyalty to its aged ministers, faith in the importance of the movement; men capable of inspiring like faith in others and of persuading them to capitalize their faith in permanent investments in behalf of the Veteran Ministers, and the widows and orphans of deceased ministers. They must be optimists who see that the times are ripe for a great church-wide movement; men who believe there never was a time in the history of the world when God had so strong a grip on the Church and the Church had so strong a grip on God as now; men who see that thoughtful Christian men were never so ready to throw their gold and silver into God's treasury for strengthening and extending his kingdom and dealing fairly and squarely with God's workmen. They must be men who believe that the gold and silver and "the cattle upon a thousand hills" belong to God, and that they are not too great a price to pay for building the kingdom or keeping the kingdom's pledge to its builders. They must know men, and be able to show them "Whose they are and Whom they serve," and that God expects them to use their resources for the proper comfortable support of those who in their strength went forth amid tears and sacrifices sowing the seeds of righteousness and laying the foundations, upon which they have builded. They should be men of such large personality as to be able to stand before any organization, or in any presence as the representatives of God and the Church, and without apology or pitiful pleas of poverty show that these sacred claims are based on scriptural authority as well as upon the most practical principles of church economy. These leaders must be men of persistent, untiring effort, ready to go anywhere or to make any sacrifice for the glory of the Church or the comfort of its Veteran Ministers, always ready to preach the blessedness of giving, to advise as to Wills and to write bequests and to solicit contributions from the people. By methods like these and a hearty cooperation of the ministers, the Pittsburgh Conference has secured during the last two quadrenniums nearly $200,000 of productive investments; besides thousands of dollars of subscriptions not yet due, and many thousands in bequests not yet in force.

To God be the praise and glory for the awakened interest in the Conference Claimants of Methodism!

W. D. SLEASE.

3119 Kelvin St., Pittsburgh, Pa.

THE MAN WITHOUT A FUTURE

Some one has said that "holding doggedly to what one believes to be strictly conscientious is acting out a farcical piece of unreasonable stubbornness."

The minister is a man who entertains a call he deems divine. He felt the call in his own heart. He heard it as did Aaron, coming from the lips of the Church. He saw it when, after years of his best endeavor, he saw the fruits of his labor. He conscientiously proved it in many ways.

He knew that the remuneration would be small. He was not looking for anything more than enough to cement body and soul. He knew the inevitable end, when he would be obliged to quit, and be set aside with no regular income, and that this would occur after he was no longer able to perform manual or brain work. He intended to spend and be spent in the labor of love. He knew he would not be permitted to take any time or energy from the charge he served and speculate as every other man can do. He gave all he had to assist some one else.

He gave his life wholly to the Church, and must work as long as life should endure. He might have stopped after he had slaved twenty years or so, before the grasshopper had become a burden, and his natural forces had abated, and have worked a few years for himself and family, but to him this would have been downright dishonesty. Had he not promised the Lord to work for Him *all his days?*

So this stubbornly conscientious man labors on, and on, and on, till the wheel breaks at the cistern. He has never had any home but a parsonage. He has no furniture except his scanty bric-a-brac, the gifts of friends through the weary years. He has no property but his dwindling library. He is retired. The Conference session ends. He has preached forty-one years and as a "necessitous case" receives $78 for the years facing him. He staggers out. He has no home, no future—but Heaven. He is a martyr, a saint, a hero!

Thank God! that this is a wrong that is being righted. In 1913 there were two dollars for him, as against one dollar five years ago, and the 1915 CAMPAIGN means that there shall be *three* dollars instead of one—$234 instead of $78.

THE 1915 CAMPAIGN

THE PROGRAM

THE REV. J. B. HINGELEY, D.D.

Corresponding Secretary Board of Conference Claimants

Many things have been said about the General Conference Board and Annual Conference organizations. We are beginning a common campaign which the Board is seeking to forward in every practicable way. At a meeting of the Ohio Conference commission, after I had presented an analysis of the situation, a bright Christian woman, member of two General Conferences, said that she thanked God for "the modern baptism of accuracy," which made it possible for the Church to measure its liabilities and resources. One reason why we can come together in such a united spirit is that we have been reading the same facts, and studying the situation in our several Conferences, and are therefore able to project the 1915 CAMPAIGN on the lines of the most intense cooperation. In the Buffalo Area there is an Area organization representing the six Conferences, which have formed an alliance for mutual help, and to see each Conference through its task. The suggestion came from Dr. F. T. Keeney, and was adopted immediately by Bishop Burt. In 1908 the Board was up against a wall of indifference or opposition, but I do not know of a Conference which is not to-day helpfully related to the Board of Conference Claimants and solicitous for its leadership.

Literature

The question of literature is a live question. Our embarrassment grows out of the fact that we have not money with which to do the necessary business. The little we had hoarded in the General Fund is exhausted. We cannot take a dollar from the Permanent Fund, or from percentages. But we have the work to do, and I am sufficient of an optimist to believe that as in the childhood of the Board, so now in its manhood the friends of the Veterans will provide funds for the 1915 CAMPAIGN. We cannot wage successful battle along the great lines laid out by this Convention unless the ammunition wagon is filled for use. The Board must have the money. The literature for the 1915 CAMPAIGN must be prepared and printed, and adapted for use in any Conference. The *Veteran Preacher* must be enlarged and issued every month, with pages devoted to the Annual Conference Campaigns, with special editions for the several Conferences. We are ready to do this, and have the plans, program and arrangements with the printer. We wait only the arrival of the "Ammunition Wagon."

We have a great intensive, extensive, cooperative campaign; and on our mailing list in Chicago must have the name of every possible contributor in every pastoral charge in Methodism. Inspirational literature, the *Veteran Preacher,* and special literature must be prepared and sent to them. Pastors must be given inspiration and information so as to present the cause to the people. Every district in Methodism must be organized for work, and skilled workers discovered and trained.

Climax of Conference Campaign

The climax of a Campaign might be handled as follows: Take a charge which has sent in one hundred names of possible contributors who have received literature from the Board and have been informed as to the needs. The pastor has presented the cause in the pulpit; five canvassers, laymen or pastors, set aside for that purpose, go to that community trained to do a certain task. Each man is to see ten persons in the morning and ten in the afternoon, and urge them to make contributions or pledges to the fund. Each of these Preachers will be met and introduced by a layman. By night every one of those one hundred possible contributors will have been personally solicited and the entire work of solicitation for that charge completed in one day. If there are thirty solicitors, then six other charges can be canvassed in one day, and six hundred possible contributors interviewed; and in ten days six thousand friends of the Veterans can be seen.

The work done will be reported to headquarters each night; an account of what has been done put into type and sent out the next morning to each possible contributor so that all may know just what has been accomplished. This will be done daily, until the canvass has been completed. Several Conferences are organizing along these lines. I am sure that such an intensive "lightning campaign," following thorough preparation, would place any Conference on the hundred per cent list during this quadrennium.

Connectional Work Merged

For the sake of greater efficiency the Board of Conference Claimants has submerged its individual interests in the larger program of the intensive, cooperative Campaign. Ten million dollars will make all the Conferences solvent, and when that is accomplished, and while it is being accomplished, there is no doubt as to the response of the Church to the special and particular needs of the Board of Conference Claimants. God is already sending to us messages laden with money. The other day one aeroplaned almost 2,000 miles and landed on my desk. We did not go after it, and never met the giver. But the Spirit of God and of Christian liberality had visited him, and he "was not disobedient to the heavenly vision." A few weeks ago an old soldier wrote, "I am an old man and have five thousand dollars in the bank, and haven't an heir this side of Scotland. I want my money to go to the old Preachers; will you take the money for them, and pay me interest on it until I die?" It cost us two postage stamps to secure that gift. Nobody knew he had a penny, but he had five thousand dollars, *and love for the old Preachers.*

Publicity

One result of this campaign will be the opening of the hearts of the people. We need only open their eyes and ears, *God will open their hearts.* They will be glad to get the suggestion of helping the old Preachers, but they will never get it if we remain silent. A clipping from the Northwestern Christian Advocate opened the way for us to receive $11,000 from an aged Christian woman. If we will only give the publicity God will wing our words with His love.

The Campaign is *cooperative, intensive* and *general.* It is ordered by the General Conference, has the leadership of the Bishops and District Superintendents, is intended to meet the full claims in every Annual Conference throughout the entire Church, and is aided, abetted, pushed and led by the Board of Conference Claimants, to whom the Church has committed the duty not only of "uniting the stronger and weaker Conferences in one general plan to secure a more equitable and general support for the Retired Preachers, especially in the more needy Conferences," and of "building up and administering a Permanent Connectional Fund"; but also that of *"increasing the revenues for the benefit of Conference Claimants,"* however distributed.

This provision to "increase revenues for Conference Claimants" has no limitations placed upon it. Wherever there is a Retired Preacher or the widow or dependent orphan of a deceased preacher there it is the duty of the Board of Conference Claimants to go and, so far as may be in its power, to see that a sufficient support is provided.

The Permanent Fund of the Board of Conference Claimants helps "necessitous cases" in all Conferences; and the funds in the hands of Annual Conference Trustees, Preachers' Aid Societies, etc., are distributed generally as annuities or pensions based on service. The more investments Annual Conferences have, the more fully can they meet their obligations to their Conference Claimants, and the less claim they will have on the Connectional Fund. On the other hand the more money that is invested by the Board of Conference Claimants, the more money it will have to assist the Annual Conferences in relieving the needs of "necessitous cases."

The 1915 CAMPAIGN, to quote the language of the General Conference, is for "The Jubilee Gift of Five Million Dollars, comprised of *all gifts* to the funds of the several Annual Conferences and also to the Permanent Fund of the Board of Conference Claimants."

By the time of the session of the next General Conference *there must be no Conference in Methodism in which the Retired Preacher does not receive in full the amount promised to him by the Discipline.*

There are many great organizations in Methodism, and our Bishops and connectional officers and ministers are greatly interested in them all, but are determined to see the fulfillment of the General Conference program for Conference Claimants.

THE 1915 CAMPAIGN

COOPERATIVE, INTENSIVE, EXTENSIVE

REV. E. C. E. DORION, D.D.
Associate Editor Zion's Herald
Member Board of Conference Claimants

The year 1915 will mark an epoch in the history of American Methodism. One need not be prophetic in vision in order to know that this will be so, for one branch of that family is awakening to the responsibility it owes its ministry. Such an awakening means a new day, the dawn of a new era for the Methodist Episcopal Church. I speak in no uncertain terms. By the token of our advance legislation, by the awakened consciousness in the industrial world, by this gathering I see the triumph of the idea for which we stand. There is the scent of victory in the air.

We are engaged in big business to-day. We are talking in dollars, but that is merely for the convenience of expression. Back of all is a great overmastering idea—the recognition on the part of the Church of its responsibility to the ministry. Even as a new attitude in the business world toward the worker has resulted in more equitable laws, and a change of industrial conditions, so the new attitude of the Church toward its ministry will bring about new conditions that will affect the preacher throughout his entire career.

Fulfilling a Compact

We are not inaugurating a campaign this day for a company of paupers; our task has not for a main purpose the relief of suffering. It is true that this fund will make it possible for us in an adequate way to take care of those in need, and that there will come relief from hardship and suffering for men who have given themselves to a life of holy service. But back of the 1915 CAMPAIGN there is something more important even than that, because it includes this and much more. It will bring about a new attitude on the part of the Church toward the men whom it has ordained. We would have the Methodist Episcopal Church live up to the obligation it took on itself when it accepted the young minister as he stood at the bar of the Conference and said to him: "Give us your life; go and preach; devote all your time and service to the ministry and we will take care of you." Let Methodism catch a glimpse of the significance of this compact, and who need fear for the success of the campaign? We may talk in dollars and cents, but this idea is back of it all—the obligation of the Church to its ministry. And this is why the year 1915 will mark an epoch in the history of American Methodism. It will result in a complete transformation of the entire ministerial question. It will affect the ministry at its source, and will cause to swell that stream of youths who will dedicate themselves in answer to God's call to them. It will affect the man who is in the strength of his power, and will inspire him to better work as he realizes that a loyal Church is back of him. It will affect the Veteran as he drops out of the firing line, knowing that a grateful Church holds him in affectionate and tangible remembrance. It will transform the entire ministry, and by the same token transform the Church itself. Of a truth we are erecting milestones along the way of American Methodism.

A Campaign

"The 1915 CAMPAIGN." Why a campaign? Not for the sake of having great gatherings or great speeches, interesting as this might be. Not that we may discourse on the unfortunate condition of the old preachers. That may come out of it, but only in an incidental way. I shall never forget when the condition of some of these old preachers first dawned on me. The son of a Methodist preacher—the third generation, in fact, in the ministry—I was ignorant of the unfortunate conditions under which some superannuates lived. I learned one day that during the week an enfeebled old preacher cobbled shoes to support himself and his aged wife; and there came to me a sense of burning shame that my Church should thus ignore its old preachers in the day when they had ceased from active service. The condition of the old preacher will come into the discussion, and we will help to arouse the Church; but that which will most impress the Church will be its responsibility to the entire ministry.

It is time we did this. The ministry as a cause has long enough been ignored. The minister gives himself, body, mind and soul, to every good cause. This has been the history and the glory of our Church. But his own cause? Over and over again it has been set aside for "a more convenient time." *That time has now come.* Loyal to the very end to every cause, let the Church now be loyal to him. This will affect the whole ministerial situation. We often think that we have a sure ministerial supply in the Methodist Episcopal Church, and that it will never exhaust itself. That is true only up to a certain point. If this is true in the general run of appointments, how about our weaker work? And how about our larger work? Every District Superintendent knows how difficult it is to secure men for the small, out-of-the way appointments—the hard places. If we are to have the men who are needed to care for all our work, then there is need of a new attitude toward the ministry on the part of the laity. I know a man who, in an hour of excitement, spoke of the minister as the "hired man" of the church. Brutal this may have been, but I fear that all too often that for which this expression frankly stands is back in the consciousness of some of our laity. No, not "hired men" are these who stand at the sacred desk, but prophets of the Most High, touched by the power of Almighty God; men who have given their lives to the Church, and to whom the Church in loyalty must give its support throughout all their years.

A Cooperative Campaign

In order to bring about this new attitude, the campaign must first of all be cooperative—that is to say, we must have the cooperation of all church agencies. Each department of Methodism has its own work and each must be honored in prosecuting it. But there comes a time when, for one reason or another, the right of way must be given to some particular agency for a special campaign. Then the sense of brotherly consideration and cooperation must come into play. Such it is with the Board of Conference Claimants at this time. The General Conference called upon this Board to raise, at some time during this quadrennium, the magnificent sum of five million dollars for the Retired Preachers. All through this period one cause or another has been given the right of way. Now, we are saying that the year 1915 belongs to the old preacher. This is the great emergency cause for that year. Nothing must be allowed to take its place.

Then again, this cooperation must be between the various agencies to which this cause has been committed—the General Conference Board of Conference Claimants and Annual Conference organizations. Some thought these agencies of necessity overlapped; but nothing of the kind exists and must not appear to. Cooperation between the General Conference Board and the coordinating agencies is the word, and all friends of the Veterans must strike hands together throughout Methodism. We are told of the battle-line in Europe that stretches over four hundred miles and more. The various detachments are unable to keep in touch one with another; yet there is no isolation, for back of the battle-line are the master minds and back still further the master mind; so that the skirmish here, and the artillery duel yonder, and the infantry charge become parts of one great general plan. There must be a like coordination of the forces of every Conference in Methodism, from Maine to California, all cooperating with the Board in carrying out the one program.

Intensive Campaign

It is to be an intensive campaign—that is, intensive in the several Conferences. We may till the field at large, but in order to do so successfully we must first of all till in particular. Every furrow must be turned and every acre cultivated. We must work well each individual Conference. In order to do that, there must be the organizing of our local forces. Now and then we are led to think we have too much organization. That is true if the organization be useless, but it is not so if the organization has a purpose. In organizing Annual Conferences for the 1915 CAMPAIGN we must lay the burden on the laity. The laity can make this program go; and are ready to do it. This idea that we are trying to make dominant is already recognized in industrial circles. The laymen recognize the right of the worker to his hire, and are carrying this over into the realm of the Church.

An Extensive Campaign

It must be an extensive campaign. It must swing into line all the Church's resources and activities. It must swing the Bishops into line. They have much to do, and are continually called upon for service; but it was for this purpose they were elected to their high office, that they might be the great leaders in every great and good cause. We rejoice to-day in the knowledge that the Bishops have already entered enthusiastically into the 1915 CAMPAIGN. There must be the most earnest cooperation of the District Superintendents, those who represent "the applied end of the Episcopacy," the local Bishops, by whom the Church swings to victory. They are the key men of our Methodism, and every one of them must get into line down to the last man. Then we must secure the individual support of the preacher—not for himself, but for the great cause, into which he must throw himself with utter abandon. The importance of the press to the success of the 1915 CAMPAIGN cannot be overstated. We are inclined to think at times that the press has lost much of its influence. But did you notice that no sooner had war broken out in Europe than every nation began appealing to the American press that it might secure its influence? The influence of the press! It can hardly be overestimated. It was never greater than at the present time. Our denominational press must be in line with this campaign for the old preacher. I know what I say when I assert that every editor in the Church is interested, intensely interested, in this great cause.

As we look at this task and consider the conditions, we may be discouraged at times, wondering if, after all, we can succeed against so many obstacles? The old story comes to mind, of the drummer boy who, ordered to beat the retreat, answered that he knew not how. "But I can beat a charge that will bring the dead to life." And victory took the place of despair. Let the representatives of Methodism beat a charge that will bring the dead to life. Then secure not five million dollars, nor ten million dollars for Conference Claimants, but millions enough to make the future of the Methodist ministry secure.

Methodism, rise and march to victory!

Boston, Mass. E. C. E. Dorion.

A FAMILY AFFAIR

"ROUND ROBIN" FROM THE GENERAL OFFICERS

PUBLISHING AGENTS

George P. Mains

Publishing Agent Methodist Book Concern, New York

There is no benevolence in the entire Church more worthy in itself, none more meriting universal and enthusiastic cooperation by the entire Church, than the Veteran Preachers' interest. My entire conviction and sympathy are with this cause, and I wish you the largest possible success in its promotion.

H. C. Jennings

General Agent Methodist Book Concern

The Kingdom which the Methodist preacher is helping to bring, so far as he is concerned, is a Kingdom built upon sacrifice. It is often said that preachers are not good business men, but it is safe to say that any man who can take successful charge of a church; be the general manager of not only all the religious services, but of the church debts and the building committees; and the raising of funds for all manner of causes, often on an insufficient living salary, and keep his business credit in perfect order, is a man who if he had given himself to it would have made a successful business man. Knowing the almost certain poverty of old age in the Christian ministry, this preacher listens to the higher call and becomes a preacher of the gospel, resigning his opportunities for money-making into the hands of those who do not hear the same call to higher service. These other men in business life whose homes and whose opportunities are conserved by the sacrificing preacher who brings the better moral tone into the community are under obligations most binding to see that the preacher of righteousness is maintained in decent comfort when he is, through disability, beyond the power of earning. It is therefore a simple justice to see that his old age is cared for. The 1915 CAMPAIGN is founded upon justice, and ought to win, and it will win.

E. R. Graham

Publishing Agent Methodist Book Concern, Chicago

Why a "Retired Minister"? Because he has given freely of his life forces to help to establish the Kingdom here on earth, and he is, therefore, an agent in making the world better and bringing men into touch with Him who gave the command—"Go ye into all the world and preach the gospel to every creature." He did not consider himself but the cause he was presenting to a sinful world. He gladly responded to every call, day or night, sick or well; and this faithful work brought the world under obligations to him. By devotion to duty he overtaxed the physical or mental man so that he became a broken force with nothing laid by for a day like this. Shall we pay the debt which the world owes him, or shall he suffer alone and in silence? For he neither chides nor complains.

J. H. Race

Publishing Agent Methodist Book Concern, Cincinnati

What could be finer than a denomination-wide campaign for our Retired Ministers—these deserving Veterans of Methodism! We all know that each one deserves a comfortable support. Endowment funds should be adequate so that each of these heroes may depend definitely upon his annual income. May Militant Methodism respond to the call!

EDITORS

W. V. Kelley

Editor Methodist Review

To those men, who have given themselves and their all to the Church in lavish service through many years, the Church should say, in their years of Retirement, *Freely ye have given, freely ye shall receive.*

George P. Eckman

Editor The Christian Advocate

Every reason one can think of for supporting a minister of the gospel while he is in active service is also a reason for

W. V. KELLEY
LEVI GILBERT
R. H. HUGHES
F. M. LARKIN

J. M. BUCKLEY
E. R. ZARING
D. B. BRUMMITT
H. H. MEYER

G. P. ECKMAN
C. B. SPENCER
D. G. DOWNEY
J. R. JOY

taking care of him when through age or infirmity he can no longer fulfill his public ministry. Because in his youth he turned away from all the means of gaining a livelihood, the Church undertook to provide him with sustenance. When he finishes his work the obligation to care for him is not relinquished. On the contrary it is increased. The financial opportunities which other men possess have never come to him. The claims upon his income have always equalled and usually surpassed his ability to respond to them. He gave all for the Church, and the Church is morally bound to protect him from want. The campaign which Dr. Joseph B. Hingeley is conducting under the authority of the General Conference, and the simultaneous movements in the same direction by the several Annual Conferences of Methodism, have not begun too soon, nor do they aim too high. The Church will not be comfortable until the interests of the Conference Claimants have been made secure.

H. H. Meyer
Editor Sunday School Publications

The campaign for the better support of our Retired Ministers is worthy the attention and active cooperation of every one. No benevolence or missionary enterprise has a juster claim upon our moral and financial support than has this fund. It should be promptly and adequately endowed and thereby placed upon a sound business basis, lifting the support of the Retired Ministers out of the realm of benevolences into that of recognized and deserved pensions.

J. J. Wallace
Editor Pittsburgh Christian Advocate

The very best service the preacher can render with no thought of reward or claim for wages is involved in the Divine call to the Ministry. The minimum of return for such service which God calls the Church to render is adequate provision for the preacher's needs and comfort as long as God leaves him on earth. The Campaign for Retired Preachers is a timely and worthy attempt to make feasible the realization of ideals in the Methodist Episcopal Church.

Levi Gilbert

Editor Western Christian Advocate

I believe that the Church will never be satisfied until the pensioning of her honored Retired Ministers is put upon a logical basis. The disciplinary legislation upon the subject seems very well thought out on reasonable lines. We need to push forward to the full realization of these statutes. It is but just that our aged and broken-down men should receive the full support for their old age which the legislation contemplates. To put them off with only a percentage of it is not particularly creditable to us as a great and powerful denomination. There is no lack of money to finance this project if only our laymen will awake to the full necessity of it, and I have long been of the strong opinion that no Veteran should be compelled to plead his poverty or need in order to get his full claim, nor should he think that because he has been a little forehanded and has endeavored to put aside some savings during his years, that he ought to be expected to give up his claim, perhaps to have his portion given over into the hands of some one who has more recklessly used his money.

A. J. Nast

Editor Der Christliche Apologete

The Campaign of 1915 to raise a Fund of Five Million Dollars for the Conference Claimants of the Methodist Episcopal Church will find a hearty response in the breast of every Methodist who appreciates the great debt the Church owes to those noble messengers of the Cross, who, obeying the call of their Master, have counted all things but loss for the excellency of the knowledge of Jesus Christ, their Lord, and for the privilege of spreading abroad the honor of His Name to a world redeemed by His Blood.

The proper provision for their temporal comfort in the old age is but a recognition of God's ordinance that "those who preach the gospel should live of the gospel." "Should it be thought a great thing," the Apostle Paul exclaims, "if we, who have sown unto you spiritual things, should reap your carnal things?" The spiritual debt we owe to the great army of faithful ministers of Jesus Christ can never be fully paid in gold or silver; but to withhold the gold and silver would be the height of niggardliness and dishonor.

A. J. Bucher
Editor Haus und Herd

Even under the Old Testament dispensation ministers were well provided for, who gave themselves wholly and for life to the service of the sanctuary. Could the Church to-day wish to do less? Her provision must extend over the whole of that period in the life of her faithful ministers, in which they are utterly unable to provide for themselves. If a man of God has given his all to the Church in his best years, the Church during his worst years should give him at least what he needs.

E. R. Zaring
Editor Northwestern Christian Advocate

The cause of the Retired Minister in the Methodist Episcopal Church in reality needs no defence. We all agree that in taking his ministerial vows to go wherever he may be sent, the minister earns the gratitude of the Church to the extent that he should be provided for in his declining days. The average Methodist Episcopal Preacher's salary is small and the demands made upon him are many. He is generous to the fault. He is a soldier and is earning his pension just as soldiers in the standing army of the Nation are earning their pensions. The Methodist Episcopal Minister went to the front when there were others who did not answer the call. Can we afford not to provide for him? Is not his claim a just one?

C. B. Spencer
Editor Central Christian Advocate

I hope the 1915 CAMPAIGN for five million will end in exultant triumph. The endeavor for Annual Conference organizations strikes near home and to it the people will respond, but we need also the wider or connectional view that builds up a strong treasury independent of Conference lines. Really there is nothing that will prove such a strong connectional tie as a great Connectional Fund administered by a connectional society. Success to you. Our heroes need you; and we too who will be coming along presently.

R. E. Jones
Editor Southwestern Christian Advocate

When a man enters the ministry of the Methodist Episcopal Church he solemnly agrees to go cheerfully wherever he is sent. And often in the interest of the work, ministers are put in strategic places where they suffer inconvenience and discomfiture both for themselves and their families. When they surrender themselves thus to the denomination for the good of the denomination it is only just and equitable that they should be provided for in their old age. For this reason, the work of the Board of Conference Claimants is carrying forward an imperial task of the Church. The Board is meeting an obligation that is brotherly, just, equitable and thoroughly in line with modern humanitarian movements. If he who gives himself to the country is worthy of a pension; no less worthy is he who gives himself to the Church; for often in our stead he suffers privation and inconvenience, therefore, we should share with him some comforts of life in his old age.

R. H. Hughes
Editor Pacific Christian Advocate

As I have gone to the Conferences year after year, the one thing that has astonished me above everything else as a layman, is the absolute unselfishness of a vast majority of the Methodist Preachers. They receive only a meager allowance; a very large percentage of them tithe, and then at Conference they give, and give until it really hurts, for the causes presented. I have often said that a collection would be much more appropriate than asking them to contribute. But one of the prime requisites of a follower of Jesus is unselfishness.

Then what about the day of retirement for the sacrificing minister? The laymen should provide against that day. The campaign for $5,000,000 is one of the most vital before the Church to-day. May it succeed, and may God speed the day when the "Old Veterans" may spend their declining years in the comforting assurance that the great Church they unselfishly served will see that they want naught.

Dan B. Brummitt
Editor The Epworth Herald

One thing the Methodist Episcopal Church needs to do just now with regard to the Retired Preacher is to make his lot as comfortable relatively in one part of the Church as in another. If we are connectional at all we surely should be in our dealings with the men who have made us a connection. It is not the fault of any Retired Preacher that he happens to be in a Conference whose funds are scant; and it is not fair that the Conference of the scant funds should be blamed more than other Conferences for its treatment of the Veterans. If the Board of Conference Claimants does nothing more than level up this particular form of inequality and inequity, it will justify the purposes of its existence. I believe it will do much more than that.

F. M. Larkin
Editor California Christian Advocate

It would be difficult to improve on the Discipline of the Church in what it says in reference to the cause of the Veteran Preacher. If the Church succeeds in carrying out the plan suggested by the Board of Conference Claimants and the law of the Church as found in the Discipline very much will be accomplished in the redemption of the pledges of the Methodist Episcopal Church which have been a part of the law from the beginning, to provide a comfortable support for every Retired Minister. Let every Conference apportion the full amount and give the laymen the opportunity of meeting it. This is the first and most important step in securing an adequate support for our Retired Ministers.

J. J. Manker
Editor Methodist Advocate Journal

The campaign inaugurated by the Board of Conference Claimants, with the endorsement and cooperation of the

Bishops, for securing a more adequate support for the Retired Ministers and the widows and orphan children of our deceased ministers, is worthy of all praise and merits the hearty cooperation of all ministers and laymen.

The ministers now on the Retired list labored under greater difficulties and received smaller compensations for their services than most of those now in service, and they are consequently more in need of help in their declining years. Their very necessities appeal to us who are yet on the "firing line" and on the score of justice and generosity touch our nobler nature and call us to do our best in their behalf.

We who are to-day bearing the burden and heat of the struggle soon will be laid aside ourselves, and then the very beneficence that we are now providing for others will inure to our benefit in our time of need. As we now do unto others, even so by and by will it be done unto us. Thus we shall be doubly blessed, having the consciousness of having done the right and worthy thing for worthy and needy brethren, and having the assurance that when the dark and cloudy day shall come to us there shall be light and cheer for us.

David G. Downey

Book Editor Methodist Episcopal Church

The cause of the Veteran Preacher! Need we say more? There is every reason in the world why we should be proudly anxious and glad to help these noble men. By their years of devotion, by their days of old age, by their love for us and our love for them the appeal is made strong and irresistible. God speed the 1915 CAMPAIGN in behalf of these, our elder brothers!

CORRESPONDING SECRETARIES

S. Earl Taylor

Corresponding Secretary Board of Foreign Missions

We of the Board of Foreign Missions can well understand the urgency which prompts your Board to undertake a movement for the better care of the Retired Preacher, because we ourselves are facing new conditions which make it necessary for us to make better provision for our retired missionaries, and to secure those larger sums which are necessary for the furtherance of our world-wide work. We wish you Godspeed in your great effort.

W. F. Oldham

Corresponding Secretary Board of Foreign Missions

What concerns me much in providing suitably for our Veteran Preachers is that failure at this point cuts the tap root of enthusiasm for entering the Ministry. This is true, not so much on the part of the eager young candidates as of their parents and friends who seeing the distressing conditions under which old age and feebleness find our Veterans, may be pardoned for trying to keep their sons from so uninviting a prospect. We cannot hope for the enrollment of a steady stream of capable and spiritually trained men at the front doors of our Conferences if the back doors open upon poverty and distress.

F. M. North

Corresponding Secretary Board of Foreign Missions

Your favor followed me across the Pacific, and reached me when I was occupied with travel and close work in our fields here. I feel quite sure that you need no new expression of my interest in this matter. It has been a satisfaction to me that I was able in the beginning of the quadrennium to give your Campaign a push forward.

A. B. Leonard

Secretary Emeritus Board of Foreign Missions

The campaign you are so vigorously and successfully leading for a more generous support of Retired Ministers, their widows and orphans, is worthy of the generous support of the entire Church.

Its success will not only give good cheer to preachers already retired, but will greatly hearten many now in the active ranks, poorly supported, who are looking forward to retirement in the oncoming years. Best wishes for highest success.

Ward Platt

Corresponding Secretary Board of Home Missions and Church Extension

It is a paramount claim. He has more than earned it. He has invested his life for the Church and the Kingdom; and the Church cannot do less than provide for him when he retires from a life service out of which he was able to bring little or nothing for the time when he might most need it.

C. M. Boswell

Corresponding Secretary Board of Home Missions and Church Extension

The 1915 CAMPAIGN for the Retired Preachers conducted by the Board of Conference Claimants merits the most liberal support of Ministers and laymen. The amount asked for the cause will not only aid in making Veteran Ministers comfortable in their sunsetting years but will also assure the young minister, entering upon his life's work, of a supporting provision for his latter years if he shall fully dedicate his life and talents to the work of the ministry.

F. D. Bovard

Corresponding Secretary Board of Home Missions and Church Extension

The campaign for the support of the Retired Ministers of the Methodist Episcopal Church should have the hearty cooperation of all the departments of the Church. Adequate support for the Retired Preachers will greatly strengthen the ranks of the itineracy. Success to your most worthy cause.

Robert Forbes

Corresponding Secretary Board of Home Missions and Church Extension

The amount paid to a Conference Claimant is an *equity, not a charity*. The superannuated man gave his life to the service of the Church on a *mere support,* while others were making money. Robert Burns said that Age and Want are an "ill-matched pair." Let honored age in the Methodist

Ministry be free from want. The Conference Claimants' Fund is the most sacred of all funds.

P. J. Maveety

Corresponding Secretary Freedmen's Aid Society

I am tremendously interested in the effort which is being put forth to raise a fund whose income shall make comfortable the last years of our Retired Ministers and their wives. There is no cause in the whole Church which has a louder call than that of the men who did the pioneer work of establishing and building churches, and making possible the wealth and prosperity of our whole Methodist membership. In my early ministry I was frequently solicited by Retired Ministers, whose only means of support was canvassing for books, and at that time I sincerely hoped that the day would not be far distant when a man, who had given his life to the moral and spiritual enrichment of his fellow men, should not be in abject poverty himself in his old age. As the inheritors of the fruits of the labors of these men and women, we of the younger generation should at least provide against the poverty and suffering of the makers of our riches in their old age. We are well able to do this, and are going to do it. This movement must succeed.

Thomas Nicholson

Corresponding Secretary Board of Education

I thoroughly believe in the effort to provide amply for the Retired Ministers of our Church. In this day when railroads and corporations are pensioning their faithful employees, when almost every State in the Union is making some provision for a pension fund for its teachers, and when the rewards of business are constantly becoming ample enough to enable the employees to provide for themselves, it seems to me that the Church should show due liberality toward her Veteran Ministers. It seems to me that there are two movements to which Methodism should give itself with its whole heart: First, to raise the minimum salary for a preacher in every Conference so that every acceptable Minister will have a living wage, and then to provide a sufficient retiring allowance to enable that man to give himself unreservedly to his work without distraction through the necessity of making money to provide for his declining years.

Edgar Blake

Corresponding Secretary Board of Sunday Schools

The Methodist Episcopal Church owes it to the Veteran Preacher to make his support sufficient for his needs, and to stop the policy of giving him the crumbs that fall from others' tables. His claim should be the first to be raised in full. If any man must lack, let it not be he. The 1915 CAMPAIGN of the Board of Conference Claimants is the most comprehensive and statesmanlike procedure that has ever been attempted in behalf of Veteran Preachers in the history of Methodism. May it succeed beyond even the fondest hopes of the Corresponding Secretary and his colaborers.

J. B. Hingeley

Corresponding Secretary Board of Conference Claimants

"Whatsoever things are Honest, whatsoever things are Just, whatsoever things are Pure, whatsoever things are Lovely, whatsoever things are of Good Report; if there be any Virtue and if there be any Praise, think on these things"; and remember that the Veterans of the Cross were "honest," "just," "pure," "lovely," "of good report," examples of "virtue" and worthy of "praise," and that the Church which neglects them cannot itself remain "honest," "just," "pure" or "lovely," nor can it be "of good report," for "virtue" in a world which in so many ways recognizes and praises the pension competency for old age.

W. F. Sheridan

General Secretary Epworth League

The Church owes a debt to its Retired Preachers which it never can repay. These men are the hidden pillars upon which the Church of to-day stands. They have laid broad and deep the foundations of the Church's present prosperity. I trust that you will be gloriously successful in raising funds adequate to the needs of these Heroes of the Cross.

Clarence T. Wilson

Corresponding Secretary Temperance Society

I am greatly stirred and thoroughly grateful to hear of your proposed plan to endow the great movement for the support of the Conference Claimants. These men have purchased the lots, built our churches, won our members, organized our colleges, paid our debts, started our beneficent enterprises, made our civilization, reformed our abuses and suffered for every good cause. Is it not time we were doing something worthy for them and something worthy of ourselves?

When they volunteered for this service, we put them up before the Conference and made them vow to go where sent, to live on what was given them and to make no complaints. They have carried out their part of the contract; and what is our part but to see that when the field work is done, the pension is adequate to support them in comfort until the end? There ought to be millions in your treasury to supplement the meager offerings of the Conferences and hold up the hands of these representatives of the cross.

W. S. Bovard

General Secretary Methodist Brotherhood

I congratulate the Methodist Episcopal Church upon the plan and progress of the campaign for a suitable sum of money with which to care for the Veteran Ministers. No cause making its appeal to the Church meets with more general and more hearty response than the appeal for these funds. The Church is seeing that it is not simply a benefit to the Retired Ministers, but a great stimulus to men looking toward the ministry or now bearing its burdens. The Church is also seeing that the laymen are serving themselves by protecting the ministry against the temptation to remain in the active ranks after they should be upon the pension roll. Success is bound to crown your efforts.

D. W. Howell

Corresponding Secretary General Deaconess Board

I sincerely trust that the Campaign of 1915 will be all that you desire. It seems to me that if the preachers give the strength of their manhood to the development of the Kingdom that the Church should amply provide for them in old age. The only proper and honorable care that the Church should offer to the Retired Preachers is a care-free old age.

"WHY DON'T YOU SPEAK FOR YOURSELF, JOHN?"

BY A METHODIST PRISCILLA TO JOHN, THE PREACHER

Hoarse? Yes, hoarse from shouting
For the brown men of Japan;
Sore-throated from long preaching
On the lost in Palawan;
Vocal cords all rasping
From lambasting Holy Rome;—
And not a breath for whispering
For the Brownies in your home.

Tired? Yes, tired from working
For the mothers in Ceylon;
For the foot-bound Chinese mothers
Limping, hobbling in Canton
Far away and distant,
Under minaret and dome;—
Tired? Too tired for thinking
Of the Mother in your home.

Pleading? Tears a-streaming
Down your cheek; with sobbing voice,
For the alien and stranger,
That they make your heaven their choice?
Anxious for the Hindu children
Far away across the foam;—
What about these orphan children
Of your Pastor here at home?

Out of patience with the Veteran
Who will not lie down and die?
With the Widow and the Orphan
Who distract you with their cry?
No? Forgive you? You don't mean it?
Far away you will not roam?
You repent? *Then sure will care for*
Those who dwell within your home.

WE'LL DO IT!

BISHOP W. F. OLDHAM

Corresponding Secretary Board of Foreign Missions

"They took us for life—let them see us thru," was the homely but unmistakably clear putting of the case by the Rev. Varnum A. Cooper, D.D., to the New England Conference. It is true. It is reasonable. It is just.

When the young man after years of rigorous and expensive training stood at the door of the Annual Conference he approached the Church of his choice with mingled feelings of high hope and utter abandon. His hope was that opportunity would be given him to preach Christ's Gospel, which he felt with glow of soul to be "the Power of God unto Salvation." He was eager to be at it and asked few questions, if any, about his earthly compensations. He expected to marry and in due course to welcome the children God might send him. But his was no prudent calculation of the exact means for the support of himself and those dear ones whom in his young enthusiasm and other-worldly devotion he committed to the care of the church, at whose altars he was converted, under whose fostering care he had grown, and to whose service he was consecrating his talents, his labors, his family, his life, his all.

Because of his eager youth, his fine preparedness, his enthusiasm and his quality, the Church received him gladly. When he was presented to the Conference, and the Board of Examiners reported on his case, and the District Superintendent followed in a brief statement, closing with the words, "Bishop, there is nothing against him," the older men saw again the picture of their own youthful days, and their eyes were moist while they cried aloud, "Amen! Amen!"

And so the Church took the young minister for life; and for thirty, forty or it might be fifty years he has given to it the best there was in him. Unstintedly he has poured himself out. He has been "in labors abundant." His sermons have been on every possible subject that can engage human attention. He has appeared before every kind of Society, from the Masons bedecked in solemn pomp, and the Grand Army of the Republic, with its pathetic group of feeble but grand old men, to the "Sisters of the Maccabees" and the children of the "Loyal Legion"—and to all of them he has spoken the fitting, Christly word. He has been ceaseless in pastoral and community labors; advising the careless, counseling the perplexed, stimulating the indolent, urging the timid. He has sent scores of young people to high school and college, advised others in their choice of a life work; has married the youths, baptized the babies, visited the sick, watched by the dying, buried the dead—and above all has yearned over the wayward, has pleaded with the erring, and has brought many to a saving knowledge of Jesus Christ.

Meanwhile financial matters have pressed upon him. A family has come; the children have had to be schooled and suitably kept; there have been books to buy, and endless social duties to meet. He has contributed to every collection and has often been the mainstay of "the benevolences." His home has been headquarters for church guests, and he has never turned away from the poor. He is often blamed for lack of thrift; but the money he spends on others is the only money he has really "laid up."

Meanwhile the boys and girls whose education has always kept the preacher-couple at the borders of want are scattered and gone. They are now in those efforts in getting started in life which are the common experience of the children of the parsonage.

And now it comes towards evening. His hair is frosted, and his pastoral feet do not trip readily from door to door. His sermons, too, though packed with the weighty advices of a lifetime, are not as merrily full of cheer as those of his less knowing youth. It has been hard for several years to place him. The fact is that the preacher has grown old, and must give place to younger men.

Where is he to turn for shelter and food as evening gathers about him? Will the Church, that took him in his youth, and to whom he has given unstintedly the strength of his manhood years, with material compensations far below the level achieved by others of his parts and training in other vocations of life, now reassure him as he comes towards the end of his active days? Was not that the implied covenant through all the strenuous and poorly paid years? Was not he to give the best he had and was not the Church in its turn to see that his outpoured life was to be sacredly guarded from the most dreaded of stalking ghosts—an old age of feebleness and penury? And besides, there's the old preacher's wife, and what he might bear for himself, how shall he bear for her?

Is it not a refinement of cruelty as well as a breach of implied trust for the Church in the end to fail this man? It is true he has not been a close financier. He has not painfully counted or pinched the pennies he drew from his pocket; he has been too busy trying to persuade others to follow him in the support of every good cause. And, truth to tell, the margin between respectable living demanded of him and the last dollar of salary was never noticeably wide.

And so, to return to the question, what will the Church say to this anxious man as he now for the first time inquires, and justly, as to what provision is being made for his remaining days? He is now, in the telling phrase of the older day, "A Worn Out Minister." Will not the Church, in whose service he wore himself out, fulfill its part of the contract?

Surely our laymen—men of the market, the shop, the court-house, the office and the farm—need only look at this question in its broader aspects to determine at once what a square deal calls for.

"They took us for life—let them see us through."

The retired minister must be provided with a modest competency. Shame must not be brought upon the Church, nor heart-break to the old preacher and his loved companion by failure at this point. And it can so easily be done. Let pastors give the people the *actual* facts *without apology.* Then let us all pull together to raise the *ten million dollar endowment.* It needs to be done only *once for all.*

Kindness, Thoughtfulness, Gratitude, Justice, Fair Play, all say, "*Do it.*" What shall be the answer of the individual pastor—what the reply of the individual layman? May there not be a quick, glad response from all: *We'll do it!*

WILLIAM F. OLDHAM.

THE HERO FUND

"Some day a millionaire may establish a 'hero fund' for country ministers who spend their lives in the service of the community, not only ministering weekly to their congregations, but marrying the young people, visiting the sick, burying the dead and responding to every call. Not the least part of their heroism consists in their willingness to serve for the pitiful salaries paid in some small towns, salaries smaller than the wages of a carpenter or a blacksmith and less than a day laborer gets in cities."—*Youth's Companion.*

C. H. McRea

Youth's fire had faded from his face,
And Time had wrinkles sent him;
The crown of age, the hoary head,
The other world has lent him.
His step is slow, his eye is dim;
There is no hero fund for him.

When first he heard the trumpet call
To preach the glad evangel,
His heart, responsive, said, "I will,"
As might a strong archangel.
He preached that mighty word with vim—
But there's no hero fund for him.

By day and night, through flood and fire,
O'er dying sinners yearning;
He pulled the sinking from the tide,
The brands from out the burning;
Desire is dying now, and dim
The hope of hero fund for him.

The meanness of the narrow souls,
Who starved him in the service,
Is fearful now—when health is gone—
That wealth might make him nervous.
The claimant's dole is spare and slim.
There is no hero fund for him.

But O, the chariots of God
Are ready to move straightway
To bear the conquering hero home
Whene'er he sights the gateway!
'Tis sunset o'er the world's red rim,
The hero fund is full for him.

PART III. THE CLAIM SUPREME

CHAPTER III. AGENCIES

HENRY C. JENNINGS

GEORGE P. MAINS

JOHN H. RACE

EDWIN R. GRAHAM

CLAIMANTS' GREAT ASSET

THE BOOK CONCERN

THE REV. GEORGE P. MAINS, D.D., LL.D
Publishing Agent Methodist Episcopal Church

I would like to emphasize two facts about the Book Concern, and also make a suggestion which I hope may be received with large hospitality.

FIRST. While I cheerfully recognize the large service which the Book Concern has been able to render to the Retired Ministers, I nevertheless think that there is some danger that this specific mission may be unduly emphasized at the expense of what is fundamentally and really its great mission, namely, that of furnishing the Church with the best literature at the most reasonable cost to the consumer. I yield to no person in my interest in the welfare of the Retired Preacher, and believe that he should not only receive the largest recognition of sympathy and approval from the Church, but that it is a supreme duty of the Church to see that his old age is ministered to in comfort by a support that shall be adequate to his needs. In the thought of many observers it is an anomalous thing that the Methodist Episcopal Church should subsidize its literature in the interest of making dividends to the Annual Conferences in behalf of the Veteran and Retired Preachers. I do not myself quarrel with the proposition that from its surplus earnings the Book Concern shall make generous bestowments in their interests. I simply have a feeling that at present we are unduly emphasizing the function of the Book Concern in this particular relation. There are some people who seem to be in danger of losing sight, pretty much altogether, of the real mission for which the Book Concern was established. I know personally men of prominence who are continually urging upon us the necessity of earning large amounts of money in order that we may make generous dividends to the worn-out preachers, yet, if I were entirely frank, I would be bound to say that from the lips of several of these men I have never heard one single suggestion with reference to the supreme importance that the Book Concern shall consider it to be its primary mission to furnish to our great constituency the best Church literature possible at the lowest sustaining costs.

When the Book Concern was first founded its promoters were all poor. The best of them received only a meager, living support. It was a very natural and legitimate thing that if any earnings were made by the publication house in excess of the real needs of the business, such earnings should be divided among the traveling preachers of that early day. Our present condition, however, is widely different from that which then prevailed. We now have a great and wealthy Church with a lay membership rapidly approximating four millions; a Church from whose prosperity the creation of a fund which would be adequate to give comfort to all our Retired Ministers, if entered upon dutifully and cheerfully, would hardly call for an appreciable reduction of current resources. It is my very firm conviction that whatever the Book Concern may now do, or may be able to do for this interest in the future, the Church as a whole should respond to the summons of the General Conference by the establishment of a fund which shall place the Methodist Veteran in his old age on a basis of financial support not excelled by any other Church in Christendom.

SECOND. The aid which the Book Concern has already rendered to the Conference Claimants funds represents a great fact, worthy of all emphasis. I understand from the Corresponding Secretary of the Board of Conference Claimants that an effort is now to be made to raise an endowment fund of five million dollars, the proceeds of which shall be devoted *in perpetuo* to supplementing the present provisions for the support of Retired Preachers. I might very properly congratulate the secretary upon the fact that before a dollar of this proposed fund shall have been raised there is already provided a sustaining fund of nearly six million dollars, which has been utilized for this purpose. The Methodist Book Concern to-day has assets amounting to very nearly this sum, from the earnings of which during this very year we are paying over to Annual Conferences the magnificent sum of three hundred thousand dollars. By a law that is pretty definitely ascertained in the experience of the financial world, the most conservative securities can be reckoned upon to return an interest revenue of only about four per cent. This seems to be a pretty well demonstrated fact under normal financial conditions; but this year we are actually paying to the Annual Conferences from our earnings a cash dividend of five per cent on our capital of six million dollars, really a little more than five per cent on our actual capital.

In the history of the Book Concern there have been long periods when, because of obligations incurred in other directions, no dividends from earnings have been paid to the Annual Conferences. I need not here enter into a statement as to the reasons for the large diversions which during some considerable periods have been made from the earnings of the Book Concern to causes other than to benefactions for the worn-out preachers. I call your attention, however, to what has been done in recent years in this connection. Previous to the year 1883 there were paid altogether as dividends to the Annual Conferences, $344,066. Since 1883, including the current year 1914, we have paid $3,254,000, thus making a total of dividends from the earnings of the Book Concern of $3,598,066. Undoubtedly the total dividends of the present quadrennium will exceed a million dollars. I challenge you with the statement that this magnificent result is without parallel in the history of any other denomination in Christendom. It is something for which the Church as a whole may cherish a sense of profound gratitude. With continued loyalty to its increasing publishing interests, I see no reason why the Book Concern should not prove a source of unceasing and increasing benefactions to our Retired Ministers.

Third. I would like to make a suggestion that the Board of Conference Claimants should enter into arrangements with the Book Concern as to life annuities, in which work we have an advantage over any other existing organizations. I can see no reason why the income from such a fund should not be placed for administration with the Board of Conference Claimants; but I am very clearly of the conviction that a great annuity fund could be secured by compliance with the suggestion. I congratulate the Church upon the prospects of enlarging success in this honorable enterprise.

150 Fifth Ave., New York. George P. Mains.

STORY OF THE SADDLEBAGS

The Rev. C. M. Adams

"The saddlebags were tied on behind the saddle when full, otherwise thrown over the seat of saddle. They were often used as a pillow at night in the open, with a camp fire at the feet, at which coffee had been boiled and bacon fried.

"The outfit consisted of horse, saddle, saddlebags, quirt, lariat and frying-pan, food, Bible and hymn book. Preaching places were school houses or the Court House. School houses were of logs with openings, but without windows and

doors, with dirt floors, fire places and slabs for benches. The parsonage had been sold for fifty dollars as I had no bird for the nest. It was loaded on to a lumber wagon, without being torn down, and drawn ten miles to a mining camp. My salary was $150 a year. Board was $3 per week, or $156 a year. The hospitality of the people knew no bounds."

METHODISM'S OLDEST INSTITUTION
THE CHARTERED FUND

THE REV. ELWIN HITCHCOCK, D.D.
Secretary Preachers' Aid Society
New Hampshire Conference

There is no fellowship that surpasses that of Methodist preachers. It is not merely poetry or sentiment that we sing at Annual Conference:

> "We share our mutual woes,
> Our mutual burdens bear.
> And often for each other flows
> The sympathizing tear."

It is "what we have felt and known." This was true a hundred and fifty years ago and it is true to-day. The spirit of other denominations toward Methodism at that time was not what it is to-day. Methodists were looked at askance as those that were turning the theological world "upside down." Because of this and other conditions many of the preachers were frequently sent to fields that tried soul and body, to meet opposition and not infrequently persecution. Their salaries were uncertain and meager, so that a *distressed* traveling preacher was not an unknown quantity, and the superannuate or worn-out preacher was not cared for as he had a right to expect; for he had given his life to the Church and was not the Church under moral obligations to care for him in his old age?

At an early date it became apparent, not only to the preachers but also to the Church, that relief must be found for these men in their old age; and with this in view the General Conference of 1796 established the Chartered Fund, and the Presiding Elders and pastors were appointed agents to solicit and receive subscriptions for the same, the money to be invested by Trustees chosen by the General Conference. It was ordered that the income be divided into as many equal parts as there were Annual Conferences in the United States, and applied for the benefit of the distressed effective preachers and Retired Ministers and their families.

The Chartered Fund has not been a failure, although it has not accomplished all that was hoped for. If it has not brought permanent relief for those for whom it was established, it has brought temporary help and joy into many a preacher's home. The annual dividend from the Chartered Fund at present amounts to thirty dollars for each Annual Conference.

Because the Chartered Fund was not equal to the emergencies, Preachers' Aid Societies, Relief Associations, and kindred organizations were started, which have frequently failed to do all that was expected, because the Presiding Elders and preachers, who were depended upon to solicit the funds already had multiplying cares which taxed their time and bodies. Such organizations lacked the essential requisite for efficiency, namely, an executive head charged with the duty of making the movement go.

The Methodist Church has at last struck the trail that will lead us to the goal of a sufficient support for all Conference Claimants. With our Campaign cry of five million dollars for permanent funds, and with Bishops, District Superintendents, Preachers, Corresponding Secretary and Conference representatives all joining in the shout and giving this cause the right of way for 1915, the time is near when Veteran Preachers and their wives will be assured a comfortable support, which neither they nor the Church will consider to be a charity, but an honorable claim to be honorably met.

ELWIN HITCHCOCK.

Bradford, Mass.

ANNUAL CONFERENCE ENDOWMENTS

THE REV. S. J. GREENFIELD, D.D.
Field Secretary of Preachers' Permanent Fund Commission, Northern New York Conference

The denomination to which we belong possesses the unique distinction of being the only branch of Protestantism, with the exception of the Methodist Episcopal Church, South, which has had local endowment funds of any considerable size for the benefit of Retired Ministers, widows and orphans.

Endowment funds are generally denominational rather than local; as for instance, those in the Presbyterian, Baptist, Congregational and Protestant Episcopal Churches; also those of Methodism in Canada, England and Australia. In these bodies endowment funds are secured and managed by general boards instead of by local organizations. Many of our Annual Conference organizations have existed for years, but it was not until 1908 that the General Board of Conference Claimants was organized. Up to that time the general endowment funds for the benefit of Conference Claimants were held by the Trustees of the Methodist Episcopal Church and by the Chartered Fund. Had the Board of Conference Claimants been brought into existence decades ago a general fund might have been established sufficient by this time to provide an adequate support for all Conference Claimants.

These two methods, that of a general board and that of local boards, are widely different and suggest the question as to which is the better plan; and much might be said in favor of each. A central fund held in trust and administered by a general board would be in agreement with our polity, for our other denominational interests are in the hands of general boards and have been for many years. A general board would secure centralization of work and responsibility; it would insure a more equitable distribution of the funds to those who are to be benefited by them; it would tend to remove restiveness on the part of the ministry, and conduce to a greater contentment among the members of the smaller and weaker Annual Conferences; it might also be less expensive to administer one general fund than one hundred or more local funds; and it is possible, also, that as funds would be invested on a larger scale, they could be invested to greater advantage. These considerations, I think, may all be urged in support of one endowment fund for the whole Church. But there are other considerations which may be urged in favor of local endowments. There is, for instance, the fact that a local fund appeals more strongly to the people within a given Conference. Such a fund is for the direct benefit of ministers and widows with whose names and work and faces the people of the Annual Conference are familiar. There are also the ties of pastoral relationships which bind the membership to their own ministers, and the appeal in behalf of the Retired Ministers and those dependent upon them is an appeal in behalf of people who are known; and, of course, such an appeal is likely to be more effective than a more general one.

Then a local fund makes a stronger appeal to the ministers since it is their own fund raised and administered for and by themselves. The average minister, as well as the average church member, will be likely to take more pride in and give more liberally to such a fund than to one which is to be administered by a general board; and as the chief consideration is the securing of the funds this fact is very important. At the present time, too, such Conference funds are administered economically; for except the special representative the officers do not receive compensation for their labor.

That Annual Conference Endowment Funds for the benefit of Conference Claimants appeal strongly to our people is evidenced from the number and the size of them now in existence. Eighty-two Annual Conferences have endowment funds, the largest of which is about $350,000 and the smallest is about $500. Altogether the funds now owned and managed by the Annual Conferences amount to about $4,000,000; an amount which is far from being adequate to meet the just dues of 7,000 Conference Claimants, half of whom are Retired Ministers. Reducing the claims of the widows (one half of their husbands' claims) and those of the dependent orphans (one fifth of their fathers' claims) to the basis of the full annuity claim of a Retired Minister, we find that the total problem is the same as if there were 5,000 Veteran Preachers for whom the Disciplinary rate of one seventieth of the average salary of the effective ministers of the Conference for each year of service was to be provided. The total $4,000,000 divided by 5,000 would give only an endowment of $800 for each, the annual interest on which would amount to only $40. The total legal claims are $1,600,000 annually which represents five per cent on $32,000,000. The annual dividends of The Book Concern, the Board of Conference Claimants and the Chartered Fund amount to $330,000, equal to five per cent on $6,600,000. The direct contributions from the pastoral charges exceed $550,000, or five per cent on $11,000,000, so that when Methodism shall have added $10,400,000, to its present invested funds all claims will be met.

Many Annual Conferences have undertaken to raise large amounts for their endowments, those amounts in the fall Conferences alone reaching beyond five millions of dollars; but the ultimate goal is far beyond the total of the figures already set, and that distant goal must be reached, before the Retired Minister or widow can be certain of a comfortable support in retirement.

The Northern New York Conference has 100 Conference Claimants. To give them an average of $400 a year we need $40,000. From the connectional dividends, annual collections, and our present endowments, they get $13,000 leaving a deficit of $27,000 to be provided out of future endowments. So that we need to increase our present endowment to at least $500,000.

Various methods are used in securing funds for Annual Conference Endowments; cash gifts, pledges payable in annual installments, the issuance of life annuity bonds, the establishment of memorial funds, bequests of money or devises of real estate, apportionments made to the pastoral charges, assessments on the ministers, etc. Many Conferences have committees, commissions or incorporated organizations, some composed of ministers alone and others of ministers and laymen. The latter is preferable because it secures the active support of strong church members, which is an asset of great value in such work, and places also at the service of the commission the business foresight and experience and judgment of successful business men, and gives confidence to the people in the undertaking itself and also in the proper care and investment of the funds after they have been secured. Many Annual Conferences have set apart a member of the Conference who devotes all his time to this work and becomes the official representative of his Conference, presenting the cause in the churches and in personal solicitation; devising means for carrying on the work, keeping up the correspondence, looking after the collection of pledges and cultivating the interest of the people generally; acting as an official of the Conference by the appointment of the presiding bishop. That the labor of such a representative is necessary is shown by the fact that only those Conferences which have such a representative in the field succeed to any marked degree. During the three years immediately preceding the appointment of a field representative in the Northern New York Conference, two hundred charges and as many pastors gave to the endowment fund an average of $103 per year. But during the next three years the same churches and pastors paid to the endowment fund over $30,000, an average of $10,000 a year, with fully as much more provided for in pledges and bequests. But the cash result of such labor is not all. In addressing a congregation in behalf of the cause, and in showing its merits he can speak out more candidly and frankly than the pastors feel at liberty to do. Incidentally also, his appeals make clear the need of a more adequate support for the ministers in the effective ranks and lead the people to appreciate the value of the pastorate.

The basis of distribution for the incomes from the endowment funds is not the same in each Conference. The differences are numerous, and indicate a great variety of opinions as to which is the more equitable. There are, however, two methods, which are more or less general. One method provides for distribution on a basis of necessity; the other method is based on years of service. Some Conferences have two funds, distributed separately.

The Methodist Church in Canada has two such funds. With us, however, the Annual Conference can distribute money to meet necessities, if it so desires. The charity element in the necessitous distribution is highly objectionable to self-respecting ministers. For a person accustomed to associate, as a minister and wife, with people who never depend upon charity for their support, this difficulty is prohibitive. The sympathies of our people should be aroused but not at the expense of their sense of equity and gratitude.

The distribution based on years of service is free from the element of "charity" and *makes no infringement on self-respect.* Under this method Retired Ministers or widows do not have to disclose their financial condition or to prove their poverty. Pension systems of other institutions do not make poverty a condition of receiving benefit. The government does not pension a veteran soldier or a civil servant because of his penury. The Carnegie Fund does not pension professors on proof of poverty. The Pennsylvania or any other great railroad or corporation does not pension employees because they are living under the shadow of the poorhouse; and it is not going too far to say that ministers should not be compelled to prove poverty to a grateful Church. True, much money is contributed by the churches for benevolent purposes, but the support of the ministry must never be viewed in the light of a benevolence. One has said, "The laborer is worthy of his hire"; and another has written, "The Lord hath ordained that they that preach the gospel should live of the gospel"; and later, with a touch of irony, wrote, "If we have sown unto you spiritual things, *is it a great thing if we shall reap your carnal things?*" The support of the ministry can no more be regarded as a benevolence than can the support of the physician, who receives fees, or the mechanic who is paid wages. To regard it as a benevolence is to weaken the Church before the world, to turn the effective minister into a mendicant and the Retired Minister into a pauper.

In Canadian Methodism the support of the Retired Ministry is based wholly upon years of service; though a small fund is reserved to meet special needs. At its recent General Conference the pension rate was raised from ten to twelve dollars for each year of service, the amount to be paid in semi-annual installments. An appeal on this basis is an appeal to our people's sense of equity, justice and gratitude, rather than to their sympathy; and they will respond through gratitude for the holy services of men and women, the character of whose work entitles them to *a life-time of support in return for a life-time of service.*

Utica, N. Y. S. J. Greenfield.

ANNUAL CONFERENCE REPRESENTATIVES

J. C. North	Robert Stephens	S. A. Morse
J. B. Green	S. J. Greenfield	J. A. Sargent
C. A. Kelley	Stedman Applegate	J. W. Robinson
G. W. Kepler	C. M. Shepherd	U. G. Humphrey

CLAIMANTS' GREATEST ASSET

CONTRIBUTIONS FROM CHURCHES—APPORTIONMENTS

THE REV. E. C. CLEMANS, D.D.
Field Representative Board of Conference Claimants

One of the early problems that confronted American Methodism was the care of "worn-out" preachers and those dependent upon them. The people were poor, collections were small and smaller still were the salaries of the preachers. The Book Concern was organized; also the Chartered Fund, the first permanent investment fund for Conference Claimants. But the main source of revenue was the "Fifth Collection." At the first quarterly meeting a collection was taken for the preacher, the Presiding Elder and the Bishops; at the second quarterly meeting a second collection was taken; at the third quarterly meeting a third collection; and at the fourth quarterly meeting a fourth collection. After these four collections had secured about all the money in sight, a *fifth collection* was taken for the "worn-out preachers and widows."

The number of claimants being large and the funds small, the Conference stewards were compelled to reduce each claimant to a necessitous basis, the motion generally being, "I move that Brother Brown be granted a superannuated relation and be referred to the stewards for favorable consideration"; and all superannuates were so referred. The stewards were compelled to scrutinize carefully the material condition of each claimant, for if one claimant had more means than another, he would need and receive less. To be reduced to such a basis was so humiliating, that preachers in the active ranks dreaded the day of superannuation and prayed to be taken away before they were called to humiliating penury.

Just when the Conferences commenced to make an apportionment to the pastoral charges for the support of superannuated preachers is uncertain, but it was at about the time when the benevolent causes were apportioned to the Church. The Annual Conference made the apportionment for superannuates; the Presiding Elders apportioned it to the pastoral charges and the pastors were supposed to raise the amount apportioned. There was no sense of responsibility, no prorating, no pressure brought to bear on the stewards, and the pastors took the collection as they minded. If superannuation was near, they felt the necessity of raising the full apportionment. If other causes were pressing, the claim of the superannuate suffered. So that during all these years hardly sixty per cent of the amount apportioned was raised; the greatest amount, about $300,000, being raised in 1908.

The General Conference of 1908 made a great advance in the legislation in regard to the support of Conference Claimants. At that time the support of Conference Claimants became one of the four items of ministerial support, and the pastoral charges were required to pro rate the claims of the Pastor, District Superintendent, Bishop and Conference Claimants. Previously the cause of the claimants had been considered a benevolence and the people were appealed to to give money to it out of charity; but the new legislation, by making their claim a part of ministerial support, took it out of the benevolences and placed it on the salary basis, so that now the charges must raise this money in the salary budget.

Then the law of prorating was established. In accordance with this law the Pastor, the District Superintendent or the Bishop cannot be paid in full, unless the Conference Claimants are paid in full; all ministers are to receive the same proportion of the total amount paid as their several claims bear to the total budget for ministerial support. The law of prorating means simply that neither of the four shall receive more than his proportionate share of the total support.

The basis for the apportionment is usually the cash salary paid to the pastors, the percentage in many Conferences being seven per cent. It is the duty of the Conference stewards to recommend the apportionment (¶ 326 of the Discipline), which, however, must be approved by the Conference before it becomes effective. The stewards by referring to the Conference Minutes determine what is the average salary of the preachers in the effective ranks. This average salary is divided by two, because every Retired Preacher after thirty-five years of service in the "effective relation" is entitled to an amount equal to one half of the average salary of the effective members of the Conference. This half salary divided by thirty-five gives the *legal annuity rate for one year's service.* The stewards then find the total number of the annuity years of all the Retired Preachers, widows and dependent orphans, which, multiplied by the legal annuity rate, gives the amount required for annuities. To this must be added what will be necessary for "necessitous cases," that is, those claimants whose condition is such as to require more than their annuity.

The sum of the amount required for annuities, or pensions, and for necessitous cases makes the *total claims* for the Conference Claimants, or the total liability of the Annual Conference. In order to determine what amount should be provided by the pastoral charges, the total income derived from other sources—connectional dividends, interest of Conference investments, etc.—is subtracted from the total claims, and the remainder, plus 5%, must be apportioned the several pastoral charges of the Conference, to be raised as a part of the budget for ministerial support. In 1913 the total amount raised through such apportionment was about $500,-000, being only one third of the toal amount needed.

The intensive 1915 CAMPAIGN will greatly increase the investment income; also there will be a steady increase in the dividends of The Book Concern and the Board of Conference Claimants; but in order to meet the full liability of the entire Church, $1,600,000, the total amount to be raised by apportionments to the pastoral charges should be $700,000, an increase of $200,000; and for many years to come the amounts received annually from the churches will continue to be the "greatest asset of Conference Claimants."

And this ought to be so. There never should be a time in the history of Methodism when Methodists should not be raising money for the support of claimants. We love those whom we help. We forget those for whom we are not concerned, and the Church cannot afford to forget its honored Veterans. Their claim should remain one of the items of ministerial support; and for its own good, as well as for their care, the Church should always have an apportionment for the support of its Retired Preachers and other Conference Claimants.

Minneapolis, Minn. EZRA C. CLEMANS.

ANNUAL CONFERENCE REPRESENTATIVES

G. F. Hopkins
J. W. Bissell
A. G. Schafer
T. E. Green

J. W. Pruen
J. M. Leonard
John Collins
J. W. Cain

F. M. Van Treese
John Mayer
W. H. Pope
J. C. Kendrick

METHODISM'S YOUNGEST INSTITUTION

THE BOARD OF CONFERENCE CLAIMANTS

THE REV. JAMES HAMILTON, D.D.

Conference Claimants Comm'ssion and Board

With this youngest institution of Methodism I have been related since its birth, and also closely identified with its strenuous career. Miss Willard declared that the best time to begin training a child was a hundred years before it was born. This child of the Church has been in prenatal training about that long, but more particularly since 1878, when the Rev. J. S. Smart, a big-hearted, robust character, led in the fight to have the profits of the Book Concern go to the support of Conference Claimants, as originally designed, instead of to paying Bishops' salaries, General Conference expenses and other items. Later Dr. J. Benson Hamilton took a prominent part in the training.

At the Cleveland General Conference, 1896, the first forward step was taken to put the claim of the superannuates upon a self-respecting basis; that is, on years of service instead of penury. Three things were accomplished by the advanced legislation: (1) A declaration was made defining Conference Claimants; (2) The annual observance of Conference Claimants' Day was ordered, with the presentation of the claim and a collection; (3) An annuity distribution was provided. It is a matter of personal gratification to be able to say that this advance was copied almost verbatim from what was then known as the Michigan Conference Plan, which was the Canadian Plan modified to meet American exigencies. Had the whole plan gone into the Discipline at that time, we would have had, substantially, the plan of to-day.

The Chicago General Conference, 1900, left the chapter on Conference Claimants without change, but the discussion and agitation of the subject went forward with increasing momentum, so that at the Los Angeles General Conference, 1904, the entire Church was ready for pronounced action. Dr.

Buckley voiced this sentiment in a motion made on the first day of the session asking for the appointment of a special committee to take up the question and report at an early date. The Committee was appointed, but before it could convene, the action was reconsidered and all papers referring to the subject were referred to the Committee on Temporal Economy. A further delay in appointing the sub-committee to work out the plan made it impossible to report until very late in the session, when the delegates were getting anxious to return to their homes. There was also a minority report, and finally a Commission was appointed to study the question during the quadrennium and to report later.

It was my privilege to have been a member of the Special Committee, and of the Commission, and also of the subcommittee which drafted the plan submitted at Los Angeles. While I have had my share of honors in the Church, I never felt more highly complimented than by that assignment. Bishop Cranston, Dr. Wilder and Mr. Robert T. Miller were fine types of the episcopacy, the pastorate and the laity, who served on the Commission. I will never forget the devotion and faithfulness of my associates to the sacred work committed to their hands. Soon Bishop Joyce, who would have been appointed Chairman, was taken away, but not until he had written a letter whose pathos and consecration inspired and enthused all hearts. Bishop Walden was appointed chairman, and in due time the plan was published.

At the Baltimore General Conference, 1908, we had the help of Drs. J. R. Day, C. J. Little and Frank Mason North in putting the finishing touches to the immortal document. It remained for our Corresponding Secretary, then and now Secretary of the General Conference, to move an amendment providing for the creation of the Board of Conference Claimants and the election of a Corresponding Secretary to work the plan. He had the idea that although an axe may be a good tool, yet it is not worth much without a man to swing it. I had a like proposition "up my sleeve" intending to present it when the plan had carried. There was opposition to the multiplication of benevolent boards, and I was afraid to have the idea of a board with a corresponding secretary, incorporated in the legislation, lest the instrument upon which we had spent so much time and care should be put in jeopardy. In this conviction I was sustained by the others. But Dr. Hingeley made it appear so reasonable and necessary that the entire plan went through with little opposition, and the child was born.

Well was it for the child that there was some one to care for it; for no infant was ever left in a worse plight. No provision had been made for clothing or sustenance. My indignation waxes hot as I recall the situation. Think of it! A great Connectional Church Board was brought into existence and given all the rights and privileges of the other benevolent boards, and not a dollar provided with which it could inaugurate its work. The Hebrew slaves were called on to make bricks without straw. But that was not a circumstance compared with this. They at least had the *mud,* but our Board had nothing. Then too some of the older sisters did not take any too kindly to the youngster. Of course, they couldn't help liking him; but why should he demand recognition and his share of the family income? It was a little distressing, especially since there was not any too much to go around. But he was there to stay and to have his rights recognized.

And now look for a moment at the miracle of finance which placed this institution on its feet. It was said of Alexander Hamilton that he "struck the rock of our national resources and abundant streams of revenue gushed forth." But Hamilton had the authority to strike. Not so Marvin Campbell, the treasurer; but he struck, and the treasury was filled. Our big, elder brother, the Book Concern, had faith in our integrity and future usefulness and granted us a loan which put us on our feet until our Corresponding Secretary could state the case to the Church.

Now hear the story of a financial achievement. Having absolutely no assured income, save the "Conference percentages," not a cent of which could be touched for expenses, the Board has distributed to the Conferences, or has on hand for such distribution, $175,000; has a Permanent Fund amounting to $250,000; has a good office equipment; has paid all bills when due and has spent for the common good, for literature and publicity, $40,000. If the Board had done nothing more than supply inspirational literature, it would have abundantly justified its creation. At this point we touch the greatest achievement of the Board—the successful leadership of the entire Church in increasing its annual distribution by $500,000, and in adding $3,000,000 to endowment funds. For me to have contributed in any way to this magnificent result is abundant honor.

The whole attitude of the Church has been changed by the persistent championship of the Veterans' cause. "Prorating," for instance, instead of being regarded as a matter of easy convenience, is now recognized as an honest effort to do right. Had the Board from the beginning received the generous support that it deserved and which it now receives, it would be able by this time to provide for all the necessitous cases; which would have produced the ideal condition: The Board of Conference Claimants caring for all "necessitous cases," leaving Annual Conferences free to pay the full annuity rate. With such a record, why should not the Board receive the praise and hearty support of the entire Church?

No words of praise can do justice to the officers of the Board of Conference Claimants. We challenge any Board to show a better record. Dr. Hingeley has shown himself to the "manor born," and master of the most difficult situations. The services of Judge Oliver H. Horton, chairman of the executive committee, a man of profound legal ability, have been invaluable. Dr. J. A. Mulfinger, the careful and painstaking recording secretary, has kept us straight from start to finish. Dr. Clemans, the field representative, is a regular Boanerges, and stirs up enthusiasm wherever he goes. Our Episcopal chairman, Bishop McDowell, by his devotion to the cause and his enthusiasm in the work has demonstrated that he is in the royal apostolic succession of the saintly Asbury, who carried about with him a subscription book for the relief of his aged and needy brethren; and now that the whole Board of Bishops has pledged leadership in this holy cause the 1915 CAMPAIGN isalready assured.

Years ago a friend asked Dr. Arnold of the Detroit Conference, who had been driving Dr. Thompson's fast horse, how far it was to the fair grounds. "Two miles," said Dr. Arnold, "but with Thompson's horse *you are there already.*"

With all the Bishops and District Superintendents in line, we are at the $5,000,000 milestone already, and the $10,000,000 milestone is not far ahead.

Grand Rapids, Mich. JAMES HAMILTON.

THE VETERANS OF THE CROSS FELLOWSHIP

THE REV. VARNUM A. COOPER, D.D.
President and Organizer of the Fellowship

THE VETERANS OF THE CROSS FELLOWSHIP is not a secret society with pass-words and grips, but is a fellowship into which we enter and find Jesus is in the midst. The Fellowship represents almost seven thousand—seven regiments—Conference Claimants who are asking in what way they can cooperate in this Church-wide movement in their behalf?

1. Some men are born to wealth; some men achieve wealth; some men have wealth thrust upon them. Here and there are Veterans with wealth, or a competency. I need not point out the way for them to cooperate. A few examples of liberality on their part would inflame the whole Church! We can cooperate by practicing what we preach; by being ourselves generous givers to the extent of our ability.

2. The 1915 CAMPAIGN is not a revolution but an evolution; a change in the sentiment of the Church from the thought of charity to that of justice and gratitude in its dealings with Retired Ministers and other Claimants. Whatever softens prejudice, stimulates honor or creates sympathy will strengthen the claims of justice. We utter no complaints. Through the long years in which we have received a pitiful dole of charity, we might have complained, but at this stage of the evolution if our just claim—declared by the Indianapolis Convention to be the Supreme Claim—is not fully met, we will continue to endure hardness as good soldiers of the Cross; practicing self-denial with patience and strengthening the hand so intelligently employed in our behalf.

3. In every way possible we will show our gratitude. It is beyond value that by a great Emancipation Proclamation the cause has been taken from beneath the ægis of Charity and placed in the scales of Justice; that the Methodist Episcopal

Church has declared that our claim to a comfortable support *inheres in the gospel ministry,* and that retirement is only an incident and in no sense invalidates our claim. We have lived long in the Church and love it. Let us rejoice and be glad that the great record now being transcribed on the pages of Methodist history is a record of justice. True it ought to have been written long ago; but thank God! the Recording Angel has his pen in hand and the record reads, "Methodism has pledged itself to the payment of the full claims of its Veteran Ministers, and their Supreme Claim has been given the supreme place." Let us manifest gratitude to the Board of Conference Claimants for leadership which has enabled us already to receive such relief as never known before, and to the Bishops for pledging themselves and the Church to the 1915 CAMPAIGN. Our vision may not be as clear as it once was, but we are not so blind that we cannot see that the day is near at hand when every claim will be paid, every necessity met, and from a grateful Church we will receive a comfortable support.

4. There is no Retired Minister who during his long ministry has not made and retained the confidence and esteem of one or more friends who are able to help in this supreme effort of the Church. Write a letter to those friends. In words that you well know how to utter, and which God can set on fire by His Spirit, place the cause on their hearts. Think of it! three thousand or more such letters! What a result would such a written appeal or a personal visit bring!

5. Veterans of the Cross are past masters in the art of prayer. We are familiar with strong crying and tears at the throne of grace. We are practiced in wielding the sword of the Spirit and in the exercise of faith, the power that "moves the hand that moves the world." Comrades of the Cross! If we could unite the prayers of thirty-five hundred seasoned Veterans and of as many widows of our brothers gone before, all used to seeing miracles of grace, crooked paths would be made straight, and mountains of difficulty "cast into the midst of the sea." If we will accompany the intensive 1915 CAMPAIGN for funds with an *intensive campaign of prayer,* no power can prevail against us. I summon you to this cooperation of prayer.

6. But after all, brethren, if every claim were paid, every

necessity met, and each had a "comfortable support," money is not all we need. When we think of the intense activities of the itinerant minister's life, the multiplied functions he fills, and organizations for which he is responsible and for which he is charged every year by his Annual Conference to do his utmost, and then realize that by one touch of the lever, one show of hands his active career is stopped, what a shock it is! Suddenly and with a sickening dull thud, he drops out of all *official* responsibility. From thirty to forty years he has been the magnetic center of a Church and congregation, the dynamo of all its responsibilities, and the leader of all its enterprises; but "in a moment, in the twinkling of an eye," at what seems to him to be "the last trump," he is separated from it all, and for the first time in his itinerant life has his destiny in his own hands. For there is no Bishop to read the Retired Minister's appointment. He is through, not with his ministry nor his call to preach, but is through with his work; and must set himself down *alone* wherever his stipend will best serve him. He is *retired.*

Retired means "withdrawn from public view, separated from some place, position, association, function or responsibility in which he has been a factor." A Retired Methodist Minister has withdrawn or separated, not only from the high office of preacher in charge with superintendents over him and parishioners under him, but also from the parsonage home, and must house himself in an upstairs or downstairs tenement, a cottage on a side street, or be absorbed into the family of relatives, where his headship fades away. He is separated from the presidency of the official board, from stewards with whom he could confer daily, from the ladies' aid society to which his wife could confidently bring every want, from leadership of prayer meetings and class meetings, from all the multiplied responsibilities and functions with which his restless, intense life has been full. He looks forward to the Annual Conference with no feeling of official responsibility. He has no reports to present, no committee work to do and nothing to say. He takes an humble seat at the grand review, irregularly responds to the roll-call for a few years and then sinks out of sight; though here and there among them are stars of first magnitude whom no night but death can dim.

7. These Veterans are scattered throughout the Conference bounds, and often far beyond it. They are of courageous spirit; can suffer, and make no sign; and, like their Master, can bear the cross or wear a crown of thorns and never cry out. Grace may reconcile them to scant fare and lack of the necessities and the conveniences to which they were accustomed. But there are wants of the soul; heart desires and longing for fellowship which alone can bring "the contentedness of seventy years." Money cannot buy it. There is need of that official recognition which they have always had, a longing for some responsibility which they are expected to meet and of some *organized* useful work which will be suited to their strength, and, most of all, an absence of all appearance of just being tolerated in the work to which they are occasionally assigned. It would be better if such an organization of Retired Ministers should not run on a separate pulley, but rather be geared into the machinery of the great Church, receiving that inspirational help which, in a connectional Church, can only come from being recognized, fostered and guided by the supreme authority.

8. To meet in some measure these conditions, to open a door of usefulness for themselves, to afford the means of expressing to the Church not only their gratitude but also their opinions and views, and to protect their recognized claims, believing that the Veteran Ministers had earned the right to be heard, the Veterans of the Cross Fellowship was organized on March 7, 1910, in old Bromfield Street Church, Boston. The Fellowship served one year on trial and, having proved itself worthy, was cordially received into full connection by the New England Conference in 1911. A pronouncement of aims and purposes was made, the work for the year was reported, and we were adopted into the Conference family of fraternal societies and given space in the Minutes.

9. The purposes and aims of the VETERANS OF THE CROSS FELLOWSHIP are set forth in a brief constitution consisting of three articles.

Article I reads: "This association shall be called *The Veterans of the Cross Fellowship* of the Methodist Episcopal Church." Considerable time and attention was given to the question of a suitable name. The Church at that time called us superannuated ministers. A few, through age and infirmities, were such; but the majority of us were not. The word itself has been given a superannuated relation, and no longer appears in the Discipline. Few of us had ever liked *that* name. The term "*Retired* Minister" was proposed; but we did not fancy that term either. The old preacher had not retired—"gone to bed." But there was a word which suited us all because it included us all. We were "*Veterans.*" We had served long in the cause. That is what makes a veteran. We had long served the cause of the Methodist Episcopal Church, under the banner of the cross. The General Conference had designated our day in the Church calendar, "Veterans' Day." So we took the name, "Veterans of the Cross."

But what should we call ourselves; a society? That was meaningless. The world is as full of societies as an ancient garret of cobwebs; and many of them just as flimsy. Associations? That was not much better. There are all kinds of associations. We desired a word expressive of the true inwardness of our longings and aims. The days of our activities had passed, but not the days of our loving fellowship, thank God. These fellowships had become stronger and sweeter and dearer. In the ritual for receiving members into the Church there is one of the most expressive and beautiful words to be found in the Word of God: "That you may have FELLOWSHIP with us," and truly, "OUR FELLOWSHIP is with the Father and with his Son, Jesus Christ." "If ye walk in the light as He is in the light, WE HAVE FELLOWSHIP ONE WITH ANOTHER." So "VETERANS OF THE CROSS FELLOWSHIP" was adopted for the Church.

Article II states the object of the Fellowship: (1) To create a solidarity and special fellowship; and (2) to render comfort and help to the sick, infirm or otherwise disabled Retired Ministers, and the widows and the orphan children of deceased ministers; to express our relations to the universal Church, the duties we owe to it, and our obligations to render to it loyalty and gratitude.

Article III defines the membership: Any Veteran Methodist Minister who shall sign the constitution. The membership was limited to ministers because one object was the cultivation of closer fellowship among the members of the Conference, and because of the desire to render service and to extend courtesies to our faithful co-laborers.

10. The By-Laws indicate the character of the work of the Fellowship: Annual and special meetings; correspondence with those who cannot meet with us; extending fraternal greetings to the widows of the Conference, and to other claimants living within the Conference bounds; visiting or writing to sick or disabled ministers; and in case of death to attend the funeral and, when permitted, perform a brief ritual service expressive of the peculiar fellowship the veteran "brave feel in circumstances they cannot control."

Annual and special meetings may be made both profitable and delightfully interesting. Numbers cannot be large. An interested pastor invites the Fellowship and the ladies' aid society provides the dinner. We enter into some retired room, and the door is shut to all but the Veterans and their Master. A brief devotional service kindles the altar fires until they glow. At the banquet some special invited guest helps to make the dinner a "feast of reason and a flow of soul." Dinner over, we resume the Altar Fire service, taking our guest in with us, or a trip is taken to some place of interest; and we go home happy.

The 1915 CAMPAIGN, *cooperative, intensive, extensive,* for ten million dollars is on, and with it the placing of the Veteran Ministers before the Church and the world in their exalted and true character; no longer as "worn-out" or *superannuated* or even *retired,* but as Veterans of the Cross of the Methodist Episcopal Church. The Board of Conference Claimants has adopted the VETERANS OF THE CROSS FELLOWSHIP and in every way has put the Veteran of the Cross to the front as the living remnant of the conquering host which brought the Church to its present greatness of numbers and achievement. We need no longer orate about destitution and sufferings, but only to tell the truth about their character, their dauntless courage and their heroic deeds, emblazoned on every page of Methodist history.

Hyde Park, Mass. V. A. COOPER.

NOTE. The Rev. Varnum A. Cooper, D.D., writer of this article, has been appointed by the Board of Conference Claimants as general Organizer of the Veterans of the Cross Fellowship. For information or literature address, Dr. V. A. Cooper, 1 Kensington Park, Roxbury, Mass.—*J. B. H.*

PART III. THE CLAIM SUPREME

CHAPTER IV. HISTORICAL

AGED PASTORS MUST BE PROVIDED FOR

Shall the old minister be shot?

This question was asked and answered by the Rev. Dr. George P. Eckman at the Rock River Conference.

The present age, Dr. Eckman said, demands young men to fill the pulpits. If churches want that sort of a thing let them pay the price. Let them support the Retired Ministers comfortably so that they can have only young men.

As far as the old man is concerned, the office of an executioner would be welcomed kindly enough, but he has a wife and a family to support. He cannot be treated as they treat the old in India, where they are thrown upon the funeral pyre, or in Africa, where they are thrown into the trenches.

The age is exacting on the minister in the work he is put to do. It is exhausting. This is expensive business and the Church must pay for it. An engine constantly driven over the road soon wears out. After becoming unfit for the long routes it becomes a switch engine, and then is consigned to the scrap heap. After hammering ministers out on the road of life, shall we consign them to the scrap heap?

One of the reasons why so many young men hesitate to enter the ministry is because of this precarious support in old age. Ministers would like to have money, but they cannot take time to earn it, nor can they save it, if they give themselves to their work as they ought to do.

The support of Retired Ministers is not a charity, it is a debt. What is paid in old age is a part of what was withheld in the early years of a minister's life. The minister is a preferred creditor. He is not a mendicant.

The pulpit is the freest place in our day so far as independence of character or of utterance is concerned. It is more free than the newspaper or business. The preaching of the gospel is the salvation of this country from anarchy.

Whenever I hear a Socialist speaking I feel like saying, "Stop, thief!" for his doctrines are largely those of Christ. Without the safeguards of religion the wealthy men of the country could not have made their money or kept it.

Carnegie might well endow the ministry as he has libraries. Rockefeller would do well if he considered this cause.

THE VETERAN'S RANK AND RIGHTS RESTORED

THE REV. FREDERICK T. KEENEY, D.D.

The Methodist Itinerancy began as a fraternity of hearts. Common hardships, perils and sacrifices bound the circuit riders of the wilderness together as brothers in the Methodist household of faith. There was no high, no low; no rich, no poor; no grade or rank in all their borders. All were one, and all were brethren in Christ Jesus. At the close of the New York Conference in 1791 Bishop Asbury declared: "There were about thirty preachers present and the most perfect harmony. Not a frown, not a sign of a sour temper or an unkind word was seen or heard among us."

The law of the Church governing the support of the early ministry was that each should share alike. From the Christmas Conference of 1784 to 1800, the uniform allowance was $64 per year for bishops, presiding elders, pastors, superannuated ministers and the widows of ministers. In 1800 this annual allowance was increased to $80, and it remained at that figure until 1816, when the Church became rich enough and sufficiently generous to grant an annual support of $100 to the itinerant, an additional allowance of $100 for his wife, and an allowance of $16 for the support of each child under seven years of age, and $24 for each child from seven to fourteen years. Through all these years the principle maintained that every man in the ranks, from bishop to superannuate, as well as the widows of deceased ministers, should share equally. When Bishop Asbury was charged with using his position to increase his own income, he demanded an investigation, saying that he had received but $64 and traveling expenses, "the same as any other preacher."

In 1808 a Brother Frye, of the Genesee Conference, received $16.18½ above his allowance of $80, and the record tells of his sending the surplus to Conference to help out the deficit of his less fortunate brethren. The Bishops during these years experienced the same hardships as the humblest minister. When Bishop Hedding, who was a giant in stature and intellect, moved his family into a certain Connecticut town, where they might find a home during his absence among the Conferences, the Town Fathers were at once called together and the family was officially "warned out." The law of Connecticut at that time was that if any family came to town without a visible means of support the councilmen might order them to leave the place. This order did not necessitate their removal. But if, after having been "warned out," they should become dependent on the community for the necessities of life, the town was free from any obligation for their support. The Town Fathers therefore thought it expedient, in view of Bishop Hedding's limited income, to protect themselves against the possibility of being chargeable with the care of his family during his absence.

The average length of service in the effective relation of the heroes of these early days was *only seven years*. With some, their fervent zeal, accompanied with numerous hardships and frequent exposure, caused life's candle to be burned out at both ends and to be soon extinguished; while others were starved out of the itinerancy, that they might provide food for their families. In reply to the question, "When are men justified in superannuating?" Mr. Wesley answered: "If they are not strong enough to preach four or five times a week, let them superannuate." Some of these heroes never came to superannuation as is evidenced by the request sent to the Bishop presiding in the Genesee Conference in 1811: "Send us a pastor this year who can swim. The preacher you sent us last year got drowned trying to cross the river."

There were heroes in those days. Occasionally a Peter Cartwright would live to give the Church sixty-five years in the effective relation, fifty of them as presiding elder; and preach four hundred sermons a year. Charles Giles, the first Methodist itinerant to preach in Syracuse, Seth Mattison and Isaac Puffer, each went down with a half century of royal service to their credit. But a host of others were mustered out through failure either of health or purse, before their sun had reached the meridian. One cannot forget Ebenezer White, of whom it was beautifully said that "he never carried sand instead of salt, nor flowers instead of fruit"; or Benjamin Bidlock, a soldier of the Revolution, who was known as the "warrior" preacher, and who fought the devil as valiantly as he fought King George; or Valentine Cook, who gave to Methodism that piece of furniture more highly prized than any other, the "Mourners Bench." Heroes all, with hearts and zeal too large to be measured, who spelled brotherhood and service in the same terms as did Christ.

In 1848 the General Conference authorized the quarterly conference committee on each charge, to estimate the cost of the pastor's table expenses and fuel; which should be a claim on the church *in addition to the annual allowance fixed by the Discipline* for pastoral support. After sixty-four years of history this was the beginning of a new basis of support; which should make it possible for one minister, through the generosity of his church, to receive more than another. Not, however, until 1860 was there a complete break with the past in this respect, when for the first time the General Conference authorized a quarterly conference committee on each charge to estimate a "comfortable support" for the pastor. This provision stands to-day without material modification.

During the past sixty-six years the support of bishops, presiding elders and pastors has materially increased throughout the entire Church. According to the Methodist Year Book, the Bishops now receive twenty-five times as much as they did in 1848. The District Superintendents receive an average of ten times as much as did the presiding elders sixty-six years ago, and pastors four and one-half times as much. The progress which these figures show in ability and generosity is cause for gratification. But the retired itinerant, who in other days bared his breast to the foe, now marches at the rear of this procession of advance. In 1908 one third of the Conference Claimants received not one penny more than did the Claimant in 1848. Less than two thirds of the entire number received twice as much, and only one tenth received three times as much. And this meager amount was doled out to them not as to honored brothers of equal rank, but as to paupers, on the basis of necessity.

The last five years have witnessed the dawning of a new day for the Veterans of the Cross in the army of our Methodist itinerancy, where their rank and rights are being both recognized and restored. No longer is the veteran's claim based on necessity, but on the years of service rendered. No longer is the offering for his support counted as a "benevolence," but as a part of "ministerial support," in which his claim is as valid as that of a pastor, district superintendent or bishop. At last the veteran stands beside the men now in the effective ranks as their honored brother, and receives with them the support which a generous Church provides for all.

The last General Conference made provision, fixing the annuity rate, so that each minister's claim, who has been in the effective relation for thirty-five years, shall be one half of the average cash salary received by the members of his Conference. For a number of years many Conferences had been working toward the goal set by the New York East Conference, namely: To pay each minister on retirement ten dollars for each year of effective service. Investigation, however, disclosed the fact that a more equitable basis should be established for the entire Church. For, in some Conferences, if a minister who had preached fifty years should receive on retiring ten dollars for each year of effective service, he would receive much more than the active pastors were receiving. There are eleven Conferences in American Methodism where the average salary is $300 or less; and twenty-two Conferences, where the average salary does not exceed $400. The average salary received by members of the Central New York Conference is $1,050; which amount fixes the Disciplinary claim of a Retired Minister who has preached thirty-five years, at $525, or $15 for each year of active service.

The whole Church, with great heartiness and unanimity, has said that this new basis is right. The laymen have spoken with their gifts as well as with their lips. In five years there has been a gain in moneys contributed for annual distribution of nearly one hundred per cent. Five years ago the entire Church had only $600,000 to distribute among the six thousand Conference Claimants of Methodism. This year she has almost $1,100,000 for distribution. The present basis, which makes the Claimant a pensioner rather than a pauper, is in harmony with the spirit of the times. Corporations, municipalities and Boards of Education are coming to recognize the principle that has long obtained in the army, the navy and the courts, that every faithful toiler has a claim upon those whom he has served through many years, beyond that of his salary or wage during the term of his active service.

The growth of interest and funds in the Central New York Conference is of surpassing interest. In 1869 the Permanent Fund was $9,000, but so little interest attached to it that it required twenty-four years to add the next thousand dollars; and eleven years more to add the next six thousand dollars to the principal. This amount was doubled during the next five years, and during the last five years has increased six-fold.

The following figures indicate this increase.

1869..............	$9,000	1911..............	$116,295
1893..............	10,361	1912..............	132,906
1904..............	16,923	1913..............	150,879
1910..............	35,151	1914..............	200,000

The further program is, 1915, $300,000; 1916, $500,000.

These results would not have been possible but for the magnificent gift of $50,000, made in 1911 by a son of the parsonage, Mr. George H. Maxwell, whose honored father, Joseph Maxwell, spent his life serving small charges. The challenge of Mr. Maxwell's generosity quickened the heart-beat of the entire Conference, and the momentum acquired in matching his gift in a single year with more than $50,000 in cash and subscriptions has carried us on to the still larger results, and made possible the adoption last year of the slogan "Three Hundred Thousand Dollars for the Permanent Fund by October 1, 1915." The Conference has not yet reached the goal, but both ministers and laymen have said unanimously that the present year shall record the Jubilee of achievement. Five years ago twenty-eight Conferences surpassed us in invested funds. To-day only six Conferences have a larger Permanent Fund; and to-morrow we shall be still nearer the head of the column. Each District is to be intrusted with raising $25,000, have charge of its own campaign, and determine both the time and methods of its prosecution.

The Conference campaign is greatly stimulated by the general movement projected by the last General Conference to raise $5,000,000 for Conference Claimants throughout the entire Church during the quadrennium. The Bishops are heartily and unanimously supporting this movement; which each, in his own Episcopal Area, is to direct. Bishop Burt was the first to call representatives of the Conferences in the Buffalo Area to confer together concerning the establishment of a Permanent Fund in each Conference; with the result that the Conferences of this Episcopal Area have each set a goal for themselves. The formal inauguration of the 1915 CAMPAIGN in Washington, at which time the Bishops delivered their "ADDRESS AND APPEAL TO THE CHURCH," has added enthusiasm to the Campaign in all the Conferences. The Bishops and District Superintendents have said that for 1915 the Veterans' Cause shall have right of way, and shall be the one financial appeal on which supreme emphasis shall be placed. The general movement will make available both literature and speakers for Conference campaigns; and by an interchange of ideas, methods and workers each Conference will receive help from the others in an intensive movement which will reach every pastor and charge through the mails, group meetings and team work; in all of which the pastors and District Superintendents will be assisted by a committee of carefully chosen laymen from each district.

While the Permanent Fund is being secured, and until the full $300,000 shall have become productive, the Annual Conference unanimously voted to apportion to the several pastoral charges for the regular Conference Claimants' collection the amount necessary *to meet the full annuity claims.* If the income from $300,000 was immediately available we could at once pay the full annuity rate of $15 for each year of effective service, without increasing the apportionment. But it may be some time before we can receive full returns from the Permanent Fund. Our annual apportionment for Conference Claimants was therefore increased from $10,000 to $16,000; which, added to the Book Concern dividend, the dividend from the Board of Conference Claimants, interest on investments, etc., will make it possible to pay all claims in full beginning with October, 1915, and to give to the Retired Ministers their rightful support. This will be quite a large advance, but it is within reason and ability. The amount is no more than the Conference, in 1868, apportioned and enforced the apportionment by resolving that: "Any preacher failing to report the full amount apportioned to his charge, shall be called upon to give satisfactory reasons for such failure."

Claimants have not properly shared in the general advance the Church has made since 1868. In 1869 the Central New York Conference contributed 58 cents per capita for Missions. In 1913 this had increased to $1.29 per member, a gain of 122 per cent; none too much for churches as favorably situated as are ours. But during the same period the apportionment for Conference Claimants *decreased* from 35 cents per member to less than 22 cents. It is the plain duty of the Conference to ask for the full amount needed, as the Discipline directs. By so doing the responsibility is transferred to the laymen; many of whom in meeting the smaller apportionment have supposed that they were paying the full claim, not knowing that the apportionment to the churches was less than two thirds of what was really needed. If the pastors fail to acquaint the laymen with the facts, can they escape responsibility in the consequent result? Can the men in the effective ranks, who last year received more than 99 per cent of their claims, do less than ask, with loving, persistent emphasis, that the Veterans, who now receive but 55 per cent of their due, shall receive at least as large a proportion of their claim as do the effective members? It is not necessary to raise the question of pro-rating. The law is clear, and our pastors and laymen are *not* lawless. Of every dollar received for ministerial support the average division would be approximately, 85 cents for the pastor, 2 cents for the Episcopal Fund, 6 cents for the District Superintendents, and 7 cents for Conference Claimants. When the disciplinary provisions are followed questions involved in pro-rating take care of themselves.

The laymen are making more generous estimates for the support of their pastors than forty years ago, and are generally paying the claim in full. In 1870 the churches of this Conference defaulted payment of six per cent of the pastors' salaries. Last year the deficit was less than one-half of one per cent; a decrease of deficit of 87 per cent. If the pastors were to contribute the amount thus added to their income through the quickened conscience of the Church the full annuity claim for the Retired Ministers would be met.

Although in the practical working out of this plan it may

be difficult for the first year to meet the increased apportionment, still the pastor who is called upon to sacrifice in effort or purse may find comfort not only in the thought that he is helping the Veterans to their just claim, too long withheld, but also in the knowledge that the provisions made to meet the full annuity claim are equivalent to adding $300 a year to the invested capital of every pastor; the income from which at five per cent will be paid him and his family without possible loss or shrinkage from the time of his retirement until his death. The annuity claim for a Minister who has preached forty years is better than an investment of $12,000 to one's credit. Although the establishment of proper standards may mean heroic effort, it is certainly worth while, in view of the far-reaching and beneficent results. In most cases the pastor who finds it hardest to meet the full apportionment while in the active work, will be the one who will find the fund thus established of greatest benefit at the time of his retirement.

The payment of the full annuity claim cannot fail to hearten every pastor who is struggling to make ends meet on an all too meager salary. Men will go to the weak charges with better heart for the hard tasks, and will be more content to remain in the fields where the remuneration is small, but the importance of the work is large, in the knowledge it gives that Methodism appreciates their heroism and will care for them to the end. Every pastor, in whatever field, will sleep better by night and will work with lighter heart by day in the consciousness that the Church, to whom he is giving his life, has made adequate provision for his family and himself as an honorable return for his labor; and that, whatever financial reverses may come to him, his spirit will not be crushed on retiring by being compelled to receive the dole of a pauper, which only prolongs the agony of starvation.

Dr. B. I. Ives, the invincible hero of a thousand battles, used to say: *"Whatever ought to be done can be done."* Today as the Church faces the opportunity and obligation of providing adequately for the honored Veterans of Methodism, I make bold to declare, not only that we ought to reach the goal in 1915, and that we can reach it; but, that with hearty cooperation and God's blessing, we will reach it.

Syracuse, N. Y. FREDERICK T. KEENEY.

STEWARDSHIP IN EARLY METHODISM

THE REV. HARVEY REEVES CALKINS
Stewardship Secretary

By permission of the Rev. Harvey Reeves Calkins, D.D., author of the recent illuminating book *A Man and His Money,* we reproduce in part the chapter on "Early Stewardship in America." There is a temptation to include much more, but the book itself is accessible. The early idea concerning the support of the ministry is still reflected in the legislation of the Church, but has yielded gradually to the spirit of the age and to contact with other denominations, whose pastors have a salary which can be enforced at court, until at present the duty of supporting the entire ministry is recognized by the laity; and Bishops, District Superintendents, Pastors and Retired Preachers are provided from a common budget. The principle is now fully recognized that the duty of the ministers to minister to the people involves the duty of the people to support the ministers. —J. B. H.

Until the death of its first Bishop, the Methodist Episcopal Church is responsible for this strange anomaly—a Pentecostal movement of unprecedented power and, with it, a meager, parsimonious, and wholly unworthy program of stewardship.

Nor did this come from mere chance or neglect, for Methodist leaders were never negligent. It was the unhappy and unexpected result of a deliberate policy, whose main purpose was to produce a race of heroic preachers. And the logical result followed. With amazing swiftness a continental Church was created, notably strong and elastic in administration; but the multitudes that made up its membership, the very bone and sinew of American Christianity, never realized the vastness of the responsibility of stewardship that inevitably must be laid upon them. . . . The exalted dispensation of the gospel, which was committed to the Methodists, demanded an equally exalted program of stewardship, and herein their failure in those momentous days of the beginning proved nothing less than a calamity. The purpose of the fathers, unto this hour, has been in part defeated, because, in their mighty program of advance, they failed to develop a sufficient base to carry to completion their vast designs. No one will misconstrue us. . . . But this we say: Had American Methodists recognized in the beginning their responsible stewardship of property, as was their right, this day would behold, in vaster measure than we can estimate, the triumph of Christianity and the glory of the Son of God. The Methodist people themselves were not culpable for the neglect of Christian stewardship in those days of the beginnings. The fathers made mistakes. The heroic Asbury recognized but one commanding necessity: the creation of an itinerant ministry, ready to march at command for the conquering of a continent. And Asbury realized his ideal. What a mighty race of preachers rallied to the banner of early Methodism! Brave, indomitable, Godly, they threaded every forest, they forded every river, they subdued every wilderness. The record of their deathless devotion is in the heart of the nation.

But the creation of a race of preachers is not the whole of apostolic counsel. Bishop Asbury was tireless in leading forth a band of burden-bearing ministers, but, judging from preserved records, Bishop Asbury seemed little concerned in raising up a body of burden-bearing laymen, and herein he seems to have erred grievously. As we contemplate those days of the foundations, when hundreds of congregations were being knit together in close organic connection, and, at the same time, were loosely left both to find and to fix their own standards of stewardship, it is difficult to explain this misjudgment of the responsible leadership of the Church. It came to pass again and again that brave ministers, those, indeed, who could least be spared from the active work, were forced by dire poverty to abandon the active ministry.

Even so gentle a spirit as Nathan Bangs, who understood whereof he spoke, wrote in 1839: "The defect of Bishop Asbury's administration, as I think, was not encouraging the people sufficiently in making provision for their ministers, particularly for men of families. He seemed to fear that, if they were too well off as respects this world's goods, they would lose their zeal and spirituality, and thus cease to be useful; and it was very congenial to the covetous disposition, so natural to men, to withhold when they were not compelled to pay.

"Bishop Asbury considered the itinerant ministry, under God, as the grand instrument of the world's salvation; to support this therefore, in all its vigor and spirituality, he bent all his energies. Hence, to prevent a catastrophe which must come upon the Church by the substitution of a 'located' for a 'traveling' ministry, he thought it essential to keep it aloof from the world, by preventing it from accumulating worldly property. Yet it may be questioned whether more have not been induced to locate from a feeling or fear of poverty than by the enjoyment of a competency. Had a competent provision been made for the support of itinerant ministers, and for the suitable education of their children, I have no doubt we should have been far stronger every way—in wisdom, in numbers, in ministerial talent and usefulness, if not also in holiness and general prosperity." These weighty words were written while the heroic days of the fathers were fresh in the memory of a host of living men. . . .

Keen historic insight cannot forget those hundreds of located preachers, the flower of the army, forced out of the ranks in those very days when American Methodism was laying down the lines for its future development. As early as the year 1799, when there were two hundred and sixty-nine "traveling" preachers in the actual work, Jesse Lee is authority for the astounding statement that there were eight hundred and fifty "located" preachers, many of them the most commanding leaders of the Church. That is to say, men who had completed their probation, tested men, were compelled to step aside for young and untried men.

It is an astonishment and a grief to recall some of the noble men, who ate out their hearts in lonely separation from their brethren, when to preach the gospel was their very breath of life. There was Valentine Cook, the one great product of the ill-fated Cokesbury College, a leader of profound spiritual insight as well as of genuine culture. . . . In 1800 he turned heavily from the ministry to feed a dependent family, and as a school teacher earned his living.

There was Russell Bigelow, whom Bishop Thomson described as "a perfect gentleman," who preached with such majesty of thought and such beauty of diction that his audiences "were well nigh paralyzed beneath the avalanche of thought that descended upon them." Of him a chief justice remarked, "It is one of the greatest regrets of my life that I did not know him better; we were a wild people when he was among us and we never duly appreciated him." And yet Russell Bigelow, the Bishop Simpson of the first Methodists, and absolutely needed by the Church in those crude frontier days, turned broken-hearted from the ministry, which he loved with such passion, to provide bread for his wife and children. He died in extreme poverty, neglected and alone.

There were Caleb Boyer and Ignatius Pigman, of whom Bishop Whatcoat said he had not heard their equal, except . . . Wesley and Fletcher. There was Edward Dromgoole, whose practical wisdom prevented the disruption of the early societies and made possible the organization of Episcopal Methodism. There was Ira Ellis, of whom Asbury himself said he had "abilities not inferior to a Jefferson or a Madison." There were James Cromwell, Jonathan Forrest, Lemuel Green, John Hagerty. Yet these ordained ministers of God, all of them, and scores and hundreds of others besides, were compelled to withdraw from the active ministry of the Church whose altars they had builded.

This unconscionable sacrifice of leaders, when leadership was above the price of rubies, is almost incredible. Why was it necessary? In the large majority of cases because stern duty compelled it; because Methodist ministers had to turn from the ministry in order to provide food for their dependent families. Because, forsooth, Francis Asbury inflexibly demanded that Methodist preachers should provide for their expenses on a stipend of $64 a year! In 1800 an increase of $16 a year was permitted, but, until the death of the immovable Bishop, to whom the itinerancy was more worth than the itinerant, Methodist preachers received lodgings among the people and $80 a year "and no more," for their salary.

Of course a family could not be maintained on this pittance, nor was a family in the program of the itinerancy.

When godly men had announced their purpose of marriage the good Bishop petulantly exclaimed, "The devil and the women are getting after my preachers!" not seeming to perceive that God had a larger purpose, even for "The Itinerancy," when faithful ministers made covenant bonds with holy women. A remnant were indeed able to maintain their ministry unto the end, and some great names survive out of that first eventful and crucial generation. But who were they?—Richard Whatcoat, Jesse Lee, William McKendree, Beverly Waugh—men who, like Asbury himself, were able to remain bachelors and live the camp life of a soldier, and who were, therefore, able to continue in the Methodist ministry. Freeborn Garrettson married a lady of wealth, as well as piety, so he too was able to hold his place of leadership. These and a few other names are held in abiding honor, for their works do follow them. But of the many brave men who died, unfamed and forgotten, their life tragedy is recorded in the early Conference Minutes. One word reveals it all: "Located."

Let it not be supposed that the Methodist people were loath to support their ministers, or begrudged them a competent allowance. They loved their pastors and never was a people more loyal than the people called Methodists. But they were trained to believe that the work of God would be impeded if their ministers should receive the comforts of temporal prosperity; they would then be unwilling to "travel." It was in reality a discounting of the very manhood and consecration of Methodist preachers themselves. Bishop Asbury thought he knew human nature, and the rule respecting a minister's salary remained in force. That the Methodist people themselves were ready to respond with liberal contributions is apparent, for they built and equipped Cokesbury College. When it was burned and the second Cokesbury College was consumed, Dr. Coke exclaimed, "O that all this money had been laid out for a married ministry!" But it was not to be. The married preachers were "located," and striplings took their places.

Stewardship started on a high level and might have been conspicuous from the beginning, for the preachers and the people were ready. But the vision of Coke was not shared by Bishop Asbury. Alas! two generations were to pass before that neglected vision would come again.

It can never be well when the responsible leaders of the Church undertake to set at naught, for any reason, the divine word, "Thou shalt not muzzle the mouth of the ox that treadeth out the corn." From the time the holy tithe of the Jewish people was set apart for the support of the tribe of Levi it was ordained, "They that minister about holy things live of the things of the temple." Even so, "They which preach the gospel should live of the gospel." If Asbury neglected to follow this ancient command, other apostles before him had fallen into the same mistake. The church at Corinth failed to provide a support for the apostle Paul when he labored among them; and Paul gloried that he worked with his own hands, lest he should become burdensome unto them. This seems like great magnanimity and worthy of high praise. Nevertheless, when Paul beheld that same church "straitened in their own affections," when they might have been "enlarged," he remembered that he himself had omitted to train them in personal lessons of stewardship; and he wrote, "Forgive me this wrong." Could the spirit of Asbury travel again those pioneer circuits of a vanished generation, would he not utter the lament of the great and sorrowing apostle?

It is congenial to our ingrained hero-worship to magnify the men who hazarded their lives for the gospel; it is not congenial to lay upon them the blame for an unready Church. Yet what shall we say? In March, 1816, Bishop Asbury died. In May the General Conference met in Baltimore. One of the most significant acts of the General Conference of 1816 was the recasting of the Church law for the support of the ministry. The salary of "traveling" preachers was increased to a fair competency, and a worthy plan inaugurated for reaching Methodist people with a larger program of stewardship. But the reform had come too late. Thirty-two years had passed since the organization of the Church, and an entire generation were entrenched in the financial doctrines of Asbury. It was an arduous undertaking to change inwrought convictions and lifelong habits. "A penny a week and a shilling a quarter" had provided sufficient living for the mighty men of the beginning; who were these later preachers, that they should expect more? Thus ever has incompetency glorified a golden age that is past!

Evanston, Ill. HARVEY R. CALKINS.

EZEKIEL COOPER AND JOHN DICKINS

THE REV. JOHN KRANTZ, D.D.
General Sales Agent of The Methodist Book Concern

John Dickins and Ezekiel Cooper were leaders of the Methodist publishing propaganda whose products and profits have done so much for the intellectual, spiritual and financial welfare of the Methodist ministry. They started that magnificent flow of dividends which annually pours into the treasury of the claimants' fund.

At the Conference in 1789 the plan was proposed for the establishment of a book-making institution, and the Rev. John Dickins was appointed "Book Steward," afterward known as superintendent of the printing and book business. It was one thing to project such an enterprise by vote, and was quite another to launch it safely on the sea of uncertainty. In this crisis Mr. Dickins generously offered to loan the business the savings of a lifetime, six hundred dollars, an act of heroic faith and far-seeing vision. He was not afraid of mortgaging the future, of subtracting much of himself from himself in order to carry on a tremendously useful work for God.

John Dickins, Book Steward, was required at first to take a pastoral charge, and was not only burdened with the cares of a parish, but he was editor, proof reader, business manager, bookkeeper, salesman and shipping clerk of the infant publishing house. In addition, he faced serious embarrassments in the publishing business, since he had to depend for the distribution and sale of his goods on a few ministers who were weighted down already with numerous burdens, and had to travel great distances over rough ways and often through overflowing streams. Both the clergy and the laity were poor, and very little cash was at command. So he had to trust out most of the merchandise. He had no experience in printing or publishing and was without precedent or model to guide him. Is it any wonder that the commencement of the publishing interests of the Church soon became a matter of grave concern to Mr. Dickins and his counselors! They had to be *concerned* about it day and night in order to keep the enterprise alive; from which manifested care originated the title "Book *Concern*," which name first appears in the Conference Minutes of 1792. After three years Mr. Dickins was released from pastoral work that he might give his entire time to his duties as superintendent of the Book Business. The sum of $666.33 1-3 was the "estimate" for his salary and house rent.

The first payment to the superannuate fund was $307.29. During his term of office he published 114,000 volumes. Notwithstanding the many hindrances in the way his administration was wise, prudent, safe and economical. By the blessing of God upon this one man's pioneer labors, he created influences whose vibrations are now reaching the uttermost parts of the earth. He was a man of small stature but of great spirit; of quick apprehension and sound judgment; just and generous. He died at his post in 1798 during a yellow fever plague. Stricken in the city he refused to leave it, even when urged by his friends by word and example. With his own hands he ministered to the sick and dying until he himself fell a victim to the pestilential ravages. His last words were, "Glory to Jesus! I have not felt in seven years so much like trusting and praising Him." He was a notable figure among the fathers of Methodism. He was faithful in the pulpit, "a thundering Methodist," and his loss was deeply felt by the Church. "According to his time and opportunity he was one of the greatest characters that ever graced the pulpit or adorned the society of Methodists."

At the time of Dickins's death the Rev. Ezekiel Cooper, who was the chairman of the Publishing Committee, was so shocked that he questioned whether another man could be found, qualified to take his place. An appeal from Bishop Asbury finally persuaded Mr. Cooper against his wishes to take up the work of the fallen leader; but consented to his appointment and election only on condition that it be "year by year." The result showed that the mantle of Elijah had fallen on the shoulders of Elisha. Mr. Cooper found the business crippled by debt, and collections badly in arrears. Mr. Dickins was an Englishman, slow in thought and movement, steady, easy and indulgent. Ezekiel Cooper was an American born, sharp, quick, aggressive man of affairs, and an expert in details. He infused new energy and introduced new methods. He stirred up the clergy and membership of the Church by setting forth clearly the aims and possibilities of the Book Concern. He began the custom of Conference visitation, and impressed on the preachers the fact of their ownership of and agency for the publishing interests. Consignments of books and supplies for sale and distribution were sent out to the presiding elders and pastors, who had to give an account of their stewardship and report collections and circulation to the Annual Conferences. The preachers worked the machinery and commercial advantages of this unique institution for all they were worth, and very soon the Book Concern became a fountain of revenue; a hint to us, their living successors, that if we will loyally, industriously and thoroughly utilize the benefits of this educational, benevolent and money-making organization, we will reap an annual harvest of half a million dollars for Conference Claimants. So energetic and effective was Mr. Cooper's work that he advanced the business capital from nothing to nearly $50,000.

During a sermon preached by Freeborn Garrettson to a company of Revolutionary soldiers his attention was attracted by the thoughtful, absorbing aspect of a boy thirteen years of age who was leaning against the gate. That boy became the illustrious Ezekiel Cooper. Early in life he gave promise of remarkable gifts and powers. At the age of twenty he was sent out as a circuit preacher. He was only thirty years old when he was appointed presiding elder of the Boston District. At thirty-six he was elected Publishing Agent. Mr. Cooper was an eloquent preacher, a very learned man, possessed of such a diversity of information that they called him the "walking encyclopedia." I can do but scant justice to these mighty princes in Israel. In fact, very little comparatively is written about them; they are famous through their works which follow them. They need no elaborate biography, bronze tablets, towering monuments or glowing panegyrics to perpetuate their memory. The publishing house of the Methodist Episcopal Church, of which they were the founders, is their enduring monument.

150 Fifth Ave., New York. JOHN KRANTZ.

ANNUAL CONFERENCE REPRESENTATIVES

J. B. Gibson
W. H. Miller
F. E. Bauchop
John Sweet

W. G. Koons
R. S. Borland
W. K. Beans
G. Raihle

L. E. Lennox
E. C. Bass
George Hartung
G. C. Wilding

JOHN STREET CHURCH, NEW YORK

THE REV. J. WESLEY JOHNSTON, D.D.

New York East Conference

Just as at Plymouth Rock certain figures come into prominence and their names from henceforth are imperishable, so in the early history of John Street Church there are those to whom Methodism is under obligations which will outlast the generations.

Perhaps the first of these is Philip Embury, who was intimately associated with the beginnings of Methodism in New York. Of Irish birth, for he was born in the south of Ireland, but of German blood, he combined some of the qualities of both races, being warm in spirit, fervid of soul, eloquent of speech, yet cautious, careful and singularly prudent in matters of business. In every way—temperament, habit, home training—Embury was eminently qualified for leadership. A man of less buoyancy would have failed in the years of discouragement; one of less prudence, in the years of prosperity.

Under the preaching of Wesley, who visited Ireland in 1752, Embury was deeply stirred, and ere long entered into a gracious religious experience. His gifts as a speaker were soon recognized and he was appointed class leader, then local preacher, and at the Limerick Conference in 1758, where Wesley presided, he was recommended as an itinerant preacher and placed on the reserve list.

In 1760 Embury emigrated to New York and for a time resided in John Street. At that time New York was a small city with a population of about twenty thousand, with no signs of immediate growth; for when a benevolent man offered six acres of ground, at Canal Street and Broadway, to the trustees of a Lutheran church, they declined the gift, saying that the land was not worth fencing in! John Street, where Embury lived, was a suburb in the "North Ward."

But, though New York was small as compared with the New York of to-day, relatively it was perhaps even more wicked. For the presence of a large body of British troops, officered by men of profligate tastes, among whom gambling, drunkenness and vicious pursuits were common, affected the people generally and resulted in the coarsest forms of dissipation and sin. Either through natural diffidence, or because of the strangeness of his surroundings, as far as we can ascertain, Embury made no serious attempt to rally his fellow Christians until the spring of 1766.

This introduces another character, the far-famed Barbara Heck, a woman of rare piety and courage, through whom God began a work which not only continues to this day but with each succeeding year widens in influence and power. Like Embury, Barbara Heck too came from Ireland, and like him she was a Methodist; but, unlike him, she was not diffident, neither was she restrained by those around her. Hence, with characteristic fearlessness, she entered the room where a company of men were playing cards, and instantly she rebuked them for what, to her, seemed a sin against God. Then gathering up the cards from the tables she flung them into the fire, meantime exhorting the men to abandon forever such abominable pursuits. Her next step was to seek Philip Embury to whom she said with intense feeling:

"You must preach to us, or we shall all go to hell, and God will require our blood at your hands."

"How can I preach, for I have neither a place nor a congregation?"

"You can preach in your own house," she promptly answered. And so he did—to a congregation of five—his wife, Paul and Barbara Heck, John Lawrence and Betty, a colored servant of Mr. Heck.

Such was the beginning of American Methodism in October, 1766. Just think of then and now! Then five persons to hear the first sermon; now five millions, and more, assemble in Methodist churches every Sunday to hear "the gospel of the grace of God." Then the little company met in a private house, now twice ten thousand churches would not accommodate the mighty host. The Methodist Church in America is a miracle of miracles.

The third person in this historic and immortal group is

Captain Thomas Webb, whose entrance on the scene was both dramatic and startling. One day when the little company had assembled for worship a stranger appeared dressed in full military uniform. All eyes turned anxiously to him. Why had he come? Did he mean to persecute them, to interrupt their service, to prohibit them from meeting together? But when they saw his earnest, devotional spirit, and the gladness with which he united in the service their fears were at once allayed and they gave him cordial welcome. When the service was over he introduced himself as, "Captain Thomas Webb, of Albany, a soldier of the cross and a spiritual son of John Wesley." A thrill of gladness was felt by all present, for the coming of such a man, an officer in the king's army, meant a great deal to them. At that time Methodism was bitterly denounced almost everywhere. It was made the topic of ribald songs, sung on the streets and in the theaters. Sermons were preached against it in the leading pulpits. To be a Methodist was to incur ridicule. To have a man of the high rank of Captain Webb unite with the little Church at this time was, therefore, like the incoming of reenforcements to a beleaguered garrison. And, humanly speaking, the coming of no other man could have been more opportune. Hearty, earnest, popular in speech, courageous to a high degree, as many a battlefield bore witness, wonderfully effective as a preacher and with a zeal which never faltered or declined, Captain Webb was preeminently qualified to be one of the leading spirits in the founding of American Methodism.

After the coming of Captain Webb, the room which Embury had hired became too small for the rapidly increasing congregation. So in 1767 a rigging loft was rented, on what is now known as William Street. The rigging loft was a long narrow room fitted up with plain benches, with a rude pulpit made by Embury himself. But God wonderfully honored this unpretentious place. Every service was a season of gracious visitation. Divine favor rested on the word of the preacher. Conversions were frequent. Soon it became manifest that a larger place must be found. But where? And if found where was the money with which to erect a building. Those in that rigging loft society, with the exception of Captain Webb, were of the most humble conditions in life. But Barbara Heck, with the splendid faith of a heroic woman, insisted that the work was of God and that He would open their way, provided that they had the courage to follow His leadings. And so it proved; for in a way assuredly providential a lot was secured on what is now John Street, then known as Golden Hill; and here was built, on this site on which the present John Street Church now stands, the first Methodist church in America.

Like the rigging loft, only much more commodious, John Street Church was a plain, simple stone building, with galleries which at first were accessible only by ladders. The interior walls remained in their original rough plaster and the seats had no backs; the floor, however, had a coating of fine white sand. To meet the requirements of the law then prevailing in the colonies, which provided that no religious services could be held in churches other than those properly legalized, a fireplace and chimney were placed in the new edifice, thus technically making it a dwelling house. This was a bit of legal fiction to which dissenters at that time were forced to resort. Having no Bishop or distinguished church official to assist in the service of dedication, the privilege fell to Philip Embury, who, from a pulpit made by his own hands, preached the dedicatory sermon.

And now the miracle of the rigging loft repeated itself. The same divine favor which had been manifested so wonderfully there crowded the services of the new church, so that the congregations overflowed the building, at times filling the area in front of it. It was seen that Embury must have help, so in response to an urgent appeal Wesley sent Richard Boardman and Joseph Pilmoor. Robert Williams, however, eager for work in the new world, hastened to the port where a dear friend was about to sail, sold his horse to pay his debts, and carrying his saddle-bags on his arm, set off for the ship with a loaf of bread, a bottle of milk, but no money to pay his passage. His friend and fellow passenger, Mr. Ashton, met the expense, and on arriving in New York Robert Williams became the first regularly appointed minister of John Street Church.

In 1771 Francis Asbury came as pastor. He refers to this in his journal, and a tablet giving something of Asbury's record may be found on the walls of the present John Street Church.

It is significant that during the years of the Revolution John Street Church was strangely delivered from either sacrilege or destruction. A fire in 1776, which started near Whitehall and destroyed one quarter of the city, consuming Trinity Church, the Lutheran church, and fifteen hundred dwelling houses near by, left John Street Church unscathed. And when the British army was using New York as its headquarters, the churches generally were taken for military purposes; as, for example, the Dutch church on Nassau Street, which was occupied as a prison, John Street Church suffered no violation whatever. All of the Presbyterian churches were occupied by the military; the Baptist church was converted into a stable; the Quaker meetinghouse on Pearl Street was used as a hospital; and the Dutch church on William Street was made a jail for liberty-loving Americans; and yet John Street Church experienced no inconvenience, save that on Sunday morning it was occupied by the Hessians for services conducted by their own chaplains; the Methodists using it at night, and at such other times as they desired for the worship of God. This is most remarkable, and it is something to remember with profound gratitude that for all these years, without a single Sunday's intermission, the gospel of the grace of God has been preached in old John Street Church.

At the Conference of 1789 held in John Street Church John Dickins, a former pastor, and who had the honor of giving the Methodist Society the title of "Methodist Episcopal Church," was appointed Book Steward. The Methodist Book Concern was therefore born in John Street Church, for John Dickins with a borrowed capital of six hundred dollars, at once took up the work assigned him.

In 1817 the first church gave way to one very much larger, and better adapted for the needs of the constantly increasing congregations, and the service of dedication was conducted by Nathan Bangs, Samuel Merwin, and Joshua Soule, later a Bishop of the Methodist Episcopal Church, South. In this church John Summerfield preached his first sermon on his arrival from Ireland, and some time afterward served it as pastor. For years John Street Church was the stronghold of Methodism in New York; but in time business began to make serious inroads in that section of the city, so much so that in 1854 the trustees voted to sell the property and erect a new building on Madison Square. This led to a struggle worthy of Revolutionary days, for there was a defiance of law on the part of the downtown portion of the membership equal to that of the colonists. They literally entrenched themselves in the church building, eating in it, sleeping in it, holding services in it; finally arousing such a general sentiment against the sale that the proceedings had to be abandoned.

The present church building is practically as it was when dedicated in 1841, and though the site on which it stands is one of the most valuable in New York, yet no board of trustees would suggest even the possibility of a sale. John Street Church does not belong to any trustee board, nor to any Annual Conference, nor to any General Conference, however august the body may be. John Street Church is the property of worldwide Methodism: the Methodism of the past, present and future. What Plymouth Rock meant to the Pilgrim fathers, what Bunker Hill meant to the heroes of the Revolution, what Gettysburg means to this republic, old John Street Church means to Methodism, for it stands as the rock where our Church first had a foundation, it stands as a symbol of the battle that was fought against religious intolerance and persecution, it stands as the pledge and promise of God's favor for the generations to come.

J. Wesley Johnston.

1320 Forty-eighth St., Brooklyn, N. Y.

WILLS ARE UNCERTAIN

The old lady sent for her lawyer to make her will.

"I wish to explain to you," she said weakly, "about my property."

The lawyer was sympathetic. "There, there, don't worry about it. Just leave it to me."

"O, well," said the old lady resignedly. "I suppose I might as well. You'll get it anyway."

If you would rather have the old preacher get it than the lawyer, buy Life Annuity Bonds.

ST. GEORGE'S CHURCH, PHILADELPHIA

THE REV. J. S. HUGHES, D.D., PASTOR

Corresponding Secretary Preachers Aid Society
Philadelphia Conference

To Captain Thomas Webb belongs the honor of unfurling the banner of Methodism in Philadelphia. He was an officer of the British Army, a man of good social position and of unstinted means, who had been converted under John Wesley, and was a licensed local preacher. In 1768 he visited Philadelphia, and began to preach in a sail-loft near the drawbridge, which spanned Dock Creek. Here a class of seven persons was formed, Mr. Emerson being chosen leader, and among the first converts was Mr. Croft, the owner of the room in which the meetings were first held. After a time the meeting-place was changed to a house in Loxley's Court, a small thoroughfare east of Fourth Street running from Arch Street to Cherry Street.

On October 21, 1769, Richard Boardman and Joseph Pilmoor, missionaries sent to America by John Wesley, arrived in Philadelphia, and not knowing that there were any Methodists in the city, purposed making their way immediately to New York. But they met a man who had seen Mr. Boardman in Ireland, and who told them that, having heard of the arrival of two preachers, he was out looking for them. He informed them of the little company of Methodists and introduced them to Captain Webb. In a day or two Mr. Boardman went to New York as he had intended, while Mr. Pilmoor remained in Philadelphia. He preached in the regular place of meeting above mentioned, not only on Sabbath but frequently during the week; frequently at five o'clock in the morning. He also preached to immense congregations at the race-course, now Franklin Square, which at that time was considered to be quite out of town. The race-course gave Race Street its name. Large audiences gathered to hear him preach in Potter's Field, now Washington Square.

The room in Loxley's Court soon became much too small for the constantly increasing congregation, and more ample accommodations were locked for. About this time an unfinished church building, located on Fourth Street near Story (now New Street), was sold at public sale. It had been erected by members of the High Dutch Reformed Church, who, becoming financially embarrassed in the project, were imprisoned for debt. It is said that some of their friends, surprised at finding them in prison, and asking for an explanation were told: "We are in prison for building a church." The Provincial Assembly passed an Act authorizing the sale of the building in order to satisfy the creditors. While the public auction was in progress, a feeble-minded young man by the name of Hockley, entered the room, and by some singular impulse bid 700 pounds. This being the highest, some say the only bid, he was declared to be the buyer. His father, unwilling to reflect on his son by taking legal measures to show his irresponsibility, paid the amount for which it was sold, and immediately began to inquire for a purchaser. Hearing that the Methodists were desiring a larger place of worship, he offered to sell them his newly purchased building. In a day or two, Mr. Miles Pennington, a prominent member of the Society, bought it for 650 pounds. It is said that the building had cost 2,000 pounds. The purchase price did not include the ground, which had been taken up on an annual ground rent of 24 pounds, redeemable within ten years by the payment of 400 pounds. The size of the lot was the same as that now occupied by the church and the Conference building on New Street. The church, which is 55 by 85, was regarded as of immense proportions, and its size was a matter of comment everywhere.

The Methodists of Philadelphia of that period seem to have been quite prompt in their church movements. On Thursday, Nov. 23, 1769, the purchase was agreed upon, though the deed was not delivered till some months later. On the next morning Mr. Pilmoor preached in the church, and dedicated it to the worship of God. His text was Zech. 4. 7: "Who art thou, O great mountain? before Zerubbabel thou shalt become a plain; and he shall bring forth the head stone thereof with shoutings, crying Grace, grace unto it." The feeble congregation must have had great faith in

God to have dedicated the building before having received the deed, and before having paid anything on the property, for there is no record that anything had been paid previous to this event. The owner of the premises must have had the utmost confidence, also, in the success of this struggling band. The first Sabbath in the new place of worship was a great day to the rejoicing congregation. Captain Webb preached in the morning and Mr. Pilmoor in the evening. A collection was taken at the evening service for the payment of the church, amounting to over 16 pounds. This was regarded as a large and generous offering. In a short time a section of the room was floored and provided with cheap benches, the discomfort of which gave their occupants but little temptation to drowsiness. The unfinished condition of the room made it difficult for the congregation to keep comfortable in the winter season, and the women were accustomed to bring little "wooden stoves" for the feet, such as were used in the markets. Notwithstanding all these inconveniences, the Lord was with His people in a marvelous manner and added daily to their number.

The deed for the property, dated Sept. 11, 1770, was given in the names of Miles Pennington, Richard Boardman, Joseph Pilmoor, Thomas Webb, Edward Evans, Daniel Montgomery, John Dowers, Edmund Beach, Robert Fitzgerald and James Emerson. The following is the "Trust clause" in the deed:

"Nevertheless upon special trust and confidence, and to the intent that they and the survivors of them and the trustees for the time being, do and shall permit John Wesley, late of Lincoln College, Oxford, Clerk, and such other persons as he from time to time, and at all times during his natural life shall appoint, and no other persons, to have and enjoy the free use and benefit of said premises, so that the said John Wesley and such persons as he appoints, may therein preach and expound God's holy word; and after his decease, upon further trust and confidence, and to the intent that the said trustees and survivors of them, and the trustees for the time being, do and shall permit Charles Wesley, late of Christ Church College, Oxford, Clerk, and such other persons as he from time to time, and at all times during his life shall appoint, and no others, to have and enjoy the free use and benefit of the said premises for the purposes aforesaid.

"And after the decease of the survivors of them, the said John Wesley and Charles Wesley, then upon further trust and confidence, and to the intent that the said Richard Boardman (and others mentioned above) and the survivors of them and the trustees for the time being, shall and do from time to time, and at all times, hereafter forever permit such persons as shall be appointed at the Yearly Conference of the people called Methodists in London, Bristol and Leeds, and no others, to have and to enjoy the free use and benefit of the said premises for the purposes aforesaid; provided, always that the said persons preach no other doctrine than is contained in the said John Wesley's Notes upon the New Testament, and four volumes of sermons. Provided also that they preach in the said house in the mornings and evenings of Sundays and of such other days of the week as by custom of the Methodists, may from time to time be set apart for that purpose. And upon this further trust and confidence that as often as any of them, the said trustees or of the trustees for the time being, shall die or cease to be a member of the Society commonly called Methodists, the rest of the said trustees or of the trustees for the time being, shall as conveniently may be, choose another trustee or trustees in order to keep up the number of nine trustees forever."

In 1777, after the battle of Brandywine, when the British Army occupied Philadelphia, the church was used, for a while, as a hospital and afterward "as a riding school" for the cavalry. Long after peace had been declared implements of war lay around the building. During the Revolutionary struggle the church was greatly distracted if not demoralized. The building, which it was thought had fallen so providentially into the possession of the needy society, was now closed against its members, and used for military purposes. At the close of the war the membership was reorganized with about forty or fifty persons and Freeborn Garrettson was appointed preacher in charge. The building was plastered in 1784, fitted up with galleries in 1790 and in 1837, under the successful pastorate of Charles Pitman, was remodeled, and a basement constructed for Sabbath school and other purposes. For several years the edifice was not called St. George's, but was usually referred to by Mr. Asbury as "our preaching house in Philadelphia."

Francis Asbury, the first Methodist Bishop ordained in America, was always greatly interested in St. George's. He attended services in it on the evening of the day he arrived in America, and preached his first sermon in this country within its walls. He was its third pastor for a period of four months, which was about the limit of a pastorate at that time. He collected money for it in different parts of the country; in 1772, 150 pounds, and ten years later 270 pounds. Dr. Coke spent his first Sabbath in America in St. George's, preaching in the evening.

For fifty years it was the largest Methodist church in America, and was regarded as the cathedral of our denomination. From its distinguished line of pastors, four at least, have been elected Bishops: Francis Asbury, Richard Whatcoat, Robert R. Roberts and Levi Scott.

The first Methodist Conference in America was held at St. George's, commencing July 14, 1773. The second Conference in 1774, and the third in 1775, were held in the same place. This building is the oldest Methodist church edifice, used continuously for worship, in the world. City Road Chapel, London, was commenced April, 1777, and opened Nov. 1, 1778. The present John Street Church, New York City, was erected in recent years.

No church in this country has done more for its denomination than St. George's has done for Methodism. Revival fires began to burn on its altars on the very day of dedication, and for a hundred years these altars were almost constantly filled with penitents. Multitudes have been converted within its walls, among them many of the most stalwart characters of American Methodism. In a great revival in the pastorate of Charles Pitman, more than 1,300 persons professed conversion, from whom, it is said, at least fifty-five young men entered the itinerant ministry.

For many years in the early history of Philadelphia Methodism, every new Church of our denomination, with one or two exceptions, was organized and fostered by St. George's.

For thirty years the society has been struggling with downtown conditions, but is resolved to keep the doors of the old temple forever wide open to one of the most needy communities to be found in any city.

Philadelphia, Pa. J. S. Hughes.

AN AGED GOVERNMENT PENSIONER

Thirty years ago the War Department learned that there was a white mule named Mexique, which had been for many years in the service of the United States, but which had been ordered sold. The officers of the post desired permission to purchase the animal and care for it at their own expense.

Major Guenther reported that the mule was originally left at Key West barracks in 1848 at the close of the war with Mexico. He added:

"During the time that I served at Key West the mule did not miss a day's work. He is very old and has been worn out by his long service in the quartermaster's department. If there is any way to provide for him, I should be glad to have it done."

The petition went through the regular channels until it reached the Quartermaster General, who indorsed it as follows:

"To promote the sentiment of kindness toward animals that are so intimately connected with military men, it is recommended that this mule be kept in the department, and left to the care of those whose kindly feelings are so deeply enlisted in its behalf."

General Sherman submitted the case with the following report:

"I have seen the mule, and whether true or not, the soldiers believe it was left at Big Spring, the time General Jackson's army encamped there. Tradition says that it was once a sorrel, but now it is white from age. The quartermaster's department will be chargeable with ingratitude if the mule is sold or the care or maintenance of it thrown on the charitable officers of the post. I advise that it be kept in the department, fed and maintained until death."

The Secretary of War thereupon made the following order: *"Let the mule be kept and well cared for as long as he lives."*

DEFERRED PAYMENTS TO VETERAN PREACHERS

THE REV. E. L. WATSON, D.D.
Baltimore Conference

The claim of the Retired Preacher is often put on the basis of sentiment. I prefer to put the five-million-dollar endowment on the ground of the payment of a debt long due the Preacher. The figures can be secured with sufficient accuracy to prove that a $5,000,000 fund would be but a part payment of what the Church owes the Preachers for the unpaid salaries which have accrued during the years.

You will find some interesting matters in Bishop McKendree's diary, which I hold in my hands. Up to 1800 he was paid $64 a year; after 1800, $80. This little book shows that in 1799 about one third of his sixty-four dollars was not paid. When he was given a pair of socks he carefully charged himself $1.50 to $1.80 per pair. All such gifts were subtracted from his salary, so that in that year he had only $40 in cash, and gave ten dollars of that to the poor, leaving $30 for the year. His expenses, exclusive of traveling expenses, were fifteen pounds ten and a half pence. He was serving the Church without any net income whatsoever. When he went on the Western District in 1800 his salary was raised from $64 to $80 a year. During the first quarter he received $3, the second quarter, $2; $20 in all for the first year. In 1802 the deficit was $36.23 out of the total salary of $80.

Deficit

I have gone over the statistics of the Baltimore Conference, and find that during the forty-two years from 1872 to 1914, there was a total deficiency in the Preachers' salaries of $232,654; an average deficit of $5,539 each year. I asked a Baltimore expert accountant, Mr. Wilmer Black, the son of a Methodist Preacher, to tell me what would be the present value of an investment of five thousand dollars a year for fifty years with compound interest, and his figures were $613,827.48. In this calculation the deficits of seventy-five other years are not included, and only the support of pastors is included; not that of Presiding Elders, Superannuates or Bishops. Had all the items been included during the entire history of the Baltimore Conference, the total deficit would have been at least $2,000,000; a sum which, if invested at five per cent, would give $100,000 annually to be divided among the eighty-eight Conference Claimants, or more than one thousand one hundred dollars each.

This statement covers only one Conference. I am told by a member of the Central Pennsylvania Conference that their deficiencies exceed $500,000. So in every Conference, especially in the older Conferences, there are sufficient deficiencies due the preachers to make it true beyond a doubt that the 1915 CAMPAIGN is based on equity, and that it is not a charity but the tardy return to the Preachers to-day of what was justly due the fathers. It is the Veterans' right.

Asbury's Last Pen Stroke

I hold in my hand a remarkable document; the last pen stroke of the dying Asbury, a page from his journal, which reads in this fashion:

Francis Asbury's Account with the nine Annual Conferences for the year 1816.

January 1st, to balance of 1815, $27.34¾.
1816, to my allowance for the present year, $80.
To sundries, while lying sick 18 days in Cypress, $13.
To allowance to J. W. Bond as traveling companion, $20.
To cash paid to J. W. Bond for road expense, $7.
March 21st, to cash J. W. Bond, Quarterage, $20.
" 29th, to cash to J. W. Bond for road expenses, $10.

He died on March 31, 1816; so that was his last entry, made only two days before his death.

On the debtor side we read,

By cash received January 1st from South Carolina Conference, $40.

By cash from the Virginia Conference, $30.

Compounding the interest on just this part of Asbury's salary from January 1st to the close of March, 1816, the total indebtedness would amount to $52,000.

Hundredth Anniversary of Asbury's Death

I have a suggestion to make. There is a difference of opinion concerning the proper date for the origin of American Methodism. In Baltimore we say that the original meeting place was in Maryland, and we are now celebrating the Sesqui-Centennial of American Methodism. But there is no doubt of the fact that on March 31, 1916, will occur the one hundredth anniversary of the death of Francis Asbury. With others who have the historic spirit I have been desirous that here in Washington there should be an equestrian statue of Francis Asbury, with his saddlebags, seated on his gray mare. The Presbyterians have a statue of Witherspoon, and the Lutherans, a statue of Martin Luther. Was it not President Roosevelt who declared that the Methodist Episcopal Church was the most American in type of any Protestant body? And there is no greater force making for American liberty than the Methodism that is represented in this Convention. A statue of Asbury on his horse, as he was when threading the intricacies of the eastern coast from Maine to Florida and from the Atlantic to the Mississippi would be eminently fitting—the payment of a debt due to him and to the great Church he created. The little monument on the Bishops' lot at Mount Olivet, Baltimore, where four Bishops lie, the humble shaft of marble reared there by the Church of the past generation, is not a sufficient monument to the representative of the greatest religious factor in the making of America. The forces emanating from John Street and Sam's Creek have had more to do with the spiritual upbuilding of American Protestantism than those which came from Plymouth Rock. It is the Methodist, and not the Puritan, who has won out in the struggle for religious leadership in these lands; and therefore, recognizing that we owe him $52,000 by the accretion of the years, might we not invest at least that much to his memory and to spur the Church to Christly sacrifice?

While we are doing this may we not bring the 1915 CAM-

PAIGN to a triumphant climax on March 31, 1916, the one hundredth anniversary of the death of this, the greatest of American Preachers! For the largest factor in the conserving of the itinerancy, the greatest force in pushing the Preacher from the city into the rural districts, was Francis Asbury. The movement for the conservation of rural life, in many respects the greatest movement of our times, must date from this great prophet who, seeing that the salvation of Methodism and the evangelization of the continent was in the conquest of the country, provided for the coming of the itinerant Ministry. We never can pay the debt we owe him, but this recognition of debt cannot be given too soon. Why should not this great Convention, greater in its wider meaning beyond the walls of this building even than within them, determine that the time when we shall bring to a fitting climax this ten-million-dollar campaign and bring honors to his name who has been so little honored, shall be the one hundredth anniversary of the death of the immortal Asbury?

Baltimore, Md. E. L. WATSON.

DISCIPLINARY PROVISIONS FOR SUPPORT OF CONFERENCE CLAIMANTS IN THE METHODIST EPISCOPAL CHURCH

LEGISLATION FOR CONFERENCE CLAIMANTS; INCLUDING RETIRED MINISTERS, AND WIDOWS AND DEPENDENT ORPHANS

The paragraphs are those of the Discipline.

I. THE CLAIM (¶ 323)

The claim to a comfortable support inheres in the Gospel Ministry and rightfully inures to the benefit of the Preacher in the Methodist Episcopal Church, when he is admitted to membership in an Annual Conference. Such claim is not invalidated by his being retired, and at his death passes to the dependent members of his family.

Retired Ministers, the widows of deceased Ministers (during their widowhood, and while they remain members of the Methodist Episcopal Church), and their children under sixteen years of age, are Conference Claimants and beneficiaries of the moneys hereinafter provided. For a year at a time and without prejudice to their rights, such Claimants may voluntarily relinquish their claim; or on recommendation of the Conference Stewards the claim may be disallowed by action of the Annual Conference, taken after opportunity to be heard has been given.

II. Permanent Endowment (¶ 324)

Moneys for the permanent endowment of the Conference Claimants of the entire Church shall be held by the Board of Conference Claimants located at Chicago, Illinois, and shall be administered through its Connectional Permanent Fund. The Board of Conference Claimants shall also administer all gifts and bequests the custody of which is not otherwise designated, the income of which is intended for the use of Conference Claimants.

Annual Conferences are authorized to establish and maintain investment Funds, Preachers' Aid Societies, and organizations and funds of similar character, under such names, plans, rules, and regulations as they may determine, the income from which shall be applied for the support of Conference Claimants. It is recommended that each Annual Conference provide for an incorporated Board to administer its permanent funds.

III. Conference Stewards (¶ 329)

Each Annual Conference shall elect Conference Stewards, who may be either preachers or laymen, arranged in classes so that one third of the members shall be elected each year.

The Conference Stewards shall ascertain what Claimants are in special need (that is, *whose needs require more than can be paid to them from the Annuity Distribution*) and, using as a general basis the estimates received from the Quarterly Conferences and other available information, shall make an equitable allowance to them, which shall be paid *pro rata* from moneys available for that purpose.

Upon the recommendation of the Annual Conference, the Conference Stewards may consider and act upon any claim which the Quarterly Conference may have overlooked.

Each Annual Conference shall determine whether or not its Conference Stewards shall make a preliminary report; and, if so, whether or not it shall be read in open Conference or the action of the Conference Stewards be final.

An Annual Conference shall have authority to recognize as Claimants the widow and minor children of a former member, by agreement with the Conference of which he was a member at the time of his death.

IV. Methods of Distribution (¶¶ 330-333)

1. The Annual Conference Annuity Distribution shall be made to Conference Claimants by the Conference Stewards according to the following regulations:

The annuity claim of a Retired Minister who has been in the effective relation for thirty-five years as a member of an Annual Conference shall not be less than one half of the average annual salary paid to the effective members of his Annual Conference, House Rent excluded.

The annuity claim of any Retired Minister, determined by this standard, shall not be less than one seventieth (1-70) of the average salary of the effective members of his Conference multiplied by the number of years of his effective service, including two years on trial.

The annuity claim of a widow shall be determined by the number of years during which she was the wife of a preacher while he was in the effective relation, as a member of an Annual Conference, and shall be one half of the annuity claim of a Retired Minister for such term of years.

The term of a father's effective service shall determine the annuity claim of his child, which shall be one fifth of the claim of a Retired Minister for such term.

Moneys designated for Annuity Distribution shall be distributed on the BASIS OF SERVICE, and shall consist of:

(1) The dividends of the Book Concern and the Chartered Fund.

(2) The income from any investments made by the Annual Conference for Annuity Distribution and held in trust for this purpose.

(3) Such gifts and bequests as are made for Annuity Distribution.

(4) Such part of the annual support of Conference Claimants furnished by the pastoral charges as the Annual Conference may determine.

2. The Annual Conference Necessitous Distribution Shall be

on the BASIS OF SPECIAL NEED, and shall consist of:

(1) The annual Dividend for Connectional Relief paid to the Annual Conference by the Board of Conference Claimants.

(2) Such part of the support of Conference Claimants furnished by the Pastoral Charges, as the Annual Conference may determine.

(3) The income from such gifts and bequests as are made for necessitous distribution.

(4) Gifts and bequests made for immediate distribution.

(5) Income arising from investments made by Relief and Aid Societies of Annual Conferences, if so determined by them.

3. Connectional Relief Distribution Shall be

to Annual Conferences by the Board of Conference Claimants.

Board of Conference Claimants (¶¶ 469-473)

1. Authorization and Officers

There shall be a Board of Conference Claimants nominated by the Bishops and elected by the General Conference, consisting of one effective Bishop, seven Ministers, and seven Laymen. No Annual Conference shall have more than one representative on the Board.

The Board of Conference Claimants shall be duly and legally incorporated, according to the laws of the State of Illinois, with such powers and prerogatives as shall be needful for the accomplishing of the objects of the Board as herein stated. This Board is authorized to adopt such measures as in its judgment are necessary to build up and administer a Connectional Permanent Fund which is hereby established, and to increase the revenues for the benefit of Conference Claimants, provided, however, that it shall not have authority to make any apportionment whatever, either to the Annual Conferences or to the pastoral charges. Seven members shall constitute a quorum. The office of the Board shall be in Chicago, Illinois.

The expenses of administration shall be taken from the two per cent of collections from Pastoral charges, and any other funds in the hands of the Board not otherwise designated.

The term of service of the members of this Board shall be four years, or until their successors are duly elected and qualified. Vacancies occurring during the interval of the General Conference shall be filled by the Board upon nomination by the Bishops.

II. Corresponding Secretary

There shall be a Corresponding Secretary who shall be elected by the General Conference, and shall be the chief executive officer of the Board. Under the provisions of the Discipline and the authority, direction, and control of the Board, of which he shall be an advisory member, he shall conduct the correspondence and business. His time shall be employed in conducting the affairs and promoting the general interests for which the Board was created.

III. Connectional Relief

Connectional Relief for Conference Claimants is established that the Preachers and people of the stronger Annual Conferences may be united with those of the weaker Conferences in one connectional or general plan in order that, by such cooperation, a more equitable and general support may be secured for Retired Ministers and other Conference Claimants, especially for those in the more needy Conferences.

Such Connectional Relief shall consist of:

(1) The three per cent of the annual collections for Conference Claimants forwarded from the Annual Conferences.

(2) The income from all other sources the use of which is not otherwise designated and which is not required for the maintenance of the Board.

Moneys for Connectional Relief shall be distributed by the Board of Conference Claimants at its Annual Meeting, to the Annual Conferences severally and not to the individual claimant.

The Board of Conference Claimants, in determining the Dividend for Connectional Relief, shall ascertain from the authorized reports of the Conference Stewards of the several Annual Conferences what Conferences are in need of Connectional Relief, and shall make the distribution to such Conferences according to their need as this shall appear from such reports.

The Remainder of the available funds shall be distributed among the other Conferences as the Board of Conference Claimants may determine to be wise and equitable in view of all the data in its possession.

No Conference shall receive Connectional Relief unless its share of the annual collections shall have been paid into the Board of Conference Claimants.

IV. Reports

The Treasurer of the Board of Conference Claimants shall send to the Treasurer of the Annual Conference a draft for the Dividend for Connectional Relief, together with the last Annual Report of the Board; in which shall be shown the resources of the Board, the amount and distribution of its income, and such other information concerning the work of the Church in behalf of Conference Claimants as the Board may obtain.

The Conference Stewards shall forward to the Board of Conference Claimants a certified copy of their Report, made on blanks furnished by the Board of Conference Claimants, in which shall be shown the annuities and allowances made to each Conference Claimant, together with additional data for the guidance of the Board of Conference Claimants in making its Dividend for Connectional Relief and in preparing its Annual Report.

STEEL PENSIONERS GOT $511,967 IN 1914

The fourth annual report of the United States Steel and Carnegie Pension Fund shows the total disbursements for the year were $511,967, as compared with $422,815 in 1913, $358,780 in 1912, and $281,457 in 1911, making a grand total of $1,575,021 for the four years.

The greatest disbursement was at the plants of the Carnegie Steel Company, where $122,914 were distributed. During the year 2,704 employees were on the pension list, an increase of 612 during the year. During the year 183 cases were discontinued, so that on December 31, 2,521 remained on the rolls.

The averages for cases added during 1914 were: Age 63.33 years; service, 28.76 years; monthly pension, $20.40.

ANNUAL CONFERENCE REPRESENTATIVES

H. L. Jacobs, J. S. Hughes, L. O. Sherburne
W. H. Hughes, Elwin Hitchcock, W. L. Slease

VETERANS OF THE MINNESOTA CONFERENCE

Wm. McKinley, W. C. Rice, Henry Bilbie, W. K. Marshall, E. R. Lathrop, E. H. Bronson

PART IV

THE CLAIM ILLUSTRATED

FACT, STORY, SONG

Fact, Story and Song illustrate the Struggles, Triumphs and Needs of the Veteran Ministers and make a large appeal to all. The Scriptures state the Relationships underlying the Principle of a Retiring Competency for the Aged Servants of God and His Church; the Press, both secular and religious, demands the Recognition of their Services, while The Story of their Devotion lends itself readily to Sentiments expressed in Poetry and Song.

CHAPTER I. SCRIPTURAL TREATMENT

THE OLD ARAB PRIEST AND THE OLD PREACHER

Rev. J. D. Maddox, M.D.

An aged Arab priest who had ridden with his people over rocks and burning sands in search of pasture and water for fourscore years is about to take his last ride. See him, with form still erect, leaning on his staff, his hair and beard white as snow. He stands apart turning his eyes, dim with age, toward the shoreless desert and the rising sun. His Arabian steed, with heavy flowing mane and tail clean and white as linen, seems to know that some bereavement has come into his life.

Do you see that group of men standing at a distance in earnest conference? The old man knows what it means. Having grown old to the point of helplessness and dependence he knows that he must be dealt with according to the ancient custom of his people. The lots are cast and two men withdraw and saddle their steeds. Another saddles the beautiful steed of the old man who sadly but silently yields to their ministrations. They bathe him after their manner, and put on him clean apparel. All others have disappeared in their tents. The old man is silently and gently lifted into the saddle and those who drew the lots ride up, one on either side of him. Without parley or "good-bys," at once and in silence, the three ride straight into the desert, from "early morn till high noon." Then as if by appointment they stop.

The attendants dismount and gently lift the old man from his steed, and spreading a beautifully colored cloth on the sand, lay the old man not unlovingly upon it. Leaving him a crust and a bone, they take his staff, mount their steeds in silence, take the leading-strap of the old man's steed and ride back to the camp. No questions were asked.

I had thought of making an application of this story. But I cannot, it is too suggestive; and it makes its own application. I need not.

HELPFUL HOMILETIC HINTS

THE REV. HENRY H. SWEETS

Secretary Ministerial Relief, Louisville, Ky.

I

Deut. 10. 8, 9. At that time the Lord separated the tribe of Levi, to bear the ark of the covenant of the Lord, to stand before the Lord to minister unto him, and to bless in his name, unto this day. Wherefore Levi hath no part nor inheritance with his brethren; the Lord is his inheritance, according as the Lord thy God promised him.

The Hebrew economy was in advance of anything that has thus far characterized the Christian Church. The Levites, set apart to the service of the sanctuary, were provided for on a magnificent scale. Having no proper inheritance among the Children of Israel, they nevertheless were assured from any possible want from cradle to grave, and their widows and orphans after them. The abundant tithes and offerings, the levitical cities and their suburbs, and the sacredness of their calling, assured to all those who stood before the Lord to minister to him, the most ample, continuous and unfailing supply of all their wants.—*Rev. Arthur Pierson, D.D.*

The Assembly believes that of all the duties, not to say privileges belonging to the Church of Jesus Christ, there is none more sacred and tender than that of making suitable provision for those who have worn themselves out in her service, and for the lonely, dependent ones who have been left without any means of support.

II

Num. 18. 24. But the tithes of the children of Israel, which they offer as an heave offering unto the Lord, *I have given to the Levites* to inherit: therefore I have said unto them, among the children of Israel they shall have no inheritance.

The veteran is entitled to rest, even when his strength

remains. The tenderest of care should be his when his strength has gone with his years.

It is the duty and responsibility of the Church quite as much to look after the workers as the work; and its work will be better done if it does look after the worker. There is not a man living who will not throw himself more heartily into the work, no matter how hard and difficult it is, or how poor the place, if he feels that behind him is the help of the Church when he is wounded or falls by the wayside.—*Dr. Alfred J. P. McClure.*

III

Num. 35. 2. Command the children of Israel, that they give unto the Levites of the inheritance of their possession cities to dwell in; and ye shall give also unto the Levites suburbs for the cities around about them.

There are men who see to it that even the aged, worn-out beast of burden is provided for. Shall we be found less considerate of human beings?

The ministry may not contribute directly to the creation of wealth, but they do render society service absolutely invaluable. The pay is contemptibly inadequate. Seven hundred dollars was the sum which a church in Philadelphia recently thought ample for a faithful pastor to live and keep a family on a year, and even that is considerably above the average salary. The Bishop was right when he imputed to the dreary outlook for old age the disinclination of young men to enter the ministry.—*The Philadelphia Public Ledger.*

IV

Deut. 12. 19. Take heed to thyself that thou forsake not the Levite as long as thou livest upon the earth.

Shall we pension the soldier, and fail to provide for the preacher?

On June 30, 1914, there were on the pension rolls of the United States 785,239 army and navy pensioners. To these the sum of $172,417,546 was paid in one year. Since 1866 $4,633,511,926 has been paid to pensioners.

The cause of Ministerial Relief has languished for many years because our ministers have been modestly reticent.

This is not begging; it is counsel to do right, counsel that the people need, counsel for the lack of which the Church is daily forfeiting the precious blessings of duty done. Shake off your false modesty. Help the Church to do right. You know that many of your aged brethren are suffering through a neglect for which the people are not responsible, since they do not know the facts. It is in your power to make the facts known. Therefore, take these words to heart: "Who so seeth his brother have need, and shutteth up his compassion from him, how dwelleth the love of God in him?"—*Dr. Fulton.*

V

Deut. 14. 27. And the Levite that is within thy gates; thou shalt not forsake him; for he hath no part nor inheritance with thee.

Queen Elizabeth requested a merchant to go abroad on her service, and when he mentioned that his own business would be ruined, she replied, "You mind my business and I will mind yours."

When the Church ordains a man to the Gospel Ministry, she says to him, "You minister to us in spiritual things and we will care for you in material things." This is the day of opportunity. If the Church does not act promptly, not only will the cause of Ministerial Relief suffer, but also the supply of candidates for the ministry will be seriously affected. If the father lies wounded on the field of battle uncared for, can we expect the son to fill his place in the depleted ranks of the regiment?—*General Assembly.*

VI

1 Cor. 9. 13, 14. Do ye not know that they which minister about holy things live of the things of the temple? And they which wait at the altar are partakers with the altar? Even so hath the Lord ordained that they which preach the gospel should live of the gospel.

We believe God never meant the place of a minister to be ordinarily one of ample means or elegant luxury; but He does mean that no minister should be entangled in affairs of this life; and to prevent this, it is more important than any other one thing to assure every servant of God that, whatever self-denial may be incident to the days of his actual and active labor, when the day of work is over he shall not suffer want for the necessities of life; or, if prematurely called hence, shall not leave a wife and children to be cast on the charity of the very Church he has self-denyingly served.—*Dr. Pierson.*

The spirit of Christianity is beginning to permeate the national industrial, fraternal and educational circles of the world. Benefits, annuities and pensions are being provided on every hand. Some one has said: "The Church of God is disloyal to Christ and unfaithful, when she does not practice, among her own, the gospel she preaches."

VII

1 Tim. 5. 18. For the Scripture saith, Thou shalt not muzzle the ox that treadeth out the corn. And, The laborer is worthy of his reward.

Lewis Elkin left one million, seven hundred and fifty thousand dollars for pensioning the school teachers of Philadelphia. It is called the Elkin Relief Fund.

It is an insult to call this charity; it is in the very highest sense a debt, and should be so honored as an imperative obligation owed to those who use their days of strength in the service of our Lord; and no blessing can be expected on a Church which allows the veteran soldier of Christ to go down to his grave like an inmate of a poor-house, or a dependent on charity, looking for a miserable pittance bestowed as on a beggar, for the bare subsistence of life.—*Dr. Pierson.*

Many a man of the world would provide for a faithful old dog or the family horse better than the churches provide for those who have served their Master and humanity faithfully until infirmity beset them.—*Philadelphia Public Ledger.*

VIII

1 Cor. 9. 7-10. Who goeth a warfare any time at his own charges? Who planteth a vineyard, and eateth not of the fruit thereof? or who feedeth a flock, and eateth not of the milk of the flock? Say I these things as a man? or saith not the law the same also? For it is written in the law of Moses, Thou shalt not muzzle the mouth of the ox that treadeth out the corn. Doth God take care for oxen? Or saith he it altogether for our sakes? For our sakes, no doubt, this is written; that he that ploweth should plow in hope; and that he that thresheth in hope should be partaker of his hope.

"Doth God take thought for oxen?" Shall He not take

thought for these servants, who have toiled in the field through the noon-tide heat, as oxen toil in the furrow? Surely God must put it into the hearts of His people to do something toward the fund that pathetically describes itself for the relief of aged pastors.—*Margaret E. Sangster.*

Rev. J. W. Wallace said before his death, "When I came out from Kentucky I brought a good horse. He served me faithfully many years as a 'family horse.' When he got to be twenty years old, I fenced off a ten-acre lot of the best blue grass in Jackson county. I said: 'No matter how much drought I'll never let any stock in old Jake's preserves.'" The night old Jake died, he sat up all night with him.

IX

1 Sam. 30. 23, 24. Then said David, Ye shall not do so, my brethren, with that which the Lord hath given us, who hath preserved us, and delivered the company that came against us into our hand. For who will hearken unto you in this matter? But as his part is that goeth down to the battle, so shall his part be that tarrieth by the stuff; they shall part alike.

> Taught by time, my heart has learned to glow
> For others' good, and melted others' woe.—*Homer.*

Who shall have the spoils? Well, some selfish soul suggests that those treasures ought to belong to those who had been out in active service. "We did all the fighting, and we ought to have all the treasures." But David looked into the worn faces of these veterans who had stayed in the garrison, and saw how cleanly everything had been kept, and that the baggage was all safe; and knew how that these aged, wounded and crippled men would gladly enough have been at the front if they had been able, and said: "No! no! Let us have fair play; 'As his part is that goeth down to the battle, so shall his part be that tarrieth by the stuff.'"

There is high encouragement for those who once wrought mightily for Christ and the Church, but who through sickness or collapse of fortune or advanced years cannot now go to the front. These two hundred men of the text were veterans. Let that man bare his arms and show how the muscles were torn. Let him pull aside the turban and see the mark of the battle ax. Pull aside the coat and see where the spear thrust him. Would it have been fair for those men, crippled, weak and old, to have no share in the triumph?—*Talmage.*

X

Prov. 3. 27. Withhold not good from them to whom it is due, when it is in the power of thine hand to do it.

To neglect any one who needs our help is to neglect Christ Himself.—*J. R. Miller, D.D.*

What do we live for if it is not to make life less difficult for each other?—*George Eliot.*

Cornell University has a retiring pension of fifteen hundred dollars for its professors.

Withhold all eulogies when I am dead,
All noisy sorrow;
Give me the tender word to-day
Instead of tears to-morrow.

XI

1 Tim. 5. 8. But if any provide not for his own, and specially for those of his own house, he hath denied the faith, and is worse than an infidel.

Germany, Denmark, New Zealand and some other countries have pension systems for working men, of advanced years and good moral character.

The Church must face and solve the problem of proper pension and care for its disabled and superannuated ministry. Justice and Christianity both demand it. To leave the aged workers to humiliation and distress and poverty is unchristian and unwise.

The man of fifty thousand dollars who brings five, twenty, or one hundred dollars to the altar of God, and says, "This is all I have to spare," lies to God, as Ananias never did. Tens of thousands are living in luxury, spending money for vanity and pride, gluttony and sensuality, submitting a mere bagatelle to the use of the Holy Spirit.—*Bishop A. W. Wilson.*

XII

Gal. 6. 10. As we have therefore opportunity, let us do good unto all men, especially unto them who are of the household of faith.

The measure of a gift is in what is kept.—*Alexander McKenzie, D.D.*

The Roman Catholic Church guarantees to its old priests six hundred dollars annually.

Faithful soldiers are falling by the way, overcome by the burden and the heat of the day. Some linger a little while. They need our brotherly sympathy and help. Others have fallen to rise no more until the bright morning; but their dependent ones call for our tenderest care.—*Dr. Agnew.*

Help us to help each other, Lord,
  Each other's cross to bear;
Let each his friendly aid afford,
  And feel his brother's care.

XIII

1 Cor. 16. 1, 2. Now concerning the collection for the saints, as I have given order to the churches of Galatia, even so do ye. Upon the first day of the week let every one of you lay by him in store, as God has prospered him, that there be no gatherings when I come.

God sees to it that the cheerful giver never has to go out of business for lack of capital.—*The Ram's Horn.*

There is a Carnegie Relief Fund which applies to all the Carnegie iron interests for pensions and relief of iron workers. It disbursed over $250,000 in 1904.

I bring before you the small army of aged ministers. Do you see them? Their hair is thin and silvery; their faces are furrowed and their forms bent; they are feeble. Leaning upon some strong arm, each one goes forward, tottering. Soon they will be beyond our help. But they are here now. We see their hands clasped in holy prayer; we hear their tremulous voices as in union they cry out, "Cast us not off in time of old age!" That prayer ascends to heaven; it reaches the ears of the Almighty, who at once sends it back to us and bids us answer it. We are to take the Lord's place and provide for these faithful old servants.—*Dr. Peter Stryker.*

XIV

2 Cor. 8. 13, 14. For I mean not that other men be eased, and ye burdened; but by an equality, that now at this time your abundance may be a supply for their want, that their abundance also may be a supply for your want; that there may be equality.

Every Christian should label his pocketbook with the words of the Lord's lease, "Occupy till I come."

Andrew Carnegie has given ten million dollars for the pensioning of old professors and teachers in the colleges and schools of the United States.

Do you realize that there are aged and enfeebled ministers, who have broken down in the service of Christ and your Church, refined, patient, godly men who are inadequately supplied with life's necessities, or wholly unprovided for now, to-day, at this present time; while thousands of dollars are being given to objects very remotely related to the Kingdom of God, or to charities which are often unappreciated, and which accomplish little good. Some one has said, "This is a perversion of a Christian idea. It is the Church neglecting to practice among her own the gospel she preaches."—*Dr. Alfred J. P. McClure.*

XV

1 Cor. 12. 25, 26. That there should be no schism in the body; but that the members should have the same care one for another. And whether one member suffer, all the members suffer with it; or one member be honored, all the members rejoice with it.

There are scores of private firms and corporations and railroads now pensioning their employees and officers.

"Is thy cruse of comfort wasting?
Rise and share it with another,
And through all the years of famine,
It shall serve thee and thy brother."
—*Mrs. E. R. Charles.*

XVI

1 Tim. 6. 17-19. Charge them that are rich in this world, that they be not highminded, nor trust in uncertain riches, but in the living God, who giveth us richly all things to enjoy; that they do good, that they be rich in good works, ready to distribute, willing to communicate; laying up in store for themselves a good foundation against the time to come, that they may lay hold on eternal life.

There is no happiness in having and getting, but only in giving. Half the world is on the wrong scent in pursuit of happiness.—*Henry Drummond.*

The Church of Scotland, from Sustentation Funds and tithes, gives her Retired Ministers a pension of $800 to $900.

There are many needy ones who will not apply for help because the Relief Fund is so small and they feel that there are others who need the help more than they do. There was an aged and infirm Minister. The last handful had been taken from the barrel of meal. When he was asked why he had not applied for assistance, his reply was, "Because I thought there might be many of God's servants in greater need, and I knew the supply was small."—*Dr. Stryker.*

XVII

Prov. 11. 25. The liberal soul shall be made fat; and he that watereth shall be watered also himself.

In giving, a man receives more than he gives, and the more is in proportion to the worth of the thing given.—*George Macdonald.*

XVIII

Eccl. 11. 1. Cast thy bread upon the waters: for thou shalt find it after many days.

We lose what on ourselves we spend.
We have as treasure without end
Whatever, Lord, to Thee we lend.

To feed the hungry and relieve the distressed, to take care of the workers in the household of faith, when they are sick and disabled and old, is one of the fundamental duties of Christianity, and no matter what other urgent claims there may seem to be, we believe that, because this first and primary duty is neglected, the Church is poor and hopeless, and lacking in courage and brave initiative.—*Dr. McClure.*

XIX

Prov. 19. 17. He that hath pity upon the poor lendeth unto the Lord; and that which he hath given will he pay him again.

A bag that does not wax old is one that will never fail to send an income. There are men in heaven who were rich while on earth, and who in some wise beneficent ways invested their property with a view to results in another world. Ask them, "Are you getting any income from your investments down there?" "O, yes, a wonderful income. There is a continual stream of persons coming in here who were started heavenward or were helped on their way by those investments. They are beginning to come up out of all lands and tribes and kindreds and tongues." Many earthly investments pay dividends in heaven.—*William Ashmore.*

There was a man, they called him mad,
The more he gave, the more he had.

XX

2 Cor. 9. 1, 2. As touching the ministering to the saints, it is superfluous for me to write to you: for I know the forwardness of your mind, for which I boast of you to them of Macedonia, that Achaia was ready a year ago; and your zeal hath provoked very many.

The Presbyterian Church is endeavoring to increase its endowment fund to $10,000,000. In 1908 this Church contributed more than $374,000 for present needs.

During 1914 the Methodist Episcopal Church paid more than a million dollars to its aged Ministers, widows and orphans. During 1915 it will engage in a campaign for $10,000,000 as the 150th Anniversary Jubilee Gift.

XXI

2 Cor. 9. 9, 10. As it is written, He hath dispersed abroad; he hath given to the poor: his righteousness remaineth forever. Now he that ministereth seed to the sower both minister bread for your food, and multiply your seed sown, and increase the fruits of your righteousness;

For his bounty,
There was no winter in't; an autumn 'twas,
That grew the more by reaping.—*Shakespeare.*

For the heart grows rich in giving:
All its wealth is living grain;
Seeds which mildew in the garner,
Scattered, fill with gold the plain.

XXII

1 Cor. 9. 11. If we have sown unto you spiritual things, is it a great thing if we shall reap your carnal things?

Andrew Carnegie has given five millions for rewarding heroes and pensioning them. Good!

Some day a millionaire may establish a "hero fund" for

country ministers who spend their lives in the service of the community, not only ministering weekly to their congregations, but marrying the young people, visiting the sick, burying the dead, and being always ready to respond to the call of need of any kind.—*Youth's Companion.*

If the man in the pulpit helps you with his thought and speech, recognize it as you do the work of the lawyer who counsels you what course to take when Smith's cow straddles your fence and eats your corn. Recognize it as you do the work of the doctor who cures your boy who had eaten too many of your neighbor's green apples. When these bill you for services, you own your debt and pay up. But the minister will seldom ask for his. His fiber won't stand that strain; but he will beg for other and less needy institutions than his own home and study shelves.—*Chronicle, Halifax.*

XXIII

Acts 20. 35. I have showed you all things, how that so laboring ye ought to support the weak, and to remember the words of the Lord Jesus, how he said, It is more blessed to give than to receive.

There is on record an admirable prayer of Thomas Sutton, the pious founder of the Charterhouse, "O, Lord, Thou hast given me a large estate, *give me a large heart.*"

XXIV

2 Cor. 8. 9. For ye know the grace of our Lord Jesus Christ, that, though he was rich, yet for your sakes he became poor, that ye through his poverty might be rich.

You can give without loving, but you can't love without giving.—*Marion Lawrance.*

Every dictate of justice, humanity, gratitude and religion urges us to care more adequately for our worn-out Ministers, who are in need after spending their lives in most self-denying service to Christ and the Church; and to assist the widows and helpless orphans who have shared the privations of those who, having served their generation by the will of God, have "fallen asleep."

Help us to help each other, Lord,
Each other's cross to bear;
Let each his friendly aid afford,
And feel his brother's care.

XXV

Heb. 6. 10. For God is not unrighteous to forget your work and labor of love, which ye have showed toward his name, in that ye have ministered to the saints, and do minister.

The assistance which the Church gives for Ministerial Relief brings more cheer and sunshine into darkened homes than you can imagine. The gratitude of the beneficiaries is unbounded. They are constantly remembering at the Throne of Grace those who have made this help possible. Have you a place in their prayers?

> Me let the tender office long engage
> To rock the cradle of reposing age.—*Pope.*

XXVI

Gal. 6. 6. Let him that is taught in the word communicate unto Him that teacheth in all good things.

The average mechanic in New York City receives an average of $4.60 a day, which makes $1,380 a year for 300 working days.

He had some money, and instead of hoarding it, hunted up one of God's aged and disabled ministers, Paul, and used part of the money for him. The record reads thus: "The Lord give mercy unto the house of Onesiphorus, for he oft refreshed me, and was not ashamed of my chain. But when he was in Rome, he sought me out diligently and found me. The Lord grant unto him that he may find mercy of the Lord in that day."

If Onesiphorus had held on to his money and let Paul suffer, he could have enjoyed it only a few years; he parted with his money, and helped the suffering Minister of God, and it has given him nineteen hundred years of pleasure.—*Dr. Thomas E. Converse.*

XXVII

Matt. 10. 41, 42. He that receiveth a prophet in the name of a prophet shall receive a prophet's reward; and he that receiveth a righteous man in the name of a righteous man shall receive a righteous man's reward. And whosoever shall give to drink unto one of these little ones a cup of cold water only in the name of a disciple, verily I say unto you, he shall in no wise lose his reward.

Give strength, give thought, give deeds, give pelf,
Give love, give tears, and give thyself;
Give, give, be always giving,
Who gives not is not living.
The more we give,
The more we live.

These Ministers have been retired, not because of any want of courage or eagerness for the battle, but because they have grown old in the service or have been wounded in the fight. Their loneliness and want should touch every soul. This cry goes up from their hearts:

"How long, O Lord, to wait
  Beside this open gate?
My sheep with many a lamb
Have entered, and I am
  Alone, and it is late."

XXVIII

Matt. 18. 5. And whoso shall receive one such little child in my name receiveth me.

Her husband was in the ministry eighteen years, preaching to weak churches for a very small salary. Her five children were in school. She wrote: "Knights of Pythias paid for books of smaller children last term. Have managed by close economy to keep out of debt until now, but am falling behind and the future looks very gloomy. If the children have to stop school, I see nothing ahead for them." Yes, the Church is ahead of them, the almoner of God's mercy.

The Church is not a myth. She is as much an entity as the state, and she claims far more than the state; she claims to be a mother. Why not then take care of her sick and aged and children?—*G. H. McKnight.*

It is not the deed we do,
  Though the deed be ever so fair,
But the love the dear Lord looketh for,
  Hidden with lowly care
In the heart of the deed so fair.

XXIX

Mark 9. 41. For whosoever shall give you a cup of water to drink in my name, because ye belong to Christ, verily I say unto you, he shall not lose his reward.

That man may last, but never lives,
Who much receives, but nothing gives;
Whom none can love, whom none can thank.
Creation's blot, creation's blank.
—*Thomas Gibbons.*

The widows have endured hardness as they stood by the side of their husbands in the poor mission fields of our Church. They are making a brave struggle to meet the needs of their families at a time when the cost of living is greatly increasing. The beneficiaries are dying off rapidly. Help now to bring relief to the "saints" who are in need.

"To comfort and to bless,
To find a balm for woe,
To tend the lone and fatherless,
Is angels' work below."

XXX

James 1. 27. Pure religion and undefiled before God and the Father is this; to visit the fatherless and widows in their affliction, and to keep himself unspotted from the world.

Of some of the appeals for relief which come to us it might be said, "Cut the words and they would bleed." They rarely breathe any note of complaint; they are spoken in the ear in closets, but they throb with a meaning big enough to be proclaimed upon the house tops. No servant of the Cross can ask to be exempted from the obligation to endure hardness as a good soldier of Jesus Christ, but surely the Church should not wait to see how well her aged or widowed or orphaned ones can starve.

Never are kind acts done
To wipe the weeping eyes,
But like the flashes of the sun
They signal to the skies;
And up above, the angels read
How we have helped the sorer need.

XXXI

Psa. 37. 3. Trust in the Lord and do good; so shalt thou dwell in the land, and verily thou shalt be fed.

A chairman wrote concerning a beneficiary: "He is most

worthy in every way. In his work he has been faithful and zealous, successful in promoting the cause of the Gospel, and is one of Christ's sincere, patient, tender and loving disciples. I think he will never have the strength to preach again and believe that his life is drawing to a rapid close. He is resting on the promise, 'Trust in the Lord and do good; so shalt thou dwell in the land, and verily thou shalt be fed.'"

XXXII

Psa. 37. 25. I have been young, and now am old; yet have I not seen the righteous forsaken, nor his seed begging bread.

Many of the old servants of Christ and his Church have this same child-like faith in their Heavenly Father. But God does not send the ravens to feed them, as He sent to the prophet of old. He does not rain the manna from heaven, as He did to feed the children of Israel in the wilderness. He says to us, *"Give ye them to eat."*

XXXIII

Job 5. 26. Thou shalt come to thy grave in a full age, like as a shock of corn cometh in his season.

In latter days of Confederacy when boys sixteen and seventeen years of age were being sent into war, Alexander Stephens said: "We are burning up the seed-corn. The war must stop." Not so much danger of burning up seed-corn to-day in the army of God as of neglecting the ripe ear in the shock. —*Dr. J. W. Bachman.*

I'm growing fonder of my staff,
I'm growing dimmer in the eyes,
I'm growing fainter in my laugh,
I'm growing deeper in my sighs,
I'm growing careless of my dress,
I'm growing frugal of my gold,
I'm growing wise; I'm growing, yes—
I'm growing old.—*Saxe.*

XXXIV

Psa. 92. 14. They shall still bring forth fruit in old age; they shall be fat and flourishing.

Age is not all decay; it is the ripening, the swelling of the fresh life within, that withers and bursts the husk.—*George Macdonald.*

A faithful veteran, who has lost his eyesight, and because of rapidly failing health has had to give up his charge, said at a delightful communion service: "I want you to think of me, as the shadows are lengthening across my path, as still holding out the light of God's truth to guide the wanderers Home."

XXXV

Psa. 71. 18. Now also when I am old and grayheaded, O God, forsake me not; until I have showed thy strength unto this generation, and thy power to every one that is to come.

In 1913, the Pennsylvania Railroad Company had on its pension rolls 3,975 former employees to whom it paid $1,165,-996.33.

Forsake me not when I am old;
  The daylight wanes, my work is done,
My feet draw near the streets of gold,
  I wait the setting of the sun.

Forsake me not when I am old,
  When youthful vigor is no more;
When in the twilight gray and cold,
  I sit and wait the summons o'er.

XXXVI

Lev. 19. 32. Thou shalt rise up before the hoary head and honor the face of the old man, and fear thy God: I am the Lord.

Our youth we can have but today;
We must always find time to grow old.
—*Bishop Berkeley.*

I thank God for the presence of our old men, who, unable to bear the burden and the heat of the day, are praying for the peace and prosperity of Zion, and with trembling voice are bearing comfort to bereaved souls. God bless the Fathers in Israel who still tarry with us, and spare them to bless the Church of Christ with their ripe experience and consecrated wisdom, and to fill the communities and homes in which they live with the delightful fragrance of their Spirit-filled lives.—*Dr. W. H. Frazer.*

Forsake thee not when thou art old?
  Thy Father hears thy trustful prayer,
His arms of love shall thee enfold;
  His hand thy table shall prepare.

Forsake thee not when thou art old?
  We hear the call; the churches wake;
The heart that won us to the fold
  Our grateful love shall ne'er forsake.

XXXVII

Philem. 13. Whom I would have retained with me, that in thy stead he might have ministered unto me in the bonds of the gospel.

One can easily get stirred up over this matter when he begins to examine facts and figures—and yet few sermons are harder for some of the ministers to preach. If he were only a layman for that sermon! Or if it were his people, the laity, who were facing a homeless old age, and all the ministers had homes of their own, and he were preaching to them! Then how easy it would be to put fervor and heart-power into the appeal. But to seem to plead for self, for bread and clothes and shelter—no wonder many a man and his family are suffering rather than to let their wants be known.—*Church Standard.*

Not what we give, but what we share,
For the gift without the giver is bare;
Who gives himself with his alms, feeds *three*,
Himself, his hungering neighbor, and Me.
—*Lowell.*

XXXVIII

2 Tim. 4. 9, 21. Do thy diligence to come shortly unto me. Come before winter.

The Old Merchants Relief Fund of Philadelphia gives a pension of three hundred dollars to old merchants.

"And yet it never was in my soul
  To play so ill a part,
But evil is wrought by want of thought
  As well as want of heart."—*Hood.*

There is surely no want of *heart* in the Church. But many have not *thought* of this need. Have *you?*

XXXIX

The title to Psalm 71, in the American Revision reads,

"PRAYER OF AN OLD MAN FOR DELIVERANCE."

The Psalm photographs the hopes, fears, faith and prayers of a Veteran Preacher. The tone is plaintive yet trustful, but the Psalm ends in gladness, and expresses in mingled prayers and thanksgiving the pathetic history of blended joy and sorrow throughout an anxious, patient and finally triumphant life:

"In thee, O Jehovah, do I take refuge;
Let me never be put to shame.
Deliver me in thy righteousness, and rescue me:
Bow down thy ear unto me and save me.

"For thou art my hope, O Lord Jehovah:
Thou art my trust from my youth.
Cast me not off in my old age:
Forsake me not when my strength faileth."

The Aged Minister becomes jealous for the good name of Jehovah, because the world was saying that God had been unfaithful to Him.

"Mine enemies speak concerning me,
Saying, 'God hath forsaken him.'"

So the old Preacher tells his experience:

"My mouth shall tell of thy righteousness,
And thy salvation all the day.
I will come to the mighty acts of the Lord Jehovah,
I will make mention of thy righteousness, even of thine only.
O God, thou hath taught me from my youth:
And hitherto have I declared thy wondrous works,
Yea, even when I am old and gray-headed,
O God, forsake me not."

XL

Heb. 13. 16. To do good and to communicate forget not; for with such sacrifices God is well pleased.

Gal. 6. 10. Let us do good unto all men, especially unto them who are of the household of faith.

Give as you would if an angel
  Awaited your gift at the door;
Give as you would if tomorrow
  Found you where waiting is o'er;
Give as you would to the Master
  If you met His searching look;
Give as you would of your substance,
  If His hand your offering took.

Every one may have the joy of the Patriarch Job who exclaimed: "Because I delivered the poor that cried, and the fatherless, and him that had none to help him, the blessing of him that was ready to perish came upon me; and I caused the widow's heart to sing for joy. I was eyes to the blind, and feet was I to the lame. I was a father to the poor: and the cause which I knew not I searched out." Job. 29. 12-16.

XLI

Matt. 25. 34-40. Then shall the King say unto them on his right hand, Come, ye blessed of my Father, inherit the kingdom prepared for you from the foundation of the world; for I was an hungered, and ye gave me meat; I was thirsty, and ye gave me drink: I was a stranger, and ye took me in; naked, and ye clothed me: I was sick, and ye visited me: I was in prison, and ye came unto me. Then shall the righteous answer him, saying, Lord, when saw we thee an hungered, and fed thee? or thirsty, and gave thee drink? When saw we thee a stranger, and took thee in? or naked, and clothed thee? Or when saw we thee sick, or in prison, and came unto thee? And the King shall answer and say unto them, Verily I say unto you, Inasmuch as ye have done it unto one of the least of these my brethren, ye have done it unto me.

VETERANS OF THE CROSS

MISS E. E. HEWITT

All glory to our Captain, for the Veterans of the Cross!
They held aloft his banner, never counting earthly loss;
They bravely fought the battles of the right against the wrong;
They led the Lord's battalions with a hallelujah song.

For all the faithful service of the Veterans of the King,
O, let the Church they honored, glad and grateful tribute bring!
They gave their lives' devotion: let us give them, as their right,
The comforts that will fill them with contentment and delight.

Salute, O Christian soldiers, as the Veteran corps goes by;
The angels wait their coming, in the city built on high;
O, haste to render homage to these leaders, good and true,
Before the gates shall open for the final grand review.

XLII

Matt. 26. 6, 7. Now when Jesus was in Bethany in the house of Simon the Leper, there came unto him a woman having an ALABASTER BOX of very precious ointment, and poured it on his head.

Do not keep the alabaster boxes of your love and tenderness

sealed until your friends are dead. Fill their lives with its sweetness. Speak approving, cheering words while their hearts can be thrilled and made happier by them. The kind things you mean to say when they are gone say before they go. The flowers you mean to send for their coffins send to brighten and sweeten their homes.

If my friends have alabaster boxes laid away, full of fragrant perfumes of sympathy and affection, which they intend to break over my dead body, I would rather they would bring them now in my weary and troubled hours, and open them, that I may be refreshed and cheered. I would rather have a plain coffin, without a flower, a funeral without an eulogy, than a life without the sweetness of love and sympathy.

Let us learn to anoint our friends beforehand for their burial. Post-mortem kindness does not cheer the burdened spirit. Flowers on the coffin cast no fragrance backward over the weary way.

> I'd rather buy a cheap bouquet
> And give to my friend this very day,
> Than a bushel of roses, white and red,
> To put on his coffin when he's dead.

XLIII

The Widow's Mite

Mark 12. 42. And there came a certain poor widow, and she threw in two mites, which make a farthing.

"Jesus sat over against the treasury." He still sits there, watching. All our giving is in his sight.

"And beheld," not critically or with fault-finding, but delighted.

"How the people cast money into the treasury." "Flung it." They like to do it. Methodists alone "flung" in $40,-000,000 last year.

"And many that were rich cast in much." Thank God for consecrated wealth!

"And there was a certain poor widow." Nameless? Yes. But so were the *"rich."* No discrimination here.

"And she threw in," just as the saints "cast their crowns" before the throne. It's the same word. O the *Lordliness!*

the prodigality of her giving! She gave with the abandon of a spendthrift King!

"Two Mites." Is that a climax or an anti-climax? Call it a mill—the tenth part of a cent—and you exaggerate.

"And he called his disciples unto him." It was "too good to keep." He was afraid that they would not "catch on"! that the rattle of the Pharisees' gold would distract their attention.

"I say unto you that this poor widow hath cast in more than all." Relatively? Yes. But *actually "more than all."* For they quit. She is still "flinging it in."

"For all they did cast in of their abundance." "Superfluity," "overflow." I wish that the Church of Christ would do even that much—reach the standard of the Pharisees and give some of their "overflow" money to the Veteran Preachers. When that standard of giving is reached the Church will have *millions for the Retired Ministers,* for the "overflow" alone is reckoned by hundreds of millions.

"But she of her want." "Penury," contrasted with "superfluity." God bless this Princely Giver! The dictionary of your experience does not contain the word "want," but is crowded with the synonyms of "superfluity."

"Did cast in all that she had, all her living." Every coin she had in the world.

Two mites—half a mill! How small! But the collective voice of the ages cries out,

"O! Woman! Great is thy munificence!"

XLIV

"Barzillai was a very aged man; and the king said unto him, Come thou over with me, and I will sustain thee with me in Jerusalem, and whatsoever thou shalt require of me, that will I do for thee."

This is not the first time David met Barzillai. When the young king was pursued by Absalom, Barzillai "brought beds, basins, earthen vessels, wheat, barley, meal, parched grain, beans, lentils, parched pulse, honey, butter, sheep and cheese for David and the people that were with him to eat; because the people were hungry and weary and thirsty." In recognition of this service rendered years before, David provided for Barzillai in his old age, and not as a "benevolence" complainingly or grudgingly given, but as duty on the ground of the past service rendered by him in his better days.

In the same way the Veteran Ministers rendered us unselfish service in the days of their strength, and we owe them not a miserable charity, but an adequate support. The salaries of many of our Ministers are barely adequate for a livelihood. It would be truer to say, barely sufficient for subsistence. Such men when they are too old to be any longer in active service, will come to poverty unless the Church which has benefited by their work makes provision for their needs. The Church must act as fairly in this matter as did King David.

The inadequate support given to many of our Ministers during the years of their active service is not the only reason why we should provide for them in their old age. We insist that ministers shall not divert their attention from their holy work through commercial distractions. Why, then, should we not provide an adequate support for them in their declining and unproductive years?

What is good for commerce and education ought to be good for religion. Ministers are not caring to make fortunes, but they do desire the assurance that they shall not come to poverty in their old age. Shall it be said in regard to the pension system that "sons of this world are in their own generation, wiser than the sons of light"? When the Church has as sensitive a conscience on the right of preempted service as David had what may we not expect in promises for the cause of Retired Ministers!—*Dr. A. D. Batchelor, in the Butte Miner.*

MODERN PSALMS

THE REV. W. H. FOULKES, D.D.

THE FATHER OF THE FATHERLESS

The Psalm of the Widowed Mother

They were cradled in childhood when God took him; they awakened, and, lo, they were fatherless.
I held them to my heart, but it was too hot with grief.
The flood gates were opened, but my tears brought no succor.

He was strong and manly; I helped him carry the load.
When death knocked at the door, I offered myself.
It scorned my pleading and carried away my beloved.

When I awoke from the trance, I saw hungry mouths.
My precious ones called for their father's help,
My cup of grief was full of bitter dregs.

Then God sent His angels; Goodness and Mercy knocked at my door.
They entered and removed their outer garments;
They kindled the fire on my cheerless hearth.

They fed me with good things; my darlings shouted and laughed.
I sent them at length to the school of instruction.
They have grown into youth: yet their arms are still about their widowed mother.

The Father hath remembered the fatherless; He hath visited the desolate mother.
The people of God comfort me every day, they do not fail.
The thanksgiving of the widow and the fatherless arise like incense unto God.

GOD IS MY REFUGE

The Psalm of the Aged Saint

God is my refuge, I am resting in Him.
Old age has come upon me, yet I am unafraid:
Days of adversity have befallen my lot, but I am secure.

In the hour of my weakness I cried unto my Deliverer,
"Send help, I beseech Thee," and He heard my moaning.

My years of fruitful ministry have passed like a dream;
Young men have risen up to stand in my stead.

Relief has come to me from the Most High by the hands of His people.
Every morning I bless the Lord for the kindness of His servants.
Friends have ministered to me of their substance and I am filled.
Unto the end of my days my bread will not fail.

God has opened His hand and the hearts of His chosen ones.
Exult, O my soul, for I am forgotten neither of God nor of men!

THE JUDGE OF THE WIDOW

The Psalm of the Lonely Soul

Jehovah is my Judge; He only knoweth my loneliness and grief.
For thirty years we walked together, yea for two score years and ten.
The young man took me from my father's house, we builded our own altar to God.
Jehovah filled my lap with children; lo, He hath taken them away.
We only were left: I felt for my husband's hand, but I could not find it.
I am left alone, but my Redeemer is with me.
In the morning I rose to eat bitter bread, but my table was filled with goodness.
Loving hands ministered to me; my meal and my oil did not fail.
I put on sackcloth, but the people of God gave me garments of love.
I opened a little door, but it led me into a large room.
My eyes are dim and my ears are dull, yet I am full of joy.
Loving-kindness is turning my tears into pearls.
My soul is adorned as a bride for her husband.
Blessed be God who hath moved His people to visit me.
In but a little while the days of my desolation will be ended.
Jehovah is my Judge: His people are my faithful helpers and friends.

PART IV. THE CLAIM ILLUSTRATED

CHAPTER II. STORY AND SONG

THE HAPPY MAN

HENRY ALBERT COLLINS

"The Life Annuity Man"

"Well, it's just no use, nephew, I'm utterly discouraged. Sanitarium treatment may be beneficial in some cases, but it certainly aggravates my condition. I was ill when we came here, and seeing the lame, the halt and the afflicted of every nation under heaven is getting on my nerves. Why, I never knew before that there were so many afflicted people in the world."

"But you know, uncle, you've only been here a week. The doctors say that the conditions here are apt at first to affect everybody in this way, but those who persevere in these treatments usually get well or, at least, obtain relief. Besides, if you do not stay here, where can you go? You have tried all sorts of physicians and many health resorts without getting much relief and home is no longer home to you since auntie left us."

"That is true, nephew, and life is getting to be intolerable. During the best years of my life I was a devotee to business. The Genii of the Arabian fairy tales were no more slaves to the wonderful lamp than I have been to my business. I worshiped in season and out of season the great American god, Business. The goal of my ambition was wealth, and I've reached it. When I should be enjoying the fruits of my labors I have neither the capacity nor health to do so. The wise man was right when he said, 'Human life is vanity and a striving after wind.' Why, I've not seen a happy man for five years, and I don't ever expect to see another one."

"Well, there is at least one happy man in this institution, uncle. I met him yesterday and I've had my eye on him ever since."

"Oh, I suppose that it's some young fellow like yourself who does not know what the real problems of life are."

"No, uncle, his hair is as gray as yours and his step has lost the spring of youth, but his face reflects the sunshine which is within, and his laugh rings true. I think that he is certainly the happiest man I ever saw. In fact the attendants here dub him, 'The Happy Man!'"

"He must be the proprietor and sees his institution full of wrecks of humanity and hears of men and women who are burning their candle at both ends, and who in time are likely to come here. Of course he is happy. He has a fine prospect of laying by something for a 'rainy day.'"

"No, uncle, he is one of the patients and has been here several months. He has kind words and a smile for everybody. He seems to be perfectly happy. It does a fellow good to hear him talk, and you know the wise man said, 'A merry heart doeth good like a medicine.'"

"By George! nephew, I'll have to get acquainted with 'The Happy Man.' What's his name?"

"That I cannot say. I do not know his name, neither whence he comes, nor his line of business."

"Well, I'll have to get acquainted with him. He reminds me of Sir Walter Scott's story of the Eastern potentate who was afflicted with melancholia. After he had suffered many things at the hands of his doctors without avail, he took his mother-in-law's advice, to travel until he found a perfectly happy man, and to borrow and wear his shirt. By so doing he would absorb happiness and his melancholia would fly away. He traveled throughout many lands in vain, for everyone he met had troubles of his own. Coming at last to Donnybrook Fair he saw the object of his search—a carefree, happy man. He commanded his servants to seize him, strip him and secure his precious shirt. But alas! the happy man had no shirt. I wonder if your 'Happy Man' wears a shirt. If he does I would like to either beg, buy, borrow or steal it."

"You had better try your luck, Uncle, and if you are as good a trader as your competitors say you are, you will have no difficulty in securing his magic garment."

"Well, bring him to me, nephew. I would like to see one happy man in this institution."

"Let's go out on the veranda, uncle. A while ago I saw him taking a sun bath out there. I know him well enough to give you a sanitarium introduction, and I am sure that he will be glad to meet you."

They found the "Happy Man," and the nephew excused himself, going to the gymnasium.

The uncle seated himself beside "The Happy Man," and began questioning him. He said, "I have been told that the helpers at this sanitarium call you, 'The Happy Man.' I don't know what they call me, but if they should call me 'The Miserable Man,' they would not miss the mark."

"My dear sir, why should a man be miserable in such a beautiful world as this?"

"As for its beauty, I have no eye to see it. Wherever I look I see misery, and whenever I listen I hear moans. The world calls me a successful man. Men usually found it hard to overreach me in a business way, and I have secured a goodly portion of this world's goods, and that's the world's idea of success. In fact it was my own idea until recently. My wife is dead, I have no children living to inherit my wealth or to perpetuate my name, and I have few personal friends. I have two houses furnished with all the comforts of life, but no home. I lost my health in the pursuit of wealth and now I am of all men the most miserable."

"But, sir, you have a nephew who seems to be a fine young man. I know that he is very fond of you."

"Oh yes, he may be in a way, but he has no business ability. If I should leave him my money I can already see his finish. He would not only lose all the money but would ruin himself. Let me tell you a little of his history. He was a clerk in a large commission house. One day he came to me and said, 'Uncle, I have a chance to buy out the business of my employer who wants to retire. There is another young man connected with the house who is willing to put in twenty thousand dollars if I will put in fifty-five thousand dollars. That will give me the controlling interest in a splendid business. Will you please let me have the money?' I knew that he was a good, clean, young fellow and without any question gave him the fifty-five thousand dollars. In less than three months he was back again and asked me to give him twenty thousand dollars so that he could buy out his partner's interest. I gave it to him, and it was not long until he wanted twenty-five thousand dollars more to make some improvements in his place of business. I let him have the money. When he asked me for another twenty-five thousand dollars I began to think it was time for me to investigate and under my questioning he made a clean breast of the matter. He had been speculating, and had gotten on the wrong side of the market and had lost all the money.

"So my money is not doing me much good and has not done my nephew any good. I'm here to be treated and I have some little hope of being cured, but even were I well again I could not go into business with the old time vim and energy, for my illusions have perished. Yes, I am truly a miserable old man."

"My dear sir," said "The Happy Man," "your case interests me greatly. In many respects it is like my own. I, too, lost my health through too close application to business. My children passed away in their childhood. My wife and I are growing old, but notwithstanding that fact we are happy because we have found our mission in life."

"May I ask what is your mission?"

"Certainly. You said the helpers of this sanitarium call me, 'The Happy Man.' I am more often called, 'The Annuity Man.' My mission is to preach the gospel of life annuities."

"Oh, I see, you sell life annuities."

"No, sir. I have nothing to sell, but I have bought some Life Annuity Bonds. My mission in life is to teach prospective annuitants the value of these bonds. When I persuade a man to invest in Life Annuity Bonds I feel that I have conferred a great favor upon him which he can only repay by enlisting others in this excellent work. The old proverb says, 'A man cannot eat his goose and have it, too,' but the Life Annuity system enables us to do that very thing. We can eat our goose, and have it, too, when we invest our money in Life Annuity Bonds."

"Go on. I begin to see what you are driving at."

"The Happy Man" continued, "If a man is a true Christian, God is a silent partner in all of his business enterprises. He is, as St. Paul says, 'A laborer together with God, God's husbandry, and God's building.' If we are His building He ought to dwell in us. If we are His husbandry we should bring to Him the increase. To be a co-laborer with Him is man's greatest privilege, and it is my desire to avail myself of it to the utmost. By buying Life Annuity Bonds of Christian institutions, I insure my own living; by preaching the gospel of Life Annuities to others I perpetuate my influence. Therefore, you see that I am cooperating with Him in building His kingdom on earth now, and my money invested in Christian institutions will continue the work after I have gone home. If you would find true happiness go thou and do likewise.

"I have no patent on this plan and would like to see you give it a fair trial. Would you 'put on immortality' while here on earth, then put your work and your money into institutions designed to help mankind."

The miserable man shrugged his shoulders and shifted his chair as he answered, "Oh, that's like life insurance. I carry policies in several first-class life insurance companies, but I can't say I ever got much happiness out of them. The only reason I continue to pay premiums on them is that it is the only way I can escape from them without great loss. I must pay until I die, and I must die to win. If that's your recipe for happiness it don't take much to make you happy."

"No, sir, you are mistaken, Life Annuity is very different and very much better than life insurance. When a man insures his life he does it usually so that those dependent upon him may be assured of an income after he is dead. Life insurance tends to shorten life, because a man who loses his health or fails in business and cannot keep up the payments on his policies is often tempted to commit suicide so that his family may get his insurance before the policy lapses. You rarely pick up a newspaper without reading of some one being murdered for his or her life insurance money. This is the great difference between life insurance and Life Annuities. Life insurance *shortens* one's life; Life Annuities *lengthen it* because in the life insurance game you must die to win, but in case of Life Annuities you have to *live to win.* A Life Annuity Bond does not insure your life but it *insures your living,* because you must live to win, and that tends to prolong your life."

"Oh, I see, sir, there is a difference between insuring your life and insuring your living. I know that life insurance has in it the danger you refer to. I knew a young lawyer, a bright manly fellow, in my home city. He had a wife and three fine children and a splendid practice. He got the political bee in his bonnet, became a candidate for governor and made a strenuous and expensive campaign for the nomination, but was defeated. His defeat brought on a nervous attack and in a moment of delirium he committed suicide. His life was heavily insured, and suicide seemed to him to be the only way for him to provide a living for his family. I see that life insurance often has a tendency to shorten life. You said that Life Annuity Bonds lengthen life. Can you prove it?"

"Certainly. Macaulay said, *'Annuitants are notoriously long lived.'* The reasons for this are obvious. The annuitant has insured his living. He is free from the labor and cares that are incident to making a livelihood in these days of keen competition, hence he can live his life on natural lines, which tends to prolong his days."

"This is a new business proposition to me and it is certainly interesting and worth looking into. Tell me more about this Life Annuity business. How old is it?"

"About twenty-five hundred years," replied "The Happy Man," "but it is only during the past one hundred years that the business has assumed its present magnitude. The system is older than all forms of life insurance. It is on a strictly scientific basis, and is as reliable as anything human can be."

"What induced you to put your money into life annuities?"

"My wife and I for many years have been interested in benevolent Christian organizations. We have, from time to time, given a few dollars to worthy institutions. Having a small income and being in poor health I was not able to earn much money, so could not give largely to any one object. We needed the interest from our principal for our daily needs. When the life annuity system, which had been adopted by certain organizations, was brought to our attention we found that we were able to place our money with them and be assured of our interest being promptly paid. The first hundred-dollar Life Annuity Bond which we bought proved so satisfactory that since that time we have placed nearly all our money out on Life Annuity Bonds."

"Who are issuing these Life Annuity Bonds?"

"Well, I have Life Annuity Bonds in Christian colleges, missionary societies, church building societies, hospitals, orphanages, and homes for the aged, and similar organizations connected with the Baptist, Christian, Congregational, Methodist and Presbyterian denominations. I invested money with them after carefully investigating their business methods and their work, and thus know more about their lines of good work than persons who have made no such investigations. I am interested in their work for God and humanity."

"So you give them the money in a lump sum and then they pay you a regular income as long as you or your wife shall live? What becomes of the investment at your death?"

With a bright smile on his face and a cheerful tone in his voice "The Happy Man" replied, "It goes on doing good while I am resting in heaven. That's what the Bible means when it says, 'They rest from their labors; and *their works do follow them.*' And that's just what I mean by eating my goose and having it too. There are Methodist institutions for the care of Aged Ministers which are holding intact to-day moneys which were given by men who 'rested from their labors' a hundred years ago, and their works follow them as dividends to help Christ's Ministers to-day; and such works will continue to follow them as long as Methodism and the Republic exist. The Life Annuity Bond is not only the best bond in the market but, in fact, it is the only bond worth having. My Life Annuity Bonds pay me dividends in two worlds. That's why I am 'The Happy Man' in spite of poor health."

"But these organizations can't pay you any very high rate of interest and have anything left for their work, and when you pay the taxes on these annuity bonds there will not be very much profit left for you, either."

"That's another good thing about Life Annuity Bonds. They pay a very satisfactory rate of income, and there are no taxes, commissions or medical examinations. The organization invests the money carefully, assumes all the risk and does all the work. I get the interest as long as I have any need of it, and then the money goes into the treasury of these organizations and continues to do good work as long as the world endures. How could one make a better investment?"

"You said these institutions you selected were all safe and sound, now why did you put your money into so many organizations? Why did you not pick out the one you liked best and put all the money into that one?"

"When I was a boy I was told, 'It is not wise to put all

your eggs in one basket.' I believe that Christianity is not confined to denominational lines. We are told to 'Sow beside *all* waters,' and as I am interested in all these various causes I want to have a share in their work."

"That's a common sense way of looking at the matter. Whom do you advise to invest in Life Annuity Bonds?"

"Everyone who can afford to do so, but more especially men like you and me. I have known men who were once shrewd business men, but who lost all their property in their old age, and died paupers. The clock does not always strike twelve. Neither is a man always at his best intellectually. He may have made a fortune when his powers were at their best, but has lost it when his powers began to decline, and courts will often pronounce such a man incompetent to do business or even to make a will. I once knew a man and his wife, farmers, who began their married life without any of this world's goods, but by the time they were sixty years old by diligent work amid many hardships were able to pay for a splendid farm of three hundred and twenty acres. They had two children, a daughter who never married and a son who left home and drifted to the city. Soon after the farm was clear of debt the old folks moved to the city to spend the remainder of their days in comfort and ease. The farmer had never handled large sums of money and had no experience in making investments, and so fell an easy prey of unscrupulous men who swindled him out of all his money. How much better it would have been for him if he had put his money into Life Annuity Bonds with some reliable organizations. It would not only have been a good thing for himself, wife and daughter, but he would not now be sleeping in a pauper's grave at the county poor farm."

"My friend," said "The Miserable Man," "I do not wish to pry into your business affairs, but I do want to ask you an important question. In case you had more money to invest would you put it into Life Annuity Bonds?"

"Yes, indeed, I would. That is what we are doing every year with the surplus of our income. My wife is just as anxious as I to place our money with these worthy organizations during our lifetime so that we may see the enlarged work which they are able to do because we have lent a hand in their good works.

"Now let me ask you a question. Have you ever talked with other people who are holding Life Annuity Bonds?"

"No, sir. I never have."

"Then you have missed a great pleasure, because it is a fact that the most enthusiastic friends of the Life Annuity Bonds are those who have tested them."

"I thank you for this information, and now may I ask, do you know whether there is any way by which I can provide an income for my nieces and nephews after I am dead? Two of my nieces are sorely afflicted and the brother of this nephew has no better business judgment than himself."

"Yes, sir. There are Life Annuity Bonds from one hundred dollars and up which will suit all classes and conditions of people."

The uncle said, "Since I lost my health I have been of no service to myself nor, to tell the truth, to anyone else. But since talking with you I have gained a new viewpoint of the possibilities and responsibilities of life, and I am glad that it is not too late for me to be of some service in the world."

"I am glad to hear you say so. Of course you can be of service. Besides investing in Life Annuity Bonds for yourself, nieces and nephews, you can be the means of inducing other people to put their money into Life Annuity Bonds."

"Yes, indeed, I can. I know several persons who should provide for one or more of their relatives or friends on this plan. I'll be so glad when I am well enough to go and see some of these people and tell them what a comfort and pleasure Life Annuity Bonds give the holder. You said a prospective annuitant had to apply for these bonds. Will you please tell me how to get a number of them?"

"Indeed, I will. Wherever I go I find that the annuity system appeals to people like yourself. They take a new, personal interest in the organizations which have adopted this plan for securing money. But you will have to excuse me now, for I see my nurse is coming to take me to the treatment rooms. I'll see you right after my treatment. Meanwhile you might take down the address of the Rev. J. B. Hingeley, Corresponding Secretary of the Board of Conference Claimants, 1018 South Wabash Avenue, Chicago."

NOTE—For names of organizations which issue Life Annuity Bonds see page 289.

"IS HE WORTH IT?"

In one of our Presbyterian exchanges there is a display advertisement headed "Is He Worth It?" which goes on to say: "One of our aged ministers, in answer to a letter from the Board of Relief and Sustentation, writes that he has been in the Presbyterian ministry fifty-eight years; has sent his three sons into that ministry; his average salary has been less than $450; he is now eighty-eight years old, and receives from the Board $150 a year, though entitled to $400.

"Is he worth it?" asks the paper, and continues, "When you have answered that question, ask another, *'Is the Presbyterian Church worthy of him and his ministry?'* "

It is some relief to us, as Methodists, to find that other Churches are in the same situation and under similar condemnation with the Methodist Episcopal Church in relation to its Retired Ministers. Certainly there must be an awakening of conscience in all Churches in regard to this. It is not charity or sentimentality, but simple justice and humanity. Our laymen must see the question in the broad light of doing the right and square thing by men who have made every sacrifice for the Church, the higher life of the Nation, and Christ's cause on earth.

In answer to the question, "Is he worth it?" there should be a unanimous and emphatic reply, "Yes."—*Western Christian Advocate.*

HOPE FOR THE SUPERANNUATES

Every Methodist preacher, old or young, and every friend of the preachers has reason to rejoice over the really great and successful efforts put forth by the Board of Conference Claimants to provide a comfortable support for the Conference Claimants. Better provision for the old preachers will put extra vim into the younger and relieve them of painful anxiety about their own future. It will also remove one cause of hesitancy on the part of young men who feel called to the ministry and yet have felt unwilling to devote their lives to a service which pointed to an old age of poverty.

OLD PREACHER'S SOLILOQUY

THE REV. C. C. BROWN, D.D.

It was a little home in the country, three miles from a thriving county seat town. Sometimes the Sunday bells could be heard across the hills. A few plain pieces of furniture were set against the walls of the living-room, and in one corner were two shelves of books, resting on a box. The frost had already nipped the green foliage, and the air was sharp and biting. An old man, his feet in carpet slippers, sat beside a table on which a lamp was burning. Close to the hearth, in an easy chair, sat his wife, her hair as white as the cap that crowned her head. A widowed daughter, the sole dependence of the aged couple, was stirring about in the pantry and kitchen, getting ready tea and bread for the coming meal.

"Wife, is there food enough?" the old man asked.

"I hope so," she replied; "but even if there is not, we must not complain. In some way or other, the Lord will provide."

"O, I am not complaining—not complaining. I will not now, in these last days, go back on the teaching of my whole life. I spent many years trying to abate the anxieties of the people to whom I gave the gospel, telling them to trust and not be afraid. Now I am trying to practice what once I preached."

The old man's mind and tongue were set going, and looking up toward a faded picture above the mantelpiece, he said:

"But it does seem hard—hard to have come to want in old age, to be turned out on the grass because no longer able to work. Sometimes I wonder if it is really a sin to grow old. I call God to witness"—and his eyes filled up—"that for fifty years in the ministry, I did not spare myself. People sometimes said of me, as they said of others, that I was preaching for money. But where is it? Not even a home of my own—

no bonds nor stocks, nothing at all, but rather I am daily faced by the vexing problem of bread. I remember now some work I did—the churches I built in the face of many trials. One at Deep Creek, one in Mayburn, one at Oak Hill, one at Layton, besides those years of mission work in the lower country, where the fever took me and laid me up so long. That sickness was the beginning of the end. It does seem—now that I am in want—that I ought to have gotten some sort of pay for all of this work. In those days, when I gave away half of my living, and never thought to lay up a cent, I was only striving to accomplish what was before me. I did not look far enough ahead maybe. Surely I did not see the coming of any day like this, when you or I should have to wonder if we could get bread for another day. I have never known till now what these simple words in the prayer meant, 'Give us this day our daily bread.' And then the children—"

"Now, dear," interposed the wife, "why lament the children that God took? Maybe they went away to escape evil days."

"O you misunderstood me! I am not referring to the children of our flesh and blood. I gave them to God long ago, and I don't think that I ever have had a rebellious thought against Him for taking them. But my children in the gospel —I am talking of them. Where are they? How many have told me, weeping for joy, that they would never forget me! Do you remember that meeting at Deep Creek in the summer of '70? What a time of refreshing that was! The easiest thing I had to do was to preach and tell the story. And it was just a year later that we had the great revival at Oak Hill. And then think of the long list of names of those who came into the Church through the long years!

"Now that we have come to this sore strait, is it not natural for me to ask for my spiritual children, and to demand some help from them? Can it be that they have forgotten me? Paul, you know, seemed to think he had some claim on Timothy, because he was his son in the gospel, and it does look to me as if my children should remember their old, worn-out father. But they do not, and I think I can now see the end. If my thin blood refuses to flow, and I go down before long, as surely I must, I want to be buried over yonder at Oak Hill, where I labored and spent the very best years of my life. I guess they will remember me when you carry my body back, and will want to put flowers on my coffin or on my grave. Yes, I hear them now singing about the old soldier and the warfare through which he passed. But, wife, flowers on my grave or in my stiff fingers are not as good as bread on an old man's table, and warm clothes on his back these winter days. To be alone in the world is not the worst solitude. The worst is that which we are suffering now—the sense that we are forgotten and that nobody cares for us, because we are old and cannot work any more. I know it is true that our life should be like the days, more beautiful in the evening, or like the summer, aglow with promise, or the autumn, rich with golden sheaves, when good deeds and good works have ripened on the field. But want may beget bitterness, and I am afraid I will become bitter.

"If I preached for money where is it? I had the burden on me of caring for hundreds of people, visiting them in their sickness, looking them up when they strayed from the church, marrying the living and burying the dead. I had to keep the Sunday schools alive, and work up the missionary enterprises, and I held inquiry meetings, and wrote letters, and sat day and night beside the sick—sometimes only to hold the hand of the dying, who said they wanted me with them to the end. I tried to do it all. I followed many of them till their feet touched Jordan, and it seems to me that the love I bore for my children in the gospel would have made me willing to go on over Jordan with them. It was my joy to put their hands into the hands of Jesus, and bid them goodby for His better keeping.

"Then there were the letters I had to write, the begging I had to do, the weak churches to visit, the quarrels to adjust, the poor to feed, the erring ones to reclaim, the visitors to entertain. I don't know, wife, how we stood it all. But I have nothing to regret. I would not undo any of it. I only wish I had been stronger and braver, and that the Master had loaded on more for me to carry. But to be as we are now after the work is over—this is the pinch. The house not ours, the land a stranger's, the pantry empty, our only child a servant and cook. I don't think God will censure me for asking, where are my children? Jesus cleansed ten lepers, and when only one returned to give thanks, he asked,

'Where are the nine?' Ah, Master, it makes the rough path a little smoother, now that I see thou hast even gone this way before me. I am not alone in knowing the dagger-thrust of ingratitude."

Just then a clear voice, in undertone, sounded out from the dining-room as the cheerful daughter sang:

> **Must Jesus bear the cross alone,**
> **And all the world go free?**
> **No, there's a cross for every one,**
> **And there's a cross for me.**

"Yes, yes," the old man said; "there's a cross for me."

In the corner under a bookshelf was a box with a hinged top, and upon this the old man fastened his eyes. That box contained his sermons, but for two years it had not been opened. He had no use for them now. He gazed steadily for a few moments, and then said:

"There's the old box of sermons! What a record of the history of a human mind and heart! The mind was small, maybe, but the heart—bless God!—was large. The heart-beats that are in those sermons will never be counted in this world. My hope, my love, my warmest aspirations toward God were all poured out in those sermons. It was honest labor. However faulty and imperfect my life, I was pure and honest when I wrote those sermons. They may be nothing but ashes now for others, but once they contained all the fire of my being. Some of them were born in joy, some in agony. Some hung struggling on my pen, some flowed like a swelling stream of fire. Some of them flamed in the pulpit, some of them were dead and cold and languishing. But there they are—fifteen hundred weeks of my life packed away in a box. Maybe it would be good to bury them. I think I could preach their funeral. Soul-thrilling memories, let them rest!

"The village church bell is ringing in my ear. I can see the people crossing the green. I am once more in the old pulpit. There before me are the forms I love. A soft harmonious song fills the air, and I climb up on it as on a ladder to talk with God, while they sing. Then the reading and prayer, and the Holy Spirit comes down upon us all. I am living it all over again. I see Brother Brayton sitting there on the corner of the first bench, weeping, and dear old Sister Dunn—her eyes float around in a sea of delight."

The old man had arisen to his feet, half staggering. Rubbing his hands across his eyes, he continued:

"Well, maybe this is age and weakness, and reason may be going; but these thoughts are worth to me all the toil and pain I have ever endured. I know I am poor, but I have bread to eat that ye know not of. Memories of those days surge through my brain, and I can live them over, if it is only in thought. I am happy that I can think of the souls born to God, of all the churches, of the happy homes once open to me, of the daily greetings with pilgrims who were on the journey home. Yes, I can hold again, if only in memory, the hand of the dying." He rested one hand in the other, and stopped as if to gather a thought. But the thought had come. "I wonder, wife, who will hold our hands when we are dying, now that we are old and forsaken by the friends of other and better days?"

His wife looked up, her eyes red with weeping. "Ah, dear," she said, "there is no good fruit to come of this. Let us cast ourselves again upon the good mercy of God. It is not far away to the grave. After we have made the little journey, all the problems will be solved and the enigmas made plain. *The righteous will not be forsaken.* This is the sure word of Him who never forgets His people's labor of love, and I have a faith which says that some heart and hand will yet open to us to supply our need."

At the table, after the scanty supper, the old man recited a psalm, and the little family bowed their heads in prayer. That night, after retiring, when his head was pillowed for sleep, a sweet peace came down upon him, and the kind Master gave him refreshing rest. But when the morning came, and the breakfast table offered so little to tempt a weak appetite, he found that the harassing problem was still there—whence is my bread to come? Nor was it ever finally removed till life's sun paled away and set forever. Then the old man had bread and to spare, for he sat daily at the Master's table, in a land of plenty—the only land where problems never come to preachers.

Beaufort, S. C. C. C. Brown.

THE REV. NOWKNOWSBETTER TO HIS WIFE
(Confidential letter.)

DEAR LIZZIE:

Have you read the poem, "If I Should Die To-night"? Well, don't. It is not very cheerful, and it has almost used me up. I read it last night and had a bad dream: I was dead, you a widow, and the children, orphans; and it made my bones rattle when I realized what a hard proposition you must face.

It was hard enough when we were together and had $1,200 a year and a parsonage; but had it not been for your skill and economy the $1,200 never would have provided for our large family; for it was hard to live on $100 a month when the people expected us to live at the rate of $250 a month, and complained if our children did not look as well as the children of Jones, who draws $500 a month. How did you ever do it? We might have laid up something; but receiving $1,200 a year, if we had lived on $1,000 a year we would have been sent to an $800 charge, as was Foster, because "not stylish enough for such a high-toned charge." Besides the old Church is doing better by its claimants, and I thought that before the time came for me to retire there would be funds.

But as I think of it now, I never did much to help the Cause. I was too busy looking after the heathen and the schools. I never put myself out to raise the Jubilee Gift, and had an idea that some day a good-natured layman would plank down Five Million Dollars and do the work. My stewards placed the apportionment in the budget, so that I was not bothered with *pro-rating*.

But now, alas! my widow is a Claimant and my orphan children dependent, and I have defaulted duty and opportunity! Your hands are empty. To get a stamp to send the catalogue of your poverty to the Conference stewards you must rob Margaret's bank of her pennies.

While awaiting my turn to interview St. Peter I have been trying to recall how our widows fared last year. It was shocking! They received only an average of $83.25 each. Why did we transfer from the old Conference, for there the widows received an average of $118.49; $35.24 more! I never knew that a dollar looked so big. It will look like a cart wheel to you before the year closes, and the fault is mine and that of the other preachers. There is absolutely no call for your present need. Laymen always responded to everything we asked for the old preachers. But we have held telescopes to our eyes to spy out new lands and create new sunrises for distant people, and have forgotten that our own old preachers and widows here at home are sitting in the evening shadows of neglect and poverty.

It looks as though hard times were ahead of you, my Dear, and I cannot help you. No, worse than that, I might have helped you had I had the true perspective. There are claims and claims, and there are causes and causes, but the *Outstanding Claim and the Cause of all Causes* is that the Veteran and the Widow should be provided for. Could my brother Ministers see this as I now see it, they would become deaf and blind and dumb to every other cause until their aged brethren have been provided for, and the old age *of their loved ones.* Laymen listening to the call of to-morrow have laid up for themselves treasures on earth, but the Preacher, who inspired them, has lamentably failed to do so.

You cannot imagine how I feel! I have troubles of my own. I tried to enter, but Peter stopped me and said, "You belong to that Conference which paid the old Ministers $160 and the widows $83.27 and you were deaf and blind and dumb to their needs. Young man, it's a good thing that Paul isn't on duty, or you'd never get in. For Paul is notional on this subject and declares that a man 'who careth not for his own has denied the faith and is *worse* than an infidel.' You know just where Paul would send *you.* Surely the Lord knew what He was about when He put me on guard. I denied Him, and swore, and am still a little rooster-shy, so I'm not inclined to be too inquisitive; but it strikes me that a man who is as foolish as you are and didn't have sense enough to convert the loving loyalty of the laymen into the coin of the realm for your widow and children, is too big a fool to make much difference which way he goes. You can take the elevator or shoot the chutes. It makes no difference which; but don't touch those halos. They are all *men's size.*"

I am not sure which route I took, but the trip ended with a thump, and, thank the Lord! I'm awake and my wife is *not* a widow, and my children are not orphans. But henceforth, "*first* things *first.*" I'll be home soon, and, first of all, we'll raise $1,000 for the *permanent endowment fund.* Then we will see Deacon Thompson and have him fulfill his promise to bequeath $10,000 to the Preachers' Aid Society. And then there is dear old Sister Green, worrying about that $5,000 her sister left her. I will see that she puts it into a Life Annuity Bond of the Board of Conference Claimants, which will give her an income of $30 a month as regularly as a government pension, so that she will be free to do what she so much loves to do, contribute liberally to missions and other benevolences.

Good-bye for to-day. I'll be home to-morrow and get busy. I know I'll have a job, "Keeping up with Lizzie." I'm glad I'm not dead. No obituary in mine. No Abner epitaph, "Abner died as a fool dieth," on my headstone. I'm glad you're not a widow (though you always did look well in black.) I'm glad the kiddies are not "the poor orphan children of a Methodist preacher," and heirs of Sammy and Susie Jones's cast-offs.

Lovingly yours,

John Alden Nowknowsbetter.

(One John who has learned to "speak for himself.")

METHODISTS SEEK $10,000,000 MINISTERS' PENSIONS

Campaign Extending Through Year Will Be One of Most Remarkable Ever Undertaken by the Denomination—Plea Based on Business Principles.

By J. R. Hildebrand

In Washington this week will be launched one of the most remarkable campaigns ever undertaken by a religious denomination.

Methodists intend to make a campaign to raise $10,000,000 within a year as a ministers' retirement fund.

Following the examples of great corporations, and giving an object lesson to Uncle Sam, who now makes no provision for his aged employees, this Church body hopes to raise a Permanent Fund for pensioning every retired minister, every minister's widow and ministers' dependent children.

Heading this unique example of religious efficiency is the Rev. Dr. Hingeley, of Chicago, who outlined the plans.

Ten million dollars for a ministers' retirement fund!

Startling, perhaps, but here is the real surprise of this campaign. This money is to be raised without a single "hard-luck" tale, without a tear-compelling story, with no vivid pictures of ministerial derelicts, suffering widows or penniless orphans. And nary an "over the hill to the poorhouse" touch.

The campaign for that fund is to be launched in Washington this week, where Government clerks are fighting for civil pensions, and where school teachers are pleading for a retirement fund.

Clergymen and prominent laymen of the Methodist Church will go about this great undertaking on business principles. They will base their appeal on good business arguments and pleas for higher efficiency. They hope to avoid any "sob" efforts and to avert any misguided pathos.

By way of emphasizing this point they have included on their program pension experts of several great corporations, for example, the Pennsylvania Railroad Company and the Youngstown (Ohio) Steel Company; and before the assembled Bishops, leading clergymen and noted laymen of the Methodist Church, leaders of the ministers' retirement movement will urge the application of sound business principles.

Harrowing Tales Obsolete

Talk for a few minutes to the leader of this great movement, the Rev. Dr. Joseph B. Hingeley, secretary of the Board of Conference Claimants, and you will realize why this is to be no campaign of perfervid and lachrymal oratory. Dr. Hingeley possesses the personality, the forceful bearing, the concise speech, the penetrating glance of the successful business man.

"The day of harrowing tales of superannuated ministers has passed for our denomination," he said. "In 1908, in Baltimore a system of pensions was worked out. It now remains for us to secure the money to insure the fulfillment of the pledges under that system.

"And we consider those pledges as binding as those made to an active minister or an active Bishop. It is as much a congregation's business to pay its retired clergyman as it is to pay the salary of its pastor.

"Before 1908 each Conference was the scene of sad stories about clergymen, their widows and their children. These men were entitled to pensions, but were merely tendered 'help.' The man who told the most pitiful story would get the most 'help.' "

Average Salaries Basis

Under the present arrangement clergymen who have served thirty-five years are entitled to a pension of half the average annual salary paid by their Conference. In the Baltimore Conference the average salary paid Methodist ministers is $1,050. Therefore, a clergyman retiring in this territory receives $525. Ministers having served less than thirty-five years are allowed $15 annually for each year's service.

In the Northern Minnesota Conference, the average is $1,400. It is believed this arrangement is equitable because it takes into consideration the cost of living in the locality where the minister is retired. Widows of clergymen are paid one half of the ratio, and each child under sixteen years receives one fifth of his father's claim.

In special cases the Conference has a right to increase these pensions to meet special needs. If a clergyman is crippled after only a few years' service his pension would not be adequate for his support.

At present the full pensions due under this arrangement cannot always be paid for lack of funds. Last year $1,100,000 was paid out, although $1,600,000 was needed to meet all obligations. A $10,000,000 fund, in addition to present resources, will afford interest sufficient to meet this obligation in full.

During 1915, Methodists in all parts of the land will give their united efforts to raise this sum. The undertaking is heavy, but leaders of the movement express confidence in the outcome.—*The Washington Times.*

"SUPERANNUATED"

"No, I don't believe in these 'worn-out preachers' yarns,' such as the preacher sprung on us this morning. A superannuated preacher ought to be like a superannuated business man—able to take care of himself."

"How about your old friend Jones?" mildly asked his wife. "He is a superannuated business man and he's in the poorhouse."

"Humph! Lack of business sagacity."

"But," continued the wife, "suppose a hard-working preacher receives, while in his strength of body and mind, only enough to keep soul and body together. What is he to do when he is old?"

"Why—eh? Say, wife, I've got to go north on business to-morrow. Want to go along? You will have to run your own chances, for I do not know what sort of a place it is."

"It may be that jumping-off place to the poorhouse," suggested his wife.

At six o'clock the next evening they found themselves in a scrubby town.

"There is no hotel here!" exclaimed the wife. But after looking around they directed their steps to the most neatly kept house in town where a feeble, kindly-faced old lady answered their knock.

"Good woman," said the business man, "we are obliged to remain in town over night. Can you give us lodging? We will pay you well for your trouble."

"If you can put up with what we have we will be glad to keep you. Shall we not, husband?"

"Certainly," came a cheery voice from within. "We turn no stranger from our door."

For supper they had the shredded leg of a chicken made into a delicious gravy, faultlessly cooked potato, the proverbial pinch of salt, and water. A repetition of their supper constituted their breakfast.

"We are poor," explained the kindly-faced woman, "and are obliged to make a chicken go a long way," she said, laughing. "Husband is feeble, and I am not much better; but so far the good Lord has provided for all of our necessities."

"Amen!" responded the gray-haired man at the table.

"But where did you sleep last night?" asked the business man's wife.

"We have but one bed," answered the gray-haired man. "Wife and I took to our old rocking-chairs, and passed a very comfortable night of it. You see, we have plenty of wood."

"And who are you?" asked the business man, while he tried to find something in his eye which very much troubled him.

"My name is ——— ———."

"What! Not my father's old pastor?" exclaimed the business man's wife.

"The same."

"And you baptized me?"

"Yes."

"And preached my mother's and father's funeral sermons?"

"Husband!"

But the business man did not answer. He was having trouble now with *both* eyes. He had out his pocketbook, and, counting out a generous sum of money, handed it over to the superannuated minister and his wife.

Then the old pastor took the blessed Book and with a quavering voice read a joyous psalm of thanksgiving:

> "Bless the Lord, O my soul;
> And all that is within me, bless his holy name.
> Bless the Lord, O my soul,
> And forget not all his benefits."

The next Sunday the business man united with his home church, and ever after saw to it that the superannuated preachers' apportionment was pressed down and running over.—*Michigan Christian Advocate.*

OUR VETERANS

THE REV. S. J. GREENFIELD, D.D.

Yes, that is what they are, "*Our* Veterans." Do you ask why we call them "Our Veterans"? Well, I will tell you. Years ago they gave themselves to us, and we accepted the gift and have made use of it. Long ago, when in the vigor of early manhood, when ambition fired the blood, when many alluring voices called to them from different directions, when professional, commercial and industrial careers opened before them, they turned away from them and offered themselves to us for the work "of God, and the Church and the ministry." From that moment to this they have been ours. They have been our "servants for Christ's sake," bearing the burdens, facing the difficulties, and solving the problems that fall to the lot of a Methodist pastor. They have done our bidding, gone wherever sent, taught the flock "publicly and from house to house"; they have led many of us and our sons and daughters into the fold of Christ, and have done it all without murmuring; yes, done it till the yet willing soul found itself imprisoned in a feeble body. Surely they are ours.

Grown Old in Service

They are our *"Veterans,"* too, for they have "grown old in the service and are entitled to consideration and allowance on account of it." Such is the dictionary definition of a "Veteran," and the Methodist Church cannot afford to have a definition that means less. They have grown old in the service, so old that they are practically unfitted for any other work by which to earn a living. If any Veterans in the world were ever entitled "to consideration and allowance" from those they had faithfully served, surely these must be. Warriors are they in the age-long struggle between right and wrong; laborers in the Lord's harvest field gathering precious sheaves into His garner; wise builders patiently adding stone by stone to characters that shall witness through all eternity to their fidelity to their sacred trust. Say you not, then, Brother, that they are worthy of "consideration and allowance"?

A Soulless Corporation

When at a summer resort there was pointed out to me a cozy little cottage overlooking the far-famed beauties of the majestic St. Lawrence. My companion told me that this was the summer home of one who had grown old in the service of a great railroad. When failing sight unfitted him to hold safely any longer the throttle of the mighty locomotive, the company retired him on a pension of fifty dollars a month for life, the company stating that this pension was a recognition of "long and faithful service." There instantly ran through my mind the recollection of not a few members of the Methodist ministry who had, under all circumstances, faithfully guided onward the churches committed to their care till physical infirmity compelled retirement, but who have never received from the great Church they served fifty dollars a month; in some cases not fifty dollars a year as a recognition of "long and faithful service." Yet that was a "soulless" corporation and we are a Christian Church.

Utica, N. Y. S. J. Greenfield.

THE LIGHT BRIGADE

When an effort was made in London to raise a fund for the survivors of the heroic charge at Balaklava only about a hundred dollars was collected. The veterans called on Tennyson, and he aroused the country to action with his pen. But much of the money raised went to other purposes—to Ireland, to the Society for Prevention of Cruelty to Animals. The incident called forth the following lines from Kipling:

THE LAST OF THE LIGHT BRIGADE

RUDYARD KIPLING

There were thirty million English that talked of England's Might:
There were twenty broken troopers that lacked a bed for the night:
They had neither food nor money, they had neither work nor trade,
They were only shiftless soldiers, the last of the Light Brigade.

They felt that Life was fleeting; they knew that Art was long,
That though they were dying of famine they lived in deathless song;
They asked for a little money to keep the wolf from the door,
And the thirty million English sent twenty pounds and four.

They laid their heads together, that were scarred and lined with gray—
Keen were the Russian sabers, but want was keener than they—
And the old troop sergeant muttered: "Let's go to the man who writes
The things on Balaklava the kiddies at school recites."

They went without band or colors, a regiment ten file strong,
To look for the Master Singer, who had crowned them all in his song;
And waiting his servant's order, by the garden gate they stayed,
A desolate little cluster, the last of the Light Brigade.

They strove to stand to attention, to straighten the toil-worn back;
They drilled on empty stomachs, the loose knit files fell slack.
With stooping of weary shoulders, in garments tattered and frayed,
They shambled into his presence, the last of the Light Brigade.

The old troop sergeant was spokesman, and "Beggin' your pardon," he said,
"You wrote o' the Light Brigade, sir. Here's all that isn't dead.
And it's all come true what you wrote, sir, regardin' the Mouth o' Hell,
For we're all of us nigh the work-house, an' we thought we'd call an' tell.

"No, thank you, we don't want alms, sir, but couldn't you take an' write
A sort o' 'to-be-continued,' and 'see-next-page' o' the fight?
We think that some one has blundered, an' couldn't you tell 'em how?
You wrote we was heroes once, sir—please write we are starving now."

The poor little army departed, limping and lean and forlorn,
And the heart of the Master Singer grew hot with the scorn of scorn,
And he wrote for them wondrous verses that swept the land like flame,
Till the fatted souls of the English were scourged with the thing called shame.

They sent a check to the felon that sprang from an Irish bog.
They healed the spavined cab horse, they housed the homeless dog;
And they sent (you may call me a liar) when rebel and beast were paid,
A check for enough to live on to the last of the Light Brigade.

O thirty million English, that babble of England's Might,
Behold there are twenty heroes, who lack their food to-night;
Our children's children are lisping to honor the charge they made,
But we leave to the streets and work-house the last of the Light Brigade.

WHO FORGETS?

A ragged, poor and friendless Chicago boy was asked, "Do you not think that if there were a God he would tell somebody to give you clothes and other things that you need?"

"He does tell somebody," replied the boy, "but somebody forgets."

All around us are God's children, in need of a kind word of sympathy, in want of temporary assistance. But we forget.

And how about the faithful veterans of the ministry who have literally worn themselves out in the service of Christ and the Church; who are unable to serve longer, whose salaries are cut off and who are in need?

How about the widows and little orphan children who have shared the privations of these self-denying ministers?

"Doth God care for oxen?" Then he cannot forget his saints.

But somebody forgets. Is your memory good?

Have you forgotten?

VETERANS!

Rev. Alfred J. Hough

[Read before the Veterans of Vermont Annual Conference.]

"Veterans!" That's a name of honor, borne by men who wrought and taught
That their fellows might be lifted to high planes of life and thought.
Not that age has lowered a pulse-beat, dimmed one radiant ideal,
Clouded any goal before them, or toned down their ardent zeal;
But the years of service rendered in the Master's holy cause
Give them right to relaxation and the blessing of a pause!
Looking backward, forward, standing on the heights, serene and fair,
Won by life-long aspiration and the upward life of prayer,
While the memories sweet and tender from the far-off years arise,
Filling with unclouded splendor all the sweep of evening skies.

How they sweetened noisome places, succored souls when tempest-tossed;
How they lightened shadowed faces, soothed the sorrowing, saved the lost!
How they laid the sure foundations, gardens out of deserts made,
Spoke the truth without evasion, opened heaven as they prayed.
When the world's long Roll of Honor angel hands at last unroll,
Then these ministers of Jesus will stand highest on the scroll.
Veterans, ere you leave us, swinging in bright chariots through the air,
Give us back the old-time singing, give us back the power of prayer!
Give us, ere you go, the secret of that preaching art of yours,
Which sent home the Gospel message, saving sinners by the scores!

If the church regains her prestige in the fight with sin, 'tis plain
She must bugle-call her Veterans to the firing-line again!
Talk of empty churches, drifting, why, a flock of sheep will go
Over fences to the neighbors when their feed is running low!
O beloved, you have spoken words that to the people showed
Where the heavenly bread was broken, where the living waters flowed,
How a soul by sin defeated could find mercy's open door,
Hear the Master's words repeated: "Go thy way, and sin no more!"
These the men that went forth weeping, sowing fields with precious grain
For the harvests we are reaping—shall we see their like again?

From the world your names may perish, for the world forgets its best,
But your memories souls will cherish that you guided home to rest.

Some day—may that day come swiftly!—this great Church of ours will heed,
And munificently answer, every veteran's sigh of need!
How her spires rise up, unnumbered, to the sun, in every State,
But she seems to have forgotten those who made her strong and great!
It may be our risen Master will rare gifts of grace withhold
Till the Church to her old pastors pays her debt of love in gold—
Till their widows and their orphans stand as mendicants no more,
Heeded not, while wealth and plenty walk through every church's door.

Listen! for these words of chiding, from the pen God wrote with, fell:
"He, not for his house providing, is far worse than infidel!"
And we read that when God's storehouse holds the tithes that are its due,
He will open heaven's windows and let boundless blessings through.
When the Church pays her long owing for divinest ministers,
There will be a sound of going in those blessed mulberry trees;
On the floor of every Conference may the Veterans' pleadings win;
For the Lord, with all His loving, hates a stingy Church like sin,
But just loves to pour out blessings on the church that loves to give
Of its bounty, countless treasure that the Veterans may live.

THE DIFFERENT WAYS WE TREAT THEM

MILDRED WELCH

I want to tell you about two soldiers, one, a gray-haired Confederate veteran, the other a young soldier of the Southern Presbyterian Church. The veteran is growing old and feeble and it will not be long till he joins the men in gray who have "crossed over the river and rest in the shade of the trees"; the other soldier, the young Minister, has already answered the roll-call in the happy land and laid down his armor in the prime of his manhood.

They call the Confederate soldier a hero where he lives, and when a stranger comes to town he is told this story. The veteran was a young fellow when he went into the war and carried the colors of his regiment with pride and joy beating high in his heart. One day in the heat of a fierce battle his commander, General Forrest, not wishing to expose his men unnecessarily, said to him: "Give me the colors. I want to plant them there," pointing to the most dangerous position on the field. The young color-bearer drew himself up to full height and said: "I will not give you the colors, but I will *take* them anywhere you say."

"Plant them on the enemy's breastworks!" answered the general, and the color-bearer planted them where shot and shell were raining fire, and the blue and the gray falling side by side. When the men in gray saw their colors waving there they charged and in one impetuous rush carried the breastworks. And that is why we call him a hero! He does not need our money, and so in place of money we give him love, honor and the brave man's place in our hearts.

And the other, the young soldier of Jesus Christ! He was a poor boy, used to hard work, sorrow and trouble, without the good play-times of other boys. One day he heard the call of God for him to be a minister and he answered it. There were years of hard toil, struggling for an education, getting along with little money, shabby clothes and insufficient food. Then came six years as a minister in the mountains. Not in one gallant charge did the young soldier fight his battle, but through hard years, going up and down the wild mountain caves, teaching little children, visiting the sick, comforting the dying. He had barely enough to live on and out of that little he gave to the wretched mountain people, while in all the commonplaces of daily life there shone the beautiful spirit of sacrifice.

One day, the young minister's strength gave way and when he lay sick he had not money enough to pay his board. At last the Church for which he had suffered so much heard and sent help. But it came too late. A check for $40 was held before his eyes already growing dim. He smiled gratefully, and said: "It will help," and almost at once answered the roll-call as a faithful soldier in the other world.

It never would have happened if we had only *known,* would it? But let us see that it does not ever happen to any other soldier of the Cross.

AGED MINISTERS IN THE GERMAN STATE CHURCH

The shamefully inadequate provision made for the support of the aged ministers of the gospel in this country is in marked contrast with the superb provision made for them in

*

Germany. The *Christian Herald* is authority for the statement that in Germany the young minister gets a minimum salary, usually of $500 and a parsonage. This salary is increased every few years until, at sixty-five, the minister, even if he has changed his parish, receives $2,500, the largest compensation permissible, the use of a parsonage and certain fees. At sixty-five the minister can withdraw on a pension if he shall so elect or, if the parish so desire; or by consent he can continue five years longer. On retiring he receives a pension for the rest of his life of two thirds of his last and highest salary. On his death his widow receives an adequate pension for the remainder of her days, as also does each of her minor children.—*The New Orleans Picayune.*

THE CIRCUIT PREACHER

GEORGE ALFRED TOWNSEND

His thin wife's cheek grows pinched and pale with anxiousness
intense;
He sees the brethren's prayerful eyes o'er all the Conference;
He hears the bishop slowly call the long "appointment" rolls,
Where in his vineyard God would place these gatherers of souls.

Poor rugged heart, be still a pause, and you, worn wife, be meek!
Two years of banishment they read far down the Chesapeake!
"Cheer up, my girl! here Brother Riggs our circuit knows 'twill
please:
He raised three hundred dollars there, besides the marriage fees.

"The schools are good, the brethren say, and our church holds the
wheel:
The Presbyterians lost their house; the Baptists lost their zeal.
Oh, thy just will, our Lord, be done! though these eight seasons
more
We see our ague-crippled boys pine on the Eastern shore.

"Yea! some must serve on God's frontiers, and I shall fail perforce
To sow upon some better ground my most select discourse:
"Gray am I, brethren, in the work, though tough to bear my part.
It is these drooping little ones that sometimes wring my heart.

"These hairs were brown when, full of hope, ent'ring these holy
lists,
Proud of my order as a knight,—the shouting Methodists,
My nag was gray, my gig was new—fast went the sandy miles;
The eldest trustee gave me praise, the fairest sisters smiles.

"All winter long I rode the snows, rejoicing on my way;
At midnight our revival hymns rolled o'er the sobbing bay;
But larger, tenderer charities such vain debates supplant,
When the dear wife, saved by my zeal, loved the Itinerant.

"No cooing dove, of storms afeared, she shared my life's distress—
A singing Miriam, alway in God's Poor wilderness.
The wretched at her footstep smiled, the frivolous were still:
A bright path marked her pilgrimage, from Blackbird to Snowhill.

"A new face in the parsonage, at church a double pride!—
Like the Madonna and her babe they filled the "Amen side":
Crouched at my feet in the old gig, my boy, so fair and frank,
Naswongo's darkest marches cheered, and sluices of Choptank.

"My cloth drew close; too fruitful love my fruitless life outran:
The townfolk marveled, when we moved, at such a caravan!
I wonder not my lads grew wild, when, bright, without the door
Spread the ripe, luring, wanton world—and we, within, so poor!

"For, down the silent cypress aisles came shapes even me to scout,
Mocking the lean flanks of my mare, my boy's patched round-about,
And saying 'Have these starveling boors, thy congregation, souls,
That on their dull heads Heaven and thou pour forth such living coals?'

"Well! well! my brethren, it is true we should not preach for pelf;
(I would my sermon on Saint Paul the bishop heard himself!)
But this crushed wife—these boys—these hairs! they cut me to the core;—
Is it not hard, year after year, to ride the Eastern Shore?

"Next year? Yes, yes, I thank you much! Then my reward may fall!
(That is a downright fair discourse on Patmos and Saint Paul!)
So, Brother Riggs, once more my voice shall ring in the old lists.
Cheer up, sick heart, who would not die among these Methodists?"

QUITTING TOO SOON

The Conferences have had the usual number of men stepping out of the active work of the ministry into the more quiet and restful way of the superannuate. There is nearly always some touch of pathos in this process, and we believe that not many Methodist ministers ask for a superannuated relation without misgiving, wrenching of heart, or tears.

But this decision and this process is sometimes worse than pathetic; it is occasionally a tragedy—because it has been reached altogether too early in life. If some change could be made in conditions or in the trend of things that would do away with the seeming necessity for early superannuation two excellent things would result—the problem of ministerial supply would be much easier of solution, and much heart-break, bitterness, and real suffering would be spared the preacher, and in some cases the people as well.

The minister who is retiring at fifty-five, still active and vigorous, may seek to justify himself on the plea that the foolish craze of the people for young men has driven him to the wall; but he ought in all fairness to honestly question himself as to whether that way of putting the matter actually covers the whole situation. It may be true that Church members and official boards are sometimes foolishly fond of preachers under thirty, but it is worth a question whether their fancy is really for men young in years or only for those young in spirit. It is probably true that a minister who is youthful in feelings and outlook and yet has the advantage of years behind him, has a much better chance of real appreciation than the one who is both young and inexperienced.

There are two or three things that the minister who has reached middle life should set himself steadfastly to do. He should determine not to lose his grip on himself. If a man keeps fast hold of his courage, his enthusiasm, his buoyancy of spirit, and does not allow his adversities, or hardships, or disappointments to sour or embitter him, he has made one of the first and most necessary preparations for the coming on of the years.

Men sometimes foolishly think that as the hair grows gray and the years crowd on into the fifties it is a call to slacken effort. In most cases it is no such thing. There is no reason why any ordinary man should not grow and develop and advance in knowledge, ability, and usefulness in the fifties or sixties—or even the seventies, for that matter—as he did in the thirties or forties; no reason in the world, save as he allows carelessness and inertness and slothfulness to settle down upon him.

The great necessity for the middle-aged man is that he hold on to his faith and optimism and hopefulness. The man who believes in the future really never grows old; the old man is the one who believes in the past. The preacher who is ready to lead his people on into the new and better days that are always ahead will very seldom be thrust from his place; but the one who talks overmuch about the better days that are gone, and tries to lead back to them, very often will be. The old men who "dream dreams" are on an equality with the young men who "see visions."

It is really a fine thing to see middle-aged men, alert and resourceful and buoyant and keeping abreast of things and leading in the forward movements of life; and it is an especially pleasing thing when these men are in the ministry of the Christian Church.—*The Christian Guardian.*

WANTED: A MINISTER'S WIFE

Wanted, a perfect lady,
  Delicate, gentle, refined,
With every beauty of person,
  And every endowment of mind:
Fitted by early culture
  To move in fashionable life—
Please note our advertisement:
  "Wanted, a Minister's Wife!"

Wanted, a thoroughbred worker,
  Who well to her household looks;
(Shall we see our money wasted
  By extravagant Irish cooks?)
Who cuts the daily expenses
  With economy sharp as a knife,
And washes and scrubs in the kitchen:
  "Wanted, a Minister's Wife!"

A "very domestic person,"
  To "callers" she must never be "out,"
It has such a bad appearance
  For her to be gadding about;
Except to visit a parish
  Every long day of her life,
And attend all the funerals and weddings:
  "Wanted, a Minister's Wife!"

To conduct the "Ladies' Prayer Meeting,"
  The Aid's "sewing-circle" attend;
And when we "work for the soldiers,"
  Her ready assistance to lend,

To clothe the destitute children
  Where sorrow and want are rife,
And look up new Sunday school scholars:
  "Wanted, a Minister's Wife!"

With courtesy entertain strangers,
  Traveling agents and such;
Of this kind of stray "angels' visits,"
  The stewards have had far too much,
These prove so perfect a nuisance
  That they hope these plagues of their life
Can soon be sent to the parson's:
  "Wanted, a Minister's Wife!"

A perfect pattern of prudence,
  Than all others spending much less,
But never disgracing the parish
  By looking too shabby in dress;
And playing the organ on Sunday
  Would aid in our laudable strife
To save the society's money:
  "Wanted, a Minister's Wife!"

And when we have found such a person,
  We hope that by working the two,
We'll pay our old debt and build newly.
  And then do you know what we'll do?
For both will be worn out and weary,
  And needing new change in their life:
We'll advertise, "Wanted—A youngish
  New Minister and with a New Wife!"

A STRONG CHURCH

W. B. Matteson

You are a "strong" church—a "leading church" in your Conference. Your pastor is a conspicuous, influential man. You are proud of him—of the position you have given him. You pay him a "good" salary. He lives in a modest house in a respectable neighborhood. He and his family are properly clothed (you would very much resent him in a shiny coat). He has a good library to which he is constantly adding. He can occasionally "travel." He gives you back a good part of his salary—how large a part you do not realize, for he is always giving, here, there, everywhere. He never escapes any appeal—you sometimes do. He may be saving up a little money—though the chances are that he isn't; almost certainly he isn't, if he has children to educate. He is possibly carrying, with much difficulty, a little life insurance.

You love him. If he fell ill—you would be kind. If he died, you would for a while anyway, until you forgot, care for his widow and children. If he were to grow old and pass the time of real usefulness while still your pastor you might, if he had been with you for a long time, retire him with a modest pension. If he had only been with you a few years—but then you never would have been so foolish as to call an old man who might obviously in a few years become a charge upon you! In a word, you are a kind, respectable people who would wish to do what was right toward your pastor in any emergency, and would do it so far as you saw and understood.

But, because you are a strong church, you *are an exceptional church*. Do you realize that? Do you not know that where there is one church willing and able to do so much as you, there are at least ten which however willing they might be could not do as much or anything like enough?

Do you not know that where there is one pastor as comfortable as yours, there are ten whose life is a bitter struggle to secure even the most common necessities of life—whose clothes are perpetually shiny—to whom a new book is a great rarity, for whom, in case of prolonged illness or death, their churches could make no adequate provision?

Because you are a rich church and can take good care of your pastor, is it right that you should forget the others? Have you no obligation to the Church and to the ministry beyond your own church and your own pastor? How large a part of your strength came to you from small churches whose pastors lived on miserably inadequate salaries?

It is the astonishing peculiarity of the work for ministerial relief that it is precisely the strong, rich churches which are most negligent. It is doubtless because they are farther from the need. The smaller churches, the little country churches know. They send in their contribution and "wish they could make it more"; but the contributions are necessarily small and the aggregate of them quite unequal to the need. But if we ask a church which gives $5,000 to benevolences to give this cause $500 it would be simply a fair proportion—a proportion which many moderate churches cheerfully give.

The strong church is the crux of this situation. Some of them are doing all that could be fairly asked—some are doing even more than they are asked. But for the most part the strong churches fail us. When they begin to do—we do not say their "proportional" part—but even a part of the part they ought in fairness to do, all will be well.

HAS METHODISM ITS "FORGOTTEN MAN"?

As we look over the Church we find one man who makes a very pathetic picture for all whose hearts are watered by the springs of tender feeling. Bathed in the twilight of age and poverty, he sits in the silent places. He had his day. He was once the bravest, blithest toiler in the field. He now can only pray and hope and hear the jocund note of his more active brother as he tells the tale of victories achieved. He is the worn-out preacher—more euphemistically called the "superannuate."

Are we as a Church forgetting this man?

"No," you say. "See how we remember him. Not an Annual Conference passes that he does not receive his little envelope containing a check, whose denomination has been carefully figured out by a body of wise men."

Yet how small and inadequate is this stipend! In many cases it is not sufficient to support him through more than a few months of the year. In many cases it is used to pay in part the expense of the preceding year.

Yes, he is remembered by the Church *in a way*, and it is to its credit that it does remember him to this extent. We would not forget, too, that the General Conference adopted a plan for raising a fund of $5,000,000; that this plan is being pushed vigorously and wisely.

Yet, when we consider the obligations of the Church to him, his actual needs, and what he really receives, would it be a mere figure of speech to call the superannuate "Methodism's Forgotten Man"?

For the reason that we have faith in God and in his people, we look for a day when the superannuate preacher of Southern Methodism will receive from his Church that practical financial support which an old soldier receives from his government, or which a worn-out employee receives from the secular institution. The time will come when we will be unwilling as a Church to use up the energies of our men, and, when we can no longer utilize them, to bestow merely our sympathy on them. As Christian men and women, we will be unwilling to bestow our gifts on the sturdy and active, and have no gift ready for the men who once bore the heat and burden of the day.—*The Christian Advocate* (*Nashville*).

LOVE AND PET ME NOW

T. B. Larimore, in The Christian Advocate (Nashville)

Take my withered hand in yours,
  Children of my soul;
Mother's heart is craving love,
  Mother's growing old.
See the snows of many years
  Crown my furrowed brow.
As I've loved and petted you,
  Love and pet me now.

Lay your hand upon my head,
  Smooth my whitened hair;
I've been growing old the while
  You've been growing fair.
I have toiled and prayed for you—
  Ask not why or how.
As I've loved and petted you,
  Love and pet me now.

Take my withered hand in yours,
  Children of my heart.
Mother's growing old; your love
  Makes life's sweetest part.
Touch with love my faded cheeks,
  Kiss my anxious brow.
As I've loved and petted you,
  Love and pet me now.

Take my withered hands in yours,
  Hold them close and strong;
Cheer me with a fond caress,
  'Twill not be for long.
Youth immortal soon will crown
  With its wreath my brow.
As I've loved and petted you,
  Love and pet me now.

Take my withered hand in yours,
  This your heart will prove;
If you owe me anything,
  Pay the debt with love.
Press me in your strong young arms,
  Breathe a loving vow.
As I've loved and petted you,
  Love and pet me now.

MAKING MONEY FOR GOD

Alpheus Hardy, the princely benefactor of countless good causes, once told this thrilling experience:

"I am not a college man, and it was the bitter disappointment of my life that I could not go to college and become a minister. My health broke down, and, in spite of my determined hope of being able to go on, the truth was forced on me that I could not.

"To tell my disappointment is impossible. It seemed as if all my hope and purpose in life were defeated. 'I cannot be God's minister,' was the sentence that kept rolling through my mind.

"When that fact at last became certain to me, one morning—alone in my room—my distress was so great that I threw myself flat on the floor, with the voiceless cry, 'O God, I cannot be Thy minister!' Then there came to me as I lay, a vision, a new hope, a perception that I could serve God in business with the same devotion as in preaching, and that to make money for God might be my sacred calling.

"The vision of this service and its nature as a sacred ministry was so clear and joyous that I rose to my feet, and with new hope in my heart exclaimed aloud, 'O God, I *can* be Thy minister! I will go back to Boston. *I will make money for God, and that shall be my ministry.'*

"From that time I have felt myself as much appointed and ordained to make money for God as if I had been permitted to carry out my own plan and had been ordained to preach the Gospel. I am God's man, and the ministry to which God called me is to make and administer money for Him, and I consider myself responsible to discharge this ministry and to give account of it to Him."

THE OLD PACKING BOXES

Song of the Itinerant's Wife

By Mrs. E. M. McKibbin.

How dear to my heart are the old packing boxes,
  Piled out of the way in the loft of the shed,
Infested with spiders and 'broidered with cobwebs,
  They're patiently waiting high up over head.
Serenely they wait for the verdict of Conference,
  Undisturbed by the fiat "Go forth" or "Go back,"
As the days hasten on for the annual flitting
  When the Methodist preacher is ordered to pack:
The old wooden boxes, the dust-covered boxes,
  The iron-bound boxes the preacher must pack.

How often when Conf'rence is over we hasten
  To pull down the boxes and brush off the dust,
And take up the carpets and take down the curtains,
  And wrap up the dishes; for pack up we must.
Ah, me! who can tell of the work and the worry,
  The din and confusion from morning till night,
The rush and the whirl—till a well-ordered household
  Has lost its headquarters—demoralized quite:
The old wooden boxes, the iron-bound boxes,
  The old packing boxes all ready for flight.

'Tis easy to pack all the goods and the chattels,
  The old packing boxes are spacious and wide.
We can carry the bird-cage, the cat, and the chickens;
  We can ship the old cow and the horses beside;
But the friends we have known, and the hearts we have tested,
  The communion of souls that were kindred and dear,
The trust and the love that consoled in affliction,
  The words and the smiles that encourage and cheer,
Are not packed in the boxes, the old wooden boxes,
  The iron-bound boxes, at the end of the year.

These are folded away in the heart's inner recess,
  Like flowers that blossomed away from the light,
Unforgotten they yield their perfume like a censer,
  These memory-blossoms, so precious, so bright.
When the Bishop of souls makes our final appointment,
  And we make our last move from the charges of time,
We shall welcome a crown and an entrance abundant
  To mansions of glory, eternal, sublime;
Bid farewell to the boxes, the iron-bound boxes,
  That so often we packed after Conference time.

AGED MINISTERS

The need of relief for ministers of the gospel has impressed itself upon the conscience of Christian people. The difficulty does not lie so much in the illiberality of the members as in their uninformed understanding of the subject.

Almost all the people respond to a special call for relief. A few words from the pastor of each congregation is enough, if only he overcomes his natural delicacy, which should not be as great as if he were asking for himself. For instance, a congregation in an Episcopal parish in Pittsburgh increased its offerings to the general Clergy Relief Fund from $200 to $2,000 simply because the rector took the trouble to discuss the matter candidly in a sermon whose telling point was the contrast between the comfortable condition of a retired army chaplain on $1,800 a year and the insupportable lot of another clergyman of the same Church who had toiled and starved on $600 a year, and now with his library sold, decrepit and infirm was facing the problem of existence.

Many dioceses or Conferences have considerable funds to assist their own retired clergymen. Nevertheless this local arrangement works rather in the interests of the pastors of rich and influential congregations and against the ministers in the small parish or mission. Members of prosperous and wealthy congregations can hardly realize that there are many poor churches which can scarcely give the necessaries of life to their ministers, to say nothing of providing relief for their old age.

A NICKEL FOR THE LORD

He wore a rose on his coat, but when the plate was passed gave a nickel to the Lord. He had several bills in his pocket and silver change, but he hunted out this poor nickel and gave it to aid the Church militant in its fight against the world, the flesh and the devil. His silk hat was on the seat; his gloves and cane were beside it, and the nickel was on the plate, *a whole nickel.*

He met a friend; the cash register recorded $1.35, and he handed the boy a dime. A nickel to the Lord and a dime to the waiter! He had his shoes polished and handed the Greek a dime without a murmur. He had a shave and paid his check of fifteen cents and "tipped" the barber a dime. He took a box of candies to his wife, tied with a dainty ribbon. He paid fifty cents for it, and gave a nickel to the Lord.

Who is this Lord?

This nickel-giver worships Him as the Creator of the universe, the One who put the stars in order and by whose immutable decree the heavens stand—and he dropped a nickel on the plate to support his Church. The Lord being slow to anger and remembering his size did not slay this mean little fellow, but gave him his daily bread.

But the nickel *was* ashamed, if the man was not. It slunk from sight beneath the quarter given by a poor woman who washes for a living.

THE SAINTS WHO FROM THEIR LABORS REST

For all the saints who from their labors rest,
Who Thee by faith before the world confessed,
Thy name, O Jesus, be forever blest,
Alleluia!

Thou wast their rock, their fortress, and their might;
Thou, Lord, their captain in the well-fought fight;
Thou, in the darkness drear, their one true light
Alleluia!

O may Thy soldiers, faithful, true, and bold,
Fight as the saints who nobly fought of old,
And win, with them, the victors' crown of gold.
Alleluia!

The golden evening brightens in the west;
Soon, soon to faithful warriors cometh rest;
Sweet is the calm of Paradise the blest.
Alleluia!

But lo! there breaks a yet more glorious day;
The saints triumphant rise in bright array;
The King of Glory passes on His way.
Alleluia!

From earth's wide bounds, from ocean's farthest coast,
Through gates of pearl, streams in the countless host,
Singing to Father, Son, and Holy Ghost,
Alleluia!

—Bishop William W. How, 1864.

PLEA FOR THE YOUNG MINISTER

Dr. P. S. Henson

I plead not only for the battle-scarred veterans whose fighting days are over, but for the young-blooded, high-mettled, oncoming heroes, who are girding on their armor for the fray which summons them, that, unvexed by fear of future want, they may give themselves with utter abandon to that high calling with which heaven has honored them.

How many a minister in the prime of his powers is heavily handicapped by the felt necessity of making provision, while health and strength last, against the peril of poverty when the evil days come, as come they will, when heart and flesh shall fail him, and he who has spent all his powers in caring for other people's perishing souls shall find nobody to care for his perishing body.

As he looks about him at the poverty of men whose voices once rang out like a clarion call, and upon whose eloquent lips delighted thousands hung, but who are now hobbling along to humble graves with none so poor as to do them reverence, is it any wonder that he feels as if he owes it to himself and those he loves to make provision, while he may, against such pitiful experience? And who can tell how much of splendid possibility of ministerial power is sacrificed to such felt necessity?

STATESMEN AND MINISTERS

President Roosevelt:

"I have made quite a study of American history and have always been greatly interested in the thrust of our people westward across the continent, that movement which began during Revolutionary days, and which from its beginning included as the spiritual leaders of the pioneers an extraordinary proportion of preachers of the Methodist Church. It was the Methodist preacher who gave to the backwoodsmen, as they lived in their stockaded villages among the dotted clearings, the spiritual life that prevented them from going down overwhelmed in the hard materialism of their surroundings."

Vice-President Fairbanks: "The ministers, who have

given their lives in the fullest and best sense of the word to the good of their fellow men, should be bountifully provided for when the infirmities of age and other disabilities have come upon them."

SENATOR DOLLIVER: "It is the pressing duty of the Church to see to it that the old age of its faithful retired servants should not be embarrassed by poverty and want."

GOVERNOR DURBIN, OF INDIANA: "Nothing is too good for the men who have worn themselves out in the service of the Methodist Episcopal Church."

THE GRAND ARMY OF THE CHURCH

Hats off to the Grand Army of the Republic!

But where camp the men who have fought the battles of the Church in the places of hardship and danger, and who now are old? Hats off for these, the Grand Army of Aged Ministers!

Yes, and while your hats are off, pass them; pass them farther around than they have yet gone; put more into them than the pittance you have been wont to contribute.

Larger pensions for our heroes!

It is much to their credit, but it is little to the credit of the Church that so few of these heroes of the hard places die in the poorhouse.

You, reader, whose eye at this moment falls on this editorial, how much did you do last year to make it impossible for aged ministers to die in the poorhouse? Are you proud of your gift?

The Gettysburg heroes draw pensions, every man of them, even though some of them may never have smelt powder. But not one in ten of the disabled Veterans of our Grand Army of the Ministry, has a pension, and those who have one have but a beggar's pittance.

Go now, while you think of it, and get your checkbook.

Hats off for the Grand Army of the Church! And while the hats are off, pass them and fill them!

MINISTERS' SONS

The Wesleyan Methodist Church in Great Britain maintains two schools—Kingswood and Woodhouse Grove—for the education of sons of Methodist preachers. What we would call an alumni volume has recently been published, giving some account of the subsequent career of 3,221 former students, from which it appears that 515 have entered the Wesleyan ministry; 135 have taken orders in the Church of England; and forty-four have become ministers of other denominations. About eight hundred have gone into business. Two hundred and eighty-one are teachers. Medicine claims 253; pharmacy, 213; engineering, 164; law, 104; civil service, 117; and so on. Art, literature, the drama and music together employ the energies of thirty-one. Eighteen of these ministers' sons have become presidents of the Conference; four have achieved the distinction of fellowship in the Royal Society, and twenty-seven have been fellows at Oxford or Cambridge. One of the lawyers is a member of the House of Lords and has held high cabinet offices, and eleven others have been members of Parliament.

BE A BOOSTER

HOMER CLARK BENNETT, M.D.

Do you know there's lots o' people,
  Settin' 'round in every town,
Growlin' like a broody chicken,
  Knockin' every good thing down?
Don't you be that kind of cattle,
  'Cause they ain't no use on earth.
You just be a booster rooster,
  Crow an' boost for all you're worth.

If things don't just seem to suit you
  An' the world seems kinder wrong
What's the matter with a boostin',
  Just to help the thing along;
'Cause if things should stop a-goin',
  We'd be in a sorry plight,
You just keep that horn a-blowin',
  Boost 'er up with all your might.

If you see some feller tryin'
  For to make some project go,
You can boost it up a trifle,
  That's your cue to let him know
That you're not a-goin' to knock it,
  Just because it ain't your "shout,"
But you're goin' to boost a little,
  'Cause he's got "the best thing out."

THE PRESBYTERIANS

The work of relief is now carried on in the Presbyterian Church through its General Board of Relief. While the avowed basis is service and the idea of charity is strongly repudiated, help is actually conditioned by need. The Board received last year: from the churches, $122,000; from interest on endowments, $90,000; from legacies, $45,000—in all, $260,000. It gave relief to 1,197 persons.

Within a few years the Presbyterians have harked back toward their original plan and established a ministers' sustentation fund, the ministers contributing, the Church adding, with distribution as need arises. The Board having this plan in charge have raised over $100,000 in two years; 640 out of 9,000 Presbyterian ministers have joined, it is already paying benefits to eleven widows and six disabled ministers.

The Presbyterians have two "homes"—one has sixteen, the other fourteen inmates. In the home which has sixteen inmates, but one is an old minister.

OLD AGE, THE INDIAN SUMMER OF LIFE

Some one has well said that of all the seasons of the year in our American climate there is none so tender, so beautiful, so weird and unearthly, so fascinating and perfect as Indian Summer. After the buds, blossoms, heat, and harvests of summer; after the autumn fruits and frosts, when the forests are mantled in crimson, fire and gold, when chill winds and vagrant snow squalls warn of the approach of winter, then some invisible hand seizes the galloping steeds of the seasons and reins them up suddenly for a few days, while earth, air, and sky weave around the weather-beaten brow of the year the golden crown of Indian Summer. The sun pours down a soft and dreamy golden light; the sky is robed with a delicate purplish gauze that seems to float everywhere; the air is balmy and caressing. There is a bewitching charm in the unearthly spell that has been cast upon nature.

And so God designs old age to be the Indian Summer of life, the gentlest, the tenderest, the most beautiful of all of life's seasons; for he says: "And even to your old age I am He; and even to hoary hairs I will carry and will deliver you." God's special care and love for old age marks it as the Indian Summer of earth's pilgrimage.—*Baltimore Southern Methodist.*

THE SECOND MILE

THE WATCHMAN

BY STEPHEN MOORE

Whosoever shall compel thee to go a mile go with him twain.— Matt. 5. 41.

Stern Duty said, "Go walk a mile
And help thy brother bear his load.
I walked reluctant, but meanwhile
My heart grew soft with help bestowed.

Then Love said, "Go another mile."
I went, and Duty spoke no more.
But Love arose and with a smile
Took all the burden that I bore.

'Tis ever thus when Duty calls;
If we spring quickly to obey,
Love comes, and, whatsoe'er befalls,
We're glad to help another day.

The second mile we walked with joy;
Heaven's peace goes with us on the road,
So let us all our powers employ
To help our brother bear life's load.

THE VILLAGE CHAPEL

LLOYD GEORGE

No profession demands as high qualities of head and heart as the ministry. Think of the catalogue of virtues which you demand! judgment, tact, discretion, patience, sobriety, temperance—every virtue in the catalogue. In addition to that you demand knowledge and intelligence; and expect to get all these virtues for 26s. a week. Try that on the doctor! You cannot keep all those virtues alive and respectable on a pittance, because the ministers must not merely be respectable, but must look respectable, and they certainly cannot provide food, clothing, houses and doctoring for themselves and their families on the wretched pittance which they are getting at the present moment, and it is a cruelty to demand it at their hands.

And what about books? A minister is not like a carpenter or a bricklayer, who equips himself with the implements of his trade at the beginning of his trade and gets through life. He must renew them every year; he has a wily opponent to meet, and up-to-date, who has the most modern inventions, and the preacher must meet him. In the villages people read, and the days have gone when a minister could pull through with a second-hand copy of Barnes' Commentary.

THE BLIND GIRL KNOWS

I know what Mother's face is like,
Though it I cannot see:—
It's like the music of the bell;
It's like the way the roses smell;
It's like the stories fairies tell.
It's all of these to me.

I know what Father's face is like,
I'm sure I know it all:—
It's like his footstep on the stair;
It's like his whistle on the air;
It's like his arms that take such care,
Nor ever let me fall.

And I can tell what God is like,
The God whom no one sees:—
He's everything that Mother means;
He's everything that Father seems;
He's like my very sweetest dreams;
But greater than all these.

THE STORY THE SADDLEBAGS TELL

The Rev. T. F. Royal

"The saddlebags were the traveling preacher's library and wardrobe and often his larder; sometimes the bin for his horse's oats, a peck at a time. Outward bound they were always loaded with Bibles, Sunday school libraries, and other books from the 'Concern.' Inward bound, they came loaded with ham, a flitch of bacon, a chunk of fresh meat, or a dressed chicken or turkey. They have conveyed all kinds of dry goods, groceries, boots, shoes, hardware and more than once an assortment of Christmas toys. These bags have been stretched to their utmost capacity with vegetables of all kinds. They have ventured to cargo such explosives as eggs by the dozen, gallons of sauerkraut, often a whole cheese, and once a gallon of soft soap; and many a time, fruits—fresh, dried, canned and preserved. All these were usually counted on 'quarterage.'

"To the itinerant's wife the saddlebags were like a pack of Providence, and to his children their opening was like the coming of Santa Claus. Those faithful receptacles always brought some happy surprise for the whole household."

HE LEFT ALL

A Vanderbilt died a few days ago leaving an estate of forty million dollars, all of which was poured back into the coffers of his family. He will be numbered among those who reverse the truth of God to make it read, "It is more blessed to receive than to give." Having received bounteously, he failed in that final and most gracious act of returning to society a part of what he could not have secured alone. The day is coming when a man will not dare go out of the world with the epitaph: "He left $40,000,000 *behind him and not one cent before him.*"

In this case no one was disappointed, because no one expected anything different. The really sad cases are those of rich Methodists who thus die poor; "having" changed the glory of the uncorruptible God into an image made like unto corruptible man (Lincoln pennies), and to birds (eagle pennies), and four-footed beasts (buffalo nickels); who worship and serve the creature more than the Creator."

What an irony to call them "rich"! Like the rich Laodiceans they say, "I am rich and increased with goods and have need of nothing and know not that they are wretched and miserable and poor."

SOUTHERN PACIFIC RAILROAD

Since the inauguration of the Pension Department of the Southern Pacific Company, 1903, nearly one million dollars has been voluntarily disbursed among the retired employees of that corporation; the precise amount being $850,608.

The total disbursements for June were $14,010.35, divided among 420 men and women, retired employees of the Southern Pacific Company.

NEW YORK CITY FIRE DEPARTMENT PENSIONS

The New York City Fire Department Relief Fund report for 1914 shows an increase of forty-five annuitants, the smallest in many years.

There are 1,681 annuitants on the pension rolls, drawing $1,063,739.73 annually; a net increase of $27,283.33 over the amount paid during 1913.

THROWN TO THE SCRAP HEAP

At the recent session of the British Wesleyan Conference, fifty-five ministers, many of them men of ability and learning, were retired from active work. The Methodist Recorder says: "It is one of the grim ironies of our itinerant system that at a period when other skilled workers are in the prime of power, these spiritual laborers should be seeking the shades. At sixty a cabinet minister would be thought to have his most distinguished years ahead, and ministers of other Churches are steadily advancing to widest influence."

The Recorder finds an explanation of the existing conditions in the fact of "the invitations given to junior men for filling the most responsible positions," and adds that "sensitive, gifted men, when invitations fail, think they hear the 'knell of parting day.'" Whether this explanation be entirely correct we cannot say, but we are certain that it contains elements of the truth. In the Churches of America as well as those of England there is a clamor for younger men. Bishop Hoss has called it "a popular demand for greens." It is reported of Bishop Candler that when a committee told him that what they needed in their pastor was "young blood," he replied, "O, no, brethren! You are in error about that. Half the pulpits are suffering now from cholera infantum."

To cast aside a whole class of men simply because they have reached a certain age is a cruelty and a costly waste.

FORMAL PROCEEDINGS OF THE WASHINGTON CONVENTION

TUESDAY, OCTOBER 27, 1914.

The first National Convention in behalf of the Retired Ministers and other Conference Claimants met in the Metropolitan Methodist Episcopal Church, Washington, D. C., on Tuesday afternoon, October 27. Dr. James S. Montgomery, Minister, and his Board of Trustees generously placed this church, admirably adapted for holding large gatherings, at the disposal of the Convention.

Bishop Earl Cranston, D.D., LL.D., senior bishop, opened the Convention and conducted the devotional services, the Rev. George C. Wilding, D.D., of the Newark Conference leading in prayer.

BISHOP CRANSTON'S ADDRESS

Bishop Cranston addressed the Convention as follows:

"In some things we are permitted to depart from the example of the fathers, but in the spirit of our common Ministry we are bound for time and eternity. So long as we find ourselves among those to whom for the time being the cause of God and of men is committed, it behooves us to prove our loyalty and fitness not only by fidelity of speech, industry of action and reverence of spirit, but also by devising the means that may contribute immediately or remotely to the ultimate victory of Jesus Christ. In that kind of service we are engaged to-day.

"I am called away from other tasks on one of my busiest days; but I am not sorry to find myself here to invoke upon you a blessing, and to voice a prayer that God will be with you in all your counsels together, and that out of these days of communing and determining there shall come a campaign that shall issue in victory. I see that District Superintendents from the Washington Area are here. I addressed all of them individually. It was not possible for some to be here, and others will yet arrive. I am sure they do not object to what was almost an episcopal command; for the hearts of all our preachers are in this task. If we can only communicate to the Church the convictions we hold, Dr. Hingeley and the Board of Conference Claimants and his associates in the Annual Conferences will have little difficulty in achieving what they have undertaken. But the conviction must first possess us; and we must be so completely dominated by what appears to us to be the command of God to do a work of justice that we shall go courageously forward.

"On the battle-line yonder they are fighting desperately, and none can tell what the issue will be. But that is not our kind of a fight. We are engaged in setting before the Church a cause which is absolutely just. Its foundations as set forth in our book of Discipline are impregnable. I shall never be sorry that I was present when the words were first written and shall never forget that it was a great layman, Robert T. Miller, who insisted that it should go in as the fundamental proposition that *'the claim to a comfortable support inheres in the Gospel Ministry'; and that 'such is not invalidated by his being retired, and at his death passes to the dependent members of his family.'*

"On such a foundation you have been building, and on that proposition I believe the Church will be found ready to carry forward the 1915 CAMPAIGN that has been ordered by the General Conference."

The Rev. J. B. Hingeley, D.D., Corresponding Secretary of the Board of Conference Claimants, made a statement as to the business and scope of the Convention.

Officers and Committees were elected as follows: Presiding Officers to be the Bishops when they could be present.

Officers

Vice-Presidents: The Rev. E. M. Mills, D.D., Central New York Conference; the Rev. J. W. Van Cleve, D.D., Illinois Conference; the Rev. J. M. Leonard, D.D., New England Conference; the Rev. E. L. Decker, D.D., Troy Conference; and Mr. J. L. Transue, Williamson, N. Y., Central New York Conference.

Secretary: The Rev. M. E. Snyder, Ph.D., New Jersey Conference; Assistant Secretary, the Rev. J. C. Youker, Rock River Conference; the Rev. C. R. Oaten, Northern Minnesota Conference.

Publicity Secretaries: The Rev. Horace Lincoln Jacobs, D.D., Central Pennsylvania Conference; the Rev. L. M.

Chambers, D.D., and the Rev. W. L. McDowell, D.D., Baltimore Conference; the Rev. E. C. E. Dorion, D.D., New Hampshire Conference; the Rev. W. B. Norton, D.D., Rock River Conference; and the Rev. J. H. Pearce, D.D., Central New York Conference.

COMMITTEE ON NOMINATIONS AND CONVENTION WORK: The Rev. C. W. Baldwin, D.D., Baltimore Conference; the Rev. F. T. Keeney, D.D., Central New York Conference; the Rev. U. G. Humphrey, D.D., West Ohio Conference; the Rev. I. H. Lidstone, D.D., East Maine Conference; and the Rev. J. B. Hingeley, D.D., Northern Minnesota Conference.

After the organization of the Convention, the afternoon program was carried out without a single break. Every speaker was there with his paper. This was practically true of the entire program.

GREETINGS

Mr. Justice Thomas H. Anderson, one of the supreme judges of the District of Columbia and a member of the Metropolitan Church, greeted the members of the Convention and gave them a warm and hearty welcome to the National Capital, on behalf of himself and church and the Methodism of Washington. The Rev. Joseph W. Van Cleve, D.D., responded in the name of the Convention. (See page 335.)

PRESIDENT WILSON

A letter from the President of the United States was read conveying his greetings and expressing his sincere hope that "the cause of Justice and Benevolence" represented by the Convention might be successfully carried out. (See page 317.) The letter was received with great applause and by resolution, unanimously adopted, the Secretary was requested to express to the President the pleasure of the Convention upon receiving his letter and its high appreciation of his greetings and well wishes. (See page 318.)

The Rev. J. B. Hingeley, D.D., gave an address on "The Problem and Its Solution." The next three papers were under the general head of "Present Organizations" in the Methodist Episcopal Church for the support of Conference Claimants. "Methodism's Oldest Institution—The Chartered

Fund" was read by the Rev. Elwin Hitchcock, D.D., Agent of the Permanent Fund of the New Hampshire Conference. The Rev. George P. Mains, D.D., of the New York East Conference, one of the Publishing Agents of The Methodist Book Concern, read a paper on "The Claimants' Great Asset —The Book Concern Dividend." (See page 409.)

The Rev. John Krantz, D.D., Newark Conference, read a sketch of "Ezekiel Cooper and John Dickins." (See page 451.) The Rev. E. C. Clemans, D.D., Field Representative of the Board of Conference Claimants, addressed the Convention on "The Claimants' Greatest Asset—Annual Contributions by the Churches—The Apportionment" (see page 421), and the afternoon program closed with a paper by the Rev. Isaac H. Lidstone, D.D., Chairman of the Board of Stewards of the East Maine Conference, on "The Debt of the Nation to the Ministry." (See page 53.)

EVENING SESSION—TUESDAY

The Rev. E. M. Mills, D.D., Central New York Conference, took the chair at the evening session, and the Rev. L. Olin Sherburne, D.D., Vermont Conference, conducted the devotions.

Bishop William Fraser McDowell, D.D., LL.D., President of the Board of Conference Claimants, addressed the Convention on "We Shall Win." (See page 329.)

Mr. J. L. Transue, Williamson, N. Y., addressed the Convention on "Approaching a Crisis." (See page 349.)

The Rev. F. T. Keeney, D.D., of the Central New York Conference, delivered an address on "Paving the Last Mile for the Itinerant." (See page 19.)

Dr. J. B. Hingeley spoke on what the Conferences generally were doing, and the session adjourned with the Benediction by the Rev. James S. Montgomery, D.D.

MORNING SESSION—WEDNESDAY, OCTOBER 28, 1914

Bishop Thomas B. Neely presided, and the Rev. Hugh Johnston, D.D., Baltimore Conference, conducted the devotional services. The COMMITTEE ON NOMINATIONS AND CONVENTION WORK made the following nominations:

(1) COMMITTEE ON FORWARDING THE BUSINESS OF THE CONVENTION: The Rev. J. B. Hingeley, D.D., Northern

Minnesota Conference; the Rev. E. C. E. Dorion, D.D., New Hampshire Conference; and the Rev. J. W. Van Cleve, D.D., Illinois Conference. (2) COMMITTEE ON COURTESIES: The Rev. Whitford L. McDowell, D.D., and the Rev. James Shera Montgomery, D.D., Baltimore Conference; the Rev. L. O. Sherburne, D.D., Vermont Conference; the Rev. C. A. Kelley, D.D., Rock River Conference; and Messrs. W. T. Gallier, T. F. Layton and Gardnier Johnson, Washington, D. C. (3) COMMITTEE ON LITERATURE AND REGISTRATION: The Rev. E. C. Clemans, D.D., Northern Minnesota Conference; the Rev. L. M. Ferguson, Baltimore Conference; and the Rev. G. W. Kepler, D.D., West Virginia Conference. (4) COMMITTEE ON RESOLUTIONS: The Rev. F. T. Keeney, D.D., Central New York Conference; the Rev. Frank P. Parkin, D.D., Philadelphia Conference; the Rev. S. J. Greenfield, D.D., Northern New York Conference; the Rev. Allan MacRossie, D.D., New York Conference; the Rev. E. C. E. Dorion, D.D., New Hampshire Conference; the Rev. J. A. Sargent, D.D., Indiana Conference; the Rev. W. A. Layton, D.D., New York East Conference; the Rev. Horace L. Jacobs, D.D., Central Pennsylvania Conference; the Rev. S. A. Morse, D.D., Genesee Conference; the Rev. J. W. Van Cleve, D.D., Illinois Conference; and the Rev. James Hamilton, D.D., Michigan Conference. (5) COMMITTEE ON FINANCING THE CAMPAIGN: Bishop W. F. McDowell, D.D., LL.D., the Rev. W. G. Koons, D.D., Wilmington Conference; Mr. Summerfield Baldwin, Baltimore Conference; the Rev. A. B. Rich, D.D., Erie Conference; the Rev. F. T. Keeney, D.D., Central New York Conference; the Rev. M. E. Evans, D.D., North-East Ohio Conference; Mr. J. L. Transue, Central New York Conference; Mr. John Andrus, New York Conference; the Rev. John Krantz, D.D., Newark Conference; and the Rev. J. W. Van Cleve, D.D., Illinois Conference. (6) COMMITTEE ON EXPRESSING TO THE BISHOPS THE THANKS OF THE CONVENTION: The Rev. F. T. Keeney, D.D., Central New York Conference; the Rev. Joel M. Leonard, D.D., New England Conference; the Rev. Robert Stephens, Illinois Conference; the Rev. W. A. Layton, D.D., New York East Conference; the Rev. I. H. Lidstone, D.D., East Maine Conference; the Rev. W. L. McDowell, D.D., and the Rev. James S. Montgomery, D.D., Baltimore Conference.

"Methodism's Youngest Institution—The Board of Conference Claimants" was the subject of an address by the Rev. James Hamilton, D.D., of the Michigan Conference. (See page 425.)

The Rev. S. J. Greenfield, D.D., Field Secretary, Preachers' Permanent Fund Commission of the Northern New York Conference, delivered an address on "Annual Conference Endowments." (See page 415.) An address on "Cooperation Between Annual Conference Organizations and the Board of Conference Claimants" was given by the Rev. S. A. Morse, D.D., Secretary of the Permanent Fund of the Genesee Conference. (Page 369.) The Rev. C. W. Miller, A.M., of the Pittsburgh Conference, could not be present owing to ill-health, but he had forwarded his paper on "Why a Service Pension?" The paper was read by the Rev. Horace L. Jacobs, D.D., of the Central Pennsylvania Conference, and a resolution of appreciation of the address was unanimously adopted. (See page 67.)

The Committee appointed to Express the Thanks of the Convention to the Bishops presented their report which was unanimously adopted and the Committee instructed to present the report in person to the Bishops assembled in their semiannual meeting in Foundry Methodist Episcopal Church, Washington. (See page 315.)

Introductions

The Rev. John R. Stewart, D.D., Agent Superannuate Fund, Methodist Episcopal Church, South; the Rev. Alfred J. P. McClure, D.D., Treasurer and Financial Agent of the General Clergy Relief Fund of the Protestant Episcopal Church; the Rev. William B. Matteson, D.D., Financial Secretary of the Baptist Ministers' Home Society; and the Rev. S. L. Loomis, D.D., member of the Ministerial Relief Committee and Chairman of the Committee on Ministerial Annuities of the Congregational Church, were introduced and brought the greetings of their respective denominations.

The Rev. E. C. E. Dorion, D.D., Member of the Board of Conference Claimants and Associate Editor of *Zion's Herald,* gave an address on "The 1915 Campaign—Cooperative, Intensive, Extensive." (See page 383.)

The Rev. W. D. Slease, D.D., Agent Centenary Fund Society of the Pittsburgh Conference, on "Leadership of Annual Conference Agents." (See page 375.)

The Rev. Frank P. Parkin, D.D., District Superintendent Central District, Philadelphia Conference, on "Leadership of District Superintendents." (See page 367.)

The Rev. J. B. Hingeley, D.D., Corresponding Secretary of the Board of Conference Claimants, delivered an address on "The Leadership of the Board of Conference Claimants." (See page 379.)

Bishop Thomas B. Neely

The discussion was closed by Bishop Neely, who spoke on "Cooperation on the Part of the Bishops." (See page 365.)

The following resolution was unanimously adopted:

It is with peculiar pleasure and satisfaction that we have had for the presiding officer of this Wednesday morning session our beloved Bishop, the Rev. Thomas B. Neely, D.D., LL.D., whose interest in the purpose of this Convention and the challenging cause of Conference Claimants is increasingly inspiring. We rejoice in his presence among us, and in his word and leadership. Upon him we entreat the great Head of the Church to bestow his grace, health, increase of days and strength for continued service and widening usefulness to the kingdom of our Lord.

Horace L. Jacobs, *Central Pennsylvania Conference.*
W. F. Conner, *Pittsburgh Conference.*
Albert H. Rich, *Erie Conference.*

Afternoon Session—Wednesday

Group Meetings were on the program and they were held in various rooms in the church. Annual Conference Agents, Conference Representatives, District Superintendents and Board members met with the Rev. F. T. Keeney presiding. The members of the Veterans of the Cross Fellowship, Retired Ministers and other claimants met with the Rev. V. A. Cooper, D.D., New England Conference, official organizer of the Fellowship. (See resolutions, page 561.)

The Rev. Charles W. Baldwin, D.D., Baltimore Conference, presided at the afternoon meeting of the Convention, and the Rev. V. A. Cooper, D.D., led in prayer. "The Campaign in the Swedish Conferences" was the subject of an address by the Rev. Herman Young, D.D., Eastern Swedish Conference. (See page 359.)

The Rev. William H. Dean, D.D., of the Washington Conference read a paper on "The Campaign Among the Colored Conferences." (See page 363.)

The Rev. Stedman Applegate, D.D., of the New Jersey Conference, gave an address on "Old-Age, Mothers, and Government Pensions." (See page 251.) The Rev. E. L. Watson, D.D., Baltimore Conference, spoke on "Deferred Payments to Veteran Preachers." He greatly interested all by showing the last written words of Bishop Asbury, written two days before his death. (See page 467.) Two historic Churches, "John Street," New York City, and "St. George's," Philadelphia, were subjects of sketches read by the Rev. J. Wesley Johnston, D.D., New York East Conference, and the Rev. Frank P. Parkin, D.D., Philadelphia Conference. The sketch of St. George's Church was written by its pastor, the Rev. J. S. Hughes, D.D., Philadelphia Conference, but owing to sickness he was unable to be present. (See page 461.)

Evening Session—Wednesday

Three great addresses were the features of the evening program. The Rev. G. W. Kepler, D.D., West Virginia Conference, presided, and the Rev. Charles W. Baldwin, D.D., of the Baltimore Conference, led in prayer.

The Rev. L. J. Birney, D.D., New England Conference, Dean of the Boston University School of Theology, addressed the Convention on "The Retiring Competence as Related to the Call to Preach." (See page 31.)

"Savings vs. Efficiency" was the theme of an address by the Rev. J. W. Van Cleve, D.D., Illinois Conference, Vice-President of the Board of Conference Claimants of the Methodist Episcopal Church. (See page 43.)

Bishop R. J. Cooke, D.D., LL.D., was introduced and spoke on "The Justice of the Retired Preachers' Claim and Its Relation to the Permanence of Organized Religion." (See page 111.)

Morning Session—Thursday, October 29, 1914

Bishop Jos. F. Berry, D.D., LL.D., presided at the morning session, and the devotional exercises were in charge of the Rev. L. E. Lennox, D.D., Michigan Conference.

The Rev. Joel M. Leonard, D.D., New England Conference, presented the following

RESOLUTIONS ADOPTED BY VETERAN PREACHERS IN ATTENDANCE ON THE WASHINGTON CONVENTION

WHEREAS, We, the Retired Ministers and other claimants, are members of the Washington Convention by the courteous invitation of the Rev. J. B. Hingeley, D.D., Corresponding Secretary of the Board of Conference Claimants, and thereby are permitted to enjoy its privileges, purposes and aims; therefore be it

Resolved, 1. That we heartily thank Dr. Hingeley for the honor conferred and the opportunities afforded us, and for the opportunity of learning more fully about the Veterans of the Cross Fellowship.

Resolved, 2. That while we are very grateful for the benevolent contributions which we have received in the past by which we were enabled to meet in part the daily necessities of life, we appreciate beyond the power of expression the action of the General Conference of 1908 (See Discipline, ¶ 323) that we are no longer necessitous cases only, but honored Veterans of the Church and just claimants worthy of a "comfortable support." Our hearts burn within us as we contemplate the good hand of our God upon us. O, that the Church might know the gratitude we feel!

Resolved, 3. That expressing as we believe the sentiments of all Retired Ministers and other claimants, we will cooperate in all ways we can to make successful the stupendous movement of the Board of Conference Claimants to inaugurate a Campaign for Five Million Dollars, to meet the request of the General Conference of 1912, to provide sufficient permanent funds, to pay the annuities and necessities which two General Conferences have judged us worthy to receive.

Papers on "What the Railroads and Corporations are Doing," were presented. A paper on the "Pension System of the Pennsylvania Lines," prepared by Mr. John W. Renner, Secretary of the Pension Department, Pennsylvania Railroad, was read by the Rev. C. A. Kelley, D.D., of the Rock River Conference. (See page 233.)

A paper on "Pensions in Industrial Corporations" prepared by Mr. J. O. Pew, President and General Manager of the

Youngstown (Ohio) Steel Company, was presented. (See page 241.)

Bishop Jos. F. Berry, D.D., LL.D., addressed the Convention, stating that the Bishops are in hearty sympathy with the proposed Campaign in behalf of Conference Claimants.

What Other Churches Are Doing

"What Other Churches Are Doing" was considered and the Protestant Episcopal Church was represented by the Rev. Alfred J. P. McClure, D.D., Treasurer and Financial Agent of the General Clergy Relief Fund of the Protestant Episcopal Church. (See page 151.)

The Baptist Church was represented by the Rev. William B. Matteson, D.D., Financial Secretary of the Baptist Ministers' Home Society. (See page 195.)

Rev. William H. Foulkes, D.D., Secretary Ministerial Relief and Sustentation of the Presbyterian Church, spoke of the plans of his Church for the care of Retired Ministers. (See page 165.)

The Methodist Episcopal Church, South, was represented by the Rev. John R. Stewart, D.D., Agent Superannuate Fund, Methodist Episcopal Church, South. (See page 183.)

Resolutions

The following report of the Committee on Resolutions was presented and unanimously adopted:

The Laymen

In view of the widespread interest of the laymen in the "comfortable support" of Conference Claimants and the success which has attended their efforts in the Conferences where laymen's associations have been promoted, we urge that all laymen's associations enlist themselves heartily in this plan and we recommend that laymen's associations be organized in every Conference and on every district where they do not already exist, for the purpose of making the 1915 CAMPAIGN for Conference Claimants successful.

Episcopal Areas

In harmony with the action of the General Conference and the unanimous indorsement of the Board of Bishops at their spring meeting to set apart the year 1915 for the Veterans, and in view of the proposed plan of organizing the Conferences in each Episcopal Area, and of uniting them for campaign purposes, we urge the representatives of the various Conferences to cooperate with their Resident Bishop and with each other in perfecting their organizations at the earliest possible moment.

Full Apportionments

Whereas, The enactment of the rule requiring the prorating of the moneys received for ministerial support evidenced the will of the Church that no ministerial claims should be favored at the expense of any other; and

Whereas, The apportionment by Annual Conferences of less than the full amount of the claims of Conference Claimants tends directly to defeat the purpose of this rule; therefore be it

Resolved, That we urge upon all Annual Conferences and Conference Boards of Stewards the apportionment of the full amount of the claim, so that, if all the apportionments are met in full, all Retired Ministers, as well as ministers in the effective relation, shall receive the full amount of their claims.

Campaign Expenses

Whereas, A large expenditure will be required to provide for properly leading the Church in the 1915 CAMPAIGN, and

Whereas, The Funds specially secured for the general work are practically exhausted and the regular income of the Board is necessarily devoted to special uses and cannot be used in general work, and the moneys which can be applied to the general expenses of the Campaign are small, therefore be it

Resolved, That we endorse the action of the Board of Conference Claimants in projecting this Convention and thus bringing together for conference and mutual inspiration a number of the men who have the responsibilities of the canvass; that we approve of the expense incurred as a wise and profitable investment of money for the cause of Conference Claimants, and that we further endorse the plan to hold a similar Convention in the city of Chicago near the beginning of the campaign year; be it further.

Resolved, That we authorize the Corresponding Secretary

of the Board of Conference Claimants to secure by such means as may seem to him wise and proper, moneys which may be used to defray the general expenses of the Campaign.

Resolved, That we request the ministers in effective relation throughout the whole Church to contribute sums of from one to five dollars for the expense of the general campaign in which all Conferences are to share; be it further

Resolved, That we authorize the Corresponding Secretary to state the situation to such laymen as he may have reason to believe will be disposed to help in financing the campaign and secure from them gifts for this purpose.

Common Ministerial Budget

Whereas, Much difficulty and embarrassment in the collection and prorating of moneys for ministerial support arise from the raising of money for Conference Claimants in connection with the benevolences; therefore be it

Resolved, That we urge upon district superintendents, pastors and church stewards throughout the Church to raise the money for Conference Claimants in a common budget with other items of ministerial support, wherever practicable, and that in all cases it be raised separately from the benevolent collections.

Invitation to the Bishops

During the earlier part of the session, the Rev. J. B. Hingeley, D.D., visited the Bishops in their semi-annual meeting in Foundry Church and presented to them an invitation to be present in a body on Thursday evening. (See page 316.)

The Rev. M. E. Snyder, Ph.D., read a letter from the secretary of the President of the United States, in which he stated that the President had read with great appreciation the resolution adopted by the Convention at its Tuesday session.

Afternoon Session—Thursday

The members of the Convention met in Episcopal area groups to consider matters of interest concerning Conference Claimants as related to the Conferences included in the several areas. These groups were presided over as follows:

Washington Area—Rev. W. L. McDowell, D.D., Baltimore Conference.

Boston Area—Rev. J. M. Leonard, D.D., New England Conference.

New York Area—Rev. Allan MacRossie, D.D., New York Conference.

Philadelphia Area—Rev. W. G. Koons, D.D., Wilmington Conference.

Buffalo Area—Rev. S. J. Greenfield, D.D., Northern New York Conference.

After the meetings of the Area groups, the Rev. S. J. Greenfield, D.D., Northern New York Conference, took the chair, and the Rev. W. H. Miller, D.D., Ohio Conference, led in prayer.

What Other Churches Are Doing

The discussion of the general subject, "What the Other Churches Are Doing," was resumed. Presbyterian Church of the United States (Southern Presbyterian) was represented by the Rev. Henry H. Sweets, D.D., Secretary of Education and Ministerial Relief. (See page 175.)

The Rev. S. L. Loomis, D.D., member of the Ministerial Relief Committee and Chairman of the Committee on Ministerial Annuities of the Congregational Church, spoke on "What the Congregational Churches are Doing for the Relief of the Veteran Preachers." (See page 207.)

Mr. Marvin Campbell, Member of the Board of Conference Claimants, had prepared a paper on "The Layman and the Claimants." Owing to illness in his family, Mr. Campbell could not be present, but his paper was presented to the Convention. (See page 79.)

Literature

The Committee on Literature and Registration submitted the following report, which was unanimously adopted:

Whereas, Our General Secretary, the Rev. Joseph B. Hingeley, has created and put in circulation a splendid literature pertaining to the work of the Board of Conference Claimants, which covers every phase of the work for better support of Retired Ministers, and

Whereas, This literature is of great value to the field secretaries, agents of Conference funds, Boards of Stewards, and to all concerned in the work of caring for Veteran Preachers, and

WHEREAS, We believe that this splendid output of the printing press ought to be scattered like the leaves of autumn among our Methodist people; therefore be it

Resolved, That we will give this literature the widest circulation.

Resolved, That we appreciate the fact that all of the leaflets and other matter that can be used by the various Conferences are to be so arranged that they can be used for local circulation, by leaving space where may be printed matter suitable for local needs and conditions and that we recommend that the Board of Conference Claimants print and put into circulation such literature as may be printed and circulated by the secretaries of Conference organizations which may be suitable for general circulation.

We recommend that all literature published by the Board of Conference Claimants be furnished at cost to Conference agents of permanent funds and Preachers' Aid Societies.

We heartily commend the purpose of the General Secretary to arrange the *Veteran Preacher* so that each Conference may have a special edition with several pages including the cover for the publishing of any matter that may be desirable for local information.

"THE RETIRED MINISTER—HIS CLAIM"

We suggest to all concerned the very great importance of the forthcoming book, *The Retired Minister—His Claim Inherent, Foremost and Supreme,* in which the proceedings of this Convention will be published and the papers and addresses of the Convention, the Address and Appeal of the Bishops, the addresses of the Representatives of other Denominations, important documents and literature bearing on the work for better support for Conference Claimants, will furnish material for pastors who are preparing special sermons and addresses and will inform laymen as to what is being done for this great cause. A copy of the book should be in the hands of every preacher and layman.

G. W. KEPLER, L. M. FERGUSON, Committee.

Courtesies

The Committee on Courtesies presented the following resolutions, which were unanimously adopted:

We hereby express our appreciation of the many courtesies which have contributed so much to make this Convention pleasant and profitable.

Our thanks are due and are now extended to the proprietor of the National Hotel, Washington; to the Baltimore and Ohio Railway Company for its consideration in travel; to the Metropolitan Methodist Episcopal Church, its pastor, the Rev. James Shera Montgomery, D.D., and his people, for their unstinted kindness during our stay as their guests; to our genial and efficient Corresponding Secretary, the Rev. J. B. Hingeley, D.D., for his wise and untiring labors in calling this Convention and in leading it to gratifying success; to those who have taken part in the program for their inspiring and helpful addresses, especially to those who are representatives of Denominations other than our own, namely, the Rev. Alfred J. P. McClure, D.D., of the Protestant Episcopal Church; the Rev. W. B. Matteson, D.D., of the Baptist Church; the Rev. William H. Foulkes, D.D., of the Presbyterian Church; the Rev. John R. Stewart, D.D., of the Methodist Episcopal Church, South; the Rev. Henry S. Sweets, D.D., of the Southern Presbyterian Church; and the Rev. S. L. Loomis, D.D., of the Congregational Church.

We also desire to express our gratitude to the Press for their kindness in giving publicity to the work of this Convention and thus helping forward our great cause.

We also express our gratitude to the District Superintendent, the Rev. Whitford L. McDowell, D.D., and the Local Committee of the Washington Preachers' Meeting for their kindness in planning so wisely for the comfort of the Convention, and to the secretaries who have so faithfully served us.

We record our appreciation of the presence and help of the Bishops in our meetings, many of whom were on our program and gave us most helpful addresses.

F. T. Keeney, *Chairman.*

The Rev. Allan MacRossie, D.D., of the New York Conference gave an address on "The Larger Meaning of the Program." Dr. J. B. Hingeley spoke parting words as follows:

Brothers, I would not attempt to hide my gratification and delight with this Convention. The thought in calling it was that we might get together in spirit and fact throughout the entire Church; and that we might receive the inspiration, which has already come to us, from the knowledge of what the other Churches are doing, and have the opportunity of adding new inspiration to their leaders.

I presume that if we were beginning matters anew, we might not have quite so many agencies, but there is one beauty about the Methodist machine, that while there may be complications or duplications of machinery, somehow or other the product comes out, and we are doing business efficiently in many different ways, with a common result. Occasionally brethren say, "There ought to be one connectional organization, and all these funds should be under its administrative control." If we were beginning and trying to project a new institution, with the knowledge we now have, we might plan that way; but we are adapting plans of work to meet varying conditions, some of the provisions being more than threescore and ten years old, while one has passed far beyond the century mark. No one is inclined to interfere with anything that is being done, except it be to adjust the several parts, so that there may be consistency in the outcome. Sometimes I almost envy our brethren in the Presbyterian Church who have one common central organization, and I think of what it must be to be at the head of an organization which consolidates the entire movement; but it is better far to be the official head of a great organization which is closely related to 105 Conference organizations with complete unity of heart and purpose.

Great connectional dividends of the Book Concern, the Chartered Fund and the Board of Conference Claimants all have their places, and fall into the general plan like the orderly movements of sections of a great army; while Annual Conference funds, and contributions from the pastoral charges supplement what comes from the outside. The distribution to Claimants is not made by a central Board, but by Annual Conferences, which know all the conditions.

I have been delighted with the reports of our brothers of other churches. The problem of distribution is the same in every church—to provide help on the score of need, and to distribute according to service, apart from any question of need. It has been somewhat difficult to get rid of the old fashioned methods. The questions used in Annual Conferences when we began the work would almost paralyze the willingness of an intelligent, self-respecting Preacher to receive the money. But to-day there are simply two questions in order in the Methodist Episcopal Church as far as my annuity right is concerned: "What is your name? How long have you been in the effective ministry?" Anything more is an impertinence. It is nobody's business how poor I am. By the laws of the Methodist Episcopal Church my claim is determined on the basis of my years of service, and that is recorded. Methodism is, first of all, paying its debts, and then, when necessary, giving gifts. My butcher does not want me to say, "I owe you twenty dollars. I will *pay* you ten dollars, but as you are a good fellow, and your family is growing up and you have had sickness, I will *give* you ten dollars." He would tell me, "I'm not a beggar. Keep your gift for paupers and *pay me what you owe me*." The 1915 CAMPAIGN is to make it possible for every Conference to pay its Retired Ministers what the law allows, and then to give whatever else may be needed.

I was very much interested to find a letter from an Ojibway Indian Preacher, breathing his prayer that God's blessing might be upon the Convention. Eight years ago, in the wilderness of Northern Minnesota, an Ojibway medicine man, Tay-Bay-Wain-Dung, adopted me as his son, and gave to me the beautiful name of "Kee-Tche-Me-Wah-Nah-Nah-Quod." I never knew why, until that fall when I visited the Gulf Conference, and an old Preacher with shining face and glistening eye said, "You are the fellow that is making the old fellows happy!" Then I knew. For "Kee-Tche-Me-Wah-Nah-Nah-Quod" means, "A Big Cloud Full of Blessing." It is a delight when the glistening eyes of the Veterans take on new luster as they speak my name; not because of myself but because they recognize me as the representative of every one who loves the old Preacher.

The meaning of the 1915 CAMPAIGN cannot be fully

interpreted by the benefits which will come to the Retired Preachers, the widows and orphans. Its fulfillment means a "*dependable* Annuity or pension" for all the future, so that as the young Minister takes his ordination vows, he shall know that back of the promises made to him of a comfortable support there are invested sufficient funds to make the promise good. The income will not be his during his active ministerial life, but some day when he shall have fulfilled those vows, it will be his as long as he lives; and he will have the added joy of knowing that until he needs it others, his brethren, will be benefited by it, and that when his time passes others perpetually will enjoy its blessings.

As we have listened to the addresses on the influence of this movement on ministerial efficiency, we cannot doubt that the young Minister will take his vows with greater confidence, freedom and consecration, knowing that adequate provision has been made for his old age. For that is what this proposition means. It will mean a thousandfold more to the men in the strength of their ministerial manhood than to the old Preachers. I thank God that the Methodist Episcopal Church is recognizing more completely than ever before that it is the duty of the laity to support the Minister, effective and retired, just as it is the duty of the Preacher to minister in God's name, and I am glad to hear the statement repeated from the lips of the brethren of our sister churches who have spoken to-day. Let us not get away from that fact. We are not a company of Ministers seeking to help the brotherhood of Methodist Ministers to a comfortable support; we are a company of chosen leaders in the Church of God who are trying to help and inspire godly laymen to fulfill their duty of furnishing a sufficient support of the entire Ministry.

We need to understand that victory is not by might, nor by numbers, but "*by my Spirit,* saith the Lord."

The Rev. James Hamilton, D.D., of the Michigan Conference, led in prayer, and after the benediction by the Rev. J. B. Hingeley, D.D., the first National Convention in behalf of Retired Ministers adjourned without date.

Camden, N. J. M. E. Snyder, *Secretary.*

CHOOSING THE BETTER PART

The following was a Favorite Poem of the late Dr. Robert Forbes.

They came through the meadows of Childhood together, hand in hand,
And often they talked of the future that waited in Manhood's land:
And one saw ever the glory that crowns the peaks of fame
In that strange and mystical country to which no man giveth a name.
"Up to the heights whose beauty lures me by night and by day
I will sometimes find, my Comrade, with kindred souls, the way."
And because his eyes turned ever to the heights, he could not see
The beauty that was about him. Blind to it all was he!

But the other saw all the flowers that grew by the paths they trod,
He read on the hills and meadows the wordless poems of God;
He saw the sin and sorrow that was round him everywhere;
But he spoke kind words to a comrade and lightened his load of care,
"Here's work for my hands, my Brother, I find it on every side.
It may not be grand like a hero's, but I shall be satisfied
If in the lives of others I bring some hope and some cheer,
And feel that the world is better because of my being here."

The ways that their feet had followed, parted in Manhood's land;
And he whose eyes saw only the peaks far off and grand,
Strove steadily onward toward them and paused not once by the way
To help and comfort a comrade as sometimes the weakest may.
He clambered up the hills and over their summit passed from sight,
And to-day he lives in the glory that crowns those mystic heights.
But no man's heart thrills warmly when another speaks his name.
Ah! that soul hath need of pity that feeds on the husks of fame.

But he who saw all about him work for his willing hands,
Has done it faithfully, nobly, as by a King's commands.
He helped the weak and the weary, he comforted those who mourn,
And no man knoweth the number of burdens he has borne.
He sang when his heart was heavy, songs full of hope and cheer;
And his songs brought comfort and courage, and all were glad to hear,
And men and women and children speak lovingly his name:
Ah! happy is he that findeth that Love is better than fame.

The Veteran's Camp Fire.

"The time of my departure is at hand. There is laid up for me a crown."

J. B. HINGELEY.

1. I am wait-ing to-night for the Lord to come To take His chil-dren home,— To hoist the sail and say fare-well, And seek my Fa-ther's throne.
2. I have fought the fight, and have kept the faith, And stood fast in the ranks; The hosts of sin have felt my sword, Yea, to the Lord be thanks.
3. I am bear-ing to-night the cross of my Lord, But soon I'll wear that crown The Right-eous Judge will sure-ly give To those He calls "His own."
CHORUS.
Veterans of the cross, wait-ing to-night, Wait-ing for the Lord to come;
Veterans of the cross, list'ning to-night, To hear the call "Come home."
REFRAIN.
Waiting to-night,
Last v.—Resting to-night,
pray-ing to-night, rest-ing till the Lord shall come.
pray-ing to-night, (Omit.) wait-ing for the Lord's "Well Done."

Facing the Sunset.

E. E. HEWITT

CHAS. H. GABRIEL.

1. Min - is - ters of Je - sus, look-ing t'ward the west! Ye who love the Mas - ter,
2. Looking t'ward the sun-set, life will sweet-er be, If God's loy - al peo - yle
3. Widows, too, and or - phans, we will not for - get; Hast - en, Christians, hast-en,
com-fort give, and rest; With your lov - ing of-f'rings, years of toil re - pay;
yield glad min - is - try; With a will - ing spir - it, all their needs sup - ply;
pay the se - cred debt! Naught that we can ren - der can our hand with - hold
As they face the sun - set, glad - den now their way.
They have oft - en brought us bless - ings from the sky.
From God's faith-ful serv - ants, sil - ver haired and old.
CHORUS.
Fac - ing the sun - set,
heirs of glo - ry, they; Wait-ing the dawn-ing of a bet - ter day; Care for their
wel - fare, time - ly aid af - ford, Ere they pass to their re - ward.

The Aged Minister's Prayer.

"Cast me not off in the time of old age; forsake me not when my strength faileth. . . . . Now also when I am old and gray-headed, O God, forsake me not."—Ps. 71: 9, 18.

Tune, BERA.

1. For-sake me not when I am old, The day-light wanes, my work is done;
2. For-sake me not when I am old, When youthful vig- or is no more;
3. For-sake thee not when thou art old? Thy Fa-ther hears thy trust-ful pray'r,
4. For-sake thee not when thou art old? We hear the call; the church-es wake,
My feet draw near the streets of gold; I wait the set - ting of the sun.
When in the twi - light grey and cold, I sit and wait the sum - mons o'er.
His arms of love shall thee en - fold; His hand thy ta - ble shall pre - pare.
The heart that won us to the fold Our grate-ful love shall ne'er for - sake.

The leader or choir may sing the first two stanzas, and all the people the last two.

Scatter the Flowers Now.

(To God's Men.)

Mrs. C. D. Martin. W. Stillman Martin.

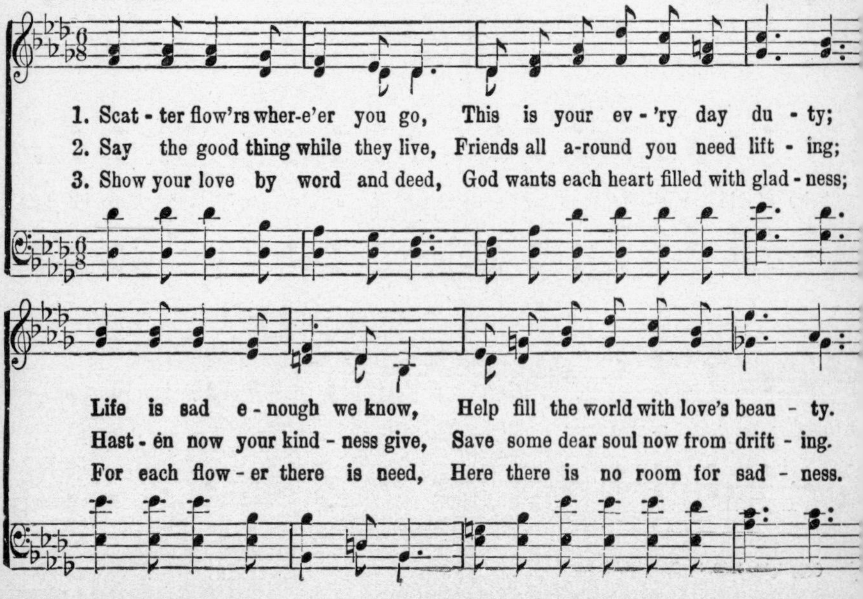
1. Scat - ter flow'rs wher-e'er you go, This is your ev - 'ry day du - ty;
2. Say the good thing while they live, Friends all a-round you need lift - ing;
3. Show your love by word and deed, God wants each heart filled with glad - ness;
Life is sad e - nough we know, Help fill the world with love's beau - ty.
Hast - en now your kind - ness give, Save some dear soul now from drift - ing.
For each flow - er there is need, Here there is no room for sad - ness.

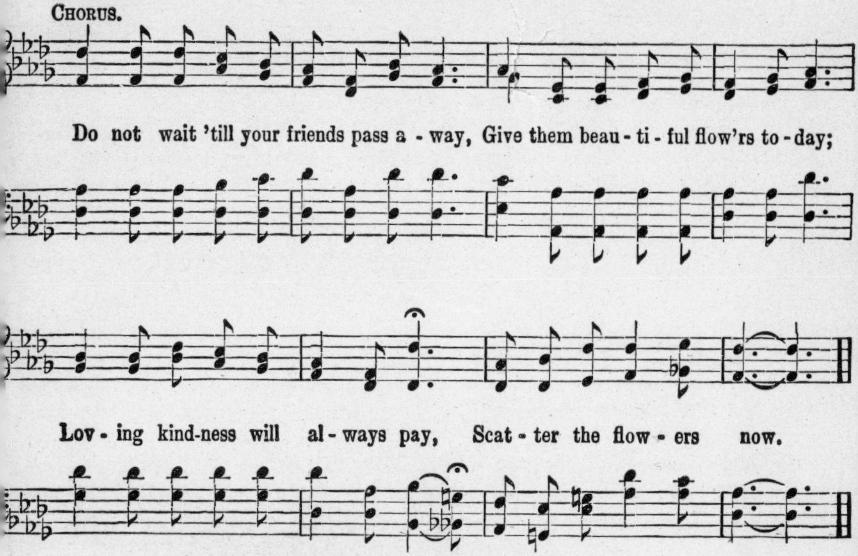
CHORUS.
Do not wait 'till your friends pass a - way, Give them beau - ti - ful flow'rs to - day;
Lov - ing kind-ness will al - ways pay, Scat - ter the flow - ers now.

THE SUN IS RISING, LET US GO

At end of Love, at end of Life,
At end of Hope, at end of Strife,
At end of all we cling to so,
The sun is setting. Must we go?

At dawn of Love, at dawn of Life,
At dawn of Peace that follows Strife,
At dawn of all we long for so,
The sun is rising. Let us go.

FINIS

INDEX

Y

Z

ILLUSTRATIONS

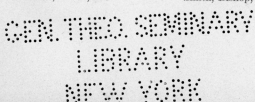